THE ASQ
ISO 9000:2000
HANDBOOK

Also available from ASQ Quality Press:

ISO 9001:2000 Explained, Second Edition
Charles A. Cianfrani, Joseph J. Tsiakals, and John E. (Jack) West

Quality Audits for ISO 9001:2000: Making Compliance Value-Added
Tim O'Hanlon

ISO 9000:2000 Quick Reference
Jeanne Ketola and Kathy Roberts

ISO Lesson Guide 2000: Pocket Guide to Q9001:2000, Second Edition
Dennis Arter and J. P. Russell

ANSI/ISO/ASQ Q9000:2000 Series Quality Standards

ISO 9000:2000 for Small and Medium Businesses
Herbert C. Monnich

The ISO 9001:2000 Auditor's Companion
Kent A. Keeney

The ISO 9001:2000 Audit Kit
Kent A. Keeney

The Practical Guide to People-Friendly Documentation
Adrienne Escoe

The Certified Quality Manager Handbook, Second Edition
Duke Okes and Russell T. Westcott, editors

To request a complimentary catalog of ASQ Quality Press publications, call
800-248-1946, or visit our Web site at www.qualitypress.asq.org .

THE ASQ
ISO 9000:2000
HANDBOOK

Charles A. Cianfrani, Joseph J. Tsiakals,
and John E. (Jack) West, Editors

ASQ Quality Press
Milwaukee, Wisconsin

The ASQ ISO 9000:2000 Handbook
Charles A. Cianfrani, Joseph J. Tsiakals, and John E. (Jack) West, Editors

Library of Congress Cataloging-in-Publication Data

The ASQ ISO 9000:2000 handbook / Charles A. Cianfrani, Joseph J.
Tsiakals, and John E. (Jack) West, editors.
   p. cm.
  Includes bibliographical references and index.
  ISBN 0-87389-522-3 (alk. paper)
  1. Quality control. 2. Total quality management. 3. Quality
control—Standards. I. Cianfrani, Charles A. II. Tsiakals, Joseph J.
III. West, Jack, 1944–

TS156 .A79 2001
658.5'62—dc21   2001006465

© 2002 by ASQ

10 9 8 7 6 5 4 3 2 1

ISBN 0-87389-522-3

Acquisitions Editor: Annemieke Koudstaal
Project Editor: Craig S. Powell
Production Administrator: Gretchen Trautman
Special Marketing Representative: Denise Cawley

ASQ Mission: The American Society for Quality advances individual, organizational,
and community excellence worldwide through learning, quality improvement, and
knowledge exchange.

Attention Bookstores, Wholesalers, Schools and Corporations: ASQ Quality Press books,
videotapes, audiotapes, and software are available at quantity discounts with bulk
purchases for business, educational, or instructional use. For information, please contact
ASQ Quality Press at 800-248-1946, or write to ASQ Quality Press, P.O. Box 3005,
Milwaukee, WI 53201-3005.

To place orders or to request a free copy of the ASQ Quality Press Publications Catalog,
including ASQ membership information, call 800-248-1946. Visit our Web site at
www.asq.org or http://qualitypress.asq.org .

Printed in the United States of America

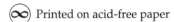 Printed on acid-free paper

American Society for Quality

Quality Press
600 N. Plankinton Avenue
Milwaukee, Wisconsin 53203
Call toll free 800-248-1946
Fax 414-272-1734
www.asq.org
http://qualitypress.asq.org
http://standardsgroup.asq.org
E-mail: authors@asq.org

Table of Contents

The following appendixes can be found on the CD accompanying this book

List of Figures and Tables

Foreword

Wouldn't it be great if we could achieve our quality goals by plugging in a quality training program and adding a dash of cheerleading from upper management? Many people have been down that road, so often in fact that they could drive it in their sleep. Sorry—results don't come that way. We need many more activities, including an infrastructure of quality-related activities. ISO 9000 provides that structure.

The ISO 9000:2000 series has two key documents: ISO 9001 and ISO 9004. ISO 9001 presents requirements for use in the certification process; ISO 9004 explains quality management principles and how they make an ISO 9000 system effective in terms of quality, cost, and cycle time.

Some say that standards documents like the ISO 9000 series tell a company how it must run itself. Not so—but these people will never be convinced. Standards help to achieve a level playing field among companies. Over 40 years ago, my review of a standards document from the U.S. Department of Defense led me to the conclusion that the document omitted certain activities necessary to make a good product. Our recommendation: make the standards tougher because (1) it is the right thing to do for the user, and (2) we want to bid on an equal basis with our competition.

For companies that already have excellent quality systems but lack sufficient documentation, ISO 9001 requires an investment for initial documentation and periodic updating. Documentation work is boring, but it must be done. Alas, updating is vital because obsolete documentation is useless.

The matter of continual improvement deserves a comment. In the 1987 version of the ISO 9000 series, the coverage of continual improvement in terms of results in products and processes was weak. The ISO 9000:2000 series places emphasis on continual improvement of the quality management system, which in turn leads to improvement in results in products and processes. This is an important step forward.

The inevitable question is this: what's the difference between ISO 9001 and national quality awards such as the Malcolm Baldrige National Quality Award and the European Quality Award?

ISO 9001 provides a structure of activities for a quality system and requires (1) objective evidence on every requirement, (2) up-to-date documentation, and (3) periodic audits to ensure continuous compliance. Certification to ISO 9001 furnishes assurance to customers that the organization has an adequate quality system. This assurance is essential for facilitating trade among countries. Thus, ISO 9001 emphasizes quality systems.

Baldrige supplies criteria for excellent systems and evidence of product quality superiority in the eyes of the customer; Baldrige is not a set of minimum standard practices. The emphasis in Baldrige is on superior product results and customer satisfaction. Baldrige provides criteria to identify those few organizations that achieve the highest level of quality and business effectiveness compared with competition.

ISO 9001 serves a different purpose than a national quality award, and it is narrower in scope. ISO 9004 covers a wider scope and greater depth than ISO 9001 and thus approaches the criteria of a national quality award. ISO 9004 thus goes beyond ISO 9001 to help organizations build on the ISO 9001 standards and start on the road to excellence that can lead to a national quality award.

On behalf of the quality profession, I want to express my gratitude to the brigade of people and their years of work on the past and current development of the ISO 9000 series. These creators of ISO 9000 did the work in addition to their regular jobs—it was an "add-on." They were still fully responsible for quality activities in their organizations. Also, thank you to the authors of this handbook, whose writings supplement the ISO standards and help us to implement ISO 9000.

The bottom line is this: achieve ISO 9001 certification but don't stop. Use ISO 9004 to become superior to competition and follow a dart-straight road to a regional or national quality award.

Frank M. Gryna
Distinguished Professor of
Industrial Engineering Emeritus,
Bradley University

Introduction

There has been tremendous worldwide growth in the use of quality management systems since the initial edition of the ISO 9001 standard was issued in 1987. Accompanying this trend is the growth of third-party certification of these systems. Much of this growth is no doubt due to the increasingly global nature of the world economy. Organizations on one continent now must rely on the quality of the products and services produced in another region of the world. Even very small organizations are becoming involved in the worldwide economy. The need for confidence in the quality of products from around the world has led consumers and businesses to seek assurance that the organizations producing those products have a management system that will ensure conformity to customer requirements. The ISO 9000 standards have successfully provided a basis for confidence that organizations have effective quality management systems.

In a very pragmatic way, the quality system has to be built to meet the needs of customers, executive leaders, and the organization's culture. Many organizations implement ISO 9001:1994 by simply documenting what they are doing without having a positive influence on the organization. In measurement theory there is a concept that you can't measure something without changing it. A similar principle applies to the management systems of an organization. Any change in one part of the system will ultimately have impact on other areas. This handbook deals with the fact that in building the quality system and fitting it into the culture of the organization, the organization will change. The challenge is to implement a system that meets requirements and achieves positive change for the organization.

But having a quality management system that can meet requirements is only part of the challenge organizations face. They must also address other needs. Customers are constantly demanding more at a lower price. Customer requirements are changing at a rate not contemplated a few years ago. These realities present a huge dilemma for many organizations. They are confused. "How," they ask, "can I comply with all these quality management system requirements and still remain competitive?" A key purpose of this handbook is to help organizations resolve this dilemma.

PURPOSE OF THE HANDBOOK

This handbook is intended as an easy-to-use reference source for those designing, implementing, and improving quality management systems.

- It describes the fundamentals of quality management and provides an easy-to-use reference for implementing quality management concepts
- It explains how to implement an effective quality management system using ISO 9001
- It is a quick reference to answer implementation questions that a practitioner or manager would likely have during an ISO 9001 implementation
- It serves as a guide for those implementing changes from the 1994 edition
- It provides ideas and describes how to go beyond ISO 9001 to create a quality management system that is both effective and efficient in addressing the needs of all stakeholders
- It describes the use of the performance improvement guidance of ISO 9004 and the use of the eight quality management principles
- It is a quick reference for those who seek to continually improve their quality management system
- It also contains sector-specific chapters that address the implementation and use of ISO in a variety of business sectors and for small and medium-size enterprises

HOW TO USE THIS HANDBOOK

The handbook is divided into nine sections. Sections 1 and 2 focus on the fundamental concepts of the quality management system and the basics of the ISO 9000 family. These sections provide useful background and are an excellent reference on the basics of quality management.

Section 3 discusses basic requirements for the quality management system and its documentation. Section 4 addresses topics related to management responsibility. Sections 5, 6, and 7 cover the core requirements found in clauses five through eight of ISO 9001. The chapters in these sections provide information on meeting the requirements of ISO 9001 and also include ideas and examples of implementation methods. Guidance for using ISO 9004:2000 to focus the quality management system on performance improvement is also included.

Section 8 discusses the application of the ISO 9000 family to achieve customer requirements and demonstrate conformance of the quality management system, and it provides ideas for efficiently achieving those objectives.

Section 9 discusses various sector applications.

The appendixes provide supplementary material including the exact text of ISO 9000, ISO 9001, and ISO 9004 and four implementation and support packages for ISO 9001. There are also useful listings of registrars, acronyms, the current and future ISO 9000 family, sources of more information, a list of contributing authors with their biographies, and a bibliography. Also in the appendixes is a copy of ISO 11462, which provides useful guidance on the systematic implementation of statistical process control. The appendixes alone have a value greater than the price of this handbook.

The handbook is intended for three categories of users:

• Those already compliant with ISO 9001:1994, ISO 9002:1994, or ISO 9003:1994 will find the discussion in chapter 8 of what is different in ISO 9001:2000 with respect to the 1994 standard to be their best starting point. A review of the two-phase revision process in chapter 7 would also provide background. It may be useful to review the process approach discussed in detail in chapter 2 and in the guideline document provided as Appendix J on the accompanying CD. A review of chapter 11, "The Quality Management System," and chapter 12, "Documenting the Quality Management System," is critical to understanding the streamlined documentation requirements of ISO 9001:2000. It is also important that those making the transition from the 1994 standards read chapter 9, on "Quality Management System Application (Clause 1.2)," and understand any impact the elimination of ISO 9002 and ISO 9003 will have on their system. The other chapters can be used as reference as the organization moves through the transition process to the new standard.

• For readers who are new to ISO 9001 and desire to achieve compliance, it would be best to start with a thorough reading of chapter 1, "Why Use the ISO 9000 Family?" Then read Section 1, "Fundamentals of Quality Management." This should include a careful study of the process approach, discussed in detail in chapter 2 and in the guideline document provided as Appendix J. Chapter 11, "The Quality Management System," and chapter 12, "Documenting the Quality Management System," should then be studied in detail. Use the rest of the handbook as a reference guide as you move through the process of gap analysis, system design, implementation, audit, and certification.

• Readers who want to develop a quality management system focused on achieving business excellence should start with a careful study of Section 1, "Fundamentals of Quality Management." You will find the discussion of the process approach in chapter 2 and in the guideline document provided as Appendix J useful. Since measurement is one key to achieving improvement and quality excellence, you should read chapter 36, "Process Analysis," and chapter 28, "Statistical Procedures Useful for Implementation of ISO 9001:2000." You will also find chapter 12, "Documenting the Quality Management System," surprisingly useful as a guide in tying the documentation of the system to improvement.

Of course all users will find the inclusion on the CD of ANSI/ISO/ASQ Q9000, Q9001, and Q9004 to be very useful and convenient. The new ISO 9000 series provides a powerful set of tools to help organizations better compete in the increasingly complex and competitive global marketplace. ISO 9000 contains a synopsis of the fundamentals of quality management systems and the "dictionary of quality terms." The new ISO 9001:2000 provides far more flexibility than did the 1994 version. ISO 9004:2000 provides updated guidance for developing a quality management system that is focused on improving the organization's performance.

The final result of the creation of the new ISO 9000 family was intended to be standards that will better meet the needs of the broad spectrum of users worldwide. This handbook's editors were personally involved in the process of creating these standards. Authors contributing to the handbook were selected based on their contributions to the writing of the new standards and/or their expertise in topics covered herein. The intention in creating this handbook was to provide users and potential users of the ISO 9000 family of standards with the best and most up-to-date thinking on the many dimensions of quality management from the minds of the people who are at the forefront of the quality profession.

ABOUT THE EDITORS

Charles A. Cianfrani is one of the U.S. expert representatives to ISO/TC 176/SC2/WG18, the working group that wrote ISO 9001:2000 and 9004:2000. He also directly participated in writing ISO 9001:1994. He is managing director of the Customer-Focused Quality Group at ARBOR, in Media, Pennsylvania, and has led implementation of ISO 9001–compliant processes on five continents. He is a fellow of ASQ, holds BS, MS, and MBA degrees, and is an ASQ CQE, CRE, and CQA, as well as a RAB-certified auditor. He is coauthor of the book *ISO 9001:2000 Explained* and of *ISO 9001:2000, An Audio Workshop and Master Slide Presentation*, both published by ASQ. He is also a founder of ISOize.com, a training consortium dedicated to providing ISO 9000 training, primarily over the Web. His Web-based course on ISO 9001:2000 is available through ASQ. (Reach him at cianfranic@aol.com.)

Joseph J. Tsiakals is one of the U.S. expert representatives to ISO/TC 176/SC2/WG18, the working group that wrote ISO 9001:2000 and 9004:2000. He previously was the lead U.S. expert representative for the development of ISO 9001:1994. He is one of the founding members of the ISO Medical Device Quality Committee and has more than 25 years of experience in quality management and engineering. He has been a member of the board of examiners of the Malcolm Baldrige National Quality Award, a judge for the Illinois Quality Award, a member of the board of directors of RAB, and a member of the board of directors for the Joint ANSI/RAB National Accreditation Program. He is senior director of corporate quality for Amgen, Inc. He is coauthor of the book *ISO 9001:2000 Explained*, published by ASQ. (Reach him at tsiakals@amgen.com.)

John E. "Jack" West is chairman of the U.S. Technical Advisory Group for ISO/TC 176 and lead U.S. delegate to the International Organization for Standardization committee responsible for the ISO 9000 family of quality management standards. In ISO/TC 176, Jack was a key player in the development of the eight quality management principles, serving as convener of the working group responsible for that project. He is a quality excellence business consultant with more than 30 years of experience in various industries around the world. He is also a member of the board of directors of the Registrar Accreditation Board (RAB). Jack has authored many papers and articles. He is coauthor of the book *ISO 9001:2000 Explained* and of *ISO 9001:2000, An Audio Workshop and Master Slide Presentation*, both published by the American Society for Quality (ASQ). (Reach him at jwest92144@aol.com.)

ABOUT THE CONTRIBUTING AUTHORS

A contributing author has written each chapter. The authors come from a variety of backgrounds, countries, cultures, and experiences. They come from different sectors of the world economy. Each has his or her own opinions regarding quality, quality management systems, and quality management systems standards. In some cases the opinion of one author may be different from that of another. The editors have not attempted to resolve these differences. In fact, differences in application and experience add to the richness of the handbook. Contributing authors' biographies are provided in Appendix E.

Section 1

The Fundamentals of Quality Management

Introduction

Joseph J. Tsiakals
Amgen, Thousand Oaks, California

Quality management is the process of establishing policy and objectives with regard to quality and then directing and controlling the activities necessary to achieve those objectives. The ISO 9000 series of standards describes in generic terms the essential elements of quality management as applied to any type of product (the ISO definition of product includes hardware, software, services, processed materials, or any combination thereof). This first section of the handbook provides the fundamental concepts of quality management.

Chapter 1, "Why Use the ISO 9000 Family?" sets the stage. William Houser and Russ Bloom explain the various reasons for an organization to use the ISO 9000-2000 series. They lead the reader through a process for establishing the needs and benefits necessary to provide direction and give support for a successful ISO 9000 implementation. They then explain how to use the standard as a business template to guide the implementation effort, making sure that each business system associated with a requirement of the standard is doing what is necessary. To a great extent this effort requires gaining understanding of your business through a process approach. This leads to chapter 2, "The Process Approach to Quality Management Systems," where Jeff Hooper explains the most significant change occurring in this revision, the restructuring of the core standards from a traditional lifecycle model to that of a process model. Why and what this process approach means is described.

In chapter 3, "The ISO 9000 Family," Klaus Petrick describes the set of standards that comprise the ISO 9000 family. With this revision there is a significant restructuring and simplification of these standards. Experienced users of these standards as well as those being newly introduced to ISO 9000 will find useful explanations about the extent and applications of these standards. Included are the definitions of quality, management, and systems and their use in ISO 9000. ISO 9000 fundamentals and the interrelationships among principles, definitions, and the core standards are explained.

Where does the ISO 9000 series fit within the array of approaches, techniques, and programs for achieving quality? In chapter 4, "The Hierarchy of Quality," Joseph Tsiakals presents the concept of a quality hierarchy to explain how the various approaches and techniques can fit together. The distinguishing characteristics are described that differentiate between the role played by a quality management systems approach and the various quality models dealing with performance excellence such as Six Sigma programs and "business excellence" award programs including the Malcolm Baldrige National Quality Award program in the United States and related quality award programs used in Europe and Asia. The quality hierarchy helps to explain the relationship between ISO 9001:2000 and ISO 9004:2000 and the rationale behind these two compatible standards.

With the 2000 revision of the ISO 9000 series there is now a clear articulation of the philosophy behind successful quality programs. Since the first revision of the standards was issued in 1994 the ISO Quality Management Committee, ISO Technical Committee 176, developed a set of eight quality management principles that describe the core values upon which these standards rest. In chapter 5, "Quality Management Principles," Jack West describes these principles and how they form the basis for the entire quality management system. As the underlying values, these principles serve as the guiding light for understanding to what end quality policy and objectives are set. These quality principles are described and explained as the primary links among the various levels of the quality hierarchy described in chapter 4.

This section ranges from an emphasis on a business success model, to the reasoning behind the process approach, to the description of the ISO 9000 family of standards, to the global view of the quality hierarchy, and finally to the underlying philosophy given by the eight principles. Section 1 gives a broad perspective that serves as a backdrop for the remainder of this handbook.

Chapter 1

Why Use the ISO 9000 Family?

William F. Houser
Integrated Productivity and Quality Systems, Spring, Texas

Russ Bloom
Smithers Quality Assessments, Akron, Ohio

The results of a study published in *Quality Progress* showed that the four most common reasons for using the ISO 9000 family of quality standards were, in order of perceived importance:

1. Customer or marketing demands.
2. Needed improvement in processes or systems.
3. Desire for global deployment.
4. Company not focused.

This same study showed that fully 85 percent of those using the ISO 9000 family of standards did so because customers or marketing suggested or demanded their use. Therefore, for most organizations the key question has seemed to be "is ISO required by our customers?" If the answer was yes, they proceeded (often reluctantly) with development and implementation. On the other hand, many organizations have avoided ISO when the answer was "no, customers don't currently require ISO."

At first glance, responding to customer demands to implement an ISO 9000–based quality system appears defensive in nature. In other words, implementing an ISO 9000 for this reason is meant to defend or maintain the status quo—the current customer position. There is nothing inherent in bowing to customer demands to become certified to ISO 9000 that will cause the gain of new business or growth of the organization. However, many companies that have implemented ISO 9000–based quality systems to meet customer requirements have found, to their delight, that they have been able to leverage additional business as a result of their certification. This additional business often flows their way from competitors unwilling or unable to meet the ISO requirements.

Taking a more offensive market posture, companies have implemented an ISO 9000–based quality system to differentiate their products or services and grow their business both globally and domestically. For example, Newport News Shipbuilding had been building aircraft carriers and submarines for the U.S. Navy and wanted to gain a foothold in global commercial shipbuilding, so they became ISO certified. After doing so, they received the first United States commercial shipbuilding order from a foreign company in 40 years.

On the domestic scene, two Packaging Corporation of America corrugated container plants found that being certified added to their credibility and helped their sales efforts considerably. They reported that customer requirements for audits before being allowed to quote were sometimes waived based on the ISO 9000 certification. They also reported that, all things being equal, customers respected the certification enough to routinely award them business. Additionally, as seen in Figure 1.1, they enjoyed significant operational improvements as a result of their ISO 9000 implementation.

While customer or marketing demands may provide the original impetus for certification, external influences do little to encourage an organization to produce anything other than the minimum system necessary to get by the registrars and obtain certification. Consequently, many organizations pursuing ISO 9000 strictly because it is demanded of them do not realize the full potential customer satisfaction and efficiency of operation benefits that an ISO 9000–based quality system can provide if a more focused and improvement-oriented approach to development and implementation is employed.

A key to getting significant internal operational benefits from an ISO 9000 development and implementation is establishing what improvements need to be achieved and targeting to make those improvements. A second key is to use the ISO 9000 family of quality standards as a template to compare against current system results, not just as a set of requirements. Organizations following this approach have achieved significant improvements, such as those realized by the Ekco aluminum mill in Clayton, New Jersey, and illustrated in Figure 1.2.

Container Plant Example 1
Waste reduced 34%.
Returns down 18%.
Productivity improved 46%.
Late delivery reduced 40%.
Volume up 40%.

Container Plant Example 2
Waste reduced 22%.
Cost of quality down 33.5%.
Productivity improved 29.7%.
OSHA recordables down 70.8%.

Figure 1.1   Results achieved in container plants.

Aluminum Rolling Mill Results
1. Internal rejects down 76%.
2. Run hours up 16 hours/month.
3. Returns down 37.5%.
4. On-time delivery improved 44%.

Figure 1.2   Results achieved in an aluminum rolling mill.

It has often been said, "If you don't know where you're going, you won't know when you get there." For those organizations wanting and needing to get the most from their ISO implementation, it is critical to focus early on where they are going and what needs to be accomplished in the process. In order to establish this focus, the needs and benefits to be derived from the ISO 9000 implementation must be identified. This step ensures that the necessary support is provided to sustain development and implementation. This support is developed by making certain that everyone sees what is in it for them if the organization becomes certified.

ESTABLISH NEEDS AND BENEFITS

The importance of precisely establishing the organization's needs and benefits to the organization of an ISO-based quality system cannot be overemphasized. This step accomplishes a couple of very important objectives: First, establishing the needs and benefits provides focus for the development and implementation effort. Second, it garners the support necessary to sustain such an effort. If there isn't support that starts with the leadership and flows throughout the organization, the entire ISO 9000 implementation is doomed to failure. Therefore, a primary objective of establishing the needs and benefits is to generate the support needed to sustain the development and implementation effort.

In establishing the needs and benefits necessary to provide direction and gain the support for a successful ISO 9000 implementation, the *push–pull exercise* has proven very valuable. The push–pull exercise consists of identifying the forces *pushing* and *pulling* the organization toward ISO. The pressures *pushing* the organization toward certification are essentially negative in nature, while the pressures *pulling* toward certification are essentially positive in nature. The push–pull exercise can be used with any group and should be used across the organization.

Identifying the pressures for certification is the first step in establishing the needs and benefits. In doing so, everyone should recognize the problems that will be faced if the organization doesn't implement a certifiable ISO 9000 quality system. In other words, what is *pushing* the organization toward certification?

A facilitator typically poses the following question to the management team and steering committee:

"What is pushing us to develop and implement a certifiable quality system?" Or, in other words, "what will happen to us if we don't implement the quality system?"

| **Forces Acting** | |
Pushing	Pulling
• Customer pressure • Lost business if competitors do it • Bosses pressuring • Etc.	• Lower scrap • Higher quality • Gain business • Advertising potential • Lower costs • Recognition • Etc.

Figure 1.3   Examples of forces acting on the organization.

The responses are solicited in a round-robin fashion so that everyone participates. As illustrated in Figure 1.3, responses are extracted and the facilitator places them on the left side of the push–pull exercise to indicate those forces that are pushing the organization toward ISO 9000.

From a distinctly different perspective, the forces pulling the organization toward implementing a certifiable quality system should also be identified. In other words, what benefits will accrue to the organization, to different functions within the organization, and to individuals within the organization by implementing an improvement-based and certifiable ISO 9000–based quality system?

This is the second question that the facilitator poses to the group:

"What is pulling us toward developing and implementing a certifiable quality system?" Or, in other words, "what will the implementation do for the business, my function, and me?"

The facilitator typically poses this question to the management team and steering committee, and again the responses are solicited in round-robin fashion so that everyone participates. Answering this second question always should and usually does take much longer than answering the first question. The answers to the second question identify and provide the motivation to sustain the support and involvement necessary to complete an ISO 9000 installation. As illustrated in Figure 1.3, as the responses are extracted, the facilitator places them on the right side of the push–pull exercise to show those positive forces that are pulling the organization toward ISO 9000.

While conducting this exercise, the participants should be closely observed, as their participation and answers to the questions will reveal if any participants are hesitant in their support of the development and implementation of the quality system. Where hesitancy is evident, separate discussions as to the benefits may be warranted.

Specific and meaningful forces pulling the organization should be sought. These can be forces that affect the entire organization, a particular function, or an individual. Forces identified at the organizational level tend to be more general than those at the individual level, and those affecting the individual are usually the most specific and powerful. These more specific forces also can provide planning information.

For example, department managers in a PACTIV plant in Plattsburgh, New York, that makes paper plates and other molded fiber products agreed that one of the forces pulling them toward ISO 9000 was the prospect of fewer nighttime phone calls to solve problems. Establishing fewer nighttime phone calls as one of the goals helped gain and maintain the support of the department managers. From a planning perspective, this goal meant the work instructions needed to go beyond simply explaining how to operate the equipment and make the necessary inspections and tests. The work instructions also needed to contain troubleshooting information to guide the night crews in solving problems themselves. Because this goal was pursued faithfully, by the time of certification all the managers agreed that nighttime phone calls had dropped dramatically, and because problems were solved more quickly, customer complaints dropped by more than 60 percent.

There are three primary end products of the push–pull exercise:

1. A management team that can see what is in it for the organization, for their functions, and for them to pursue ISO 9000.

2. A management team that is consequently motivated to support the ISO 9000 development and implementation.

3. A set of goals to assist in planning the quality system development for use in measuring the success of the installation.

The push–pull exercise should be a "live" document. In other words, the push–pull exercise should remain visible throughout the ISO 9000 installation, and as the design and implementation progress, the push-pull exercise should be updated to reflect additional forces pushing and pulling the organization toward certification. Figure 1.4 shows the organizational benefits derived from ISO implementation by two Tenneco plastics packaging plants that started the process with the push-pull exercise.

Plastics Packaging Plant Example 1
1. Credits down 36%.
2. Scrap down over 30%.
3. Stopped routine resin contamination.

Plastics Packaging Plant Example 2
1. Reduced extruder color to clear changeover scrap by 4,000 lbs.
2. Improved pallets and packaging saved $100K annually.

Figure 1.4 Results achieved in a plastics packaging plant.

USE THE ISO STANDARD AS A BUSINESS "TEMPLATE"

Having established the goals to be attained and the necessary motivation to sustain the installation, the second key to a successful improvement-based ISO implementation is to use the standard as a template to guide the improvement effort.

Using ISO 9001 as a business template requires making sure that each business system associated with a requirement of the standard is doing what is necessary. In other words, the design and implementation team needs to check the adequacy of each business system by asking the following questions:

- Does the current system meet the business needs?
- Does the current system meet the quality needs?
- Does the current system meet the cost needs?
- Does the current system meet the customer needs?
- Does the current system meet these needs each and every time?

A yes to each of these questions means that the systems meet the business, quality, cost, and customer needs each and every time. On the other hand, a no to some or all of the questions means that current business systems do not meet the business, quality, cost, or customer needs each and every time. Figure 1.5 graphically represents the steps for using the ISO standard as a business template.

If any of the systems don't meet the business, quality, cost, and customer needs each and every time, they have to be modified or redesigned to do so. Only after making certain all business needs are being met is this question asked: do these systems meet the quality system standard requirements?

It is important to ask these questions in this order, because experience has shown that systems meeting business needs will invariably meet ISO needs. But the reverse is not always true. It is very easy to fall into the trap of designing systems that meet ISO 9000 requirements but make the business noncompetitive. *The*

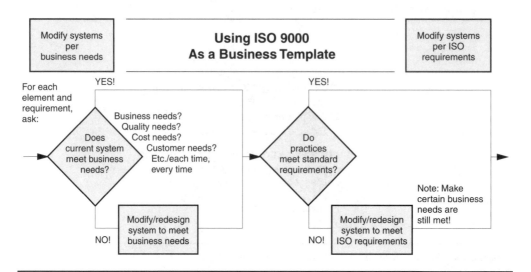

Figure 1.5   Using ISO 9000 as a business template.

Egg Carton Plant Results

1. Complaints down 39.2%.
2. Downtime reduced 32%.
3. Scrap down 32.3%.
4. Safety incident rate down 55.5%.

Figure 1.6   Results achieved in an egg carton plant.

---

implementation team must be careful not to design and implement systems that meet ISO needs but make the organization less competitive. Asking these two questions in this order will guard against this.

To save time and energy, current *practices* should be examined for all systems, whether documented or not, and compared against business *needs* first and the ISO 9000 *requirements* second. If current practices meet the needs of the business and ISO 9000, they should be documented in procedures and work instructions. However, those current practices not meeting either the business needs or those of ISO 9000 should be modified or completely changed prior to documenting in order to prevent needless rewrites and undue frustration.

Process-mapping each business system and production process is the logical first step in optimizing and documenting current practices. A high-level business process map can be used to help gain consensus regarding which individual business systems and processes cause the most quality, delivery, and cost problems, with the objective being to develop a list, in priority order, of those individual business systems and processes needing improvement, the type of improvement needed, and the beneficial impact on the operation when these improvements are made. By following this process, the PACTIV fiber egg carton producer in Macon, Georgia, achieved the results outlined in Figure 1.6.

THE AUDITOR'S REACTION

While a certification audit primarily focuses on conformance to the ISO 9000 requirements, auditors appreciate those systems that support the objectives of the organization because rational quality systems will be maintained and will continuously improve. Also, part of the audit charter is to assess the effectiveness of the quality system, and having established why the organization has implemented the quality management system makes measuring effectiveness more meaningful.

Common traits of these improvement-based ISO 9000 systems include the following:

- There is companywide enthusiasm
- Certification is viewed as validation
- The ISO system is not static but is changing and evolving
- Objectives are defined with action plans and the results monitored and recorded
- The auditors are considered as value-added partners
- The quality systems hold up to surveillance audits

SUMMARY

The difference in the impact on the organization between a compliance-based and an improvement-based ISO 9000 quality system is dramatic. The compliance-based quality system is typically an expense with little gain, while the improvement-based system is an investment yielding large returns.

Significantly, we find no more work involved in developing an improvement-based system than in installing a compliance-based quality system. There is, however, a significant difference in the *thinking* that goes into the development. A successful improvement-based quality system will never be developed unless the ISO 9000 standard is used as a thought-provoking business template.

The ideal time to rethink your business is during ISO 9000 quality system development.

Chapter 2

The Process Approach to Quality Management Systems

Jeff Hooper
Managing Vice President, Information Services,
Lucent Technologies, Warren, New Jersey

One of the most important aspects of the year 2000 revisions of ISO 9001 and ISO 9004 was the adoption of the *process approach* to quality management systems. A strong consensus for adopting the process approach formed very early in the year 2000 revision cycle. This decision had a great effect on the structure of the standards and significantly contributed to achieving many of the revision objectives. Whereas the 1994 versions of ISO 9001 and ISO 9004 contained requirements and guidance at the procedural level, with the requirements and guidance grouped into elements, the year 2000 revisions provide the guidance and requirements at the process level. Putting the guidance and requirements at the process level provides a much more generic structure, readily applicable to all sectors and sizes of organization, while at the same time allowing the requirements to be stated in language more familiar to line managers and less encumbered by quality jargon.

The new ISO Q9001:2000 and ISO 9004:2000 standards promote the adoption of a process approach when developing, implementing, and improving a quality management system (QMS). ISO 9001:2000 focuses on improving the effectiveness of a quality management system to enhance customer satisfaction by meeting customer requirements, while ISO 9004:2000 focuses on improving the effectiveness and efficiency of a quality management system to enhance interested party satisfaction by meeting interested party requirements. The common structure of these two standards (Figure 2.1) is based on the process approach.

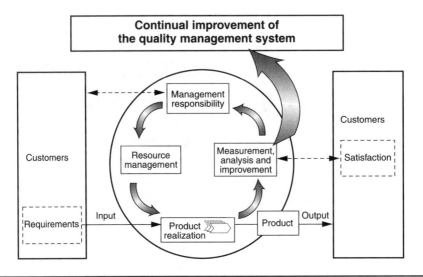

Figure 2.1 Model of a process–based quality management system.

UNDERSTANDING THE PROCESS APPROACH

The process approach is one of the eight quality management principles upon which the entire ISO 9000 series of standards is based. This quality management principle is stated as follows:

> Process Approach: *a desired result is achieved more efficiently when activities and related resources are managed as a* process, *where* process *is defined in ISO 9000:2000 clause 3.4.1 as: a set of interrelated or interacting activities which transforms inputs into outputs.*

Note 1: Inputs to a process are generally outputs of other processes.

Note 2: Processes in an organization (3.3.1) are generally planned and carried out under controlled conditions to add value.

From the principle and process definition we can see that the process approach is a powerful way of organizing and managing how work activities create value. Whereas a more traditional structure organizes and manages work activities vertically by function, with quality problems frequently occurring at the boundaries of the functional departments, the process approach organizes and manages work horizontally the way work activities create customer value. The approach directly links process inputs that come from suppliers, to the value-adding activities of the members of the organization, to the outputs of the process that go to customers. This horizontal linkage between suppliers and customers is an excellent way to manage and continually improve the effectiveness, the amount of value created for the customers, and the efficiency (the amount of resources consumed) of the process. Figure 2.2 shows these relationships.

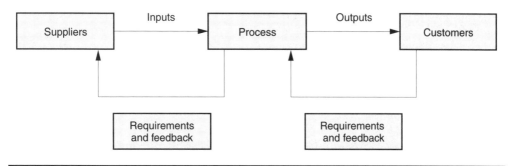

Figure 2.2   Representation of a process showing the relationships between the suppliers and customers of the process.

PROCESS MANAGEMENT AND IMPROVEMENT: A METHODOLOGY

Once the processes needed for the quality management system and their sequences and interactions have been identified (see Figure 2.1), it is necessary to establish management responsibilities and accountabilities for the performance of these processes. There are many methodologies available for managing and improving processes, but all these methodologies share some simple basic elements. In this section we will define a simple process management and improvement methodology organized in a series of steps.

Step 1: Establish the Responsibilities for Managing the Process.

- It is critical to have an overall process manager or process owner with end-to-end responsibility and accountability for all aspects of process performance. The process manager needs to understand the process from end to end and have the authority to effect changes in any part of the process.
- The process manager is responsible for forming the process management team, which includes representatives from each major part of the process.
- The process manager is responsible for ensuring that the process operates in a controlled state of predictable performance.
- The process manager is responsible for establishing process performance measures that adequately characterize the efficiency and effectiveness of the process in meeting the needs of all customers and other interested parties.
- The process manager is responsible for ensuring that all aspects of process management and improvement are performed, including necessary documentation of the process, tracking of process performance, and securing and allocating process resources.

Step 2: Define the Process

- The process manager and the process management team need to carefully define the process so that everyone working within the process has a shared understanding of how the process operates. How much process documentation is required depends on the stability and education of the workforce, the complexity of the process, and the criticality of the process, and so on.

- All the process inputs and outputs are identified along with the suppliers and customers of the process. Suppliers and customers of a process may be internal or external to the organization.

- Process steps and process flows are identified. Many quality tools are available to support these activities such as block diagrams, flowcharts, and so forth.

Step 3: Identify Customer Requirements

- Carefully gather, analyze, and document customer needs, including how they use the outputs of the process. Communicate frequently with customers to understand needs from their viewpoint.

- To the extent possible, define measurable customer needs and rank them in their order of importance.

- Directly validate needs and requirements with the customers.

Step 4: Establish Measures of Process Performance

- Translate customer needs and requirements into measures of process performance. This is one of the most important and difficult steps in process management.

- Process performance measures should include customer satisfaction, in-process measures, and measures of supplier performance.

- Process performance measures should relate to all important customer needs. For example, customer needs related to on-time performance, defect or error rates, tolerance intervals, product recyclability, worker health and safety, and so on. For this reason the process approach is one of the strongest approaches for integrating management system standards since each process must be managed and improved simultaneously for all process performance measures.

- Directly linking process performance measures with customer needs is one of the most powerful aspects of process management.

Step 5: Compare Process Performance with Customer Requirements

- Use the process performance measures to ensure that your process is operating in a stable and predictable manner.

- Compare the process performance measures with the needs and requirements of the customers.

- There are many statistical tools for analyzing process measurement data to help quantify process performance.
- Gaps in process performance versus customer needs identify critical process improvement opportunities.

These first five steps provide a basic methodology for process management. But the responsibilities of the process manager and the process management team do not end there. A significant benefit of process management is its natural fit with process improvement. Once process performance has been compared with customer requirements, process improvement is the natural next step.

Step 6: Identify Process Improvement Opportunities

- Gaps in process performance versus customer needs provide critical process improvement opportunities.
- Analysis of process performance measures provides improvement opportunities related to sources of errors and defects, process simplification opportunities, process bottlenecks, lack of adequate process controls, and so on.
- Both process effectiveness and efficiency can improve as a result of process improvement activities.
- Many process analysis tools exist to identify process improvement opportunities.

Once process improvement opportunities have been identified, any of the many quality improvement methods can be used to improve process performance. These quality improvement methods fit naturally into step 7 of the process management and improvement methodology. One quality improvement method which can be used at this step is the plan–do–check–act (PDCA) cycle.

Step 7: Improve Process Performance

- Select the process improvement opportunity(ies) to pursue. This selection should take into account the criticality of certain improvement needs, the difficulty of improvement opportunities, the resources and expertise available, and so forth.
- Establish quality improvement teams to pursue specific improvement opportunities. These quality improvement teams are established by the process manager and the process management team. The quality improvement teams report to the process manager or the process management team, and are typically disbanded once their improvement project is completed. The quality improvement teams complete the following activities.
- Clarify the improvement opportunity problem statement, schedule, and budget.
- Determine the root causes of the problem(s).
- Develop and implement countermeasures to reduce or eliminate the occurrence of the root causes.

- Stabilize the process at the new level of performance.
- Return to step 6 or step 7.

THE PROCESS APPROACH: SUPPORT FOR THE SYSTEM APPROACH TO MANAGEMENT

The process approach is an important part of the *system approach* to management. In this section we briefly explore this relationship.

The system approach to management is a quality management principle that states: identifying, understanding, and managing interrelated processes as a system contributes to the organization's effectiveness and efficiency in achieving its objectives.

Using the process approach, a quality management system is comprised of a number of interrelated processes. Figure 2.1 groups these processes into the categories of: management responsibility, resource management, product realization, measurement, analysis, and improvement. Each of these processes can be managed and improved using the process management and improvement methodology in section 2.2. But managing the interrelated processes as a system introduces additional improvement opportunites. First processes can be analyzed and improved together as mega-processes, increasing the opportunities for improvement. But we can also directly pursue the improvement of the entire quality management system using audit and self-assessment (using 9004:2000 or quality award criteria) results and the PDCA cycle as indicated in Figure 2.1. The multiple levels at which continual improvement occurs makes quality management systems based on the process approach a powerful way to manage organizations toward achieving performance excellence.

SUMMARY

There are many benefits to adopting the process approach when developing, implementing, and improving a quality management system. First, it is a very generic approach applicable to all sectors and sizes of organizations, while at the same time it is very straightforward to implement through defined methodologies such as process management and improvement. Second, the process approach directly manages the creation of value by managing horizontally across functional departments, thus reducing the quality problems that occur at department boundaries. Third, the process approach directly ties process measures of performance to customer needs and supplier performance, thereby focusing process performance on what is important to the customers. Fourth, the process approach is very strong model for continual improvement, with gaps between customer requirements and process performance providing an ideal starting place for improvement efforts. And finally, the process approach directly supports the systems approach to management, with improvements involving everyone and every level of the organization.

REFERENCES

AT&T. *Process Quality Management and Improvement Guidelines,* Issue 1.1. AT&T Quality Steering Committee, 1988.

AT&T. *PQMI: Tips, Experiences and Lessons Learned.* AT&T Quality Steering Committee, 1990.

Chapter 3
The ISO 9000 Family

Klaus Petrick
DQS German Management System Registrar, Berlin, Germany,

THE VARIOUS STANDARDS OF THE ISO 9000 FAMILY

The term *ISO 9000 family* was first used in ISO 9000-1:1994, that is, in the second edition of ISO 9000-1 (the first edition was ISO 9000-1:1987). The term was used as a collective term to address all international standards established by ISO Technical Committee 176 relating to quality management systems (QMSs) and technologies. Between 1994 and 2000 the "family" included the original nine basic standards: ISO 9000-1; ISO 9004-1; ISO 10011-1, 10011-2, and 11011-3 (guideline standards); ISO 9001, 9002, and 9003 (requirement standards); and ISO 8402 (the terminology standard). It also included several secondary standards that were added over the years to the basic ones as ISO 9000-*parts* (ISO 9000-2, 9000-3, 9000-4) and ISO 9004-*parts* (ISO 9004-2, 9004-3, and so on). The family was also extended to include the standards ISO 10005, 10006, 10007, 100012-1, 10012-2, 10013, and 10015 as well as the technical reports ISO/TR 10014 and 10017. Many users did not understand the logic or rationale behind all these standards, the less so since several of them were interrelated but were presented in completely different structures. The process for revision of the standards aimed at improving the content as well as the structure and maintaining consistency between ISO 9001 and 9004.

With the year 2000 revisions, the number of basic standards in the ISO 9000 family has been reduced. There are now four QMS "core" standards in the ISO 9000 family:

- ANSI/ISO/ASQ Q9000-2000, *Quality management systems—Fundamentals and vocabulary*
- ANSI/ISO/ASQ Q9001-2000, *Quality management systems—Requirements*
- ANSI/ISO/ASQ Q9004-2000, *Quality management systems—Guidelines for performance improvements*
- A future replacement for the auditing standards: ISO 19011, *Guidelines for quality and/or environmental management systems auditing*

Several of the secondary standards mentioned previously are now covered sufficiently by these core standards and will therefore be deleted as they come due for revision. The rest, especially those with 100xx numbers, are being revised and/or will stay as useful supporting documents with a status of international standard, technical report, or brochure-type document.

One of those brochures provides help for selection and use of the documents constituting the new ISO 9000 family. Another brochure contains the worldwide accepted eight quality management principles, which can be treated as the intellectual background of the ISO 9000 family. The third existing brochure-type document is the *Handbook*, which helps small and medium enterprises understand ISO 9001.

All documents in the ISO 9000 family are generic in nature—that is, they are applicable in the field of quality management (QM) for all categories of products and all industrial or economic sectors. It is also planned that the guideline standard on the application of ISO 9001 for IT software (ISO 9000-3) will in the future be dealt with by a committee other than ISO/TC 176 (that is, by ISO/IEC JTC 1/SC7). Sector documents applying ISO 9001 or 9004 for a specific industry or economic sector are usually prepared by ISO committees other than ISO/TC 176 or by committees or industry groups outside ISO. The only exception is ISO/TS 16949, a technical specification for the automotive industry that has been adopted by ISO/TC 176 as part of a pilot project. It would be an exception if any further sector-specific documents are developed by TC 176, and in any case, none of them would become part of the ISO 9000 family of generic QM standards.

It should be emphasized that the ISO 9000 family existing now is the result of tremendous work by many experts who cooperated during the past decade. All those people had as their aim to take advantage of experience with practical application and to adapt the original 1987 version of the ISO 9000 series of standards to modern developments in quality management. The work was done during two revision cycles that ended in 1994 and 2000 respectively. The revision work was driven by the so-called "Vision 2000: A Strategy for International Standards' Implementation in the Quality Arena During the 1990s." Vision 2000 was developed by a small group under the convenorship of Don Marquardt (United States), and it was adopted by ISO/TC 176 in 1992. Several aspects of Vision 2000 were implemented in the 1994 versions of the basic standards:

- Clarification that the ISO 9000 series relates to all kinds of product offerings for which four main categories can be distinguished: hardware, software, processed material, and service, as well as any combination thereof (it was later further clarified that a service is a product, that is, the result of activities/processes and not the activity itself, which is the process of providing a service).

- Clarification that the ISO 9000 series can be applied in all "industry/economic sectors," that is, by all groupings of suppliers whose product offerings meet similar customer needs or whose customers are closely interrelated in the marketplace. This and the previous clarification helped TC 176 express its clear strategy to avoid proliferation of product- and/or sector-related QMS standards. As proliferation cannot be avoided completely, TC 176 intends that sectors (that can justify the need for a sector document) use ISO 9001 unchanged in its entirety and that the number of additional QMS requirements is minimized.

- Clear distinction between QMS requirements and product (and related process) requirements.

- Flexibility of implementation.

- Strategic goals for the development of the standards of the ISO 9000 family: universal acceptance, current and forward compatibility (sufficient consistency among the existing standards and between the existing and revised standards), and forward flexibility (revised requirements acceptable for all sectors and product categories).

During the two revision cycles of the ISO 9000 standards, the Vision 2000 issues just cited were complemented by additional concepts and strategies:

- Use of the concept of "interested parties/stakeholders" of an organization

- Use of quality management principles, including adoption of the process approach

- Addressing organizations' self-assessment capabilities and striving for improving business performance as the basis for the new ISO 9004

- Enhancing compatibility with other management system fields and possibly achieving an integrated, single approach for the overall management system

THE IMPORTANCE OF TERMINOLOGY STANDARDS

A quotation from *The Analects* of Confucius (Book 13) is relevant:

Tzu-lu said, if the prince of Wei were waiting for you to come and administer the country for him, what would be your first measure? The Master said, It would certainly be to correct language. Tzu-lu said, Can I have heard aright? Surely what you say has nothing to do with the matter. Why should language be corrected? The Master said, Yu! How boorish you are! A gentleman, when things he does not understand are mentioned, should maintain an attitude of reserve. If language is incorrect, then what is said does not concord with what was meant; and if what is said does not concord with what was meant, what is to be done cannot be effected. If what is to be done cannot be effected, then rites and music will not flourish. If rites and music do not flourish, then mutilations and lesser punishments will go astray. And if mutilations and lesser punishments go astray, then the people have nowhere to put hand or foot.

Therefore the gentleman uses only such languages as is proper for speech, and only speaks of what it would be proper to carry into effect. The gentleman, in what he says, leaves nothing to mere chance.

As the standards of the ISO 9000 family are generic standards they should be understandable by people in all industrial and economic sectors, at all organizational levels having managerial, technical, or administrative tasks. That is a high demand that can be satisfied only by the use of clear generic concepts expressed in clear terms and definitions. The more generally applicable a terminology is meant to be, the more abstract the concepts used need to be. That demand conflicts with the wish of most people to invest only a minimum of time and effort in the study of terminology. But the abstraction is an important precondition for the necessary intellectual simplification of the very complex situations and problems encountered in practice. Learning, understanding, and practically applying a consistent QM terminology helps to facilitate successful communication within the organization and between organizations, nationally and internationally. It improves understanding and application of QM methods. It also serves to identify similar questions that arise in various practical situations and to simplify them. QM terminology should be based on a small number of basic concepts, should not cause contradictions with the common language, should avoid synonyms (several terms with one meaning), and must avoid homonyms (one term with different meanings). The narrower a technical field is, the better a high consistency in the specialist terminology can be achieved, especially if only one language is concerned. Quality management is a very wide field, and QM standardization has become a worldwide exercise where experts from many countries speaking various languages are involved. The composition of committees and working groups of TC 176 and the impact of member bodies' comments change considerably from meeting to meeting. Continuity of work is a problem. Therefore the terminology standard, ISO 9000:2000, is not an ideal result of terminology work, but progress can be identified compared with the "old" standard, ISO 8402:1994. It is hoped that the next generation of logically thinking people aim for and achieve full consistency, because the increasingly used IT software and IT hardware "think" absolutely logically.

SOME BASIC CONCEPTS

A concept can be considered a "unit of thought." Each concept is expressed by its term and its definition. To be understandable, definitions should be short and unambiguous. To achieve that, definitions should make use of terms for concepts already defined elsewhere.

The ISO 9000 vocabulary contains 85 concepts with their terms and definitions:

- Concepts relating to quality
- Concepts relating to management
- Concepts relating to organization
- Concepts relating to process and product
- Concepts relating to characteristics
- Concepts relating to conformity
- Concepts relating to document
- Concepts relating to examination

- Concepts relating to audit
- Concepts relating to quality assurance for measurement processes

The relationships between the concepts are illustrated by concept diagrams given in an annex of ISO 9000. The following discussion presents some basic concepts.

Quality

Different people usually attach very different meanings to the concept of *quality*, such as extent of fulfillment of expectations, product excellence, grade (category or rank given to requirements), fitness for purpose, or even management excellence. Fulfillment of the quality requirement (that is, for all characteristics) may be called *excellent quality*. If only some of the individual requirements for characteristics are fulfilled, the result may collectively be called *poor quality*. *Inherent characteristics* are those characteristics that are part of the product, process, or system, such as the diameter of a bolt or the waiting time at a call center. *Assigned characteristics* (for example, the price and the delivery time of a bolt) are not inherent characteristics. The definition of *quality* reflects a compromise of opinions and reads thus: "Ability of a complete set of realized inherent characteristics of a product, process, or system to fulfill requirements of customers and other interested parties."

Management, Management System, Quality Management System, Quality Management

The following concepts, along with their straightforward definitions, play a key role in the ISO 9000 family of standards:

- *Management:* coordinated activities to direct and control an organization.
- *Management system:* system to establish policy and objectives and to achieve those objectives.
- *Quality management system:* system to establish quality policy and quality objectives and to achieve those objectives.

Management is defined as an activity, but the term also may be used to refer to people; thus the latter meaning should be expressed using a clarifying qualifier, as in "top management." *Quality management* includes the establishment of quality policy and quality objectives, quality planning, quality control, quality assurance, and quality improvement (all these concepts are defined in ISO 9000). It should be mentioned here that ISO 9001:2000 and ISO 9004:2000 do not use the term *quality assurance* because in practice that term has had different meanings and because it is difficult to translate into other languages. It should also be mentioned that a definition of *quality improvement* is presented for the first time in an international standard. But the scope of ISO 9001:2000 makes it clear that the concept of quality assurance (that is, the provision of confidence in the quality capability by demonstration) is still an underlying concept of ISO 9001.

The former standard, ISO 8402, used the generic concept *entity* to describe the object of consideration. That term helped to define a concept in a general and more abstract way—that is, to make the concept applicable to all kinds of entities.

English-speaking practitioners were uncomfortable with the term *entity*, and it was replaced with "product, process, or system." Will the user of the new standard now understand that those three words should cover any object of consideration (for example, a person)?

Product

Product is defined very generically as the "result of a process." The term covers tangible products such as hardware and processed material, intangible products such as software and services, and all combinations thereof. It is useful to distinguish between products offered to customers and other products.

Test, Measurement, and Inspection

According to ISO/IEC Guide 2, *test* is defined as the determination of characteristics. The definition of *measurement* (taken from "VIM," the international vocabulary of basic and general terms in metrology) shows that measurement is a subconcept of test. Measurement is the determination of the values of a quantity (the latter being a specific category of characteristics). *Inspection*, according to ISO/IEC Guide 2, is the evaluation of conformity using measurement or test or gauging results.

A detailed discussion of the previous definitions is found in chapter 10.

QUALITY MANAGEMENT SYSTEMS AND OTHER MANAGEMENT SYSTEM FOCUSES

Positioning quality management within the overall management system of an organization is a difficult task and cannot be explained easily in words. The illustration in Figure 3.1 will help the reader understand better what is explained briefly in clause 3.11 of ISO 9000.

Figure 3.1 applies the simplest process model to a whole organization. Within the organization is a structure and a network of processes that transform inputs into outputs using resources. The outputs (that is, the results of the organization) are of interest to different parties who have their own needs, expectations, and requirements regarding the qualities, costs, and delivery times of the various outputs.

The quality management system focus of ISO 9001 is on the following:

- The achievement of offered products the quality of which satisfy customer needs, expectations, and requirements
- The achievement of confidence in the organization's ongoing quality capability to satisfy its customers

ISO 9001 requires that the organization implement a quality policy and quality objectives.

The quality management system focus of ISO 9004 is broader and can, if the organization decides, include the achievement of offered products and additional outputs (results) the quality of which satisfy additional interested parties. ISO 9004 provides guidance concerning the implementation of a broader quality policy and broader quality objectives. It also provides guidance for improving the

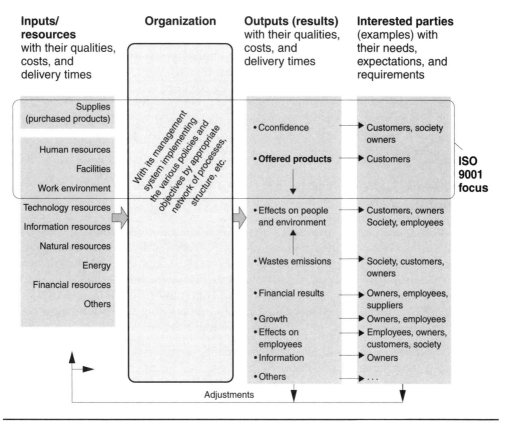

Figure 3.1   An organization's process model.

performance of the organization in achieving those objectives—more about this aspect later.

The environmental management system focus of ISO 14001 is on the following:

- The offered products, wastes, and emissions, and the effects of those outputs on the environment.

- The achievement of confidence in the organization's capability to satisfy the environment-related needs, expectations, and requirements of the relevant interested parties (for example, society, customers, owners). ISO 14001 requires that the organization implement an environmental policy and environmental objectives.

Similar considerations can be given to other management system focuses.

The foregoing explanation shows clearly that quality management (which fulfills the requirements of ISO 9001) and environmental management cannot be separated. Managing for satisfactory environmental quality of offered products is part of quality management as well as of environmental management. When realizing the environmental characteristics of the offered product, we have to indicate those characteristics as quality characteristics. The same conclusion can be drawn for occupational health and safety management because safety characteristics of offered products must be indicated as quality characteristics.

Figure 3.1 also shows that quality management does not automatically include cost management and delivery time management, although integration of all aspects is advisable. In addition, the figure illustrates the complexity of ISO 9004 and of total quality management (TQM), which aims to achieve high quality of all relevant results of the organization including the results of financial management. In the same way, excellence models aim at the excellence of the organization's overall performance.

ISO 9000 FUNDAMENTALS AND CONCEPTS IN RELATION TO QM PRINCIPLES

Quality management principles that were identified by ISO/TC 176 before embarking on the detailed revision of the ISO 9000 family of standards are reproduced in brief in the introduction to ISO 9000 as well as in ISO 9004. Those principles can be applied in management disciplines other than quality management. The principles and their influence on the contents of the basic standards—ISO 9000, 9001, and 9004—are reviewed in detail in chapter 5. The following discussion presents each principle in brief together with where it is reflected in ISO 9000.

1. *Customer focus.* Organizations depend on their customers and therefore should understand current and future customer needs, meet customer requirements, and strive to exceed customer expectations.

ISO 9000 clause 3.1 states that the main purpose of an organization's quality management system is to offer products that achieve customer satisfaction by fulfilling the customer's needs and expectations as expressed in requirements for the product characteristics. Furthermore, the customer wants to have confidence in the organization's capability to consistently fulfill requirements. Although each organization focuses on the customer, there are other interested parties—that is, parties that have an interest in or are affected by the organization's offered products or other results. The overall management system should assist the organization in achieving the optimal satisfaction of all interested parties. For example, society (government, societal groups) should be satisfied with the realized environmental characteristics of the product and with the effects of the organization's activity on the environment, and the owners should be satisfied with the financial result achieved by the organization.

2. *Leadership.* Leaders establish unity with regard to the purpose, direction, and internal environment of the organization. They create the environment in which people can become fully involved in achieving the organization's objectives.

Clause 3.6 of ISO 9000 presents those issues that must be driven within the quality management system by top management:

- Creation of an environment where people are fully involved
- Establishment of the quality policy and the quality objectives
- Customer focus and appropriate processes to fulfill customer requirements and objectives

- Establishment and maintenance of the quality management system and provision of resources
- Evaluation of achieved results and decision on necessary actions including those for quality improvement

Top management cannot delegate these responsibilities to other people in the organization. The organization cannot succeed without the engagement of top management.

3. *Involvement of people.* People at all levels are the essence of an organization, and their full involvement enables their abilities to be used for the organization's benefit.

The first point mentioned in the preceding list and taken from ISO 9000 clause 3.6 is most relevant here: top management's creation of an environment where people are fully involved.

4. *Process approach.* A desired result is achieved more efficiently when related resources and activities are managed as a process.

Clause 3.4 of ISO 9000 indicates that the process approach includes the systematic identification and management of the processes employed in the organization and particularly the interactions between such processes.

5. *System approach to management.* Identifying, understanding, and managing a system of interrelated processes for a given objective contributes to the effectiveness and efficiency of the organization.

Clause 3.3 of ISO 9000 describes the different steps for developing, implementing, and improving a quality management system. The model provided in Figure 1 of ISO 9000 helps the user understand the process and the system approach.

6. *Factual approach to decision making.* Effective decisions are based on the logical and intuitive analysis of data and information.

Clause 3.9 of ISO 9000 mentions various actions believed to continually and systematically enhance products and increase the effectiveness and efficiency of the processes used to produce and deliver them.

The principle is reflected in several of ISO 9000's clauses:

- Clause 3.5 on policy and objectives: achievement of quality objectives needs to be measurable.
- Clause 3.7 on documentation: provision of objective evidence.
- Clause 3.8 on evaluating the QMS: evaluation by auditing, reviewing, and self-assessment of activities and results in order to determine suitability, adequacy, effectiveness, and efficiency of the QMS and of the organization's performance.
- Clause 3.10 on role of statistical techniques: help to measure, describe, analyze, interpret, and model variability of data.

7. *Mutually beneficial supplier relationships.* Mutually beneficial relationships between the organization and its suppliers enhance the ability of both entities to create value.

This principle is addressed only indirectly in ISO 9000, as its Figure 1 and several clauses relate to all parties with an interest in the organization. The suppliers of the organization constitute one of those parties whose expectations and needs must be satisfied for mutual benefit.

RELATIONSHIP TO THE QUALITY HIERARCHY

As we have discussed, ISO 9004 provides guidance that may be used in a broader context than just meeting customer requirements. Indeed, it can be used to create a quality management system that focuses on all the interested parties or stakeholders of the organization. In chapter 4 we review the quality hierarchy concept. The ISO 9000 family forms a key part of that concept:

- ISO 9001 provides the baseline quality management system requirements. Its use can ensure that the quality management system is *effective* in meeting customer requirements.

- ISO 9004 not only provides a broader perspective but also focuses on *performance improvement*. It is appropriate guidance for organizations wanting to go beyond the minimum quality management system described in ISO 9001. In effect, it provides a linkage between the minimum requirements and the business excellence models given in the criteria of the European Foundation for Quality Management or the criteria for the U.S. Malcom Baldrige National Quality Award.

- ISO 9000 supports ISO 9001 and 9004 by describing the fundamentals of quality management systems and their relationship to other management systems. It also provides the concepts and vocabulary used in ISO 9001 and 9004.

Chapter 4

The Hierarchy of Quality

Joseph J. Tsiakals
Amgen, Thousand Oaks, California

What reader hasn't heard criticisms of ISO 9001?

- ISO 9000 does not ensure quality. If you specify garbage, you will get garbage.
- ISO 9000 is very expensive to implement, with questionable benefits.
- Instead of drafting useless documents for meeting standards, it is more important to analyze and improve the manufacturing process.
- We do Baldrige (the Malcolm Baldrige National Quality Award). ISO 9000 is the old paradigm of an internal, overlay quality program implying that quality costs money.
- ISO 9000's focus on conformity means that it doesn't address customer-driven quality.

Although there are grains of truth in each of the above misconceptions, these criticisms, some from supposedly informed experts, are all widely off the mark. They originate partially in the frustration that comes from unrealized or unrealistic expectations or from expectations that arise from different approaches.

From these and other criticisms, however, it became clear that a key motivation for the 2000 revision of the ISO 9000 series was to address the organizational need to ensure quality, provide for meeting customer needs and requirements, create efficient and low cost operations, and achieve marketplace success.

Paradoxically, in light of all the criticism, there are close to half a million organizations currently registered to ISO 9001. Each of these organizations has implemented a system and retains external auditors to obtain and maintain its registration. And the upward trend is continuing.

To understand why the ISO 9000 series of quality management standards has been so widely embraced, it's important to see the big picture. Only then does one understand the major driving force for change and the corresponding response of ISO Technical Committee 176 (ISO/TC 176) through development of an aligned pair of standards that are designed to be used together.

TWO MAJOR APPROACHES

The efforts of governments to lower trade barriers, along with a drive for international markets, tough competition, and customer pressures on suppliers have all resulted in great focus on quality. Many agree that quality serves as a major unifying principle of business. The many differing methods for achieving quality have coalesced into two main quality management approaches:

- *ISO 9001 quality management systems* (including ISO 9002 and ISO 9003), which focus on process management.
- *Performance excellence models,* which focus on results-oriented improvements. The various national or regional quality award programs such as the Baldrige Award, the Deming Prize, and the European Quality Award, along with efforts such as the Six Sigma process, best characterize the performance excellence models. ISO 9004:1994, as a guidance standard for quality management, also has had a focus on performance excellence. It uses ISO 9001 as the basic system and gives guidance on improving all aspects of the quality system, including achieving improved performance of the cost of quality and continual quality improvement.

Each of these two approaches, ISO 9001 and performance excellence, is legitimate. Organizations that embrace one of these approaches typically engage in many elements of the other approach. Both approaches, in fact, need to be embraced.

The real issues involve understanding the goals of each approach, the roles to be played by them in providing value to an organization and the ways in which they might be integrated into one cohesive quality system. Much of the confusion today arises because of the tendency of practitioners to promote one approach by emphasizing the differences and inadequacies of the other. Instead, it is better to embrace both approaches in a unified manner.

MASLOW'S HIERARCHY OF HUMAN NEEDS

A useful way to illustrate the relationships between ISO 9001 and performance excellence is to draw a parallel to a well-established model, namely Abraham Maslow's hierarchy of human needs (Figure 4.1).

Maslow first published his theory of human needs and incorporated it into leadership training for the U.S. Air Force during World War II. This theory attracted much interest as a basic structure for at least broadly understanding human motivation. Basically, the theory holds that individuals have a hierarchy of needs:

Figure 4.1   Maslow's hierarchy of human needs.

- Survival or basic needs
- Security or safety
- Love or belonging
- Status or esteem and self-realization or self-actualization.

The theory holds that individuals are motivated by lower order needs until these are relatively satisfied. Higher order needs are then addressed. Even so, the lower levels must be maintained. If not, their importance overshadows the reaching to self-actualization. Lower order needs must be dealt with first. It is difficult to be self-actualized if you are hungry, with no coat, and outdoors in a snowstorm. First things first.

Motivation for the lower needs is to avoid deficiency, while self-actualized people are growth oriented and continually expanding their interests and contributions to society. Fulfillment at the highest levels of the hierarchy tends to be episodic. Maslow later redefined self-actualization as a function of frequency of peak experiences.

THE QUALITY HIERARCHY

Consider ISO 9001 and performance excellence as existing in a hierarchy of quality needs parallel to the Maslow model, as shown in Figure 4.2. ISO 9001 is at the base, and everything above the base represents performance excellence. Goals differ at each level: survival or effectiveness (assure quality through an effective quality system), efficiency (minimize resource utilization), and competitive advantage (maximize shareholder value). Clearly, organizations must first meet the needs at the base. They cannot achieve and sustain higher levels in the hierarchy without the base.

Figure 4.2   The quality hierarchy–goals.

The nature of the actions differs at each level (Figure 4.3):

- Effectiveness addresses such areas as conformance to customer requirements, prevention of customer dissatisfaction, recalls and defects, and achievement of safe products

- Efficiency is concerned with such issues as using resources prudently, reducing material costs, reducing cycle times, and increasing productivity

- Competitive advantage focuses on ensuring delighted customers, increasing market share, and increasing profitability

At each level, organizations should target results that are aligned with their strategic and tactical objectives. At the base, product- and service-related processes, functions, and workers are of primary concern. At the top of the hierarchy, all processes, all functions, and all employees need to be involved.

There are other major differences between the base and the top of the hierarchy. The base is defined by a quality system consisting of a minimum set of actions that must be performed. In order to be able to provide customer confidence, the system must be able to be audited. It either complies or it doesn't. Requirements are fulfilled, or organizations are not compliant. Product is defective or acceptable. Customers either complain or don't. The base can be considered as a binary territory. Quality, at the base, deals with meeting those aspects of customer satisfaction achieved through conformance to requirements.

In sharp contrast to this is the nature of the world above the base. Above the base the world exists on a continuum. Strengthening competitiveness depends upon pursuit of operational excellence—referred to as excellent or superior or world-class quality.

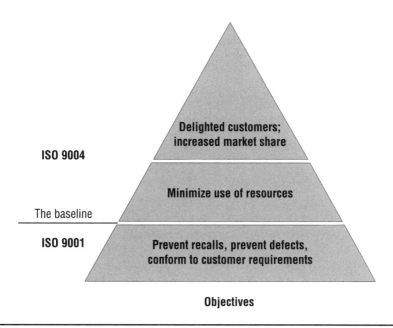

Figure 4.3   The quality hierarchy—objectives.

Organizations must look outside of themselves and benchmark for the best practices and the best results to gain understanding of what they must do. Success depends on deployment throughout the organization and ever-improving results. Above the base, organizations need concern themselves not only with present but also with future customer needs.

Whereas an organization must meet all the requirements at the base in order to pass a compliance audit and achieve registration, no organization ever fully arrives at the top of the quality hierarchy.

An Example

The earlier description of performance excellence (everything above the base) sounds enticing. Why then bother with ISO 9001? Why not just go directly for world-class quality and competitive advantage? After all, isn't there criticism that ISO 9001 does not ensure quality? Surprising to some, there is strong evidence that ISO 9001 does ensure quality, while performance excellence models may not.

Consider the fact that medical devices are among the most reliable products in the world. For critical functional characteristics, most achieve beyond six sigma levels of performance. These products are among the most critical, as evidenced by the fact that governments consider it necessary to regulate them.

As an example let's look at one type of medical device—a heart valve. Heart valves are implanted through open-heart surgery. If requirements—including those related to sterility and functionality—are not 100% fulfilled 100% of the time, a patient's death may result. In such a critical application, the adequacy of design and manufacture is paramount.

The U.S. Food and Drug Administration as well as corresponding regulatory bodies for first-world countries all regulate the design and manufacture of heart valves using the ISO 9001:1994 quality system standard (or the regulatory equivalent) as the core requirements.

ISO 9001 requires the following:

1. A thorough documentation of quality requirements, quality related processing steps, and results.
2. Implementation of controls to maintain the system.
3. Complete compliance to the defined system requirements.

Assurance of fulfillment of these requirements is achieved through internal audit, management review, and corrective or preventive action, which, as required in ISO 9001:1994, encourages continuous improvement of the system for meeting customer requirements.

The ISO 9001 quality system or its equivalent is a minimum requirement with which every single medical device manufacturer must fully comply. Compliance is a requirement to even enter the market. It doesn't guarantee marketplace success. Instead, it is used, along with enforcement actions, to ensure product safety and reliability.

Since performance excellence models do not require the rigor of a quality management system, to be sustained it is best implemented in the context of using ISO 9001. Although some might argue that not all products are as critical as medical devices, isn't it obvious that ISO 9001 should come first? A major part of the 2000 revision was the restructuring and careful crafting of ISO 9001 to be generically appropriate for all organizations and for all types of products, including services and software. The nature and extent of the specific requirements for a given quality system are dependent on the nature of the product, the size and type of organization, complexity and interaction of the processes, and competence of personnel. For example, ISO 9001 applied to a business of 25 employees is significantly different than when applied to a business of 1,000 employees, all other aspects being equal.

While ISO 9001 is necessary for assuring the meeting of quality requirements, it is not sufficient for the organization's continuing success. Through its systems approach, ISO 9001 sets the foundation for efficiency and low cost production, but it does not deal directly with cycle time reduction, low-cost material, higher productivity or any of the other means of achieving competitive advantage.

Performance excellence does deal with these needs. Executive management may use performance excellence or an equivalent approach to achieve operational excellence. By their very nature, the tools of performance excellence work best in the project-by-project mode. As projects are completed, focus tends to shift to other projects without adequate institutionalization. And so the gains may be lost.

As in the Maslow model, achievement at the highest level of the quality hierarchy tends to be episodic. It is the formal quality management system at the base that serves as the means to standardize and institutionalize the improvements that are gained from the projects.

THE CONSISTENT PAIR: ISO 9001:2000 AND ISO 9004:2000

ISO/TC 176 has attempted to address the greatest concerns of the users of ISO 9001—the desire to ensure quality and provide for marketplace success—by developing and promoting the use of a consistent pair of standards:

- ISO 9001:2000 covers quality management system requirements
- ISO 9004:2000 provides guidance for performance improvement

From the initial publication of the ISO 9000 series in 1987, ISO 9004 served as guidance for achieving improved performance. Quite naturally, with the pressure of audits for conformity to ISO 9001, ISO 9004 has been all but ignored. Few even know of its existence.

One of the changes implemented by the 1994 revision of the ISO 9000 series was alignment between ISO 9004 and ISO 9001 in order to allow integration of the two standards. The alignment will be completed with the upcoming revision by using matching clause numbers and titles to achieve a much higher degree of consistency between the two.

Additionally, a set of eight quality principles have been developed by ISO/TC 176 to serve as the necessary linkage between the base (ISO 9001) and higher levels that are above the base (ISO 9004).

WHY ISO 9000:2000?

If one were to gather representatives on quality worldwide from all types of organizations and have them describe a system to ensure quality by preventing product and service failures and field recalls, the result would be ISO 9001:2000. It encompasses the requirements at the base of the hierarchy of quality needs.

Likewise, if one were to gather representatives on quality worldwide from all types of organizations and have them describe approaches to provide for marketplace success through efficient operations and competitive advantage, an equivalent or an approximation of ISO 9004:2000 would emerge. It provides guidance for all of those activities of a quality nature that need to be considered above the base.

Chapter 7 outlines the need for the changes in the 2000 revision of the ISO 9000 family. These include the need to achieve a consistent pair of quality management system standards—ISO 9001:2000 and ISO 9004:2000. From a big picture standpoint, the new revision facilitates rapid and smooth progression from baseline quality to performance excellence.

To ensure quality and marketplace success, all organizations need to embrace both the requirements within ISO 9001 and the performance improvement guidance within ISO 9004.

Chapter 5
Quality Management Principles

John E. (Jack) West
Consultant, The Woodlands, Texas

PRACTICAL APPLICATION FIRST, THEN PRINCIPLES

Many of the most successful quality programs have started with action, not defined philosophy. Often the most successful organizations act first and only later take the time to define the basis for their actions. The same has been true of the ISO 9000 family of standards. Past editions of the ISO 9000 family have been based primarily upon practices, ideas, and concepts that have worked. This pragmatic foundation has served well, and the standards have become the most widely used in ISO's history.

The ISO 9000:2000 documents also contain a great deal of this pragmatism. On the other hand, the new standards were developed after sufficient time had elapsed to make it feasible to state the principles upon which quality management is really based. Quality management is not a topic for which the principles were laid out early on and practice has followed. Rather, the concepts of quality management have grown out of actual practice.

WHAT IS A PRINCIPLE ANYWAY?

A principle is nothing more than a fundamental belief.

Many have proposed sets of quality principles, and some of these models are quite similar to those that underpin the ISO 9000:2000 standards. Some are quite different, being quite operational in nature.

THE QUALITY MANAGEMENT PRINCIPLES

During the mid-1990s, ISO Technical Committee 176 established a working group with the charter to research the basic principles and develop a brochure to explain them. That work resulted in eight fundamental principles. These principles are intended to be the basis of the consistent pair of quality management system standards. They form the basis of the entire system.

The development of the principles was an extremely difficult task. The working group assembled a vast array of documents on the subject of quality systems. The various quality award criteria documents from around the world formed a key part of the research. Sorting through the available philosophies, conducting discussions among working group members from around the world, and attaining consensus through two international ballots consumed almost five years of work. The result was an amazingly coherent set of principles:

Principle 1—*Customer focus*
Organizations depend on their customers and therefore should understand current and future customer needs, should meet customer requirements, and strive to exceed customer expectations.

Principle 2—*Leadership*
Leaders establish unity of purpose and direction of the organization. They should create and maintain the internal environment in which people can become fully involved in achieving the organization's objectives.

Principle 3—*Involvement of people*
People at all levels are the essence of an organization, and their full involvement enables their abilities to be used for the organization's benefit.

Principle 4—*Process approach*
A desired result is achieved more efficiently when activities and related resources are managed as a process.

Principle 5—*System approach to management*
Identifying, understanding, and managing interrelated processes as a system contributes to the organization's effectiveness and efficiency in achieving its objectives.

Principle 6—*Continual improvement*
Continual improvement of the organization's overall performance should be a permanent objective of the organization.

Principle 7—*Factual approach to decision making*
Effective decisions are based on the analysis of data and information.

Principle 8—*Mutually beneficial supplier relationships*
An organization and its suppliers are interdependent, and a mutually beneficial relationship enhances the ability of both to create value.

Source: ANSI/ISO/ASQ Q9000-2000.

THE PRINCIPLES AND THE HIERARCHY

The principles apply at each level of the quality hierarchy, and their realm is not just at the top of the quality pyramid. The concept is that the principles can lead to quality excellence for an organization that is willing to continually refocus its efforts in the direction shown by following them.

Principle 1—Customer Focus

Principle 1—*Customer focus*
Organizations depend on their customers and therefore should understand current and future customer needs, should meet customer requirements, and strive to exceed customer expectations.

Source: ANSI/ISO/ASQ Q9000-2000.

Quality Control—Principle 1 at the Bottom of the Hierarchy

- There is no denying that the customer is important, no matter where an organization finds itself on the hierarchy. It is difficult to argue that any organization is not dependent upon its customer. At the quality control level, the focus is upon meeting customer requirements that are clearly spelled out or in satisfying customer needs that are understood by the organization. There may be little effort to clearly understand the customer beyond basic requirements, but the control system focuses on achieving sufficient conformity to ensure that the product or service is merchantable.

- It is much more difficult to apply the portion of the principle that deals with exceeding customer expectations to the quality control level in the hierarchy because organizations that focus only on quality control typically do not have sufficient customer knowledge to accurately target customer perceptions. In reality, it is perceptions that are addressed when an organization attempts to exceed the expectations of its customers.

Quality Management—Principle 1 in the Middle of the Hierarchy:

- At the basic quality management level, the principle applies much as it does for quality control. The fundamental difference is that at this level, the organization's focus has shifted from controlling defined characteristics to better understanding the customers' overall needs. There is a much more mature understanding of the customer requirements through a formal system of contract review. In reality, this focus on identifying customer requirements may be the single biggest value in adopting ISO 9001 as a model for developing a quality management system.

- Quality management systems typically include customer complaint or returns management systems that are linked to data analysis. These systems provide the beginnings of a systematic means to understand customer feedback. And customer feedback is one means for redefining customer needs to prevent future problems.

Total Quality Management—Principle 1 at the Top of the Hierarchy:

- At the top of the pyramid, we can imagine an organization that has complete knowledge of its customers, their current and future needs, and their perceptions. Many organizations can claim that they have this knowledge—even with no quality system at all. They might point to the sales or research and development organizations as having the customer insight needed to understand such things. And in some businesses, this is adequate. But in a real total quality management (TQM) environment, such knowledge is not just the purview of these departments; rather, it is information collected systematically throughout the organization.

- At the TQM level, sharing of customer information and data is pervasive in the organization. There is also a process to define customer perceptions of the organization's performance and drive market performance by affecting changes in customers' perceptions of how well their expectations are met.

- Ultimately, the organization is able to capture markets because it offers preferred products and services at attractive prices.

Principle 2—Leadership

Principle 2—*Leadership*
Leaders establish unity of purpose and direction of the organization. They should create and maintain the internal environment in which people can become fully involved in achieving the organization's objectives.

Source: ANSI/ISO/ASQ Q9000-2000.

Quality Control—Principle 2 at the Bottom of the Hierarchy:

- At the quality control level, leadership creates an environment where quality is sufficiently important to provide resources for its control.

Quality Management—Principle 2 in the Middle of the Hierarchy:

- At this level in the hierarchy, management establishes policy, objectives, and an environment in which processes can be controlled to ensure quality.

Total Quality Management—Principle 2 at the Top of the Hierarchy:

- In organizations near the top of the hierarchy, leadership tends to become a more personal thing, with managers providing personal examples of the behaviors that facilitate creation of high levels of customer satisfaction.

- At this level, quality is treated as a strategic issue by the organization's leaders. Target setting and management review are ongoing activities, and leaders integrate the quality and human resources plans of the organization fully with the strategic business plans.

Principle 3—Involvement of People

> **Principle 3—*Involvement of people***
> People at all levels are the essence of an organization, and their full involvement enables their abilities to be used for the organization's benefit.

Source: ANSI/ISO/ASQ Q9000-2000.

Quality Control—Principle 3 at the Bottom of the Hierarchy:

- At the very basic level, people must create and operate the basic processes of the business. Even in an organization that does not really recognize the value in establishing formal process controls, people are key. Some might point out that at the very bottom of our hierarchy, the people are even more important than at the top because processes may be less well defined.

- At this level, much work remains to be done to draw on the full talents of all employees. Processes may not be fully understood, and this makes full participation in improvement activities difficult. Managers, supervisors, or technical experts conduct virtually all improvement activities.

Quality Management—Principle 3 in the Middle of the Hierarchy:

- In the middle of our hierarchy, the system should have evolved to a point where the individuals involved in the work are fully qualified and capable to carry out the processes to which they are assigned. Training and process qualification have been mastered by the organization.

- At this stage most employees are beginning to be able to contribute to the improvement of the organization. There is a corrective action process into which most employees can make inputs. Employees may be asked to serve on teams to introduce new products or processes, improve safety, and conduct other activities.

Total Quality Management—Principle 3 at the Top of the Hierarchy:

- Organizations at this level have mastered the art of getting all employees fully engaged in their jobs and actively involved in making improvements.

- There is a consistently high level of communications between the leadership and all employees. The leaders focus on achieving full alignment between the goals of the organization and the personal goals of individual employees. Organizations at this level tend to share lots of important business data and information with all employees. They do this to make certain that everyone's daily work is aligned with the overall objectives of the organization.

Principle 4—Process Approach

> **Principle 4—*Process approach***
> A desired result is achieved more efficiently when activities and related resources are managed as a process.

Source: ANSI/ISO/ASQ Q9000-2000.

Quality Control—Principle 4 at the Bottom of the Hierarchy:

- At a basic level, the processes for quality control must be defined and executed in a manner that provides assurance that the final products or services meet requirements. Simple controlled processes for inspection and testing are common. Controlled processes for assessing service performance are used to provide feedback to customer contact personnel.

- Where statistical quality control techniques are used, the key characteristics of the product must be defined, along with the points in the production cycle where measurements should be made.

- Some of the other key elements of the ISO 9001 basic quality management system will be present, such as controls for nonconforming products.

Quality Management—Principle 4 in the Middle of the Hierarchy:

- When a basic quality management system is present, the organization will have clearly defined the processes for designing, producing, and delivering the product or service. Processes for ensuring that customer requirements are met will have been defined and implemented. Control of product and service quality will have moved "upstream" from control of only process outputs to control of the process itself.

- The organization would also have the other processes discussed in ISO 9001 for such activities as management reviews, corrective and preventive action, and audits.

Total Quality Management—Principle 4 at the Top of the Hierarchy:

- At the top of the pyramid, we see that the organization is focused on the optimization of resources in each process. There is an attitude that the processes can always be improved and activity is present in the organization to make planned improvements.

- The organization will be using process measures extensively, and there is clear understanding of process performance. Correlation between the measures of process outputs are regularly correlated with measures taken at key points in the process to help identify actions needed to make these improvements.

Principle 5—System Approach to Management

> **Principle 5—*System approach to management***
> Identifying, understanding, and managing interrelated processes as a system con-
> tributes to the organization's effectiveness and efficiency in achieving its objectives.

Source: ANSI/ISO/ASQ Q9000-2000.

Quality Control—Principle 5 at the Bottom of the Hierarchy:

- Organizations that find themselves at the bottom of the hierarchy can begin to better understand how to improve quality and its control by recognizing the need for key processes to function together. Some organizations that are at this stage actually have quite sophisticated inspection or quality control systems. Those systems are a collection of control processes that work together to make certain the product or service delivered to the customer meets requirements.

- While the processes for inspection, testing, and correcting products and services may work well as a system, these processes tend to be somewhat disconnected from the processes that actually produce the product or service. And in some organizations, there is a lot of pressure to keep it that way! Regulatory requirements for the independence of the quality function may be used as a rationale to avoid fully integrating the control processes with the processes for creating the product or service.

- At the lowest stage in the hierarchy, the system is generally characterized by the "re's"—rework, redo, rewrite, remake, and so on. The focus of the system is to get the final product "right"; it is not on efficient production or delivery of a product or service.

Quality Management—Principle 5 in the Middle of the Hierarchy:

- With the development of a basic quality management system, the organization has moved to integrate the processes for creating the product or service with those processes which verify that the product or service meets customer needs. This is a very important step for an organization.

- At this level, the emphasis is upon developing a quality management system that is suitable for the organization's situation and effective in assuring that customer requirements are met.

- The quality management system must still control those processes which verify and validate that the product or service meets customer needs. On the other hand, the focus has shifted from controlling only those verification and validation processes to the design, development, production, and delivery processes as well. This shift makes some people uneasy. They see bureaucratically implemented quality control systems spreading "documentation" and other paperwork into other parts of the organization. The trick at this level is to create an effective system with fully integrated processes while avoiding unneeded paperwork and bureaucracy.

- At this level, the purpose of the quality management system is to achieve customer satisfaction. Fully effective systems at this level use measures of customer satisfaction along with other data to perform day-to-day management and decision making. The management review process has matured and uses these data along with audit results to assess system effectiveness.

Total Quality Management—Principle 5 at the Top of the Hierarchy:

- At the top of the pyramid, the organization fully understands and manages the interactions among the various processes in the business. Processes are aligned with each other and with the goals of the organization.
- At this level, the organization is focused on achieving results by continually improving the management system. While achieving customer satisfaction remains a key driver of business success, the organization now can use data on its processes along with customer feedback for strategic decision making and overall business planning.

Principle 6—Continual Improvement

Principle 6—*Continual improvement*
Continual improvement of the organization's overall performance should be a permanent objective of the organization.

Source: ANSI/ISO/ASQ Q9000-2000.

Quality Control—Principle 6 at the Bottom of the Hierarchy:

- At this level, there is a focus on improvement of the processes used to make certain that the customer does not receive defective products or services.

Quality Management—Principle 6 in the Middle of the Hierarchy:

- At this level, there is a mature corrective and preventive action loop.
- The organization is focused on improving the effectiveness and efficiency of the quality management system.

Total Quality Management—Principle 6 at the Top of the Hierarchy:

- At this level, leaders are establishing targets and goals against key measures of customer satisfaction and internal performance. There is a drive to achieve stretch improvement goals. Leaders themselves are involved in the improvement process and provide resources to ensure that targets are met.
- The organization is focused on efficiently meeting future customer needs and on achieving business results through the quality management system.

Principle 7—Factual Approach to Decision Making

> **Principle 7—*Factual Approach to Decision Making***
> Effective decisions are based on the analysis of data and information.

Source: ANSI/ISO/ASQ Q9000-2000.

Quality Control—Principle 7 at the Bottom of the Hierarchy:

- Quality control makes use of data and facts to distinguish good products and services from those that contain nonconformities.
- Quality control also makes use of facts in the decision-making process to determine the disposition of nonconformities.
- Statistical data are used at the quality control level to ensure that products and services meet customer requirements.
- Analysis tends to be a day-to-day activity with little use of trends or indicators of performance.

Quality Management—Principle 7 in the Middle of the Hierarchy:

- Facts and data are used in the quality management system to make decisions related to the system's operations. The information used is gained from analysis of audit results, corrective actions, customer complaints, and other sources.
- Analysis tends to be focused on data that can be used to improve customer satisfaction and the effectiveness of the quality management system.

Total Quality Management—Principle 7 at the Top of the Hierarchy:

- Decisions and actions are based on the analyses of a broad range of data. Customer data are derived by using all available "listening posts" to understand what is important and make decisions that will improve the organization's market position.
- Information is derived from analysis of data and from the innovative ideas of all members of the organization. The focus is on improving productivity while eliminating waste and rework and enhancing market value.

Principle 8—Mutually Beneficial Supplier Relationships

Principle 8—*Mutually beneficial supplier relationships*
An organization and its suppliers are interdependent, and a mutually beneficial relationship enhances the ability of both to create value.

Source: ANSI/ISO/ASQ Q9000-2000.

Quality Control—Principle 8 at the Bottom of the Hierarchy:

- Suppliers are always important to the organization. At the quality control level in the hierarchy, there is typically some validation of the supplier's product or service.

Quality Management—Principle 8 in the Middle of the Hierarchy:

- With the development of a quality management system, an organization will have processes to define and document requirements to be met by suppliers. There will also be processes in place to review and evaluate suppliers' ability to meet those requirements.

- Product validation processes should be well developed and defined at this level in the hierarchy.

Total Quality Management—Principle 8 at the Top of the Hierarchy:

- At the top of the hierarchy, the processes established for the quality management system remain important. The focus tends to change as organizations establish strategic alliances or partnerships with suppliers. In many cases, organizations involve suppliers very early in defining requirements for joint development.

- Organizations work with suppliers to develop mutual trust, respect, and commitment to customer satisfaction. Mutual efforts focusing on continual improvement become common.

- Integration of the supplier quality process with other efforts related to supplier systems becomes common.

THE IMPORTANCE OF INTEGRATION—RELATIONSHIP TO THE PROCESS MODEL

Relationship to the Process Model

The process model is introduced and explained in detail in chapter 2. It should be clear, though, that there is a significant relationship between the processes in the organization and the eight principles. Indeed, two of the principles point out that all work is best managed as a part of a process and that the quality management system is really a collection of processes. The relationship of the principle of customer focus should also be clear: each process has customers with requirements that must be understood and met. The organization has suppliers who provide inputs to those processes and are critical to successful operations. And the people in the organization are the ones who should be using data along with innovation to continually improve performance. From beginning to end, the organization's success is driven by the leadership of its managers and employees.

Integration is the Key

Perhaps the most important concept the principles bring out is the notion of integration. The overall management system—its leaders, its processes, its data, its people, its suppliers—works best when it is fully integrated. The system should be far more effective working as an integrated family of processes than its parts could ever be. To some this might appear to be as simple as teamwork. But it is far more complex than just building the organization into a cohesive team.

Applying the Principles within the Quality Assurance System

Users of ISO 9001 can realize significant benefits from applying the principles in the design and improvement of their basic quality system. As each formal process is developed, the organization should ask itself whether it really uses the applicable principles. From an overall system perspective, the real issue is whether each process in the system creates value for the organization. Asking whether each process fully utilizes the quality management principles is one way to prevent the creation of non-value-added processes.

Applying the Principles to Focus on Business Excellence

The quality management principles are actually simple. But following any set of principles over the long haul is not really all that easy. Times, ideas, and even fads come and go. If the principles are truly universal, an organization should be able to rely on them over time. In reality, the principles on which an organization is grounded are often unstated. Perhaps most often, they have never been thought out by the leadership. Development of the quality management principles and their use as a key input for the ISO 9000:2000 family gives organizations an opportunity to reassess the basis for their business. So how should an organization go about such an assessment?

First, it is useful to realize that the eight quality management principles are closely related to the culture of the organization. As organizations develop, their culture may naturally give them greater strengths in some principles than in others. This may not be wrong! The organization's focus may be just right to cope with its business environment. But this should be validated.

First, it would be beneficial to conduct an assessment of the organization against the concepts in ISO 9004 or against quality award criteria such as the EFQM or Baldrige Award criteria. Once this is done and the organization has established a list of needed improvements, it is time to look at which of the eight principles really will need focus to drive the improvements. The leaders then need to establish ways to focus the organization on behaviors that will strengthen the organization's performance. The organization should plan improvements that will enhance its growth in all of the principles, but the focus should be on those that offer the best combination to drive business improvements.

Many combinations of the principles are possible. An organization may choose to focus on "involving people using facts and data to achieve a corporate habit of continual improvement." This concept becomes the core of the organization's quality policy and a key statement of the expected behaviors of all members of the organization. While this possible combination uses only three of the eight principles, it does not mean the organization ignores the others. But it does mean the organization has chosen to focus everyone's activities along a common path to improvement.

Section 2

The New Consistent Pair: An Overview of the Standards

Introduction

John E. (Jack) West
Consultant, The Woodlands, Texas

The ISO 9000 family of standards has become the most well known in the history of ISO. Their use has been driven by the trend toward increasing international trade and by the fact that they have proven their value in the global marketplace. It is probably safe to say that most of the people in the world who have heard of ISO have heard of it as a result of some contact with one of the standards in the ISO 9000 family. It is also probably safe to assume that most people who speak of ISO 9000 actually mean ISO 9001 or ISO 9002. It is these two standards that have been the most-used in the family. They are the two primary standards used as models for third-party quality assurance system certification by organizations around the world. They are the standards that are used in commerce as contractual quality system requirements between customers and suppliers. They are also the primary standards used by industrial sectors as the basis for their sector-specific documents such as QS 9000, AS 9100, and TL 9000.

With all of their success, these standards have been perceived by many as lacking in focus on the customer and on improvement. ISO 9001 and 9002 have been often criticized as representing "old" quality concepts (like inspection, testing, and documented procedures) over more modern concepts (like process management, customer focus, and continual improvement). While the standards writers can make a valid argument that the 1994 versions of ISO 9001 and 9002 cover the more modern ideas, actual practical application has sometimes ignored them. Indeed, in some cases application of the more modern practices for creating products and assuring that they meet customer needs has been judged as violating ISO 9001! ISO 9001:2000 is designed to make it clear that not only is application of modern practices permitted but it is also, to some degree at least, a requirement.

The other key standards in the ISO 9000 family have received far less use and attention. This has been particularly true for ISO 9004:1994, which was designed to help organizations develop the very modern quality systems needed in today's competitive environment. This lack of usage of ISO 9004:1994 has its roots in the design of that standard. It was not developed with the intention of making it easy to use along with ISO 9001:1994 and ISO 9002:1994.

The 2000 revisions of ISO 9001 and ISO 9004 are intended to address these issues. These two standards are called the "consistent pair" because they have been written in a way that makes them very easy to use together. The new consistent pair should encourage organizations to develop their basic quality management systems around the requirements of ISO 9001 while giving them the flexibility to use the guidance of ISO 9004 to focus that same quality management system on performance improvement.

In chapter 6, "The History of Standardization and the ISO 9000 Family," Jack West provides an overview of the history of standardization and of the ISO 9000 family. In chapter 7, "The Need for Change and the Two-Phase Revision Process," Joe Tsiakals reviews the need for changing the original 1987 version of the standards and discusses the two-phase revision process that resulted in the new ISO 9000:2000 series. In chapter 8, "Summary and Implications of Major Changes from ISO 9001:1994 to ISO 9001:2000," Charlie Cianfrani, Jack West, and Joe Dunbeck summarize the key changes from ISO 9001:1994 that have been incorporated in ISO 9001:2000.

Chapter 6

The History of Standardization and the ISO 9000 Family

John E. (Jack) West
Consultant, The Woodlands, Texas

BACKGROUND

Standards exist to help people communicate. They provide information so things can be nearly the same even when different people create them. In earlier ages, local manufacturers or service providers set standards. Village artisans set the standards for local products and sometimes for how they were to be produced. In the European craft guild system of the 12th through 15th centuries, the master craftsmen in each community set standards for final products and production methods. The qualifications of guild members and journeymen were also standardized. For a very long while, local standards sufficed. Most of the world's commerce was local. And where there was major long-distance trade, most of the products involved were naturally occurring raw materials or relatively simple manufactured items.

Expansion of trade and, ultimately, the industrial revolution changed all of this. As railroads were constructed across great distances, the need for standardized rail gauges became obvious. But it may have been the increase in the size and intensity of wars that really forced the world toward standardization. As nations rose from city-states and armies grew in size, there arose a practical need for standardization of weapons and munitions. By the end of the 18th century, Eli Whitney was experimenting with the mass production of muskets using standardized parts.

Over time, local governments began to regulate products to ensure their purity or safety. Such schemes as the French *appellation d'origine controlée* for wines evolved to ensure that products met standards of quality, purity, and origin. Such local standards often were enacted as law. Slowly, standardization shifted from unwritten norms passed down from master to apprentice to written requirements.

Standards Organizations

By the end of the 19th century, this concept had expanded as organizations were established to develop standards that could be used by entire industrial sectors. In the last quarter of the 19th century, technical societies became mechanisms to exchange ideas on a broad basis. Some of these, such as the American Society of Mechanical Engineers (ASME), grew into standards-developing organizations in their field. In many cases, the development of standards can be traced to problems. As an example, the standards of ASME can easily be traced to the need for common rules to ensure boiler safety. In short, the absence of a code for boilers did not cause boilers to blow up, but the rate of boiler explosions dropped after the introduction of the ASME boiler code early in the 20th century. Another area that received a lot of attention at the end of the 19th century was fire. In 1896, a group was established in New York to draft sprinkler standards. This group became the National Fire Protection Association (NFPA).

Some of these organizations worked on an international basis and some continue to set standards that are used around the world. For example, NFPA claims membership of over 75,000 individuals from around the world and more than 80 national trade and professional organizations. More than 6,000 representatives voluntarily serve on NFPA's nearly 250 technical committees. Several NFPA codes have reached worldwide recognition, such as the Fire Prevention Code (NFPA 1), the Life Safety Code (NFPA 101), the National Electrical Code (NFPA 70), and the National Fuel Gas Code (NFPA 54). NFPA is in the process of developing the NFPA Building Code, a central component of the full set of codes and standards for the built environment to be known as the NFPA Consensus Codes Set.[1]

National Standards Organizations

Early in the 20th century, organizations started to evolve that could provide standards for entire nations. The first of these was the British Standards Institution (BSI), founded in 1901. Over the next century, national standards bodies were established in over 100 countries.

Electricity and the International Electrotechnical Commission

With the widespread introduction of electricity, it became necessary to standardize on a more global basis. This need led to the creation in 1906 of the International Electrotechnical Commission (IEC).

International Trade and the Creation of ISO

In 1926, the International Federation of the National Standardizing Associations (ISA) was established to coordinate standardization in areas other than electrical. The ISA focused on mechanical engineering standardization until its demise at the beginning of the Second World War. In 1947, a new organization was established to take on nonelectrical international standardization. This new organization was named the International Organization for Standardization and was given the

---

ISO, A WORD, NOT AN ACRONYM

The short name ISO is not an abbreviation for the International Organization for Standardization with the letters reversed! Rather, ISO is derived from the Greek word *isos*, meaning "equal," which is not too hard to stretch into "standard."

---

short name ISO.[2] ISO published its first standard in 1951 and now has over 130 member bodies.

Earlier we pointed out that standards sometimes evolved out of problems—from safety issues such as tainted food and exploding boilers to issues of compatibility as with electrical connectors. So there are practical safety and interoperability aspects to standardization. Different nations or regions may establish different standards for the same thing. In theory, if the safety and interoperability standards of one nation are different from those in another nation, trade between the two nations would be difficult, and trading partners would find themselves having to comply with the standards of both nations. Thus such national standards can become technical barriers to trade.

The purpose of ISO is to provide the standards needed to facilitate international trade. It is a noble-sounding purpose, but there is a stark reality in the world of standardization: *it is the market that decides which standards are really used.* ISO is a federation of member bodies representing over 130 countries. It is headquartered in Geneva, Switzerland. But the staff in Geneva does not do the standards work. Instead, ISO technical committees (TCs) and subcommittees (SCs) perform the work required to develop, update, and revise the ISO standards. TC 176 is the committee responsible for the ISO 9000 family. Each TC and SC has a "secretariat," which is usually a standards body from one of the member countries. The Canadian Standards Association acts as secretariat to ISO TC 176 on behalf of the Standards Council of Canada (the official Canadian member body of ISO). ISO covers all technical fields except the electrotechnical area, which is covered by IEC.

The ISO Standards Development Process

The development process is based on the principle of consensus and voluntary involvement of all interests. The intent is to provide industrywide global solutions to satisfy users worldwide. The TCs and SCs establish working groups (WGs) to do the actual drafting work. These groups are composed of experts from member bodies that choose to participate. Drafts are prepared and circulated to members of the WG until sufficient consensus has been achieved for the responsible TC or SC to issue the document to the member bodies as a committee draft. Committee drafts are circulated for comments and balloted for elevation to the status of draft international standard (DIS). At the DIS stage, member bodies vote on adoption of the document as an international standard. After comments have been incorporated and final editing done by the Geneva staff, there is one more vote on the final draft international standard (FDIS). Once the process is completed, the document is issued as an international standard.

"National Adoption" of ISO Standards

Each member body of ISO has the privilege of "adopting" each ISO standard as a national standard. The member body may offer either the national adoption or the international version or both versions for public sale in their country. National adoption processes vary but may involve the balloting of a consensus group within the member country.

TYPES OF STANDARDS

Standards can be classified by their basic purpose, by the organization that writes them, by the subject mater covered, and by their scope and field of application. Some standards provide guidance while others specify requirements. Some standards are used in procurement while others are intended for internal application.

Requirements versus Guidance

Some standards are specifications intended to convey requirements that must be met. ISO 9001 is a specification to convey the requirements for a quality management system. Sometimes specifications are called "requirements documents."

Other standards are guidelines. ISO 9004 is a guidance document that can help organizations achieve excellence in customer satisfaction and business results. The distinction between requirements and guidance documents is not always so clear. Some standards provide guidance that is optional. Sometimes, guidance standards are intended to provide one or more alternative means to comply with requirements. In such cases, compliance with the guidance standard may actually be mandatory.

Company Standards

Standards can also be grouped by the type of organization that develops them. There are company standards that are developed by a company for use internally or by the company's suppliers. Some company standards are developed to capture a market by establishing a preferred standard during the introduction of a new product. This has been a common occurrence in the electronics industry with items such as VCRs and high-speed modems.

Consensus Standards

There are also consensus standards. These are developed by one of the standards organizations with some level of consensus among potential users and other interests.

Procurement Standards

There are procurement standards that are developed by standards organizations, companies, or governments for use as contract documents in the procurement process. There is a current trend for governments and companies to use consensus standards developed by standards organizations in their procurement activities. When procurement standards are developed by a customer organization, there is often little supplier involvement. On the other hand, if such standards are developed by a consensus standards organization, suppliers have an opportunity to participate in the process openly. This can improve the standards used in the industry and the quality of the resulting products and services. Using the consensus process can also lower costs because issues are resolved earlier during the consensus process. On the other hand, the consensus process takes time, and in many cases organizations would rather develop their own standards because they can do so more quickly.

Consensus Standards to Publicly Available Specifications—Consortia

This need for speed in the development of product and service standards coupled with the need to achieve some level of consensus has led to the development of standards "consortia" to rapidly develop documents. Normally, consortia involve key players in an industry who work together to develop needed standards. They achieve limited consensus among these key players but do not include the participation of all interested parties, as is general practice with the standards organizations. Often these consortia start out as relatively informal organizations with the purpose of developing a few standards. Some create documents and turn them over to more formal organizations for publication. Some of the standards organizations have begun to offer the services of publishing these documents as "publicly available specifications." Standards organizations have a number of different names for this type of document.

Specifications for Products and Services

Most early standards provided requirements for products and services. There are a number of different types of specifications for products and services. Some are called performance standards because they specify the performance requirements for the end item but do not include the means necessary to achieve that performance. In performance standards, features and technical details are left to be developed by the user of the standard. Other specifications for products give the design details needed to ensure that the product will be compatible with other components. For example, dimensions and shapes must be specified in an electrical connector standard so the connector will fit the socket. Other variations are possible.

Test Methods

While the earliest standards were likely product specifications, there has always been a need to determine whether a product complies with its specification requirements. In many cases, this can easily be accomplished by simple measurement of the product or by using the item. But increased product complexity, mass production, and widespread distribution have vastly increased the financial consequences if a product is found unacceptable in the marketplace. Standardized means for determining that the product complies with requirements have become a necessity.

Test methods standards give instructions for conducting tests, inspections, or analyses of materials or products. In some cases, these testing requirements are included in the specification for the product itself. In other cases, there are generic testing methods that apply to a wide variety of materials or products.

Administrative Practices

Some standards provide requirements or guidance for conducting administrative processes. Financial accounting standards can be placed in this category, as can standards that specify how to administer a training and qualification program for production or service personnel.

Management Systems

Standardization of the systems used to accomplish management activities is relatively recent. These standards provide rules for managing certain aspects of an organization. Generally, such standards provide broader coverage than standards that cover a single administrative process. Management systems standards tend to cover a family of interrelated processes that are used together to accomplish major portions of the organization's work. The ISO 9001 and 9004 standards are management systems standards. Other standards in the ISO 9000 family provide guidance for the application of quality tools and concepts.

THE QUALITY MANAGEMENT JOURNEY

As product requirements standards and the associated test methods evolved, industry began developing the infrastructure to cope with new requirements and increasing complexity. The disciplines required to ensure conformity were slowly being developed.

Conformance to Specifications

As products became standardized, there emerged a need for systematic means to ensure that they complied with the requirements. In many cases, the delineation of a testing method was sufficient. But as products and commerce became more complex, the larger and more sophisticated customers began to develop organizational units responsible for this determination. These units became inspection departments with their own staff and operating rules. By the 1930s, these organizations were beginning to use sampling and other statistical methods to make decisions on conformity.

Early Quality Systems—Inspection

By the 1950s, managers had established rules for the entire workforce covering such things as control of nonconforming items and identification of materials. Manufacturing organizations were beginning to develop management systems to ensure conformity with product specifications. In many cases, these systems were quite informal, but they often became a part of the cultural fabric of the organization. In fact, these systems became so embedded in some organizations that they often became roadblocks to improvement when more modern quality management processes became available in the mid-20th century.

Naturally, inspection systems in large organizations included the inspection of incoming materials. It became clear that the quality of incoming items might improve if the suppliers also had systematic methods to control the conformity of the products they shipped, so the internal inspection systems were often

INSPECTION

In many organizations, the quality premise has long been something like "You get what you *inspect*, not what you *expect.*"

Strangely, with all of the process controls, management measures, and employee involvement we have today, this old premise is still alive, well, and sometimes true!

transferred to key suppliers. Eventually, large organizations started requiring that suppliers inspect products prior to shipment to ensure that the products met requirements. In the early days, these requirements were subtle. Contracts may have included references to a standard containing statistical sampling plans and defined an acceptable quality level for use in applying that standard. To ensure that the goods would be acceptable on receipt by the customer, suppliers would conduct final inspections using the sampling plan.

The Foundation of ISO CASCO

In 1970, ISO created the Committee on Conformity Assessment (CASCO) to study and provide guidelines on conformity assessment processes for products. The creation of CASCO signaled a recognition that the world was changing. Even at that early date, there was recognition that without uniformity in determining conformity with standards, technical trade barriers were inevitable. At the time of CASCO's creation and until the late 1990s, its terms of reference included only the preparation of ISO/IEC guides in the area of conformity assessment. These CASCO guides are used in a wide range of conformity assessment activities. In a very real sense, ISO TC 176 is the child of CASCO. In effect, since CASCO only prepared guides, a technical committee was needed to develop ISO standards in the area of quality management.

Over the years, CASCO has produced a number of guides. It was finally realized that some of these documents would be more appropriate if they were issued

CURRENT (AS OF JUNE 2001) CASCO TERMS OF REFERENCE

• To study means of assessing the conformity of products, processes, services, and management systems to appropriate standards or other technical specifications

• To prepare international guides and international standards relating to the practice of testing, inspection, and certification of products, processes, and services, and to the assessment of management systems, testing laboratories, inspection bodies, certification bodies, accreditation bodies, and their operation and acceptance

• To promote mutual recognition and acceptance of national and regional conformity assessment systems, and the appropriate use of international standards for testing, inspection, certification, assessment, and related purposes

as ISO standards. With this recognition, CASCO was given the task of converting the appropriate guides into consensus standards. The current CASCO terms of reference include preparation of both guides and international standards.[3]

Table 6.1   List of CASCO guides and international standards.[4]

Guide or Standard Number	Subject
ISO/IEC Guide 2:1996	Standardization and related activities—General vocabulary
ISO/IEC Guide 7:1994	Guidelines for drafting of standards suitable for use for conformity assessment
ISO/IEC Guide 22:1996	General criteria for supplier's declaration of conformity
ISO/IEC Guide 23:1982	Methods of indicating conformity with standards for third-party certification systems
ISO Guide 27:1983	Guidelines for corrective action to be taken by a certification body in the event of misuse of its mark of conformity
ISO/IEC Guide 28:1982	General rules for a model third-party certification system for products
ISO/IEC Guide 43-1:1997	Proficiency testing by interlaboratory comparisons—Part 1: Development and operation of proficiency testing schemes
ISO/IEC Guide 43-2:1997	Proficiency testing by interlaboratory comparisons—Part 2: Selection and use of proficiency testing schemes by laboratory accreditation bodies
ISO/IEC Guide 53:1988	An approach to the utilization of a supplier's quality system in third party product certification
ISO/IEC Guide 58:1993	Calibration and testing laboratory accreditation systems—General requirements for operation and recognition
ISO/IEC Guide 60:1994	ISO/IEC code of good practice for conformity assessment
ISO/IEC Guide 61:1996	General requirements for assessment and accreditation of certification/registration bodies
ISO/IEC Guide 62:1996	General requirements for bodies operating assessment and certification/registration of quality systems
ISO/IEC Guide 65:1996	General requirements for bodies operating product certification systems
ISO/IEC Guide 66:1999	General requirements for bodies operating assessment and certification/registration of environmental management systems (EMS)
ISO/IEC TR 17010:1998	General requirements for bodies providing accreditation of inspection bodies
ISO/IEC 17020:1998	General criteria for the operation of various types of bodies performing inspection
ISO/IEC 17025:1999	General requirements for the competence of testing and calibration laboratories

PREDECESSORS OF THE ISO 9000 FAMILY

By the end of the 1950s, companies were specifying minimum requirements for their suppliers' inspection systems. In some countries, the military procurement process also developed descriptions of the inspections required of their contractors and suppliers. By the early 1970s, these requirements documents were common.

Military Specifications for Quality Systems

The U.S. military services issued several inspection system requirements documents in the late 1950s. These documents received a lot of development. They were finally integrated into a family of documents applicable to the procurements of all the U.S. services with the issue of MIL-I-45208A, *Inspection System Requirements*, and of MIL-Q-9858A, *Quality Program Requirements*, both issued on 16 December 1963. MIL-Q-9858A required a comprehensive quality assurance program, while MIL-I-45208A required control of all inspection and testing. A third document, issued in the procurement regulations as a standard contract clause, required controls of only final inspection and testing. This family of documents provided three levels of quality systems. The family also had other members, such as MIL-C-45662, *Calibration System Requirements*. Similar standards were developed by the militaries of other nations. Over time, some of these were integrated by NATO into the Allied Quality Assurance Publication (AQAP) series.

Early Quality System Certification Schemes

The company-specific standards and the military specifications had the advantage of conveying the customer's specific requirements to the supply base, but large numbers of suppliers served more than one customer. This meant that each supplier was subjected to the audits of several customers. During the 1970s, there were a number of efforts to simplify the approval of suppliers by creating data-sharing systems. Large participants in an industry would agree to share information on supplier quality system approvals to reduce their own and their suppliers' audit burden. While a number of these schemes were developed and used, few survived the test of time.

National Standards

In the 1970s, there began to emerge national standards for inspection systems and quality programs. Some of these were based on the earlier military documents. Prominent among these efforts were the development of the British standard BS 5750, issued in 1979, and of the Canadian CSA Z 299 series, initially issued in the mid-1970s. Both the British and Canadian offerings featured different "levels" of inspection and quality assurance system requirements. (There were three levels in the case of BS 5750, parts 1, 2, and 3, and four levels in the case of the Z 299 series.) These differing levels allowed purchasing companies to select more comprehensive system requirements for more important procurements and simpler systems for simpler buys.

In the United States, quite a different approach was adopted. ANSI/ASQC Z-1.15, *Generic guidelines for quality systems*, issued in December 1979, was written as a guideline. It was a comprehensive set of quality management and quality assurance elements from which the user could select those that applied to the business at hand. In effect, adoption of the entire Z-1.15 was not intended; rather, each organization was expected to use the document to structure exactly the right quality system for its needs. Instead of three or four levels of optional requirements, the U.S. document offered virtually infinite tailoring.

Emergence of Third-Party Quality System Certification Schemes

The introduction of BS 5750 brought with it the concept of third-party certification of quality systems. Certainly, third-party schemes for quality systems were not new with BS 5750. In fact, the American Society of Mechanical Engineers had operated such schemes for nuclear components and unfired pressure vessels for several years. But BS 5750 certification carried the third-party scheme to the national level. In the mid-1980s, organizations in the United Kingdom were beginning to seek third-party approval of these standards.

The Need for the ISO 9000 Family

During the early days of quality system standards development, most economies remained national in nature. Even as late as the early 1970s, most of the world's commerce was national. But by the 1980s this had all changed. Not only was international commerce becoming more visible to the average person, it was also changing the way in which business was conducted. In past decades, large organizations had engaged in international trade and had developed business outside their home countries. Now even very small organizations were finding it necessary—or advantageous—to compete for markets abroad. By the 1980s, some believed that the national standards for quality systems and the emerging national certification schemes could create a technical barrier to international trade. It appeared that there could be significant advantages if the various national standards could be drawn together to create a single family on a worldwide basis. The development of well-accepted international standards for quality assurance was viewed as a significant opportunity to help level the international trade playing field.

THE DEVELOPMENT OF THE 1987 VERSION OF THE ISO 9000 FAMILY

ISO TC 176 first met in 1980, nearly seven years before the issue of the 1987 edition of the ISO 9001 standard. It takes a long time to gain international consensus.

The Initial Development of the ISO 9000 Family—The 1987 Versions

There were major issues. First of all, there were definitions. The need to develop basic concepts early in the project led the committee to establish a strong subcommittee on terminology. ISO 8402 on terminology, issued in 1986, was the result of this work. But there were also major issues involving the type of quality system standards the committee would produce. The Americans favored a guideline approach like that of their own Z-1.15 because it was comprehensive yet offered great flexibility. Some countries, led by Britain and Canada, offered their national multilevel quality assurance standards as bases for a requirements standard.

There was even a great deal of debate as to whether the three-level structure favored by the British or the Canadian four-level structure was best.

What resulted was a compromise. The committee developed both a guideline document (ISO 9004) along the American pattern and a three-level set of requirements documents.

With registration schemes to support them and the emergence of their use in regulation, ISO 9001 and 9002 became the most successful documents in the series. By the time they were first revised in 1994, they had become the most widely known standards in ISO's history.

GROWTH IN POPULARITY

A good deal of the great popularity of the ISO 9000 family can be attributed to the rapid growth of schemes to certify or register organizations that comply. When applied to quality systems, the terms *certification* and *registration* are often used to mean the same activity. An organization is audited by a certification body (often called a registrar) against one of the requirements standards. If the registrar determines that the organization complies with the standard, the organization is issued a certificate and is included on the registrar's listing of compliant organizations. As this system of registration evolved, a need was recognized to ensure the adequacy of the various registrars' work. Organizations were established to accredit registrars and provide a level of confidence in their capabilities. With this system, an organization seeking to achieve quality system registration may be certain that the registrar will provide an accredited certificate, meaning that the process used for registration meets the requirements of a recognized accreditation body.

Influence of Certification on the Standards' Popularity

In some industries, companies jumped to be the first to be registered, seeing this approval as a competitive advantage. In other industries, large players began to adopt ISO 9001 or 9002 as requirements for their suppliers. A number of organizations used ISO 9000 as a follow-on to earlier quality initiatives and achieved improved business results. For some it was another opportunity to reengineer processes, something they were beginning to do anyway.

All of these things contributed to the early success of the ISO 9000 family. But it was the European Community's (EC's) effort to standardize product certification requirements among EC countries that provided the greatest surge in the use of these new standards.

EC '92 and the Push to Get Registered

In the late 1980s, a great myth circulated among businesspeople around the world. It was that, in order to do business in Europe after 1992, you would have to be registered to ISO 9000. The European Community (now the European Union, or EU) had a goal of establishing its single internal market by 1992. Among the things that needed to be done to achieve this integrated market was to create a set of new product regulations. Most who spread the myth knew little enough about ISO 9000 and almost nothing about European regulations. As it turned out, few European regulations contain requirements for ISO 9000 registration. Even

---

PRINCIPLES OF THE NEW APPROACH TO HARMONIZATION AND STANDARDIZATION

- There must be clear separation between the EU legislation (e.g., the directives) and European standardization by CEN, CENELEC, and ETSI.

- EU legislative harmonization is limited to the essential requirements (safety requirements of general interest).

- Corresponding technical specifications are left to the standardization bodies (CEN, CENELEC, and ETSI).

- Products manufactured in conformity with harmonized standards are presumed to conform to the essential requirements.

- Standards are not mandatory—they remain voluntary—but the producer has an obligation to prove conformance to the essential requirements.

- Standards must offer a guarantee of quality with regard to the essential requirements of the directives.

- Public authorities are responsible for the protection requirements on their territory, and member states must take appropriate measures to withdraw unsafe products from the market.

---

though most people discovered that registration was not really an absolute requirement before they actually went through the process, the myth had a strange effect on the use of the ISO 9000 family:

- In many cases, it was EC '92 that introduced organizations to the standards, but they became registered for other reasons.
- Some organizations studied the ISO 9000 family as a result of the EC '92 push and decided to become registered to capture potential market advantage.
- And finally, some organizations reacted to the uncertainty: better to get registered than to risk market exclusion.

It all happened because of the vague relationship between quality system registration and conformity assessment for products sold in Europe. In 1985, the European Community set a goal of full development and implementation of a family of a new kind of product-related regulation called the New Approach Directives. The New Approach to Harmonization and Standardization was adopted by European Council resolution in May 1985. The regulations produced under this new approach give "essential requirements" for protection of health and safety. They cover broad areas such as machinery and electromagnetic compatibility. This is different from the older approach of product directives that covered individual products. These rules have the force of law and are expected to be adopted by the member states of the EU to generally replace national regulations.

THE EUROPEAN STANDARDS BODIES

CEN (Comité Européen de Normalisation): CEN's mission is to promote voluntary technical harmonization in Europe in conjunction with worldwide bodies and its partners in Europe.

CENELEC (Comité Européen de Normalisation Electrotechnique): CENELEC is the European committee for electrotechnical standardization. It has been officially recognized as the European standards organization in the electrotechnical field.

ETSI (European Telecommunications Standards Institute): ETSI's mission is to produce the telecommunications standards that will be used for decades to come throughout Europe and beyond.

The European standards bodies (CEN, CENELEC, and ETSI) produce standards to support these directives.

The New Approach to Harmonization and Standardization can be viewed as fitting within the EU's Global Approach to Product Certification and Testing. This global approach includes the development of harmonized standards, a process to demonstrate the competence of certification bodies, national implementation of legislation for the EC directives, and a consistent conformity assessment process.

While quality management systems can contribute to the conformity of products, the direct tie of product conformity to the quality system has always been tenuous.

In the early days of this approach, it was often stated that the EU would include compliance with one of the ISO 9000 standards in these directives. In most cases this has not occurred. The medical devices directive is a notable exception.

Growing Acceptance around the World

Since 1993, ISO has conducted surveys of ISO 9000 certification. Since 1995, these surveys have been done on an annual basis. The 1999 survey results indicate in that year there were 100 countries that had adopted ISO 9001 as a national standard. The 1999 survey also indicated that worldwide there were over 340,000 ISO 9000 registrations and there was a 26.4 percent increase in registrations during 1999 alone. ISO 9000 certificates have been awarded in 150 countries around the world. The trend in certifications as measured by ISO is shown in Figure 6.1. The survey also indicated the rate of increase in the number of registrations was higher in 1999 than in previous years.

This gives us a good indication of the significant impact that has been made by ISO 9001 and ISO 9002, the basic requirements standards. The popularity and use of the other standards is not as easy to measure. It is possible to "count" the number of organizations achieving registration, but it is far more difficult to determine how many organizations use the guidance standards in the family. Indications are, however, that the use of the guidance standards has not been anywhere near as great as that of the requirements documents. All of these data are based, of course, on the 1987 and 1994 versions of the family. With the new ISO

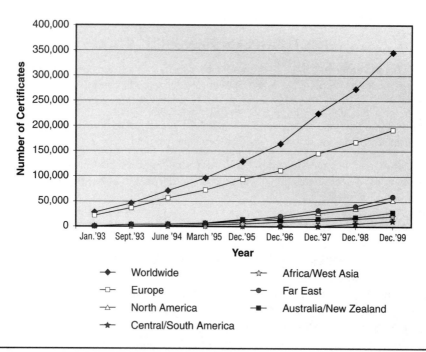

Figure 6.1   Growth in the number of ISO 9000 certificates.

Source: The ISO Survey of ISO 9000 and ISO 14000 Certificates, Ninth Cycle, up to and including 31 December 1999, http://www.iso.ch/iso/en/iso9000-14000/pdf/survey9.pdf (Accessed June 21, 2001).]

9000:2000 family, it is expected that the guidance documents may get more use. This is one of the issues that drove the changes made in the ISO 9000:2000 revisions. The full range of user needs that sparked the changes is discussed in the next chapter.

ENDNOTES

1. *An Overview of NFPA,* http://www.nfpa.org/About_NFPA/An_Overview_of_NFPA/an_overview_of_nfpa.html (Accessed 21 June 2001).
2. *What is ISO?,* http://www.iso.ch/iso/en/aboutiso/introduction/whatisISO.html (Accessed 21 June 2001).
3. *CASCO—Committee on Conformity Assessment* http://www.iso.ch/iso/en/aboutiso/isostructure/CASCO.html (Accessed 21 June 2001).
4. *List of CASCO Guides and Standards by Field of Application,* http://www.iso.ch/iso/en/comms-markets/conformity/listguides.html#TopOfPage (Accessed 21 June 2001).

Chapter 7

The Need for Change and the Two-Phase Revision Process

Joseph J. Tsiakals

Amgen, Thousand Oaks, California

Today's ISO 9000 series of quality management system standards is considerably different from the original standards issued in 1987. This chapter describes the original purpose and concepts underlying these standards to demonstrate the significance of the current changes. This chapter describes the deficiencies that became apparent after the first issuance of these standards in 1987, the improvements in content achieved in the 1994 revision, and the major needs addressed by the current edition published in December 2000.

The process of revision is particularly important when major changes are planned. Various dimensions of the process used to create the new standards are described.

THE 1987 ISO 9000 SERIES

ISO Technical Committee 176, formed in 1980, published the ISO 9000 series of international standards in 1987. An important driver of this work was the growing significance of third-party schemes for certifying quality systems based on various national, standardized approaches for inspection systems and quality programs.

Another important consideration was the desire to provide information to organizations about how to design their own quality systems based on individual company marketplace needs.

The standards in the ISO 9000 series were intended to be generic standards for quality management and quality assurance. The standards were to apply to all types of companies; they could be adapted to fit both small and large corporations in all types of businesses, including manufacturing, software, and service.

The original ISO 9000 series consisted of five standards—ISO 9000, 9001, 9002, 9003, and 9004—plus ISO 8402 (which was published in 1986 and focused on terminology). These six standards served as the core of the ISO 9000 family until additional guideline standards were issued in the early 1990s to explain applications to specific areas not otherwise adequately addressed. ISO 9000 described how to use the series.

ISO 9001:1987, 9002:1987, and 9003:1987 specify minimum requirements for quality assurance systems. They have been used by customers in contracts and also for quality system certification audits performed by third-party auditors. These three standards were "conformance," or "requirements," standards. They were referred to collectively as multilevel standards since a company or its customer would select only one of the three for use as a contract requirement or in certification. ISO 9001:1987 was the most comprehensive, including all elements of a product's lifecycle, while ISO 9002:1987 didn't include design and servicing (it was intended for use primarily by manufacturing plants), and ISO 9003:1987 dealt only with inspection and testing (it was intended for use primarily by distributors of raw materials or components—for example, timber, minerals, agricultural products, or semiconductors). As standards describing a minimum set of requirements intended for use in contractual agreements between suppliers and customers, all of the requirements set forth in the selected standard were expected to be met for a company to meet its contract requirements or pass a third-party audit for certification. The title of each of these standards included the words: *Quality systems—Model for quality assurance.* They were referred to as *external* quality assurance standards because they were used to provide confidence to the customer that the company's quality system would provide a satisfactory product or service.

ISO 9004:1987 was a guidance standard titled *Quality management and quality system elements—Guidelines.* It was referred to as an *internal* quality assurance standard and was intended to be used by all organizations for quality management purposes without regard to external contractual requirements. It has no specific requirements but contains guidance as to what a company might consider when developing its quality system. ISO 9004:1987 dealt with both effectiveness (meeting customer requirements) and efficiency (using minimum resources).

In terms of the quality hierarchy, ISO 9001:1987, 9002:1987, and 9003:1987 were foundational—they served as the base of the hierarchy. (Chapter 4 describes the various elements and concepts underlying the quality hierarchy.) Compliance with all requirements in the selected standard was required. To be registered a company needed to demonstrate that it met the quality system requirements of the standard. The standards provided customers with confidence that a quality system was in place to ensure that customer requirements were met. ISO 9004:1987, on the other hand, provided guidance as to how to meet requirements and how to do it with minimum resources. It dealt with both effectiveness and efficiency. In this regard, it contained aspects of total quality management, or TQM, and is located somewhere above the foundation of the quality hierarchy, depending on a company's success in implementing the guidance of the standard. ISO 9004:1987 was designed for use by the managers of a company for obtaining confidence that a quality system to drive all aspects of customer satisfaction was in place and that the system was working efficiently, improving the utilization of resources. Table 7.1 contrasts the concepts of ISO 9001:1987, 9002:1987, and 9003:1987 with those of ISO 9004:1987.

Table 7.1 Quality assurance requirements versus quality management guidance.	
ISO 9001:1994, 9002:1994, and 9003:1994 Concepts	**ISO 9004:1994 Concepts**
Consists of requirements, all of which must be met.	Consists of guidance. As guidance, the contents do not need to be demonstrated.
Deals with quality assurance.	Deals with all aspects of quality management.
Deals with that aspect of customer satisfaction achieved through conformance to customer requirements.	Deals with all aspects of customer satisfaction.
Concerned with conformance to written customer requirements.	Concerned with achievement of unwritten customer needs.
Intended to achieve a common understanding between a customer and a supplier by means of agreed-upon requirements.	Intended to achieve delighted customers through exceeding expectations.
Aimed at achieving a goal of 100 percent compliance to written procedures.	Aimed at achieving performance-based results such as levels of performance that are better than those of competitors, that are among the best in the world (world-class), or that are demonstrated to be the "best of the best."
Describes a quality system able to be audited. Procedures are either performed or not performed.	Describes a quality system with metrics that indicate degrees of excellence, progress to a goal, and continual improvement.
Includes minimum organizational requirements for preventing defects, product failures, and recalls.	Includes organizational requirements that maximize value-added activities, deal with competitive advantages, or focus on the continual improvement of value to customers.
Is only subtly a standard of continual improvement and only in the sense of updating procedures based on reviews and the like in order to improve the ability to meet written customer requirements.	Is a standard of continual improvement and prevention in the sense of continually improving all functions and processes to achieve superior performance and delighted customers.

THE NEED FOR CHANGE

The ISO 9000 series was popular from the start. By 1990 more than 75 countries had adopted the series as national standards, and more than 50,000 supplier facilities had been certified by third-party organizations to ISO 9001, 9002, or 9003. By 1999 more than 100 countries had adopted the series, and more than a third of a million facilities had become certified. Since the issuance of the standards in 1987, it is unlikely that any other three documents have had more impact on international trade, the relationship between suppliers and their customers, and the management of quality.

Undoubtedly much of the initial interest in the series, as reported in chapter 6, "History," was driven by the hype surrounding the European Community (now European Union) efforts in the late 1980s to achieve market integration by 1992. This effort, called "EC '92" spawned the myth that to sell products in Europe companies must be registered to ISO 9000. This interest was heightened by the role played by the series. The series embodies uniform international standards that define customer-supplier relationships for assessing quality system requirements. It was natural for customers to welcome the standards as an answer to problems with supplier variability, late deliveries, nonconforming materials, and cost overruns.

Unfortunately the standards fell short of their intent in a number of important areas. Following are the major needs for change that were partially addressed in the 1994 revision and more fully addressed in the 2000 edition of the series:

- *Meet stakeholder needs.* Registration to ISO 9000 should mean the product is of high quality. This has implications in the emerging criteria for top management involvement, focus on customer satisfaction, and achievement of continual improvement.

- *Be usable by all sizes of organizations.* Registration should not require excessive documentation bureaucracies. Small organizations should find value in following ISO 9000.

- *Be usable by all product sectors.* The product lifecycle structure of the 1987 and 1994 standards applies well only to hardware products. Software, processed materials, and service sectors are better addressed by the description of the quality system as a series of processes. This is a strong reason for the structural change of the standards to a process model from the lifecycle model.

- *Be simple and clearly understood.* Quality jargon was used throughout the 1987 standards.

- *Connect the quality management system to business processes.* With a strong emphasis on top management involvement, the registration standards needed to move to being closely aligned with ISO 9004 and needed to permit organizations to maintain the foundation of the quality hierarchy (ISO 9001) while functioning in the upper reaches of the quality hierarchy (ISO 9004). Business success requires emphasis on both effectiveness and efficiency. The *quality system/quality assurance requirements* now become the *quality management system.* A business has only one quality system, and it is a quality management system.

By 1996, when the specifications were being finalized for the 2000 revision, an additional need was identified:

- *Demonstrate enhanced usability with ISO 14000 environment management standards.* It is significantly more efficient for companies if their management systems for quality and the environment are structured and expressed in similar terms.

THE TWO-PHASE REVISION PROCESS

All ISO standards are evaluated on a five-year schedule to determine whether they remain suitable for their application or need to be revised or withdrawn. In the case of the ISO 9000:1987 series, its great visibility made its need to better address concerns of users immediately evident. To achieve a better understanding of the application of the requirements standards (ISO 9001, ISO 9002, and ISO 9003) to specific product and business sectors, work began on additional guidance standards. A number of those were issued during the early 1990s. They included guidance standards for the application of the requirements to software, services, and processed material. In addition, a handbook was prepared for use by small businesses.

At the annual ISO/TC 176 meeting in 1990 it was agreed that work on changes should begin immediately. There was debate as to the extent of change required, resolved by agreement that the revision should be done in two phases. This approach was adopted because a large base of users was familiar with the 1987 standards and would likely be resistant to major structural changes. A gradual, two-step evolution would likely be more acceptable to these users and cause less confusion. In addition, ISO/TC 176 wanted additional time to gain experience and to gain understanding of the shortcomings of the original standards before issuing major changes. In short, a controlling consideration in the first revision of the series was to maintain stability and consistency with regard to the 1987 standard. Only changes that met these criteria were considered in the phase 1 revision. The major changes to structure and content were reserved for phase 2, the year 2000 revision.

Phase 1: The 1994 Revision

The 1994 revision to ISO 9001, 9002, and 9003 was significant but did not make major changes in the requirements. The intent was to clarify the standards, offer better focus on customers and introduce the idea of improvement. The changes included:

- Inclusion of the servicing clause in 9002.
- Inclusion of the customer satisfaction concept in the scope clause.
- Significant improvement in the clarity of the clause on design control.
- Included in 9003 most of the content of 9002, excluding only clauses relating to manufacturing such as clause 4.3, Process Control.
- Restructured the previous clause on corrective and preventive action to two clauses, one for corrective action and one for preventive action, to emphasize that these are separate, required activities for improvement.
- Significantly aligned 9004 with 9001, 9002, and 9003. The 9004 terminology of supplier–organization–customer was adopted in 9001. An attempt was made to have the same or similar clause numbers and titles. This was not completely successful primarily because different working groups were assigned to each standard, a situation corrected for the current revision.
- Additional, minor changes were made to add clarity and achieve internal consistency of terminology. For example, the 1987 standards used the terms "procedures," "written procedures," and "documented procedures" interchangeably. The 1994 standards used only the term "documented procedures."

Phase 2: The Revision Process for the 2000 Standards

Actual work on the phase 2 revisions started in parallel with the work on phase 1. The basic process by which a standard is updated and rereleased is controlled by procedures developed by the International Organization for Standardization (ISO), but the ISO technical committees (or TCs)—TC 176 is responsible for ISO 9001—have some discretion regarding how the process is implemented.

The task of creating ISO 9001:2000 (and ISO 9004:2000) was assigned to Working Group 18 (WG 18) in TC 176—Subcommittee 2 (SC 2). Dr. Jeffery Hoper was appointed the project leader for the work. Each national member body of TC 176 was initially permitted to nominate two experts to this WG. Later, as the workload increased, each member body was asked to appoint a third expert. The work was shared by these member body experts and expert representatives of organizations having formal liaison relationships with the committee.

WG 18 made impressive enhancements to the process for revising a standard and for effectively reviewing and incorporating, as appropriate, the many suggestions and comments received from around the world during each stage of the revision. It is fair to say that there was more interest and involvement in the revision process of this standard by individuals and organizations worldwide than ever before. More than 200 technical experts were directly involved in the international meetings, and many more participated at home on the national delegations. The process to accomplish this work combined high technology and contemporary project management methodology with effective people utilization.

Electronic communications (e-mail) and the Internet had a profound impact on the efficiency and effectiveness of the development process. Essentially all communications between working group meetings took place by e-mail and/or via the WG 18 Web site, which made an enormous amount of information pertinent to the project readily available to all WG members.

Also, during WG meetings, there were several computers in every meeting room with state-of-the-art support equipment so that work proceeded effectively. Computer projection equipment was available for on-screen document review and editing. The Verification Task Group, for example, used multiple computer-driven projectors to review, sort, cut, and paste thousands of comments on the first committee draft (CD 1). This was done in one week just prior to each full WG meeting by investing close to a thousand intense person-hours to ensure appropriate disposition of the comments.

One of the more profound influences on this revision was the decision to manage the development of ISO 9001:2000 just like the development of any new product (that is, to follow the requirements defined in ISO 9001 clause 4.4). Participants agreed early in the development process that to achieve as "clean" a release of this new standard as possible, the process must incorporate, among many other things, robust and formal verification and validation. But other project management techniques and quality tools were important as well. One of the more important advances was using project management methodology to manage the entire development process from developing the management and project plans to customer needs analysis and communications to verification and validation, product introduction, and product support. Figure 7.1 shows a simplified overview of the revision process. This entire spectrum of activity was broken down into 27 task groups. Each task group had a carefully defined task and a task monitor to monitor and

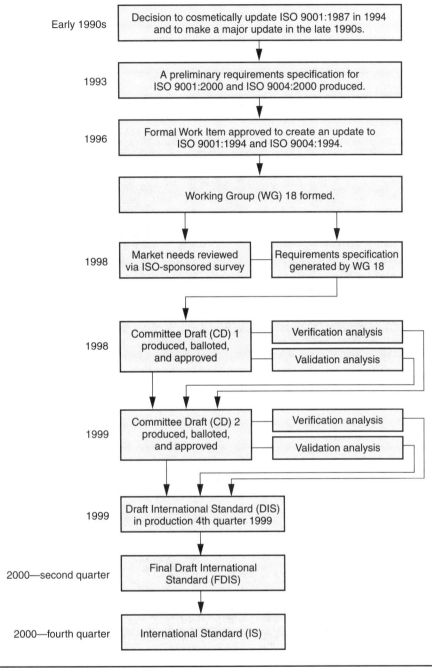

Figure 7.1   Simplified overview of ISO 9001 and ISO 9004 standards update process.[1]

help remove roadblocks; the task group was very carefully staffed with a balanced set of experts. The Planning and Operations Task Group managed the interrelationships among the task groups. See Figure 7.2 for the work breakdown structure and Figure 7.3 for the organizational structure used by WG 18.

1.0 Consistent Pair of Quality Assurance and Quality Management Standards

1.1 Project planning and operations	1.2 Customer needs analysis and communication	1.3 Key concepts for the consistent pair	1.4 Relationships to other standards	1.5 Structure of the consistent pair	1.6 Approach to drafting the consistent pair	1.7 Drafting the consistent pair	1.8 Verification and validation: consistent pair meet customer requirements	1.9 Product introduction	1.10 Product support
1.1.1 Management plan completed by POTG	1.2.1 Fast-track analysis and communication of customer needs	1.3.1 Scope of the consistent pair including the relationship between quality assurance and quality management	1.4.1 Liasons within TC 176 • 8402/9000 • 10011 • 10012			1.7.5 Drafting ISO 9001 and 9004 introductory clauses and annexes	1.8.1 Design and execute verification process for 1.5, 1.6, & 1.7	1.9.1 Develop product introduction plan for new and existing customers	
1.1.2 Project plan	1.2.2 Ongoing information analysis and communication of customer needs	1.3.2 Process model	1.4.2 Review TC 176 standards planned for merging with consistent pair in 1.7			1.7.6 Drafting 9001 management responsibility resource management	1.8.2 Design and execute validation process for 1.7 including prototypes and working draft, committee draft, and draft international standards approvals	1.9.2 Develop transition plan to consistent pair	
1.1.3 Project operations		1.3.3 Principles of vertical and horizontal integration	1.4.3 Compatibility with environmental management standards 14001/4			1.7.7 Drafting 9001 process product/service realization analysis and improvement		1.9.3 Introduce consistent pair	
						1.7.8 Drafting 9004			

Completed

In progress

Figure 7.2   Work structure breakdown design.[1]

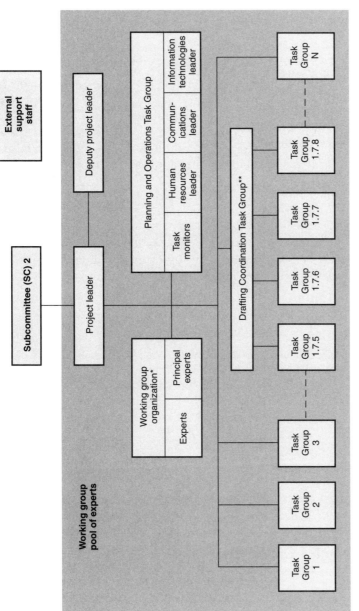

* **Responsibilities of the working group organizations**

1. Making strategic working groups decisions.
2. Providing feedback and guidance to the project leader and task groups.
3. Building consensus.
4. Sharing information.

** **Responsibilities of the Drafting Coordination Task Group**

Ensure consistency of approach, structure, content, and style among the Drafting Task Group 1.7.5–1.7.8. Drafting Task Groups 1.7.1–1.7.4 were responsible for the preparation of CD 1 9001 and CD 1 9004 and have been disbanded.

1998.01.29, Issue C, 1 Page, Authorized by John Owen, project leader.

Figure 7.3   Organization of working group 18.[1]

WG 18 structured a validation process to get direct user feedback. On a worldwide basis, several hundred organizations in over 30 countries participated in the validation process. Forty-two of these organizations were from the United States. As we have found over and over again in the industrial sector, the validation process yielded important feedback. This feedback was used to revise drafts, and it resulted in a more robust international standard.

CONCLUSION

Evolving changes reflect a growing understanding of the needs of customers in all major product and service sectors. Balance is sought with an emphasis on addressing the quality management system requirements of hardware, service, processed material, and software customers and producers. Many of the new, generic changes in the ISO 9000 series are a reflection of this migration from ISO 9001:1987 with its hardware focus to one that applies equally well to the service and software sectors.

The actual language of ISO 9001:2000 standard is biased toward compromises in the best interest of the private sector, since much of the experience base of the experts has been in industry and a vast majority of users have been in the private sector. The primary consideration in developing the 2000 revision was to address the requirements and needs of customers, the users of the standard. The goal is to create a standard that can be used to add value, lower costs, and achieve customer satisfaction.

ENDNOTE

1. C. A. Cianfrani, J. H. Hooper, J. J. Tsiakals, and J. West, "Standards Outlook—The Art of Creating a Standard," ASQ *Quality Progress* (December 1999): 59–63.

Chapter 8

Summary and Implications of Major Changes from ISO 9001:1994 to ISO 9001:2000

Charles A. Cianfrani
Managing Director, Customer-Focused Quality Group,
ARBOR, Media, Pennsylvania

John E. (Jack) West,
Consultant, The Woodlands, Texas

Joseph R. Dunbeck
Chief Executive Officer, Registrar Accreditation Board, Milwaukee, Wisconsin

BACKGROUND

An unprecedented amount of preliminary information about the anticipated changes was made available in the two years prior to the issue of ISO 9001:2000. Starting with ISO/CD2 9001:2000 in 1998, users of the ISO 9001 standard have been able to see and review draft versions of the ISO 9001:2000 standard as it was being developed. The decision to make such preliminary information widely available was not made lightly, especially in the United States. The danger of misuse of, misinterpretation of, or reliance on such preliminary information is real, but the U.S. TAG to ISO/TC 176 (U.S. Technical Advisory Group to ISO Technical Committee 176) and the ANSI ASC Z-1 Quality Management Subcommittee—the U.S. bodies responsible for bringing international standards into the U.S. system—believed that the changes were so significant that users and potential users should be afforded maximum time to review the proposed modifications, to consider the impact of the modifications on their organizations, and to provide input to the U.S. experts who were participating in writing the 2000 versions of ISO 9001 and ISO 9004.

The changes that have been incorporated into ISO 9001:2000 are indeed substantial and substantive. The impact of the changes on organizations will depend on many factors including the kind of business (for example, product, service), the market sector, the size of the organization, and the state of maturity of the current QMS (quality management system).

Anyone familiar with ISO 9001:1994 could construct a list of major changes between the 1994 and 2000 editions of ISO 9001, and no two lists would be identical. Indeed, just in progressing from DIS (draft international standard) status to FDIS (final draft international standard) status involved literally hundreds of changes in response to the thousands of comments that were received on the DIS from ISO member bodies that review and vote on the standards. There was also input from verification and validation processes that were incorporated into the development of ISO 9001:2000 by the working group responsible for creating this "new product." What one person or organization considers to be major could be of no significance to another individual or organization. There are, however, some areas of change that will affect most organizations desiring to conform to ISO 9001:2000. Those areas of major change in requirements are indicated below, and a brief general description of the change is provided to stimulate thinking about what QMS modifications, if any, should be considered by an organization.

SUMMARY OF THE MAJOR CHANGES

Here is a summary of the major changes that have been introduced in ISO 9001:2000:

- Greater focus on the customer and specific reference to customer satisfaction (numerous—see clause 8.2.1)
- A new focus on the process approach (clauses 0.2, 4.1, 5.4.2, 7.1 and 8.1)
- Clarification of requirements for continual improvement (numerous—see clause 8.5)
- Greater emphasis on the role of top management (clause 5)
- Measurable quality objectives (clause 5.4.1)
- New requirements for data collection and analysis (clause 8.4)
- Reduced emphasis on documented procedures (clause 4.2)
- Shift in emphasis from training to providing competent people (clause 6.2)
- Consistency between ISO 9001 and ISO 9004 (clause 0.3)
- Compatibility with ISO 14000 (clause 0.4)
- Elimination of ISO 9002 and ISO 9003 (clause 1.2)
- Modification of the purpose of internal audits (clause 8.2.2)

In addition to the above, many other changes have been incorporated into ISO 9001, any one of which could potentially be of great significance to an organization. However, the changes listed above are believed to be the ones that will have the most significant impact on the greatest number of organizations.

DESCRIPTION AND IMPLICATIONS OF MAJOR CHANGES

This section provides a brief discussion of each major change. It also briefly discusses some of the implications of each change for both implementing and auditing.

Greater Focus on the Customer and Specific Reference to Customer Satisfaction (Numerous—See Clause 8.2.1)

In ISO 9001:2000 there are seven specific references to customer satisfaction. In addition, clause 8.2.1 specifically requires that "as one of the measurements of the performance of the QMS the organization shall monitor information relating to customer perception as to whether the organization has fulfilled customer requirements."

Clearly the 2000 version of ISO 9001 explicitly recognizes the need for, and importance of, attention to achieving customer satisfaction as an output of the QMS. That need was identified as a result of the market research performed by the writers of ISO 9001, and it was included as an element of the requirement specification that was developed for ISO 9001:2000.

Implications for Implementation

Many organizations now comply with the requirement. On the other hand, some have no system to monitor customer satisfaction at all. Other organizations have a corporate system (in some cases very sophisticated systems) for measuring customer satisfaction but the data are not provided in a form that can be used within the quality management system. In either case, these organizations will need to address this gap. Chapter 29, "Measurement of Customer Satisfaction" addresses methods organizations can use to comply with the new requirement.

Implications for Auditing

Auditors need to verify that the organization has established measures of customer satisfaction, is collecting data, and is using the data to find opportunities to enhance customer satisfaction. Auditors need to be clear that the standard places the responsibility for determining how to do this measurement on the organization implementing the standard. There are many ways in which an organization can choose to measure customer perceptions and auditors should not get involved in making specific recommendations as to methods.

A New Focus on the Process Approach (Clause 0.2, 4.1, 5.4.2, 7.1 and 8.1)

Perhaps the most significant change introduced by ISO 9001:2000 is the transition from a lifecycle model (20 elements) to a process approach (inputs, activities, outputs) as the foundation of the QMS. Even the structures of both ISO 9001:2000 and ISO 9004:2000 use this approach. The reason for this change is the belief that "for an organization to function effectively, it has to identify and manage numerous linked activities."

Implications for Implementation

The implications of this change may be significant to an organization. The requirements embodied in ISO 9001:2000, particularly in clauses 4.1, 7.1, and 8.1, require organizations to identify, manage, and improve the processes and their interrelationships that comprise the QMS and the realization of their products (realization meaning the way the organization makes their products), including monitoring, measurement, and analysis of data. It will no longer be sufficient to document procedures to control 20 discrete elements of the organization.

The transition to a process model will require organizations to think about and plan all the processes that, when linked together, will result in products that conform to customer requirements.

Processes must be measured so that the data can be used to improve the processes and the overall effectiveness of the quality management system. There is a significant linkage between the process approach and the requirement for continual improvement discussed below. The overall system is improved by improving the processes.

Implications for Auditing

Auditors will need to look at the interaction of the processes and consider that often processes flow through several functions of the organization. Auditors will need to understand intended process outputs and determine whether the process is actually achieving them. Auditors must review the organization's approach to monitoring (and where necessary, measuring) and improving the processes.

Clarification of Requirements for Continual Improvement (Numerous—See Clause 8.5)

In ISO 9001:2000 there are seven specific references to continual improvement and many others to improvement, including clause 8.5, titled "Continual improvement." In 2000 the mandate to incorporate continual improvement in the QMS of an organization is explicit.

The 1994 edition of ISO 9001 contained provision for management review, internal audit, and corrective and preventive action. It was believed by the drafters of ISO 9001:1994 that those requirements were a clear mandate to include continual improvement in the scope of the QMS. Unfortunately, many users of the 1994 standard did not understand the significance of the linked requirements (or chose to ignore them) and, therefore, did not perceive the "clear mandate" to pursue continual improvement. Clause 8.5.1 of ISO 9001:2000 now makes this linkage clear.

Implications for Implementation

Continual improvement must be facilitated by:

- Setting a quality policy with a commitment to continual improvement of the effectiveness of the quality management system. (Clause 5.3)
- Establishing and deploying measurable objectives at the relevant levels and functions of the organization. The objectives must be set with the commitment to improvement in mind! (Clause 5.4.1)
- Monitoring customer satisfaction, monitoring and measurement of products, and processes, and conducting audits. (Clause 8.2)
- Collecting data. (Clause 8.4)
- Analyzing data. (Clause 8.4)

- Conducting meaningful management reviews to track progress, identify improvement opportunities, establish priorities, and provide resources. (Clause 5.6)
- Identifying opportunities. (Clauses 8.4 and 5.6)
- Taking corrective action by correcting the causes of nonconformities and problems. (Clause 8.5.2)
- Taking preventive action to prevent high-risk nonconformities or problems from ever occurring. (Clause 8.5.3)

These activities should be viewed as an ongoing improvement loop.

Implications for Auditing

Auditors should be looking for evidence of continual improvement as previously discussed at all times during their audits. This may require a fundamental change in the way in which auditors think and the specific questions they ask as they audit the various processes of the QMS.

Greater Emphasis on the Role of Top Management (Clause 5)

In the 2000 edition of ISO 9001, more emphasis has been placed on the role top management. That emphasis includes areas such as communicating the importance of meeting customer requirements, creating and maintaining awareness of quality policy, determining customer needs and expectations, ensuring fulfillment of customer requirements, and establishing measurable quality objectives at relevant levels in the organization.

Implications for Implementation

The implications should be clear. Top managers must be involved.

Implications for Auditing

Auditors will need to discuss these top management roles with top managers themselves. It is no longer acceptable to rely only on the discussions with the management representative to deal with top managers' responsibilities.

Measurable Quality Objectives (Clause 5.4.1)

A new, explicit feature of ISO 9001:2000 is the specific requirement for top management to ensure that quality objectives are established "at relevant functions and levels within the organization" and that those objectives ". . . shall be measurable and consistent with the quality policy."

The intent of this requirement is to ensure that responsibility and authority for key dimensions of the QMS are understood and deployed throughout the organization with the involvement of top management. Ensuring that objectives are measurable is intended to enhance improvement.

Clause 5.4.2 requires that the QMS be planned so that it meets the quality objectives. This means that the processes of the organization need to be operated, monitored, and measured with the organization's objectives in mind.

Implications for Implementation

Many organizations that implemented ISO 9001:1994 have had measurable objectives that are fully deployed. Other organizations have not addressed the need to quantify their quality objectives or recognized that objectives should be related to monitoring and measurement of the processes of the organization. Developing and implementing a process to address the establishment and deployment of measurable objectives that truly drive the effectiveness of the QMS is not a trivial task and will challenge many organizations.

Implications for Auditing

Auditors need to understand the measurable objectives of the organization and how they are deployed. They need to look for alignment of objectives across the functions and levels of the organization. Auditors should look for QMS processes (including process monitoring and measurement) that are aligned with the organization's objectives.

New Requirements for Data Collection and Analysis (Clause 8.4)

The requirements for data collection and analysis mandate that the organization define and implement monitoring, measurement, analysis, and improvement processes to demonstrate that product and/or service conforms to specified requirements, to ensure conformity of the QMS, and to continually improve the effectiveness of the QMS. Measurement requirements are explicitly mandated in ISO 9001:2000, something that was not done in ISO 9001:1994.

Implications for Implementation

Some of the specific areas requiring monitoring and/or measurement include QMS performance, perceptions of customer satisfaction, processes needed to meet customer requirements, and overall product and service performance.

Implications for Auditing

A key issue for auditors should be whether the data collection and analysis activities actually provide information on customer satisfaction, conformity to product requirements, characteristics and trends of processes, and suppliers. A more important audit issue is whether this information is actually being used to control product quality and continually improve the effectiveness of the QMS.

Reduced Emphasis on Documented Procedures (Clause 4.2)

In ISO 9001:1994 there are 18 requirements for documented procedures. In ISO 9001:2000 the requirement for documented procedures occurs for just six processes: (1) control of documents; (2) control of records; (3) planning and conducting an internal audit; (4) addressing nonconforming products; (5) corrective action; and (6) preventive action.

The diminished explicit requirements for documented procedures do not mean that ISO 9001 does not now require complete documentation of the QMS. Rather, it means that the responsibility for defining what must be documented and how to document is in the control of the organization.

Implications for Implementation

The organization now has much more flexibility to decide the documentation required to operate processes under controlled conditions and how to deploy such documentation. The notes in clause 4.2 provide good guidance on the extent to which an organization should go to document its system.

Implications for Auditing

Some organizations express the view that auditors will continue to demand documented procedures where they have no value. And some auditors state they are unable or unwilling to audit in the absence of documentation. Where documentation of a process has no value and the criteria of the notes in clause 4.2 have been met, organizations should "stand their ground" and resist creating useless paperwork. In such cases auditors need to learn to assure process effectiveness by questioning multiple individuals from top managers or supervisors to the workers who carry out the process. Auditors should determine whether the process is actually carried out as intended by the leadership. On the other hand, auditors should seriously question processes where there is a lack of such alignment.

Shift in Emphasis from Training to Providing Competent People (Clause 6.2)

ISO 9001:1994 had requirements for training. The new ISO 9001 uses a broader concept. It requires that the organization assign personnel who are competent to perform their jobs. Instead of a requirement to provide training, there is now a requirement to take whatever action is appropriate to ensure a competent workforce. The new requirement is much more focused than the 1994 standard. Emphasis has shifted from providing training to ensuring a competent workforce.

Implications for Implementation

Job requirements (in terms of required application education, training, skills, and experience) must be determined and personnel must meet those requirements. Where there are gaps, the organization must take action to close them. This action could include training, hiring of competent people, or other appropriate action. The effectiveness of this action must be evaluated.

Implications for Auditing

Auditors will need to remember that it is not their job to determine whether or not the workforce is competent. Rather they must determine whether the organization has processes in place to determine job requirements, identify gaps, and close them.

Consistency between ISO 9001 and ISO 9004 (Clause 0.3)

The structure and sequence of ISO 9001 and ISO 9004 in 2000 will be identical in order to facilitate an easy transition by users from ISO 9001 to a more comprehensive QMS (by using the guidelines contained in ISO 9004).

In 1987 and 1994, ISO 9001 and ISO 9004 coexisted as related standards but had different structures, thereby making it difficult for potential users to migrate from a QMS meeting minimum requirements (ISO 9001) to a more comprehensive QMS (ISO 9004).

Implications for Implementation

There is no requirement for organizations to use ISO 9004:2000 in developing their QMS. On the other hand, the new ISO 9004 is structured in a way that makes it easy to use it as a companion to ISO 9001:2000 to enhance the quality management system.

Implications for Auditing

Auditors must recognize that the role of ISO 9004:2000 is to help organizations implement processes that will improve performance. This means that ISO 9004 is not a guide for implementing ISO 9001:2000. Understanding this is particularly important for third party auditors.

Compatibility with ISO 14000 (Clause 0.4)

Good compatibility has existed between ISO 9001:1994 and ISO 14001:1996 (*Environmental management systems—Specification with guidance for use*). ISO 9001:2000 was developed with the specific intent to maintain and enhance this compatibility. The drafters of the two families worked together during the development of ISO 9001:2000 to ensure that compatibility. In fact, experts from ISO/TC 207, the technical committee responsible for ISO 14001, were participants in the working group that drafted ISO/DIS 9001:2000.

Considerations related to compatibility included ensuring that the structure of ISO 9001:2000 enhanced its usability with ISO 14001 and ensuring that there was no unnecessary duplication or conflicting requirements.

Implications for Implementation

The implementation of integrated management systems is facilitated by the new standard. Organizations should consider the advantages of such consolidation during the implementation of, or transition to, ISO 9001:2000.

Implications for Auditing

Consolidated third party audits of ISO 9004:1994 and ISO 14001:1996 have been conducted in the past. The new ISO 9001 further facilitates consolidation of such audits.

Elimination of ISO 9002 and ISO 9003 (Clause 1.2)

The 2000 revisions of this ISO 9000 series will contain a single requirements standard, ISO 9001:2000. That requirements standard will replace ISO 9001:1994, ISO 9002:1994, and ISO 9003:1994.

An organization will be permitted to exclude QMS requirements contained in clause 7 of the standard that do not affect the organization's ability to provide products that meet customer requirements.

Implications for Implementation

This change will have the greatest impact on organizations that have been certified to ISO 9002 but who do have design responsibility for products. To comply with ISO 9001:2000, such organizations will be required to include design in their QMS.

There is application guidance available from ISO to assist organizations in evaluating the impact of this change on an organization. It is "Guidance on ISO 9001:2000 Clause 1.2 'Applications'." This guidance is available at both of the following Web sites:

- http://www.bsi.org.uk/iso-tc176-sc2
- http://www.iso.ch/iso/en/iso9000-14000/iso9000/transition.html

Implications for Auditing

Auditors and third-party certification bodies will need to carefully review the scopes of organizations to ensure compliance with the applications clause of ISO 9001:2000.

Modification of the Purpose of Internal Audits (Clause 8.2.2)

Although the basic intent of the internal audit requirements has not changed substantially, a few of the requirements should be reviewed carefully. In ISO 9001:1994, the requirement existed for the organization to determine the effectiveness of the quality system. ISO 9001:2000 requires the organization to ensure effective implementation of the QMS. This makes it clear that top management has the responsibility for determining, as a part of management review, whether the QMS is effective.

The requirement related to independence of auditors has been liberalized: ISO 9001 now requires that the selection of internal auditors ensure "objectivity and impartiality of the audit process," which provides improved flexibility in the administration of the audit process particularly for very small organizations.

Implications for Implementation

Most organizations should have little difficulty adapting their audit program to meet ISO 9001:2000.

Implications for Auditing

Considerations other than organizational independence need to be used as audit criteria when auditing the "objectivity and impartiality" of the internal audit processes.

SUMMARY

The changes noted in this chapter relate to the content of ISO 9001 that could affect how an organization structures and implements a QMS. Many other changes have been introduced that affect the ease of use of the standard. One primary example is in the area of terminology. Considerable effort was invested in "cleaning up" the language in the standard and in ensuring that words were used consistently (for example, the words *record* and *document* are now used exclusively as nouns and not variably as nouns or verbs). Although such changes may be subtle, they nevertheless should enhance usability and understanding.

Another example is in the area of "ease of use." One criticism of ISO 9001:1994 was that it was targeted at large organizations in the manufacturing world. ISO 9001:2000 is much more "user friendly" to users in other sectors, such as software and service, and should be easier to apply in smaller organizations, or SMEs (small and medium enterprises). The changes in wording to accommodate such users may be transparent but should significantly enhance the ability of all organizations to effectively integrate the ISO model.

The brief descriptions above of potentially significant areas of change provide only an introduction to the "newness" of ISO 9001:2000 and to its potential impact on an organization. Much already has been published regarding what ISO 9001:2000 says and what it really means (a few excellent references include *ISO 9001:2000 Explained* and *ISO 9001:2000: An Audio Workshop and Master Slide Presentation,* both available from ASQ Quality Press). Much more will follow as the standard is used around the world. Such reference material, along with many of the other chapters in this handbook, will provide more insight into the standard so users can find the implementation path that makes sense for each organization.

It has been said that the more things change, the more they remain the same. And so it is with ISO 9001:2000. The ultimate objective of the standard is still to provide a framework organizations can use to operate more efficiently and effectively internally while better serving existing customers and the marketplace.

Section 3

Quality Management System— Scope, Application, Definitions, Documentation, and Records

Introduction

John E. (Jack) West,
Consultant, The Woodlands, Texas

Part 3 of the ISO directives defines the normative elements of an ISO standard as "those elements setting out the provisions to which it is necessary to conform in order to be able to claim compliance with the standard."[1] Clause 0 of ISO 9001:2000 and its subclauses are "informative" and do not form part of the requirements of the standard. On the other hand, the scope is a normative part of every standard. The rules for the scope clause are different from other parts of the normative text. Part 3 of the ISO directives specifies that the topics in clause 1 also must not contain requirements. Part 3 of the ISO directives states that the scope of a standard "shall be succinct so that it can be used as a summary for bibliographic purposes. This element shall be worded as a series of statements of fact."[2] Clause 1, therefore, does not use the word *shall*. It contains material that describes how the standard is used.

The scope clause of ISO 9001 has two subclauses: subclause 1.1, "General," and subclause 1.2, "Application." Subclause 1.1 makes it clear that the standard is intended for use by any organization that needs to demonstrate that its quality management system can consistently provide products that meet requirements. It is also clear from the scope that the focus in ISO 9001 is on achieving customer satisfaction by meeting customer requirements. Actually, this focus on customer satisfaction was also included in the scope of ISO 9001:1994, but that reference was largely ignored.

The 1994 edition of the ISO 9000 family included three requirements standards and a number of guidance documents. The 1994 requirements standards were as follows:

- ISO 9001, *Quality systems—Model for quality assurance in design, development, production, installation, and servicing*

- ISO 9002, *Quality systems—Model for quality assurance in production, installation, and servicing*

- ISO 9003, *Quality systems—Model for quality assurance in final inspection and test*

This arrangement provided a structure in which an organization could use the minimal ISO 9003 if it were appropriate to control only the detection and correction of nonconforming products. ISO 9001 could be used when all aspects of design, production, installation, and servicing were applicable, while ISO 9002 was available to organizations whose scope of operations related to products provided to customers did not include design and development.

The new 2000 revision eliminates the ISO 9002 and 9003 documents. Subclause 1.2, the application clause, provides instructions on how to accommodate the elimination of ISO 9002 and ISO 9003. Key points of the application clause are discussed by J. P. Russell in chapter 9, "Quality Management System Application (Clause 1.2)." Appendix I provides the full text of the ISO/TC 176 guidance to the application of ISO 9001:2000 clause 1.2.

Clause 2, "Normative reference," and clause 3, "Terms and definitions," are also normative portions of the standard. The only normative reference is ISO 9000. Where a term is used in ISO 9001 and is defined in ISO 9000, the definition given in ISO 9000:2000 is the one that applies. ISO 9000:2000 replaces ISO 8402:1994, *Quality management and quality assurance—Vocabulary*. In chapter 10, "International Standards Definitions," F. Craig Johnson discusses the definitions.

The nature of clause 4, "Quality management system," is also normative. It is where the actual requirements for the quality management system start. It is the first clause that uses the word *shall* to indicate mandatory compliance. The clause requires the organization to manage and document the processes that make up the quality management system. In chapter 11, "The Quality Management System," Lawrence A. Wilson discusses the general requirements for a quality management system that are given in clause 4.1. He also presents activities needed to manage its implementation. In section 1, chapter 2, Jeff Hooper discusses the use of the process approach, which is the basis for the system requirements of clause 4.1. Appendix J provides the full text of the ISO/TC 176 guidance on the process approach. In chapter 12, "Documenting the Quality Management System," Jack West describes documenting the quality management system and outlines a method that can be used by organizations to focus on improvement as they document their system.

ENDNOTES

1. ISO Directives, Part 3, 3rd ed., 1997, Clause 3.4: 16.
2. ISO Directives, Part 3, 3rd ed., 1997, Clause 6.2.1: 36.

Chapter 9

Quality Management System Application

J. P. Russell

J. P. Russell and Associates, Gulf Breeze, Florida

The principal reason for ISO 9001:2000 clause 1.2, "Application," is to provide guidance for determining the quality management system (QMS) scope and nonapplicable requirements. In prior versions of the ISO 9000 series standards, organizations were required to select the standard that fit their business. Now there is one requirement standard that is to be used by all organizations. However, when controls are not relevant, organizations are permitted to customize their QMS based on guidance in clause 1.2.

SCOPE OF ISO 9001:2000

ANSI/ISO/ASQ Q9001-2000 clause 1.2 states:

> All the requirements of this International Standard are generic and are intended to be applicable to all organizations, regardless of type, size, and product provided.

ISO 9001:2000 is written for all types of organizations, such as hardware, software, process, and service organizations. Different industries may have their own in-house terminology, but the standard is written using universal, generic terms. Whether an organization is fabricating, assembling, reacting, mixing, coding, hosting, arranging, consulting, or providing accommodations, it will benefit from the implementation of the QMS requirements contained in this standard. The 2000 version of ISO 9001:2000 is written to be more user-friendly to small businesses and service organizations yet remain useful to large manufacturing organizations.

The standard's generic controls and terminology allow it to be used by all organizations; it is not specific to any one particular organization. In all cases where the standard has been adopted by an organization, the QMS must be customized to fit organization needs.

SCOPE OF THE QUALITY MANAGEMENT SYSTEM

When the standard is used for registration purposes, the organization seeking registration must determine the scope of its QMS. The scope is the tangible and physical boundaries of the QMS. Scope may be defined in terms of physical location and products or services for which the QMS has been implemented. [Editor's note: When discussing concepts related to certification, this chapter uses the term "registration" or "registered." The term "registrar" is used in the same sense as the term "certification body." See chapter 39 for an explanation of these terms.]

The QMS scope may stipulate one location or several locations. The QMS processes (design, purchasing, operations, and so on) may be at one location (facility) or spread across several. An organization may have a headquarters with plants, branches, regions, districts, centers, stores, or terminals. Scope must include the identification of products and services being provided under the requirements of the QMS. There can be one product produced in one step or several steps. There can be multiple products that are similar or dissimilar. The scope can include one service, several services, or both services and other types of products. (See Table 9.1.)

Determining the QMS scope is an important decision. An organization may need a QMS to address regulations or statutes, customer mandates, competitive market environments, or management objectives. The ISO 9001:2000 quality management system provides stability, structure, and the means for continual improvement and achieving customer satisfaction.

Once the scope of the QMS has been defined, all the requirements of ISO 9001:2000 must be addressed. An organization cannot arbitrarily decide to limit implementation of some ISO 9001:2000 requirements as part of the scope statement. For example, an organization cannot decide to not comply with the require-

Table 9.1   Example of QMS scopes.

Organization	Manufacture	Transportation	Association	Manufacture
Location	Mytown plant	Headquarters and North American terminals	Home office and regions	H_2O plant
Product/ services	Brackets large and small	Pickup and delivery	Information and merchandise sales	Electrical grade H_2O

ments for control of customer property if it handles customer property, and it cannot decide to delete the requirements for design and development if design and development is required. For registration purposes, an organization cannot claim or imply conformance to ISO 9001:2000 if it has excluded an element of the standard that applies to it.

APPLICABILITY OF CLAUSES

ANSI/ISO/ASQ Q9001-2000 clause 1.2 states:

> *Where any requirement(s) of this International Standard cannot be applied due to the nature of an organization and its product, this can be considered for exclusion.*[1]

The starting point for determining which ISO 9001:2000 requirements apply for a registered quality management system is that all requirements must be addressed. However, it is recognized that not all the requirements of the standard will necessarily be relevant to all organizations and their processes. It is up to the organization seeking registration of its QMS to justify why some requirements do not apply to it.

If specified ISO 9001:2000 requirements are not applicable due to the nature of the organization and its product, they can be considered for exclusion. For example, design and development may not be applicable to an organization that manufactures standard marine anchors, and control of measuring and monitoring devices may not be applicable to an organization that provides a cleaning service.

GUIDELINES FOR EXCLUDING CLAUSES

ANSI/ISO/ASQ Q9001-2000 clause 1.2 states:

> *Where exclusions are made, claims of conformity to this International Standard are not acceptable unless these exclusions are limited to requirements within clause 7, and such exclusions do not affect the organization's ability, or responsibility, to provide product that meets customer, and applicable regulatory requirements.*

Only the requirements in the product realization clause (clause 7) can be considered for exclusion from the QMS. Table 9.2 shows the clauses and subclauses that may be considered for exclusion if not relevant to the organization or product.

Clause 1.2 of ISO 9001:2000 is not intended to apply only to entire clauses. There may be circumstances where specific requirements within a clause or subclause are not applicable. An example is subclause 7.5.3, where traceability requirements may be excluded but requirements regarding identification may be required.

When a clause is not applicable but regulations require control of that process or activity, the clause cannot be excluded. Requirements of ISO 9001:2000 must be met if applicable or required by regulations. *Regulatory* and *statutory requirements* take precedence over the requirements of international standards such as ISO 9001:2000. In the absence of regulatory requirements, ISO 9001:2000 requirements must be met to claim conformity.

Table 9.2   Requirements in clause 7 that may be considered for exclusion.

Clause	Situations where the clause may not be applicable
7.1 Planning of product realization	This clause applies to all the realization clauses and for practical purposes cannot be excluded except as it applies to other clauses being excluded.
7.2 Customer-related processes	Since all organizations have inputs and requirements to meet, it is difficult to envision excluding this clause. However, nontraditional business situations do exist, such as a government agency that may consider the U.S. Congress or another agency as its customer.
7.3 Design and development	When an organization is not responsible for design and development of the product or service this clause can be excluded.
7.4 Purchasing	Public and private service organizations may not purchase any materials, equipment, or services that affect the quality of their service. For example, a temporary employment service agency may exclude the purchasing clause (clause 7.4) if no services or product (parts, equipment, materials) are purchased that would affect the ability of the organization to conform to customer and regulatory requirements.
7.5.1 Control of production and service provision	This clause applies to value-added product or service being provided by the organization. The clause is fundamental to the standard and should not be excluded. Some organizations outsource or subcontract production of the product or provision of the service, but they are not absolved of the responsibility to control the process.
7.5.2 Validation of processes for production and service provision	This clause could be excluded if process outputs (product) can be verified by subsequent measuring and monitoring. For example, an organization that manufactures a product to specified dimensions may be able to justify exclusion of this clause.
7.5.3 Identification and traceability	If identification, traceability, and product (service) status are not required, this clause could be excluded. As is the case with the other clauses, it is possible that only portions of this clause are relevant.
7.5.4 Customer property	If no customer property (product, materials, proprietary information) is used in the product realization process, this clause could be considered for exclusion. Note: designs, blueprints, procedures, or drawings supplied by the customer may be intellectual property.
7.5.5 Preservation of product	Many service organizations may not store product or material needed to conform to customer or regulatory requirements. It should be noted that *product* only applies to the product intended for, or required by, a customer. (See ISO 9001:2000 clause 1.1, note.)
7.6 Control of monitoring and measuring devices	An organization may exclude this clause when conformity of the product (service) is not verified by measuring and monitoring devices. For example, some service organizations do not use inspection equipment.

JUSTIFICATION OF EXCLUSIONS

ANSI/ISO/ASQ Q9001-2000 clause 4.2.2(a) states:

The organization shall establish and maintain a quality manual that includes: a) the scope of the quality management system, including details of and justification for any exclusions (see 1.2).

When it is appropriate for an organization to exclude certain requirements in its implementation of ISO 9001:2000, such exclusions must be defined and justified in the organization's quality manual. Just as it is important to clearly define what facilities and products are included in the registered/certified QMS, it is equally important to know if an organization has excluded certain ISO 9001:2000 requirements. When an organization has properly justified excluding certain ISO 9001:2000 clauses, such exclusions must be made clear in registration documents and any other publicly distributed documents, such as marketing materials. Such declarations should not be confusing or misleading to customers and end users of the organization's product or service.

Outsourcing or *subcontracting* an activity cannot be the sole justification for exclusion of a requirement. An organization must determine who has overall responsibility for that activity regardless of outsource or subcontract status. If responsibility resides with the organization, the organization must demonstrate that it has implemented adequate controls to ensure conformance to ISO 9001:2000 requirements. The extent of the controls will depend on the nature of the outsourced activity and risk. Typically, outsourced or subcontracted activities are controlled under purchasing (clause 7.4). Control can include issuing specifications; conducting product, process, and system audits at the subcontractor or outsource facility; testing preshipment samples; source inspection; and so on. An organization can require a supplier to conform to product or service specifications as well as require conformance to ISO 9001:2000.

An outsourced or subcontracted activity may be excluded if it does not affect the organization's ability or responsibility to provide product that meets customer and applicable regulatory requirements. In many cases outsourcing decisions are based on financial reasons, resource availability, or competency requirements and not because it does not affect meeting product or service requirements.

Organizations may outsource or subcontract *activities that are outside clause 7*, such as training (clause 6.2) or measurement and monitoring of product (clause 8.2.4). Organizations are expected to maintain responsibility and control of those processes outsourced or subcontracted outside clause 7.

Lack of *regulatory requirements* cannot be used as justification for excluding requirements of ISO 9001:2000 from a QMS. There may be situations where an activity affects the organization's ability or responsibility to provide products that fulfill customer and applicable regulatory requirements but regulations do not require control. For example, an organization may design a product but design does not fall under regulatory requirements.

Previous registration of the QMS to ISO 9002 or ISO 9003 cannot be used as justification for exclusion of ISO 9001:2000 requirements. The only clauses that can be excluded are those that have no affect on conformity of the product or service to requirements. For example, an organization that does design but chooses to be registered to ISO 9002:1994 cannot exclude design to be registered to ISO 9001:2000. Previous QMS scope statements that excluded certain ISO 9000:1994 version requirements are not considered sufficient justification for exclusion of ISO 9001:2000 requirements.

EXCLUSION SUMMARY

Requirements cannot be excluded:[2]

- By declaration in the scope statement
- If the requirements are outside clause 7
- Just because they are outsourced or subcontracted
- For the sole reason that they were not included in the 1994 version QMS
- Because regulations do not require it
- When regulations do require it
- To absolve the organization from meeting customer requirements

Requirements can be excluded:

- When they are not relevant (applicable) to an organization
- If the requirements are part of clause 7
- When the clause does not affect the organization's ability or responsibility to meet requirements
- When adequately justified in the quality manual

REGISTRAR OVERSIGHT

According to a September 1999 communiqué of the IAF-ISO/TC176-ISO/CASCO[3] joint group responsible for defining transition policy:

Certification/Registration Bodies will need to take particular care in defining the scope of certificates issued to ISO 9001:2000, and the permissible exclusions[3] to the requirements of that standard.

Because there will no longer be the option to issue certificates to ISO 9002 or 9003 after 15 December 2003, a clear description of the scope of an organization's QMS and the application of the requirements of ISO 9001:2000 is very important.

Registrars are expected to pay particular attention to registration scope and the justification of any claimed exclusions. Registrars should investigate the validity of exclusions claimed by the organization. Organizations cannot claim conformance to ISO 9001:2000 unless they have met all requirements and have justified all exclusions.

The applications clause is written so that organizations can exclude ISO 9001:2000 requirements that do not apply to them, but organizations must exercise the utmost care when doing so. This clause should not be used to exclude applicable requirements (cut corners) or to deceive customers. Exclusions should be declared in the quality manual and other documents (marketing literature) provided to customers and other interested parties where conformance to ISO 9001:2000 is claimed.

EXAMPLE SUMMARIES

Table 9.3 contains summaries of examples found in ISO/TC 176/SC 2/N524R2, *Guidance on ISO 9001:2000 clause 1.2 "Application."* The guidance document and the detailed examples can be found in Appendix I. Simply scan the summaries and select the example or examples that interest you.

Table 9.3 Example summaries.

Organization	Example summary
ABC Bank	**Type:** Service organization (institutional, banking). **Scope:** ABC Bank services for online Internet banking. **QMS registration:** ISO 9001:2000. **Example note:** Customer intellectual property is highlighted.
DEF Bottling Company	**Type:** Process organization (mixing and bottling). **Scope:** DEF Bottling Company—complete line of products and packaging at Anytown. **QMS registration:** ISO 9001:2000 excluding the nonapplicable process of design and development (clause 7.3). **Example note:** Purchasing is not excluded even though purchasing is handled at corporate headquarters.
HIJ & Partners	**Type:** Service organization (personal, legal services). **Scope:** HIJ & Partners law firm—standard and customized legal services at the Anytown office. **QMS registration:** ISO 9001:2000 except the nonapplicable clause 7.6 concerning the control of measuring and monitoring devices. **Example note:** Design and development is not excluded because the organization designs customized services for clients.
XYZ Electronics	**Type:** Hardware organization (electronic devices). **Scope:** XYZ Electronics—complete line mobile phones from the Anytown facility. **QMS registration:** ISO 9001:2000 excluding the nonapplicable process of design and development (ISO 9001:2000 clause 7.3). **Example note:** The design information provided by the customer is controlled as customer property under clause 7.5.4.
KML Medical	**Type:** Hardware organization (medical devices). **Scope:** KML Medical—design and manufacture of medical devices at Anytown. **QMS registration:** ISO 9001:2000 with no exclusions. **Example note:** The company does design and claims conformity to ISO 9001:2000, so it cannot exclude design from its QMS even though regulations do not require design control.

Continued

Table 9.3 Example summaries *(continued)*.

Organization	Example summary
NOP Ltd.	**Type:** Service (maintenance of units) as part of a large organization.
	Scope: NOP Ltd. workshop—train maintenance services at Anytown facility.
	QMS registration: ISO 9001:2000 excluding the nonapplicable process of design and development (clause 7.3).
	Example note: Design and development is not applicable to the workshop facilities because it is done at headquarters. This is an example of a support function within a large organization seeking registration of its QMS. The concepts of internal customer, internal customer property, and centralized purchasing are included in this example.
TCH Enterprise	**Type:** Hardware organization (manufactured product).
	Scope: TCH Enterprise—new product.
	QMS registration: ISO 9001:2000.
	Example note: This is an example of an organization subcontracting design and manufacturing. There are no exclusions except for lack of design control for the subcontracting organization manufacturing the product.
CDH Construction Ltd.	**Type:** Service organization (construction).
	Scope: CDH Construction Ltd.—design, development, and construction building services.
	QMS registration: ISO 9001:2000.
	Example note: The organization maintains responsibility for design even though it is subcontracted (outsourced).
AKP Corp	**Type:** Hardware organization (electric motors).
	Scope: AKP Corp.—complete line of electric motors manufactured at Anytown.
	QMS registration: ISO 9001:2000 without exclusions.
	Example note: Example of a customer requiring traceability even though the organization does not. Traceability controls must be implemented to claim conformity to ISO 9001:2000.

CONCLUSION

Using the information provided here and in Appendix I, organizations should be able to determine their scope with confidence. The guidance provided is sound but cannot address every situation. The idea that an organization can exclude nonapplicable requirements is new, but it makes sense. Under the old standard, cases arose where organizations would write procedures for controls that were not relevant to their system and that did not make sense.

The general rule is to ensure that the scope makes sense. If the organization is responsible for design, then there should be design control; if it is responsible for customer property, then there should be customer property controls; and so on.

ENDNOTES

1. In the ISO/DIS version of the standard, clause 1.2 was titled "Permissible exclusions." The title was changed to "Application" in the FDIS version of ISO 9001:2000.
2. J. P. Russell, *ISO 9001:2K Delta Class,* Web-based training materials (J. P. Russell & Associates), www.QualityWBT.com (Accessed 29 June 2001).
3. The IAF-ISO/TC176-ISO/CASCO joint group is where the International Accreditation Forum (IAF), the ISO Technical Committee 176 (which is responsible for the development of the ISO 9000 standards), and the ISO Policy Committee on Conformity Assessment (ISO/CASCO) meet to coordinate their work.

Chapter 10
International Standards Definitions

F. Craig Johnson
Florida State University, Tallahassee, Florida

ISO TERMS AND DEFINITIONS

The ISO terminology standards establish the principles, theory, method, vocabulary, and application for all ISO terms and definitions. They provide guidelines for classifying and diagramming a *concept* (unit of knowledge created by a unique combination of characteristics). These *characteristics* (an abstraction of an object or set of objects) are used to classify essential concepts. Finally, delimiting characteristics differentiate the essential concepts needed to establish common terms and definitions for standards users.

- An ISO *term* is a "verbal designation of a general concept in a specific subject field." The specific subject field in ISO 9000:2000 is quality management systems.

- An ISO *definition* is a "representation of a concept by a descriptive statement which serves to differentiate it from related concepts." Ten essential concepts are differentiated into 80 terms with their ISO 9000:2000 definitions as follows:

  1. *Quality:* 5 terms and definitions
  2. *Management:* 15 terms and definitions
  3. *Organization:* 7 terms and definitions
  4. *Product and process:* 5 terms and definitions
  5. *Characteristics:* 4 terms and definitions

6. *Conformity:* 13 terms and definitions
7. *Documentation:* 6 terms and definitions
8. *Examination:* 7 terms and definitions
9. *Audit:* 12 terms and definitions
10. *Measurement process:* 6 terms and definitions

These 80 ISO 9000:2000 terms and definitions establish the required "coherent and harmonized vocabulary that is easily understood by all the potential users of quality management system standards" consisting of "generic relationships" between essential concepts and delimiting characteristics. This can take the following form:

[Definition = essential concept + delimiting characteristic]

For example, the essential concept *management* is differentiated for the functions of control and assurance as follows:

- *Quality control* is defined as "part of quality management focused on fulfilling quality requirements":

  [Quality control = quality management + fulfilling quality requirements]

- *Quality assurance* is defined as "part of quality management focused on providing confidence that requirements will be met":

  [Quality assurance = quality management + providing confidence]

ISO terminology standards also provide guidance on designations other than terms, including symbols, names, abbreviations, acronyms, initials, and combined terms. The purpose of these designations is to establish consistent usage throughout ISO standards. All these designations can be normative.

ISO terms and definitions can be arranged alphabetically, thematically, systematically, or by some combination thereof. ISO directives recommend that terms should be arranged, "according to the hierarchy of the concepts. The terms and definitions of general concepts shall precede those of less general concepts." ISO 9000:2000 accepts this recommendation and arranges the quality management system terms and definitions systematically based on the 10 essential concepts. An informative alphabetical index is also provided.

OTHER DEFINITIONS

ISO terms and definitions do not address all the needs and expectations of ISO 9000 users because ISO definitions are limited to differentiating concepts and seeking agreement for selected terms. Other definitions are needed for terms used but not defined in ISO standards. Also, organizations may wish to use operational definitions or propositions to direct and control an organization. These definitions can be included as a part of the quality management system.

UNDEFINED TERMS

ISO standards users should seek the dictionary definition for undefined terms in ISO standards when the text in the body of the standard does not make the intended meaning clear.

For example, the verb *communicate* is used in ISO 9001 and 9004 but is not defined in ISO 9000; however, the body of the standard does make the intended meaning clear. The dictionary suggested by the 1997 ISO/IEC directives, part 3 is *The Shorter Oxford English Dictionary*, which has 25 definitions of *communicate* to select from. Two of these definitions, "transmit information" and "succeed in evoking understanding with," could be interpreted as two different requirements. Guidance on using definitions selected from the concise Oxford dictionary, for undefined terms in ISO 9001:2000 and ISO 9004:2000, is available electronically to the public. (This guidance document is provided on the accompanying CD as Appendix L.)

OPERATIONAL DEFINITIONS

Operational definitions containing ISO 9000 defined terms should be technically consistent with their ISO 9000 definition. Operational definitions, often in the form of flowcharts, are used in quality management systems to create common understanding among suppliers, organizations, and customers to describe and explain the steps taken to create an object.

PROPOSITIONS

When ISO 9000 terms are used to make logical arguments, they should have the meaning agreed to in ISO 9000:2000. Propositions, similar to "real" definitions used in scientific inquiry, often are used to analyze objective evidence, to draw inferences, and to construct logical arguments. Propositions are stated as a *subject*, which is the thing about which the assertion is being made; a *verb*, which takes some form of the infinitive "to be," and the *object*, which states the assertion. Some examples of these propositions are the following:

- *Process* improvement criteria are set to satisfy requirements
- Confidence increases as *requirements* are met
- Confidence is restored by *corrective action* on root causes

ISO 9000 FAMILY

The family of quality management system standards covered by ISO 9000 includes the following:

- ISO 9000 contains technical normative terms and definitions as well as informative examples, notes, and an annex
- ISO 9001 uses technical normative terms to state provisions in the form of "requirements" for the quality management system

- ISO 9004 uses technical normative terms to state provisions in the form of "recommendations" for performance improvement related to all management systems in an organization
- Other ISO quality management system standards, technical reports, and technical specifications use technical normative terms to provide guidance on common management activities such as auditing, interpreting test results, training, and describing the quality management system

The ISO family of standards does not include definitions that specify requirements that must be fulfilled to establish the fitness for purpose of a specific product, process, or service.

ISO 9000 PURPOSE

ISO 9000 has two purposes. The first is to describe the fundamentals of quality management systems, and the second is to specify the terminology (designations belonging to special knowledge) for quality management systems. This chapter relates to the second purpose.

ISO 9001:2000 AND USERS OF THE ISO 9000 SERIES

Global acceptance of the ISO 9000 series of standards depends on a harmonized technical description of terms that facilitate international interchange of products, processes, services, and test results information. The users of ISO 9000 include:

- Organizations using quality management systems
- Organizations seeking confidence from their suppliers
- Users of products
- Suppliers
- Customers
- Regulators
- Auditors
- Certification/registration bodies
- Consultants
- Developers of related standards

ISO 9000 TERMS

Clause 3 of ISO 9000 provides the essential meaning for the way terms are used in the ISO 9000 family of quality management systems standards but does not prescribe how these concepts should be implemented. This nonprescriptive characteristic gives ISO 9000 standards wide applicability for various products and situations of use. The terms defined in ISO 9000:

- Have explicit meaning for all standards in the ISO 9000 family that cite ISO 9000:2000 in clause 2, "Normative references"

- Ensure common usage in the family
- Are translatable into different languages

The layout for each term and definition follows the directions given in ISO 10241. The order is as follows, with an example given in brackets [example] for the term *conformity* from ISO 9000:2000:

- Entry number [3.6.1]
- Preferred term(s) [conformity]
- Admitted term(s)
- Deprecated term(s) [conformance]
- Definition [fulfillment of a *requirement* (3.1.2)]
- Example(s)
- Note(s) [NOTE 1 This definition is consistent with ISO/IEC Guide 2...]

Reference to another entry is in *italic* followed by bracketed number of the entry where it is first mentioned.

The complete entry follows:

3.6.1

Conformity

fulfillment of a *requirement* (3.1.2)

NOTE 1 This definition is consistent with ISO/IEC (Guide 2) but differs from it in phrasing to fit into the ISO 9000 concepts.

NOTE 2 The term "conformance" is synonymous but deprecated.

Source: ANSI/ISO/ASQ Q9000-2000

ISO 9000 DEFINITIONS

The definitions in clause 3 of ISO 9000 do not comprise a technical language based on formal logic or scientific inquiry. Rather, quality management system concepts are based on the objective reality of the practice of quality management systems and express that reality in understandable language. ISO member bodies attested to the understandable language of ISO 9000 when they approved it.

The following are the criteria used to develop the ISO 9000 terms and definitions:

- A technical description but without the use of technical language.
- A coherent and harmonized vocabulary that is easily understood by all potential users of quality management system standards. The ISO 9000 terms and definitions are cited in clause 2 as "normative reference" in all the ISO 9000 family of standards.

For example, the following text appears in clauses 2 and 3 of both ISO 9001 and ISO 9004:

> **2 Normative reference**
>
> The following normative document contains provisions which, through reference in this text, constitute provisions of this International Standard.
>
> **3 Terms and definitions**
>
> For the purpose of this International Standard, the terms and definitions given in ISO 9000 apply.

Source: ANSI/ISO/ASQ Q9000-2000

ISO 9000 NORMATIVE REFERENCES

Confusion may arise about the use of prescriptive words like *normative* and *provisions* in nonprescriptive informative text. Simply stated, normative elements are those elements setting out the provisions with which it is necessary to comply in order to be able to claim conformity with the standard. The place of normative elements can be seen more clearly within the context of the following ISO classification for general elements of standards.

Preliminary elements identify the standard, introduce its content, and explain its background, its development, and its relationship with other standards.

Preliminary elements include:

- Title page
- Contents
- Foreword
- Introduction

Normative elements include both general and technical clauses.
The general clauses of an ISO standard include:

- Title
- Scope
- Normative references

The technical clauses of an ISO standard include:

- Definitions
- Symbols and abbreviations
- Requirements
- Sampling
- Test methods
- Classification and designations

- Marking, labeling, and packaging
- Normative annexes

Supplementary elements may be used in ISO standards to provide additional information intended to assist the understanding or use of the standard, including:

- Informative annexes
- Footnotes

The terms in clause 3 of ISO 9000 are used in ISO 9001 to state requirements and are used in ISO 9004 to provide guidance. However, ISO 9000 itself does not state requirements. This is consistent with annex C to Part 3 of the ISO/IEC Directives, clause C.1.5, "Drafting of definitions." A definition shall not take the form of, or contain, a requirement. This prevents defined terms from increasing the prescriptive nature of individual standards and from adding requirements to them.

Suggestions on how to use a term appropriately may be included in notes following a definition, but those notes are informative and not prescriptive. ISO/IEC Directives, Part 3, clause 6.5.1, contains guidance on notes and examples: "Notes and examples integrated in the text of a standard shall only be used for giving additional information intended to assist the understanding or use of the standard and shall not contain provisions to which it is necessary to conform in order to be able to claim compliance with the standard."

Terms defined in clause 3 of ISO 9000 have the same meaning in ISO 9001, 9004 and all other standards in the ISO 9000 family. For example, the term *top management* is consistently used to mean "person or group who direct and control an organization."

In ISO 9001 *top management* is used in a requirement clause: "Top management shall review the organization's quality management system, at planned intervals, to ensure its continuing suitability, adequacy, and effectiveness." In ISO 9004 top management is used in a guidance clause: "Top management should develop the management review activity beyond verification of the effectiveness and efficiency of the quality management system into a process that extends to the whole organization, and which evaluates the efficiency of the system." The term top management has the same meaning in both standards.

ISO 9000 CONCEPTS

ISO 9000 states, as a quality management principle (clause 0.2e), "Identifying, understanding, and managing interrelated processes as a system contributes to the organization's effectiveness and efficiency in achieving its objectives."

ISO 704, "Principles and methods of terminology," states "The terminology of any subject field should not be an arbitrary collection of terms, but rather a coherent terminological system corresponding to a system of concepts." It provides reasonable expectations for a terminological system to

- Serve as a means of mental ordering of knowledge
- Visualize and clarify the relationship between concepts
- Permit the optimization of unified and standardized terminology
- Establish equivalence between terminologies in different languages

ISO 9000 states, "an analysis of the relationships between concepts within the field of quality management systems and the arrangement of them within a concept system . . . was used in the development of the vocabulary in this international standard." Well-known and widely used quality management terms (see ISO 8402) were developed and arranged into a concept system by ISO/TC 176 Subcommittee 1 on Terminology. The subcommittee members were national experts in terminology with broad quality management experience. The method used in the development of the vocabulary is presented in ISO 9000 annex A. Note that annex A is *informative*.

CONCEPT DIAGRAMS

Concept diagrams are tools used by writers of vocabularies to understand the relationships among the terms defined. ISO terminology standards include an informative annex of "graphic representations" to show these relationships as:

- Generic: an essential concept plus a delimiting characteristic
- Partitive: one concept is the whole and another is a part of the whole
- Associative: a thematic relationship by virtue of experience

The following are examples of these relationships in ISO 9000:2000:

- Generic:
  - Document
  - Specification
  - Quality manual
  - Quality plan
  - Record
  - Procedure document
- Partitive:
  - Quality management
  - Quality planning
  - Quality control
  - Quality assurance
  - Quality improvement

The following is an example of a relationship among terms:

Grade . . . . Requirement
Requirement . . . . Quality
Quality . . . . Customer satisfaction
Customer satisfaction . . . Capability

The concept diagrams in annex A may be helpful to users of ISO 9000:2000 as they seek to understand the relationships among terms. Some users may find the diagrams confusing and of little value. The main reason annex A is included is to facilitate the translation of the ISO 9000 family of quality management standards into languages other than English. This is important because it is a general requirement of ISO standards that "the texts in the different official language versions shall be technically equivalent and structurally identical."

This provision ensures that contracts among organizations, their suppliers, and their customers have the same meaning, regardless of the language in which the contract is written.

Two additional provisions of ISO 9000:2000, called "universal transparency" and "the substitution rule," reinforce the intended "technically equivalent" ISO requirement. Universal transparency relies more on the concepts and the characteristics than on a literal translation.

For example the term *interested party* is defined in ISO 9000:2000 as "a person or group having an interest in the performance or success of an organization." The more common term in English is *stakeholder*. However, a literal translation of this term into some languages would be "a person or group holding a stick." Selecting the term *interested party* makes the translation more transparent but leaves the English definition awkwardly defining *interested party* as "a person or group having an interest," which comes close to being a tautology because the definition includes the term being defined. Compromises like this, reached by a consensus process, do not always satisfy all users.

The substitution rule checks the accuracy of the definition: "When a term is substituted by its definition, subject to minor syntax changes, there should be no change in the meaning."

For example, ISO 9000:2000 defines *capability* as the "ability of an *organization, system* or *process* to realize a *product* that will fulfill the *requirements* for that product." The substitution rule would expand the definition to the "ability of a group of people and facilities with an arrangement of responsibilities, authorities and relationships, a set of interrelated or interacting elements, or a set of interrelated or interacting activities which transforms inputs into outputs to realize a result of a process that will fulfill the need or expectation that is stated, generally implied, or obligatory." This is a useful check for standards writers and translators but of little interest to the typical ISO 9000:2000 user.

ISO 9000:2000 GENERIC DEFINITIONS

All 80 terms defined in ISO 9000, clause 3, are related to one of 10 quality management system concepts. These concepts and differentiating functions and their associated concepts and differentiating functions are presented following. In ISO 9000, the concept diagrams for each essential concept is presented in an informative annex A. The diagrams find their widest acceptance among users who need to translate ISO 9000 standards into their own language. The following relationships are not exact replications of the terms and definitions in ISO 9000:2000 and are presented to show the generic relationships more than a definition of terms. The exact terms and definitions can be found in ISO 9000:2000, clause 3.

ISO 9000:2000 GENERIC RELATIONSHIPS

Quality: degree to which characteristics fulfill requirements

Requirement: stated need or requirement

Grade: rank or category of requirement

Customer satisfaction: perception of degree of fulfillment

Capability: ability to realize a product to fulfill requirements

Management: coordinated activities to direct and control an organization

Top management: person or group who direct and control

Quality policy: overall direction expressed by top management

Quality objective: something sought or aimed at

Management system: to establish and achieve policy objectives

System: set of interrelated elements

Quality management system: manage system with regard to quality

Quality management: control and direct with regard to quality

Quality planning: quality management focus on objectives, processes, and resources

Quality control: focus on fulfilling requirements

Quality assurance: providing confidence that requirements will be met

Quality improvement: increasing ability to fulfill requirements

Effectiveness: extent to which planned activities are realized and results achieved

Efficiency: relationship between the result achieved and resources used

Organization: people, facilities, arranged responsibility, authority, and relationships

Organizational structure: responsibility, authority, and relationships between people

Infrastructure: system of facilities, equipment, and service

Work environment: conditions under which work is performed

Interested parties: persons having an interest in performance or success

Supplier: person that provides a product

Customer: person that receives a product

PRODUCT AND PROCESS

Process: activities that transform inputs into outputs

Product: result of a process

Procedure: way to carry out an activity or process

Project: an activity objective conforming to requirements and constraints

Design and development: processes that transform requirements into characteristics

Characteristics: distinguishing features

Dependability: characteristics related to performance and influencing factors

Traceability: ability to trace history, application, or location

Quality characteristics: characteristics related to a requirement

Conformity: fulfillment of a requirement (stated need or expectation)

Nonconformity: nonfulfillment of a requirement

Defect: nonfulfillment of a requirement related to use

Release: permission for product to proceed to the next stage

Concession: permission to release a product that does not conform

Deviation point: permission to depart from specified requirements

Correction: eliminate a detected nonconformity

Corrective action: eliminate cause of detected nonconformity

Preventive action: eliminate cause of potential nonconformity

Scrap: preclude original intended use

Rework: make a nonconforming product conform to requirements

Repair: make a nonconforming product conform to intended usage requirements

Regrade: alter the grade of a nonconforming product

DOCUMENTATION

Document: information and its supporting media

Information: meaningful data

Procedure document: a document containing a written procedure

Specification: document stating requirements

Quality manual: document specifying the quality management system of an organization

Quality plan: document specifying procedures and resources

Record: document stating results

EXAMINATION

Review: suitability, adequacy, and effectiveness of subject matter to achieve objectives

Inspection: observation and judgement

Test: determining characteristics according to procedures

Objective evidence: data supporting existence

Verification: objective evidence that the specification has been fulfilled

Validation: objective evidence that the requirements for intended use have been fulfilled

Audit: degree to which agreed criteria are fulfilled

Auditee: organization to be audited

Audit client: organization requesting an audit

Audit program: planned for specific time and purpose

Audit scope: extent and boundaries

Audit findings: result of an audit

Criteria: policies, procedures, or requirements as a reference

Audit team: persons conducting an audit

Audit evidence: facts relevant to criteria that can be cross-checked

Audit conclusions: outcome from findings

Auditor: person appointed to conduct an audit

Technical expert: person with specific knowledge

Measurement process: set of operations to determine the value of a quantity

Measurement control system: elements for metrological confirmation and control

Metrological function: responsibility for the measurement control system

Metrological confirmation: measuring equipment complying with use requirements

Metrological characteristic: distinguishing feature influencing measurement result

Measuring equipment: instruments, software, material for a measurement process

"Terms relating to quantities, units, measurement, and measuring instruments are defined in the *International Vocabulary of Basic and General Terms in Metrology* (VIM), prepared jointly by the International Bureau of Weights and Measures (BIPM), the International Organization of Legal Metrology (OIML), ISO, and IEC" (ISO directives, guide 2).

REFERENCES

ISO 10241:1992, International terminology standards—Preparation and layout

ISO 1087-1:2000, Terminology work—Vocabulary, Part 1, Theory and application.

ISO 704:1987E, Terminology work—Principles and methods of terminology.

ISO 9000:2000, Quality management systems—Fundamentals and vocabulary.

ISO/IEC Directives, Part 3, Rules for the structure and drafting of International Standards, 3rd ed., 1997.

ISO/IEC Guide 2, General vocabulary—Standardisation and related activities, 2nd ed., 1992.

Chapter 11

The Quality Management System

Lawrence A. Wilson
Lawrence A. Wilson and Associates, Atlanta, Georgia

WHAT IS A QUALITY MANAGEMENT SYSTEM?

By an obvious definition, a quality management system (QMS) is a system for managing the quality of an organization. It covers everything in the organization that relates to quality, including products and services, processes, operations, and customer satisfaction. To fully understand the QMS, it is necessary to briefly explore the basic concepts upon which the QMS of any organization is based.

UNDERSTANDING THE CONCEPTS BEHIND A QUALITY MANAGEMENT SYSTEM

Most individuals tend to measure point-in-time successes, such as activities, actions, and events. The truth is that there are few such single-point successes. Almost all successes are related to specific points *in a process* or to the operation of the process itself (the end point of the process or the achievement of its cyclic nature).

Virtually everything is accomplished by means of processes. The linear or cyclic order of a set of activities, actions, or events constitutes a process. Each process has at least one input (subprocess, material, data, action, or event); involves the accomplishment of the process focus step (the core transforming or realization activity, subprocess, action, or event) and ends with a process output (such as a product or service, material, or a report).

A process may be as simple as driving to work or it may be as complicated as designing a space vehicle. Each of these examples requires the following subprocesses:

- Determination of the applicable process inputs (driving route, time, auto, and driver, or mission, performance, materials, and cost)
- Performance of the core transforming or realization steps (the actual drive to work or the actual designing of the space vehicle)
- Attainment of the intended process goal (arrival at work or completion of the vehicle design)

As stated earlier, the nature of many processes may be cyclic. In that situation, the process output often becomes the upgraded input, or at least a more appropriate input, for the process, eventually resulting in a further improved output. When a process operates in this cyclic mode, improvement of the process is achieved on a continuous basis (for example, the drive to work or the space vehicle design may eventually be optimized).

Clearly, many processes are linked to one another. This is true on a serial linkage basis as well as on a side-linked or a branched basis. The linkages among processes result from common points or steps in two or more processes. Processes linked in this manner are regarded as interrelated or interactive processes, and the extent of this interrelationship network may involve many processes. For instance, a process dealing with customer satisfaction will obviously, as a minimum, have links with the employee training process, the sales process, the warranty process, and the customer service process. Of course, each of these processes may also link with other processes, which leads to the concept of a process network, better known as a *system*. Depending on the size of the organization and the particular aspect being reviewed, a system may be large or small. As expected, those systems that deal with the management of all or part of the organization are known as management systems.

Again, a quality management system is a set of interrelated processes that focuses on establishing and achieving the quality policy and quality objectives of an organization. The QMS is usually one of the more complex management systems within an organization, simply because the quality policy and quality objectives embrace so much of the organization, including its performance and operation, and its products and/or services. Any organization, no matter how large or how small, has a QMS. In a large organization it may be very complex while in a small organization it may be very simple.

THE PURPOSE OF A QUALITY MANAGEMENT SYSTEM

First and foremost, the QMS is a management system. Management must determine and establish the requirements for successful operational performance of the organization. The organization's overall planning process begins with the creation of management's vision, mission, and strategic and tactical objectives for the organization. Part of this planning process must involve management requirements for the quality of operational performance, the quality of products and/or services, the satisfaction of customers and other interested parties, and continual improvement. The accomplishment of these requirements is the purpose for which the QMS is established. The QMS is the tool, guidance, and control by which the organization ensures that these quality objectives are achieved. To affirm the importance of meeting these management expectations and the quality requirements they have established, members of the organization's top management must be the visible leaders of the QMS.

REQUIREMENTS FOR A QUALITY MANAGEMENT SYSTEM

As indicated earlier, all organizations have some type of quality management system. It may be based on a craftperson's pride; it may be based on nothing more than an end-of-the-line inspection; it may depend on customer inspection and acceptance; or it may be a world-class QMS. Some organizations have started with virtually no QMS and have matured their system into a very respectable ISO 9001–compliant QMS. Other organizations have started with an existing military or commercial QMS and have improved it to the point at which it approaches world-class. ISO 9004 can be used as a tool to aid in the improvement of a QMS beyond simple compliance with the basic ISO 9001 requirements.

The requirements for a successful quality management system are as follows:

- Top management must be the recognized leader of the QMS
- Top management must create an environment in which the QMS can be effective
- Top management must assure compliance with a documented QMS
- Top management must supply the resources, training, and support for employees implementing the QMS
- Top management must continually review the compliance performance of the organization
- Top management must demonstrate expectations of outstanding performance and improvement of the system
- Top management must recognize the successful efforts of the workforce
- Employees and other interested parties must be involved and must support the QMS

As can be seen, management plays the key role in ensuring that the QMS works as planned.

STRUCTURE OF THE QUALITY MANAGEMENT SYSTEM

There are no mandatory requirements for the structure of a QMS, but clearly the structure must be both effective and suitable to the needs of the organization. The QMS needs to reflect the organization itself, since it basically guides how the majority of the organization is operated. This point is quite significant but is often overlooked because of the association with the term *quality* and the assumption that the QMS relates only to that functional unit in the organization.

The operational processes and activities that are required for the performance of the organization's QMS depend on such aspects as:

- The products and/or services provided by the organization
- The facilities and equipment involved
- The size of the organization
- The training and experience level of the workforce
- The structure of the organization itself

Many QMS processes are structured as being operational and related to products and/or services or to the realization of products and/or services. QMS processes other than those for product realization are support processes. Examples of support processes include control and management-related processes focused on measurement and performance, personnel and training, environment, health and safety, and customer satisfaction. Some processes may even be limited to specific organizational functions.

Customarily, when the structure of the QMS is described, it is really the nature of the QMS documentation that is discussed. This is not inappropriate, since the QMS must be documented to the extent necessary for the operation of the QMS. Based on the fact that the QMS must be documented, and since the QMS reflects the basic operation and structure of the organization, the documentation itself tends to be a valid measure of the organization's structure. QMS documentation is examined further in chapter 12.

FACTORS THAT DRIVE THE QUALITY MANAGEMENT SYSTEM

An examination of the QMSs of successful organizations reveals that they usually encompass a common set of elements. This assumption has been validated by the contents of ISO 9001 and ISO 9004 in 1987 and again in 1994 with the "20 elements" approach used at that time. The year 2000 versions of these standards recognize that these elements are not used in a stand-alone manner but rather as parts of many processes within the QMS. Compliance with the QMS standard selected by an organization clearly is one of the main drivers of the nature of the QMS. It becomes the guidance and the "measuring stick" for successful QMS performance.

An active, involved leadership is probably the most significant driver for the establishment, implementation, operation, and improvement of an organization's QMS. As stated earlier, management creates the environment in which the QMS can successfully operate. Management review of the content of the QMS and the level of compliance (or corrected variance) with the documentation and procedures of the QMS causes all customers and other interested parties of the organization (employees, suppliers, shareholders, regulators, society, and so on) to observe and support the organization's commitment to meeting its quality-related objectives.

In addition to the internal requirements imposed by the leadership of the organization, there are other requirements imposed by customers and interested parties. These requirements are drivers and must also be incorporated into the QMS. Of course, the nature and size of the organization also tend to be reflected in the QMS.

An organization can have a relatively simple QMS if it:

- Is small and relatively uncomplicated
- Has only a single and simple product line

- Has an experienced and well-trained workforce
- Performs work to customer-supplied documents

Note, however, that a simple QMS must still address all of the processes used by the organization to satisfy its policies and commitments as well as the contracts and regulations of customers and other interested parties.

Obviously, some drivers that cause the QMS to reflect increasing complexity occur when:

- The organization becomes larger and more complex
- The product lines become multiplied and the products more complicated
- The workforce grows larger and more focused on specific rather than general tasks
- Documented procedures and work instructions have to be more detailed

ADMINISTRATION AND OPERATION OF THE QUALITY MANAGEMENT SYSTEM

There is no set method for the administration and operation of the QMS. Uniquely, QMS documentation covers the nature of its own operation. On that basis, the organization determines the best arrangement for QMS administration and incorporates the method into its approved documentation.

RESPONSIBILITY AND AUTHORITY FOR THE QUALITY MANAGEMENT SYSTEM

It is obvious from the term *quality management system* that the QMS is a management responsibility. It is conceived and driven by top management, but all management levels are directly involved in the implementation and operation of the QMS. If implemented properly, the QMS also embraces and involves all members of the organization, at all levels.

Clearly, all functions within the organization are participants in the QMS. Likewise, the QMS is a system that affects the operation of virtually every organizational process and activity.

It must be continually reinforced that the QMS is not just a functional responsibility of quality assurance but rather a system that covers the whole organization, belongs to each function, and is the responsibility of each function.

It was stated earlier that, even though the focus is on quality, the QMS basically represents and guides the way the organization operates. Since the QMS includes a set of management procedures, it is directive in nature, but it also serves as a guide to each QMS practitioner. Within the QMS document control process, there is a built-in mechanism, even a requirement, for continual improvement.

Before the benefits of a QMS can become available to an organization, it must be implemented. The responsibility for the implementation of the QMS should be assigned to an individual or individuals with experience in program management. The implementation process is essentially the operation of a program, with decisions that must be made as to what actions and resources are required, where they are required, when they are required, and so on. The achievement of an operational QMS involves the coordination of the efforts of many functions and individuals and the scheduling of activities at optimal times.

The ISO 9001 standard requires the appointment of one or more members of management to act as management representatives for the implementation (and operation) of the ISO 9001–based QMS. This assignment must go to a recognized leader who has demonstrated performance and authority and the ability to work well with multiple functions and people. Although many quality assurance (QA) management people have been assigned to this task, their frequent lack of scheduling and program management skills often causes the implementation process to be a difficult one and often results in the effort being considered a QA program. Based on observation, this author recommends handling QMS implementation from a program management approach with an experienced program manager.

While the designated management representative often continues beyond the QMS implementation role and into the caretaking or maintenance phase, the caretaking or ongoing responsibilities for the QMS can be assigned to any recognized authority within the organization. This ongoing assignment is frequently placed in the QA function. This transition tends to be derived from the control aspect of the QMS. The audit process background, normally found in the QA function, assists in this role.

VARIATIONS OF THE QUALITY MANAGEMENT SYSTEM

All organizations have some level of existing QMS. The degree of QMS maturity depends on the organization's perceived need for a mature QMS.

The perception of management on this subject may be any of the following:

- No perceived need for a QMS
- An internal need to ensure that products and/or services meet contract
- An industry or regulatory need requiring QMS variation
- Corporate-driven directives to standardize the QMS
- A need to satisfy customer-specified requirements
- A marketing need to be competitive by using expected standards

In most cases, the organization is not starting from a zero base but is upgrading the existing QMS to the point that the management of the organization has determined is necessary for success. Various tools or vehicles can be used to facilitate such a transition. The use of quality system standards or specifications is the usual vehicle for the improvement process. These documents may be specified by the customer, recommended by the industry, required to participate in a particular market, or selected by the organization's management. The organization must select one or a combination of standards to use as its template for developing a mature QMS.

Such standards may be developed by:

- The organization itself
- The related industry
- The customer base

- The regulatory and legal bodies
- An appropriate national standards agency
- The International Organization for Standardization (ISO)

All of these standards reflect what potential QMS developers perceive as being required in order to have a guide for a mature QMS. By examining the nature and content of the existing QMS, comparing that current system with the requirements of the selected standard, and identifying the variances (gap analysis), the organization can determine the actions that must be taken to achieve compliance with the selected standard.

The QMS standards discussed previously can be divided into two classes, the first of which is requirements or directive standards, such as ISO 9001. These standards are focused on the QMS processes that must be implemented in order for the organization to be able to meet the requirements stated within the standard. The second type of standard is the guidance standard or technical guidance document, such as ISO 9004. This type of standard provides guidance as to the best way to achieve a mature QMS that satisfies both the customers and other interested parties and effectively and efficiently benefits the organization itself. The minimum requirements standard seldom addresses such important things as costs and risks, while the guidance standard goes beyond minimum requirements and recognizes the need to make a profit, minimize risk to the organization, and bring benefit to customers and all its other interested parties.

IMPROVING ORGANIZATIONAL PERFORMANCE AS AN OBJECTIVE OF THE QMS

It is the responsibility of prudent management to set improvement goals for the organization. The improvement goals may be based on such operational measures as material costs, cost per unit or service block, delivery cost, unit throughput, man-hours worked, man-hours per unit, delivery/installation and warranty costs, scrap rates, and rework and repair costs. Improvements may also be focused on aspects such as increasing market share, profits, customer and interested party satisfaction, acquisitions, partnerships, and recognition of success. Whatever the measure, the action or process required for the improvement change is virtually sure to be part of the QMS.

The basic QMS, such as ISO 9001, has processes that focus on the control of nonconforming materials, corrective and preventive actions, management review, and internal quality audits. ISO 9001 also has requirements for a management-driven effort to achieve process improvement within the organization, but it does not give details as to how that should be achieved.

The ISO 9004 guidance standard for QMS performance improvement goes beyond 9001 in this area by addressing areas for improvement and methods to use to achieve improvement. The annexes in 9004 provide, first, an assessment tool/methodology for determining the maturity of the QMS, and second, a generic process improvement methodology that is capable of being used by any organization interested in process improvement. While the national and international excellence awards criteria go well beyond 9004, the tools provided by 9004 (and other documents of its caliber) can be used to move an organization toward world-class or award excellence, in fact, as far as the management wishes to take the organization.

EXAMINATION OF THE CONTROL ASPECT OF THE QMS

By itself, the QMS acts as a passive control for the management of the organization. Management has selected a requirements or guidance standard as the basis for the QMS. The standard acts as the regimen for developing a QMS that is compliant with its requirements. The methods of compliance with each of the specified processes or elements have, it is to be hoped, been optimized based on the needs and resources of the organization. In essence, the organization has tailored its methods for compliance with the standard. Continued compliance with the methods documented in the QMS ensures that by the very existence of the QMS the organization has controlled and repetitive processes.

The use of this documented QMS as a further tool or basis for evaluating compliance or noncompliance, by means of internal quality audit, self-audit by user employees, management review and oversight, and so on, permits the organization to identify areas and situations for improvement. This approach, coupled with technical, employee, and management identification of improvement targets, allows the organization to make beneficial improvements and then document the changes as a new or revised part of the QMS. The change then becomes incorporated as part of the passive control mechanism offered by compliance with the QMS.

DOCUMENTING THE QMS

The documented QMS identifies the basic methodology by which the organization operates. The QMS is derived from a review of all applicable requirements and a conscious decision on the part of the organization as to the best way to comply with the requirements. Prudent management will ensure that the means by which the requirement is met is the optimum method for the organization, based upon all of the factors specific to its needs and resources. The optimum method or process of meeting the requirement is then documented to ensure that it is repetitively applied.

BENEFITS DERIVED FROM A DOCUMENTED QMS

The documented QMS becomes the backbone of the organization by:

1. Providing the detailed guidance required for the realization of products and/or services.
2. Documenting optimized methods used by the organization to comply with the standard.
3. Providing the basis for repetitive operation of the organization at the optimum level.
4. Offering a training resource for new workers working an assignment within the QMS.

5. Deploying the policies and procedures of the organization to all QMS users.

6. Presenting a documented control mechanism against which compliance can be measured.

7. Providing a tool for auditing the QMS as part of the management review process.

8. Providing both continuity and archival records of the operations of the organization.

VARIATIONS IN QMS DOCUMENTATION

Once the methodologies of the QMS are determined, they must be documented in a method that is suitable to the needs of the organization.

QMS DOCUMENTATION FORM AND PRESENTATION

The ISO standards do not establish the nature, format, or content of documented procedures. The documentation may be in any form suitable to the needs of the users, including text, diagrams, or flowcharts. Organizations usually impose some type of format for their documentation to facilitate recognition and ease of use.

The acceptable media for presentation of the documentation are also quite variable. Examples of acceptable media are presentations in manuals or other operational paperwork, blueprints and specifications, microfiche, and computer databases or screens.

THE NATURE AND EXTENT OF QMS DOCUMENTATION

The QMS standard selected for use by the organization will specify any documentation that is mandatory. In ISO 9001, these areas of required documentation are designated in the text of the standard. These mandatory documented procedures are considered to cover topics so critical to the nature of a successful QMS that an organization cannot function properly without having them available in writing for users. An obvious example of such a topic for a mandatory documented procedure is the organization's control of quality records.

Other QMS procedures may or may not be documented at the discretion of the user organization. The usual criterion for determining whether a procedure needs to be documented is whether it must be in written form for the proper operation of the QMS. Almost all organizations have determined that some level of discretionary written procedures is necessary to consistently maintain the intended operation of the QMS. Procedures that aid in the deployment of the policies and objectives of the organization or the satisfaction of the requirements of customers and other interested parties, as well as regulatory requirements, are obvious candidates for being presented in written form.

The extent or volume of documentation is dependent upon the needs of the planned user. Normally, it is appropriate to limit the documentation to what is necessary to provide guidance on the particular policy, procedural topic, process, or task. Simple is usually better than complex, and brief is usually better than long. The terms used to describe how the documents should be written focus on being clear, concise, simple to understand, suitable for a particular need, approved for a particular use, and so on. Any transfer of information or data is more readily received if it is clear and focuses directly on the point or points being conveyed.

TYPES OF QMS DOCUMENTATION

As previously stated, the documentation of an organization is for the members of that organization to use and understand. The organization's documentation can take any structure or form that is appropriate. The following types of documentation are discussed because they are mentioned in ISO 9001, but even that standard permits the types of documentation to be in stand-alone or combined form, in manuals or in databases, and so forth, as long as the end result is suitable for proper use. In some small organizations, the entire documentation of the organization may be in one manual or on the hard drive of one computer.

The ISO 9001 standard requires that the management of the organization create and deploy a controlled quality policy that establishes the environment, commitment, and quality mission for the organization. The quality policy is required to be documented to aid in its deployment.

Using the quality policy as the basis, the ISO 9001–specified planning process indicates that the organization must develop a set of measurable quality objectives. These objectives should be incorporated as part of the organization's strategic plans.

Ordinarily, the mandatory system procedures, or the requirements for other procedures, are specified in standards with just a general subject or a brief content list noted as the basis for the requirement. The detail of suitable procedural content on the subject is the responsibility of the organization. ISO 9001 specifies only six mandatory documented procedures, but there are many other requirements stated for which the organization must decide whether a documented procedure is needed. The determining point for whether a procedure is to be documented or not, is whether it is required in that form by the organization in order to successfully comply with the standard and the content of the QMS.

The most likely type of document to be in written form is the work instruction. These documents are to be used by the workforce to aid in performing detailed tasks. Since these tasks must be performed in the same manner each time, often with intervals between applications, written work instructions for proper performance are necessary. The extent of detail offered in this type of document is usually based on the training and experience level of the employees of the organization.

Many other types of documentation support the QMS, such as product and/or service specifications, drawings and plans, forms, and tags. These are also essential for the organization and are often referenced in the procedures and work instructions.

The typical organization develops a planning package for the realization of the products and/or services it desires to offer for sale. The production realization package includes all of the documentation required by the operators, technicians, and engineers, along with identification of tools, equipment, and materials. A similar package is developed for each product and/or service offered, usually with as much commonality of processing as possible. Frequently, the organization develops and sells its products and/or services at a more competitive cost when a limited number of processes can be operated for product and/or service realization.

A *quality plan* is a special set of specifications, procedures, and processes that is quite different from the normal planning package used for the typical products and/or services of the organization, and it may be required by the customer. A quality plan may be needed because of a unique design, prototype, or material. Products affected by this type of contract requirement must be processed under controlled conditions, and they usually go beyond the requirements in the organization's basic planning packages.

THE NEED FOR RECORDS AND DATA

The majority of process documentation is directive, causative, or guiding in nature. The documentation is used to tell or show people what is required to achieve the desired result. Often the documentation provides detail as to what methods, tools, equipment, or path the person must use to arrive at the product that is desired. With a well-developed set of procedures or work instructions, a trained individual should be capable of completing the assigned task or process with success, thereby meeting the technical product requirements specified as well as complying with the QMS.

Customers, interested parties, and regulators, like the managers of the organization, cannot always be in attendance at each workstation or site to judge or ensure compliance with the documentation. The QMS standards require that the organization must have objective evidence of such compliance. Many work documents that have been used to accomplish the planned tasks or processes become records when they are completed and signed/stamped or electronically accepted/closed by approved members of the organization as meeting all requirements. In many instances, similar acceptance of the product and/or service is based on the collection of measurements and/or test data that offer objective evidence of the organization's compliance with specifications.

Many of these records have been identified by the organization, or the customer, as being necessary for presentation or acceptance of the product and/or service. Many products and/or services may not be physically capable of being determined as acceptable because of the nature of the processing (as in the cases of painting and plating). Proper records may be used in lieu of detailed verification, and the product and/or service can be subsequently transferred to the customer.

Many records are identified for retention by the organization. In addition to the product or service completed and delivered, the records may serve to demonstrate the compliance of purchased materials, qualifications of personnel, compliant equipment performance, satisfactory test results, in-process and final testing or inspection, successful field demonstrations, and so on. They are retained as evidence of compliance by the organization and may be of value as archival resources in reviews, studies, or litigation. The period of controlled record retention may be specified by the customer, set by the organization, or determined by regulatory requirements. Often the period for retention coincides with the expected useful life of the product and/or service.

THE DOCUMENT AND DATA CONTROL PROCESS

One of the requirements of the ISO 9001 standard is to ensure that the people of the organization are working to the latest/appropriate revision of the particular document governing their activities. In order to accomplish this requirement, there must be a document control process or system that clearly identifies the latest version or issue of the document. Processes that change the revision letter or revision number on the document each time the document is revised or changed are the most commonly used. Other less common revision control processes may involve the use of set periods of application or date control for the documentation. The coding of the document permits the potential user to access and examine the master revision list to ensure that the most current version is selected for use.

A distribution process for the new revisions and a process to prevent the unintended use of obsolete documents must be included in the organization's document control process. The distribution of new or revised documents may be by physical replacement of the obsolete documents in manuals, mailing within the organization, provision at a document center, and so forth. Collection may be by the same methods or there may be user destruction of the expired document. Many organizations mail out the new documents within the organization with a receipt form address label that retains the recipient's identity and can be used to mail the expired or obsolete document back to the distribution center to ensure positive removal and destruction. Small organizations use much simpler methods.

Revision control also ensures that the latest specifications, test procedures, and other data are provided to the users within the organization. Changes to these documents are just as critical to the integrity of the product and/or service as are the procedural documents.

There are times when spare parts for older existing products are to be produced, which requires the use of documentation that may not be the latest currently released. The revision control system permits the organization to match the appropriate archived documentation to the task.

Although the implication is that the organization will have one document and data control process, many organizations have elected to maintain document control by function. Frequently, the engineering function may have a separate process for its technical data and then join the rest of the organization for control of the basic QMS documentation.

A document control method that is rapidly becoming the preferred approach for ensuring the use of the appropriate version of applicable documents is the electronic approach. First, all revision-controlled documents are placed in an electronic or computer database. Documents are sorted into convenient categories by process, function, and so on. Computers are made available at convenient sites within the organization. Security codes may be used if desired. When a document is revised, a simple database revision ensures that only the updated revision is displayed or available throughout the organization. Often, organizations require that any necessary printout of the document be coded as usable for only the day of printing. Using the above approach, no longer should there be a concern about the use of outdated documents.

USE OF ISO 9001 AND ISO 9004 AS THE QMS TEMPLATE

Other quality management system standards are available to the world community, but the QMS standards that have received the most worldwide use in the last decade are the basic family of ISO 9000 standards: ISO 9000, *QMS—Fundamentals and vocabulary*, ISO 9001, *QMS—Requirements*, and ISO 9004, *QMS—Guidance for performance improvement*.

THE SELECTED ISO 9000 CORE QMS STANDARDS FOR 2000

In addition to ISO 9000, ISO 9001, and ISO 9004, ISO 10011 (to be replaced by ISO 19011) on auditing, and ISO 10012 on metrology and measurement assurance, have been selected for inclusion in the list of core standards. Core standards are those that are the most crucial to the organization in the development of a successful QMS. All of these standards have recently undergone or are undergoing revision.

The rest of the ISO 9000 family guidance standards are scheduled for disposition by cancellation, conversion to technical reports, or incorporation of the essence of their content into one or more of the core documents. These planned actions are summarized in Appendix N, provided on the accompanying CD.

CONSIDERATION OF THE "CONSISTENT PAIR" OF QMS STANDARDS

The year 2000 revisions of ISO 9001 and ISO 9004 have been developed as a consistent pair of standards. Although quite suitable for use independently, they are best applied as a pair of standards. They have been revised based on a set of design standards that were balloted and accepted by the members of ISO TC 176. Both documents have essentially the same structure for ease of understanding and use, but each has a different scope.

ISO 9004 is the guideline standard for a complete QMS. It offers guidance to the management of organizations for proper implementation of a QMS, which can provide the organization with the capability and tools for effectively and efficiently improving its performance, to the benefit of all interested parties of the organization. It offers QMS guidance and choices. It is not a requirements document and it is not intended for use in any certification scheme.

ISO 9001 is clearly a directive or requirements standard designed to cover that portion of a QMS focusing on the satisfaction of specified customer requirements. It provides the minimum requirements for an acceptable QMS. The requirements of ISO 9001 are stated in such a way as to permit the organization's compliance with each requirement. It is therefore capable of being used for third-party certification or registration of compliance to ISO 9001 by the organization.

Although an organization can start its implementation of an acceptable QMS with either standard, the majority of organizations have started by moving their existing quality activities toward compliance with the minimum QMS requirements stated in ISO 9001. Once at that level, most organizations look for ways to improve their performance to the benefit of all interested parties, and they move to the guidance and improvement tools available in ISO 9004. The guidance and tools in ISO 9004 are presented in such a way as to be usable by management for moving the organization as far toward world-class status as is appropriate to its needs.

Since these two standards have essentially the same structure, the user can first examine the minimum QMS requirements stated in 9001, then look at the guidance for going beyond just the minimum to see what is offered by 9004 for beneficial performance improvement of the organization. For instance, ISO 9004 examines effective cost and profit considerations, while 9001 does not address these factors except to require "suitable" resources.

ARE DIFFERENCES BETWEEN ISO 9001:1994 AND ISO 9001:2000 NEW REQUIREMENTS?

There are many differences in the structure and presentation of the content in the new revision. The process approach is new. However, all 20 elements that existed in the 1994 version can be placed within the process model presented in ISO 9001:2000. Additionally, the wording in the new version has been modified to accommodate use by service- and software-related organizations. In spite of these obvious changes, are there really new requirements?

The following key points have been "identified as new requirements":

- Placing of QMS elements in process format to better reflect actual use by organizations
- Identification of customer satisfaction as a significant output of the QMS
- Identification of continual improvement as a management responsibility/obligation
- Recognition that QMS compatibility with other management system standards, such as ISO 14001 is needed
- Allowing of exclusions from clause 7 of ISO 9001:2000 requirements and canceling ISO 9002:1994 and ISO 9003:1994
- Use of *organization* instead of previous term *supplier* to denote user of standard
- More liberal requirements for documentation of QMS, including user discretion
- Identification of competency as an output of the organization's training process
- Identification and management of the human and physical factors in the workplace that affect quality
- Two-way communication with the customer (and internal communication)

Virtually all of the apparent new requirements listed above:

- Existed in the 1994 version and have been reworded for clarity of intent
- Are a simple change due to the way the 1994 requirements have been interpreted by users
- Are assumed to be a reasonable part of an earlier QMS requirement

On that basis, the method and extent of the organization's implementation of the 1994 standard will determine what is a new requirement to them. Clearly, if they have not included customer satisfaction, employee competency, and communication as part of their QMS, then the impact of the 2000 revision will be greater than for those organizations that did include them. Although the term was not used in 1994, continual improvement was always built into the requirements of such elements as internal quality audit, corrective and preventive action, and management review. Exclusions were a part of the ISO 9002/3 usage, and many organizations had to request an exemption from elements that did not apply to them, even with the use of ISO 9001.

For a discussion of the major changes and their implications for implementation and auditing see chapter 8.

IMPLEMENTING ISO 9001:2000

First of all, the organization's management, and therefore the people in the organization, should not panic about implementing a standard. As of this writing, there will be a three-year period after the publication and release of the new standard in which to implement it and, if desired, get your organization's registration upgraded—or obtain the organization's initial registration. Additionally, the registrar with whom you are affiliated has committed to perform the mandatory reviews of your current registration against those portions of the new standard where your compliance is changing over to meet the new standard.

The "apparent" new requirements actually come from the need to be able to present objective evidence of compliance with existing requirements. If the interpretations used in 1994 were minimal or incorrect, then both the process and the related documentation will require revision. The 2000 standard clearly states that the organization should not have to rewrite its documentation in the format and structure of the new standard, but interim use of cross-reference matrices of both sets of requirements, documentation, and so on will likely give way to some rewriting eventually. With the need for the majority of documentation now being left up to the organization, a good case can be made that this revision is an opportunity to "streamline" documentation, leaving only what is currently required for satisfactory operation of the QMS.

The organization should start its movement toward compliance with the new revision by becoming familiar with the new document. Each requirement should be reviewed to see whether the organization complies and to identify those areas where further work is needed. The organization should then systematically review the work package and develop an action plan to mitigate the concerns, within the organization's frame of reference. Finally, assignments and schedules should be established. Nothing should be done that does not benefit the organization, customers, or other interested parties. Compliance is not a penalty but rather a chance to optimize processes. The organization should embrace the process approach in the standard, since that is the way all organizations have been operating all along. Once that is acknowledged and promulgated, then achieving understanding and compliance will become quite simple.

USE OF ISO 9004:2000 AS AN ALLY IN YOUR CONVERSION TO ISO 9001:2000

The new ISO 9004:2000 standard has been significantly revised from the version of 1994. As with the earlier version, ISO 9004:2000 is not a guide for the implementation of ISO 9001:2000. As noted earlier, both standards now have the same structure and the same major QMS processes. Since ISO 9004 is a guidance document for a complete QMS and ISO 9001 is a requirements document for a minimum QMS designed for meeting specified customer requirements, the content of clauses, even those with the same basic title, is quite different. ISO 9004:2000 goes beyond the minimum QMS required by ISO 9001 to provide the user with a management look at the clause content and then a look at how the organization can derive additional benefits in the subject area for all its interested parties, including customers. Tools are provided for the user organization in the form of (1) a generic self-assessment approach that is capable of determining the organization's position against a QMS improvement matrix and (2) a generic process improvement approach applicable to all QMS processes. These tools are vital to the management of an organization wishing to use performance improvement as the vehicle to move toward recognized excellence.

As an organization undertakes the implementation of ISO 9001:2000, significant benefit may be derived by examining the requirement clause in both the ISO 9001 and the ISO 9004 frameworks. In many cases, the organization will gain advantage by implementing some or all aspects of the ISO 9004 guidance as easily as it does by implementing the minimum requirements of ISO 9001. Since the organization will eventually wish to go beyond the ISO 9001 minimum to achieve both effectiveness and efficiency in the QMS, and since ISO 9001 does not address efficiency, any upward step over the ISO 9001 minimums is well considered. In addition, ISO 9004 is business oriented, meaning that both the customer and the organization will benefit from its operations, whereas ISO 9001 does not address the "bottom line."

As you may recall from earlier discussion, ISO 9004:2000 has within its text pages all of the requirement content of ISO 9001:2000. The ISO 9001 content is separately identified as such and is placed within boxes. The boxes are placed as near the corresponding clause in ISO 9004 as practical, thus permitting the user of ISO 9004 the opportunity to refer to the ISO 9001 requirements content at any time. Although this placement of ISO 9001 clauses within ISO 9004 would appear to render ISO 9004 a guideline for the former, ISO 9004 is not an implementation guide and is best used by the ISO 9001 user to determine where the organization has the opportunity to go beyond the ISO 9001 minimums.

ISO 9001:2000 COMPONENT PROCESSES FOR A GENERIC QMS

ISO 9001:2000 requires the implementation of the quality management system as four basic generic QMS processes. The specified requirements in each of the four are also presented in a process format, to better represent the actual manner in which organizations operate. All of the four processes can be placed within the generic process model offered in the standard, demonstrating the relationship of each process to the system and of all the processes to one another. The process approach presented in the model is only one of many examples that could have been used to represent a generic QMS.

The four main clauses in ISO 9001:2000 will be briefly critiqued in the following paragraphs. Even though some QMS-related observations will be provided, this brief examination is not meant to be an analysis of the standard. In-depth analysis of the requirements of ISO 9001:2000 is provided elsewhere in the literature.

THE MANAGEMENT RESPONSIBILITY PROCESS (CLAUSE 5.0 IN ISO 9001:2000)

The management responsibility clause offers an excellent view of how requirements can be stated as a process. This management-based process can be demonstrated by simply listing its process steps, as follows:

1. Obtaining the visible involvement and commitment of management
2. Establishing direction and policies for the organization, or quality policy
3. Initiating the planning subprocess and the creation of objectives
4. Ensuring that the administration, responsibilities, and authorities for the QMS are clear
5. Appointing a management representative as the focal point for the QMS operation
6. Establishing the nature of communication and documentation for the QMS
7. Ensuring that the organization has document and record control processes
8. Developing a management review process to evaluate success or identify course correction

Each of the steps listed above is actually a subprocess of the total management responsibility process. While step 8 is a feedback to step 1 and causes the entire process to recycle, each step in the above list offers within it the same feedback concept.

Since it is a management process, it is clear that the organization's response to the requirements of this clause will apply to all other QMS requirements stated in the rest of the standard.

Mandatory requirements for specific types of documentation (such as clause 5.5.5, "Quality manual") and documented (written) procedures (such as clause 5.5.6, "Control of documents") are stated in the standard. As noted earlier, if not stated to be mandatory, the documentation of procedures is at the discretion of the organization.

In this clause for management responsibility, the main hurdle for the implementing organization will likely be the presentation of objective evidence of the effectiveness of all the required management activities described. To cite one example, clause 5.5.4, "Internal communication," requires that communication be ensured among the organization's various levels and functions. There would likely be difficulty in auditing the process and its effectiveness. The organization would need to establish acceptable parameters for effective internal communication, ensuring that its approach meets the standard. The organization would need to document the parameters, and then implement them. Auditing would then determine compliance to the acceptable documentation rather than directly to the standard (clearly a more practical approach).

THE RESOURCE MANAGEMENT PROCESS (CLAUSE 6.0 IN ISO 9001:2000)

This clause presents the process for the provisioning of resources, so as to ensure the proper operation of the QMS to the requirements. It covers all types of resources, but it only addresses a few in detail. (ISO 9004:2000 examines many more, and many other resources are examined or specified under clause 7, "Product realization," which follows.)

Certainly the provisioning of resources is a management responsibility that is required before the QMS can be fully operative for realization of products and/or services. On that basis, it is well placed in the overall QMS process, as represented by the order of the contents of the standard.

The human resources clause (6.2) covers a factor not fully explored in the earlier version of ISO 9001, which is worker "competency." The 1994 version essentially stated that the employee ought to be capable of satisfactorily performing the assigned task. The new version replaces that statement with "shall be competent, on the basis of appropriate education, training, skills and experience." This requirement implies that all four categories must be considered to establish competency and is an unnecessary detail, since any one of the four may be sufficient to make the individual competent to perform the assigned task. The organization will need to clarify this requirement in its own "needs analysis" procedure and then work *and* audit to that document to determine its QMS compliance.

In clause 6.4, "Work environment," there is a requirement to determine and manage the work environment needed to achieve conformity of product. Again, the organization will have to define the factors to be controlled.

PRODUCT REALIZATION (CLAUSE 7.0 IN ISO 9001:2000)

As would be expected, since this clause specifies all the QMS requirements for the realization of products and/or services from concept to delivery, it is by far the most lengthy clause in the standard. All other processes are developed to support product realization. Those processes directly related to the creation of value-added products or services are called realization processes and may even form a complex net of processes that may also reach out to the organization's product and service suppliers.

In addition, there are many supporting processes, that in themselves do not create products and services but are essential to the product and service realization process. Examples of supporting processes are human resource processes, financial processes, and maintenance processes.

The overall process represented by the requirements stated in this clause includes the following steps:

1. Planning the capability instruments necessary for realization of products and/or services.
2. Obtaining input of product/service requirements from both customers and the organization.
3. Defining and planning the identified design and/or development requirements.
4. Performing design and development in accordance with plans and expectations.
5. Reviewing the design and development process to ensure achievement of requirements.
6. Performing product and/or service verification and validation of input requirements.
7. Identifying and controlling purchasing processes to ensure conformity of purchases.
8. Controlling production and service operations/processes in accordance with plans.
9. Qualifying or validating processes, products/services, personnel, and documentation.
10. Controlling measuring and monitoring devices to ensure accuracy of device results.

Clearly, these steps or subprocesses are linear in order and still constitute a process. The actual evaluation of the final success of the realization process in clause 7 is determined by the measurement requirements in clause 8 in the 2000 revision of the standard. Clause 8 then provides feedback to the realization process in clause 7. Clause 8 is examined in the next section of this chapter.

Although presented differently, the basic requirements in clause 7 of the new revision of ISO 9001 are not very different from those in the 1994 version. In clause 8, the need to identify and plan what needs to be done to satisfy the specified requirements and then determine at various stages whether it has been accomplished is conveyed throughout the clause. This documented input/output indication of an ongoing process provides a virtual checklist for determining success. The requirements for documentation in clause 7 are generally less strenuous than those required in the 1994 version of 9001.

Since the basic requirements in this ISO 9001:2000 clause do not vary greatly from the earlier version of the 9001, the users of the earlier standard should have few problems adapting to comply with it. As clause 7 covers much of the content of the total QMS, and it has not changed greatly in basic content, the conversion task is greatly simplified.

MEASUREMENT, ANALYSIS, AND IMPROVEMENT PROCESS (CLAUSE 8 IN ISO 9001:2000)

This clause in the new 2000 standard pulls together all of the check and control elements found in the 1994 version of 9001. Added to this clause are the methods for improvement of the QMS.

As with most processes, clause 8 begins by addressing the planning of the activities for measurement, analysis, and improvement. The 2000 version also has a general subclause (8.1) that makes planning for continual improvement a requirement. The tools that are listed for use in the continual improvement subclause are essentially the same as those found in the 1994 version (quality policy, objectives, internal audit results, analysis of data, corrective action, preventive action, and management review). One could draw the conclusion that the only new requirement is really the "planning and managing for improvement" requirement.

The measuring and monitoring of products and processes are covered very briefly. The extensive product inspection and test coverage in the 1994 version has been reduced to only seven lines that essentially say to ensure conformity and have records to prove it. Although the measuring and monitoring of processes was intended in the 1994 version, it is stated clearly for the first time in ISO 9001:2000, albeit in only four lines.

Another clearly stated requirement is the three-line requirement for customer satisfaction. Although this was likely presumed in the 1994 version, it was never stated. Meeting customer requirements was the 1994 objective. In ISO 9001:2000, the requirement is to monitor information on customer satisfaction; the term *measuring customer satisfaction* has been carefully left to the more comprehensive ISO 9004:2000. However, under clause 8.4, "Analysis of data," in the new version it is stated that the organization shall collect and analyze data to provide, among other things, information on customer satisfaction. This way of expressing it was chosen over the term *level of customer satisfaction,* used in ISO 9004:2000.

Although the clause for internal audit is somewhat reduced, as with virtually all of clause 8 in ISO 9001:2000, there are requirements for documented procedures. Documented procedures are required for the following clauses:

- Clause 8.2.2, "Internal audit"
- Clause 8.3, "Control of nonconformity"
- Clause 8.5.2, "Corrective action"
- Clause 8.5.3, "Preventive action"

QMS GUIDANCE FOR PERFORMANCE IMPROVEMENT: ISO 9004:2000

As indicated earlier, the ISO 9001:2000 standard states the minimum requirements for a quality management system. ISO 9004:2000 goes well beyond this basic approach and focuses on guidance for management to pursue performance improvement for the organization by using the QMS as the primary tool for achieving effective and efficient improvements. Although the basic structure of the two documents is the same, ISO 9004 builds on the ISO 9001 requirements. First, the minimum requirements of ISO 9001 are listed in boxes or blocks at each related clause within the text of ISO 9004 for the convenience of the user. Second, at each clause, ISO 9004 offers to management "heads up" guidance as to those aspects of the subject clause that need to have special management attention. Third, again at each clause, ISO 9004 provides management with guidance as to how the organization's performance can be improved by moving the subject/content of the clause well beyond the minimum requirements of ISO 9001 and toward excellence.

One example of how the management of an organization could use the guidance supplied at each clause involves customer satisfaction. The minimum requirements are to monitor customer satisfaction, whereas ISO 9004 provides guidance on meeting the needs and expectations of the customer and other interested parties.

This movement toward improvement can be accomplished by using tools in ISO 9004 to:

- Proactively determine the needs and expectations of customers and other interested parties
- Collect and analyze data related to the satisfaction of customers and other interested parties
- Actively pursue the improvement of the level of customer satisfaction as well as the satisfaction of other interested parties
- Collect feedback on successful improvement and initiate additional actions

ISO 9004 provides tools such as a self-assessment approach, a QMS maturity matrix (both in annex A), and a process improvement tool (in annex B). These tools can be exercised by management, to the extent necessary for achieving the desired level of performance improvement. Improving the maturity of the quality management system can be the vehicle for moving the organization to the quality award level, if that is what the management of the organization has set as an objective.

The quality management system is capable of being a remarkable management tool!

Chapter 12

Documenting the Quality Management System

John E. (Jack) West
Consultant, The Woodlands, Texas

QUALITY MANAGEMENT PRINCIPLES AND DOCUMENTATION

It is useful to review the relationship between documentation and quality management principles, which are covered in more detail in chapter 5. First we will discuss the relationship of quality management principles to the process of preparing documentation of a quality management system. Four principles are involved in this relationship:

• *Leadership.* The organization's leaders must develop an environment in which people can fully participate in the development of the quality management system and its documentation. Establishing such an environment requires leaders to provide the training and resources people need to become involved. In addition, leaders establish the organization's quality policy and objectives, which are the top-level documents required by ANSI/ISO/ASQ Q9001-2000.

• *People.* The people who operate the processes of the system are in the best position to describe how they accomplish the work. This means that the people of the organization should help identify the organization's processes and their interactions. It is also important that they be directly involved in defining the activities of each process.

• *System approach to management.* The organization needs to define how it will manage the interrelated processes that make up the system. The processes of the system must be defined and their interactions clearly understood. Processes of the system should relate to attaining the established quality objectives. It is the people of the organization working with the organization's leaders who define the quality management system processes and their interactions. The quality manual is created to describe the key processes of the system and how they are interrelated.

• *Process approach.* The process approach involves management of the process and associated resources to achieve a given objective. It is not useful to create processes for their own sake. They should be developed to achieve an objective. This implies that each process in the quality management system should tie directly to the achievement of one or more of the organization's quality objectives. The people of the organization should map each of the system's processes for meeting these objectives. These processes are candidates for inclusion in the list of processes that will be covered in the documented procedures. Determinations must be made as to which processes must be included in the documented procedures. This determination should be based on the requirements of ISO 9001:2000, the complexity of the processes, the complexity of the interactions with other processes, the knowledge and skills of those who operate the processes, and other factors as defined by the organization.

Figure 12.1 shows the relationship of these four principles to the documentation requirement of ISO 9001:2000.

Even more important than the relationship of the principles to the documentation process is the relationship between documentation and the notion of continual improvement. ISO 9001:2000 requires that the organization plan for

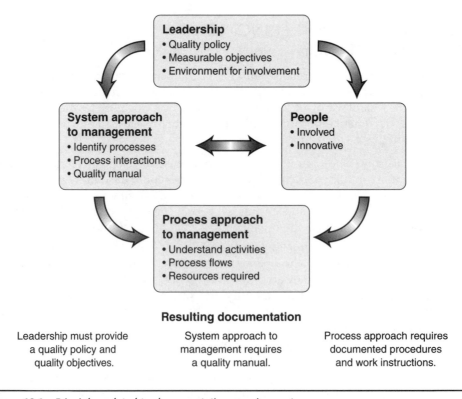

Figure 12.1 Principles related to documentation requirements.

continual improvement of the effectiveness of the quality management system. Organizations have recognized that one of the key benefits from using ANSI/ISO/ASQC Q9001-1994 is standardization of the manner in which processes are operated. Standardized processes have resulted in everyone in the organization performing the same activities using the same procedure. This reduces variation (time-to-time variation, variation due to different shifts or operators, and so on). But standardized processes can also provide the "baseline" for improving the system. If a process has been standardized and carefully documented, it is easy for the organization to understand and correct problems with the process or to analyze the process for potential problems. Having good process documentation can facilitate these analyses:

- For known problems where the result does not meet quality objectives, analyzing the process to determine the *corrective action* required to fulfill requirements
- Analyzing processes to define the risks associated with potential problems so that appropriate *preventive action* can be taken
- Assessing improvement opportunities

Documentation may also be viewed in terms of its relationship to four of the quality management principles:

- *Leadership.* The organization's leaders not only set objectives and policy but also review progress. They must conduct periodic management reviews focused on defining opportunities for improvement.
- *People.* It is the people in the organization who use the documentation every day. They see the organization's issues and opportunities for improvement on a frontline basis. The organization's people should be involved not only in the preparation and use of the processes and associated documentation but also in their improvement.
- *Factual approach to decision making.* Processes and products must be measured. The metrics applied should be related to the organization's measurable quality objectives. Appropriate data must be analyzed to provide information on customer satisfaction as well as product and process performance. This information may then be used to decide what action to take to improve effectiveness.
- *Continual improvement.* The objective is to continually improve the effectiveness (and if the organization desires, efficiency) of the quality management system. The organization must take appropriate corrective and preventive actions to achieve these improvements. It is critical to understand that the objective is not to continually improve the documentation; rather it should be to use the documentation to continually improve the processes that make up the quality management system.

It is important to understand from the beginning that not all processes need to be included in the documented procedures or other documentation. ISO 9001 clearly gives the organization flexibility when it comes to documentation. Figure 12.2 illustrates how the process approach may result in both documented and undocumented procedures.

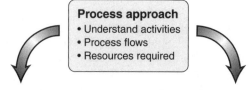

Process approach
• Understand activities
• Process flows
• Resources required

Documented procedures or work instructions required when:

• It is one of the six required documented procedures
• The process is complex
• Interactions are complex
• Lack of documentation could cause nonconformity

Documented procedures or work instructions not required when:

• None of the conditions at left apply
• The process is simple
• Interactions are simple
• Worker competence is high

Figure 12.2 Documented and undocumented procedures.

ISO 9001:2000 REQUIREMENTS FOR DOCUMENTATION

The basic requirement for a quality management system is provided in clause 4.1 of ISO 9001:2000, which states that the organization must identify and manage the family of processes needed to ensure conformity. The quality management system ensures compliance with the quality policy and that quality objectives are met. Organizations should not lose sight of this basic concept. It is easy to get so absorbed in documenting a system that the basic concept is lost. *While documentation is important, the primary emphasis should be on developing and implementing effective processes for a quality management system.*

It is critical to understand the difference between managing a system and documenting a system. Clause 4.1 does not directly address documentation; rather, it requires that processes be developed and implemented to make up the overall system. It also requires that processes be managed and continually improved. These improvement activities must include monitoring, measurement, and analysis of the processes. This is at the heart of the process approach and represents one of the major changes in focus from ISO 9001:1994.

The activities that organizations will need to consider include the following:

• Identification of processes and their interactions

• Establishment of criteria and means to effectively operate, control, measure, and analyze the processes

• Improvement of the quality management system, which includes improvement of these processes

• Provision of controls for any quality management system processes that are outsourced to another organization

Understanding and using this process approach is critical to compliance with ISO 9001:2000 because the requirements for documented procedures have been dramatically reduced. Clause 4.2 of ISO 9001:2000 provides the general documentation requirements. The organization is required to establish, document, maintain, and improve the quality management system. It is clearly management's responsibility to facilitate establishment of the system. The documented system must reflect actual activities that are performed to ensure conformity.

The perceived requirement for an excessive number of documented procedures has been one of the most criticized aspects of ISO 9001:1994. ISO 9001:2000 gives organizations much greater flexibility. The emphasis has shifted from documenting procedures that address 20 elements to managing a system of processes to achieve specific quality objectives. It is the process management described earlier that is important. Organizations have always had freedom to determine the extent of documentation that is appropriate. With ISO 9001:2000, they will now have even more flexibility to select documentation methods and structures that are appropriate for the organization's needs.

The extent of the quality management system documentation for an organization is dependent on the organization's situation. At minimum, the documentation must include an appropriate combination of the following documents:

• Documents that describe the quality policy required by clause 5.3 and giving the quality objectives required by clause 5.4.1.

• A quality manual that describes the sequence and interaction of the processes in the quality management system. The quality manual must meet certain specific requirements as detailed in clause 4.2.2 (discussed later in this chapter) and must either contain or reference the documented procedures that give greater detail of the system's processes.

• Documented procedures that describe the system. These procedures must either be included as a part of, or referenced in, the quality manual. ISO 9001:2000 specifically requires "documented procedures" in only six places, but remember that the organization must also have documentation of the system's processes and their interactions. Once the processes of the quality management system have been defined and their interactions established, the key processes should be described in documented procedures. Along with the quality manual, these documented procedures provide a mechanism for communication of the processes to the organization. A well-prepared quality manual along with easily understood procedures is a means to ensure all employees understand the quality management system.

ISO 9001:2000 has far fewer specific requirements for documented procedures than ISO 9001:1994. Table 12.1 illustrates the differences. It is important to remember that clause 4.2.1(d) requires the organization to identify and prepare any documents necessary for the effective planning and operation of the quality management system. Organizations typically need additional documentation to fully describe the quality management system.

• Other system documentation is required as necessary to describe the sequences and activities needed to operate the system. In addition to the quality manual and the documented procedures that describe the overall processes of the quality management system, organizations are specifically required to prepare other documentation needed for control of processes. The type and extent of these documents must be determined by the organization. This documentation is typically in the form of written procedures or work instructions.

Table 12.1 Comparison of requirements for documented procedures.

BSR/ISO/ASQ Q9001-2000		ANSI/ISO/ASQC Q9001-1994	
Clause	**Documented procedure required**	**Clause**	**Documented procedure required**
		4.3.1	Contract review
1	Design control		
4.2.3	Control of documents	4.5.6	Document and data control
		4.6.1	Purchasing
		4.7	Customer supplied product
		4.8	Product identification and traceability
		4.9	Process control
		4.10.1	Inspection and testing
		4.11.1	Control of measuring and test equipment
		4.12	Inspection and test status
8.3	Control of nonconforming product	4.13.1	Control of nonconforming product
8.5.2	Corrective action	4.14.1	Corrective and preventive action
8.5.3	Preventive action	4.15.1	Handling, storage, packaging, preservation, and delivery of product
4.2.4	Control of quality records	4.16	Control of quality records
8.2.2	Internal quality audits	4.17	Internal quality audits
		4.18	Training
		4.19	Servicing
		4.20	Statistical techniques
		4.21	

PLANNING THE QUALITY MANAGEMENT SYSTEM

Clauses 5.3 and 5.4 of ISO 9001:2000 cover development of the quality policy and planning of the quality management system. These activities are discussed in greater detail in chapters 13 and 14. They will be covered here only as input to the process of documenting the system.

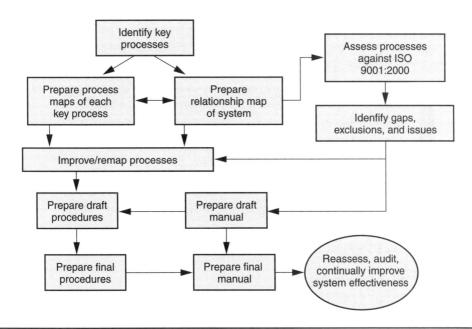

Figure 12.3   Developing the quality management system processes and their documentation.

The quality policy should be established by top management and must meet the criteria given in clause 5.3. Once it is developed, that policy must be included in the documentation of the quality management system as required in clause 4.2.1. The policy should be controlled to make it available to all employees and provide assurance that only the current version is available. It is quite normal for organizations to post the quality policy in prominent places so that it is easily accessible or print it on business cards or even on employee badges.

The quality objectives must also be developed. It is a role of top management to develop and deploy in appropriate functions and at appropriate levels the organization's quality objectives as required by clause 5.4.1.

Once the policy and objectives have been developed, it is necessary to plan the processes of the quality management system. One possible process for developing the processes and their documentation is shown in Figure 12.3. These processes should be developed to drive achievement of the quality objectives. This planning is required by clauses 5.4.2 and 4.1. It is necessary to identify the processes of the organization that fulfill the requirements of ISO 9001 and to understand how these processes work and interact with each other. This implies a need to develop basic process maps or flow diagrams or charts of key processes and a relationship map showing how these key processes relate to each other.

Developing the Quality Manual

The quality manual flows from the quality system planning. That planning should have identified the key processes of the organization and the basic interrelationships among those processes. Each of these key processes should then be mapped before the quality manual is prepared. Once this mapping has been completed, the processes should be compared to ISO 9001:2000 to determine compliance. Gaps should be identified and processes or activities developed to close them. Development of the quality manual has five basic steps:

1. Develop the process flows or descriptions of the key processes. This includes mapping or describing each process and identifying resources.
2. Compare the initial process maps and descriptions to ISO 9001:2000 to determine any gaps in compliance, and then develop plans to close any identified gaps.
3. Prepare draft manual text to describe the overall system and each process.
4. Define which of the key processes of the system need detailed documented procedures.
5. Prepare a final manual after the detailed procedures have been written.

Content of the Quality Manual

In most cases, the text describing each key process should be general in nature. The standard permits either including or referencing the detailed procedures within the manual. Obviously, if the organization chooses to include the procedures, the manual will need to cover the details. If the detailed procedures are separate documents, the manual need not be a step-by-step procedure for accomplishing the activities of the process. On the other hand, the text should be complete enough to provide a good understanding of how each process works and how it interrelates with the other processes of the system.

Continual Improvement of Processes

Continual improvement should be an objective of all organizations. The development and documentation of the quality management system processes offers an outstanding opportunity for improvement. We have already discussed the development of process maps or flowcharts for each of the key processes that will comprise the system. These maps are useful for several purposes:

- They help enhance our understanding the degree of complexity of each process and its interactions. This is a big help in determining which of the processes must be covered in documented procedures.
- They help us to understand the process so that preparation of documented procedures is easier.
- They offer the opportunity to further study each process to determine opportunities for improving both effectiveness and efficiency.

This last opportunity has three components: correcting processes that do not flow properly, improving the effectiveness with which the process meets its goals, and improving process efficiency so that it meets its goals faster or with fewer resources. Most organizations do flowcharting to ensure correct process flow. In fact, many organizations consider this to be a major benefit of implementing an ISO 9001–based quality management system; they have eliminated many process problems with conventional flowcharting.

But organizations often miss other opportunities. Improving process effectiveness and efficiency requires the use of more data than just the flowchart itself. Process mapping encourages incorporating measurement into the process. There is no requirement that all processes be measured or that the measures be included on the actual flowcharts. On the other hand, developing measurement as a part of the process mapping process has several advantages:

- The measures can provide greater visibility of process performance
- The measures can help identify opportunities for improvement
- Measurement gets us thinking about how the activities within the process act together to create the required output

Analyzing the Processes—Improving Process Effectiveness

Processes are developed to achieve specific results. To understand process effectiveness, the organization must measure process results. Before starting process flowcharting, the organization should write down the results expected from each process and determine the measures of process performance that will be used to determine effectiveness. First the outputs of the process should be defined: Who are the customers? What do they require? How can the output be measured against those requirements? What have been the results? Then the organization should ask the same questions for the inputs to the process: Who are the suppliers? What are their inputs? How can those inputs be measured? What do the measures say about suppliers' performance? By starting with this exercise, the organization can already begin to define areas where the process may be in need of improvement. The data on inputs and outputs should be recorded on the process map so that they are clearly evident during process analysis. When the process inputs and outputs are clearly understood, the process itself can be flowcharted. It is advisable to do this twice: once in the "as-is" condition and again after improvements have been made. Once the initial process flowchart has been developed, data should be collected to determine how effectively each process meets its quality objectives. For those processes that do not meet objectives, the organization should develop improvement plans. Some of these improvements may be clear from studying the initial flow. Others may require later accumulation of data before process changes can be defined. If process results are generally good, opportunities for improvement can be listed and prioritized during management reviews as the system matures. If process results are very poor, the organization should seriously consider collecting the additional data and making the needed process improvements before finalizing the process documentation. The initial objective should be a documented system that is at least minimally effective in meeting its objectives.

Analyzing the Processes—Improving Process Efficiency

Addressing process effectiveness is a requirement of ISO 9001:2000, but the standard does not require organizations to address the efficiency of their processes. On the other hand, organizations should not miss the opportunity to look for efficiencies in their processes as they develop the documentation. Often, some opportunities to improve efficiency are clear just from a review of the process flows. For example, analysis of the process flow may vividly display process steps that can easily be eliminated or combined with other steps without compromising process effectiveness. Every organization should take advantage of this type of opportunity. But even greater benefit can be derived through more detailed analysis of the individual subprocesses or activities within the process. In addition to the measures of process effectiveness previously discussed, organizations should also consider targets for process efficiency. For each important subprocess or activity, appropriate data may be available or can be estimated, including resources applied, cycle time, scrap rates, rework costs, or other data relevant to process efficiency. As the data are determined, they should also be displayed on the evolving process map. These data can be used to define problem areas that can be subjected to root cause analysis. Once corrections are found to the causes of the identified issues, the solutions can be incorporated into the process documentation.

Analyzing the Processes—Process Reengineering

The previous discussion of analyzing processes to improve efficiency and effectiveness also applies in cases where acceptable process results can be achieved by solving problems or making relatively small changes within the existing process. Sometimes the initial analysis reveals that overall process results are unacceptable but the process and its activities are stable, with few opportunities for internal improvement. If this is the case, the organization should consider reengineering the process completely. This may mean developing new ways of accomplishing the overall process, applying new technology to it, or generally "thinking outside the box." Sometimes a process must be reengineered before it can effectively achieve its quality objectives. More often, reengineering is needed because the process is not meeting targets for efficiency.

Using the Preventive Action Concept

ISO 9001:2000 clause 8.5.3 requires that there be a process for preventive action. In fact, clause 8.5.3 is one of the six clauses that require documented procedures. Preventive action is often misunderstood. The organization must determine actions to eliminate the causes of potential nonconformities. There is no better time to do this than during the development of the processes. As the processes are being analyzed, it is useful to ask questions that can identify opportunities to prevent future problems. It is often impractical to prevent all possible failures, but in most organizations, it is worthwhile to address the most important ones. To do this, organizations should ask the following questions:

- What can go wrong in the process? What are the things that have a potential to fail? How likely is it for these potential failures to reach a customer?
- What is the probability that these failures will actually occur?
- How serious would these failures be if they did occur?
- Can this information be used elsewhere in the organization?

With some thought, the organization should be able to identify the important items and make process changes to prevent them from happening.

Involving the People

There are several reasons for involving the people who work in each process in its mapping and improvement. It is often true that they know the most about the processes and thus can contribute greatly to understanding the "as-is" situation. These people may also have insight as to how the process may be improved. But the most important reason for involving them is to make certain they understand the changes that are made and are committed to them.

DEVELOPING THE FINAL PROCESS MAPS AND SYSTEM RELATIONSHIP MAP

After the processes have been improved, the organization should prepare a new set of process maps and a new system relationship map. These maps can be used to record the before and after process data for use as a record of the process improvements made. They can also form a baseline for further improvements over time. The maps without the data can be included in the quality manual and procedures as appropriate to enhance understanding of the system and its processes.

DEVELOPING THE DOCUMENTED PROCEDURES OF THE SYSTEM

Writing Process and Style

Procedures should always be written with the reader and user in mind and should use simple language. In fact, it is generally best if the same people who prepared the process map also prepare the procedure. If these are the people responsible for carrying out the process, so much the better. Most procedures should be relatively short documents and should include only information that is relevant to the process being described.

Content

Every organization has the flexibility to select the format and structure of the documented procedures that best suit their needs. Each procedure normally has administrative elements to provide for document control. These normally include a *number* to identify the document, indication of the *revision status* and *process verification* or *signature*.

Title

The procedure title should state the process being covered in very few words. The name of the process being documented may be used as the initial title at the start of drafting. The final title should be selected after the purpose and scope of the procedure has been fully developed. It is a good idea to reverify that the title is correct when the procedure has been completed and is ready for review.

Purpose

Development of the procedure's purpose starts with the process map. In fact, it should start with the process output statements. The purpose statement should crisply capture the valuable output this process exists to provide. The purpose statement should be very short—no more than a couple of sentences.

Sometimes it is very difficult to distill the process and its intended outputs down to a few words. There are two possible reasons for this. First, it may be that the organization has not yet fully understood the process. In this case, the process map should be reviewed again. Second, the writer may have a process that is too "big" or complex to cover in one procedure. In this case, the organization should consider the reason for the complexity. Is the process really two or more processes, each of which should have its own documentation? Is the process overly complex, and should it be further simplified or reengineered? When the procedure is completed, it is always a good idea to return to the purpose and ensure that the procedure fulfills its objective.

Scope

While the purpose tells what the procedure will accomplish, the scope tells the extent of its application. Scope answers the questions of where the process starts and where it stops. Scope should clearly define which parts of the organization are included. As an example, an organization may have more than one preventive action procedure. The preventive action process for product development may focus on prevention of product design–related failures. The procedure for preventive action for service delivery may be quite different. Each process may be valid for its application but use unique tools. The scope of each procedure should clearly indicate what parts of the organization are covered.

If a procedure is used for a single product line or even a single customer, the scope statement should include this information. As an example, the recording of specific product traceability may be required for only certain components of a single product line. The scope statement in the traceability procedure should make this clear.

References

Any reference material that may be needed by or helpful to users should be listed. It is generally important to reference other procedures that have direct interrelationships with the procedure being developed.

Definitions

Some organizations may find it useful to include definitions of key terms that are used in the process. This may be helpful to new people if the organization or its industry has a "language" of its own. Definitions also may help standardize understanding of key concepts. On the other hand, it is best to avoid a long list of definitions. If the organization has many unique definitions, consider publishing them separately.

Procedure Requirements

Developing the actual statements of requirements starts with the flowchart portion of the process map. It is best to include the flowchart as an annex or figure in the procedure to enhance understanding. In many cases, the process steps on the flowchart can be numbered and directly referenced in the text to enhance clarity. The written requirements of the procedure should be more than just a restating of what is on the process map. For each key part of the process, the procedure writer should answer the following questions:

- What is required?
- How is it to be done?
- Any special tools, material, or equipment needed?
- Who is responsible?
- How do we know whether conformity has been achieved?
- (Perhaps) What do we do if the process is not producing acceptable results (or where do we go to get help)?
- What records do we need to maintain?

The procedure text should be derived from the answers to the questions. Each requirement should be stated simply and in language that is easy to understand. The writer should consider the conditions under which the procedure will actually be used.

Annexes and Other Appended Material

This section should include material that will help the user understand and use the procedure. It may include a copy of the process flowchart, tables of data the user will need to carry out the procedure, or other information users may require.

Forms

Forms to be filled out may also be included as figures in the requirements section or as an annex. There are at least two ways to do this. The forms may be shown exactly as they are to be used. This means that if a decision is made to change a specific form, there must be a revision to the documented procedure because it is the procedure that controls form revisions. Alternatively, the forms may be shown as "typical" and some other mechanism may be used to ensure that the correct form revision or version is always used. In the past, control through the procedure has proven to be cumbersome for some organizations because a procedure revision is required for even minor form modifications. With computer technology being applied to development, control, and issue of documentation, either method should be fairly easy to control. Organizations should consider how form revisions will be controlled and are most likely to be better off if they adopt a single method for the whole organization. Alternatively, a forms annex containing all forms referenced in policies, procedures, and work instructions can be included in the quality manual.

DEVELOPING WORK INSTRUCTIONS

Work instructions should be consistent with the needs of the organization and the people who will use them. A wide variety of options exist for work instructions. In fact, the variety is constrained only by the imaginations of the people in the organization. There are three basic questions the organization should answer in developing work instructions:

- What processes or activities should be covered by work instructions?
- How detailed must the instructions be?
- What type of work instructions is best for each circumstance?

Work instructions should exist when the process or process interactions are complex, when worker skill levels are low, and when the absence of such instructions would compromise the organization's ability to meet requirements. Similar considerations apply to the detail needed. If the process is simple and the workers are highly trained, work instructions probably need little detail. Choosing the type of work instructions appropriate to each circumstance is likely to be the most important decision. Some organizations select only one type, such as written operating procedures, and attempt to fit this type to all processes, activities, and circumstances. But there are many types of work instruction formats, both verbal and written. Examples include:

- Written
  - Shop routers
  - Standard process instructions
  - Documented operating procedures
  - Service manuals
- Visual aids
  - Workmanship standards
  - Product samples
  - Videos
  - Pictures
  - Color-coded schematics or layouts

REVIEW APPROVAL AND REVISIONS

Clause 4.2.3 requires that each document be reviewed for adequacy prior to issue. Each document should be reviewed by the departments that must comply and by key top managers. There should be a record of this review and of the actions taken to resolve issues raised by the reviewers. A final approval process should exist for each document. As revisions to the documents become necessary, it is important to go back to the process maps. The maps are a mechanism to understand the potential effects of a change before it is made.

ELECTRONIC DOCUMENTATION SYSTEMS

The technology to fully develop and maintain quality management system documentation in an online computer system has been available for a number of years. Organizations implementing ISO 9001:2000 will find the requirements to be easily applied in an electronic environment. Development of systems in which there are no paper copies of the documentation has many advantages. Documents can be developed, reviewed, and approved in an online environment. Once approved, documents can be made available to all users via internal networks or webs. It is now practical to almost completely eliminate paper copies if all users have online access to the documents. An organization should determine the following when designing an electronic documentation system:

- What types of documents and which document control activities are to be included in the electronic system.

- How users will view and use each type of document included in the system. If paper copies are to be permitted in the system, provisions are needed for their control. In any event, organizations implementing electronic documentation systems need to carefully consider revision control as a part of the system design.

- What document control activities will be automated? This may range from just maintaining an automated listing of the current document revisions to full automation of all aspects of document development, review, approval, and dissemination.

- Whether the electronic system will include the records of the system as well as the documents describing the processes. Inclusion of online records is a considerable undertaking but may have significant value for future analysis of data and automation of the audit process.

- How document distribution is to be controlled, particularly when there are multiple locations using the same document or when different locations or different contracts may require use of different revisions of the same document.

SUMMARY

If the system documentation is prepared properly, it can be a valuable asset to the organization. It is a mechanism for standardizing the way the organization functions. It can be a key element for institutionalizing best practices. Documentation can also form an important baseline for continually improving the effectiveness and efficiency of the organization.

Section 4
Management Responsibility

Introduction

Charles A. Cianfrani
Managing Director, Customer-Focused Quality Group,
ARBOR, Media, Pennsylvania

The purpose of the ISO 9001-2000 clause on management responsibility is to clearly articulate the role that management in general, and top management in particular, must assume to ensure the successful design, development, and deployment of an effective quality management system (QMS). This section of the handbook describes critical topics that represent the minimum areas that management must address to provide the foundation for an organization's QMS.

Recognizing the "globalization of quality," the chapters in section 4 present the viewpoints of thought leaders from around the world on various dimensions of management's responsibility for defining and participating in managing quality in organizations. The contents of this section include the following:

• In clause 5.2 of ISO 9001:2000, top management is charged with the responsibility to "ensure that customer requirements are determined and are met with the aim of enhancing customer satisfaction." Chapter 13, "Understanding Customers," by Blanton Godfrey and Joseph D. Moore, addresses this management responsibility by exploring how competition, the shift in power from the supplier to the customer, and the need for rapid response and quick delivery to customers has affected organizations. This chapter also describes approaches to uncovering how an organization can determine the requirements of customers in a way that provides competitive advantage. Readers will be interested to see that just meeting customers' stated requirements and specifications may not be good enough to meet the needs of the contemporary marketplace.

• Central to any QMS are the issues related to quality policy, quality objectives, and planning (clauses 5.3 and 5.4). In chapter 14, "Quality Policy, Quality Objectives, and Planning," Yoshinori Iizuka provides insight into the intent of these requirements, a description of the differences from the 1994 standard, and valuable insight into how to effectively comply with the requirements. This chapter also includes examples of quality policies that can foster creative thinking about what to include in a quality policy and advice on developing quality objectives. Many readers will also find the material for proceeding beyond the requirements of ISO 9001 particularly valuable.

- From the time of the initial release of ISO 9001 in 1987, quality professionals have recognized that management review is a powerful tool for driving improvement in organizations. In chapter 15, "Management Review," Chris Hakes explores the challenges of deploying ISO 9001:2000 in the context of creating a world-class management review process. Although the intent of clause 5.6 is unchanged from 1994 (and indeed from 1987), this chapter delves into how the emphasis on the process approach and continual improvement can be used to address requirements in an efficient and strategically beneficial way.

It is of paramount importance to understand that the requirements contained in clause 5 are among the most critical requirements of ISO 9001:2000. They establish the basis for the entire QMS. It is only when management takes complete ownership of, commitment to, and involvement in the QMS that the organization has the opportunity to implement a truly effective system—one that is in complete harmony with the strategic and tactical objectives of the organization. The chapters in section 4 will help readers address the issues related to management responsibility.

If the reader reads and heeds no other section of this handbook, this section on management responsibility should be read, absorbed, contemplated, and applied in a way that supports the goals of the organization.

Chapter 13

Understanding Customers

Blanton Godfrey
Dean, College of Textiles, North Carolina State University,
Raleigh, North Carolina

Joseph D. Moore
Distinguished University Professor,
College of Textiles, North Carolina State University,
Raleigh, North Carolina

INTRODUCTION

In the past 30 years the science of quality in the United States has changed dramatically. Old ideas have proved misguided or wrong, and many new ideas, or fundamental concepts, have emerged. During most of these changes we have created new names for the new concepts, methods, and tools; and then, slowly, these names have been absorbed into a more total or holistic approach. In this chapter we attempt to describe one of the most fundamental of these new ideas—that of understanding customers.

These changes were not the result of any new theory or thinking from our universities or quality professionals; they were for the most part driven by three realities our companies had to face. The first was competition, both internal and external. The fierce competition from Asia and Europe forced many industries to question their current business practices. As companies in the United States reacted to this international competition, they changed at different rates. Some quickly became world-class competitors themselves, putting even more pressure on those slower to change. For some industries the competition came more from newly developing nations with companies or plants of other companies that used labor rates often less than 10 percent of their U.S. competitors' rates. For those companies with labor-intensive products this competition, often from China, Southeast Asia, Mexico, or South America, provided a strong stimulus to change.

The second reason for these rapid changes was the shift in power from the supplier to the customer. There were many reasons for this shift, but a few stand out clearly. The most obvious change was driven by the emergence of the super-store. Superstores (Wal-Mart, Home Depot, K-Mart, Target, Gap) now buy and sell extraordinarily high percentages of many classes of goods. As they grew, their buying power grew, as did their ability to demand higher quality, lower costs, and more frequent deliveries from their suppliers. They often competed with each other and other similar companies on price and became the representatives of the consumer, ensuring wide varieties of product from all over the world and offering large discounts. Other large customers were more hidden in the complex supply chain but had equal effects. An example is the automotive companies. As their own competition among each other and with Japanese, European, and now Korean competitors became fierce, they put increasing pressures on their suppliers for higher quality, lower costs, and reduced cycle times.

The consumer also became more demanding—in part because of the growth of the superstores and their wide range of low-cost goods, but even more because of the information revolution that provided detailed product rankings, prices, and availability even to consumers located in tiny villages throughout the country. The Internet may be the most discussed part of this information revolution, but television advertising and the hundreds of magazines published giving product information, rankings, and comparative prices probably have had the greater impact. It is almost impossible to name a single product or service in the United States today that does not have readily accessible an incredible amount of information about its quality, price, and availability. With the Internet one can quickly get the specifications from the manufacturer's site and then click on another site that will search all sites for best price, shipping costs, and time to delivery.

The third force driving these changes was the need for speed. As most manufacturing companies moved toward lower inventories and *kanban* or just-in-time inventory systems, the requirements for rapid response and quick delivery by their suppliers intensified. As consumers compared product qualities, prices, and delivery times, the ability to deliver quickly to the consumer's door became a competitive advantage. Overnight delivery companies such as Federal Express and United Parcel Service (UPS) became some of our most rapidly growing companies.

THE CONCEPT OF CUSTOMER

As the science of quality rapidly evolved, the concept of customer evolved. The first question was "who is a customer?" Many companies quickly adopted Joseph Juran's definition: "a customer is anyone who receives or is affected by the product or process." This definition included both internal and external customers. This expansion of thinking caused many changes in the management of quality. One such change in thinking was that quality is multidimensional. What internal customers want and need may be entirely different from their external customers' wants and needs. And the multitude of external customers also has a plethora of wants and needs.

We also began to realize that each of these high-level wants and needs was supported by many other dimensions of quality underneath each high-level dimension. The first reaction to that realization was the rapid adoption of quality function deployment (Mizuno and Akao 1994). For the first time many companies now had a formal methodology for collecting customer wants and needs and dividing them into the secondary and tertiary wants and needs. A simple example of the tree diagrams often used in this step is given in Figure 13.1.

The new ISO 9001 standard (American National Standard ANSI/ISO/ASQ Q9001-2000) states clearly that "top management shall ensure that customer requirements are determined and are met with the aim of enhancing customer satisfaction." The standard goes on to state (clause 7.2.1) that the organization shall determine the requirements specified by the customer including requirements for delivery and postdelivery activities. The organization must also determine requirements not stated by the customer but necessary for intended use and all statutory and regulatory requirements related to the product. The standard also mentions "any additional requirements determined by the organization." It is this last category on which we shall focus. The subject of this chapter is using our understanding of the customer for competitive advantage. Just meeting customers' stated requirements and specifications is never enough. After all, the competitors also know the stated requirements and specifications.

The second realization was that not all customers are the same. Different customers may weight the different dimensions of quality quite differently. In the example in Figure 13.1, some may feel that light weight in a laptop computer is quite important. Others may feel that speed is more important. Still others may put performance as their highest priority and rank that as the most important. This was an important change in our thinking about customers. We began to create different customer segments and began to identify their wants and needs and how important they feel each of those wants and needs is.

There are many different strata of customers in most markets. Some companies now believe that each customer is unique. But most try to stratify the customers into several groups and target each group separately or select only a few groups to target from the entire set.

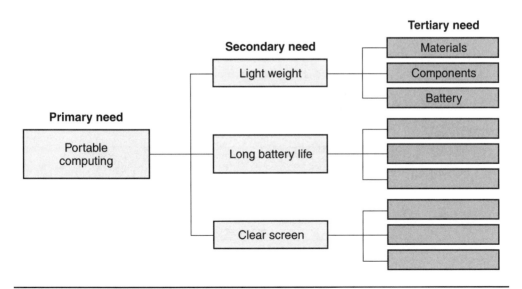

Figure 13.1   Determining customer wants and needs.

These different strata of customers have different priorities. This means they have different weights for each feature. In automobiles, for example, some may be interested in operating performance and style, others may be far more interested in economy, durability, and reliability. Still others may be most interested in cargo space and seating. As an example, we can use the dimensions of quality for notebook (laptop) computers identified in a recent issue of a leading magazine on personal computing, *PC World*, January 2000. The nine dimensions were price, base configuration, design and ease of use, performance, battery life, weight, reliability, support and warranty, and extra features. The weights the magazine assigned to these nine dimensions were 10 percent, 5 percent, 10 percent, 14 percent, 8 percent, 8 percent, 20 percent, 15 percent, and 10 percent.

For simplicity in this example, we'll collapse these to five dimensions: price; performance and features; weight; battery life; and reliability, support, and warranty. To these five dimensions we'll assign the weights shown in Table 13.1 using the magazine's weightings.

But we now realize that not all customer segments have exactly the same needs as the magazine editors. Let's assume we have identified seven different customer strata and found different weights for each of these five dimensions. The first customer segment agrees with the magazine editors on the weights for the five dimensions of quality, but the other six customer segments differ in their weights (see Figure 13.2).

The third major change in thinking about customers was the realization that each customer has many choices. This means that quality is relative. It does not matter what we offer in an absolute sense; it matters what we offer compared with our competitors. We are not the only ones in the marketplace. Our competitors are trying to offer better features and fewer deficiencies to capture the same customer segments. And to make life even more interesting, the world around us is constantly changing. As soon as we have a competitive advantage, our competitors copy it and offer similar features. Customers' incomes, lifestyles, and desires change, and our successful product of last year is this year's failure. In our example we have five major quality dimensions and seven important strata of customers. Let us also assume that we can measure accurately how well both we and our competitors perform on each of these dimensions.

We also assume we know the number of customers in each strata, and that we know the weights they give each dimension of quality in their buying decisions. We are also going to assume they act rationally. This implies they have knowledge

Table 13.1 Dimensions and weights.	
Price	20%
Performance and features	30%
Weight	10%
Battery life	10%
Reliability, support, and warranty	30%

of our products and our competitors, they know how well we perform in each dimension, and they make intelligent purchases. We will assume for this example that we have three competitors and that we are able to measure their performance on each of these dimensions of quality.

We can now create a five-by-four matrix. The five rows are the five dimensions of quality, and the four columns are our scores on these dimensions and the scores of our three competitors. We will call this five-by-four matrix K (see Figure 13.3).

We can now multiply $W \times K$ to create our seven-by-four market matrix M. The market matrix gives us the performance scores for the four competitors (the columns) for the seven customer strata (the rows). The market matrix shows us the scores for each competitor in the eyes of each customer segment (see Figure 13.4).

$$
\begin{bmatrix}
.20 & .30 & .10 & .10 & .30 \\
.30 & .20 & .20 & .10 & .20 \\
.40 & .10 & .30 & .10 & .10 \\
.10 & .40 & .20 & .10 & .20 \\
.10 & .30 & .10 & .30 & .20 \\
.20 & .20 & .20 & .20 & .20 \\
.60 & .10 & .10 & .10 & .10
\end{bmatrix}
$$

Next we determine the weights each customer segment gives each quality dimension. We have a matrix W, seven by five.

Figure 13.2 Customer weights on dimensions.

$$
\begin{bmatrix}
10 & 20 & 30 & 20 \\
20 & 30 & 20 & 10 \\
40 & 30 & 20 & 20 \\
50 & 20 & 20 & 40 \\
20 & 30 & 30 & 50
\end{bmatrix}
$$

Let us assume we can measure how well we perform (column 1) with respect to each of the five dimensions and how well each of our three competitors performs. We call this five-by-four matrix K.

Figure 13.3 Dimensions and scores.

$$
\begin{bmatrix}
23 & 27 & 26 & 28 \\
24 & 26 & 27 & 26 \\
25 & 25 & 28 & 24 \\
26 & 28 & 25 & 24 \\
30 & 26 & 24 & 29 \\
33 & 28 & 28 & 32 \\
19 & 23 & 28 & 24
\end{bmatrix}
$$

Then multiplying $W \times K$ gives us the market matrix, the matrix of scores M. This matrix is seven by four (seven customer segments and four competitors).

Figure 13.4 The market matrix.

Now we can examine the matrix to understand which competitor wins which customer segment. If we assume a winner-takes-all model, meaning that all customers in a given strata buy only from the competitor with the highest score, our matrix reduces to a matrix of zeros and ones. The ones indicate where a particular competitor was the highest rated for a particular customer segment, and the zeros indicate the losers (see Figure 13.5).

We can now multiply this new market matrix M times the one-by-seven vector N containing the number of customers in each strata (see Figure 13.6).

The resulting one-by-four vector gives the number of customers each competitor captures. From this vector we can easily calculate our market share of 20 percent (see Figure 13.7).

Now we understand our market share with the existing product, the customers' weights on the dimensions of our product, and the current quality levels of our competitors. A next step is to explore how we might improve our market position by improving our product. Assume we improve only one dimension (see

$$
\begin{bmatrix}
0 & 0 & 0 & 1 \\
0 & 0 & 1 & 0 \\
0 & 0 & 1 & 0 \\
0 & 1 & 0 & 0 \\
1 & 0 & 0 & 0 \\
1 & 0 & 0 & 0 \\
0 & 0 & 1 & 0
\end{bmatrix}
$$

Assuming winner takes all, the market matrix M looks like this.

Figure 13.5   Winner's matrix.

$$
\begin{bmatrix}
35, 20, 15, 5, 10, 10, 5
\end{bmatrix}
$$

The vector N contains the numbers of customers in each of the seven segments (numbers in millions).

Figure 13.6   Number of customers.

Market share is then easily calculated. By multiplying $N \times M$, we get a one-by-four vector that gives the number of customers for each of the competitors.

In our example, $N \times M = \begin{bmatrix} 20, 5, 40, 35 \end{bmatrix}$.

Our market share is thus 20 percent.

Figure 13.7   Market share.

Figure 13.8). In our example, let's assume we improve the second dimension and improve our score to 30.

Then we can multiply the changed matrices to calculate our new market matrix (see Figure 13.9).

The new winners' matrix is calculated as before. We now have the best results in three rows rather than two rows, and our winners' matrix is shown in Figure 13.10.

We can then do the multiplication of the winners' matrix and the vector with the number of customers to find our new market share (see Figure 13.11).

We see that our new market share is 25 percent. With the success of our improvement in market share we can once again examine the matrices and choose to improve a second score (see Figure 13.12). This time we choose the fifth dimension (for example, reliability, support, and warranty) and improve our score to 30.

$$
\begin{bmatrix}
10 & 20 & 30 & 20 \\
\mathbf{30} & 30 & 20 & 10 \\
40 & 30 & 20 & 20 \\
50 & 20 & 20 & 40 \\
20 & 30 & 20 & 40
\end{bmatrix}
$$

One thing we can do is to improve the quality of one dimension. For example, let's assume we improve the performance of the second dimension and raise its score from 20 to 30.

Figure 13.8 Improving one dimension.

$$
\begin{bmatrix}
26 & 27 & 26 & 28 \\
26 & 26 & 27 & 26 \\
26 & 25 & 28 & 24 \\
30 & 28 & 25 & 24 \\
33 & 26 & 24 & 29 \\
35 & 28 & 28 & 32 \\
20 & 23 & 28 & 24
\end{bmatrix}
$$

Then multiplying $W \times K$ gives us the new market matrix of scores M. This matrix is seven by four (seven customer segments and four competitors).

Figure 13.9 New market matrix.

$$
\begin{bmatrix}
0 & 0 & 0 & 1 \\
0 & 0 & 1 & 0 \\
0 & 0 & 0 & 0 \\
1 & 0 & 0 & 0 \\
1 & 0 & 0 & 1 \\
1 & 0 & 0 & 0 \\
0 & 0 & 0 & 0
\end{bmatrix}
$$

Now our market matrix M looks like this.

Figure 13.10 New winners' matrix.

Our new market share is then calculated by multiplying $N \times M$, where M is our new market matrix after we have improved one of the quality dimensions.

In our new example, $N \times M = \begin{bmatrix} 25,\ 0,\ 40,\ 35 \end{bmatrix}$.

Our market share is now 25 percent.

Figure 13.11   New market share.

$$\begin{bmatrix} 10 & 20 & 30 & 20 \\ \mathit{30} & 30 & 20 & 10 \\ 40 & 30 & 20 & 20 \\ 50 & 20 & 20 & 40 \\ \mathit{30} & 30 & 20 & 40 \end{bmatrix}$$

Now let's assume we improve the quality of a second dimension (for example, reliability, warranty, and support).

Figure 13.12   Changing a second score.

Then, multiplying the matrices once again, we can create a second market matrix (see Figure 13.13). This time we notice that we lead in five of the seven customer segments.

Then we can quickly turn this into a "winners' matrix" and use this to determine our new market share (see Figure 13.14).

We now see that we have 80 percent market share. This, of course, assumes that our competitors have been standing still. But if our competitors are also changing their performance in one or more of these dimensions, we can use the same method of analysis to examine the threat and plan counteractions (see Figure 13.15).

This same methodology is useful for examining new market opportunities. Prior to entering a new market (for example, a country in which we have not previously done business), we can calculate our expected market share given the current level of performance of the existing competitors. For example, assume there is a country with two existing competitors and we estimate their performance scores for each quality dimension. We compare our scores with theirs, and using estimates of the population segments and market research to estimate the weights each customer segment places on each of the quality dimensions, we can estimate how well we should do in this market (see Figure 13.16).

We must remember, though, an important assumption we made earlier. All customers have equal knowledge of the performance of each competitor and act rationally (that is, pick the best product). In new markets this will not be the case. We will be unknown to many potential customers and will have no existing reputation. We must make sure to add an additional dimension of reputation (if not

$$\begin{bmatrix} 29 & 27 & 26 & 28 \\ 28 & 26 & 27 & 26 \\ 27 & 25 & 28 & 24 \\ 32 & 28 & 25 & 24 \\ 35 & 26 & 24 & 29 \\ 37 & 28 & 28 & 32 \\ 21 & 23 & 28 & 24 \end{bmatrix}$$

Then multiplying $W \times K$ gives us our second new market matrix. We now see that we lead in five of the seven customer segments.

Figure 13.13   Second new market matrix.

$$\begin{bmatrix} 1 & 0 & 0 & 0 \\ 1 & 0 & 0 & 0 \\ 0 & 0 & 1 & 0 \\ 1 & 0 & 0 & 0 \\ 1 & 0 & 0 & 0 \\ 1 & 0 & 0 & 0 \\ 0 & 0 & 1 & 0 \end{bmatrix}$$

Now our winners' matrix M looks like this.

Figure 13.14   Second new winner's matrix.

Our new market share is again calculated by just multiplying $N \times M$, where M is our new winners' matrix after we have improved a second quality dimension.

In our new example, $N \times M = \begin{bmatrix} 80, 0, 20, 0 \end{bmatrix}$.

Our market share is now 80 percent.

Figure 13.15   Second new market share.

$$\begin{bmatrix} 60 & 50 & 40 \\ 40 & 50 & 70 \\ 30 & 60 & 20 \\ 90 & 30 & 40 \\ 70 & 50 & 40 \end{bmatrix}$$

Another strategy is to enter new markets where we have distinctive competitive advantages. The scores for our new competitors are in columns two and three.

Figure 13.16   Entering new markets.

$$\begin{bmatrix} 60 & 70 & 50 & 90 \\ 40 & 30 & 70 & 60 \\ 30 & 20 & 20 & 40 \\ 20 & 90 & 80 & 20 \\ 10 & 10 & 20 & 30 \\ 50 & 0 & 0 & 0 \\ 90 & 0 & 0 & 0 \\ 80 & 0 & 0 & 0 \end{bmatrix}$$

A third thing we can do is to create new dimensions of quality. When we are first to market with these new dimensions, we get positive scores and our competitors get zeros.

Figure 13.17   Adding new dimensions.

already included) and invest in advertising, direct sales, and other means to gain customer knowledge and acceptance even if our product is superior.

Another means of gaining market share is to add new dimensions of quality before our competitors. This is one of the time-honored methods of gaining market share. Several years ago the Saturn automobile company was losing sales of its two-door coupe. Although the styling was quite attractive to singles and young couples, they found the back seat almost unusable even for groceries and other packages. Saturn added a small door on the driver's side. This made it very easy to use the back seat. They increased sales 13 percent the first year. In automobiles we see this approach used every year. Minivans have added doors on both sides, and pickup trucks now have three or even four doors. Almost all cars, even modestly priced sedans, now have cup holders, CD players, remote locking systems, garage door openers, sunglasses holders, remote rearview mirror adjustments, cruise control, side air bags, and ABS braking systems.

We see almost the same frenzy in adding new features to desktop and laptop computers. They now have read/write CD drives, DVDs, many software packages included, and optional RAM and hard-drive capacity that we only dreamed of a few years ago. When these added dimensions of quality add true value for customers (or even for segments of customers), they can add significant market share (see Figure 13.17). We have positive scores for each of these dimensions, and our competitors have zeros.

SUMMARY

We have introduced a simple but quite powerful methodology for analyzing and estimating market potential. The math is not difficult—it can be done on spreadsheet software or using many different packages of mathematical or statistical software. It is just matrix algebra. What is difficult is collecting the data. Population data are easy to come by, but determining customer weights for different quality dimensions requires good market research. And customers change their minds often. Our competitors will not stand still either. They will constantly improve their performance in key dimensions, often introducing new dimensions themselves.

We have also assumed that customers have perfect market information. While this may be reasonable for some big-ticket items where much information is available in consumers' magazines and online systems, for many products the customers will be only partially informed. We have also used a simple winner-takes-all model where even a small difference in performance gives 100 percent share of that customer segment. In reality we need to use a probabilistic model where the percent of a customer segment gained is proportional to the gap between our performance and the competitors'. We could build this into the model quite simply by assuming close scores were ties, a certain gap changed the proportions by half, and so forth.

REFERENCES

Abernathy, F. H., J. T. Dunlop, J. H. Hammond, and D. Weil. *A Stitch in Time—Lean Retailing and the Transformation of Manufacturing—Lessons from the Apparel and Textile Industries.* Oxford: Oxford University Press, 1999.

American National Standard. *Quality Management Systems—Requirements,* ANSI/ISO/ASQ Q9001-2000. Milwaukee: American Society for Quality, 2000.

Collins, J. C., and J. I. Porras. *Built to Last: Successful Habits of Visionary Companies.* New York: Harper Business Division, HarperCollins, 1994.

Conti, T. *Building Total Quality.* New York: Chapman and Hall, 1993.

Godfrey, A. B. "Customer Satisfaction, Customer Retention, or Customer Loyalty?" In *Proceedings of the 1993 Trustee Series.* 24 February 1993. New York: The Conference Board.

———. "Beyond Satisfaction." *Quality.* 1996.

———. "Customer Loyalty." *Quality Digest* 16, no. 1 (January 1996): 15.

Juran, J. M. *Juran on Planning for Quality.* New York: The Free Press, 1988.

———. *Juran on Quality by Design.* New York: The Free Press, 1992.

Juran, J. M., and A. B. Godfrey. *Juran's Quality Handbook.* 5th ed. New York: McGraw-Hill, 1999.

Juran, J. M., and F. M. Gryna. *Quality Planning and Analysis.* 3d ed. New York: McGraw-Hill, 1993.

Mizuno, S., and Y. Akao, eds. *QFD—The Customer-Driven Approach to Quality Planning and Deployment.* Tokyo: Asian Productivity Organization, 1994.

Peppers, D., and M. Rogers. *The One-to-One Future: Building Relationships One Customer at a Time.* New York: Currency Doubleday, 1993.

Reichheld, F. F. *The Loyalty Effect.* Boston, MA: Harvard Business School Press, 1996.

Reichheld, F. F., and W. E. Sasser Jr. "Zero Defections: Quality Comes to Services." *Harvard Business Review* (September–October 1990): 105–11.

Wadsworth, H. M., Jr., ed. *Handbook of Statistical Methods for Engineers and Scientists.* 2nd ed. New York: McGraw-Hill, 1998.

Wadsworth, H. M., K. S. Stephens, and A. B. Godfrey. *Modern Methods for Quality Control and Improvement.* New York: John Wiley and Sons, 1986.

———. Forthcoming. "Robust design." In *Modern Methods for Quality Control and Improvement.* 2nd ed. New York: John Wiley and Sons.

Chapter 14

Quality Policy, Quality Objectives, and Planning

Yoshinori Iizuka

The University of Tokyo, Tokyo

ISO 9001 REQUIREMENTS AND ASSOCIATED TERMS DEFINED IN ISO 9000

This section summarizes the requirements of the clauses of ISO 9001:2000 that provide the requirements for the quality policy, the quality objectives, and planning. For the full text of these clauses in ISO 9001:2000, see Appendix G, provided on the accompanying CD. For the full definition of the terms, see Appendix F, provided on the accompanying CD.

MAIN POINTS OF THE REQUIREMENTS—ISO 9001:2000 CLAUSES 5.3 AND 5.4

Requirements of Clause 5.3   Quality Policy

Top management shall ensure the following items concerning quality policy:

a. Appropriateness to the organization's purpose

b. Commitment to compliance with requirements and continual improvement of the effectiveness of the quality management system

c. Provision of framework for establishment and review of quality objectives

d. Communication and understanding within the organization

e. Review for continuing suitability

Requirements of Clause 5.4   Planning

Requirements of Clause 5.4.1   Quality Objectives

Top management shall ensure quality objectives are established at relevant functions and levels. The quality objectives shall be measurable. Also, they shall be consistent with the quality policy.

Requirements of Clause 5.4.2   Quality Management System Planning

Top management shall ensure that:

    a. Quality management system planning is carried out to meet 4.1 requirements and the quality objectives

    b. The integrity of the quality management system is maintained when changed.

MEANINGS OF TERMS

Top Management

The term *top management* is defined in clause 3.2.7 of ANSI/ISO/ASQ Q9000:2000 (see Appendix F).

Top management is a person or a group of people who has the authority and responsibility to direct and control the quality management system of an organization at the highest level. When the *organization* is the entire company, the top management is regarded as a person or group at the highest level of management, such as the chief executive officer or the chief operating officer. When the *organization* is a division of a company, the top management can be the head of the division or group.

The corresponding term used in the 1994 edition is *the supplier's management with executive responsibility*. Even though a different term is used, there is no difference in the meaning.

Quality Policy

The term *quality policy* is defined in clause 3.2.4 of ISO 9000:2000 (see Appendix F).

A quality policy is the overall intention and direction for quality within an organization, which is formally expressed by top management. As a matter of course, a quality policy should be in line with the overall policy of the organization. A quality policy could be based on the eight quality management principles given in the ISO 9000 family standards.

Commitment

Commitment is not defined in ISO 9000:2000, but the ISO Technical Committee 176 (ISO/TC 176) *Introduction and Support Package—Terminology* (provided as Appendix L on the accompanying CD) explains that the intended meaning is "obligation." A commitment, or obligation, can be considered a pledge, a promise, an oath, or a vow to do something, and accordingly, the undertaking of a duty or a responsibility in the areas concerned. As a result of commitment, a person or a group will generally get involved, participate in, take part in, join, be implicated in, devote oneself to, concentrate on, dedicate oneself to, be strongly interested in, or be concerned about a particular matter.

ISO 9001 requires the commitment of top management to the quality management system as specified in clause 5.1 of ISO 9001.

Clause 5.1   Management commitment

Top management shall provide evidence of its commitment to the development and implementation of the quality management system and continually improving its effectiveness by:

   a) communicating to the organization the importance of meeting customer as well as statutory and regulatory requirements,

   b) establishing the quality policy,

   c) ensuring that quality objectives are established,

   d) conducting management reviews, and

   e) ensuring the availability of resources.

Source: ANSI/ISO/ASQ Q9001-2000

Clause 5.3 requires that the quality policy include commitment of the organization to compliance with requirements and continual improvement.

Effectiveness

The term *effectiveness* is defined in clause 3.2.14 of ISO 9000:2000 (see Appendix F).

Effectiveness relates to good and desired results. The effectiveness of quality management system relates to a quality management system that can produce a product meeting the relevant product requirements. Accordingly, the continual improvement of the effectiveness of the quality management system involves both continual improvement in meeting product requirements and also continual improvement of the quality management system processes. A typical improvement could be a decrease in ratio of nonconforming products by improvement of the product realization processes.

Quality Objective

The term *quality objective* is defined in clause 3.2.5 of ISO 9000:2000 (see Appendix F).

Quality objectives are what are "sought, or aimed for, related to quality." They are generally established based on quality policy. The quality objectives can be product-related and quality management system–related, as needed. Also, quality objectives are generally broken down from the quality policy and cascaded to relevant functions and levels within the organization.

Relationship between Quality Policy and Quality Objectives

Some explanations of the relationship between quality policy and quality objectives are given in clause 2.5 of ISO 9000:2000 (see Appendix F).

Both quality policy and quality objectives are established to direct an organization. Quality policy is a higher-level concept than quality objectives. Therefore, quality policy is required to provide a framework for establishing and reviewing quality objectives. As a matter of course, quality objectives should be consistent with quality policy.

Communicated and Understood

To *communicate* sometimes means to "transmit, report, or notify information in one-way manner." The ISO/TC 176 *Introduction and Support Package—Terminology* (see Appendix L) explains that the intended meaning is "exchange of information." However, clause 5.3 states that the quality policy must not only be communicated but also understood. This implies a two-way communication, through transmitting information, intention, and expectation in a two-way manner. As a result, ideas, thoughts, real intentions, true meanings, significance, and even feelings are conveyed to all concerned people.

Also, *understanding* here implies not only grasping the meaning of and comprehending something but also knowing thoroughly the details, including substantial points, and further, agreeing with the matter concerned and having the will to implement it.

Suitability

Suitability is a state where something is appropriate for a purpose, goal, objective, aim, intention, or opportunity, as well as proper for conditions, situations, or circumstances. What is needed here is a suitability of a quality policy; therefore, the quality policy should be kept appropriate for the purposes of the organization and proper for its business management circumstances.

Review

The term *review* is defined in clause 3.8.7 of ISO 9000:2000 (see Appendix F).

The review for continuing suitability of the quality policy will be generally implemented in management review, as specified in clause 5.6.

Measurable

The ISO/TC 176 *Introduction and Support Package—Terminology* (see Appendix L) explains that the intended meaning is "able to be measured or perceived; susceptible to measurement or computation." When considering the purpose of being measurable, a main point here is whether a basis for judgment is given or not. The intended meaning therefore is that the quality objectives be measurable in not only quantitative but also qualitative ways.

Planning

Planning a quality management system generally covers the following:

• *Planning of product realization:* setting quality objectives and requirements for the product and specifying processes and resources to be applied to realize a specific product. The phrase "including those needed to meet requirements for product [see clause 7.1(a)]" in clause 5.4.1 implies that there can be quality objectives for a product as well as those related to a quality management system. Clause 7.1 specifies "planning of product realization," and item (a) is "quality objectives and requirements for the product," where those items, including (a), should be determined, as appropriate, in planning of product realization. The output of this planning could be a quality plan, the definition of which is given in ISO 9000 clause 3.7.5. The definition of *quality planning* is also given in ISO 9000 clause 3.2.9.

• *Planning of quality management system*: setting quality objectives related to the quality management system and specifying necessary operational processes in the quality management system and related resources to fulfill the quality objectives.

Clause 5.4 mainly focuses on planning the quality management system, while planning product realization is addressed in clause 7.1.

Integrity

The ISO/TC 176 *Introduction and Support Package—Terminology* (see Appendix L) explains that the intended meaning of *integrity* is "condition of having no part or element taken away or lacking, undivided state, or completeness." It is a state of being absolutely perfect, flawless, and entire. The integrity of the quality management system is maintained when the quality management system is kept perfect and entire, even when changes to the quality management system are planned and implemented.

INTENT OF THE REQUIREMENTS

5.3   Quality Policy

Top management is required to establish a quality policy (the same as in the 1994 standard), as specified in clause 5.1. This clause specifies the contents of the quality policy [items (a) through (c)] and a way of handling quality policy [items (d) and (e)].

The intent of the requirements included in items (a) through (e) is as follows:

• *Purpose of the organization.* As required in item (a) and explained in note 1 of clause 3.2.4 of ISO 9000, quality policy should be appropriate to the purpose of the organization and therefore consistent with the overall policy of the organization. This was also required in ISO 9001:1994. Needless to say, there is no sense in having a quality policy that is inconsistent with the purpose of the organization.

• *Compliance with requirements and continual improvement.* Item (b) requires that the quality policy shall include a commitment to compliance with requirements and continual improvement of the effectiveness of the quality management system.

It is not clear what requirements are meant by the term *requirements* here. There can be two possibilities: customer requirements, or any requirements related to the quality management system, including requirements of ISO 9001. The minimum is customer requirements, but if an organization seeks a better quality management system, *requirements* here can be read as all requirements for the quality management system. A commitment to comply with requirements is a declaration by top management to meeting the requirements coupled with its leadership.

The quality policy shall also include a commitment to continual improvement of the effectiveness of the quality management system. What is meant by "the effectiveness of the quality management system?" The effectiveness of the quality management system relates to a quality management system that can produce a product that meets requirements. Typical improvement is a decrease in the ratio of nonconforming products.

• *Framework for quality objectives.* This requires that the quality policy shall provide a framework for establishing quality objectives. In the 1994 edition, the supplier's management with executive responsibility is required to define and document its policy for quality, including objectives for quality and its commitment to quality. In the 2000 revision, top management is required to provide a framework for establishing and reviewing quality objectives.

This is a reflection of a reality where it will not be appropriate for top management to set out all the objectives needed throughout the organization. In fact, it will be more effective to establish and review quality objectives at relevant functions. In the 2000 revision, quality policy should make it possible to establish quality objectives at relevant functions and levels within the organization.

• *Communicated and understood.* This requirement is related to the handling of quality policy. It is required that the quality policy be communicated and understood throughout the organization. The 1994 edition requires that the quality policy be understood, implemented, and maintained at all levels of the organization. Some registered organizations might have dealt with this requirement by having its employees keep a card describing the quality policy. Part of communication of policy within an organization can be achieved by this practice, but it is hard to say that the policy is understood.

The 2000 revision may require that personnel be able to tell the aims of the quality policy and more. The 1994 edition accepts a policy in the form of a slogan, and the organization can prove that its personnel understand the policy by showing that the personnel can say the slogan. However, in the 2000 revision, the contents of the quality policy will be increased and expanded. Top management therefore should explain what is meant by *understood*.

• *Suitability.* Top management must ensure that there is a review of the suitability of the quality policy. The suitability could be reviewed in management review, in accordance with the requirement specified in clause 5.6.1 of ISO 9001: "Top management shall review the organization's quality management system, at planned intervals, to ensure its continuing suitability, adequacy and effectiveness. This review shall include assessing opportunities for improvement and the need for changes to the quality management system, including the quality policy and quality objectives."

5.4 Planning

5.4.1 Quality Objectives

Quality objectives are established based on quality policy; they are generally broken down from the quality policy and cascaded down within the organization. There can be two kinds of quality objectives:

• Organizational quality objectives at relevant functions and at relevant levels within the organization (see clause 5.4.1)

• Quality objectives specific to a product and project [see clause 7.1(a)]

Relevant functions and levels within the organization should establish quality objectives related to both the quality management system and the product, as necessary.

Quality objectives for the product are important. However, at some functions within the organization, there can be no product-related quality objectives. This is why the phrase "including those needed to meet requirements for product [see clause 7.1(a)]" is inserted.

The quality objectives should be measurable, so that the achievement of the objectives can be determined.

5.4.2 Quality Management System Planning

The intent of the requirements included in items (a) and (b) is as follows:

- *Item (a), "Planning."*

Item (a) requires two planning activities:

- Planning of the quality management system to meet the requirements given in 4.1
- Planning of the quality management system to meet the quality objectives

For the first planning activity, it is recommended to identify what should be established (for example, a quality management system diagram, a quality assurance system diagram, process flowcharts, inspection standards, documented procedures, and any other process standards). For the second planning activity, the organization should establish a concrete implementation plan to achieve the quality objectives.

The requirement specified in item (a) seems a bit strange. When an organization is assessed by a third-party registration body, the organization's quality management system must have already been established. If the third-party auditor detects any nonconformity for the quality management system being assessed, it could be concluded that there is nonconformity against this planning requirement. However, since the quality management system has already been established, there could not be any meaningful corrective actions. Indeed, it is no use crying over spilled milk, or what is done cannot be undone. "Changes" to the quality management system become of primary importance. The relevant requirement is given in item (b). Actually, when any changes to the quality management system are planned, the planning should follow the requirement of item (a).

- *Item (b) changes.*

Item (b) requires that even when any changes to the quality management system are carried out, the requirements of the quality management system, including customer requirements, should still be met.

The meaning of *integrity* is explained in the section of this chapter titled "Meanings of Terms." As far as the integrity of changes to a quality management system, the term actually means:

- Planned changes have proved to be adequate
- Planned changes are actually implemented as planned

- Unchanged elements of the quality management system are maintained as they should be

- Implemented changes are demonstrated to be adequate

To ensure integrity, the organization should identify changes needed, establish a plan for implementation of those changes, implement changes as planned, and carry out the validation of the changes.

DIFFERENCES FROM THE 1994 EDITION

Table 14.1 shows a correspondence between ISO 9001:2000 and ISO 9001:1994.

5.3   Quality Policy

Substantial requirements for "quality policy" are the same as those specified in the 1994 edition; that is, top management shall establish the quality policy.

In the 2000 revision, what should be included in quality policy are specified in items (a) through (c). Item (a) is the same as in the 1994 edition, while items (b) and (c) are new requirements. Regarding item (b), it should be ensured that the quality policy includes a commitment to continual improvement. The 2000 revision specifies documented statements of quality policy and quality objectives. It may be good to issue an independent document drafted by top management addressing quality policy and quality objectives that includes a commitment to the quality management system.

Item (e) relating to review for suitability was not required in the 1994 edition. However, many organizations establish procedures for reviewing their quality policy when using the 1994 edition. This item should not pose an implementation issue.

5.4   Planning

5.4.1   Quality Objectives
The 1994 edition requires that the quality policy include quality objectives, which are established by management with executive responsibility (top management). The 2000 revision requires that quality objectives be established at relevant functions and levels within the organization. The highest level of quality objectives may be established by top management and be directly related to the quality policy. In addition, those quality objectives should be broken down into relevant functions within the organization. This way of managing and controlling objectives will be more effective to meet the organization's purpose.

The requirement that the quality objectives be measurable is a new requirement. This requirement is natural and reasonable for the effective management of quality objectives.

5.4.2   Quality Management System Planning
The term *quality planning* is not used in the requirements specified in the 2000 revision. Instead, the term *planning* is used. The meaning is substantially the same, because ISO 9001 is a "quality" management system standard. By the way, the term *quality plan* is used in note 1 of clause 7.1, with the same meaning in the 1994 edition.

Table 14.1   Correspondence between ISO 9001:2000 and ISO 9001:1994.

ISO 9001:2000	ISO 9001:1994
5.3 Quality policy Top management shall ensure that the quality policy: a) is appropriate to the purpose of the organization, b) includes a commitment to comply with requirements and continually improve the effectiveness of the quality management system, c) provides a framework for establishing and reviewing quality objectives, d) is communicated and understood within the organization, and e) is reviewed for continuing suitability	**4.1.1 Quality policy** The supplier's management with executive responsibility shall define and document its policy for quality, including objectives for quality and its commitment to quality. The quality policy shall be relevant to the supplier's organizational goals and the expectations and needs of its customers. The supplier shall ensure that this policy is understood, implemented and maintained at all levels of the organization.
5.4 Planning *5.4.1 Quality objectives* Top management shall ensure that quality objectives, including those needed to meet requirements for product [see clause 7.1 (a)], are established at relevant functions and levels within the organization. The quality objectives shall be measurable and consistent with the quality policy.	**4.2.3 Quality planning** **4.1.1 Quality policy** The supplier's management with executive responsibility shall define and document its policy for quality, including objectives for quality and its commitment to quality.
5.4.2 Quality management system planning Top management shall ensure that: a) the planning of the quality management system is carried out in order to meet the requirements given in 4.1, as well as the quality objectives, and b) the integrity of the quality management system is maintained when changes to the quality management system are planned and implemented.	

7.1   Planning of product realization

NOTE 1 (relating to quality plans): A document specifying the processes of the quality management system (including the product realization processes) and the resources to be applied to a specific product, project or contract, can be referred to as a quality plan.

Source: ANSI/ISO/ASQ Q9001-2000

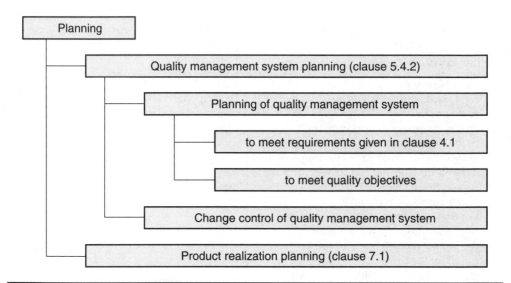

Figure 14.1 Structure of planning.

In the 1994 edition, quality planning covers planning of procedures and associated resources to be applied to a specific project, product, or contract. In the 2000 revision, the concept of planning in the quality management system has been clarified, and two kinds of planning are required:

- Planning of quality management system (clause 5.4.2)
- Planning of product realization process (clause 7.1)

The second kind is the quality planning covered in the 1994 edition, and the first one is a new requirement, which is specified in items (a) and (b) of clause 5.4.2 of ISO 9001.

The ISO 9001 requirements on "planning" are structured as shown in Figure 14.1.

IMPLEMENTING THE ISO 9001 REQUIREMENTS

Establishing the Quality Policy

It is important that the quality policy clearly express the organization's overall intention and direction. The quality policy should be aligned with the organization's purposes and be concrete, realizable, and understandable.

The ISO 9001 standard specifies that the following should be included in the quality policy:

- Commitment to compliance with requirements
- Commitment to continual improvement of the effectiveness of the quality management system
- Framework for establishing and reviewing quality objectives

When establishing a quality policy, the eight quality management principles will give general guidelines on what should be sought related to the quality management of an organization.

Because ISO 9001 requires documented statements of quality policy and quality objectives, an organization should consider issuing an independent document, drafted by top management, of quality policy and quality objectives, including a commitment to the quality management system.

Examples of Quality Policies

Examples of quality policies for imaginary organizations are shown in Tables 14.2 through 14.5.

Table 14.2   An example of quality policy—ABC Clocks and Watches.

Quality Policy

Management Philosophy (Organizational Purpose)
1. Establish a profitable organizational constitution.
2. Contribute to society through sustained organizational prosperity.

Quality Policy
1. We will promote compliance with customer requirements and continual improvement of the effectiveness of our quality management system.
2. We will provide products that are "loved" by our customers by grasping the preference of the market.
3. We will pursue coexistence and mutual prosperity with our suppliers.

Table 14.3   An example of quality policy—DEF Foods.

Quality Policy

Fundamental Ideas
In producing our products, we will devote ourselves to safety and quality control and provide products that satisfy direct customers and consumers, as well as establish the quality management system based on ISO 9001 and HACCP and continually improve its effectiveness.

Policies
We will:
• Understand the requirements of customers, including consumers, and meet their requirements
• Identify critical points in production processes to prevent nonconforming products
• Establish a traceability system to ensure quick reaction against problems
• Ensure sanitary condition of employees and workplaces

Table 14.4 An example of quality policy—GHI Construction.

Quality Policy

We will do our best for reliable construction and aim at customer satisfaction, happiness of our employees, sustained growth of our company, and growth of regional community.

To achieve this, we, the president and all employees, will establish a quality management system based on ISO 9001 and continually improve its effectiveness, as well as positively aim at clarification of responsibility and authority and standardized work processes.

We will:
- Meet customer and regulatory requirements and requirements specified in ISO 9001 to achieve customer satisfaction
- Clearly determine inspection criteria at relevant steps of construction to meet customer satisfaction
- Consider quality and safety control as the most important issues, and thoroughly implement regular quality and safety patrol
- Enhance the technological and managerial abilities of employees
- Continually improve the quality management system by analyzing and reviewing information from customers and suppliers and inspection data on constructed products

Table 14.5 An example of quality policy—JKL Chemicals.

Quality Policy

Our customers will evaluate the quality of our products, while we are responsible for the quality of our products.

1. We will meet any applicable regulatory and statutory requirements.
2. We will establish quality objectives, regularly review them, and enhance continual improvement.
3. We will reduce any nonconformity occurring in the processes.
4. We will maintain the effectiveness of the quality management system.
5. We will provide the number one quality of the product to our customers.
6. We will reflect customers' needs into product development.

Establishing Quality Objectives

Quality objectives are goals, targets, or aims concerning product, process, or system related to quality. In the 1994 edition, the subject aimed at is somewhat ambiguous, but in the 2000 revision, it is clear that quality objectives related to the following should be established:

- Quality objectives related to the quality management system such as the total number of customer complaints, an index of customer satisfaction and dissatisfaction, or occurrence ratio of nonconforming product

- Quality objectives related to a specific product or project (or a specific product category or project), such as the percent defective for a specific product

When establishing quality objectives, consideration should be given to the following:

- *Deployment of the objectives.* Quality policy and quality objectives should be broken down at relevant functions and levels of the organization. It is therefore important to identify which functions and levels are responsible for relevant objectives.

- *Contribution of relevant personnel.* As item (d) of clause 6.2.2, "Competence, awareness and training," specifies "the organization shall ensure that its personnel are aware of the relevance and importance of their activities and how they contribute to the achievement of the quality objectives." It is necessary to identify how relevant personnel achieve the relevant objectives.

- *Confirmation of the achievement.* Because ISO 9001 specifies that "the quality objectives shall be measurable," it is necessary to clearly determine whether the quality objectives are achieved or not, in whatever way, either in a quantitative or qualitative manner.

- *Consistency with the quality policy.* As a matter of course, the quality objectives are established based on quality policy or the commitment of top management. Therefore, the contents of the quality objectives should be consistent with the quality policy or management, and it is necessary to pay attention to that consistency.

Procedures for Quality Policy and Quality Objectives

Table 14.6 shows an example of a procedure for establishing quality policy and quality objectives.

Table 14.6 An example of a procedure for establishing quality policy and quality objectives.

Procedure for establishing quality policy and quality objectives

1. Purpose

    This document specifies procedures for setting quality policy and quality objectives, and for communicating quality policy based on the quality manual.

2. Scope

    This rule applies to the processes of setting quality policy and quality objectives, and for communicating quality policy in MNO division of PQR Company.

3. Setting quality policy

3.1 The head of the MNO division shall establish quality policy. Consideration shall be given to the following when setting the quality policy:
  • The quality policy is appropriate to the purpose of the MNO division
  • The quality policy includes a commitment of the division head to comply with requirements and continually improve the effectiveness of the quality system
  • The quality policy provides a framework for establishing and reviewing quality objectives
3.2 The quality policy shall be issued upon approval of the division head.
3.3 The division head shall assess the need for change to the quality policy at the regular management reviews. When the need for changes to the quality policy is suggested through the process of internal quality audits, corrective actions, and preventive actions, the division head shall review the quality policy.
3.4 When the need for changes to the quality policy is determined upon the review of the division head, the quality policy shall be revised. The revised quality policy shall be issued upon approval of the division head.

4. Setting quality objectives

4.1 The division head shall establish quality objectives in the *hoshin* (policy) statement in the hoshin process. Consideration shall be given to the following when establishing the quality objectives:
  • The quality objectives are consistent with the quality policy
  • The quality objectives are measurable to enable the determination of the extent of achievement
4.2 The policy statement of the division head, including the quality objectives, shall be issued upon approval of the division head.
4.3 Each department shall deploy the policy statement of the division head into the implementation plan for the hoshin process. The deployment shall be made following the rules for hoshin (policy) operation.
4.4 The division head shall assess the need for changes to the quality objectives at the regular management reviews. When the need for changes to the quality objectives is suggested through the process of internal quality audits, corrective actions, and preventive actions, the division head shall review the quality objectives.
4.5 When the need for changes to the quality objectives is determined upon the review of the division head, the policy statement of the division head shall be revised. The revised policy statement shall be issued upon approval of the division head.
4.6 When the policy statement of the division head is revised, each department shall examine the need for changes to its implementation plan for the hoshin process. The needed revision to the implementation plan shall be done following the rules for hoshin (policy) operation.

5. Communicating the quality policy

5.1 The quality policy statement shall be circulated to all personnel. The quality policy shall be well communicated and understood.
5.2 Managers at all departments shall communicate the quality policy with personnel at their departments through any opportunity to make them understand the policy.

Planning a Quality Management System

An approach to developing and implementing a quality management system is shown in ISO 9000. Particularly, a set of steps for developing and implementing a quality management system provides a good guideline for implementing clauses 5.3 through 5.4 of ISO 9001.

ISO 9000 clause 2.3   Quality management system approach

An approach to developing and implementing a quality management system consists of several steps, including the following:

a) determining the needs and expectations of customers and other interested parties

b) establishing the quality policy and quality objectives of the organization

c) determining the processes and responsibilities necessary to attain the quality objectives

d) determining and providing the resources necessary to attain the quality objectives

e) establishing methods to measure the effectiveness and efficiency of each process

f) applying these measures to determine the effectiveness and efficiency of each process

g) determining means of preventing nonconformities and eliminating their causes

h) establishing and applying a process for continual improvement of the quality management system

Such an approach is also applicable to maintaining and improving an existing quality management system.

An organization that adopts the above approach creates confidence in the capability of its processes and the quality of its products, and it provides a basis for continual improvement. This can lead to increased satisfaction of customers and other interested parties and to the success of the organization.

Figure 14.2 shows an outline of the quality management system planning flow of a manufacturing company. The top management directs the heads of divisions and departments to prepare the relevant quality management system plan. The quality director, who is the management representative, specifies the implementation of the quality management system in the quality manual based on this flow. All heads of divisions and departments prepare their own implementation plans to achieve their allocated quality objectives. They control any changes to the quality management system with the greatest care to maintain its integrity.

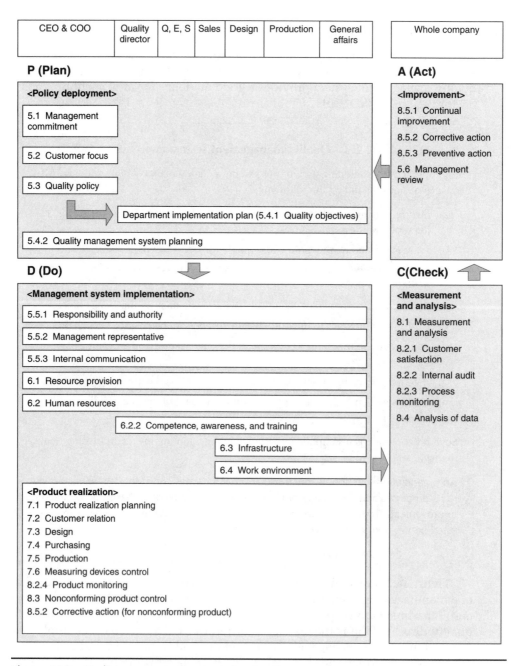

Figure 14.2 Quality management system planning flow.

BEYOND ISO 9001 COMPLIANCE

Learning from ISO 9004

Appendix H (included on the accompanying CD) provides the full text of ANSI/ISO/ASQ Q9004-2000. The main points where the guidelines given in ISO 9004:2000 expand and deepen the requirements given in ISO 9001:2000 are as follows:

5.3 Quality Policy

- A quality policy, consistent with the organization's overall policies and strategy, should be used as means of performance improvement.
- In establishing a quality policy, analyses of "needs" (needs and expectations of customers and interested parties) and "seeds" (the organization's technological ability, resources, people, suppliers, and partners) are essential.
- For effective use of quality policy, considerations should be given to its administration, such as consistency with the organization's vision and strategy, full understanding throughout the organization, provision of adequate resources, strong leadership of top management, and continual efforts for improvement.

5.4 Planning

5.4.1 Quality Objectives

- For the effective setting of quality objectives, what is stated in the quality policy is crucial.
- Quality objectives should be established for seeking the organization's performance improvement.
- When establishing quality objectives, consideration should be given to current and future status (market needs, interested parties' satisfaction, product and process performance, management review results, self-assessment results, and benchmarking) and to resources needed to achieve objectives.
- Quality objectives should be adequately deployed within the organization to enable people to contribute to their achievement.

5.4.2 Quality Planning

- Management should play an important role in the quality planning of the organization.
- Inputs for planning include higher-level objectives (organization's strategies, organizational objectives), what is wanted (needs and expectations of customers and interested parties, statutory and regulatory), results (performance of products and processes, experiences), and possibilities (opportunities, risks).
- What should be decided through quality planning includes the organization's ability (skills and knowledge, financial and other resources) and an improvement plan (responsibility and authority, metrics, methods and tools).

Strategic Business Planning

Quality policy plays an essential role in a quality management system, because the quality policy is actually a starting point for any planning of the quality management system. In this sense, a quality policy should be placed at the highest position in quality management. However, a quality management system is a part of an organization's business management system, where quality is not an ultimate goal, although it is a key weapon for great success in business. Organizations have their own purpose, policy, and strategy, and quality is (or should be) typically a core value. Therefore, top management should ensure that the quality policy is at the core of the organization's overall business strategy and policy. In the ISO 9000 registration, only quality policy is concerned, but the quality policy should be established as part of overall business planning.

To build a sound constitution, an organization should have a vision. An organization in modern society generally establishes mission, vision, and strategy as a basis for its existence. The vision statement tells interested parties about the organization's philosophy or "values," future goals and direction, and what the organization desires to realize. A quality policy should be developed to express a goal or an aim for quality (Q), as well as cost (C) and delivery time and production volume (D) based on the vision statement. A quality policy then should be established based on a business plan and the output of analyses of the needs and expectations of customers, market trends, the competitive situation, and the organization's ability.

When analyzing the business environment in strategic business planning, there are some useful viewpoints:

- *3C:* customer, competitor, and company.
- *Needs and seeds:* what is wanted and what will make it possible; needs and technology.
- *Circumstances and oneself:* the environment surrounding the organization and the organization itself.
- *Business profitability:* the ability to produce profit; the source of competitive advantage.

To identify opportunities and risks, the following should be studied:

- *Circumstances:* analyzing customers, market, society, economics, politics, international situations, technology, industry, and competitors.
- *The organization:* understanding quality, cost, and delivery time of its products; management resources, such as technology, people's abilities, financials, and infrastructure; and maturity level of its management system, such as product planning, design and development, and production engineering, purchasing, sales, and servicing.

When developing a strategic plan for a specific business domain, the following steps are recommended:

- *Environment analysis—grasping attractiveness of the business:* study the trend of the business environment, structure and characteristics of the industry, and the attractiveness of the business.

- *Product analysis—benchmarking the products:* compare the quality and price of products with competitors', and determine their advantages.
- *Market analysis—grasping users' needs:* study customer needs and purchasing motivation factors, and identify the competitive advantage of the organization in a relevant market segment.
- *Product and market analysis—understanding product positioning and competition situation:* integrate the results of the product analysis and the market analysis, and understand how the product meets customer needs and expectations.
- *Product portfolio analysis—prioritizing products:* study advantages of the organization's products in a market, and prioritize them.
- *Strategic factor analysis—determining strategic advantages factors:* identify key factors for business strategies, and develop a basis for strategic plans.
- *Resource allocation analysis—allocating resources on priority basis:* allocate resources (people, goods, money, and time) adequately to achieve strategic goals.

HOSHIN PROCESS

All organizations set out policies and objectives, so it should be easy to establish a quality policy and quality objectives if their effectiveness is not questioned. Management by objectives (MBO) points out the importance of organizational activity for achieving the organization's objectives and provides an effective methodology. Specific features of the MBO process are expressing clearly the objectives of each individual by breaking the high-level objectives down into concrete objectives to be sought by each individual and ensuring the achievement of the objectives by using incentives such as an appraisal system.

Hoshin kanri (or the *hoshin* process, management by policy, policy management, or policy deployment), which was developed in Japan as a tool for Japanese total quality control (TQC), has the same aims as MBO. Its specific features are in deployment of objectives giving consideration to its feasibility, deployment of objectives into means or measures to achieve them, application of the principle of "process control" during the implementation phase, and the deepest analysis of discrepancy from the expectation. Now, the MBO process has changed, being influenced by hoshin kanri.

Points for the success of hoshin kanri are as follows:

- *Establishment of policy:* establishing and prioritizing a reasonable and clear policy for the whole organization.
- *Deployment of policy:* deploying the policy to all departments and all levels of the organization with full communication and understanding.
- *Implementation plan:* developing concrete means and measures to achieve the policy.
- *Process control:* checking the progress during implementation to determine need for follow-up actions.
- *Reflection (problem solving):* making the deepest analysis of causes for differences from the targets.

All these points are important for successful management of policy. However, as a basis for success, systems for "day-to-day management" and a "scientific problem-solving approach" are essential.

Table 14.7 shows the steps for the hoshin kanri.

Table 14.7 Steps of hoshin kanri.

1. Establishing a policy
   Inputs from:
   - Midterm/long-term plan,
   - Analysis of business environment, and
   - Reflection of the previous year's results.

2. Deploying the policy
   Breaking it down into:
   - Subobjectives
   - Means and measures to achieve the objectives
   Harmonizing deployed policies:
   - "Catch ball" between levels of the organization
   - Careful adjustment
   - Harmonizing top-down and bottom-up manners

3. Implementing the policy
   Preparing a feasible implementation plan:
   - Identifying and analyzing problems to achieve upper-level objectives
   - Determining action items, control items, control level, and person(s) in charge
   - Determining the schedule
   Implementing the plan

4. Checking the status
   Checking the status regularly:
   - Daily, weekly, or monthly
   - "Quality diagnosis" by top management
   Process-oriented analysis of causes for unattained targets

5. Reacting against the discrepancies
   Immediate actions (how should we react to the problem that has occurred?):
   - Investing human resources, goods, and money
   - Changing the plan
   Corrective actions depend on the causes:
   - Technological difficulties
   - Changes in the environment
   - Poor management system

6. Looking to the next year (reflection, review):
   - Analyzing causes for unattainable targets
   - Reviewing the hoshin process

Actually, it is not easy to achieve an established policy. A policy cannot be achieved if it is deployed superficially. It is obviously not a final goal for a policy merely to be set out, but it must be set out before it can be achieved. To establish a meaningful policy and achieve it without fail and to improve the process for the management of policy, such activities as shown in Table 14.7 are necessary. Sound management of a quality policy requires not only that it be deployed, "communicated and understood," but also that it be broken down into objectives and means and be controlled in the true meaning of the PDCA (Plan, Do, Check, Act) way.

Chapter 15

Management Review

Chris Hakes
BQC Performance Management, Ipswich, Suffolk, United Kingdom

Globalization, price pressure, industry consolidation, decreasing geographic boundaries, and lower barriers to marketplace entry are continually reshaping the business models by which many organizations operate (see Figure 15.1). Stakeholder expectations of the return from the "world of work" continue to increase with increasing global affluence. Survival and thereby a sustained future depend on balancing these demanding and sometimes competing needs in a very responsive way. It is a complex equation, shifting on a daily basis and demanding flexibility, efficiency, consistency, effectiveness, innovation, and agility. These and a host of other virtues are the consistent features of any effective management review process.

This chapter starts with a brief summary of the ISO 9001:2000 changes. It then discusses the challenges of deploying ISO 9001:2000 in the context of creating a world-class management review process.

The ISO 9001:2000 approach to management review is designed to help you look systematically at your business and highlight key improvement areas. It will show you where your strengths are so that you can build on the good practices that already exist, and it will give you a clear indication of improvement opportunities that are appropriate for your organization.

Compared to previous versions of the ISO9000 series standards, the review principles are essentially unchanged. However, the following additions to the standard will likely influence our thinking on management review:

Figure 15.1 Change like never before.

- A new process-oriented structure
- A continual improvement process as an important step to enhance the quality management systems
- Increased emphasis on the role of top management, which includes their commitment to the development and improvement of the quality management system
 - Consideration of legal and regulatory requirements, and the establishment of measurable objectives at relevant functions and levels
- A requirement for the organization to monitor information on customer satisfaction and/or dissatisfaction as a measure of system performance
- Increased compatibility with environmental management system standards

In compliance terms, a management review must show that an organization has reviewed a range of "inputs" and that a series of "outputs" has been created. An organization must be able to demonstrate that it has addressed the following subclauses to clause 5.6 related to review input and output:

- Input-related subclauses:
  - Audit and prior reviews
  - Customer feedback
  - Process performance and product conformance
  - Status of preventive, and corrective actions
  - Follow-up actions from previous reviews
  - Changes that could affect the quality management system
  - Recommendations for improvement
- Output-related subclauses:
  - Improvement of the quality management system and its processes
  - Improvement of product related to customer requirements
  - Resource plans and needs

The challenge is how to address these requirements in an efficient and strategically beneficial way. An effective process for compliance with clause 5.6 management review subclauses will be highly dependent on how you choose to operate your key strategy formulation and deployment processes. Here are some typical inputs (clause 5.6.2; * = essential):

- Key strategic goals and objectives (your policy deployment process)
- Monitors of operational decisions
- Benchmark data
- Process performance data*
- Product conformity data*
- Internal and external audits*
- Suggestions and recommendations*
- Customer feedback*
- Other stakeholder feedback
- Complaints*
- Analysis of failures and preventive/corrective actions*

The following are desirable outputs (clause 5.6.3; * = essential):

- Process improvement plans*
- Product improvement plans*
- Resource plans and needs*
- Actions to improve the quality management system*
- Strategic initiatives and course corrections
- Internal and external performance summaries

However, the key issue to consider is not how long to make such lists but how short, concise, and effective they can be. World-class organizations are answering such questions by clearly defining the purpose of their measurements and review architectures.[1,2] So how do you focus your thinking?

A key aspect of many excellent organizations is their ability to know what drives their bottom-line results. With this in mind, current strategic thinking has emphasized the relevance of the internal origins of competitive advantage. Thus, it is now as important to identify and measure the "enablers," (key determinants or performance drivers) of future shareholder and stakeholder value as it is to measure shareholder value itself. In this context, the factors that can demonstrate the effectiveness and responsiveness of your policy deployment processes may be critical and may form a structural input into your management review process. The following are some key factors to consider in evaluating the success of your strategic processes:

- Sensing risk and opportunity quickly
- Deploying goals and alignment methods rapidly
- Maintaining clear, consistent, and transferable key business processes
- Having everyone committed to the challenges you face

Good-practice organizations are also elevating key organizational performance measures, such as key process cycle times, to an equal status with more traditional financial measures. Obtaining a balance of outcome, action, and diagnostic measurements and their related monitoring processes is often at the heart of a well-designed management review process. The measurements are defined as follows:

- *Outcome measures,* as their name suggests, measure the outcome of something. As a result, they tend to lag the events that lead to the outcome.

- *Action measures* (or performance drivers) are designed to measure activities that lead to desired outcomes.

- *Diagnostic measures* give insight into why an outcome or action measure is at its current level. Typically, they measure components of the outcome or action measure.

A recent European benchmarking study (see note 1) found that developing balanced and aligned goal deployment and measurement systems was crucial to the success of many good-practice organizations. Thus linking performance indicators and review programs into causal "chains" is the source of success of any effective management review process (see Figure 15.2).

Figure 15.2 Organizing performance indicators into "chains."

A simple but powerfully consistent message from good-practice companies is that key measurement and review activities *must* be aligned and integrated. Only you can diagnose your organization's linkages, but without such an analysis, any performance review process will be less than perfect. ISO 9001:2000 specifically demands that you consider certain inputs and outputs, but your use of these analyses will never be fully effective unless you place them in the context of a holistic, integrated, and aligned approach.

Finally, to test your thinking on the appropriateness of your review processes, consider the following questions, which are based on input from good-practice companies (see notes 1 and 2):

Does your review process . . .

- Cover all appropriate stakeholders?
- Show a cause-and-effect link between the results you obtain or intend and the approaches you use to achieve those results?
- Measure the outcomes of your key approaches and the factors that monitor their deployment?
- Allow analysis of relevant trends of performance? If yes, for how long?
- Have targets? If yes, are the targets achieved?
- Have comparisons with others, for example competitors, industry averages, or "best in class"? If yes, do you compare well with others?
- Give a holistic picture in an effective way?

If you have positive answers to all these questions, congratulations. You will not only have met the requirements of ISO 9001:2000 but have the basis of a world-class quality management system.

POSTSCRIPT

One last thought: Boiling a frog is a challenge; if you throw a frog into boiling water, it will jump out (everyone, even frogs, can sense the big problems). To carry out the task effectively, you put the frog in cold water and gradually raise the temperature (not everyone can sense the smaller issues or opportunities). The frog feels warm and comfortable and eventually falls (permanently) asleep. The key factors are that the progress is slow (but not entirely unpleasant) and the outcome is often not recognized until it is too late—an appropriate metaphor for the lack of timely and *sensitive* review processes?

ENDNOTES

1. *Using Models As Strategy Formulation and Deployment—Results of an EFQM/BQC Performance Management Benchmarking Study Project.* Available at http://www.efqm.org/publications/welcome.htm and download the benchmarking publications pdf, ISBN 905236-417-6
2. C. Hakes, *The Excellence Routefinder.* Ipswich, Suffolk, U. K.: BQC Performance Management, 1999. Available at www.bqc-network.com/publications2.htm ISBN 1-902169-05-0.

Section 5

Resource Management

Introduction

Charles A. Cianfrani
Managing Director, Customer-Focused Quality Group,
ARBOR, Media, Pennsylvania

W ork is a process that involves inputs and value-adding activities that produce outputs to obtain desired results (for example, a product or service to satisfy a user want, need, or requirement). Value-adding activities require resources—people resources, capital resources, or both. Clause 6 of ISO 9001:2000 contains the requirements for an organization to provide the resources necessary to achieve customer satisfaction, to implement and maintain an effective quality management system (QMS), and to continually improve its effectiveness.

If organizations do not address competency and training of its people and the need for equipment, then no amount of attention to product realization processes will yield long-term customer satisfaction. Organizations must also identify and manage those factors of the work environment necessary to ensure conformity of product.

Conversely, if an organization selects competent people and has a process for understanding and providing required training and equipment, then effectively achieving long-term customer satisfaction is possible.

Chapter 16 in this handbook, "Human Resources," by Gordon Staples with Jim Gildersleeve addresses critical activities related to ensuring that the people doing work in an organization are competent. The management of the organization should continually appraise the competence of its people in relationship to evolving internal needs and external customer requirements and expectations. Further, the requirements for providing the training necessary for people and the organization to be successful in meeting internal and external needs (clause 6.2.2) are discussed.

The requirements for having appropriate infrastructure available when and where needed, such as workspaces, communications equipment, and necessary product realization hardware and software are described by Jack West in chapter 17, "Management of Infrastructure and Work Environment." The requirements (ISO 9001 Clauses 6.3 and 6.4) are not intended to be prescriptive to organizations. On the other hand, the standard is making the point that it is essential for management to provide the people in the organization with the equipment and work environment necessary to achieve effective satisfaction of customer requirements.

Chapter 16

Human Resources: An Integral Part of Continual Improvement

Gordon Staples
Excel Partnership, Nantwich, Cheshire, United Kingdom

with contributions from
Jim Gildersleeve
Publisher, *The Informed Outlook* Newsletter, Montclair, Virginia

Trite sayings such as "people are our most valuable asset" are commonplace, but this author would argue that people are an organization's only assets. Among an organization's resources, the human part is key. Consequently, to talk about training issues rather than human resource development concerns is to denigrate the role that people play in an organization.

THE ISSUE OF COMPETENCE

ISO 9001:1994 had requirements related to human resources. There were requirements for ensuring the availability of adequate resources, knowing customers' needs, understanding the quality policy at all levels, identifying where training was necessary and carrying it out, and so on. ISO 9001:2000 introduced the idea of competence into the standard.

ISO 9001:2000 requires the availability of necessary resources; the determination of customers' needs as requirements; an understanding of the quality policy; the identification of and planning for resources needed; the availability of competent human resources on the basis of appropriate education, training, skills, and experience; the identification of necessary competence of personnel and the provision of training or of other actions to satisfy the needs for competence; an evaluation of the effectiveness of training; the verification that employees are aware of the relevance of their activities; and so on.

The perception of what organizational and individual competence is and whether or not it has been achieved are determined by the organization's leaders and will vary greatly from organization to organization. Simply put, an organization has to identify its forward goals and put plans in place to meet those goals. The plans must ensure that employees have the necessary competence based on education, skills, experience, or training. Where they do not, then action is needed to close the identified gaps. That action can involve reassigning work to individuals who possess the needed competence, or it can involve training. But it can also involve other activities such as changing individuals' job assignments or hiring personnel with the required competence. Whatever action is needed, the effectiveness has to be measured. The concept is illustrated in Figure 16.1.

The organization must be able to produce evidence showing that the competence required of employees has been determined and that their actual competence has been compared against that requirement. If the organization has a view that organizational and individual competence is displayed when work is being done at normal levels of proficiency, then the assessment of competence can be a simple and straightforward process. Visiting auditors can verify that the organization has assessed its needs and has provided a record of that assessment.

The effort required for an organization to achieve the needed levels of competence depends on the organization's leaders and the goals they set. Often, reward systems in companies actually prevent managers and staff from achieving greater levels of organizational competence because an environment of compliance with rules exists.

Organizations that are very hierarchically structured and have many clearly defined levels of senior and junior management, divisional and departmental budgets, and so on, tend to stifle anything that may "rock the boat." Organizational competence, let alone divisional, departmental, and personal competencies, never challenges goals in such an environment, and stagnates.

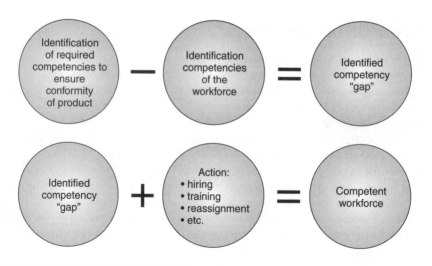

Figure 16.1   Identifying and closing competency gaps.

BREAKING NEW GROUND WITH ISO 9001:2000

It could be argued that the intentions of ISO 9001:1994 and ISO 9001:2000 are very similar. However, ISO 9001:1994 did not say quite as definitively as does ISO 9001:2000 that resources include all human resources. Neither did it specifically say that people needed to have applicable training, education, and skills, or that training effectiveness had to be measured. Presumably, many companies didn't bother to ask how management knew whether the training had been effective, even as a form of preventive (or corrective) action, nor did the companies' auditors.

There are several examples in ISO 9001:2000 of requirements that some may consider as "breaking new ground" but were obviously applicable within ISO 9001:1994. Annex B of ISO 9001:2000, the "Correspondence between ISO 9001:2000 and ISO 9001:1994" lists only three items where there is no correspondence:

1. Clause 5.6.2   (Management) Review input
2. Clause 5.6.3   Management review output
3. Clause 8.2.1   Customer satisfaction

The real lack of correspondence arises from the detail. Thus, ISO 9001:2000 includes the following requirements that were not as clearly specified in ISO 9001:1994:

1. Clause 4.1(d) requires "availability of resources and information necessary." Previously, the emphasis was on the need for documented procedures in production, installation, and service only. The emphasis now is clearly on human needs (as yet, only humans use information).

2. Clauses 4.2.3 and 4.2.4 both require (as do clauses 8.2.2, 8.3, 8.5.2, and 8.5.3) documented procedures. It appears strange to this writer that documented procedures are required in the six activities noted but not for the main business processes—how to sell, design, purchase, make, test, dispatch, invoice, service, and so on. On the one hand, ISO 9001:2000 demands fewer documented procedures than did ISO 9001:1994. Presumably, the reason for this is a realization that quality and documented procedures are not synonymous. The emphasis on quality in ISO 9001:2000 will, therefore, be on the people involved, which is a good thing. On the other hand, how can the documented procedures that the standard requires be logical? There is no explanation given in ISO 9000, ISO 9001, or ISO 9004; nor is there help in any of the other documents issued as guides by ISO (for example, quality management principles and ISO 9000 selection and use).

MANAGEMENT RESPONSIBILITY

Throughout clause 5, "Management responsibility," reference is made to top management, defined as "those who direct and control an organization at the highest level." The extent of the use of the term *top management* thus emphasizes their roles within the management system much more so than was the case in ISO 9001:1994. It also follows that for top management to fulfill their roles, they are going to have to be personally and directly involved to a greater extent than was even implied by ISO 9001:1994. Although clause 5.1, "Management commitment," is a new clause and contains five broad requirements (a to e) that were implicit in ISO 9001:1994, none particularly emphasizes human resource development.

Clause 5.2, "Customer focus," is a new clause that emphasizes the enhancement of customer satisfaction. This requirement should cause an organization to think about what customers want in the units of measurement that customers use. How can an organization enhance customer satisfaction without the customer perceiving an improvement? Such techniques as quality function deployment (QFD) were designed to enable all personnel in an organization to do just what this requirement is demanding; QFD use will doubtless become more widespread.

Clause 5.3, "Quality policy," existed previously but now has more detailed requirements attached, like ensuring that the policy is appropriate to the purpose of the company. This surely requires the company to clearly state its purpose. There is also a requirement that the policy include a commitment to comply with requirements and continually improve the effectiveness of the quality management system. Some commentators suggest that this statement—often printed, framed, and displayed in a company's visitor reception area (and perhaps in other areas) with the title "Quality Policy"—must therefore contain words such as *comply with requirements, continually improve the effectiveness*, and *quality objectives*. Some auditors have even stated that they would issue a nonconformity if these words were not there. Perhaps these people misunderstand the intent of the standard. Information about "comply with requirements," "continually improve," and so on might preferably appear in other parts of policy documents—for example, in a company's quality manual, purchase orders, or annual report.

Clause 5.4.1, "Quality objectives," requires that objectives be consistent with the policy and are measurable. The objectives must also be established at the relevant levels and functions of the organization.

Clause 5.5.4, "Internal communication," should demand that the organization establish and use appropriate processes for communication. The word *communication*, however, has become trite. No doubt a company will state that its intranet enables everyone to contact (communicate with) everyone else, regardless of whether the telephone or even face-to-face conversation would be a much more appropriate method.

HUMAN RESOURCES

Clause 6.2.1, "Human resources—General," states, "Personnel performing work affecting product quality shall be competent on the basis of appropriate education, training, skills, and experience." Why only *product* quality? Personnel competence is based not only on education, training, skills, and experience but also on awareness, attitude, and behavior, besides the effect of the prevailing work environment.

Clause 6.2.2, "Competence, awareness, and training," complements what has been said previously, but for some reason clause 6.2.2(a) requires the determination of "the necessary competence for personnel performing work affecting *product* quality." Clause 6.2.2(d) includes a requirement that the organization ensure "that its personnel are aware of the relevance and importance of their activities and how they contribute to the achievement of the quality objectives." Here perhaps is some greater emphasis on the human resource and its value and development, as well as recognition of its true place in the organization's resources.

Throughout clause 8, "Measurement, analysis, and improvement," are many requirements related to the use of real data (and thus valid information) in the measurement of processes. ISO 9001:1994 was very limited in this area; consequently, many corrective actions were taken that did not identify root causes and subsequently never closed out the problems. This, of course, was not a problem with the standard per se, only with its application by organizations. ISO 9001:2000 puts no greater emphasis than did ISO 9001:1994 on identifying the most appropriate remedies.

Perhaps not surprisingly in a standard mandating activities in organizations, the extent to which human resources are mentioned is limited. Such a standard is not likely to be concerned with such things. Historically, such standards have not considered the human resource to be primary in assuring quality. Rather, human resources have been treated as only one of the many resources required. There have always been documents produced as complementary or auxiliary to the requirements documents, but in earlier times they were guides for implementing the standards rather than what ISO 9004:2000 is—a guideline for performance improvements.

HUMAN RESOURCE DEVELOPMENT

In this section, we use examples to discuss how the standard can encourage organizations to develop their management systems in the best way rather than solely to meet third-party auditor requirements. We discuss these examples within the context of human resource development.

ISO 9000:2000 refers to the following eight quality management principles, upon which ISO 9001:2000 is purported to be based:

1. Customer focus.
2. Leadership.
3. Involvement of people.
4. Process approach.
5. System approach to management.
6. Continual improvement.
7. Factual approach to decision making.
8. Mutually beneficial supplier relationship.

The principles are covered in detail in chapter 2. In the context of human resource development, principles 2 and 3 above (especially 3) would appear to be relevant. We have considered already that the clause 5 requirement for top management to be involved and show leadership should instigate human interaction; but, however one analyzes ISO 9001:2000, it is very difficult to see how the standard encourages the application of principle 3. In various company analyses, the author has found that ISO 9001:2000 may encourage the application of certain of the quality management principles but most assuredly does not encourage each equally. For example, customer focus receives much more attention (10 clauses mention "customer") than involvement of people (2 clauses mention "personnel").

For ISO 9000 to become of serious interest to top management, it has to assist them in achieving the goals by which they are measured. Most of these goals are financial, such as profit, return on investment, value of company shares, and so on. It is well proved by others (J. M. Juran and W. Edwards Deming, for example) that to improve profit, return on investment, and value of company stock, organizations must do three fundamental things:

- Sell more
- Raise prices
- Reduce costs

Companies that sell more are perceived to provide better service; this justifies premium pricing. Only companies who are efficient will be able to reduce costs without affecting value, as seen by customers. Companies whose services are perceived to be best may keep prices level with or lower than competitors' and still make greater profits.

The human resources—that is, the employees—have goals also, such as secure employment, job satisfaction and pride in their work, and adequate financial compensation. All of these can occur to the greatest extent only when a company is successful in business.

GUIDELINES FOR PERFORMANCE IMPROVEMENT

It follows that if ISO 9004:2000 is to assist in the process for improving the performance of a business, then it has to assist in attaining the above and related goals. The following sections of ISO 9004:2000 recommend some of the principles stated.

Clause 5.2.2, "Needs and expectations (of interested parties)," says, "The organization should identify its people's needs and expectations for recognition, work satisfaction and personal development. Such attention helps to ensure that the involvement and motivation of people are as strong as possible."

Clause 5.3, "Quality policy," states, "In establishing the quality policy, top management should consider . . . the development of people in the organization."

Clause 5.4.2, "Quality planning," states, "Outputs of quality planning for the organization should define the product realization and support processes needed in terms such as skills and knowledge needed."

Clause 5.5.3, "Internal communication," states, "The management of the organization should define and implement an effective and efficient process for communicating the quality policy. Providing such information can aid in the organization's performance improvement and directly involves its people in the achievement of quality objectives." Management should actively encourage feedback and communication from people in the organization as a means of involving them. Activities for communicating include:

- Management-led communication in work areas
- Team briefings and other meetings such as for recognition of achievement
- Notice boards, in-house journals, and magazines
- Audiovisual and electronic media, such as e-mail and Web sites
- Employee surveys and suggestion schemes

Clause 6.1, "Resource management," states (in clause 6.1.2, "Issues to be considered"), "Consideration should be given to resources to improve the performance of the organization, such as: . . .

- intangible resources such as intellectual property; . . .
- enhancement of competence via focused training, education and learning;
- development of leadership skills and profiles for the future managers of the organization."

Clause 6.2, "People," states (in clause 6.2.1, "Involvement of people"), "Management should improve both the effectiveness and efficiency of the organization . . . through the involvement and support of people. As an aid to achieving its performance improvement objectives, the organization should encourage the involvement and development of its people by:

- providing ongoing training and career planning;
- recognizing and rewarding;
- facilitating the open, two-way communication of information;
- continually reviewing the needs of its people;
- creating conditions to encourage innovation;
- ensuring effective teamwork;
- communicating suggestions and opinions;
- using measurements of its people's satisfaction;
- investigating the reasons why people join and leave the organization."

Clause 6.2.2.1, "Competence," states, "Consideration of the need for competence includes sources such as: . . .

- anticipated management and workforce succession needs; . . .
- evaluation of the competence of individual people to perform defined activities."

Clause 6.2.2.2, "Awareness and training," states, "Planning for education and training needs should take account of change caused by . . . the stages of development of people and the culture of the organization. The objective is to provide people with knowledge and skills that, together with experience, improve their competence. . . . [P]lanning for education and training should consider:

- experience of people;
- tacit and explicit knowledge;
- leadership and management skills; . . .
- team building; . . .
- communication skills; . . .
- culture and social behavior; . . .
- creating and innovation.

"To facilitate the involvement of people, education and training also include: . . .

- benefits from creativity and innovation ...
- introductory programs for new people, and
- periodic refresher programs for people already trained.

"Training plans should include . . . evaluation in terms of enhanced competence of people."

Clause 6.4, "Work environment," states, "Creation of a suitable work environment, as a combination of human and physical factors, should include consideration of:

- creative work methods and opportunities for greater involvement to realize the potential of people in the organization; . . .
- social interaction;
- facilities for people in the organization."

Clause 6.5, "Information," states, "In order to manage information, the organization should . . . evaluate the benefits derived from use of the information in order to improve managing information and knowledge."

Clause 7, "Product realization," states (in clause 7.1.2, "Issues to be considered"), "The role of the people within the processes should be evaluated in order to:

- ensure the health and safety of people;
- ensure that the necessary skills exist;
- provide for input from people in process analysis;
- promote innovation from people."

Clause 7.1.3, "Managing processes," states, "Examples of support processes include . . . training of people."

Clause 7.1.3.2, "Process inputs, outputs and review," states, "Examples of input issues to consider include competence of people."

Clause 8.2.4, "Measurement and monitoring the satisfaction of interested parties," states, "The organization should identify the measurement information required to meet the needs of interested parties (other than customers). . . . Such information should include measurements relating to the people in the organization. . . . Measurement examples are as follows:

a) For people in the organization, the organization should:

- survey the options of its people regarding how well the organization satisfies their needs and expectations;
- assess individual and collective performances and their contribution to organizational results."

Clause 8.4, "Analysis of data," states, "For an effective evaluation . . .of the total performance . . . data and information . . . should be analyzed. The results can be used . . . to determine . . . satisfaction of . . . interested parties."

Clause 8.5.4, "Continual improvement of the organization," states, "Management should create a culture that involves people actively seeking opportunities for improvement. . . . To involve people, top management should create an environment . . . so that people are empowered. . . . This can be achieved by activities such as: . . .

- recognition and reward for achievement; . . .
- suggestion schemes."

The foregoing fairly exhaustive list shows us that ISO 9004:2000 is trying hard to provide real guidelines for organizations to improve both effectiveness (achieving objectives) and efficiency (achievement with minimum waste). All the references cited here have a focus on the human resource; it is clear, therefore, that ISO 9004:2000 recognizes the importance of human input.

EXAMPLE FROM THE SERVICE INDUSTRY

Perhaps an example of what a particular sector of commerce has achieved in terms of performance improvement will allow some comparison.

Initiatives in the service industry (banks and insurance companies) regarding development of their human resources are worth some mention. Although the organizational changes were driven by merger and the need to manage the consequential changes in culture, many used the opportunity to some benefit.

Bankco, a large bank, recognized it had to transform the way that its human resource (HR) department had been managed in the past. The aim was to make HR a strategic business partner, closely involved in the overall strategic aims of the company, enabling change and helping to drive the business forward. Primary vehicles developed to deliver human resources (personnel and training) included:

- Group strategy
- Defined business projects
- Managed service agreements

The group strategy vehicle ensured that HR was part of development of the strategic goals. The wider HR strategy was considered as well as industry and legislative requirements. With this approach, the HR group was involved from the beginning as new products and services were developed, and they could ensure that the appropriate long- and short-term education and training were carried out. The HR group also directed negotiations and consultation with unions and representative staff bodies.

To enable the management of appropriate business projects, a project office was established to facilitate various projects (of strategic and tactical issues). This aligned people, systems, technology, and structure around a project-based culture.

Many of the projects concerned aspects associated with the "internal customer/supplier concept" and focused on strengthening the service-level agreements among the different functions and groups. These service-level agreements developed function-to-function but were gradually cascaded down to interpersonal levels. It was recognized that establishing the agreements and the criteria was all very well, but both changed over time. Reviews were established in a formal way to ensure that the requirements were established, to validate that the requirements were the right ones, and to determine the extent to which they were still being met.

In ISO 9001:2000 terms, the development of communications among groups and between personnel has been well developed (clause 5.5.3). The awareness of customer requirements was constantly the case (clause 5.2) as projects were put into practice to further develop the system and procedures. The sequence of processes came under constant scrutiny. Measurement systems were put into place not only for the results of the processes themselves (clause 8.2.3) but also for determining the extent of real improvement (clause 8.5.1). In its first year, Bankco saved $13 million. Actions included removing redundancy in systems, removing double and triple loops of checking and approval (also removing different management levels of approvals), giving groups and people a greater degree of self-control over their jobs, and using the released manpower to create new business. By any standard, the continual improvement generated has been impressive.

The example given here illustrates very clearly how one company followed the intents of ISO 9001 and ISO 9004 to great effect. (Its staff were, however, totally unaware of the standard.)

PERFORMANCE IMPROVEMENT

Achieving these results required training beyond that required for the people of the organization to perform their jobs adequately. They were also provided with a great deal of training in project management, problem solving, teamwork, basic statistical techniques, flowcharting, and process analysis, among other things. Early training (of the board and nominated senior executives) was carried out off-site. The rest was conducted on the job. This was deliberately done so that the techniques being taught could be immediately used by the personnel involved with data from real issues in their day-to-day work.

The foregoing examples dealt with approaches to HR development in particular environments and in the use of technology. Undoubtedly, technology will play an even greater part in the future. Web-based training, using either the Internet or a company's own intranet, is a very exciting new method for developing human resources. Programs are now available that allow training and other group activities to take place simultaneously around the world if necessary. Using multiway audio conferencing (and videos, if wished), groups of people can take part in training and discussion without leaving their desks. The design of this kind of training package and other modules assumes greater importance. Training can be broken down into small modules of one to two hours so that the learners can take part in a crisp and concise session and then get on with their work. The sessions can be run on a public basis or be custom designed for a company's in-house use. The program allows attendees to "raise their hand," agree or disagree, ask questions, and receive immediate answers.

One problem that has arisen in more-traditional organizations is that insufficient or even inadequate training is provided. One of the greatest spurs to changing this has been the realization in many companies that perhaps if personnel were able to participate in the setting of standards, in determining what support they need to achieve those standards, then perhaps the HR development system could be improved.

Some companies go even further. We have seen companies whose training and development policy is one part—a subset—of its mission and vision statements. Some organizations do not mind publicizing such a statement, and they make a point of ensuring that the policy is fully discussed at all levels in the organization so that everyone can see their part. As a result, anyone in the company will be able to explain in their own words what the company is trying to achieve.

The development of an environment in which everyone can say how he or she contributes to the company's success is a big step forward. Traditionally, it was not even possible to expect such an understanding at the functional or departmental level because that is how the management systems, reward scales, and so on were designed—that is, departmental or functional goals were not fully aligned with those of the organization as a whole.

PLANNING FOR TRAINING AND DEVELOPMENT

To return to the mission statement mentioned earlier, this commitment to training and development is translated into organizational goals and targets. These goals and targets require both planning and resources. The plan must define the training and development needs, among other things.

Planning needs to take place at each level of the organization. An effective way that organizations have found to do this is to discuss at each reporting level what the organizational targets are and what the "local" targets are to assist in meeting the organizational targets. Then a plan is set to meet those targets in terms of time resources, training, and so on.

As with any business plan, it must be flexible enough to alter as markets, technology, and other external factors change. Both the overall and the local plan must change as development occurs and people's needs change at individual or departmental levels.

Clear objectives can now be set at organizational, team, and individual levels. These objectives need to specify the desired performance and improvements in terms of what is expected from training and development (knowledge, skills, and behavior). Once everyone in the company begins to share a common understanding of overall and local objectives, the reasons for the training and development can be more fully understood. Each participant can now have a real part in determining the organization's success.

Here, technologically based training such as that described earlier can be most valuable, enabling people to take the training without being away from the office or home for nights on end. To attend a traditional ISO 9000 lead auditor course may require leaving home on a Sunday, traveling to the venue, residing close to the course venue, staying for the five days of the course, and perhaps not returning home until the following Saturday.

It is essential and valuable for employees to assist in setting their own standards and participating in the process of agreeing on training and development objectives. Often personnel will set far higher standards than their boss will. The boss needs to ensure that such standards are not only achievable but also are compatible with team and organizational goals.

This process will similarly undergo constant review. As we know, training can occur in many ways other than formal classroom sessions or even logging onto Web-based training. Periodically, a review must ask, "what does 'effective' look like?" Are perceptions of effectiveness the same for both personnel and managers regarding each other as well as of any training that has occurred?

Managers should, indeed must, take responsibility for coaching, briefing, and mentoring staff continually to enable real achievement in meeting goals. Having managers constantly search for the best types of support to give and having them constantly reconsider how they can ensure that their staff can improve their knowledge, skills, and behavior are all key facets of this process.

For instance, a manager may decide to be directly involved in coaching (as teacher or copupil) or may consider it worthwhile to brief the staff before a training session to clarify how all parties—staff, department, and organization—might benefit from the training. Certainly, the outcome of the training needs to be discussed with the staff and further opportunities for development identified.

Keeping employees fully advised about the opportunities available to them, regardless of age, seniority, and length of service, is also important. It must be clear to whom they can go for advice. Furthermore, they need to know whether the advice is always actionable.

Employees have a responsibility to identify both needs and opportunities. Policy should allow for time and access to peruse, for example, trade journals, distance learning materials, and evening classes.

Even with the best intentions, it is not always possible to meet all apparent needs immediately. Managers or employees may propose specific activities that will not be doable. Whatever the reason for not going ahead, it must be explained to those proposing the activity.

Consider the situation where top management asks for suggestions from employees and then acts on some but does not acknowledge others. Within a short period, employees will stop making suggestions.

The impact of training on knowledge, skills, and behavior needs to be evaluated, as stated, and there are many means: questionnaires, tests, follow-up discussions, performance reviews, team meetings, surveys, or monitoring direct results. A key feature must be whether the improvement is *sustainable* in the workplace. This means that the learner gains in knowledge or skills or improves in behavior—that the gain is recognized and valued by the employee, manager, and company alike and it is a permanent gain. *Sustainable* must also mean that the improvement can be used as a model for the future. To go further, specific questions need to be asked, including in what ways has it improved the individual's performance and in what ways has it improved departmental and therefore organizational performance? Has it lowered costs? How have training and development contributed to this?

The reality is that training and development cost money. Although it may not be seen in this way, investing in training, like many a quality cost (preventative) is an act of faith—pay now, benefit later. Dependence on belief can be reduced by good planning and monitoring, but the faith aspect remains to some degree.

Both the job and the training contain aspects that can be improved. No processes are exempt from improvement opportunity. This is a long-term process. A company must continually look for ways to use training and development so its employees are learning at least as quickly as the company and its markets are changing. Of course, we must not forget that if the company does it correctly, it can gain ISO 9001 registration, too.

APPROACHES TO WORLD-CLASS STATUS

What kind of approach should companies take if they really want to ge
class status? One interesting way is to use the concept of "the learning organization." This concept is not new. In the 1930s and 1940s, Reginald Revans, the
acknowledged father of action learning, was inculcating learning-to-learn values
into people working in the health service and mining industries. He stated, "A workforce comprising a high proportion of people with well-honed self-development
and learning-to-learn skills is indicative of the learning organization."

K. Ross[1] discusses the work of Argyris and Schon and their concepts of single-
loop and double-loop learning:

> They argue that organizational learning involves the detection and correction of
> error. When such detection and correction enables the organization to continue
> with current policies and objectives, the result is single-loop learning. Double-
> loop learning, on the other hand, is generated by detection–correction activities
> that modify the organization's fundamental norms and aims, often through chal-
> lenging traditional norms and values and resolving subsequent conflict.

R. Hill[2] points out that in essence, double-loop learning is about raising the
learning mechanism of a company from the operational to the strategic level.
While many organizations can and do achieve single-loop learning, the more
valuable learning engendered through questioning and challenging the norm is
more difficult to accomplish. The process of continually questioning and challenging the strategic norm is the norm within a learning organization.

According to T. J. Peters and R. H. Waterman[3], the learning organization is:

> the truly adaptive organization [that] evolves in a very Darwinian way. The
> company is trying lots of things, experimenting, making the right sort of mis-
> takes; that is to say, it is fostering its own mutations. The adaptive corporation
> has learned quickly to kill off the dumb mutations and invest heavily in the ones
> that work.

Peters and Waterman's assertion underpins the need for an organization to
adopt a collaborative, action-oriented approach to learning; make mistakes without apportioning blame; and acquire an almost innate ability to recognize and discard what either will not or will no longer work.

M. Pedler et al.[4] suggest, "The learning company is a vision of what might be
possible. It is not brought about simply by training individuals; it can only happen as a result of learning at the whole organizational level." They go on to qualify this by saying, "The learning company is an organization that facilitates the
learning of all its members and continuously transforms itself."

Conceptualizing the learning organization as an amorphous vision where
learning must be the concern of everyone necessitates the requirements for learning values to be built into the company's strategic and operational thinking. In
providing an environment conducive to the learning of all its people, the company
must also find a mechanism to harness all the ensuing energy and return it to the
organization as a cohesive and effective whole. If this is not done, organizational
learning is diminished and valuable opportunities for transformation to a yet

higher order are missed. In further substantiation of this argument, Argyris and Schon (see note 1) argue that learning experienced by individuals may not be transferred or encoded into the memory of the organization, resulting in many organizations knowing less than their members.

The learning organization is inherently committed to improvement. J. S. Oakland[5] claims that the three basic principles of never-ending improvement are to focus on the customer, understand the process, and involve the people. On the aspect of customer focus, he also says that "an organization must recognize throughout its ranks that the purpose of all work and all effort to make improvements is to serve better the customer."

Clearly, the learning organization has a culture that supports the ethos of learning. It stimulates learning awareness in individuals and creates openings for dialogue about the organization's prevailing and desired learning climate. The desired state becomes the vision (the organization's preferred destination), and the gap generates the energy and motivation to change. The organization then maps out its journey and selects the best method for getting there.

P. M. Senge[6] writes about personal mastery, giving us a means to make the link between individual and organizational learning. He refers to the "discipline of personal growth and learning." He also says, "People with high levels of personal mastery are continually expanding their ability to create the results in life they truly seek. From their quest for continual learning comes the spirit of the learning organization."

In relating this last sentence to the concept of *organizational* mastery, R. Hill (see note 2) identifies "a prerequisite of which the organization is to be acutely aware, and in touch with: the individual and collective learning worth of its people." Hill goes on to say:

> *Articulating, understanding, and promoting the spirit of the learning organization in congruence with personal and organizational awareness would seem a wholly sensible and pragmatic step towards helping the organization to meet its quintessential, and perhaps most complex challenge: that of discovering, assessing, directing, and maintaining learning worth at least in line with the rate of change in both its internal and external environments."*

ENDNOTES

1. K. Ross, "The Learning Company," *Training and Development* (July 1992): 64.
2. R. Hill, *A Measure of the Learning Organization* (a section of R. Hill's thesis in support of her doctorate).
3. T. J. Peters and R. H. Waterman, *In Search of Excellence* (New York: HarperCollins, 1993): 78–79.
4. M. Pedlar, et.al., *Action Learning in Practice*, 2nd ed. (London: Gower, 1991): 146–149.
5. J. S. Oakland, *Total Quality Management* (New York: Butterworth Heinmann, 1992): 18–24, 94–99.
6. P. M. Senge, *The Fifth Discipline: The Art and Practice of the Learning Organization* (London: Century Business, 1993): 71–72, 86, 95, 108.

Chapter 17

Management of Infrastructure and Work Environment

John E. (Jack) West
Consultant, The Woodlands, Texas

COMPLIANCE WITH ISO 9001:2000

General Infrastructure and Facilities

Common sense dictates that physical resources are required to produce a product or deliver a service. Clause 6.3, "Infrastructure," encompasses all of the physical resources needed to create the product and to provide it to the customer, except personnel. The requirements for personnel are covered in clause 6.2, which addresses human resources. Included in clause 6.3 are requirements to identify, provide, and maintain the infrastructure needed to achieve conformity of product. *Infrastructure* is broadly defined to encompass the buildings, workspace, equipment, and support services.

"Infrastructure" is one of the clauses under resource management. The significance of separating it from the old process control clause should be recognized. The organization must identify, provide, and maintain appropriate infrastructure for all the processes within the quality management system. This goes beyond production and service operations and beyond even the realization processes to include the management processes; other resource processes (training, in particular); and the measurement, analysis, and improvement processes. Quality management system records should indicate that the requirements of this clause have been considered and addressed.

Work Environment

The work environment of an organization can be considered a combination of human and physical factors. Examples of human factors in the work environment that may affect conformity of product include the following:

- Work methods
- Safety rules and guidance, including use of protective equipment
- Ergonomics

Physical factors can also affect the ability to achieve conforming product. It is important to control those factors that affect product quality characteristics because they have a direct impact on the ability of the product to conform to specifications. Physical factors affecting the work environment may include the following:

- Heat
- Hygiene
- Vibration
- Noise
- Humidity
- Pollution
- Light
- Cleanliness
- Air flow

If the organization determines that it is necessary to control work areas for physical factors, it is common to do the following:

- Identify standards to be maintained
- Assure that the facility meets the standards
- Train personnel on standards pertaining to their work
- Prohibit unauthorized access to the work area
- Implement and maintain desired physical conditions
- Maintain records of the conditions as a means of demonstrating compliance to the standards

Tables 17.1 and 17.2 provide some implementation examples for the requirements related to work environment.

WHAT IS DIFFERENT FROM THE 1994 EDITION?

General Infrastructure and Facilities

There is now a clear statement that facilities and associated infrastructure elements are within the domain of this standard. Although ISO 9001:1994 does not explicitly state requirements for facilities and workspace, it has been widely

Table 17.1 Implementation examples for services and computer software.

Type of Service Organization	Examples of Infrastructure Considerations	Examples of Work Environment Considerations
Warehousing	• Warehouse location • Warehouse capabilities • Loading and unloading equipment	• Heating, ventilation, and air conditioning to preserve product in storage
Delivery service	• Availability of delivery vehicles • Loading and unloading equipment	• Air conditioning, heating, insulation, or other methods to preserve items being delivered
Electric motor repair	• Appropriate diagnostic instruments • Tools and equipment for making repairs	• Cleanliness of reassembly area • Personal protection for workers who coat the motor windings
Food service	• Appropriate kitchens and kitchen equipment • Delivery vehicles	• Personal hygiene • Hair nets and gloves for cooks to protect food from contamination
Computer software development	• Appropriate workrooms • Appropriate programming tools • Appropriate computer processors	• Temperature controls for computer processing equipment

Table 17.2 Implementation examples for hardware and processed materials.

Type of Service Organization	Examples of Infrastructure Considerations	Examples of Work Environment Considerations
Painting	• Spray equipment • Brushes • Positioning equipment, ladders, or paint booths	• Ambient humidity • Ambient temperature • Protective clothing, masks, or respirators for painters
Electronic components	• Production process equipment • Handling equipment	• Cleanliness may require "clean rooms"
Medical devices	• Special production equipment	• Clean-room environments • Sterile conditions
Chemicals	• Process reactors, tanks, and piping • Control systems • Special shipping and handling equipment	• Protective equipment • Protective clothing • Ventilation
Ship or building construction	• Building docks • Outfitting piers • Lifting and handling equipment	• Personal protective equipment for welders • Considerations for painting (see above) • Provision of clean environment for installation of critical equipment

understood that these were at least partially addressed in ISO 9001:1994, clause 4.9, "Process control," which does require "suitable production, installation and servicing equipment." Sector-specific standards that contain additional requirements provide details of the facility requirements under clause 4.9.

Work Environment

Clause 6.4 is not a new requirement. The requirement that "a suitable working environment" be provided is contained in ISO 9001:1994, clause 4.9, "Process control." Including the requirement for work environment in the resource management clause applies this concept to all the processes of the quality management system needed to achieve conformity of product. This is a broader application than in 1994.

BEYOND ISO 9001 COMPLIANCE

Goals, Objectives, and Capital Performance

A key tactic for moving beyond the requirements of ISO 9001 is to tie the infrastructure, equipment, and facilities planning very tightly to the objectives of the organization. This is particularly important when planning for future infrastructure needs. One key is to tie plans for future capital expenditures to objectives. It is all too common for an organization to set goals and objectives that are not fully supported by future capital plans. It is also common to base capital projects on project objectives that are not fully tied to the overall objectives of the organization. An organization should also measure the effectiveness of new projects in achieving both capital project goals and the organization's overall objectives for quality, cost, productivity, throughput, and other important considerations.

Maintenance Systems

Basic maintenance of equipment is needed to ensure that the organization has "suitable" production equipment, but ISO 9001 does not contain any specific maintenance system requirements. All organizations should consider integrated maintenance management systems. Such a system provides for control of maintenance work items, preventive maintenance planning, maintenance work order control, and other activities to ensure an effective maintenance system.

When critical production equipment must have relatively low downtime, organizations should go further and consider establishing maintenance requirements based on potential failure modes and actual reliability data. Such systems consider the lifecycle cost of equipment and may involve long-term equipment upgrade and replacement strategies that are tied to organizational improvement objectives.

When it is not practical or cost-effective to provide such maintenance processes within the organization, consideration should be given to outsourcing.

Work Environment

The requirements for control of the work environment found in ISO 9001 involve ensuring that the environment is suitable for achieving product conformity. ISO 9004:2000 provides a number of recommendations for moving beyond these minimum requirements to provide a work environment that positively influences those working within it. Work environment management is one area where organizations can get real value from integrating the management of quality, environment, and worker health and safety considerations. Organizations can identify elements of the work environment requiring control in all three areas and manage those controls in an integrated manner.

SUMMARY

Although the clauses containing requirements for infrastructure and work environment may appear to be narrow in scope, they nevertheless are important and should not be ignored by organizations. Their message is simple but important: organizations need to provide the physical and capital resources necessary to fulfill customer requirements and to support continual improvement of processes.

Section 6
Product Realization

Introduction

Joseph J. Tsiakals
Amgen, Thousand Oaks, California

In section 6 you'll find chapters that explain the requirements for the product-related processes of ISO 9001:2000. These requirements form various parts of clause 7, "Product realization." Product realization is one of the four major processes of the ISO 9000 quality management system, previously described in Figure 2.1. The other three are management responsibility, resource management and measurement, and analysis and improvement.

Clause 7 contains the requirements for all the work that must be done to achieve or realize the product; hence the uncommon phrase *product realization.* Considerable debate and discussion took place in the drafting committee for a better, more common term that would be an appropriate descriptor for this section. Why not *product lifecycle*? After all, these are the processes of the product lifecycle. But *product lifecycle* is at odds with the underlying emphasis on a generic approach to apply to all product sectors. It was thought that this is a product hardware term and not at all appropriate for services. Dr. J. M. Juran for 50 years has described many of these processes as the "spiral of quality" covering the processes from research to the customer. Actually, *spiral of quality* is a concept that applies to more than just the product realization processes since it includes customer feedback. Moreover, it is not a phrase that translates well and would not be meaningful to those unfamiliar with Juran's work. Earlier drafts of the standard named this section "Process management." But that is even more confusing because the entire standard deals with process management. Product realization was accepted as the most appropriate term. The term is expressive of these processes and is translatable into other languages.

To many, product realization is the heart of ISO 9001. It is through the activities described here that requirements are defined, designs created, software produced, products manufactured, services provided, goods stored, and items delivered. These are the work processes that create what we provide to our customers.

A number of major themes are evident in clause 7 as well as present in some of the other parts of ISO 9001:2000. These represent a major enhancement of the ISO 9000 series over the 1994 standard:

- The process approach
- Process planning and development
- Customer-related processes for developing customer requirements
- Generic text appropriate for service and software organizations
- Greater flexibility for documentation and applications by small businesses
- A bias for results

Even though most of the far-reaching changes found in ISO 9001:2000 are in the clauses treating the quality management system, management responsibility and measurement, and analysis and improvement, some changes are evident in clause 7 as well.

Section 6 is rich with perspectives from a variety of international authors—representative of major contributors to the content of the corresponding part of the ISO standard. The authors maintain a consistency with the major themes as they present slightly different views from their vantage points; views that differ in emphasis and example.

- In chapter 18, "General Planning of Product Realization," Joe Tsiakals discusses the planning of product realization in a way that will prove useful regardless of the product, the industry, or the size of the organization.

- Processes to determine customer requirements are discussed by Dr. Nigel H. Croft in chapter 19, "Customer-Related Processes."

- Application of the requirements of clause 7.3 on design and development is somewhat different for each of the three basic product categories. Knud E. Jensen discusses design and development from the perspective of hardware manufacturers in chapter 20, "Design and Development—Hardware." In chapter 21, "Design and Development—Software," Frank Houston discusses this critical topic from the point of view of software developers. Finally, Diane Baguley covers the application of these concepts in the service sector in chapter 22, "Design and Development—Services."

- The roles of purchasing, purchasing processes, and advanced implementation practices are covered by R. Dan Reid in chapter 23, "Purchasing."

- As with design and development, the production and service operations can vary considerably according to the type of product. For hardware, these topics are covered by Elio DiMaggio and Ennio Nicoloso in chapter 24, "Production and Service Provision for Hardware." Frank Houston discusses software aspects in chapter 25, "Production and Service Provision for Software." Aspects related to services are covered by Diane Baguley in chapter 26, "Production and Service Provision for Service."

- Dan Harper addresses the many aspects of controlling measurements, monitoring and measuring devices, measurement equipment, and calibration in chapter 27, "Control of Monitoring and Measuring Devices."

Effective implementation of the requirements of ISO 9001:2000 clause 7 is essential to achieving compliance. That clause covers the core processes for meeting customer requirements. The chapters in this section are an excellent resource to help readers achieve effective implementation in an efficient manner—a manner that improves the overall performance of the organization.

Chapter 18

General Planning of Product Realization

Joseph J. Tsiakals
Amgen, Thousand Oaks, California

INTRODUCTION

The planning described in this chapter is directly related to the product realization processes. This chapter describes the minimum requirements given in clause 7.1 of ISO 9001:2000 for the product planning that is expected of an organization. This includes discussion of how these requirements have changed since the 1994 standard and what an organization might consider when desiring to improve the value of product realization planning.

Although clause 7.1 consists of only three short paragraphs, it is one of the most important clauses in ISO 9001:2000. Along with clauses 4.1 and 8.1, clause 7.1 provides the essentials of using the process approach. It requires organizations to think about and plan all the processes that, when operating together, will result in the delivery of products that will conform to customer requirements, create customer satisfaction, and foster continual improvement.

LINKED REQUIREMENTS AND PLANNING

For clarity and simplicity, the requirements associated with quality management systems, documentation, quality policy, quality objectives, and quality planning are linked and cross-referenced rather than occurring throughout ISO 9001:2000. These requirements apply but are not repeated under product realization planning.

Planning is a process. A process is a collection of interrelated or interacting activities that transforms inputs into outputs or results (see definition 3.4.1 of ISO 9000:2000). The output of product realization planning is the plans to be fulfilled for developing and implementing the product realization processes contained within clause 7 of ISO 9001:2000.

Planning is also an explicit aspect of the process approach as used in the ISO 9000 series. This is the *plan* of the plan–do–check–act (PDCA) cycle. ISO 9001:2000 clause 7.1, "Planning of product realization," can be considered the *plan* step of PDCA for each of the clauses of clause 7, "Product realization." The process approach and a description of PDCA are given in clause 0.2 of ISO 9001:2000. Jeff Hooper in chapter 2 describes the process model in much greater detail.

An important indicator of the effectiveness of a quality management system is whether complete PDCA cycles are evident for each of the product realization processes. For example, the organization should *plan* (clause 7.1) how to determine customer requirements. Actually determining the customer requirements (clause 7.2.1) is the *do* of the PDCA cycle. Reviewing the requirements (clause 7.2.2) is the *check*. Taking action based on this review as required at the end of clause 7.2.2 is the *act*.

The fact that multiple, overlapping PDCA cycles can occur, with some applying to individual processes and others applying to sets of interacting processes for different products and different functions, can make this concept somewhat complex and confusing. For the example given earlier, the organization might find that as it is determining customer requirements, it needs to go into greater depth in understanding regulatory requirements. This becomes an embedded PDCA cycle at the determination stage (or *do* stage) of the first cycle. Hard rules for these applications of PDCA cannot be set. Only the organization's management should decide what is appropriate and needed.

ISO 9001:2000 REQUIREMENTS

ISO 9001:2000 clause 7.1 states: "The organization shall plan and develop the processes needed for product realization."

The planning described in this chapter is directly related to the activities associated with all aspects of achieving, delivering, and maintaining a product for a customer. These activities are called "product realization processes" and they include the following:

- Customer-related processes
- Design and development
- Purchasing
- Production and delivery of product
- Service provision
- Control of monitoring and measuring devices

With the exception of the last clause of "Product realization" (that is, clause 7.6, "Control of monitoring and measuring devices") the results of these processes are the items, materials, services, and software that are provided to customers. The planning requirements of this section apply to all product categories—hardware, software, processed materials, and services—although the emphasis may be different for the various types of products.

Two of the product realization processes described in clause 7 have planning requirements that go beyond what is required in clause 7.1.

Clause 7.3.1, "Design and development planning," requires that design and development stages be defined. Additionally, the organization needs to plan for design and development reviews, verifications, and validations and to define personnel responsibilities and authorities for design and development work. The organization is required to determine how it will manage interfaces between different functions and groups involved in design and development and how it will manage effective communications and assignment of responsibilities between these groups.

Clause 7.5.1, "Control of production and service provision," requires the organization to specifically plan how it will control its production and service provision processes. In developing its plans for control of these processes, the organization needs to take the following into account:

- Information on the important characteristics of the product
- Work instructions, as appropriate
- Suitable equipment
- Monitoring and measuring devices
- Implementation of monitoring and measuring
- Implementation of release, delivery, and postdelivery activities

It should be obvious that planning for these lifecycle activities makes sense only for those activities that are relevant to an organization and its product. The planning would include those activities within the scope of the organization's quality management system. (See chapter 9 "Quality Management System Application (Clause 1.2)," for discussion of exclusions from the quality management system.)

A manufacturing facility that does not perform product designs would not be required to plan for the design development work associated with its products. However, the senior organization to which the facility belongs could be responsible. But this is tricky, and determining what planning is needed should be decided on a case-by-case basis by an organization's top management. A manufacturing facility might be a contract manufacturer for a corporate entity other than its own. Planning and other activities required to fully achieve and implement the customer-related processes (clause 7.2) would need to be performed by the contractor's organization—if not at the manufacturing plant then at some other location, such as corporate headquarters.

The last clause in clause 7, clause 7.6, "Control of monitoring and measuring devices," appears out of place in a list of the stages of a product's lifecycle. It is included at the end of clause 7 in recognition that under some circumstances or for some types of product all the requirements under this clause are not relevant. For example, having measurement instruments calibrated and traceable to international or national measurement standards doesn't make sense for many service and software organizations. How would this apply to the service provided by a waiter or to the many other qualitative measurements that are common to the service and software sectors? Permitted exclusion of requirements, due to the nature of an organization and its product as detailed in clause 1.2, are limited to the requirements of ISO 9001:2000 clause 7. For this reason clause 7.6, "Control of monitoring and measuring devices," is added to the end of clause 7. Planning for these devices must meet the requirements of clause 7.1.

ISO 9001:2000 clause 7.1 states: "Planning of product realization shall be consistent with the requirements of the other processes of the quality management system (see 4.1)."

There are generic quality management system requirements (clause 4.1) that pertain to every process covered in ISO 9001:2000. The organization is required to do the following when planning its product realization processes:

- Identify the needed processes
- Determine their sequence and interaction
- Determine criteria and methods needed for their operation and control
- Ensure the availability of resources and information necessary for their operation and monitoring
- Provide for monitoring, measurement, and analysis
- Provide for actions for achieving results and continual improvement of these processes

If plans identify outsourced product realization processes, the organization needs to determine how it will ensure control over those processes.

ISO 9001:2000 clause 7.1 states: "In planning product realization, the organization shall determine the following, as appropriate:

(a) quality objectives and requirements for the product"

The first step in planning the product realization processes requires determining what must be achieved, that is, what objectives must be met. Top management must make sure that quality objectives needed to meet requirements for product are established, are measurable, and are consistent with the quality policy (clause 5.3). Likewise, top management must make sure that planning of the quality management system is performed so that the requirements of clauses 4.1 and 5.4.1 are met.

Whether planning for hardware products, services, software, or processed materials, the early phases of quality planning include the identification of customers and determination of their needs. These are translated into customer requirements. The customer requirements must be transformed into specific product requirements.

General requirements for planning (clause 5.4) of the product realization processes include requirements for quality objectives (clause 5.4.1) and for quality management system planning (clause 5.4.2). Yoshinori Iizuka explains in greater detail in chapter 14 the planning requirements addressed in clause 5.4 of ISO 9001:2000.

ISO 9001:2000 clause 7.1 states: "In planning product realization, the organization shall determine the following, as appropriate:

(b) the need to establish processes, documents, and provide resources specific to the product"

The requirement to establish processes, documents, and provide resources reinforces the importance of planning for and developing the product-related processes. These product realization processes are the core processes of any organization. Organizations exist to satisfy customers. These are the processes that provide the products that are intended to satisfy customers. The organization must evaluate if new processes need to be established or old processes modified in order to meet the new product, contract, or project requirements. There might be a need for new product specifications, modified manufacturing procedures, new capital equipment, or new work instructions. Additional personnel may need to be hired or existing personnel retrained.

ISO 9001:2000 clause 7.1 states: "In planning product realization, the organization shall determine the following, as appropriate:

(c) required verification, validation, monitoring, inspection and test activities specific to the product and the criteria for product acceptance"

In addition to evaluating the need to establish new processes or considering how old processes might need to be modified, the organization must concern itself with the adequacy of the product to meet customer requirements. New products will be designed and developed under the requirements of clause 7.3, "Design and development," and the verification and validation requirements of that clause would apply. However, clause 7.3 does not apply to an order for an existing product. When there is an intention to use existing products, the organization needs to consider during product planning if verification and validation activities are required. An issue could be whether existing products can fulfill the customer requirements specified in the new order, contract, or project. Do they require redesign or modification or addition of features?

The requirement to monitor and measure product is established in clause 8.2.4, "Monitoring and measurement of product." Clause 8.2.4 requires that these activities be carried out at appropriate stages of the product realization process in accordance with planned arrangements, and it specifically references clause 7.1. Here, in clause 7.1, the planned arrangements for the monitoring, inspection, testing, and product acceptance criteria need to be determined, as appropriate. For new products there might need to be entirely new tests and inspections. Current procedures may require modification. For orders of existing products the current methods might still be applied. New sampling plans may need to be established. Whatever is decided, the point is that the organization should review its current approaches and, as appropriate, establish plans for measuring and determining conformance to product requirements.

ISO 9001:2000 clause 7.1 states: "In planning product realization, the organization shall determine the following, as appropriate:

(d) records needed to provide evidence that the realization processes and resulting product meet requirements (see 4.2.4)"

The type and amount of documents required to show the results achieved or providing evidence of activities performed vary widely depending on the need and use for the records. The organization needs to plan to establish these records. This need differs from one product sector to another, and the level of detail contained in records is affected by considerations such as customer or contractual record requirements, the complexity and criticality of the product, the size of the organization, and special regulatory requirements. A large division of a multinational electronics firm will have very different product record requirements than will a small testing service. An electronics manufacturer for consumer markets will have significantly less traceability record requirements than a manufacturer of an implantable medical device. A contract testing laboratory will have different records requirements than will a restaurant.

Even though needs for such records vary widely, as does the form of the records, ISO 9001:2000 requires a certain minimum set of records for the product-related processes of all organizations. Chapter 11 describes what these are for the quality management system as a whole. The other chapters in section 6 discuss records needed for the product realization processes. When considering planning for records, organizations should carefully consider issues such as protection of intellectual property and product liability prevention.

ISO 9001:2000 clause 7.1 states: "The output of this planning shall be in a form suitable for the organization's method of operations. Note 1: A document specifying the processes of the quality management system (including the product realization processes) and the resources to be applied to a specific product, project or contract, can be referred to as a quality plan."

The clause includes no requirements for specific product realization planning documents. The organization's management must determine what quality planning records are needed. The clause for documentation requirements (clause 4.2) states that the organization needs to develop whatever documents are necessary to ensure effective planning, operation, and control of its processes.

The output of product realization planning is important for effective operation and control of the realization processes. Many industries refer to these as plans of one type or another: quality plans, control plans, manufacturing plans, development plans, and so on. Few plans are standardized for a product sector. The exception is control plans. Control plans are commonly required in some industries, including automotive and aerospace. They apply to the many different suppliers of these two industries and thus involve numerous product sectors. Control plans contain the processes, important quality characteristics, and methods used to minimize product and process variation. They document the controls specified for the critical product and process characteristics.

In an ISO requirements standard, the content of notes is informational. Notes are not requirements. Note 1 contains guidance about quality plans, but quality plans are not required. Planning for the product realization processes involves determining how the organization will meet contract requirements, will develop a new product program, or will execute a product-related project. In keeping with the terminology used in ISO 9001:1994, "quality plan" is identified in the note as the name often given to the document containing this information. Quality plans describe the planned activities to be implemented including those having to do with personnel, material, equipment, measurement, and facility resources.

ISO 9001:2000 clause 7.1 states: "Note 2: The organization may also apply the requirements given in 7.3 to the development of product realization processes."

This note offers the advice that an organization should consider using the same planning approach when designing product realization processes that it uses to design new hardware or service products. Surprising to many in the hardware sectors, ISO 9001:2000 does not detail specific requirements for designing and developing the product realization processes. A great deal of discussion during early drafts of the 2000 revision was directed to whether the product design and development requirements should apply to the product realization processes as well. This note is the result of that discussion. While it was agreed that the contents of clause 7.3 can be applied to the design and development of the product-related processes for many hardware items, software, and processed materials, it is not common practice in the service sector. Applying clause 7.3 universally would cause considerable confusion and would necessitate explanatory documents. Nevertheless, as noted in the following section, ISO 9001:2000 has made considerable progress beyond the 1994 version in emphasizing the importance of designing and developing processes. From the viewpoint of operating effectiveness, it is strongly suggested that an organization consider applying the design and development controls to its realization processes with the same rigor it dedicates to products, even though this is not a requirement of ISO 9001.

DIFFERENCES FROM ISO 9001:1994

Much of the content of clause 7.1 was developed from various clauses of ISO 9001:1994 (for example, clauses 4.2.3, 4.9, 4.10, 4.12, 4.15, and 4.19). The requirements were generally defined more narrowly in 1994 except for the sweeping mandate in clause 4.9 that required processes that directly affect quality to be carried out under controlled conditions.

The planning activity required by clause 7.1 may not be a trivial exercise. Fewer documented procedures may be required than in the past, and no specific format is dictated, but ISO 9001:2000 demands that the organization better understand the processes needed to deliver conforming products to customers. These processes must be understood not only with respect to the products themselves but also in the broader context of the objectives of the organization and any other requirements of the quality management system.

Many organizations will have little problem conforming to these requirements since processes and documentation already exist to address them. For others, this will require some careful thought. Perhaps flowcharts or process mapping will be appropriate to ensure that all process steps are addressed in terms of the availability of documentation, facilities, personnel, and any other required resources.

ISO 9004:2000: BEYOND 9001 FOR PERFORMANCE EXCELLENCE

Organizations must, as a first priority, be effective in meeting customer requirements. The quality management system requirements of ISO 9001:2000 are designed with that as a focus. But to survive, organizations must be concerned with the labor, materials, and time required to meet the customer's requirements. Customer requirements must be achieved as efficiently as possible. The quality management system guidance of ISO 9004:2000 is designed with that as its focus.

Organizations should have only one quality management system. The system should be both effective and efficient. For this reason, ISO 9001:2000 (which focuses on effectiveness) and ISO 9004:2000 (which focuses on efficiency) were developed as a consistent pair. They were prepared so as to be used in a complementary fashion in support of an organization's single quality management system. They have similar structures, aligning by clause title and number. An organization meeting the requirements of ISO 9001:2000 and following the guidance of ISO 9004:2000 should continually improve customer satisfaction and gain performance excellence.

ISO 9004:2000 offers considerable guidance for an organization that is planning the product realization processes:

- Define inputs and outputs of processes necessary for effective and efficient performance
- Treat processes as a network with the output of one serving as the input for another
- Use both process verification and validation results as inputs for achieving continual improvement
- Document processes in order to support effective and efficient operation:
  - Features of processes
  - Training of operators
  - Process knowledge sharing with teams
  - Measurement and audit of processes
  - Analysis, review, and improvement of processes
- Evaluate the role of people within the process
  - Ensure health and safety
  - Ensure necessary skills
  - Provide process analysis input
  - Promote innovation

ISO 9004:2000 recommends the preparation of an operating plan for managing processes that includes:

- Input and output requirements
- Activities within the processes
- Verification and validation of processes and products
- Process analysis including dependability
- Corrective and preventive actions
- Control of process changes

Examples of process inputs and outputs are listed in ISO 9004:2000, including the need for identification of critical features of products and processes in order to develop effective and efficient plans for controlling and monitoring the activities within the processes.

Validation is recommended for processes:

- For high-value and safety-critical products
- Where deficiency in product will only be apparent in use
- That cannot be repeated, and where verification of product is not possible

Plans should be developed for the prevention of failures. Computer-simulation techniques can be useful. Risk assessment should be undertaken to assess the potential for and the effect of possible failures or faults in processes. Risk assessment tools include:

- Failure mode and effects analysis
- Fault tree analysis
- Relationship diagrams
- Simulation techniques
- Reliability prediction

SUMMARY

The planning activity for product realization processes must address the quality objectives and requirements of the product; the need to establish appropriate processes and documentation; the need to provide resources; required verification, validation, monitoring, inspection, and test activities; and the criteria for acceptability of the product. The organization is also required to determine what records are necessary to provide confidence that the processes and resulting product conform to requirements. Presented altogether in clause 7.1 and linked by reference to other clauses, the explicit product realization planning requirements will be considered by many to be fresh and powerful new additions to ISO 9001. An organization's ISO 9001–based product realization processes, when planned and developed and supported with the guidance of ISO 9004, will produce superior results and achieve competitive advantage, and will do so through effective and efficient processes.

Chapter 19

Customer-Related Processes

Nigel H. Croft
International Standardized Testing Organization A.G., Zug, Switzerland

INTRODUCTION

This chapter provides an overview of the concepts surrounding customer-related processes, discusses the detailed requirements of ISO 9001:2000 for those processes, and describes how an organization can choose to go beyond the minimum compliance with the ISO 9001:2000 requirements to improve its overall performance. Monitoring of customer satisfaction is, of course, an important component of the overall process but will be discussed only superficially in this chapter. For a more detailed analysis, readers are referred to chapter 29.

THE CONCEPT OF CUSTOMER-RELATED PROCESSES

Before discussing the detailed requirements of ISO 9001:2000, it is appropriate to begin with a more basic and philosophical analysis of the organization and its products, processes, customers, and interested parties. Many organizations have a tendency to "dive headfirst" into the development of their quality management systems without first addressing apparently simple questions, many of which necessitate complex analyses with far-reaching implications. These questions include the following:

- Who are we? *(What is our organization?)*
- What do we do? *(What is our product?)*
- Who are our customers? *(Who receives our product?)*

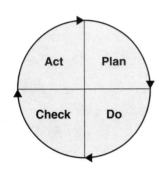

Plan:
Establish the objectives and processes necessary to deliver results in accordance with customer requirements and the organization's policies

Do:
Implement the processes

Check:
Monitor and measure processes and product against policies, objectives, and requirements for the product and report the results

Act:
Take actions to continually improve process

Figure 19.1 The plan–do–check–act cycle applied to processes.

- What do our customers want? *(What are the requirements related to the product?)*
- Can we provide what the customer wants? *(Are we capable of meeting customer and applicable statutory or regulatory requirements for the product?)*
- How do we know our customers got what they wanted? *(Are our customers satisfied?)*

As discussed later in this chapter, a clear understanding of these issues is extremely beneficial in helping the organization to define for itself what customer-related processes are needed for its quality management system. No all-embracing "recipe" covers all situations for all organizations—a theme that will become more apparent as we discuss examples later in this chapter. Each organization is different (what a boring world this would be if that were not the case!). Although the use of the plan–do–check–act (PDCA) cycle is not a formal *requirement* of ISO 9001:2000, its presence is implicit in all quality management systems and their component processes. Successful organizations use the PDCA cycle, either systematically or intuitively, consciously or subconsciously, in the day-to-day running of their business and in the management of their processes. Customer-related processes should be no exception.

The note in clause 0.2 of ISO 9001:2000 explains how the PDCA cycle can be applied to processes shown in Figure 19.1. Further information regarding the use of the PDCA cycle within a process approach to quality management systems may be found in the ISO 9000:2000, *Introduction and support package—Guidance on the process approach to quality management systems.*

Question 1: Who Are We?

ISO 9000:2000 clause 3.3.1 defines *organization* as a "group of people and facilities with an arrangement of responsibilities, authorities and relationships." Examples given in ISO 9000:2000 include a company, corporation, firm, enterprise, institution, charity, sole trader, association, or parts or combinations thereof.

Each kind of organization has different characteristics, products, and kinds of customers and therefore different needs in terms of the definition and control of its

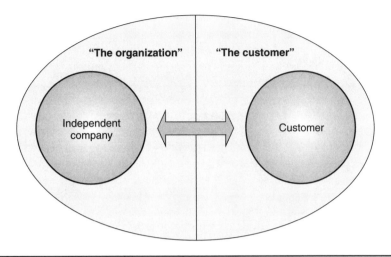

Figure 19.2a The organization—independent company—and the customer.

customer-related processes. So when we ask the question "who are we?" the intent is to define the nature of the organization and the boundaries of the quality management system within that organization. This is often called the *scope* of the quality management system. Within the defined scope (and as discussed in chapter 9) the requirements of ISO 9001:2000 are generic and are intended to apply to all organizations, regardless of type, size, and product provided.

The *organization* to which the quality management system refers may be any of the following:

1. An independent company providing products or services to other companies in a business-to-business contractual situation. This is perhaps the most common, traditional kind of organization to which ISO 9000 has been applied, and all customer-related processes are typically carried out at the interface between the appropriate functions within the company and its customers (see Figure 19.2a).

   Typical examples of this kind of organization include:

   • An independent consulting company providing technical or financial services to a manufacturing company

   • A cement manufacturer selling its products to a construction company

   • A steel forging plant selling its products to a manufacturer of components for use in the aerospace industry

   • A law firm providing services to a major corporation

2. An autonomous business unit of a larger corporation, supplying products or providing services to another organization, or directly to the end user (see Figure 19.2b). Note that in this case, it may be necessary to include some applicable corporate functions within the scope of the quality management system, even though customer-related processes are carried out directly at the interface between the business unit and the customer. Typical examples may include:

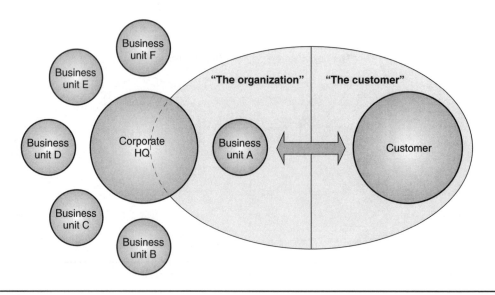

Figure 19.2b The organization–business unit–and the customer.

- The Washington branch of a major car rental company whose customers are the end users (consumers)
- The London office of a multinational financial auditing company providing services to U.K. organizations
- The hamburger restaurant on South Tamiami Trail in Sarasota, Florida, that is part of a major chain of fast-food restaurants selling its burgers to locals and tourists
- The São Paulo business unit of a major aluminum can manufacturer providing products to the Brazilian soft drinks industry

3. An entire corporation, with multiple locations, supplying products or providing services to consumers (see Figure 19.2c). In this case, multiple and complex customer-related processes may exist between various functions within the corporation and the customer. Typical examples include:

- A beer and soft drinks manufacturer, with multiple manufacturing locations and a corporate logistics and distribution function, supplying outlets nationwide, such as supermarkets and bars
- A certification body or registrar providing a multinational corporation with ISO 9000 registration at its various operational units around the world
- A large engineering contractor constructing a nuclear power plant for a French energy consortium on a "turnkey project" basis
- A software development organization providing computer operating systems for worldwide distribution
- A mass transit urban railway, with over 50 stations, providing its service to commuters

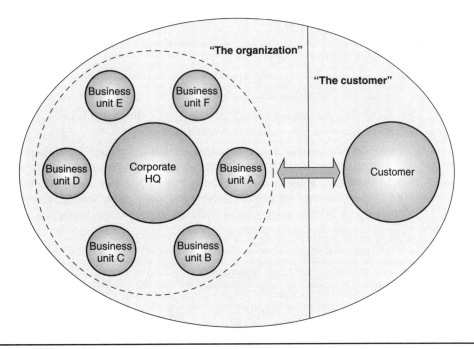

Figure 19.2c   The organization—multi-location corporation—and the customer.

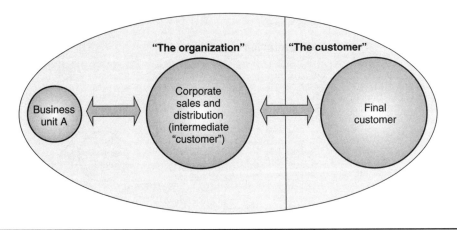

Figure 19.2d   The organization—business unit plus sales and distribution—and the customer.

4. A manufacturing or operations division of a larger corporation, providing products for distribution via the corporation's own sales and distribution network (see Figure 19.2d). In this case, it may be convenient to consider the sales and distribution network as an "intermediate customer" of the manufacturing division, with the customer-related processes being carried out at both the manufacturing unit/sales and distribution interface as well as the sales and distribution/final customer interface. Typical examples include:

- A Singapore manufacturing plant for a computer hardware company, providing its products for sale via the corporate marketing function located in Hong Kong
- An Argentinean manufacturer of beef selling its products to the United States via its corporate export department
- A German producer of specialty steels exporting its products worldwide via the group trading company

5. A support function (such as a maintenance or information technology department) providing services to the rest of the corporation (see Figure 19.2e). In this case, the customer-related processes are carried out between the support function and its customers, who are in fact "internal customers" with respect to the corporation as a whole. Typical examples include:

- The maintenance depot of a railway, providing services to the operations departments
- The corporate training department of a multisite manufacturer of oil-field equipment, providing training to employees at the various sites
- The information technology department of an Asian securities and futures commission, providing support to the rest of the organization

Clearly, these are only a few of the many possible combinations but are included here to stimulate readers to analyze carefully their particular organizations.

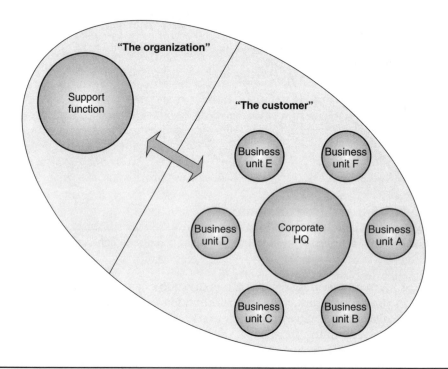

Figure 19.2e The organization—support function—and internal customers.

Question 2: What Do We Do?

ISO 9000:2000 clause 3.4.2 defines *product* as the "result of a process." Therefore, the organization's *product* is a result of the organization's *processes*. According to ISO 9000:2000, the products of most organizations comprise elements belonging to the following generic product categories:

- Services (for example, transport, provision of advice, or leisure activities)
- Software (for example, a computer program, an instruction manual, or a dictionary)
- Hardware (for example, a mechanical part or a piece of equipment)
- Processed materials (materials produced in bulk, such as lubricants, ores, or some chemical products)

Because a *service* is the result of at least one activity necessarily performed at the interface between the organization and its customer, customer-related processes in service organizations may often be more complex and diffuse than for organizations providing tangible products. So when we ask the question "what do we do?" the intent is for the organization to think about what tangible or intangible products it actually provides to its customers and therefore must be included in the customer-related processes.

In many organizations, the product is quite clearly defined and simple to understand. Examples may include:

- An electronics company selling personal stereos
- A chemicals manufacturer selling sulfuric acid
- A consultant providing financial advice
- A software developer providing a new suite of programs

In other situations, a definition of the product may be more complex. For example, what is the product of a school, a hospital, a public transport system, a local government bureau of works, or a car dealership? It is not the intent of this chapter to provide answers to these questions but instead to stimulate organizations to think about the various types and components of the products they provide. This leads to the next "simple" question in the logical sequence.

Question 3: Who Are Our Customers?

ISO 9000:2000 clause 3.3.5 defines *customer* as the "organization or person that receives a product." The customer may be internal or external to the organization, and typical examples include consumers, clients, end users, retailers, beneficiaries, and purchasers. Some organizations have very clearly defined customers (particularly in the more traditional business-to-business transactions that were the focus of earlier versions of the ISO 9000 series of standards). However, in the same way that an organization may have numerous products, it may have any number of different customers for each of those products, in different geographical locations, each with very specific needs and expectations and subject to different statutory and regulatory requirements. This can result in an extremely large and complex permutation of individual requirements for the product, even though the overall customer-related *processes* can often be simplified and consolidated.

With the worldwide application of ISO 9000 as a model for quality management systems in different kinds of organizations, and its increased use in service provision and business-to-consumer transactions, the emphasis on defining "who are our customers?" takes on an added importance. For example, a mobile telephone manufacturer might have only one basic product, but that product can be used by businesspeople, athletes, students, retired persons, people with special needs, and others; it can be used for legal or illegal purposes (beyond the control of the organization); there might be specific statutory or regulatory requirements (depending on where the product is sold or intended to be used), product liability issues to be considered, and so on.

It is also pertinent to think about the needs and expectations of interested parties other than customers. ISO 9000:2000 clause 3.3.7 defines *interested party* as a "person or group having an interest in the performance or success of an organization." This includes owners, people within the organization, suppliers, bankers, unions, partners, or society. Although meeting the needs and expectations of other interested parties is the focus of the ISO 9004:2000 guidelines and not a requirement of ISO 9001:2000, the difference between the *customer* and *other interested parties* can sometimes be rather diffuse, even in very specific circumstances.

For example, in the case of someone being admitted to a hospital, who is the customer? Who receives the product of that organization? Is it the patient receiving the treatment; the patient's family (is the patient then "customer property"?); the patient's physician, insurance company, or employer; or society as a whole (if, for example, the service is being paid for out of public funds)? Some of these issues are addressed in an ISO international workshop agreement ISO/IWA 1:2001, *Guidelines for process improvements in health service organizations*, but it is clear that there is no simple answer to the question.

In the case of a school, who is the customer? Who receives the output of *that* organization? Is it the student? (In that case, there would doubtless be a high degree of "customer satisfaction" if classes were held only two days a week, vacations lasted 10 weeks, and there was no homework.) What about the parents, future employers, society? Again, there is no simple answer, and it would be naive to try to provide one.

It is up to each individual organization to analyze its specific circumstances, to think about the customer within the context of its business, and then to manage its customer-related processes using a PDCA approach.

Question 4: What Do Our Customers Want?

I know what I want, as a customer, when I am looking to purchase a particular product. I want the best possible product, at the lowest price, with zero-interest financing for 10 years, no repayments for the first two years, a no-hassle lifetime guarantee, and so on. Oh, and a cash rebate would be nice, too! If the organization selling that product were to meet all my desires, the result would no doubt be one very satisfied customer—and one very bankrupt organization! So we have to be realistic. As a *potential* customer, I have to recognize that the organization is not obliged to meet all my requirements, and, in most cases, I am certainly not obliged to buy from the organization.

What I really want is that, once my requirements have been analyzed by the organization, negotiated, and agreed to, I will in fact receive the product or service I expected to receive, according to the terms of our agreement.

The organization cannot necessarily expect to satisfy all its *potential* customers all the time. For example, I have a favorite brand of draft beer. If I go to a bar and find that it doesn't serve that brand, I have the option of choosing another kind of beer or going to another bar. If I choose to stay and enjoy a different brand of beer, I am no longer only a potential customer but a very real one. A transaction has been agreed on and is taking place. As a *customer*, I should expect my beer to be served cold, in a clean glass, in a timely manner, and (preferably) with a smile. It may not taste as good as my favorite brand, but I get what was implicitly agreed on before making the transaction.

In some situations, I may express my needs and expectations formally, using a written specification that the organization agrees to meet by accepting my business. In other circumstances, the organization may have its own detailed specification of the product that it offers for sale. This is often the case for proprietary (brand name) products or services and in Internet or mail-order sales. Some details of the transaction may be in the form of implicit or regulatory requirements. In some cases, "customized" versions of a standard product may be available to meet individual customer requirements (extra-thick crust, heavy on the pepperoni, and hold the anchovies, please!).

Again we see that there can be no simple "recipe" for understanding customer requirements, which holds true for all organizations. It is a pity that many organizations lose out on the benefits that a profound evaluation of the question "what do our customers want?" can bring to the organization during the implementation of its quality management system. This should not be something that is done "because it is a requirement of ISO 9000" but because it is something that can bring significant benefits to the bottom line.

Question 5: Can We Provide What the Customer Wants?

This basic question has to be answered before the organization agrees to supply a product or provide a service to its customers. It is also the primary focus of ISO 9001:2000 clause 7.2, "Customer-related processes." If an organization knows who its customers are, knows what they want, and is able to provide the product or service according to what was agreed, this is the basis for achieving customer satisfaction (not necessarily *delight*, just satisfaction). To quote one of the first paragraphs of ISO 9000:2000 (clause 2.1, "Rationale for quality management systems"): *"The quality management system approach encourages organizations to analyze customer requirements, define the processes that contribute to the achievement of a product which is acceptable to the customer, and keep these processes under control."*

There is a popular saying in Brazil, "if the ball is square when you receive it, you'll never make it round." Customer-related processes within the quality management system include processes where the organization receives the "ball." If the reservations agent, salesperson, hospital receptionist, or telephone sales agent does not understand the customer's requirements and/or does not check the organization's ability to meet those requirements, then the "ball" will start off "square," and it will be virtually impossible for the subsequent product realization processes, however well managed, to make it "round." Too often, organizations will put a lot of time, effort, and money into making a product or providing a service that is exactly according to the internal sales order but does not reflect what the customer really wanted to purchase!

Gryna (1988a) discusses the strategies and tools for determining the needs of both internal and external customers. These include real needs (which may be different from the stated needs), perceived needs, and cultural needs, all of which may need to be translated from the customer's language into the language of the organization.

Question 6: How Do We Know Our Customers Got What They Wanted?

ISO 9000:2000 clause 3.1.4 defines *customer satisfaction* as the "customer's perception of the degree to which the customer's requirements have been fulfilled." The most effective way to answer the question "did our customers get what they wanted?" is by maintaining effective communication with customers. The most effective means of communication will vary greatly depending on the size and nature of the organization and of its customers, and the type and complexity of the product provided. In some cases, when, for example, a large organization is supplying a complex product to a large customer, there may be many different functions involved in the communication process in both organizations and a subsequent need to establish formal, clearly defined channels. For a two-person "organization" selling hot dogs outside the ballpark, obtaining feedback from the customers may be no less important, but it is likely to be approached in a much less formal, more direct manner. It is up to each organization to determine what works best for its circumstances, products, and customer base. Again, the emphasis should be on the effectiveness of the communication. The concept of monitoring customer satisfaction will be discussed in significantly more detail in chapter 29.

ISO 9001 REQUIREMENTS FOR CUSTOMER-RELATED PROCESSES

What Is a Customer-Related Process?

ISO 9000:2000 clause 3.4.1 defines *process* as a "set of interrelated or interacting activities which transforms inputs into outputs." We can therefore consider customer-related processes to be sets of interrelated or interacting activities that are related to the customer and transform inputs into outputs. Examples of customer-related processes include the following:

- Marketing, whereby the organization provides customers and potential customers with information about new or existing products
- Sales and order handling, where the organization has to receive information relating to the customer's needs and expectations and then "translate" this information from the "language of the customer" into the "language of the organization" (Gryna 1988a)
- Processing of changes to existing orders or contracts

- Communication relating to:
  - Product design and development (including input, review, validation, and change)
  - Order status and delivery forecasts
  - Requests for concession
  - Customer inspections at the organization's premises
  - Customer feedback (including complaints)
  - Warranties

Figures 19.3a through 19.3d show schematically the four possible combinations of input to and output from these processes. In all cases, it is important that there be a "process owner" with overall responsibility to ensure that each component activity is carried out in a timely and effective manner. This can be defined based on the nature of the process or could be specific to the customer, product, or region.

Some Examples of Customer-Related Processes

In Figure 19.3a, the input is received from the customer and processed via a series of interrelated or interacting activities within the organization, and the output is returned to the customer. This would typically be the case for the analysis of a customer inquiry or a customer complaint.

- In the case of a customer inquiry, department A could typically be sales, and departments B and C could be product engineering and manufacturing, respectively.
- In the case of a customer complaint, department A could typically be customer service, with departments B and C being quality and operations, respectively.

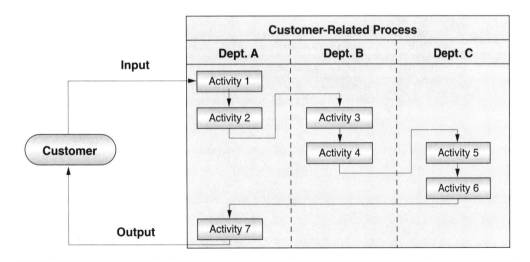

Figure 19.3a   Customer–related processes.

In Figure 19.3b, the input is received from the customer, and the output is provided to another process within the organization. An example would be the handling of a new order, or a change to an existing order. In both these cases, department A would typically be sales, with participation from planning or logistics (department B) and operations (department C).

In Figure 19.3c, the input is received in the form of output from an internal process within the organization and is processed via a series of interrelated or interacting activities both within the organization and at the organization/ customer interface. The output then returns to the organization. This would be the case for a request for concession for a nonconforming product or as part of the monitoring of customer satisfaction, for example:

- In the request for a concession, for example, the initiating department may be manufacturing, (department A), with subsequent participation of the quality and sales departments in the process (departments B and C, respectively)

- For the monitoring of customer satisfaction, department A might be the customer service department, with both quality (department B) and sales (department C) involved.

In Figure 19.3d, the input is received in the form of output from an internal process within the organization, and the output of the customer-related process goes to the customer. An example would be a marketing activity that gives the customer details of a new product developed by the organization. Department A could be the research and development department, department B the marketing department, and department C public relations.

Again, it is important to stress that these are only examples and that each organization must define what processes are important for its own quality management system and the interfunctional involvement in those processes.

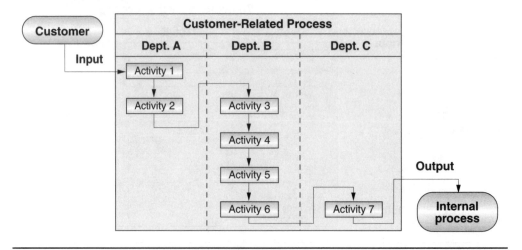

Figure 19.3b Customer input–internal output.

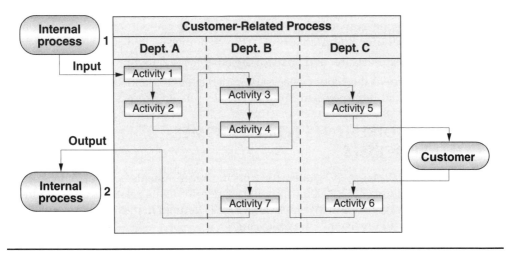

Figure 19.3c   Input from the output of internal processes.

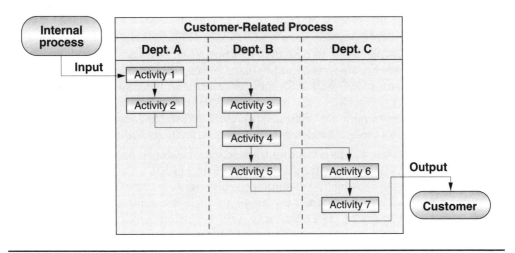

Figure 19.3d   Internal input–output to the customer.

GENERAL REQUIREMENTS FOR CUSTOMER-RELATED PROCESSES

As with any process that is needed for the quality management system, ISO 9001:2000 clause 4.1, "General requirements," applies to customer-related processes. This means that the organization has to:

- Determine the sequence and interaction of the customer-related processes with other quality management system processes, such as design and development, planning of product realization, monitoring and measurement, management review, and others

- Determine criteria and methods needed to ensure that both the operation and control of the customer-related processes are effective

- Ensure the availability of resources and information necessary to support the operation and monitoring of the customer-related processes
- Monitor, measure, and analyze the customer-related processes
- Implement the actions necessary to achieve the planned results and continual improvement of the customer-related processes

SPECIFIC REQUIREMENTS FOR CUSTOMER-RELATED PROCESSES

ISO 9001:2000 clause 7.2 states the specific requirements for customer-related processes. Clause 7.2.1, "Determination of requirements related to the product," requires the organization to *determine* (which is defined in the dictionary as "ascertain, or fix with precision") the following:

1. The requirements specified by the customer, including the requirements for delivery and postdelivery activities.

   - Has the customer (or, more correctly, the *potential* customer) provided the information necessary for the organization to understand what is wanted? (Quantity, type, grade, size, time, and so on.)

   - It is interesting to note that, in a business-to-business transaction, if the customer also has a quality management system that meets the requirements of ISO 9001:2000, the customer should ensure that this does in fact occur. One of the outputs from the customer's purchasing process (according to ISO 9001:2000 clause 7.4) forms the input to the organization's process for determining requirements related to the product.

   - In business-to-consumer transactions, however, or business-to-business transactions where the customer has no systematic approach to purchasing, the customer requirements may not be clearly defined, and it may be necessary to initiate further communications with the customer to "ascertain, or fix with precision" what is actually wanted. This does not necessarily imply a formal bureaucratic process. It may be as simple as the customer saying to a hotel reservations agent, "I need a room for the night," to which the reservations agent may respond by asking questions such as, "How many people?" "Smoking or non-smoking?" and providing information regarding the different categories of rooms available.

   - It is also important not to forget about requirements for delivery or postdelivery activities (or indeed any other requirement that the customer may choose to specify). These may include factors such as:

     - Delivery schedule or stock availability

     - Packing requirements and/or special transport or handling needs

     - Documentation requirements (particularly important for export orders)

     - Second- or third-party inspection requirements prior to shipment

     - Product installation

- Penalty clauses for late delivery
- Delivery and/or invoice address (years ago, I witnessed a truck driver trying in vain to deliver a 15-ton steel forging to the 12th floor of an office block, which was, as you've probably guessed, the address for the *invoice*)

2. Requirements not stated by the customer but necessary for specified or intended use, where known.

   - These are the so-called implicit requirements. If I buy a portion of french fries, I expect them to be hot; if I buy a beer, I expect it to be cold; if I buy a camera, I expect an instruction manual; and so on. I once heard the following story that illustrates this point quite nicely: Two friends walk into a bar and they ask the bartender for two cold beers. One of the friends is particularly fastidious and adds, "make sure my glass is clean!" In a short while, the bartender returns with the two beers and asks "which one of you asked for the clean glass?"

   - No one expects the organization to have a crystal ball that allows it to know all the intended uses (and abuses) of its product by the customer. However, when the intended use of the product *is* known or is stated by the customer, then any requirements related to this intended use must be determined by the organization. A simple example would be an American couple planning to visit friends in England and wanting to purchase a prerecorded videotape of their home town to show to their friends. Unless the couple specifically mentions that the videotape is to be shown in England (where the imaging system is PAL-G), the salesperson cannot be blamed for selling them a videotape in NTSC (U.S.) format, which will not be compatible with the English system. Had the couple commented, "our friends in England will love this," or made it clear in some other way that the videotape would be taken overseas, then the intended use would be known, and would have to be addressed by the supplier.

3. Statutory and regulatory requirements related to the product.

   - Here are a couple of simple dictionary definitions:
     - *Statutory*: "required by the *written* law of legislative body"
     - *Regulatory*: "controlled by rules; subject to restrictions"
   - The critical phrase is *"related to the product."* Clearly, it is highly desirable for an organization to comply with statutory and regulatory requirements that are relevant to *all* its activities, but, as stated in clause 0.4 of ISO 9001:2000, "this international standard does not include requirements specific to other management systems, such as those particular to environmental management, occupational health and safety management, financial management or risk management." Unless there are product specifications or specific customer requirements that oblige an organization to address statutory and regulatory requirements that are *not* directly related to the product, then it is *not* a requirement of ISO 9001:2000 that the organization do so.

- Some examples of statutory and regulatory requirements that are related to the product include:
  - Nonsmoking statutes in restaurants and concert halls
  - Federal Aviation Administration (FAA) regulations for air transport
  - Food and Drug Administration (FDA) regulations for the pharmaceutical or food industry
  - American Petroleum Institute (API) regulations for the oil and gas industry
  - American Society of Mechanical Engineers (ASME) regulations for pressure vessel manufacture
  - European standard (EN) requirements for certain product categories
- Particular care has to be taken in cases where an organization exports its products or where there may be different statutory and regulatory requirements from one state to another. In a business-to-business transaction, the organization's review of requirements related to the product (see later in this chapter) might include communication and dialogue with its customers regarding the applicable requirements in the destination market. Other valuable sources of information include international chambers of commerce, U.S. commercial delegations, industry or trade associations, and commercially available market surveys. With an ever-increasing global economy and the tendency for global sourcing, meeting many different statutory and regulatory requirements simultaneously for different markets represents a significant challenge for the organization, but it is one that has to be met.
- It is also important to recognize that this requirement is linked to the previous requirement regarding "specified or intended use, where known." The organization can only be expected to address the statutory and regulatory requirements for the intended market, or for the markets specified by the customer. In some cases, when the organization's customer is a distributor or retailer, products could be sold to other geographical regions without the organization's knowledge, so it may be prudent to clarify these issues as part of the review of requirements related to the product. This is particularly true for export sales to the European Economic Community, where a large number of separate countries coexist within a relatively small geographical area.

4. Any additional requirements determined by the organization.
   - These may include requirements such as:
     - Those defined as a result of the product design and development process to meet customer performance requirements
     - Requirements defined to provide a competitive advantage over competitors (see ISO 9004:2000 clause 7.2)

- Additional requirements for the product as preventive or corrective actions to avoid the occurrence or repetition of customer complaints
- Requirements defined to provide improved maintainability or to facilitate manufacturing operations

Clause 7.2.2 of ISO 9001:2000, "Review of requirements related to the product," requires the organization to ensure that, prior to its commitment to supply a product to the customer, it understands the product requirements (see clause 7.2.1), has resolved any ambiguities or conflicts, and has the ability to provide the product in accordance with those requirements. This raises the question: at what point does the organization commit to supplying the customer with its product? This will clearly be different for every organization, depending on the nature of its activities and its interface with the customer. The following examples, though not exhaustive, offer insight into the factors to be considered:

- In traditional business-to-business transactions, the customer requests a quotation, the organization provides the quotation, and if the order is placed within the validity of the quotation, the transaction is consummated. In other words, the commitment to supply is made by the organization when it submits its proposal, unless the proposal clearly states otherwise (for example, "delivery schedule to be confirmed at the time of order placement" or "subject to availability of stock at time of order").
- For business-to-consumer transactions, a similar sequence of events usually follows, though often in a much less formal manner. By contacting a car rental company's reservations agent, I am, in effect, requesting a quotation. The rental-car company then makes its proposal and is at that moment committing to provide a service. The transaction is verbal, but the organization needs to be sure that it has understood the customer's requirements and is able to meet them. Exceptions could include disclaimers of the type "we reserve the right to provide a similar model of car at the time of rental."
- For orders of off-the-shelf or commodity items, the commitment to sell may be characterized by the organization providing a written confirmation to its customer. It is important in these cases that any product literature, such as brochures or catalogs, make it clear to the customer that the order is subject to confirmation.
- ISO 9001:2000 mentions some specific situations, such as Internet sales, in which it may not be practical for the organization to review each individual order before acceptance. In these cases, the commitment to supply is actually made by the organization before the customer enters the site by the very fact that the product or service is listed for sale. The review of requirements in these cases has to cover the relevant product information provided up front by the organization to the customer, so that the latter can make an informed decision as to the suitability of that product for his or her needs.

- Very often the commitment to provide the product is implicit in a transaction and not so clearly defined. A gas station commits to provide a product by the very fact that it is open for business and its pumps are working. As soon as I pull up at the pump and start pumping gas, a transaction is consummated. When I go to a restaurant, however, it may be that some of the items on the menu have sold out early that evening, and so the commitment to supply is characterized only when the waitperson confirms my order.

As we have seen so many times before, the situation will most probably be different from one industry sector to another, from one geographical region to another, from one culture to another, and from one organization to another. Each organization is strongly advised to think and analyze "at what point do I commit myself to providing my product to the customer?"

Clause 7.2.2(a) of ISO 9001:2000 requires the organization to ensure that product requirements are defined. These requirements may be explicit or implicit and may have been defined by the customer, by statutory or regulatory bodies, by a franchiser, or by the organization itself.

It is pertinent at this stage to think about *how* the product requirements are stated and to remember the definition given in ISO 9000:2000 clause 3.4.4 for "design and development," according to which *product* design and development is: the "set of processes that transforms *product requirements* into specified *product characteristics* or into the specification of a product."

If the requirements provided by the customer, by the statutory or regulatory body, or by the franchiser define the *characteristics* of the product to be provided, then the product design and development process is not the responsibility of the organization. If, on the other hand, it is up to the organization to transform functional or performance-related requirements stated by the customer (or others) into specified product characteristics, then this is, by definition, design and development and must be addressed by the organization in accordance with clause 7.3 of ISO 9001:2000.

There may also be specific situations in which overall responsibility for product design and development is within the organization's parent company, but is not directly applicable to the organization itself. In these cases (in which the organization could be a manufacturing division of a consumer electronics corporation, producing TV sets or cars according to well-established designs, or a specific hamburger restaurant providing food according to corporate specifications, for example), it is important to define clearly the responsibilities and interfaces between the organization and its parent company with regard to design and development activities. This is particularly relevant as far as design and development *changes* are concerned, and the extent to which the organization may respond to specific customer requirements by changing product characteristics without consulting the appropriate corporate design function. Clearly there is a very close interaction between the customer-related process of "review of requirements related to the product" and that of design and development changes. In most practical situations, it is common for organizations to define "trigger" criteria, beyond which a "customized" order to meet specific customer requirements must be considered a "design change." For example, is a hamburger made to meet a customer's request for no pickle *really* a "product design change"?! It would probably be overzealous to consider it as such.

We must face the fact that organizations are, in general, very wary of the process known as design and development, which conjures up notions of sophisticated research laboratories and scientists in white coats. If, instead of asking an organization the question "are you responsible for design and development?" we ask "who defines the characteristics of the product or service you provide?" the conclusions we draw are likely to be entirely different. A common answer is, "ah, but I only have a very simple product," to which the reply should be, "so you only need a very simple design and development process."

The concepts and ISO 9001:2000 requirements for design and development are discussed in much greater detail in chapters 20–22. They are important here mainly because the *output* from the customer-related processes constitutes a very important *input* into the design and development process within the overall quality management system.

Clause 7.2.2(b) of ISO 9001:2000 requires the organization to ensure that any contract or order requirements that differ from those previously expressed are resolved. Typical examples may include the following:

- The customer orders a product by phone from a catalog, and the item requested is sold out.

- Instead of placing an order for 10 tons of steel, which was quoted, the customer requires 50 tons. This may affect delivery schedules.

- The customer mentions in a purchase order some new requirements (third-party inspection, penalty clauses, and so on), which had not previously been included in the quotation.

- The customer shows up to pick up a rental car and is less than 25 years old, despite having been advised that the rental agreement is only for drivers age 25 or older.

In real-world business-to-business transactions, some customers are notorious for not sending formal purchase orders in "real time." Some purchase orders arrive only after the order is produced and ready to be shipped. To meet the delivery schedule, however, you have already gone ahead based on a verbal commitment from the customer's purchasing agent that the requirements are "the same as last time." When the official purchase order arrives, however, the story may be different. Sound familiar? Great care must be taken in these cases. If you want this type of customer's business, you have to "go with the flow" (particularly if you're the small guy and they are a mighty corporation), and insisting on a formal purchase order before beginning production could cost you the account. Was it Groucho Marx who said that "a verbal agreement ain't worth the paper it's written on"? Well, let's not get into the legal implications here, but it comes back to the question, "When do you, the organization, make the commitment to supply?" Be preemptive. Send an order confirmation as soon as you receive the verbal order. Use the PDCA approach. You will very quickly realize who are the serious, organized customers you can rely on to uphold a verbal commitment, and who are the ones that will mess you around. It then becomes a strategic business decision as to how much you need them as customers.

Clause 7.2.2(c) of ISO 9001:2000 requires the organization to ensure that it has the ability to meet the defined requirements. This means that the organization must check:

- Product definition (customer, statutory, and regulatory requirements)
- Availability/delivery schedule
- Price and other commercial conditions
- Shipment details or location of service provision
- Any other contractual requirements

In some organizations and some contractual situations, it may be possible to carry out this process immediately with the involvement of only the salesperson and/or a computer terminal. Examples might include an airline reservations agent, a telephone sales executive for an insurance company, or a shopkeeper. For other organizations and more-complex transactions, however, this could necessitate a complex interfunctional process requiring the participation of sales, engineering, quality, production planning, manufacturing, legal, financial, and top management and take several weeks to complete. Examples might include a multimillion-dollar turnkey construction project, the provision of a new information system in a multinational corporation, or a major consultancy contract.

Clause 7.2 requires the organization to maintain records of the results of the review of requirements and any actions taken arising from the review. These records may be in any form or medium, such as paper, computer records (including e-mails), or recordings (in the case of telephone sales). There is no prescribed format, and what may be appropriate for a large multinational manufacturing organization would probably be excessive for a five-person fast-food restaurant.

Clause 7.2 also requires the organization to confirm customer requirements before acceptance in situations where the customer provides no documented statement of requirement. For some organizations, it may be most effective to provide this confirmation in writing, but the standard does not explicitly require this, and in some situations a verbal confirmation is more appropriate. This is very often the case when I take my kids and their friends to a pizza restaurant. When the server arrives, mayhem usually ensues about who wants what, whether we should have deep-pan or thin-crust, who likes pepperoni or onions and who doesn't, who wants a large diet drink or a medium regular soda, and so on, and so on. After listening patiently for five minutes, the server will take a deep breath and confirm our order: "So, just to confirm, that's two large deep pan pizzas with extra pepperoni and no onions, one order of garlic bread without mozzarella, three large diet sodas, one medium soda, and a large beer for Dad, right?" "Right!" "The garlic bread will be out in about seven minutes, and the pizza will take 10 to 15 minutes, OK?" "OK!" (You've all been through this at some time, I assume.) The server ticks off the little boxes on the order pad, and we're done. An excellent example of meeting all the requirements of ISO 9001:2000 clause 7.2.2 in a standardized, quick, simple, nonbureaucratic, and (usually) effective manner, complete with records.

Clause 7.2.2 further requires the organization to ensure that, when product requirements are changed, the relevant documents are amended and the relevant personnel are made aware of the changed requirements. It is implicit that any such changed requirements must be subject to review according to clauses 7.2.2(a), (b), and (c) prior to their acceptance, but there is usually an added urgency because the clock is ticking. Here are some examples of when this may occur:

- The customer changes some requirements after production or service delivery has begun. If the changes are likely to affect later activities in the product realization process, it is important that the changed requirements are communicated immediately to the relevant personnel within the organization. In some cases, this might involve the suspension of production until the changes can be properly reviewed, and may have commercial implications. In some cases, it may be too late to accept the changes requested by the customer, because the order has already been produced or the stage of the product realization process affected by the change has already been carried out.

- Statutory or regulatory requirements change. This rarely happens instantaneously, and organizations are recommended to keep abreast of any proposed changes in the requirements that affect their activities. For example, it is doubtful that any U.S. airline has accepted reservations for smoking seats on flights in or out of the United States after the FAA introduced 100 percent nonsmoking regulations. Some foreign airlines may have been caught unawares, however, even though the regulations also apply to their "products."

- The organization itself may change some requirements as a result of corrective actions arising from product nonconformities or customer complaints.

Clause 7.2.3 of ISO 9001:2000, "Customer communication," requires the organization to "determine and implement effective arrangements for communicating with the customer." If we plug in the ISO 9000:2000 definition of *effective*, this means that the arrangements for communicating with the customer must be capable of achieving the planned results. There is no specific requirement for the organization to have documented procedures addressing customer communications, although some larger or more-complex organizations may need these for the communications process to be effective. Small organizations can achieve extremely effective communications with customers with virtually no formality. Again, the use of a PDCA approach to the customer communication process is to be encouraged. What is the nature of the interface between the organization and its customers? How are communications planned? Is there a need for documented procedures? What do the results tell us? Is there any indication of problems (product nonconformities, customer complaints, delays) caused by the communication process *not* being effective?

What are the planned results that the communication process should achieve? Results are defined in the following subclauses and can be related back to the schematic diagrams shown in Figure 19.3, remembering that communication takes place in two directions.

Clause 7.2.3(a) relates to product information.

- How does the organization communicate information about its products to the customer (or, more correctly, to the *potential* customer)? This is particularly important for Internet, catalog, or mail-order sales, where the customer will base the purchasing decision on the information provided.
- Is the information transmitted in an effective manner?
- Does the information provide the customer with the amount of detail necessary to take a purchasing decision? Examples might include:
  - Technical information about a tangible product such as a roller bearing, a laptop computer, a washing machine (specifications, performance, application, and so on)
  - Details of an intangible product, such as a vacation package described in a catalog or on a Web site, or a training course

Clause 7.2.3(b) relates to inquiries and contract or order handling, including amendments.

- What is the nature of the organization and its customers (complexity, degree of formality, corporate culture, geographical proximity, and so on)?
- How does the organization facilitate the bilateral communication that is often necessary in these cases?
- Is the communication centralized in one function (for example, sales), or is communication between the organization's and the customer's technical functions encouraged? (There is no "prescribed" way of carrying out this kind of communication; what is important is its *effectiveness*.)
- Are there any problems (such as product nonconformities or customer complaints) that indicate these processes are *not* effective?

Clause 7.2.3(c) relates to customer feedback, including customer complaints.

- Gryna (1988b) describes a series of simple tools for collecting information from the customer, including the following:
  - *Warranty cards.* An important source of information about the condition of the product as it was received by the customer.
  - *Telephone calls to the customer.* A simple and effective technique for providing general customer perceptions about the quality of the product.
  - *Visits to individual customers.* Made by engineering or marketing functions not only as a response to complaints but also to learn about customer experiences with the product.
  - *Mail surveys.* Requesting information on an "absolute" basis (excellent, very good, good, fair, or poor) or compared to competitors' performance.
  - *Special arrangements with individual customers.* A simple but effective way of gaining in-depth information about the product by developing quality partnerships with key customers.
  - *Focus groups.* May involve average customers, noncustomers, or special customers; they can pinpoint quickly and at low cost specific information on quality matters and identify issues that need to be explored with quantitative or other techniques.

- It is unfortunate to think that many organizations will probably try to deal with the ISO 9001:2000 requirement to monitor customer satisfaction by simply sending customers a boring questionnaire and then trying to justify to the registrar that the customers are satisfied because they didn't respond. Where is the communication? Customer feedback is a valuable source of information that can give an organization a decisive advantage over its competitors. Remember that some large organizations may have several hundred suppliers, many of whom will be registered to ISO 9001:2000. If all those suppliers decide to inundate the poor purchasing agent with a questionnaire every quarter, then the reply (if any) could well turn out to be, "Yes, I *love* your product, but *please* don't send me any more darned questionnaires!"

- Many customers (in particular consumers) may need to be encouraged to fill out questionnaires related to the product. This can be done by offering incentives, such as "vouchers" good for the next purchase of consumer goods, "mileage credits" for airline customers, prize draws for car purchasers, and so on. Good communication doesn't usually happen by coincidence.

COMPARISON TO ISO 9001:1994 REQUIREMENTS

Clause 7.2 of ISO 9001:2000 is based on the old contract review (clause 4.3) of ISO 9001:1994. The main changes and implications are as follows:

- The adoption of the process approach, which is common throughout the ISO 9001:2000 standard. The focus is on *defining* the customer-related processes needed by the organization for its quality management system to be effective and then *managing* those processes using the PDCA cycle.

- The elimination of the requirement for the organization to have a documented procedure. However, it may be that many organizations find it necessary to maintain such procedures (possibly in the form of checklists or self-inducing records) to ensure that the customer-related processes are effective. Further guidance on the documentation requirements of ISO 9001:2000 may be found in the corresponding guidance module of the ISO 9000:2000 *Introduction and support package* published by ISO/TC176.

- The requirements of clause 7.2.1 are essentially new requirements, although many would argue that these were implicit requirements of the 1994 version of the standard. Specifically, the organization is now required to determine:

  - Requirements not specifically stated by the customer but necessary for specified or intended use, where known

  - Statutory and regulatory requirements related to the product

  - Any additional requirements determined by the organization itself

- The requirements of clause 7.2.2 of ISO 9001:2000 are virtually identical to those of clause 4.3 of ISO 9001:1994.

- The requirements of clause 7.2.3 of ISO 9001:2000 are new.

LOOKING BEYOND ISO 9001:2000 COMPLIANCE

A truly excellent organization will not implement a process simply because ISO 9001:2000 requires it to do so. The questions that they will always ask (in a constructive sense) are "What's in it for us?" "How can we improve our performance by doing this?" "How can we transform this into a competitive advantage?" "What's the most efficient way to do this?" This is also true of customer-related processes. Meeting the ISO 9001:2000 requirements using a holistic approach can provide significant insight into the customer's needs and expectations, which can then be related to and verified for compatibility with the needs and expectations of the other interested parties.

ISO 9004:2000 provides some guidance in this respect and recommends that organizations:

- Carry out market research, including sector-specific data and data from end users
- Compare performance with that of competitors
- Conduct benchmarking activities

Some examples of the techniques used by best-in-class organizations to define customer requirements, ensure their full understanding, and verify that they will be met include:

- Listening to the "voice of the customer"
- Clearly defining targets and customer service pledges
- Offering discussion forums
- Using customer feedback in a "balanced scorecard" approach
- Involving the customer in defining future needs and expectations for the product

In short, excellent organizations throughout the world have one thing in common: excellent two-way communication with their customers.

REFERENCES

Gryna, F. M., Jr. "Administrative and Support Operations." In *Juran's Quality Control Handbook*, 4th ed., ed. by J. M. Juran and F. M. Gryna. New York: McGraw-Hill, 1988a.
———. "Field Intelligence." In *Juran's Quality Control Handbook*, 4th ed., ed. by J. M. Juran and F. M. Gryna. New York: McGraw-Hill, 1988b.
ISO 9000:2000, *Introduction and support package—Guidance on the process approach to quality management systems*. Document ISO/TC176/SC2/N544R.2001 Geneva, Switzerland: International Organization for Standardization. See Appendix J, provided on the accompanying CD.
ISO 9000:2000, *Introduction and support package—Guidance on the documentation requirements of ISO 9001:2000*. Document ISO/TC176/SC2/N525R.2001 Geneva, Switzerland: International Organization for Standardization. See Appendix K, provided on the accompanying CD.
ISO/IWA 1:2001, *Guidelines for process improvements in health service organizations*. Due for publication July 2001. Geneva, Switzerland: International Organization for Standardization.

Chapter 20

Design and Development for Hardware

Knud E. Jensen
TQM—Team Quality Management I/S, Hovedgaard, Denmark

INTRODUCTION

In the last millennium more than 50 percent of the users of the ISO 9000 series of international standards were not concerned about the design and development phase of the product lifecycle encompassed by these standards. With the changes incorporated in the year 2000 edition of the ISO 9000 series, the number of companies that will address the sections in ISO 9001 and ISO 9004 on design and development will increase greatly, due to the withdrawal of the ISO 9002:1994 standard. That is, many organizations that performed design activities but chose to comply with ISO 9002 will now be required to include the design and development activities in the scope of the quality management system.

One of the key concepts behind this change is that an organization that desires to comply with the requirements of ISO 9001:2000 when providing products to its customers is responsible for all aspects of quality of such products, including design and development. For the benefit of those organizations where this can be proven not to be the case, instructions on the application of the standard are given in the scope section of ISO 9001:2000. Where product design and development is proven not to be applicable to an organization, the requirements concerning control of product design and development changes are, however, most likely applicable anyway.

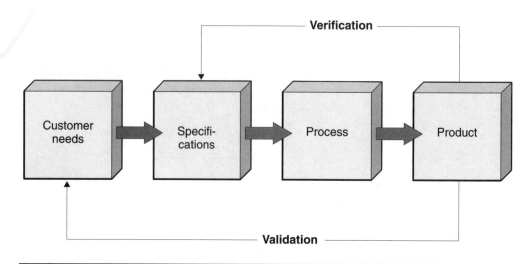

Figure 20.1 Verification and validation.

ISO 9001:2000 COMPLIANCE INFORMATION TERMINOLOGY

The two terms *design* and *development* are used in the ISO 9000 series of standards as one combined term, *design and development*. There are two very different reasons for this:

- Because of different use of the individual terms by industry sectors and major language and/or cultural differences as to the distinction between the two, consensus on definitions of the two terms could not be reached in ISO/TC 176

- Almost all, if not all, of the requirements in ISO 9001 apply as well to the design processes as to the development processes

The terms *verification* and *validation* are used strictly according to the definitions given in ISO 9000:2000, but because some major industry sectors use these two terms with varying definitions, Figure 20.1 is used to illustrate their meaning and application. This figure was originally developed by TC 176/SC2/WG18 to illustrate that committee's development process for the ISO 9001:2000 and ISO 9004:2000 standards.

DESIGN AND DEVELOPMENT—A SET OF PROCESSES

The activities in the design and development phase, when planned and controlled according to the requirements of ISO 9001:2000, can be viewed as a set of processes. This viewpoint is independent of the number and complexity of activities involved in the design and development of hardware products. This viewpoint can also be used whether the activities are organized in a strictly sequential way or with some activities being carried on concurrently. The process approach view also allows the requirements of ISO 9001:2000 for design and development to be applied in a very flexible way and to fit into any product development project structure. In addition, when the product to be designed and developed includes elements of different generic product categories—for example, a hardware product with some software control element included—the process approach accommodates such processes even though they may include major generic differences.

The process approach network for design and development activities can be initiated by identifying and defining the following elements for each of the activities (see Figure 20.2):

- Input to the process
- Output from the process
- Resources required
- Management (control) activities

Some academic dispute may arise as to whether an entity is an input or a resource, and the organization may have to devise internal rules for this distinction.

When the individual processes have been defined as just described, they can be combined into the network, which as a whole comprises the design and development process. The principles of this are shown in Figure 20.3. For the sake of clarity, resources are not shown on this figure.

Observe that the output of one process may be either:

- The input of another process
- The management (control mechanism) of another process
- The resource related to another process
- Any combination of these

When the process network is developed, it is advisable to check that:

- All inputs required by individual processes are available
- All outputs are used
- No closed loops exist that will go on forever

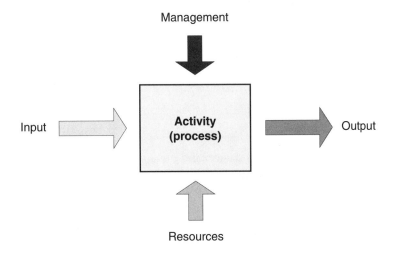

Figure 20.2   Defining the process.

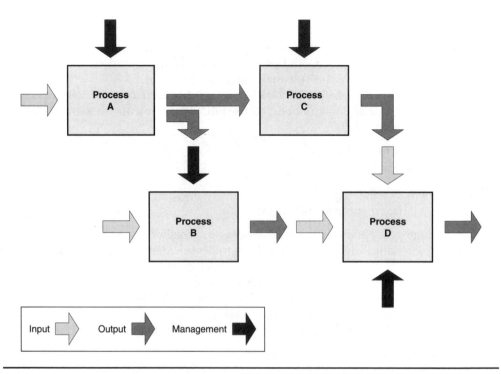

Figure 20.3 Process network.

If any of these situations occurs, you have to revisit the definition of the involved individual processes and make the necessary adjustments.

The following section on how organizations meet each of the requirements of ISO 9001:2000 will present examples of the identification and definition just described.

MEETING EACH DESIGN AND DEVELOPMENT REQUIREMENT FOR HARDWARE

Design and Development Planning (Clause 7.3.1)

The opening requirement of clause 7.3.1 in ISO 9001:2000 includes a combination of requirements for processes: "shall plan and control." These are treated separately as follows:

"Shall Plan"

Activity:
Perform planning of product design and development and determine the required design and development output process.

Input:
- Authorization of product design and development
- Predicted marketplace needs/requirements
- Competitor actions

- Customer wants/needs/requirements
- Technology advancements
- Need for updating of planning output as design and development progresses

Output:

- Definition of the design and development stages, including the review, verification, and validation appropriate for each stage
- Definition of the responsibilities and authorities for design and development
- Assignment of resources required by the design and development process planned

Note: The output may form a "product design and development quality plan," but ISO 9001:2000 does not require such a format or label.

Management:

- Budgets
- Quality objectives and other objectives for product design and development
- Quality policy and other policies

Resources:

- Budgets
- Company model for product design and development
- Control of the design and development of product

"Shall Control"

Activity:
Control (manage) the product and development processes.

Input:

- Design and development planning outputs
- Monitoring/measuring results of the design and development process

Output:

- Control of the design and development of product, including necessary actions required to maintain control
- Management of interfaces between different groups involved in design and development to ensure effective communication and clear assignment of responsibility

Management:

- The product design and development plans
- Budgets
- Quality objectives and other objectives for product design and development
- Quality policy and other policies

Resources:
- Product design and development project leader
- Company model for product design and development

Design and Development Inputs (Clause 7.3.2):

Activity:
Review of design and development input for adequacy.

Input:
- From sales and marketing specifications and so on:
  - Functional and performance requirements
  - Applicable statutory and regulatory requirements
  - Other requirements essential for design and development
- From the knowledge base in the organization (whatever form it takes):
  - Information derived from previous similar designs
  - Other requirements essential for design and development

Output:
- The product design and development specifications defining the inputs relating to product requirements (see previous items). The requirements shall be complete, unambiguous, and not in conflict with each other.
- Records of the product design and development input.

Management:
- The product design and development plans
- A company model for product design and development (could be an element of an overall product lifecycle model)
- Budgets
- Quality and other objectives for product design and development
- Quality and other policies

Resources:
Defined by the product design and development planning output.

Product Design and Development Outputs (Clause 7.3.3)

In clause 7.3.3 ISO 9001:2000 presents requirements for provision of output (but not expressed in a process format). The required product and development processes are unique to the individual organization and are determined during the product design and development planning process. This also means that part of the text that follows overlaps with what was presented earlier under "shall control."

Activity:
Design and development of the product including approval prior to release of the required output.

Input:
The product design and development specifications.

Output:

Shall be provided in a form that enables verification against the product design and development specifications; shall be approved prior to release and shall include the following:

- Results that meet the input requirements for design and development
- Specification of the characteristics of the product that are essential for its safe and proper use
- Appropriate information for purchasing, production, and service provision
- Product acceptance criteria or reference to these

Management:

- The product design and development plans
- Company model for product design and development
- Budgets
- Quality and other objectives for product design and development
- Quality and other policies

Resources:

Defined by the product design and development planning output.

Design and Development Review (Clause 7.3.4)

Activity:

Performance of systematic reviews of design and development in accordance with planned arrangements.

Input:

Results of the design and development processes as defined by the product design and development plans.

Output:

- Results of review indicating the ability of the results of design and development to meet requirements
- Reporting of any problems identified as the result of the review and the proposed necessary actions
- Records of the other outputs

Management:

- The product design and development plans
- Company model for product design and development
- Budgets
- Quality and other objectives for product design and development
- Quality and other policies

Resources:

- Defined by the product design and development planning output; shall include representatives of functions concerned with the design and development stage(s) being reviewed

- May include customer representatives
- May include representatives of external partners—for example, those responsible for outsourced activities

Design and Development Verification (Clause 7.3.5)

Activity:
Verification performed in accordance with planned arrangements to ensure that the design and development outputs have met the requirements defined in the design and development input specifications.

Input:
Design and development output, nonverified.

Output:
- Verified design and development outputs
- Records of the results of the verification and any necessary actions

Management:
- The product design and development plans
- Company model for product design and development
- Budgets
- Quality and other objectives for product design and development
- Quality and other policies

Resources:
Defined by the product design and development planning output

Design and Development Validation (Clause 7.3.6)

Activity:
Validation performed in accordance with planned arrangements to ensure that the resulting product is capable of meeting the requirements for the specified application or intended use where known.

Input:
Product resulting from design and development and/or models and elements of the product. Models and elements may include models (of forms as well as of functions), descriptions, and other forms representative of the resulting product if suitable for timely validation of such elements.

Output:
- Validated design and development output
- Records of the results of the validation and any necessary actions

Management:
- Wherever practicable, validation shall be completed prior to the delivery or implementation of the product. To facilitate this, validation of prototypes, models, or elements of the resulting product may be performed at earlier stages.

- The product design and development plans.
- Company model for product design and development.
- Budgets.
- Quality and other objectives for product design and development.
- Quality and other policies.

Resources:

- Defined by the product design and development planning output
- May include customer and/or end user and their resources in order to facilitate the specified application or intended use
- May include external parties and their resources—for example, distributors and others in the product supply chain toward the customer/end user in order to facilitate the specified application or intended use

Control of Design and Development Changes (Clause 7.3.7)

Activities:

- Identification of design and development changes
- Maintenance of records of identified changes
- Review, verification, and validation of changes as appropriate
- Evaluation of the effect of the changes on constituent parts
- Evaluation of the effect of the changes on product already delivered
- Approval of changes before implementation

Input:

The request for or the need of change to the product design and/or development.

Output:

- Approved changes to the product design and/or development
- Records of identified changes
- Records of the results of the review of changes and any necessary actions
- Initiation of necessary actions if required

Management:

- The product design and development plans
- Company model for product design and development
- Budgets
- Quality and other objectives for product design and development
- Quality and other policies
- When the request for or need of design and/or development change happens after the specific product design and development activities have been closed, special management provisions may have to be established and implemented

Resources:

- Defined by the product design and development planning output.

- When the request for or need of design and/or development change happens after the specific product design and development activities have been closed, special resource provisions may have to be established and implemented.

- The process of handling product design and development changes for complex products or market situations may require the organization to establish and implement a configuration management system. Such a system may be needed in order to facilitate the evaluation of the effect of the changes on constituent parts and product already delivered and to control the necessary actions initiated by the approved changes.

DIFFERENCES FROM ISO 9001:1994

What Is to Be Done Differently versus the 1994 Edition

The new requirements in clause 7.3 are as follows:

- A change in clause 7.3.7, "Control of design and development changes" to clarify the requirement that changes shall be reviewed, verified and validated, as appropriate, and approved before implementation.

- Some reformulated requirements in clause 7.3.6 related to design and development validation.

- New requirements in clause 7.3.6, "Design and development validation," and 7.3.7, "Control of design and development changes"—that is, "records of results shall be maintained."

- Clauses 7.3.4 to 7.3.7 include the requirement that a "record of the result shall be maintained." A new requirement has been added stating, "and (record of) any necessary actions (concerning the results) shall be maintained." There was previous discussion about whether this was an embedded part of the requirement concerning "records of results," but now it is clear that both are required.

The changes in the rest of clause 7.3, "Design and development," are few and should not require an organization to do anything differently from what it has already implemented to comply with ISO 9001:1994.

The formulation of the requirements relating to design and development validation in clause 7.3.6 has been improved when seen from a practical implementation viewpoint. Organizations that have had problems in the past with implementation of measures to meet this requirement should definitely revisit the new wording, and will most likely find that their problems have been resolved.

The requirements for control of design and development changes in clause 7.3.7 include new requirements when compared with ISO 9001:1994, and at the same time the changes from 1994 will require those organizations that previously used ISO 9002:1994 to carefully examine the requirements in this clause.

Although an organization is able to justify that all other requirements in clause 7.3, "Design and development," may be excluded in their situation, that does not in itself justify the exclusion of 7.3.7, "Control of design and development changes." It is common for organizations delivering a hardware product to implement changes to the product without recognizing that these changes are really a part of design and development. This can be a serious and even dangerous practice in cases where the producer does not have adequate knowledge of the product's intended use or design basis.

Organizations delivering products according to the customer's detailed drawings and specifications may not have knowledge of the application and use of the products delivered. In such cases the organization should resolve with the customer how the requirement in 7.3.7 stating "review of design and development changes shall include evaluation of the effect of the change on constituent part and products already delivered" has to be accommodated.

The new requirements in clause 7.3.7 are as follows:

- The changes (to the product design and development) shall be reviewed, verified, validated as appropriate, and approved before implementation

- The review shall include evaluation of the effect of the change on constituent parts

- The review shall include evaluation of the effect of the change on products already delivered

- A record of the results of the review shall be maintained

- A record of any necessary actions concerning the results of the review shall be maintained

To comply with the requirement to evaluate the effect of the change on products already delivered, many organizations will have to establish and implement some kind of configuration management. Although this requirement originally was aimed at organizations delivering software products, organizations manufacturing/delivering hardware products constituted of discrete parts may have to use configuration management in order to meet this new requirement—examples of a few such product categories are automobiles, complex machinery, complex electronic equipment, and so on (please do not consider this list at all complete).

In addition, there are new requirements in other clauses of ISO 9001:2000 that may be seen indirectly as new requirements for design and development. Here are the major areas to consider:

- Measurable quality objectives at relevant functions and levels (clause 5.4.1)

- Ensuring that personnel are aware of how they contribute to the quality objectives (clause 6.2.2[d])

- Monitoring and measurement of processes (clause 8.2.3)

- Analysis of data (clause 8.4)

USING 9004 TO GO BEYOND 9001 COMPLIANCE

Use of the Concepts Given in ISO 9001 and ISO 9004 to Design and Develop Products that Delight Customers

The concepts presented in ISO 9001:2000 and ISO 9004:2000 provide the opportunity for an organization to design and develop products that delight the customer and end user. Such an opportunity is likely to be used by many organizations in the coming years as they see their ability to delight customer and end user as the generic key to survival in the marketplace. Which product and product characteristics the customer and end user consider "top quality" within a product group is in most cases determined by the organization that can provide its customers and end users with the products they require and at the same time provide a product that delights the customer. The delight may be due to one or more of several different provisions—following are examples:

- Better value/price ratio
- More reliable or robust product
- Added features servicing customer needs
- Image-oriented features of the product

The delight experienced by the customer or end user is usually generated by exceeding his or her expectations and expressed requirements. This basic concept leads, however, to the fact that the delight will deteriorate over time—within a short time, competitors that want to stay in business will claim "me, too" and service the market in similar ways. To counteract this, organizations that wish to go on servicing their market with products that delight their customers and end users have to find systematic ways to innovate in this respect. One of the more effective ways is to incorporate such measures in the product design and development process.

Here are some examples of such measures:

- In the "monitoring of customer satisfaction" process required by ISO 9001:2000 (clause 8.2.1), include monitoring of the delight aspect and use methods that survey potential customer/end user needs even before the customer/end user perceives them. Several different techniques are available, such as customer focus groups; identification and use of front-edge trend groups of customers; and quality function deployment (QFD). (See also chapter 29.) In addition, the organization has to ensure that information on these aspects is constantly forwarded in a timely way to the product design and development process.

- Involve key customer/end user representatives in the product design and development review process and/or in the product design and development validation process.

- Use QFD in the product design and development input process.

- Use reliability engineering in the product design and development work and reliability testing in the product design and development verification process to enhance product reliability.

- Use design of experiments (for example, the Taguchi method) in the product design and development work and in the product design and development validation process to enhance product robustness.

CONCURRENT DESIGN OF PRODUCT

Product design and development can be a time-consuming process. As organizations work to delight customers with outstanding products they risk losing customers to those who are faster. During the time from the start of design and development planning to completion of successful verification and validation, the requirements, needs, and expectations of the customer or end user may have changed. Such change may take place because of new products introduced by competitors or for other reasons such as general or specific changes in the society or the market.

To counteract such risks, some of the best companies in the world have introduced what is known as "concurrent engineering," and by that method they have obtained a dramatic shortening of the calendar time needed from product idea to introduction in the marketplace.

Because of the process approach embodied in ISO 9001:2000 and ISO 9004:2000, the concepts given in these standards are as applicable to concurrent engineering as to more traditional ways of performing product design and development in an organization. The process approach enables the organization to break the design and development processes down, and optimize them with respect to resources and time as well as effectiveness.

APPLYING THE DESIGN AND DEVELOPMENT PROCESS TO THE DEVELOPMENT OF PROCESSES

ISO 9001:2000 clause 7.1 requires the organization to plan and develop the processes needed for product realization. Note 2 of the same clause states that the organization may apply the requirements in clause 7.3 regarding design and development to the development of the product realization processes.

Even though the explanation of note 2 goes beyond the requirements of ISO 9001:2000, the method is advisable. In many organizations the fundamental realization processes and their interaction have developed over some length of time, and the kind of proliferation that has taken place in this way is not necessarily in its totality (the process network) the most efficient setup.

Process reengineering of the realization process using the concepts and requirements of clause 7.3 regarding design and development can be used to achieve one or more of the following types of improvements:

- Reduced realization cost
- Reduced time needed for realization
- Less variations in the cost and time aspects of realization

The method may be used on one or more of the realization processes individually—for example, the purchasing process—as a pilot project, but to obtain the full potential impact, the reengineering process may have to be applied to the realization process as a whole.

Part of the potential improvement is clarity as to process ownership. Of course, such a revision of process ownership may include organizational adjustments as to responsibility and authority in the organization.

One area where the application of clause 7.3 to development of the product realization process goes beyond the requirement of ISO 9001:2000 is in the application of design and development validation to all the realization processes. However, representatives of world-class hardware manufacturers from the automotive industry to the medical equipment industry claim that this is one of the more efficient methods by which to obtain smooth, reliable, robust, and cost-effective processes throughout the whole realization process.

OUTSOURCING THE PRODUCT DESIGN AND DEVELOPMENT PROCESS

When an organization wishes to outsource its product design and development process—in whole or partially—it has to establish the same level of control over this process as if it were performing it itself and be able to give the same kind of demonstration of such control—see ISO 9001:2000 clause 4.1.

This may be established by requiring the partner to which the task is outsourced to demonstrate conformance to ISO 9001:2000, either by establishing and maintaining accredited registration or by demonstration to the outsourcing organization when auditing the partner's operation and facilities.

Other methods are applicable if the outsourcing organization can demonstrate the required control.

No matter which method is used, a key element in the control required may be obtained through participation in selected reviews during the design and development phase in the subcontracting partner's processes.

To obtain the most efficient results from outsourcing, the organization will have to go beyond the requirement of ISO 9001:2000 on purchasing and into the partnership-oriented principles presented in ISO 9004:2000 in order to establish processes mutually beneficial to both parties.

SUMMARY

On the surface, the changes in ISO 9001:2000 regarding design and development are few. But these few changes, along with the process approach applied throughout the standard, provide an excellent framework for setting up a quality management system for product design and development that will fit the needs and objectives of an organization regardless of its type, size, and complexity.

Due to the "consistent pair of standards" concept, ISO 9004:2000 at the same time gives valuable guidance on how to develop the quality management system for product design and development beyond the requirements of ISO 9001:2000.

Combined, these standards provide an excellent opportunity for an organization to delight its customers not only by meeting their requirements but also by exceeding their needs and expectations.

Chapter 21

Design and Development for Software

Frank Houston
EduQuest, Hyattstown, Maryland

THE ROLE OF QUALITY PLANNING AND QUALITY PLANS IN SOFTWARE DEVELOPMENT

Quality planning and quality plans play a vital role in software development. In particular, the development plan must allocate enough time and effort to determine the quality attributes and characteristics (requirements) of the software. The plan must also allow for reviews, evaluations, and tests to determine whether each development task produces outputs that conform (or support conformance) to the quality attributes.

Unlike most other products, software cannot be tested completely in a reasonable time. In fact, some software is so complex that all the users may not exercise the whole system in all the years they use it. Lacking complete testing, software, more than any other technology, must have designed-in quality, and quality activities must be integral to every task and process of design and development.

Software project plans must include evaluations needed to ensure software quality, and one evaluates by four criteria:

1. The quality attributes of the system are identified and recorded

2. The design of the system is capable of meeting the quality attributes, both the software and hardware elements

3. Both the implementation and configuration of the software and hardware elements conform to the system design

4. The deployed system conforms to its quality attributes to the degree of certainty attainable by practical verification methods

These four evaluation criteria infuse the whole of software development, and together they make up the process of software verification and validation. Software verification and validation are not separate stages of development, nor are they parallel activities. To be effective, verification and validation must be tightly integrated with every stage of the development process, and quality planning must account for the necessary time and resources. The good news is that when verification and validation become an integral part of software development, they reduce the level of effort needed to complete software projects (Clark 1997). Furthermore, the finished product of development with verification and validation typically requires less support than a product developed under a less rigorous process.

CLAUSE 7.3.1, SOFTWARE DEVELOPMENT LIFECYCLE MODELS FOR SOFTWARE QUALITY PLANNING

Software development lifecycles and methodologies are highly simplified process descriptions, idealized models used to illustrate the sequencing of various development tasks and processes. They support clause 7.3.1, being useful for identifying the stages of design and development, the sorts of activities that go on within each stage, and to some degree the interfaces between technical groups.

Three basic models and two methodologies are well known. The models are the waterfall, the V, and the spiral. The methodologies are rapid application development (RAD) and concurrent development. Each of the models and methodologies has its unique advantages, but if they are managed properly, all can promote compliance with ISO 9001:2000.

The grandfather of all software development lifecycle models is the waterfall. This model divides development into eight stages including operation/maintenance and retirement (see Figure 21.1).

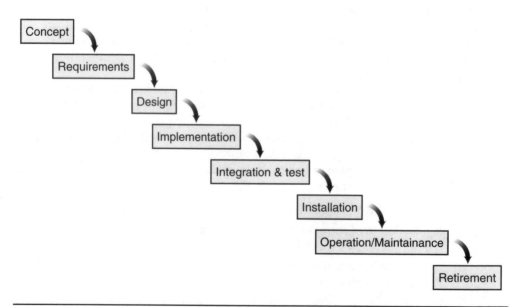

Figure 21.1 Waterfall model of software development lifecycle.

The following are the advantages of the waterfall model:

1. It fits well with Gantt charts used in project planning
2. The structure of the model encourages a linear approach to software design and development, including an evaluation of readiness for the transitions between each stage
3. Each of the first six stages is associated with a particular sort of documented output, such as requirements or design
4. The stage transitions also signal transfer of responsibility from one group to another, such as from software engineers to programmers between the design and implementation stages

The waterfall model has its critics due to notable weaknesses; in particular, the model does not portray the way software is usually developed. In customary practice, the concept, requirements, design, implementation, and often testing proceed concurrently, not in separate stages of the project. Nevertheless, the waterfall model is a good one when the functions and parameters of a system are well understood and few new issues are anticipated.

The V model of software development is essentially a waterfall model bent upward at the implementation stage. Although the model presents a linear, step-by-step view of software development, it is really designed to illustrate linked processes, not the order of execution (see Figure 21.2).

The simplified version presented here identifies 10 linked processes. Arrows mean the output of one process drives the work at the target end. Arrows pointing opposite ways indicate processes that require a great deal of communication.

The following are the advantages of the V model:

1. It identifies test development processes that can go on in parallel with the main process of system development.

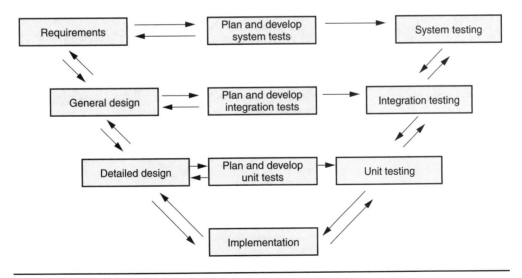

Figure 21.2 Simplified V model of software development lifecycle.

2. It clearly identifies the sources of information for each process and illustrates the primary lines of communication between processes.

3. It shows links between system development and test development processes that are only implied by the waterfall model.

The following are the disadvantages of the V model:

1. The way the processes are shown in a line may be misconstrued as the mandatory order of performance, when the intent is to illustrate concurrent activities.

2. The model can become very complex and hard to interpret when applied to the detailed list of processes and activities associated with large projects.

The V model is a good model to use when the functions and parameters of a system are well understood and it is important to maintain a complete record of software verification and validation.

The spiral model of software development represents a recursive approach in which requirements, design, implementation, and evaluation are repeated in successive stages until the quality attributes, the design, and the final product converge. The system then undergoes a final abbreviated "waterfall" process to establish a baseline configuration (see Figure 21.3).

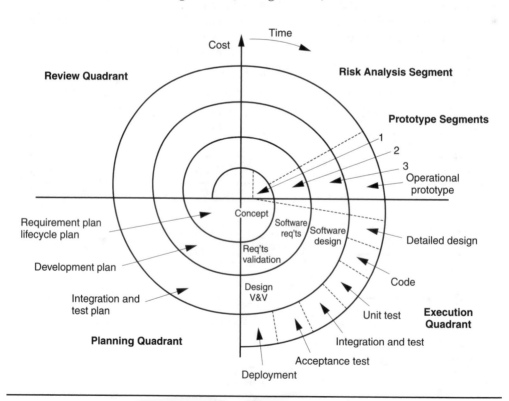

Figure 21.3 Spiral model of software development lifecycle.

The spiral model divides development into five recurring stages or processes represented as segments or quadrants on the diagram: risk analysis, prototyping, execution, planning, and review. In theory, the processes do not change, only the participants and the scope of inputs and outputs change. The outstanding feature of this model is the inclusion of a risk analysis process. In this context, the word *risk* refers to project risk, that is, the prognosis for success or failure. Risk analysis provides an opportunity to halt or redirect development if the risks of failure outweigh the benefits of success.

The following are the advantages of the spiral model:

1. Project risk analysis is explicit in the model
2. It is a more accurate representation of customary software development
3. It reduces development to five processes: risk analysis, prototyping, execution, planning, and review

The following are the disadvantages of the spiral model:

1. In spite of the reduced number of processes, the model is complex in that all five processes are repeated in every stage of development
2. The model is not as clear about technical and management interfaces as the other models
3. The model itself is unfamiliar to many software developers, although most unknowingly use it

Nevertheless, the spiral model is a good representation of software development when the scope, functions, and parameters of a system are not well understood and development requires an experimental approach.

Two methodologies were named earlier, RAD and concurrent development. These methodologies are both similar to the spiral model. RAD emphasizes speed of implementation and neglects objective functional requirements and structured verification processes. Concurrent development also emphasizes speed but is not as lax about requirements. By emphasizing speed, both methods compromise the verification processes. The proverb "haste makes waste" applies to software perhaps more than any other design undertaking.

SOFTWARE MODELING TOOLS

Tools for modeling software include but are not limited to the following: context diagrams, input–process–output (IPO) diagrams, entity–relationship diagrams (ERDs), data flow diagrams (DFDs), state–event diagrams (sometimes simply called state diagrams), state–event tables, hierarchical subroutine/function call charts, flowcharts, ladder logic diagrams, and flow graphs. These are just the well-known tools.

There is not enough space to explain these tools in this chapter, but there are a number of good texts that supply the necessary background. The following paragraphs discuss these tools in the context of the standard clauses that they support.

MODELING TOOLS FOR CLAUSE 7.3.2, DESIGN AND DEVELOPMENT INPUTS

Software design and development inputs must:

1. Set the boundaries and identify the interfaces between computerized and noncomputerized activities
2. Identify the required input data and their origins
3. Identify the required output data and their destinations
4. Establish the rules for computerized processes, including performance requirements if applicable
5. Estimate the initial size and speed requirements and the growth potential of the system with respect to anticipated inputs, outputs, and storage
6. Identify requirements outside the control of the developers and strategies for meeting them, such as company policies, industry standards, and government regulations
7. Identify constraints imposed on the developers, such as budget, manpower, and existing hardware/software infrastructure
8. Define objective criteria for success and failure with respect to all the previous seven items

On the one hand, some design inputs do not need great detail. The design inputs need not define every last aspect of the data inputs and outputs, and designers need only a logical description of the processing and handling rules. Size and speed requirements need only be order-of-magnitude estimates in the beginning. Equipment constraints may be very detailed, but usually the information is readily available.

On the other hand, other design inputs may require considerable detail to enable designers to define the right system. This is particularly true for definitions of the system boundaries, externally imposed requirements, and criteria for success and failure. Fuzzy boundaries and vague evaluation criteria usually lead to unstable systems that are expensive to deploy and maintain.

Useful tools for documenting design and development inputs include context diagrams, input–process–output diagrams, flowcharts, and written specifications.

Context diagrams are typically used to document the design concept of a whole computerized system. As the name suggests, they illustrate the context or business process in which a computer system functions. A context diagram shows a sequence of process steps, the points at which the computer acquires data or delivers information, the manual processes, and the automated processes.

A very good context diagram supplies considerable detail regarding the data and information used by the system. A good context diagram also separates automated and manual process tracks. The technique utilizes meaningful pictures or icons to symbolize processes and equipment, so the symbol set is essentially unlimited.

Since context diagrams allow for the use of meaningful icons, context diagrams are best used to flesh out and document the system concept. The resulting diagrams tend to be easier for users and managers to interpret. They are very good for identifying the system boundaries and interfaces. For example, a process of keyboard entry, report generation, and hard copy filing could be represented by the context diagram in Figure 21.4

Another useful design input device is the data flow diagram, or DFD. As the name indicates, a data flow diagram documents the flow, processing, and transformation of data within a system. In a data flow diagram, there are five basic symbols: processes, data stores, external entities, comments, and arcs. The simplicity of this symbol set enables great flexibility and ease of use.

The symbols may illustrate both physical and virtual elements of a system. (In this context, the term *virtual* is used to describe something that exists or takes place within the computer hardware.) This can lead to confusion if the physical and virtual system elements are not clearly labeled.

DFDs are good for identifying computerized functions that need definition and for qualitative estimates of storage requirements. For instance: a process of keyboard entry, report generation, and hard copy filing could be represented by the Yourdon-DeMarco DFD in Figure 21.5.

DFDs can also be used in later project stages to record the system design in greater detail—for instance, to illustrate the internal design of a function or process.

Composed of labels and only two symbols, input–process–output diagrams, or process diagrams, are the simplest of all tools for documenting a design. They are most useful for recording the necessary inputs to and outputs from a process and are frequently used to define business and manufacturing processes. They can also be used to refine complex system concepts but not to document computer program designs in detail.

A process diagram consists of labeled process symbols (boxes or circles) and labeled arcs. Being lists of the necessary inputs and outputs of each process, the

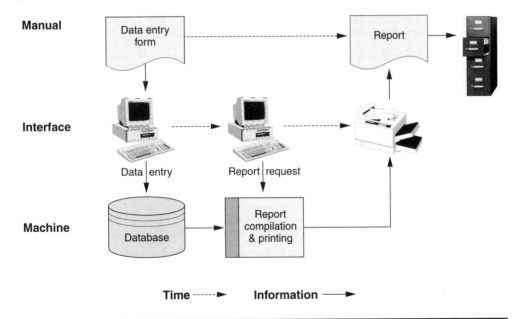

Figure 21.4 Example context diagram for keyboard entry–report generation–hard copy filing.

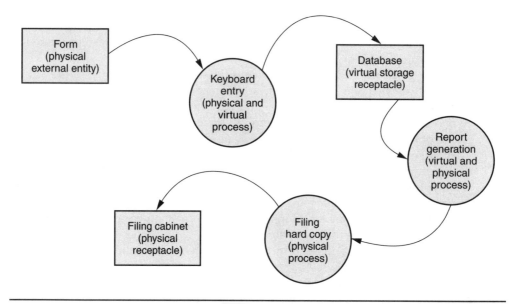

Figure 21.5 Example Yourdon–DeMarco data flow diagram for keyboard entry–report generation–hard copy filing.

labels are the most important element of these diagrams. In computer systems, they are useful to identify data items or parameters that must be passed to a process (inputs) or returned by it (outputs). Process diagrams are also useful for identifying the functions and processes for which rules must be developed. A process diagram of a process of keyboard entry, report generation, and hard copy filing is illustrated in Figure 21.6.

Flowcharts have been around so long that the standard symbols include such input media as punch cards and such storage devices as magnetic drums. Nevertheless, flowcharts are still used and still useful. Flowcharts are familiar to almost everyone involved with computers. They can be used to describe manual and automated processes. There is a rich set of process and object-specific symbols that yields very descriptive documentation.

Like data flow diagrams, flowcharts can be used to describe system concepts as well as more detailed software designs. Flowcharts are good for defining process rules. Figure 21.7 illustrates a flowchart representation of a process of keyboard entry, report generation, and hard copy filing.

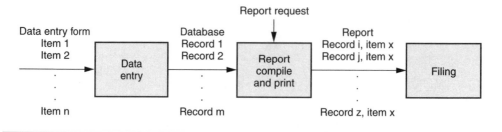

Figure 21.6 Example process diagram for keyboard entry–report generation–hard copy filing.

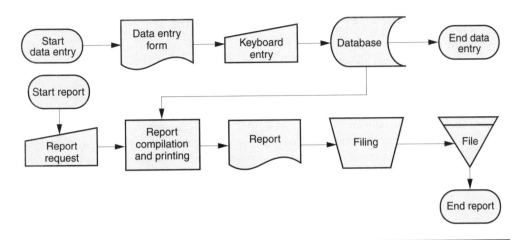

Figure 21.7   Example flowchart for keyboard entry–report generation–hard copy filing.

As a design input, written specifications have no adequate substitute. Pictures are good for defining processes and data flows, but there is always some program design information that only words can communicate. Such information includes the purpose of the system, the functions of system parts, and the content and form of data inputs and outputs.

Further, nobody has devised a graphical way to describe system constraints such as standards, government regulations, or limitations of equipment. Most of all, the design inputs must include objective criteria that define success and failure for the system, and these are most readily described in words.

Most of the written specifications concern the data to be used. It is not necessary to provide great detail at this point, but it is important to identify each item, specify useful ranges if applicable, and describe how the computer uses it. Data formats are details that may be postponed to the next stage of the design process. Data can often be described in tables, which are more economical in terms of time and words than the narrative form.

TRACEABILITY OF DESIGN INPUTS

Each design input serves as the ultimate reference for all subsequent review, verification, and validation activities. To link design inputs and outputs one must give every design input a unique identity. This is done by establishing document control and identifiers for specifications and drawings and by numbering paragraphs and figures in the specification documents. Frequently requirements documents and specifications documents contain information other than requirements, so one gives the requirement statements a special code number to set them apart—for instance, "R1234."

Clause 7.3.2 Summary

Many software models support clause 7.3.2 very nicely. To aid in the review and approval process, there is a range of models that all participants in the review process can understand. Using several software models is a good idea. By taking advantage of their unique strengths one can ensure clear, complete, and unambiguous communication of the design and development inputs.

For software the scope of 7.3.3(a) encompasses (b), (c), (d), and more, for it requires an objective verification and validation process, as discussed earlier in this chapter. The process must provide the information needed for production, quality control, and servicing; then it must provide assurance that the information is appropriate and correct; and finally it must provide objective assurance that the product meets fundamental requirements that were, in theory, established by customers. Complying with requirements (b), (c), and (d) is easy compared to (a).

Clause 7.3.3(b) simply requires the design and development process to yield information for production and servicing. To meet the standard, one documents precisely and completely all the components and processes necessary to build and deploy the software. For commercial, off-the-shelf software, one documents a list of materials, components, and equipment including the following:

- Hardware and software of the target system
- Software replication equipment and process to be used
- Distribution media
- The exact identity of the master program file(s)

For custom software, one includes a detailed specification of the target system, plans and protocols for testing and deploying the software, and the exact identity of the master files or load sets. The same information applies to configurable systems.

Clause 7.3.3(b) also requires information for servicing the product. For nonsoftware products, one prepares parts lists, electrical schematics, and mechanical drawings. For software, the appropriate outputs are design documents and source code. For verification and validation the design outputs must include a traceability instrument—a way to link each function, feature, and test back to the design input that spawned it. Traceability is essential for objective validation and change control.

The traceability matrix is one technique; however, it is cumbersome to document on paper. A software application is a necessity to document all but the simplest designs.

Another way to achieve traceability is to include it in the design documentation, code, and test cases. By this method, one labels the design output text or figure with the identification of the input requirement or requirements to which it is linked. The advantages are that one can get along without separate traceability documentation, and nobody needs to be trained to use an extra software tool. The disadvantages are that more information must be included in the design, code, and test documents, and the chances are greater that one may miss an important connection.

Clause 7.3.3(d) requires the design outputs to indicate clearly the essential product characteristics for safe and proper use. One does this by identifying critical software requirements. For computer systems, ensuring and preserving data integrity are always critical requirements.

MODELS FOR CLAUSE 7.3.3, DESIGN AND DEVELOPMENT OUTPUTS

Other models besides flowcharts and data flow diagrams are useful for documenting software design. When documenting, one must recognize that each model represents only a particular aspect of the software. As in electromechanical design, several illustrations or "views" are needed to render the design completely. A discussion of some of the most common tools follows.

Entity–relationship diagrams are intended to show the relationships between data objects (for example, tables in a database system). Data relationships come in four types: one-to-one, one-to-many, many-to-one, and many-to-many. ERDs illustrate pairs of tables that are linked to each other, and they identify the link, a data item or attribute common to both members of each pair. One uses this model to document the structure of database tables, and one can use it to document more generalized relationships in object-oriented design methodologies. It is good to use in the early stages of design, and it should be maintained as a reference through the maintenance stage in case tables are changed.

State–event diagrams and *state–event tables* are intended to show system transitions from one state or process to another. Circles usually represent the beginning and end states and an arc or line the transition between them. One labels the line to identify the event that starts the transition. State-event tables are another way of presenting the same information in three columns: beginning state, event, and end state. This model is good for documenting programs with many interactive screens, views, and dialogs. State diagrams are also a good way to specify access controls, such as security functions; and they are excellent when specifying the use of data values or conditions to invoke new functions or screens, as in Web pages.

Hierarchy or *call charts* are used to identify how the modules of a computer program call or invoke each other. They are usually best for programs with a limited number of well-defined functions or processes that are composed of functions that are more primitive. A typical use might be to document the code running an operator–screen dialog. Call charts are good for identifying the complex and primitive functions of a system in the early design stages. (In this context, primitive functions are like components of other "complex functions.") Call charts are also good references for change control. Using them one can detect when changes may affect more than one software module and avoid introducing new errors when fixing old ones.

The text equivalent of the call chart is the *called-by/calls table*. This table consists of the following columns: program, program called, parameters passed, program called by, and parameters returned. The chart is particularly useful for tracing the potential effects of code changes in modular software.

Ladder logic diagrams are specialized tools used to code and document process control systems. They are like very detailed state-event diagrams in that they define states of a control system that trigger individual actions. Ladder logic diagrams are specialized in that they comprise both the source code and the detailed specification of the program logic.

Computer programs are available to implement these software models. The programs' functionality ranges from just providing the graphics for making drawings all the way to simultaneous programming and design documentation.

7.3.4 DESIGN AND DEVELOPMENT REVIEW

Reviews are a vital part of the software development process because the effectiveness of software testing is so limited. Design reviews for software are in most respects very similar to design reviews for electromechanical designs. Where design reviews differ is in the care taken to be sure the input requirements are complete, consistent, and objective (conforming to the guidance in 7.3.2); and the design outputs are traceable to one or more input requirements. Analysis of the design for correctness and reasonableness is a given in any development venue.

The review of design inputs must necessarily be somewhat subjective, but one must determine that the inputs yield objective criteria by which one can evaluate the outputs of the design process and the finished system.

The review participants may change as design and development proceeds. Table 21.1 gives a rough idea of the essential composition of the review teams at several stages of design and development. There are several roles in an official review, namely, moderator or chairman, presenter, recorder, and reviewers. The originator or author of the reviewed item may attend or not, and he or she may present or not. The role titles describe the expected kind of participation. Refer to a good engineering management text for more discussion of engineering reviews.

Code review is unique to software development. It has three objectives. In descending order of importance they are (1) to find programming errors, (2) to identify ways to improve the code under review, and (3) to ensure consistency of format and conformance to naming conventions.

The code review process is very good at finding errors. Using fewer resources and less time, code reviews discover about 80 percent of the errors usually found in testing. This increases the efficiency of the testing process by eliminating a huge chunk of the troubleshooting and corrections that would otherwise be needed.

For software, unit test plans and results may be considered during code reviews. Lack of unit test records is a chronic problem of software development, and it could be solved by joining unit testing with the code review process. Integration testing could be streamlined too by reviewing code and data to ensure compatibility among modules.

There is a design output associated with review. In the simplest case, it consists of a running history of the action items identified during all reviews. The record of

Table 21.1 Design and development review time line and participants.

Concept and Early Design	Detailed Design	Coding	Integration and Test	Deployment Test
Users	Designers	Designers	Testers	Users
Designers	Coders	Coders	Coders	Testers
Testers	Testers	Testers	Designers	Designers
			Users	

each action item includes the date identified, the party(ies) responsible for resolving the item, the action taken, and the date of closure. Of course, the review records can be divided according to development stages, and in most cases they are.

MODELS FOR 7.3.4   DESIGN AND DEVELOPMENT REVIEW

All the models discussed to this point are useful either for planning design and development review or as review objects. Another software model, the *flow graph*, is particularly effective in the code review process.

Flow graphs map the decision pathways of a computer program. Sometimes called directed graphs, they consist of two symbols: circles (nodes) and arcs. They are similar to flowcharts, but they do not contain as much symbolic information.

For test planning and design review, flow graphs indicate likely paths to undesirable results, allowing one to identify the conditions that "steer" a program along such paths. Knowing the pathways to adverse results, one can devise program safeguards and create challenging test cases and data sets.

Another use of flow graphs in design review consists of measuring program complexity in an objective way. Flow graphs enable one to determine the number of decision nodes in a program module and to calculate an index believed to correlate positively with the probability of logical program errors. This technique, the *cyclomatic complexity metric,* can be used to identify modules needing improvement or extra care in testing.

7.3.5   DESIGN AND DEVELOPMENT VERIFICATION

Design and development verification comes in three flavors: review, test, and process monitoring. The review aspect of verification has been discussed. This section will concentrate on testing and process monitoring.

For software, the most obvious form of verification is dynamic testing. Testing is part of the coding process from the start. The programmer writes code and then executes it. He or she makes up test input data if necessary.

There is a problem with this process. Computer programming tends to be a solitary activity, and under time pressure a programmer may "test for success." He or she may overlook conditions and data sets that would expose coding errors and wrong assumptions. The same could be said of a single software engineer integrating modules into a large program. One needs the perspective of several experienced people to devise adequate dynamic tests.

Test documentation is a big issue because the standard demands it at the most inconvenient time for most projects. Dynamic testing happens when the project is already behind schedule and "busting" the budget, so every extra task becomes a burden. The project sponsors ask, "Why should the test cases be written?" and "Why must the results be recorded?"

The short answer is: "For the future." Very few, if any, software systems remain unchanged, and they are usually maintained and modified by people other than the original designers and programmers. Proven dynamic tests are the last line of defense against maintenance-induced errors and burdensome maintenance costs.

Monitoring the process is a simple but often overlooked aspect of design and development. It is not, as the comedians say, "rocket science." This task is nothing more than checking the project records for objective evidence of the following:

- Conformance to the quality plan and all defined software development lifecycle (SDLC) processes
- Satisfactory completion of all defined tests
- Satisfactory closure of all review action items
- Assurance that no process exceptions compromise the quality of the software as defined by the design and development inputs

7.3.6   DESIGN AND DEVELOPMENT VALIDATION

Where software is concerned, clause 7.3.6 could mislead. It seems to imply that validation is a separate process with separate records. In fact, as mentioned at the beginning of this chapter, good software engineering practice demands integration of development, verification, and validation.

With good software engineering practices in place, the validation record for software and the record of the software development process become one and the same. The verification task discussed earlier, process monitoring, can be regarded as the process of confirming software validation.

Clause 7.3.6 includes a requirement to complete validation before distribution or deployment "wherever practicable." Validation is practicable when one has objective, testable system requirements, a well-documented design, traceability of requirements, and systematic review and testing. This can nearly always be done if system cost and completion schedule are not allowed to take precedence over quality concerns.

Time pressure is the enemy of software validation. It is especially pernicious when applied in the early stages of software development. Every man-hour taken away from the system definition process may add as many as 100 man-hours to testing and deployment. For this reason, the planning process must allow all stakeholders plenty of time for verification and validation tasks, especially during system definition and the early part of design.

For custom and configurable systems, user participation is vital. Users, that is, customers of the system, must participate fully in developing requirements and reviewing system functions. Too often systems fall short because the users fail to take seriously the development of requirements at the beginning. The planning process must identify and obtain substantial user support. For commercial software the required level of user commitment is nearly impossible to attain, so a commercial software development company needs orderly processes for identifying and quantifying the needs of its customers as well as for developing software. Quality function deployment methods such as "house of quality" can help.

CLAUSE 7.3.6 SUMMARY

Software validation is practicable when one has reasonable schedules and systematic development processes. For custom and configurable systems, one also needs committed users. At the end of the day, software validation is nothing more than good software engineering practice.

FIRMWARE

The distribution media and installation methods are the only differences between software and firmware. Firmware comprises executable programs distributed as integrated circuits, that is, read-only memory (ROM) or hard-wired but programmable logic, installed in some equipment or instrument. Many think of such components as hardware. They are not. Firmware, like any other computer program, should be developed using good software engineering practices.

Current developments have blurred the line between firmware and other software. Erasable, reprogrammable ROMs (electronically erasable programmable read-only memory, or EEPROM) have been available for some time, so now one can change an embedded program without removing the memory chip. With changes becoming so convenient, it will be tempting to customize instruments and equipment for each customer. Good software engineering practice is a way to keep this process under control.

7.3.7 CONTROL OF DESIGN AND DEVELOPMENT CHANGES

Clause 7.3.7 requires changes to be "reviewed, verified and validated, as appropriate, and approved before implementation." Change control and configuration management are the mechanisms for meeting this requirement.

It may seem awkward to put these requirements in the design and development clause, but there is good reason. For an existing software product or system, every change is a miniature development project. Further, even in development, changes should be evaluated for their effects on the system and the project. Finally one must make sure all developers have the correct information for their part of the project at all times.

What do the terms mean? *Change control,* in a few words, means organizing and managing the processes of changing a product or system, including the following:

- Initiation
- Review
- Formulation
- Evaluation
- Deployment

Configuration management can be defined by breaking down the phrase. Configuration means the parts and structure of a product or system. Configuration management then means planning, directing, and controlling the system configuration. The output of these tasks is a record that logs the current and past configurations of a product or system.

Change control and configuration management must be approached with care in the early stages of a project. One does not want to put unnecessary obstacles in the way of creating software that meets the needs of the customer. During development, there should be one guiding principle: the information required for every stage should come from one source. The designers should have one coherent set of design inputs; the programmers should have one approved software design specification; and so forth. The reviewers and testers who evaluate each output should use the same inputs as the individuals who are responsible for realizing the outputs. During development, therefore, the number one goal of change control and configuration management is to ensure that all participants have the latest correct information for their tasks at all times. Almost as important is the number two goal, to ensure that the final description of the product or system "as built" includes all the changes and adjustments made during the product realization processes.

In practical terms, this means that at all times there can be only one master source of the following:

- System requirements
- System design specifications
- Software design specifications (including databases)
- System development files, such as source code
- Executable code files
- Test cases with acceptance criteria

These items should be linked by a traceability instrument to ensure that all changes are inserted at the proper place in the information stream of the development process. If a change represents a new requirement, then the requirement is added to the design inputs. If a change represents a better way to meet an existing requirement, then it is inserted in the design. If a change means deleting a requirement, then it is deleted from the design input. A traceability instrument enables one to map how each change propagates through the master information files. This helps when evaluating the effects of changes, as clause 7.3.7 requires.

It is important during development to keep change records as simple as possible. Ideally, changes and records would be managed entirely by means of official reviews, but in large projects, control that is more formal may be necessary to ensure conformance and accountability.

Archiving is very important during system development as insurance against the loss of important work. Conscientious maintenance of a secure and current archive is the heart of disaster recovery. There will be more discussion of archiving and configuration management later in this section.

After the software is released, there should be a process for making changes. The ideal process consists of four stages, each a process in itself:

1. Request
2. Needs and effects analysis
3. Realization
4. Deployment

The initiation process should define who might initiate a request, and by what route problem reports and found errors may be escalated to the change request level. After-release testing and error reports are, after all, the main source of software changes. The output of the initiation process should be a formal change request. The request may arise from error investigations, "discovered" functional requirements, or ideas for system improvements; but regardless of their origin, change requests are inputs to a triage process, that is, the needs and effects analysis.

One should analyze the need for and the effects of the requested change. This analysis is different from the error investigation that may have launched the request. On the one hand, there may be an error, but one may wish to defer action because the problem is small and the change is too minor to justify the expense of verifying, validating, and deploying it. On the other hand, the error may be significant, requiring immediate action, and its effects may propagate throughout the system. The output of the needs and effects analysis should determine the change priority, catalog the scope of its effects, identify its traceability links, and authorize the realization process for top-priority changes.

The change realization process should emulate the software development process but be scaled to match the scope and effects of the change. Depending on the effects of the change, the outputs of this process may include some or all of the following: draft changes to system documentation, action item records from reviews, revised source code or configuration files, revised and tested executable programs, problem resolutions, and revised or new test cases. The outputs of this process must include the change authorization and the deployment plan.

The deployment process includes the following tasks: establishing new master files using the items revised in the realization process, notifying affected users, distributing revised program files and related documentation, installing revised programs, and monitoring for change-related problems.

Configuration management plays a large role in the deployment of changes. The configuration management process is where the changed items receive identifiers to distinguish them from old editions. Configuration management includes the archiving and cataloging of old editions, necessary in case one must reverse or back out of a change. Finally, the process includes establishing new master editions and recording the new system "baseline."

DIFFERENCES

Clause 7.3 does not require anything new or different in the way of good software engineering practices. The main differences are that (1) the 2000 edition emphasizes process and (2) it contains less detail, thereby shifting the burden of explanation to guideline documents.

ISO 9000-3:1991 applies to ISO 9001:2000 as well as it did to ISO 9001:1994, and it contains considerable detail on how to comply. ISO 9004:2000 is very much in accord with ISO 9000-3:1991, but it does not contain the software-specific detail. At the end of the day, ISO 9000-3 is still a good guide to compliant software development. Table 21.2 shows some direct correlations between requirements of 9001:2000 clause 7.3 and the guidance of 9000-3:1991.

Table 21.2 Concordance of ISO 9000:2000 clause 7.3 and ISO 9000–3:1991 guidelines.

ISO 9001:2000 Requirement	ISO 9000-3:1991 Guideline
7.3.1(a)	5.4.1(c), 5.4.2.1(a)
7.3.1(b)	5.4.1(d), 5.4.2.1(d), 5.4.6, 5.5.2(c)
7.3.1(c)	5.4.1(b), 5.4.2.2(c), 5.5.2(e)
7.3.1 next to last sentence	5.4.2.2(d)
7.3.1 last sentence	5.4.1 last sentence
7.3.2 first sentence	5.4.4
7.3.2(a), (b), & (d)	5.3.1
7.3.2(c)	5.4.5(e), 5.6.2(c)
7.3.2 last sentence	5.4.4
7.3.3 first sentence	5.4.5 first paragraph
7.3.3(a)	5.4.5(a)
7.3.3(b)	5.9
7.3.3(c)	5.4.5(b)
7.3.3(d)	5.4.5(d)
7.3.4 first sentence	5.4.3, 5.4.6(a), 5.6.4
7.3.4(a) & (b)	5.4.6 last paragraph, 5.6.4
7.3.4 last paragraph	5.4.2.2(c), 5.4.6 first sentence, 5.5.2(e), 5.6.4
7.3.5	5.4.6, 5.7
7.3.6	5.7.4, 5.7.5
7.3.7	5.4.6 last paragraph, 6.1.3.1(c) & (d), 6.1.3.2

REFERENCES

Clark, B. K. *The Effects of Software Process Maturity on Software Development Effort* (1997): 67. (A dissertation presented to the faculty of the Graduate School University of Southern California in partial fulfillment of the requirements for the degree Doctor of Philosophy—Computer Science).

Humphrey, W. S. *Managing the Software Process.* Boston, MA: Addison-Wesley, 1989.

Leveson, N. *Safeware, System Safety, and Computers.* Boston, MA: Addison-Wesley, 1995.

McDermid, J., ed. *Software Engineer's Reference Book.* Boca Raton, FL: CRC Press, 1991.

Sigfried, S. *Understanding Object-Oriented Software Engineering.* New York: IEEE Press, 1996.

Chapter 22

Design and Development for Services

Diane M. Baguley
Beca Carter Hollings & Ferner, Auckland, New Zealand

INTRODUCTION

Use of the ISO 9000 family of standards has increased substantially in the service sector in recent years. Services form a significant part of the economy and are traded internationally to a greater extent than previously. In many instances they have been subject to increasing regulatory and consumer scrutiny. The situation has enhanced awareness of the need for effective systems for the management of service quality, including the development of both service products and service delivery.

A service is characterized by being intangible (even though the service transaction may involve tangible products) and generated in a way that it must be performed, at least in part, at the interface between the supplier and the customer. The interface between supplier and customer may not be limited to service delivery. Particularly where services are designed to meet individual customer needs, the customer may be involved in development as well as service provision processes. Further, development and provision processes may run simultaneously or in close relationship to each other.

This has led to some debate about the application of the design and development sections in ISO 9001:2000 and ISO 9004:2000 to service. Do they apply to the development of the service as a whole or to the service provided to a specific customer? Are there cases in which they should apply to the development of service delivery processes? When can the requirements of ISO 9001:2000 be excluded and the process controlled simply as a service operation?

The first step, then, is to understand the meaning of design and development in relation to the service sector.

SERVICE DESIGN AND SERVICE DEVELOPMENT

Are design and development different or are they just different words for the same thing? If they are different, is it important for service?

The term *design and development* is used as a collective term in ISO 9000:2000. This is done to avoid confusion, since the terms are sometimes used interchangeably and sometimes to describe different phases of an overall process. However, an understanding of design and development as sequential activities may assist service organizations in determining the processes that need to be controlled.

Design can be defined as a set of processes that transforms requirements into specified characteristics. Development uses the output of a design phase as part of its inputs and can be defined as a set of processes that transforms specified characteristics into a new or unique product or process.

Services may involve design alone, development alone, a sequence of design and development, or an iterative sequence of a number of design and development activities. In the service sector, the overall term *service development* frequently is used to cover all such elements.

The service may include design but not development—for example, architectural or engineering design, resulting in drawings and associated specifications supplied to a customer. Other services may exclude design but include development. For example, in the case where a customer provides a service contract defining the performance requirements for facilities maintenance, the service includes development activities to turn those performance specifications into process requirements. The process requirements then provide the basis for service provision.

For many services, there is a design phase during which the organization works with the customer to translate the customer's needs into a "service specification," prior to the development phase and subsequent service delivery. It is easy to overlook such a design phase and regard it simply as a customer input to development. However, the translation of needs into requirements can be the most critical stage in achieving customer satisfaction and may need to be recognized as a crucial part of the process sequence.

Figure 22.1 shows how a development phase may follow a design phase in an overall service design and development process.

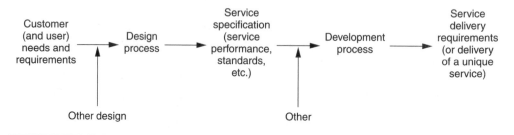

Figure 22.1 Design and development as sequential activities.

THE DESIGN AND DEVELOPMENT SEQUENCE

Illustrating Design and Development

The design process starts with customer needs and specified requirements (including regulatory and other requirements). It translates these into a service specification. A simple example is translating "I don't want to be kept waiting" into "queue length at each counter no more than three customers."

The development process starts with the service specification. In the above example, the development would establish the functional requirements to deliver the service—for example, the roster systems and other staffing arrangements to maintain the planned service standard for queue length.

The design and development sequence may contain a number of stages, some of which will run parallel to one another. The boxed example illustrates this by outlining four of the stages in the development of community health services—a feasibility study, the development of facilities, the development of service delivery processes, and the development of treatment of an individual patient.

Clause 5.1   Management commitment

Top management shall provide evidence of its commitment to the development and implementation of the quality management system and continually improving its effectiveness by:

Example: Developing Community Health Services

a. *The Feasibility Study.* The feasibility study is a project to deliver the findings of an investigation as a basis for a substantial strategic decision.

   The design phase results in the specification of the project, including the scope of the study and the methodology to be used. The development phase is the investigation and reporting of the feasibility study, based on the project specification. The output of the development project needs to be suitable for strategic decision making.

b. *Establishment of Clinic Facilities.* Prior to, or parallel to, the establishment of service delivery mechanisms, there may be a project to design and develop the clinic facilities—the building and infrastructure. The architectural and engineering design output will comprise drawings and related information to be used in the subsequent development of the facility.

c. *Establishment of Service Delivery.* The design of service delivery mechanisms produces the service specification, including the definition of services offered and the service standards to be achieved. The development phase defines how the requirements of that specification are to be met.

(continued)

---

d. *Providing Health Services to Clients.* Design and development of individual health services involves the client and may include other parties such as family members. The process of defining health service requirements (design) may include diagnostic investigation as well as discussion and examination. The findings may be provided to different providers (for example, medical specialist, nurse, physiotherapist) as a basis for treatment planning and delivery.

Each service provider may then develop a treatment plan. Depending on criticality, the development output may be highly specified or left largely to the judgment of a competent professional as part of his or her operational management. The development phase may continue throughout the delivery of services, as client progress is evaluated.

Relationship to Service Operations

For some services, design and development (for new or "one-off" services) are readily differentiated and clearly separate from service operations.

Example: A Postal Service

Design—External service specification (e.g., days for delivery to different destinations for each class). Internal specification (e.g., standards for care and protection of mail).

Development—Establishment of mail collection, security, sorting, distribution, and delivery processes to achieve the specified services.

Service operations—Implementation of the service in accordance with the above.

For some other services, design and development may run parallel to operational aspects of service provision. The differentiation between design, development, and operations may assist in clarifying objectives to be achieved and risks to be managed.

Example: A Consultancy Service

Design—Establishment of service agreement including specification.

Development—Development of service deliverables (e.g., report, advisory services).

Service operations—Job management of service processes, including activities such as team management, progress control, records management, and client satisfaction review.

COMPLIANCE WITH ISO 9001

Application of Design and Development

Three main situations call for the application of ISO 9001:2000 design and development requirements to a service:

1. Providing a service that, by its nature, includes design or development, or both. For example:

   • Services such as financial planning, management consultancy, or legal services, where the level of design and development may be from minor (for routine services) to major

   • Services such as architecture, where design is the major activity

2. Establishing a new service. For example:

   • Developing new educational programs and courses

   • Designing an Internet banking service—where the characteristics of the service and the user interface for service delivery must be specified as an input to design and development of the associated software, hardware, and internal processes

3. Developing a service delivery process. The design and development of service provision processes needs to be included for compliance with ISO 9001:2000 where:

   • They form part of the service product (for example, a project management service)

   • They cannot otherwise be validated as capable of meeting customer requirements (for example, development of certain health services).

Under ISO 9001:2000, conformity cannot be claimed if design and development requirements are excluded unless those processes do not affect the ability to meet customer and regulatory requirements. This is not necessarily a clear-cut requirement for services.

Services generally include at least some customer- or service-specific design and development. However, in some situations the level of risk and complexity is so low that it is reasonable to exclude ISO 9001:2000 design and development requirements.

Where customer needs and the services provided to meet them are reasonably standard, the quality of such services can be readily controlled during provision processes (that is, under clause 7.5 of ISO 9001:2000). There may be no benefit in distinguishing design and development processes. General administrative, wholesaling, retailing, and accounting services often fall into this category.

Some services are more individual but still are suitable for control under a service provision process. The design of a travel itinerary, for example, may be controlled by a suitably trained person (that is, by qualification of personnel as in ISO 9001 clause 7.5.5) provided with appropriate information and other resources. In such cases it should be immaterial whether the organization excludes ISO 9001 requirements for design and development or covers design and development within service provision processes. What is important is the identification and appropriate control of design and development risks within the service.

Where there is doubt if the design and development requirements need apply, it is advisable to assume they do and then work through clause 7.3 of ISO 9001 to determine how they apply. Then a practical way of meeting the requirements can be established.

Design and Development Processes

Planning

The processes involving significant design or development first need to be identified, in particular taking account of situations where:

- The organization has more than one application of design and development requirements—for example, both development of new services and development of a particular service to meet customer-specific needs

- The differentiation of service development and service provision is not obvious—for example, when both are carried out at the customer interface

Second, design and development activities need to be broken down into manageable stages. Stages often are defined around major verification and validation milestones. The output of one stage may be used as an input to a subsequent stage or stages.

In simple service development, all activities may be managed as a single stage. On the other hand, complex services such as engineering design may have a number of major stages (for example, conceptual design and detailed design milestones) each having a number of minor stages, or design packages, running parallel or sequentially. Both major and minor stages may have unique responsibility, authority, and resourcing considerations.

Judging the level of detail is a practical issue in planning service design and development. A service such as financial planning advice may range from straightforward advisory assistance customized to individuals to designing financial programs to meet complex institutional requirements. A generic design plan may be used to define minimum requirements for responsibilities and authorities, for review, and for verification points. For example, a one-page form may be sufficient to prompt personnel to consider each of these aspects. The form alone may be sufficient for simple services, while for complex situations it may provide the framework for a service-specific design plan.

Inputs

ISO 9001:2000 outlines the design and development inputs that are to be defined and documented. In the case of services, some functional requirements may be developed and defined in conjunction with customers over the period of service development and provision. It is not the intention of ISO 9001 to stifle creativity and responsiveness to customers. The system for dealing with customer-defined inputs needs to be flexible for both staff and customers. However, where customer inputs are added progressively, particular attention must be paid to resolving incomplete, ambiguous, or conflicting requirements.

Outputs

Design and development outputs need to be recorded in a manner that enables verification against the relevant inputs. At least part of the documentation of service design and development outputs may be provided to the customer for its use or reference. The needs of the customer may thus determine the style of documentation, as well as the need for verification against inputs.

Approval of design and development outputs prior to release sometimes presents difficulties, or appears to present difficulties, in the service environment. Services may be designed in conjunction with customers to meet their individual needs. However, dealing with this situation is generally a matter of process planning so that, where necessary, authority to release can be controlled at the point of delivery.

Review

The concept of design or development review as described in ISO 9001 clause 7.3.4 is straightforward. However, the complexity of review varies according to the complexity of the design or development process. It is important that the need for review is not turned into a bureaucratic overlay of activities that do not add value to the process.

Two different levels of review are illustrated in the boxed example, developing a healthcare treatment plan.

Example 1: Healthcare Treatment Plan—Sole Practitioner

A sole medical practitioner develops a treatment plan for a patient. The situation is one where the medical practitioner is competent to decide, plan, and approve treatment herself. She does not think of it as "development" because it is an everyday process. However, there are inputs (medical history, symptoms, examination findings, test results) and outputs (a plan for therapy of the condition). She conducts a self-review of the plan, if necessary consulting references such as information on possible drug interactions that could affect the outcome.

Example 2: Healthcare Treatment Plan—Hospital Admission

A patient is admitted to the hospital with an acute illness. There is an integrated service team comprising doctors, nurses, a physiotherapist, a dietitian, and a pharmacist. Immediate action is taken in accordance with standard practice. Each discipline within the team develops and records its treatment plans, consulting with others where appropriate. Regular review meetings are held where treatment plans for patients under the team are discussed and coordinated. Special review meetings are arranged for cases where there are particularly difficult management issues or where additional expertise is called for. Records of review meetings are kept and agreed-upon actions are monitored.

It is important that representatives of the different functions involved in the design or development stage or stages under review can participate in the review activity. Otherwise, important relationships between different aspects of the service can be overlooked.

Verification

Verification refers to actions to ensure that design and development outputs meet the requirements of design and development inputs. This generally involves, at a minimum, a systematic checking activity comparing records of outputs with records of inputs, carried out at the end of design and development stages. It depends on both the inputs and outputs of the particular stage being complete and unambiguous.

Verification also can involve activities such as deriving outputs by a different method—for example, alternative engineering calculations or comparing with known similar designs, to check if the same or similar result is obtained. There may need to be a trial of the service output in order to check consistency with input requirements.

The number of verification steps often depends on the way in which design and development is broken down in the planning stage. There also may be several verification activities at one stage, carried out by people with different expertise examining different parts of the particular design or development output. In that case, care must be taken to avoid conflicting changes as a result of the verification.

Verification may be needed at points other than those defined at the initial planning stage. Design and development planning needs to be under continual review to ensure that all aspects of verification are covered at appropriate times in the process.

Verification needs to be carried out by appropriately qualified personnel. Self-verification of work can be acceptable—independence is not a requirement of ISO 9001:2000. Where an independent person or persons carry out the verification, they should be at least as well qualified as those that carried out the design or development activity. Judgment on the level of independence and expertise required for verification should be based on the risk involved.

Customers of the service (or their customers or agents) may be involved in verification activities. This may occur at agreed-to points of consultation or approval, or through the verification point also being the point of service delivery. It is important to recognize that involvement of the customer does not relieve the organization of the responsibility to verify that the output meets input requirements.

ISO 9001:1994 requires that the results of verification and any required actions are recorded. This often can be carried out by simple methods such as annotating design and development documents and signaling completion by signing and dating. Separate verification records are, however, sometimes appropriate, particularly where they are used for communication of the required changes or where they are logged for data collection purposes.

Validation

Validation aims to ensure that the service as developed is capable of meeting its intended application. ISO 9001:2000 requires validation to be completed prior to service delivery wherever practicable.

For some services, validation may not be practicable at the time of delivery of the service, while for others validation can only be partial. Some services can, however, be validated at the completion of development. The boxed examples illustrate different situations.

Example 1: Full Validation

Full validation can be performed where the service is standardized, even though there may be variations in the outcome of its application. For example, the service of issuing a driver's license can be fully developed to comply with statutory and regulatory requirements, plus the practical requirements of driver testing. The method can be tested adequately to prove its effectiveness. This does not mean that all who pass such testing are necessarily competent drivers, but it does mean that they have passed the prerequisites for licensing.

Example 2: Partial Validation by Pilot Testing

A marketing organization prepares advertising material for a client. It may be practical for the organization to carry out a test of the material—for example, using a focus group to represent the target audience. If the organization does not intend some form of partial validation of the material, it should clarify that prior to finalizing its agreement with the client.

Example 3: Partial Validation by Simulation

Some services can be simulated, either physically or by computer modeling. This can be particularly valuable where the implementation of the service will be associated with the development of physical facilities that will be costly to modify.

Example 4: Partial Validation by Review

Where the service cannot be tested prior to delivery, it may be appropriate to carry out a structured review against user needs. This may be done by a number of methods, such as involvement of people representing users, using a panel with expertise in judging application to intended users, or using a review method that stimulates consideration of users. While user needs always should be considered as well as specified requirements, those closely involved in design and development activities often are focused on defined requirements. Group review is common practice in review of planned medical treatments, which cannot be full; validated except by application to the individual patient. Approval of new tertiary educational courses commonly involves a panel of experienced people other than those who developed the intended course.

Control of Change

Changes implemented in the course of design and development need to be identified and recorded. The changes need to be reviewed, verified, and validated as appropriate to the scope and stage of the change. Customer approval may be required as well as approval within the development team. Changes and their approval need to be recorded.

Changes introduced after commencement of service design and development easily can introduce unintended effects. Changes to one part of a service may have an impact on another part. Methods for change control therefore need to ensure that such impacts are detected and resolved.

Lack of communication of change is also a major problem, especially where the requirements for a service are defined progressively with a customer. The person with prime responsibility for communication with the customer's representative needs to have a process established for distribution of change information.

Where the number of changes is small, recording of design and development changes does not need to be complex. In a complex project where there may be tens or hundreds of changes, a more formal method is needed. Change control forms may be used to record the nature of the change, the reason for it, the result of the change, the planned actions, and the relevant approvals required. A table or spreadsheet can be set up as a change register to assist in monitoring completion of required approvals and actions.

WHAT IS DIFFERENT FROM THE 1994 EDITION?

The most significant change from the 1994 version is that requirements of ISO 9001:2000 clause 7.3 need to be applied unless design and development processes are either not carried out or do not affect the ability to meet customer requirements. In addition, the general requirements for process management in clause 7.1 apply to management of design and development processes.

The wording of requirements is framed in a more generic fashion than in the 1994 version so as to take account of the wide range of applications envisaged. The requirements are not lessened, but they are more flexible.

The requirement for documented procedures in ISO 9001:2000 is covered in clause 4.2.1 rather than in the design control clauses of the 1994 version. Thus the need for documentation of design and development processes must be determined by the organization itself. This determination should take account of factors such as the complexity of the processes and the skills of the staff carrying out the work. The flexibility that this permits is helpful for the service sector, where minor development (for example, customizing a service to meet individual requirements) is commonly carried out as an activity in service provision.

Review, verification, and validation of design and development are somewhat more clearly described in ISO 9001:2000 than in the 1994 version, but again the differences are in wording rather than actual requirements.

Clause 7.3.7 is more explicit about control of changes than clause 4.4.9 in the 1994 version. It requires the organization to determine the effect of changes, listing potential interactions and effects. This is an expansion of this important area rather than a change to the intent of the standard.

BEYOND ISO 9001 COMPLIANCE

Of all the processes involved in service realization, design and development processes can potentially bring the most benefit from going beyond compliance with ISO 9001. For many organizations, design and development processes offer opportunities to establish closer communication with customers and other interested parties, achieve innovative solutions, avoid future risks, reduce the costs of service provision, and improve both customer and staff satisfaction.

The ways in which such benefits can be achieved will depend to some extent on the scope of design and development, the organization's role in using the output of the process, and the relationship to future users of the service. The following are some of the points that may add value to design and development activities.

Emphasis on Planning

ISO 9004:2000 outlines a planned approach to design and development. As with other processes involved in service provision, the effectiveness of planning has an enormous impact on achieving a successful outcome. Those involved in design and development often are eager to solve problems and develop innovative solutions. They may not welcome spending time on defining objectives, determining key stages and review activities, planning verification and validation, ensuring adequate resources, and establishing communication paths. However, experience repeatedly has shown the benefit of a disciplined approach to planning, not only in avoiding mistakes and wasted work, but in providing a basis for effective communication and work satisfaction.

Preservation of Creativity

One of the benefits of good planning is the preservation of creativity. Understanding design and development objectives and setting out the key constraints allow opportunities for innovation to be identified. Key stages and review points can be planned so that there is room for creative thinking.

Some professionals, such as architects, are particularly conscious of the need for preservation of creative thinking in quality management systems. They rightly fear that a narrowly conceived approach to compliance with ISO 9001 will restrict their service to their clients. However, it is not compliance with ISO 9001 that is the threat. The danger is a focus on setting up the controls (such as review and verification steps) without having first understood the "big picture" of customer needs and the opportunities for lateral thinking.

A Risk Focus

ISO 9004:2000 highlights the importance of identifying and mitigating risk within the design and development process. It gives examples of risk assessment tools that may be used. Risks to all stakeholders need to be considered—risks to the customer, the user of the service, and other parties who may be affected by it, as well as to the organization providing the service. Risks to be considered may include environmental and health, and safety in employment.

In the case of design and development of services, risk needs to be considered at the interface with the customer as well as from the service product itself. One example is in the development of educational services, where some risks at the teacher–pupil interface are distinct from the risks of success or failure of the educational service.

A Team Approach

A strong team approach is important for two main reasons: first, because of the importance of communication across design and development interfaces, and second, because of the potential it presents for involvement of wider stakeholder interests.

There are several mechanisms for involving stakeholders in design and development of services. In some cases a project partnering structure may be used to establish participation of different parties across normal contractual or purchasing boundaries under some form of agreed-upon charter. In other cases—for example, in community health service organizations—stakeholder groups are formed to fulfill a variety of advisory and review functions, including design and development.

Use of Communication Technologies

The importance of both communication and change control means that intranet and Internet technologies can be very powerful in design and development. Access-protected project Internet sites have been used very successfully in engineering design and could be useful in many complex projects. Such sites can accommodate appropriate levels of access by the design and development team or teams, customer personnel, and future users of the results of the service. A wide range of information can be made available, including development plans, project status reports, design and development inputs and outputs, and financial control data. Document distribution and changes can be readily controlled.

Widening the Scope of Application

ISO 9001:2000 mandates the application of design and development requirements to the product. Their application to service provision processes is required only if such processes form part of the product. However, widening the scope of application to include service provision processes has great potential to improve their efficiency. The potential for improvement may be particularly important in the introduction of new services, where customer confidence can be crucially at risk.

Chapter 23

Purchasing

R. Dan Reid
General Motors Corporation, Detroit, Michigan

PURCHASING ROLE AND ORGANIZATION

The primary tasks of the purchasing function are to select sources and establish prices. The purchasing function must address both direct product and indirect materials. Typically *direct product* is material that the organization incorporates directly into its product. Both direct and indirect purchased materials are critical to the success of the organization. *Indirect material* covers a wide range of items and varies by industry. Some examples of indirect material are office furniture and supplies, tooling used to fabricate materials for incorporation into the product, facility equipment, and material-handling equipment such as fork trucks.

The organization of the purchasing function is critical in order to optimize the selection of sources and the establishment of prices. Organizations should "leverage" volumes and purchase opportunities to their advantage. To accomplish this, organizations typically buy by commodity, or product type. Purchasing can be set up within broad categories such as chemical, electrical, and metallic and/or more specifically by component name such as doors, switches, lubricants, and so on. To fulfill the purpose of the organization in the most effective and efficient manner (ISO 9004:2000 clause 0.1), the purchasing function should be organized, or at a minimum managed, centrally to take advantage of economies of scale—for example, combining volumes on like-purchased product or consolidating similar-purchased products on one request for quote.

Many organizations now use a project management approach for new product development and introduction. Less emphasis is placed on the organizational chart, and more emphasis is placed on "how work is done" as a process through the organization. Classic pyramid organizational structures are more often being replaced with matrix organizations, wherein an employee reports to more than one supervisor to ensure that all the organizational objectives are met.

GENERAL REQUIREMENTS PERTAINING TO PURCHASING

Note that the general requirements in ISO 9001:2000 apply to the whole organization, including the purchasing function. In ISO 9001:2000, clause 4.1 requires the organization to do the following:

- Identify the needed processes
- Determine how those processes interact
- Determine criteria and methods required to effectively operate and control the processes
- Ensure the availability of necessary information for process operation and monitoring
- Review and analyze the processes and then implement necessary action to achieve planned results and cause continual improvement

These general requirements as they apply to purchasing are discussed in more detail later in the chapter.

ISO 9004:2000 clause 4.1 adds that success should result from implementing a system that is designed to continually improve performance by addressing the needs of all interested parties. ISO 9000:2000 (clause 3.3.7) includes both employees and suppliers as examples under the definition of "interested party." ISO 9000:2000 (clauses 3.3.5 and 3.3.6) further indicates that customers and suppliers can be both internal and external to the organization. The purchasing function is a key internal supplier to the organization. Operations related to production and service provision (ISO 9001:2000 clause 7.5) are the primary customers of the purchasing function.

PLANNING

The process approach (see ISO 9001:2000 clause 0.2) to quality management has been previously discussed in chapter 2. One of the more common models is the plan–do–check–act (PDCA) cycle, also known as the Deming cycle. ISO 9001:2000 Figure 1 incorporates the concept from that model. The PDCA model is particularly relevant to the purchasing process.

Planning is of particular importance to the purchasing function. The organization's ability to positively influence both cost and quality is much greater earlier in the process. The carpenter's principle "measure twice, cut once" rings true for most organizations. For this reason, purchasing should be involved in the product realization process as early as possible. Some purchasing items have long lead times in relation to the organization's product realization cycle.

Purchased materials must be received by the organization in time to incorporate them into the product. Failure typically has high costs. These can include lost or dissatisfied customers, interruption of internal operations, and premium freight costs to expedite the purchased material. For some industries, downtime can cost hundreds to thousands of dollars per minute. In healthcare, lack of critical supplies can produce an unexpected or undesired result, even death. Thus significant efforts are undertaken by organizations to ensure the timely receipt of purchased materials.

For some industries—for example, computer and telecommunications—being "fast to market" is essential to survival. That means product development cycles are short. Carefully planning and executing the purchasing function becomes more critical as the lead time to market becomes shorter.

The guidance in ISO 9004:2000 clause 5.4.2 calls for quality planning to define the processes needed to meet the organization's quality requirements and objectives. The following are among the primary quality planning inputs:

- Customer and interested party needs and expectations
- Product and process performance
- Lessons learned
- Risk assessment (see ISO 9004:2000 clause 7.3.1)

The lessons learned should be documented for organizational memory. Experience with suppliers, good or bad, should be recorded for use going forward. Suppliers vary in their ability to meet specified requirements, and individual supplier performance is likely to vary over time in regard to the same purchased product. The quality of the purchased product has a direct impact on the quality of the organization's product.

Suppliers vary for a number of reasons, including leadership, management, and/or workforce competency; quality of tooling, machinery, and/or equipment; design tools used (for example, computer-aided design [CAD]/computer-aided engineering [CAE] systems); and quality of the design and implementation of the quality management system. Any specific supplier can have sporadic problems or experience variation that can lead to chronic quality problems. This can occur when the supplier's sales volume goes significantly up or down and the quality management system is not revised accordingly to accomodate the change.

Risk management is a fundamental need of all organizations; thus risk assessment and mitigation is included in the primary inputs of quality planning in ISO 9004:2000. Appropriate tools and models are available and should be considered for use at the relevant stages of product realization (ISO 9004:2000 clause 7). Risk related to purchased product is present at several levels: the supplier, the supplier's process, and the purchased product itself.

At the supplier level, a number of trends need to be considered in risk assessment. There has been a significant increase in company mergers, takeovers, and joint ventures in the last decade. The purchasing function should initiate efforts to understand the ownership and interested stakeholders of the organization's potential and current suppliers. There are various ways to determine that information (for example, supplier interviews, Dun and Bradstreet records).

Another trend of significant customer concern is the increase in the number of suppliers going out of business due to bankruptcy. When that occurs, a number of adverse consequences can ensue, including these:

- Purchased product cost increases (for example, short-term "spot buys," premium freight, new tooling where existing tooling was not properly maintained or is not compatible with the new supplier's process).

- Organizational costs increase (for example, there are higher legal fees; more buyers, more material schedulers, more operations personnel, more accounts payable personnel and more receivable clerks, supplier quality resources required to find alternate suppliers; costs of relocation of any customer-owned tooling; costs of revalidation of purchased product in a new production environment).

Early identification of financially troubled suppliers should be considered as a purchasing objective. That can be difficult to do, but there are several occurrences that should be monitored: (a) increase or trend in past-due deliveries, (b) increase or trend in premium transportation charges due to supplier fault, (c) supplier requests for change in purchase order (PO) terms and conditions affecting timing of payment of material, and (d) urgent supplier requests for price increases.

ADVANCED PRODUCT QUALITY PLANNING

Given the critical importance of up-front quality planning, organizations should use a disciplined approach to advanced product quality planning. Chrysler, Ford, and General Motors have used such a process with great success since 1994, when the manual *Advanced Product Quality Planning (APQP) and Control Plan* was published. That manual provides a generic template for planning and executing new products in alignment with the customer new launch programs. Guidance is provided in the following areas: planning and defining the program, product design and development, process design and development, product and process validation, feedback, assessment, corrective action, control plan methodology, product quality planning checklists, and analytical techniques. One of the more beneficial features of this work is the checklists. Checklists are one form of mistake-proofing. The APQP manual provides checklists that should be used by automotive suppliers to customers when planning or completing the following: failure mode and effects analysis (FMEA) forms; new production, tooling, or test equipment; new or revised products, processes, or floor plans; flowcharts; and control plans. The APQP requirements have become mandatory in much of the automotive industry, and for many automotive suppliers, the APQP manual must be rigorously applied. On the other hand, the APQP concepts can be applied in most industries. APQP provides a benefit by ensuring that specified and needed activities are performed in a multidisciplinary manner at appropriate stages of the product realization, starting very early in the process. It also provides tools (for example, checklists) to use. Thus APQP provides a how-to for addressing ISO 9001 and 9004:2000 clause 7.3, "Design and development."

In many hardware industries, control plan forms have been used to aid in the manufacture of quality products to customer requirements. Control plans can document the methods used to minimize product and process variation. They are not meant to replace work instructions (see ISO 9001:2000 clause 7.5.1[b]). They can be used in a wide range of processes and technologies. Control plans document the controls specified for all the critical product and process characteristics (see ISO 9001:2000 clauses 7.2.1, 7.3.3, 7.5.1, and 8.2.4 and ISO 9004:2000 clauses 5.2.2, 7.1.3.3, 7.3.2[c], and 8.2.3). When used, they should be a "living document"—that is, they should be revised and updated over time as appropriate. They also should be linked at the characteristic level to the design record, the FMEAs, and the work instructions so that these documents function as a system for product and process quality assurance. As in the development of other documents (for example, FMEAs), control plans are most effective when completed by multiple functions in the organization.

FMEAs also have been used by a number of organizations in various hardware sectors since the 1960s. An FMEA documents activities intended to identify and evaluate the potential failure of a product or process, the effect such a failure may have, and actions to eliminate or reduce the risk of the failure occurring. FMEAs are one method of risk assessment and mitigation (see ISO 9004:2000 clauses 5.4.2 and 7.3.1). They should also be "living" documents and efforts should be planned and implemented to further reduce the potential for failure after the initial calculation of risk.

PURCHASING AND DOCUMENT CONTROL

Control of documents is discussed in ISO 9001:2000 clause 4.2.3 and in ISO 9004:2000 clause 4.2. The ISO 9001 requirement for document control has been reported in a number of surveys as one of the more troublesome requirements for organizations seeking third-party certification to ISO 9000. Clearly, internal documents such as purchasing policies and procedures, engineering releases, or change authorizations must be controlled documents. Simply stated, the purpose of document control is to ensure that everyone who "needs to know" is informed, and those who do not need to know are excluded. An ISO 9000–compliant system also prevents the unauthorized use of obsolete documents. Methods to implement document control can be simple, but to be effective any method used must be implemented and maintained with organizational discipline and rigor. ISO 9001:2000 clause 7.4.2 refers to purchasing documents and lists their requirements. Such documents include the PO, the request for quotation (RFQ), engineered drawings or math data files, and engineering specifications. These should all be controlled documents. Some organizations use PO acknowledgments, which they require suppliers to return to verify their receipt of the PO.

This is another area where the use of electronic media is very helpful. As more documentation is available in electronic format, the master copy can be released as a "read-only" file, such as a PDF file, and hard-copy versions can be designated as "uncontrolled copies" in order to maintain control. Further, the same type of control can be applied to electronic commerce with suppliers. As organizations migrate to use of electronic media, it is important to implement appropriate data security measures such as controlled access to sensitive files and automatic "log-off" provisions for inactive personal computers.

PURCHASING AND PRODUCT REALIZATION

The purchasing process is one of the product realization processes discussed in ISO 9001:2000 clause 7.1. That clause requires the organization to have the following as appropriate:

- Quality objectives
- Processes, process documentation
- Resources, including product-specific facilities
- Activities for verification and validation with acceptance criteria
- Records necessary to document product and process conformity

The organization should develop a high-level plan for new product introduction that denotes when necessary activities need to be completed in order to meet required objectives (ISO 9001:2000 clause 5.4.1) including cost and timing. Purchasing activities must be part of this plan. In most hardware and software organizations, purchasing should develop a sourcing plan to support new product introduction. Based on past experience, long-lead-time and high-risk items (see ISO 9004:2000 clause 7.3.1) should be identified for early sourcing. Tooling commitments and potential supplier evaluations should be completed early enough in the product realization process to support the new product/program timing requirements.

As with the previous version of the ISO 9000 family (ISO 9000:2000 clause 2.7.5), the use of quality plans remains an option. ISO 9001:2000 clause 7.1 does obligate the organization to use some form of appropriate documentation for product realization.

The ISO 9000 family has consistently used the term *purchasing documents* in its various editions. The primary purchasing documents are the PO and the RFQ. Most organizations have developed standard PO contracts and a number of standard or conditional PO terms and conditions for their buyers to use in defining the organization's requirements. With the trend toward electronic commerce (e-commerce), the PO, RFQ, and the various clauses can be set up in electronic files and supporting databases that allow the buyer flexibility to choose the appropriate clauses to add to the purchasing documents. When those are used with math data files (discussed subsequently) and electronic specifications, the speed of doing business is dramatically increased as suppliers get the information faster and have it in a format that they can distribute internally much faster for review and response to the customer.

In hardware sectors, product requirements have traditionally been defined, documented, and communicated in the form of engineered drawings, or blueprints. In the last decade, some organizations have migrated to the use of math data files generated by CAD or CAE programs to replace or supplement those drawings. The use of math data provides advantages such as (1) reduced cycle time, as tooling to fabricate parts can be made by digitally communicating information from the math data file directly to tool fabrication machines, and (2) quality, by allowing for (a) computer simulation or modeling for such things as optimization and validation of part designs or facility designs prior to making commitments (for example, fabricating tooling) and (b) better control for fabricating tooling to tighter tolerances.

Additional purchasing requirements can be defined, documented, and communicated in supplemental specifications. These specifications can be used to contain a number of additional requirements that can then be referenced as requirements on the drawing or math data files. Those can include requirements for items such as painting, plating, inspection or test, and approved supplier lists.

Clause 7.1 also refers to verification and validation activities. Many organizations use a product qualification process to verify that purchased product meets specified requirements. The military and aerospace industries use a "first article" inspection process. This process requires the supplier to submit a number of production part "samples" to the customer, who then inspects them for conformity to product requirements. Where the purchased product has a large number of part characteristics, the customer may choose to verify conformance of the critical or key product characteristics only.

In the automotive industry, Chrysler, Ford, and General Motors developed the production part approval process (PPAP) in 1990 as a common supplier requirement for part qualification. This process adds a number of other requirements for documentation to provide the customer with confidence that the purchased product conforms to the specified requirements. PPAP calls for short-term statistical studies to be completed to determine the process potential for supplying conforming product going forward. Other industry sectors (for example, heavy truck and office furniture) have adopted most or all of the PPAP requirements for their suppliers as well.

PURCHASING AND RESOURCE MANAGEMENT

ISO 9004:2000 clause 6.6 lists a number of ways that organizations can work with suppliers and partners for mutual benefit. Among these are:

- Supplier rationalization or optimization
- Establishing appropriate communications contacts at both the supplier and the organization
- Monitoring supplier quality
- Encouraging suppliers to implement continual improvement activities
- Partnering with suppliers in the design or development phase (or both) to ensure eventual product quality and manufacturability
- Providing recognition or rewarding efforts for supplier/partner achievements

A unique type of partnership that has grown in popularity in the last decade is cooperation between competing customers in noncompetitive areas for the mutual benefit of the supply chain. The development of QS-9000 and other ISO 9001–related sector-specific documents are examples of this. Several primary customers in the aerospace industry several years ago also developed a common second-party supplier assessment process to share data and avoid redundant audits of common suppliers. The elements of their process included a common survey instrument, common auditor training, and a shared database for information storage and retrieval. Thus when one customer involved in the process conducted a quality audit of a supplier, that information could be used by all the other customer organizations. DaimlerChrysler, Ford, and General Motors, at the time of this writing, announced a new, unprecedented alliance to provide the world's largest virtual marketplace—a new Internet company that is to be a business-to-business integrated supplier exchange. This enables suppliers to these companies to use one system for conducting e-commerce with all three. The new "marketplace" is to be open to other auto manufacturers around the world also. Services to be provided include catalog purchases, bidding and price quotes, and online sourcing and auctions. Other existing supplier chain management functions such as capacity planning, demand forecasting, production planning, payment, and logistics will continue and may be expanded. That follows agreement by the same companies to use a common year-2000 supplier remediation process, which also was used by other automotive manufacturers worldwide. It is likely that such cooperative ventures will continue where there is mutual benefit and even include joint activities with some government agencies going forward.

With rising pressure on cost control in various sectors, management of the supply chain is critical. Supplier rationalization, or using the optimum number of suppliers, discussed later, is only one element of this. Some organizations have found that by working with their suppliers to conduct a "value-added" analysis of the supply chain for a given purchased product, they have achieved tremendous savings and improved time to market. In such an exercise, an analysis is conducted of purchased components from the time that the raw materials are dug from the ground or fabricated until the materials are eventually incorporated into the customer's product. Analysis is conducted at each step of the supply chain to determine (1) how long the material stays at each stage; (2) what percent of that time is used "adding value" to the component or material; (3) the transportation, handling, and/or logistics costs associated with the material movement required; and (4) the cost of adding value at each stage. In these exercises, time that components or material spend in inventory or in transit is considered "non-value-added," and is potential for reduction or elimination from the process. By reviewing options, a supplier may find that by changing subcontractors at the tier-two or tier-three level of the supply chain, it can avoid significant cost or lead time, benefits that can be shared with the customer to improve customer satisfaction.

Communicating effectively within and across organizations always has been difficult. One trend in working with suppliers is the establishing of communications contacts between the customer and supplier. Such contacts typically have defined communications responsibility as part of the organization's quality management system. This is one method of controlling the purchasing processes, and some form of control is required by ISO 9001. In the course of a contract relationship, communication of some information is critical—for example, change in (a) scheduling information, (b) PO terms and conditions, and (c) contact names. When points of contact can be established and used to communicate, the customer and supplier can be assured that all those that "need to know" are informed. The larger and more complex the organization becomes, the harder it is to effectively communicate, and the more it will need some plan to make that happen.

Partnering with suppliers in the product and process design and development phases has proven to be a successful initiative for many organizations.

Beginning with its L/H car years ago, Chrysler Corporation began to work closely with suppliers "up front," and its success in partnering with suppliers has been well documented since. Involving suppliers in the design and development phases provides the organization with information that allows the engineer to design to the supplier's manufacturing strengths and tolerances, as well as to the organization's manufacturability and assembly of the purchased product. Computer-aided tools such as design for manufacturability and design for assembly have been used for a number of years to achieve significant cost and quality improvements (for example, fewer components needed for a product and "snap fit" designs to replace fasteners).

Providing recognition to suppliers for significant achievement is another recommendation of clause 7.4.1. There are many ways to provide such recognition. An organization can design levels of recognition for increasing levels of accomplishment. A traditional form of supplier recognition is to award the supplier a flag and/or plaque suitable for display as a result of reaching a specified level with its quality system. A growing trend is to provide a similar award for environmental system maturity and employee safety record. Letters of appreciation or recognition from the customer CEO or quality director are another common form of recognition. Some of the larger organizations have published top suppliers in major daily newspapers or held elaborate regional or international "supplier of the year" conferences. The Internet is an emerging tool for providing recognition via the customer home page as well.

Coupled with supplier recognition, some organizations have implemented a shared risk/reward program with suppliers. This has evolved to where a supplier and customer agree up front on the product and/or process quality metrics and specified levels of reward, typically financial, for various levels of achievement toward quality targets (for example, parts per million [ppm], warranty returns). Such agreements can be used to provide incentive to suppliers to improve the system, product, and process quality.

MONITORING AND MEASURING PURCHASING

The "check" step in the PDCA cycle is also critical to the purchasing function. ISO 9001:2000 addresses this in detail in clause 8, "Measurement, analysis, and improvement." Monitoring of supplier performance is critical. Metrics of supplier performance should cover quality, service, and price. Supplier technology metrics should be included where innovation is an organizational objective.

Examples of quality metrics are customer complaints, product returns, warranty claims, ppm calculations, defects per unit, and problems per 100 or per 1000. Other measures are specific to a given sector, such as the number of medical errors resulting in accidental death in the healthcare sector. There are also a number of trade associations and independent consumer research organizations—for example, J. D. Power—that provide information on industry sectors, companies, and/or products that can be used as externally generated metrics for the organization. The organization is obligated to determine the appropriate quality metrics by ISO 9001:2000 clauses 8.1 and 8.2.4. It is certainly appropriate that supplier quality metrics be included. The organization has freedom in determining what those measures should be.

Examples of service metrics are percent of on-time delivery, incidents of premium freight required, cost of premium freight shipments, percent of lead time, or cycle time reduction. The organization is obligated to determine the appropriate supplier delivery metrics by ISO 9001:2000 clauses 8.1 and 8.2.3, which include purchasing.

Examples of cost metrics are number of price increases requested, number of increases granted, number of price decreases submitted, number of cost reduction ideas submitted, number of cost reduction ideas implemented, and percent of price increase/decrease per year. Customers can recommend other measures—for example, salary expense per net revenue dollar, labor cost as a percent of net revenue—to service suppliers looking for advice for cost metrics to use internally. Cost-of-quality metrics, discussed earlier, also should be used by suppliers to help identify waste and opportunities for improvement, including cost reductions that can be shared with customers. These include the value of scrap, rework, returns, and warranty, as well as structural costs (for example, salaries of quality managers, lab, inspection, and test personnel and time spent on activities such as FMEA or control plan preparation).

Examples of supplier technology metrics are number of ideas submitted, number of ideas implemented, rate of increase of submission of new technology ideas, research and development spending as a percent of sales, and number of patents granted.

A common mistake some organizations make is to combine several supplier metrics into one number. That is usually an oversimplification. The organization will need to measure the suppliers in a number of areas as suggested above. Individual suppliers will have various strengths and weaknesses across the metrics, and the organization should use that information to optimize its sourcing in pursuit of organizational goals and objectives.

Recognizing the importance of the use of this type of metrics approach, Ford Motor Company has since 1996 required its suppliers to use the Ford QOS, or quality operating system, which is a disciplined approach to the use of standardized metrics developed by Ford. Ford also uses a 10-point supplier metric system to determine Q1 status of suppliers, which has been a requirement for doing business with Ford even prior to the adoption of QOS.

In ISO 9001:2000 clause 8.4 the organization is required to analyze data to provide information on suppliers. This emphasizes the importance of supplier information to the success of any organization. In sectors where ISO 9000 has not been widely used, this is an area of tremendous opportunity for improvement. In healthcare, for example, various accreditation body prescriptive criteria must be met, but specified requirements for the control of purchased product are less than is required by ISO 9001.

SPECIFIC ISO 9001:2000 REQUIREMENTS FOR PURCHASING

One of the key changes in this version of ISO 9000 is the terminology used to describe the supply chain (see ISO 9001:2000 clause 3). The previous version referred to the organization as the supplier, and the supplier as the subcontractor. This change was made to reflect the current usage by organizations.

ISO 9001:2000 clause 7.4 establishes the minimum requirements for the purchasing function of the fundamental quality system. There are three elements in this clause.

7.4.1   Purchasing Process

This clause requires the organization to control its purchasing processes to ensure conformity to requirements. The type and extent of control is to be dependent on the effect of the purchased product on subsequent processes of the organization. Suppliers are to be evaluated and selected based on their ability to supply product conforming to the organization (customer) requirements. The organization must specify criteria for supplier selection and define criteria for periodic supplier evaluation. Supplier evaluations, including any follow-up actions, must be a quality record and subject to control specified in clause 4.2.4.

7.4.2   Purchasing Information

This clause requires the organization to ensure the adequacy of purchasing documents that (must) describe the product to be purchased prior to release. Requirements to be specified in the documents include, as appropriate, quality system, product and/or process approval, or qualification requirements, and any requirements for procedures, equipment, or personnel as well.

7.4.3   Verification of Purchased Product

This clause requires that the organization verify the purchased product. When the organization or its customer wants to perform product verification at the supplier's facility, the organization must specify the planned arrangements in the purchasing documents, including the method of product release.

COMPARISON WITH ISO 9001:1994 PURCHASING— SPECIFIC REQUIREMENTS

In ISO 9001:1994, clause 4.6, "Purchasing" had four sections.

ISO 9001:1994, 4.6.1   General

Clause 4.6.1 required the organization to have documented procedures to ensure purchased product conformance. The requirement for documented procedures was removed from ISO 9001:2000, however the new clause 4 does require documentation to ensure the effective operation and control of processes, which includes purchasing. This documentation can be in the form of various types of documents—for example, a combination of documents including the quality manual (ISO 9001:2000 clause 4.2.2), procedures, and/or work instructions.

ISO 9001:1994, 4.6.2   Evaluation of Subcontractors

Clause 4.6.2 included three subclauses that required the organization to do the following:

(a) Evaluate and select suppliers based on their ability to meet contract requirements.

(b) Define the type and extent of control to be exercised over suppliers, and this was to be dependent on the type of product, the impact of the purchased product on the quality of the organization's product, and where applicable, information from supplier evaluations and/or records of past supplier capability and performance.

(c) Have records of acceptable suppliers.

ISO 9001:1994, 4.6.3   Purchasing Data

Clause 4.6.3 required the organization to clearly describe the product ordered. This could include, as applicable, product identification; any specifications, drawings, or other relevant technical data including requirements for approval or qualification of the product, procedures, process equipment, and personnel; and the quality system standard to be used.

This clause also required the organization to approve purchasing documents for adequacy prior to release.

ISO 9001:1994, 4.6.4   Verification of Purchased Product

Clause 4.6.4 had two subclauses:

- *Subclause 4.6.4.1.* When the organization wanted to verify purchased product at the supplier's facility, the organization had to specify in the purchasing documents the planned arrangements and the method of product release.

- *Subclause 4.6.4.2.* When specified in the contract, the organization's customer had to be allowed to verify the purchased product at both the supplier's and the organization's facilities. If applicable, this could not be used by the organization as evidence of effective control of supplier quality. Further, this could not relieve the organization of the ongoing responsibility to provide acceptable product to the customer, and it did not preclude customer rejection of future shipments of the product.

In the 1994 edition, ISO 9001 clause 4.6 referred to *quality audit reports,* whereas the new term used is *evaluations,* or *periodic evaluations.* When considered with the new ISO 9001 clause 8.4, it is clear that information on suppliers, and potential new suppliers, must be collected, monitored, and used by the organization, but supplier audits or assessments by the organization are not required. The requirement for supplier evaluations could be satisfied by use of second- or third-party supplier audits however. The new notion pertaining to the audits is that criteria for periodic evaluation must be defined. There was no ongoing aspect of audits or evaluations in the previous edition. The 2000 revision requirement to record the results of the evaluations and any follow-up actions is a replacement for the need for records of acceptable suppliers. There was a common misconception associated with this ISO 9001:1994 requirement in that there was not a requirement for an "acceptable subcontractor list," although certification bodies conducting an ISO 9001 audit frequently asked for that.

The requirement for definition of supplier selection criteria is a new requirement in ISO 9001:2000 clause 7.4.1. In the 1994 version, suppliers had only to be selected based on their ability to meet the organization's requirements.

There is also a new requirement in ISO 9001:2000 clause 7.4.2, which addresses purchasing information. There is a requirement for information in the purchasing documents for process approval or qualification where appropriate.

In summary, the changes in ISO 9001:2000 to the purchasing-specific element are of minimal impact to the organization and are very evolutionary in nature.

PURCHASING-SPECIFIC GUIDANCE IN ISO 9004:2000

ISO 9004:2000 clause 7.4.1 introduces the subject of total cost of purchased product. In the clause, purchasing processes are to consider performance, price, and delivery as part of total cost. Sourcing traditionally takes into account the piece or unit price, unique tooling cost if any, shipping, handling, and other delivery cost. Many organizations are now using supplier cost engineering (for example, cost-breakdown analysis) to better understand the purchased product cost elements. Suppliers bidding on a given request for quote may take very different approaches to building up their quoted price. By requesting the detail from suppliers on the cost elements that make up their price, the buyer will have better information to use in making the award decision. With the trend toward globalization, the currency used for the quote and the contract becomes an issue that should be carefully managed. Leveraging the currency exchange can provide an advantage for the organization, especially for large awards.

The organization should use a cost-of-quality program, where quality costs are tracked, at a minimum, for costs of poor quality—which typically consist of internal and external failure costs, such as scrap, warranty, or returns. More sophisticated programs should address costs of conformance, which include prevention and appraisal costs. Cost-of-quality programs have proven to be an effective way for organizations to translate the language of quality into the language of management—money! Another early discovery organizations make when implementing such a program is the enormous cost of poor quality as a percent of sales. Cost-of-quality metrics can be used to successfully drive continual improvement.

Among the other initiatives that the organization should consider in reducing cost is supplier rationalization. The number of suppliers to any organization drives cost to the organization in the purchasing, operations, financial, production control, and logistics areas. The greater the number of suppliers, the more organizational resources are needed to maintain the accounts (for example, buyers, material schedulers and expediters, plant receiving, accounts payable and receivables managers). Further, if a contract is awarded to a supplier on the basis of unit price alone, and the supplier has a poor history of quality or delivery performance, the cost to the organization can go up significantly through additional ongoing remedial actions required by purchasing, supplier quality, production control, and/or operations personnel.

Another trend to control cost that has emerged over the past decade or so is the use of long-term contracts. Traditionally, customers would use annual contracts, supplemented with spot-buy POs for infrequent purchases. These annual contracts then usually would be requoted annually prior to re-award, or "carryover." For organizations with a significant number of purchased products, that can be a labor-intensive exercise. It also provides no incentive to the supplier to reinvest in the business to make improvements in quality and cost. For purchased products with a long expected use, the use of long-term agreements can provide this incentive and avoid the internal costs of requoting the business one or more times. When a significant percentage of the organization's purchased product is on long-term contracts, the organization can better plan its use of resources going forward as future costs are now known, thus eliminating the risk of future cost increases and their potential impact on the organization.

That also indicates to the supplier that the organization is willing to partner with it over the long term—a codependency that also fosters loyalty to the customer. This often translates into the supplier's bringing new ideas and/or passing on cost savings first to these customers. Such long-term agreements can be for any mutually agreed upon time frame, typically three or more years. The ultimate example of the long-term contract is the "lifetime" contract, which awards the business for a specific component, service, or material for the life of the organization's use.

ISO 9004:2000 clause 7.4.1 also introduces the need for contract administration in the purchasing processes. Commodities on the metal market and precious metals often have material escalation/de-escalation clauses in the contract. The need for ongoing revisions to the contracts drives cost. Recently there has been a significant move toward the use of e-commerce using the Internet. Organizations and their suppliers are implementing use of e-mail communications and electronic files for purchase documents to a greater degree. This can provide savings in time to process the orders as well as handling and postage costs for shipping large packages of drawings, specifications, and purchase documents. Internet sites are now available for the purpose of facilitating customer-supplier commerce electronically. They can be used by organizations that have no Web site or electronic commerce capability.

Clause 7.4.1 also mentions ordering of material. Traditionally that was done by forecasting future demand and then placing a spot buy or releasing an order against an existing PO. An alternative method has emerged and is growing in use. Replenishing material based on a forecast of future demand has become known as a *push* method of inventory management. That is being replaced by many organizations with a *pull* system. A pull system is based on replacing material as it is consumed. To implement a pull system, the organization has to determine the optimal amount of inventory for each item to have on hand and the optimal time to reorder based on the supplier and delivery lead times. A pull system also uses a visually managed trigger mechanism to place the order, such as the notice that banks include in check orders to notify customers when it is time to reorder more checks. Pull systems optimize the cost of inventory and minimize out-of-stock conditions.

Clause 7.4.1 also indicates that purchasing processes should treat the issue of nonconforming purchased product. Ideally, the supplier should implement a quality management system that prevents the manufacture of nonconforming product. Where the quality management system is not capable of this, then it should at a minimum be set up to detect and contain the nonconforming material at the supplier's facility—preventing shipment of nonconforming purchased product to the customer. The failure of many ISO 9000–certified companies to do this has been a detriment to the third-party ISO 9000 process for a number of years. A customer quickly loses confidence in a supplier and a certification body when shipments of nonconforming product become chronic. The organization should use a disciplined problem-solving process incorporating the steps listed in ISO 9001:2000 clause 8.5.2 for corrective action and clause 8.5.3 for preventive action. The organization should allocate the necessary resources and establish appropriate metrics (see ISO 9001:2000 clause 8.1) to ensure conformity.

The foregoing discussions of clause 7.4.1 and clause 7.4.2 emphasize that purchasing processes should include supplier development. This is important for reducing and controlling costs and improving quality. Supplier development can include many initiatives, such as remedial actions for poor-quality deliveries, quality system assessments with corrective action and follow-up as appropriate, third-party quality system certification requirements, and training. Probably one of the more successful supplier development initiatives is the waste reduction workshops of the past 5 to 10 years. They have been called by various names such as *kaizen*, "PICOS," and value analysis/value engineering workshops, but they all focus on reducing waste. Typical metrics associated with such workshops include productivity improvements, reduction in floor space required, reduction in inventory, and reduction in lead time. These workshops point out that "waste" is present in every organization, but if equipped with the right tools and knowledge, the right team can make dramatic improvements in a very short amount of time. Workshops also can focus on product or process quality improvement, supply chain analysis, or advanced product quality planning.

Chapter 24

Production and Service Provision for Hardware

Elio DiMaggio
ENI SpA, Milan, Italy

Ennio Nicoloso
Sistemi Qualità, Roma, Italy

GENERAL

Any organization that has already adopted a quality management system (QMS) conforming to ISO 9001:1994 or ISO 9002:1994 will not encounter any particular difficulties in the transition to ISO 9001:2000 if the QMS has been implemented knowingly and correctly. This is even more valid if the organization has properly implemented the "process control" requirements in clause 4.9 of ISO 9001:1994, in addition to the other product-related requirements concerning control of customer-supplied product, inspection and test status, identification, traceability, handling, storage, packaging, preservation, and delivery dealt with in clauses 4.7, 4.8, 4.12, and 4.15.

ISO 9001:2000 has now incorporated all these activities under "production operations" in clause 7.5 to streamline the approach and clarify the interconnections between them. The resulting set of requirements for product operations appears now to be even less stringent than before, which is in keeping with the philosophy of the new standard to allow organizations to establish the scope of their QMS beyond the requirements of the standard to meet their specific needs.

7.1 PLANNING

The requirements in ISO 9001:2000 concerning production operations are not limited to the specific clause (7.5) of the new standard. General requirements in clause 7.1 concerning all realization processes are applicable also to production operations.

The planning of processes and activities represents the starting base for managing and controlling activities. All the other requirements in clause 7.5 are, in a sense, just details of the planning process.

"Establishing quality objectives and requirements for products" (quoting from clause 7.1 of the standard) means, in fact, determining the goals the production is aiming at, goals that shall be based on the quality policy of the organization and on the customer's and legal/regulatory requirements.

"Providing resources and facilities specific to the product" is a simple but clear message: production operation cannot be performed without the necessary means. Adequate facilities, support services, specific equipment, tools, measurement/monitoring devices, sufficiently competent persons, an adequate information system, intranet systems, and so on, are all resources that shall be available in a timely manner.

"Verification and validation activities" shall be planned integrally in the production planning (like any other operation), and the related criteria for acceptability shall be known in advance to evaluate conformity of processes and products. The need to document achieved results, another specific requirement under clause 7.1, calls for the timely preparation of adequate forms that will then be completed as the need arises. Doing so provides evidence of activities and records the related data. Preparing forms requires, by the way, a good knowledge of the involved processes and techniques and can take a lot of time. Planning is really the starting base for production activities.

7.5.1 CONTROL OF PRODUCTION AND SERVICE PROVISION

Let's look more closely at the specific requirements of production operations. Subclause 7.5.1, "Control of production and service provision," is the most important requirement, dealing with the core process for producing the hardware itself.

Information Specifying the Characteristics of the Hardware

To begin with, hardware production requires the availability of the necessary information. Design and development activities shall define the characteristics of the hardware to be produced, transforming the external requirements into internal requirements, adding the specific knowledge of the organization, and preparing the specifications for hardware realization processes.

Hardware production usually involves different and sometimes interrelated production lines and processes, progressive assembling of components, and inspections and testing. All these stages and activities need to be properly and timely planned and supported by adequate information. The production management is responsible for insisting on, where necessary, the availability of the required information.

In addition to the basic information, it can be useful to have other supplementary information. Such information may include a general understanding of the organization's objectives, an understanding of basic customer requirements, a clear understanding of market needs and expectations, knowledge of the destination of the hardware, and so on. This information can help to organize the work and solve unexpected problems. For example, in nuclear power plant construction, knowledge that a pipe conveys radioactive waste to a drain tank can help one avoid choosing a pipe route that creates liquid pockets outside the controlled area.

The communications system (see requirements in subclause 5.5.3) should be the tool for exchanging and providing all this information. Communications should involve all the relevant functions of the organization.

Correspondence with ISO 9001:1994

The requirement for "information on the characteristics of the product" is new and has no corresponding requirement in ISO 9001:1994.

Correspondence with ISO 9004:2000

No specific reference to information about product characteristics is made in ISO 9004:2000, which states only that the organization has the opportunity to review its communications system.

Availability of Work Instructions

Instructions, as related to the control of production and service provision, are all information, documentation, data, and the like presented in any suitable form to aid and direct the activities of the production processes. The instructions usually contain technical details about how to perform an activity. (They are sometimes called "procedures," a term that in the QMS is usually associated with the management aspects of an activity). Each organization shall identify the work instructions that are necessary for its activities and determine their type, presentation, and details.

According to ISO 9000:2000 any organization may establish its own appropriate work instructions. The general requirement associated with work instructions is included in clause 4.2, which states that the organization shall prepare the "documentation required to ensure effective operation and control of its processes." In selecting work instructions, the organization should not only consider this need to give adequate information about how to perform the activities, but also consider the opportunity to establish or improve its base of knowledge. This body of knowledge can be useful as well for training purposes, to minimize problems with the turnover or reallocation of personnel. The quantity of work instructions should be limited to cover real necessities, avoiding useless paperwork that may endanger the credibility of the QMS.

There are many ways to present instructions. Keeping in mind that instructions are there to "instruct" people, they should be presented in the way that best fits operators' needs and in a form appropriate for easy understanding. Instructions presented in the form of tables, drawings, sketches, posters, synopses, checklists, short sentences, or in any other simple way can often be more appreciated and helpful than long texts or descriptions. Verbal instructions can also be given—but remember, "verba volant scripta manent" (that is, "speeches fly, writings remain").

The content and presentation of instructions may vary significantly, depending on the level of consolidation of the activities, the type of production (mass production or other), the skill of the operators, the level of automation of the processes, regulatory requirements, and so on. Instructions for automatic production lines should help control the process and resolve anticipated situations, rather than give technical details about production.

Instructions are not to be limited to manufacturing activities. Inspection activities represent another important area where instructions can help personnel make objective evaluations. Evaluating acceptability of products (for example, castings) or of processes (for example, welds on electronic cards) may be well supported by instructions in the form of photographic or graphical references.

Instructions can also be useful for resolving predictable nonconformities (that should nevertheless be documented).

Instructions relevant to the maintenance of production equipment should be based on the manufacturer's handbooks, unless such handbooks give sufficient details to perform related maintenance.

Correspondence with ISO 9001:1994

ISO 9001:1994's only reference to "instructions" is made in a note to subclause 4.2.2 (which deals with the preparation and implementation of documented procedures). The note makes reference to "work instructions" as a possible support to the documented procedures when performing an activity (not necessarily limited to production operations). Clause 4.9 in ISO 9001:1994, however, makes reference to suitable "documented procedures" defining the manner of production, installation, and servicing, where the absence of such procedures could adversely affect quality. The change from "documented procedures" to "instructions" is in line with the guiding principle of the new standard, which in clause 7 deliberately makes no mention of "documented procedures," confining them to the management of the system. From a practical point of view the requirement for documented procedures in ISO 9001:1994 clause 4.9 can be considered equivalent to the requirement for work instructions mentioned in subclause 7.5.1 of the new standard, the main difference being that the latter do not necessarily have to be "documented."

Correspondence with ISO 9004:2000

No specific reference is made in ISO 9004:2000 to "instructions for production operations."

Use of Suitable Equipment

The suitability of equipment for its intended use is paramount. The requirements for the proper selection of production equipment (including the associated disposition and layout) are formally specified in clause 6, "Resource management," but their compliance usually involves both design and operation experts. Ways and results of this selection may vary depending on the kind of production dealt with by the organization.

Establishing a production line in a workshop requires an approach other than selecting equipment for installation activities or for inspections and testing activities. However, experience may well contribute in both cases to identification of possible improvements in the effectiveness of the equipment. The need for appropriate selection, correct use, and adequate maintenance of the equipment should be extended also to the associated facilities, services, utilities, and any other support equipment that can play an important role in the effectiveness of the production.

Specific reference is also made in subclause 7.5.1 (and in clause 7.6) to measuring and monitoring devices, which must be considered an integral part of the production equipment.

The requirement of this clause implies an adequate planning of maintenance activities. The organization should select for each type of its equipment the most appropriate approach to maintenance and maintenance planning (preventive, predictive, routine, breakdown, and so on) taking into account quality needs and other aspects of concern (safety, production reliability, equipment availability, budget, investments protection, and so on).

Maintaining the effectiveness of equipment is important not only for ensuring conformance to technical requirements. Unforeseen failures of equipment (especially equipment included in a production line) may have direct economic impact on the organization and also jeopardize compliance with customer requirements such as delivery terms or the amount of products made available. (This reference highlights that the QMS of the organization should comply not only with the technical requirements but also with the other contractual conditions agreed to with the customer).

Correspondence with ISO 9001:1994

Reference to the use and maintenance of equipment for production, installation, and assistance is included in ISO 9001:1994 clause 4.9, "Process control," which lists all the conditions required to ensure the control of processes. These conditions include, among others, two specific bulleted items, one on the use of appropriate equipment and the other on the maintenance of equipment. Organizations already implementing a QMS complying with ISO 9001:1994 will notice the new standard has no additional requirements in this specific area.

Availability and Use of Monitoring and Measurement Devices; Implementation of Monitoring Activities

This reference to the need for monitoring and measurement devices has been introduced in subclause 7.5.1, together with the implementation of monitoring activities, as part of the control activities over production and service operations.

This reference reminds the organization that monitoring and measurement activities should be regarded as an integral part of the "product provision processes." The "suitability" of the monitoring and measurement devices, or the process that leads to it, is dealt with in a specific clause of the new standard, clause 7.6, which includes requirements related to the identification, calibration, adjustment, protection, and use of such devices.

For production operations concerning hardware products, the "measurement" component usually prevails over the "monitoring" component, and the monitoring seldom uses devices requiring calibration, adjustments, protection, and the like, in their usual meaning.

Correspondence with ISO 9001:1994

In ISO 9001:1994 monitoring and measurement activities are dealt with in different clauses and have only limited contact points with similar activities in the new standard. "Monitoring and control of suitable process parameters and product characteristics" is a requirement included in ISO 9001:1994 clause 4.9, "Process control," whilst the "measurement" aspects are implicitly mentioned in clause 4.10, "Inspection and testing." Specific reference to inspection, measuring, and test equipment concerning its selection, calibration, control, and so on, is made in clause 4.11, "Control of measuring equipment" (corresponding to clause 7.6 of the new standard).

Correspondence with ISO 9004:2000

The corresponding clause of ISO 9004:2000 does not mention the specific need for monitoring and measurement devices.

Implementation of Processes for Release, Delivery, and Postdelivery Activities

The need to ensure compliance with the requirements, needs, and expectations of the customer implies not only the correct manufacture of products but also the control of subsequent activities or processes, from product release to customer assistance. Control of the hardware provision processes should therefore cover all these phases.

Release of the product (see subclause 8.2.4) shall be authorized by an identified responsible authority after verification that the requirements—those of the customer and those established by the organization itself—have been complied with. The requirement to identify the inspection authority responsible for the release of the product is also found in ISO 9001:1994 clause 4.10.5.

Delivery of the product includes, among other things, activities such as product identification, packaging, handling, protection, and transportation (at least to the extent required by the contractual agreements). Each product, of course, has its own needs. Certain products may require clear identification (to such a level as to ensure their traceability), and others may require special packaging (glass or fragile products, radioactive sources, palletized products, and so on) or special trucks for transportation (big alternator stators, chemical reactors, automobiles, and so forth). Others will need protection from physical conditions such as heat (deep-frozen foods), humidity (cement, electric/electronic components), vibration (sensitive instrumentation) and so on. Subclause 7.5.4 of the standard includes requirements for product preservation that may be applicable to delivery as well, in a more general sense.

Delivery of a product may have specific contractual implications not only in terms of technical and schedule requirements but also in terms of responsibilities. Establishing when the delivery has been completed and a product is handed over to the customer may involve great responsibilities, particularly when health, safety, environmental, or security implications exist.

Postdelivery is another term that can include multiple activities, such as maintenance and repair services, spare parts trade, customer assistance service, and so on. All durable products need forms of assistance that may or may not be included in the initial purchase contract. The "customer satisfaction" requirements introduced in this revision of the standard cannot be limited conceptually to the bare purchase contract. No customer likes to be forced to dispose of a defective durable product just because the manufacturer is not able or willing to restore its normal usability. These kinds of activities can be so important as to warrant a specific and autonomous QMS for the branch of the organization that deals with them. (This QMS should comply, of course, not only with the hint of the requirement of this clause but also with all applicable requirements of the standard).

Correspondence with ISO 9001:1994

In ISO 9001:2000 only subclause 7.5.1 makes reference to postdelivery activities, since they are anyhow part of the "realization processes" and therefore subject to the applicable general requirements of the standard. In ISO 9001:1994 the corresponding requirements were included in clause 4.19, "Servicing," one of the 20 elements of the standard. This clause requires an organization "to establish and maintain documented procedures for performing, verifying and reporting that the servicing meets the specified requirements." Apart from the adoption of the term *servicing* instead of the more comprehensive *postdelivery*, the only noticeable change is that the requirement for establishing and maintaining documented procedures has been formally dropped in ISO 9001:2000. In this case, as in many others, the need for procedures (documented or not) or work instructions shall be established by the organization itself in relation to its specific activities.

Correspondence with ISO 9004:2000

No significant mention is made in ISO 9004:2000 to release, delivery, and post-delivery activities. Subclause 7.5.1 suggests that to meet the needs and expectations of interested parties, consideration be given to, among other things, "post-realization activities," which certainly include postdelivery activities.

7.5.2 VALIDATION OF PROCESSES FOR PRODUCTION AND SERVICE PROVISION

Determine Processes Requiring Validation

Validation is defined as the "confirmation, through the provision of objective evidence that the requirements for a specific intended use or application have been fulfilled" (see ISO 9000:2000). It should be noted, however, that when applied to processes, validation does apply to a selected number of the processes adopted by the organization, and that the same clause (clause 7.5.2) specifies the criteria for selecting these processes.

From a practical point of view, processes requiring validation should be extended to include those processes that may have an impact on the quality of the product (in terms of performance, safety, environment, and so on) and that meet the following criteria:

- Processes that because of their intrinsic nature and/or for significant economic reasons do not allow performance of the measuring and monitoring activities required to verify compliance with relevant acceptability criteria

- Processes where measuring and monitoring activities are not sufficient to ensure correct performance of the product during subsequent use thereof

- Processes where possible nonconformities or malfunctioning can be evidenced only during usage by the customer or by the users

- Processes that can be performed only by personnel with special skills, experience, and qualifications (such as welding and nondestructive testing)

Validation is itself a process that aims at evidencing in advance, by recording, that the way a process is performed gives adequate confidence that the results will conform to established requirements. The acceptability criteria for the validation should be established taking into account the "ignorance" associated with the involved process.

Examples of processes that may require validation are listed in Table 24.1, but it should be stressed that the same type of process may or may not require validation depending on the importance of the process itself in ensuring quality of the product.

In selecting which processes require validation, the organization shall consider elements such as the following:

- Customer requirements
- Applicable legal and regulatory requirements
- The feasibility of the necessary measures and verifications
- The novelty of the process concerned
- How much is known about possible future effects of the process on the reliability of the hardware

The evaluations concerning the last three items listed, and the relevant decisions about whether a process should be validated, are a typical responsibility of the organization, which should adopt a balanced approach to avoid both useless validations and oversimplification of the problem.

Correspondence with ISO 9001:1994

Clause 4.9 in ISO 9001:1994 contains specific requirements concerning the "qualification" of processes (the so-called "special processes"). The criteria for the qualification of processes are essentially the same as those covered in subclause 7.5.5 of ISO 9001:2000 for the validation of processes.

Table 24.1 Examples of processes that may require validation.

Thermal treatments of metallic materials (steel, aluminum/magnesium/titanium alloys; quenching, annealing, normalizing, tempering, case hardening; etc.)

Welding processes (arc, TIG, MAG, electronic, laser, resistance, braze, wave, etc.)

Surfacing (flame, welding, cladding, plasma, etc.)

Manufacturing processes (concrete mixing and pouring, threading, cable crimping, electrical discharge machining, etc.)

Chemical/electrochemical surface treatments (surface preparations, silvering, goldening, etc.)

Composite materials (carbon fibers, glass fibers, casting of epoxy/phenolic resins, etc.)

Painting (surface preparation, primer, finishing, etc.)

Nondestructive testing (LP, MP, RX, UT, AE, etc.)

However, this difference in terminology should be noted: *qualification* (see ISO 8402:1994) refers only to a demonstration of conformance to "specified" requirements, while *validation* refers to "a specific intended use or application." This change is in line with the general aim of the standard to satisfy customers and users, but it can be said that if the quality system adopted by an organization has correctly implemented the requirements in ISO 9001:1994 clause 4.9, the organization should have no particular problems complying with the requirements of the new ISO 9001:2000.

Correspondence with ISO 9004:2000

ISO 9004:2000 subclause 7.1.3.3, "Product and process validation and changes," goes into much greater detail regarding validation. It provides guidance for both product and process validation and discusses the importance of revalidating when changes affect product characteristics or product-related processes. It broadens the application of process validation and recommends performing validations for high-value and safety-critical products, where product deficiencies will only be apparent in use, as well as when verification of the product is not possible. Process validation should be carried out at appropriate intervals to ensure timely reaction to changes affecting the process.

Arrangements for Validation

Validation is a process that requires due planning, preparation, and analysis of results and may involve quite different arrangements, approaches, and techniques, depending on the type of process to be validated. Validation, as used in subclause 7.5.5, is a comprehensive term covering different possible activities, and it implies, as necessary, qualification of the process, the equipment, the personnel, and combinations thereof.

Elements to be considered when defining and establishing how to perform the validation process include:

- The definition of the operational parameters and tolerances in the control process
- The preparation and use of the necessary procedures or work instructions
- The availability of the necessary tools and infrastructures, such as manufacturing equipment, instrumentation, devices, and so on
- Preparations for documenting and recording the validation activities in order to demonstrate that the process has the capability to achieve planned results

The reference to "re-validation" (the last bulleted item in subclause 7.5.2) recalls, on the one hand, that the validation can be a trial-and-error process before achieving its expected results. The organization should also be ready, as the need arises, to reexamine the validity of the validation process based on feedback from the process or from product use.

Correspondence with ISO 9001:1994

ISO 9001:1994 clause 4.9 reminds us that the requirements for the *qualification* process, including associated equipment and personnel, shall be specified and that records shall be maintained of the qualified processes, equipment, and personnel.

In ISO 9001:2000 these requirements are only implied, which is in line with the general trend of the new standard to minimize requirements. There is no doubt, though, that *validation* implies the need to specify the method of performance thereof and to document the relevant results.

Correspondence with ISO 9004:2000

ISO 9004:2000 goes into greater detail regarding validation in subclause 7.1.3.3, "Product and process validation and changes," and ties validation to change control and risk assessment. It recommends that the organization implement a process for effective and efficient control of changes to ensure that product or process changes benefit the organization and satisfy the needs and expectations of interested parties. It suggests that simulation techniques can be used to plan for the prevention of failures or faults in processes. Risk assessments are recommended for assessing potential failures or faults in processes.

7.5.3   IDENTIFICATION AND TRACEABILITY

Identification of Products by Suitable Means Throughout Product Realization

Identification is a very general term that can be applied to many different entities and used in many different situations:

- It can be required for products, processes, personnel, documentation, and so on
- It can be imposed by the customer and/or regulatory requirements
- It can meet an organization's internal and external needs

To avoid useless and burdensome applications, the standard clearly specifies that identification is needed only *where appropriate*.

Product identification may range from identifying single parts to identifying batches of production. Steel plates for pressure vessels require identification in accordance with codes and/or regulatory requirements. If a plate is cut into different pieces and the pieces will have the same use, the plate's identification marks shall be transferred to each piece. Identification in this case is needed to trace back the characteristics of the plates and to allow for correlation with the manufacturing processes and the testing results. In the electronics industry (and others) the identification can be difficult or impossible for single, small components to be assembled in modules. So the identification usually refers, when required, to each module.

Batch or time identification is usually adopted when each element of a series has been produced under the same conditions and manufacturing processes (for example, metal products coming from the same pouring or food or pharmaceuticals requiring definite expiry dates) or just for grouping together products with similar or common characteristics (for example, in assembly lines for mass production, preliminary identification of different sets of parts having a similar range of tolerances can be necessary for a consequent correct matching of parts).

Internal needs for identification are usually associated with production and operation processes, while external needs are associated with postdelivery activities. The automotive industry, for example, needs to identify with a specific code all components, assemblies, or modules of its production (cars, lorries, and so on) not only for its production needs but also to be able to provide assistance to its customers, ensuring spare parts having the same physical and performance characteristics as the original components.

Identification of products can also be required for legal or administrative reasons, as in the case of the engine and/or the body of a car, identification of which is required for car registration, or in the case of rifles and firearms. Identification requirements also may concern special equipment, such as measuring equipment and monitoring devices requiring calibration. But in this case a specific clause of the standard (clause 7.6) applies.

Identification of processes is sometimes required. Correlation between production processes and personnel performing them may be useful or necessary for possible improvements. This is the case, for example, in many "special processes" where the skill of the operator is essential, such as in manual steel-welding processes. The defects rate associated with a specific welder (under the same general conditions) allows the identification of the best welders and/or the need for improving the skill of other welders. In this case identification shall be extended to the welds under consideration, to the nondestructive testing records of such welds, and to the welder concerned in order to allow for a correlation among all these parameters.

Identification can be an expensive activity (and that's the reason the application of this requirement is mitigated by the phrase "where required"). Apart from the need to comply with customer or regulatory requirements, the organization shall determine the extent of identification based on cost-benefit considerations. In this evaluation, the elements to be considered should include direct, indirect, and potential benefits, such as, among other things, feeding products for production lines, the advantages of a correct management of the warehouses, and the coverage for product liability.

There are many different ways to ensure product identification; these vary according to specific needs. Physical identification can be attached or marked directly on single products. That's the case, for example, with steel plates for pressure vessels, or in general, with any item where the need for its unique identification is not ensured by alternative means (for example, through records). Modern information technology makes available advanced equipment for controlling identification and traceability. The bar code identification is commonly adopted both in trade business (such as supermarkets) and for management of warehouses, where its capability and flexibility cover many other important needs, such as inventory and stock control.

Correspondence with ISO 9001:1994

The corresponding identification requirements in ISO 9001:1994 are included in a specific clause, 4.8, which requires the organization, where appropriate (as in ISO 9001:2000), "to establish and maintain documented procedures." This requirement has been reduced to a more generic need to adopt "suitable means." What seems to be, and in a certain way is, a new flexibility in effect transfers to the organization the decisions for selecting, in response to real needs, the most adequate means (which could be either more complex or simpler than a documented procedure).

Correspondence with ISO 9004:2000

ISO 9004:2000, Subclause 7.5.3 offers no additional guidance regarding identification and traceability. ISO 9004:2000 gives instead a list of possible reasons for establishing identification and traceability that includes status of products, contractual or statutory requirements, intended use of products, hazardous materials, and risk mitigation needs.

Identification of the Status of the Product with Respect to Monitoring and Measurement

ISO 9001:2000 offers a simplified version of the requirements of clause 4.12 of ISO 9001:1994 concerning "inspection and test status." The essential message of this requirement is that measurement and monitoring activities shall be documented, results included, to ensure that, finally, all such activities have been performed and that their results comply with the relevant requirements.

Correspondence with ISO 9001:1994

The simplicity of this requirement in ISO 9001:2000, compared with the corresponding one in ISO 9001:1994, should not be considered a reduction in scope. As mentioned earlier, the missing references to "documented procedures" and "quality plan" should be interpreted as a wish for the organization itself to decide the need and/or best way to identify the status of the product. And some expressions have been either transferred to other clauses or deleted to avoid useless repetition and unnecessary detail, which is in keeping with the more generic style of the new standard. The need to "identify the inspection and test status . . . throughout production, installation and servicing of the product" has been transferred in ISO 9001:2000 to subclause 8.2.4, where it is stated that monitoring and measurement "shall be carried out at appropriate stages of the product realization process."

Correspondence with ISO 9004:2000

No specific reference is made in ISO 9004:2000 to identification of the status of the product with respect to measurement and monitoring. "Status of products, including component parts" is only listed as one of the possible reasons for the need for identification as well as traceability. See also the previous reference to ISO 9004:2000.

Traceability, Where Required, of Product

While identification means the act of identifying or just the mark imposed on a product, traceability is defined as "the ability to trace the history, application or location of that which is under consideration." The two terms are strictly connected in that identification is a preliminary, and necessary, condition for ensuring traceability. Like identification, traceability can be required for products, processes, personnel, documentation, and so on. It can be imposed by the customer and/or regulatory requirements. It can also be in response to the organization's internal and external needs.

Traceability of a product and/or its components may derive from many different needs. One of the more important and typical occasions for traceability, which has a significant safety role, is the possibility to trace back a product's (such as materials for nuclear reactors or for high-stressed constructions) peculiar characteristics, either as a means for improving knowledge, for solving problems, or for the sake of "lessons learned." Knowledge about the characteristics (chemical, nuclear, physical, technological, and so on) of certain materials can be essential (for example, in nuclear plants for safety reasons and for evaluating trends of properties during reactor operation), and this is possible only through an adequate traceability scheme and program.

Traceability can also be necessary for postproduction activities. For example, to ensure adequate postdelivery servicing, manufacturers of durable goods such as cars, household appliances, and the like need not only to identify their products' numbers but also to correlate them to elements such as physical and/or chemical characteristics, production period, manufacturing process, production plant, personnel involved, and suppliers. A typical case where traceability is necessary is the need to recall cars for modifications, rework, or parts substitutions.

Correspondence with ISO 9001:1994

Clause 4.8 in ISO 9001:1994 requires that for traceability purposes, where and to the extent required, the organization shall *establish and maintain documented procedures* for identifying individual products or batches, and that identification shall be recorded. While the need to record the unique identification is still a requirement of ISO 9001:2000, no mention is made of documented procedures; the organization itself should establish the most convenient ways to control traceability, should it be required.

Correspondence with ISO 9004:2000

See the previous reference to ISO 9004:2000.

7.5.4 CUSTOMER PROPERTY

Care of Customer Properties

The requirement to exercise due care with customer properties seems so logical that one can ask why it has been included (in effect many of the requirements of the standard are just good-sense rules). One reason for maintaining this requirement (as well as many others) is to ensure a smooth transition to the new standard. From a practical point of view, the requirement has a simple and major implication: the organization shall manage and use customer (and other third-party) properties under its control with the same care it devotes to its products and equipment.

This requirement can be applied to many different customer products while they are under the organization's control or being used by the organization. Examples of such products are materials, instruments, devices, and the like that will be incorporated in or installed on the product; the packaging to be used to better protect the product during handling and delivery; customer properties (cars, electrical households, gas equipment, and so on) handed to the organization for maintenance activities; the products received by the organization for processing; special tools, equipment, instrumentation, and so on, handed over by the customer for measures and controls.

A special note added to this clause points out that customer property also includes *intellectual properties*, and care in this case should consist of due diligence and protection to avoid any possible disclosure to competitors and to avoid privacy violations.

Although subclause 7.5.4 deals with customer "property," it should be noted that no reference is made to the "customer" himself and to possible injuries or damages he may suffer when directly involved in the organization's activities (such as, for example, public transportation). But there is no doubt that the organization shall pay specific attention to the health and safety of its customers, clients, and users when under the responsibility of the organization. There is no doubt, as well, that a reference to this situation would have been appropriate in the standard, which has "customer satisfaction" as one of its declared aims.

Correspondence with ISO 9001:1994

In ISO 9001:1994 a specific clause, clause 4.7, addresses the *control of customer-supplied products*. The general meaning is the same in both editions of the standard, but the 1994 edition is tougher, requiring the organization to "establish and maintain documented procedures" covering verification, storage, and maintenance of customer-supplied products.

Correspondence with ISO 9004:2000

Subclause 7.5.3 in ISO 9004:2000 essentially gives examples of properties (including the interested parties' properties) that may require attention and control. This list may help the organization to understand different situations where due control is required in dealing with properties of third parties.

A clear reference (lacking in the corresponding clause in 9001:2000) is made to the assignment of responsibility for the control of customer (and interested parties') properties. There is no doubt, however, that this assignment of responsibility is covered in 9001:2000 by clause 5.5.1, "Responsibility and authority."

Customer Property Identification, Verification, Protection, and Maintenance

Subclause 7.5.4 specifies the kinds of activities that the organization shall provide to ensure due care is taken with customer properties. *Identification* may be necessary when there is a danger of exchanging properties. This is particularly important, for example, in service organizations repairing, maintaining, and upgrading products; or packaging, collecting, storing, transporting, and delivering products.

Verification and *protection* of customer properties can easily be seen as an extension of the verification and protection activities a good organization is already performing for its own properties. When necessary, it is appropriate to obtain sufficient information from the customer if the organization is not familiar with the customer's properties.

Maintenance, perhaps, requires even greater attention, because of the possible economic consequences. Although not addressed directly in the subclause, a customer's property should be included in the maintenance programs of the organization's properties. The organization is responsible for obtaining from the customer or someone else the necessary documentation on the use and maintenance of the customer's equipment. Where appropriate, obtaining the assistance of qualified personnel or outsourcing related activities may be convenient. The performed maintenance, related test results, encountered problems, and so on should be documented.

Correspondence with ISO 9001:1994

See the previous reference to ISO 9001:1994 for general comparison. In addition, clause 4.7 reminds us (and this is not covered by 9001:2000) that verification performed by the organization does not relieve the customer from providing acceptable products.

Correspondence with ISO 9004:2000

See the previous reference to ISO 9004:2000.

Reporting Lost, Damaged, or Unsuitable Customer Properties

Requirements concerning recording and reporting to the customer any anomaly regarding its property under the control of the organization are intended to meet different needs. If the involved property is to be incorporated into the product, it is impossible to ensure its conformity to the customer's requirements if the component is unsuitable or damaged (and it has not been previously repaired or replaced). Similar situations can arise if the customer's property consists of equipment used by the organization for process operations: the damaged equipment should be either repaired or replaced when found unsuitable. Other customer properties may have an indirect impact on the conformity of the product, such as in the case of damaged or unsuitable packaging, which can jeopardize the safety of the product during its handling or delivery.

Any damage to or unsuitability of customer properties may be recognized at different stages of production and should be dealt with as any other nonconformity—by adopting the same or an equivalent approach (for example, using the same procedure). But an organization would be very wise to verify the suitability and integrity of customer properties as it would products procured from a supplier, when those properties come under the organization's control.

Reporting such anomalies to the customer represents a good approach to maintaining an open relationship, and it responds to the need to involve the customer in decisions in the most convenient way to resolve the encountered problem. There can also be important economic drawbacks and/or time delays, additional good reasons for reporting to the customer any identified problems.

Correspondence with ISO 9001:1994

The requirements in ISO 9001:1994 concerning recording and reporting to the customer the anomalies in its properties are exactly the same as those in 9001:2000.

Correspondence with ISO 9004:2000

No reference is made to damaged, lost, or unsuitable customer properties.

7.5.5 Preservation of Product

The quality of a product and of its components shall be preserved throughout the production process and maintained as long as the organization is held responsible for the product's integrity.

The organization is in fact responsible for establishing, based on customer requirements, if any, the needs to identify, handle, package, store, and protect the product during its internal processing and to what extent the organization remains responsible for preservation.

Preservation includes a variety of possible aspects such as, for example, the storage of materials, components, semifinished products, and customer properties; the handling of materials and products during the manufacturing processes and phases; the protection and packaging, either during processing or during preparation for delivery; the transportation and delivery of products up to the final destination (if these activities are under the responsibility of the organization).

Identifying when the organization is still held responsible for the product's integrity can be very important from a contractual point of view. Situations may arise, for example, where the customer is the owner of the product but still assigns to the organization the duty to preserve and maintain it (with the related implications and responsibilities), or vice versa—that is, where the product has not been officially transferred to the customer, but the customer has agreed to be held responsible for its operation and preservation. Situations of this type are common in plant construction, preoperation, commissioning, and start-up, and care should be taken to ensure that the assignment of responsibilities between customer and organization is clearly established and documented in the contractual agreements.

Some useful (and still valid) indications concerning the preservation of products are included in an interesting document published in 1978, ANSI N45.2.2, *Packaging, shipping, receiving, storage and handling of items for nuclear power plants.* The N (indicating "nuclear") in the title of the document should not deceive; the document still offers a wide range of good suggestions and the possibility to select the most appropriate solution for any kind of product or preservation.

Correspondence with ISO 9001:1994

Clause 4.15 in ISO 9001:1994, with its six subclauses, covers the same issues that ISO 9001:2000 subclause 7.5.5 deals with in only four lines. But in practice the only evident reduction is the deletion of the requirement for "documented procedures." None of the other requirements in ISO 9001:1994 differ in essence from the new requirements, apart from a reduced number of details (mainly on "how to do" things) and a difference in meaning of the term *preservation*, used now not as *one* of the activities but as the *totality* of activities concerning identification, handling, packaging, storage, protection, and delivery of product. An organization that has correctly applied the ISO 9001:1994 requirements will find no difference in applying the new requirements concerning preservation, which now shall expressly be extended to include the constituent parts of a product as well.

Correspondence with ISO 9004:2000

The corresponding clause in ISO 9004:2000 offers some useful information on preservation activities. Consideration should be given to any special preservation requirements associated with the nature of the product or with special needs concerning preservation for electronic media, software, hazardous materials, unique or irreplaceable product or materials, and also for specialist personnel, should it be required. Reference is also made to the importance of identifying the resources needed to maintain the product throughout its *lifecycle* and to provide customers and interested parties with information about how to facilitate preservation actions. In general, subclause 7.5.5 in ISO 9004:2000 contains additional information that organizations adopting ISO 9001:2000 can use in setting up their preservation activities.

Chapter 25

Production and Service Provision for Software

Frank Houston
EduQuest, Hyattstown, Maryland

INTRODUCTION

This chapter provides guidance for producing and servicing software in compliance with ISO 9001:2000 clause 7.5, "Production and service provision." For the purpose of this discussion, software is divided into two groups: commercial off-the-shelf (COTS) and custom software.

The COTS group consists of software distributed as-is and installed with minimal assistance from the producing organization. Typical "warranty" service for COTS software includes free access to a help office, no-cost updates (patches), and no-cost upgrades, all for a limited time. Some organizations allow the buyer to purchase contracts that extend the warranty services for a set term.

Custom software comprises all software developed or tailored for the customer. This category includes everything from configurable database systems to software custom-developed from scratch. Custom software requires a greater supplier commitment than COTS software for support and assistance throughout development, production, and servicing.

Configurable systems are usually put together from libraries of objects or modules, which are selected and assembled to match the customer's needs. Library software is developed in the same way as COTS software, but a configurable system is not equivalent to a COTS software system. The supplier specifies, verifies, and validates functionality of the library modules, but the purchaser must jointly develop the final system configuration with the supplier or a third party, starting with system requirements. The application of configurable systems, such as database engines, is equivalent to system development, but little, if any, new code is required.

An organization designs and builds custom software for a specific customer. Libraries may be used for common functions, such as filing, printing, and communications; but custom software contains a significant amount of unique code produced to the customer's specifications. Production of custom software includes software development activities as well as production, installation, and servicing, and it always requires joint participation of the purchaser and the supplier.

Software production can cover a wide range of activities, as previously mentioned. At the end of the day, though, one essential principle applies to the quality of all software, no matter how it is acquired: the software deployed for use must conform to a master copy, or "instance," that has been evaluated and tested against established requirements.

Where software production and servicing include development activities, the reader should refer to chapter 21, which discusses clause 7.3, "Design and development." On the assumption that software development proceeds according to clause 7.3, the current chapter will discuss only the activities and requirements unique to replication, installation, and servicing.

Table 25.1 shows the relationship between clause 7.5 of ISO 9000:2000 and ISO 9000-3:1991.

COMPLYING WITH ISO 9001:2000, 7.5

7.5.1   Control of Production and Service Provision

The first subclause deals with control. Evidence of control means having the information needed to monitor and maintain the software. To comply with paragraph (a), organizations should have the work items or deliverables discussed in ISO 9000-3:1991 parts 5.10.1 and 5.10.3. In particular, the producer and the servicing organization must possess or have access to the following:

- Programs (both source and executable)
- Data structure design and description
- Specifications, including program requirements and functional descriptions
- User manuals
- Change control and configuration management processes
- Configuration of the original release (baseline)
- Present configuration
- Other up-to-date servicing information, such as service release or update history

Evidence of control means the organization has instructions and information for production and servicing, as stipulated in subclause 7.5.1(b). ISO 9000-3:1991 clauses 5.9.1, 5.9.3(f), 5.10.1(e), and 5.10.2 discuss the information needed to comply. For software production, this should include the following categories:

- Production orders:
  - Number of copies to be made, delivered, or deployed

Table 25.1 Concordance of ISO 9001:2000 clause 7.5 and ISO 9000-3:1991.

ISO 9001:2000	ISO 9000-3:1991
7.5.1, first paragraph	5.10, 6.1
7.5.1(a)	5.10.1, 5.10.3
7.5.1(b)	5.9.1, 5.9.3(f), 5.10.1(e)
7.5.1(c)	5.9.1(b), 5.9.3(d)
7.5.1(d)	5.10.6(a), 5.6.10(e), 6.4.1
7.5.1(e)	5.10.6(a), 5.6.10(e), 6.4.1
7.5.1(f)	5.9.2, 5.9.3, 5.10.1–5.10.7
7.5.2, first paragraph	5.7.4, 5.9.3(e), 5.10.7
7.5.2, second paragraph	5.6, 6.5, 6.6
7.5.2(a)	5.8.2(d), 5.9.2, 5.10.7(d)
7.5.2(b)	5.7.2(g), 5.8.2(c), 5.9.3(c), 5.9.3(d)
7.5.2(c)	5.7.2(a)–(d); 5.9.3(f); 5.10.7; 6.1.3.1, last paragraph; 6.1.3.2
7.5.2(d)	5.7.3(e), 5.10.2(e), 5.10.6, 5.10.7(e), 6.1.3
7.5.2(e)	5.7.3(c); 5.7.4; 5.10.7(d); 6.1.3.2, second paragraph
7.5.3, first paragraph	5.7.3(c), 5.9.1, 6.1
7.5.3, second paragraph	5.10.3, 5.10.6
7.5.3, third paragraph	5.7.3(c), 5.10.7(c), 6.1.3.1
7.5.4	6.8
7.5.5	5.9

- Required documentation, such as manuals and user guides
- Packaging if applicable
- Process instructions:
  - Work instructions for replicating or deploying the software
  - Work instructions for packing and shipping if applicable
- Quality control:
  - Instructions for verifying the software replication or deployment
  - Instructions for managing problems discovered in replication or deployment
  - Approval process for release or deployment

For software servicing, the following additional information is needed:

- Instructions for capturing, evaluating, and prioritizing service requests
- Change management instructions

Compliance with subclause 7.5.1(c) for production of COTS software is straightforward. It requires only that the replication equipment be appropriate for the distribution media, as implied by clause 5.9.1(b) of ISO 9000-3:1991. In the case of electronic distribution, including deployment of adaptable software, this requires a trustworthy technique for copy verification, such as error-correcting communication "handshakes."

All computer equipment used for testing and servicing must be as similar to the target system as possible. For configurable and custom software, both production and servicing require access to the customer's hardware, per clause 5.9.3(d) of ISO 9000-3:1991.

First-rate organizations comply with subclause 7.5.1(d) and (e) by monitoring the integrity of software replication or deployment. This means they devise and use information feedback from the replication or deployment to keep a record of successes and failures. The monitoring and measuring devices used are not physical instruments. They are statistical methods that help identify problem causes and measure the effectiveness of improvements.

In software servicing, statistical methods also take the place of instruments. The monitoring and measuring process starts with three basic steps: capture the problem reports, classify the problems, and count the problems in each class. A Pareto analysis on the problem classes will show where corrective actions should reduce the most problems. The art of problem analysis is in defining useful classifications to promote long-term improvements in software. It is assumed that severe functional problems will be corrected promptly.

Performance metrics, such as response time and "traffic," can be measured or counted and then analyzed using control charts to establish rational performance expectations, identify trends, and recognize potential for improvement. Again, Pareto analysis of performance histograms can show where or when performance is at its best and worst.

First-rate organizations plan their release, delivery, and post-delivery activities to comply with subclause 7.5.1(f). The planned activities include delivery, installation, and servicing.

For COTS software, delivery comprises replication and distribution. Copies are verified as they are replicated. Installation is controlled through programs on the distribution media. To conform to the standard, COTS producers must verify and validate the installation programs. Verification techniques and validation will be part of the discussion of subclause 7.5.2. Servicing typically comprises a help office and provision of updates. COTS suppliers must train help staff to assist customers with installation problems, augmenting and training the staff for new releases, updates, and corrections.

Subclause 7.5.1(f) for Custom Software

Production of a configurable system is not mass production. It is an installation process, where installation includes copying a verified system instance into a production environment. At least two and sometimes three or more parties may be involved in the production, installation, and servicing/maintenance of custom software systems. The contracts among these parties must specify the work of each. This work is described in the following paragraphs.

For configurable systems, the copying process must be verified, and the same verification techniques used for COTS can be used, for instance, to compare the copy with the original. The directory structure of the installed software should also be verified against the system specifications. After replication is verified, the functionality of the system must be tested under controlled conditions, typically a test of navigation and predefined functions. Predefined functions include but are not limited to sorts and searches (views and queries, in database terminology), counts, and calculations. Finally, the system must be monitored and evaluated, preferably in normal use. If it is not possible to perform monitoring and evaluation in normal use, then normal use should be simulated during a trial period. During the monitoring and evaluation period, the organization must follow its change control processes when correcting system problems.

7.5.2   Validation of Processes for Production and Service Provision

Production and servicing require six basic processes: installation, qualification, deployment, monitoring, correction, and decommissioning. The first three comprise production, and the latter make up servicing.

Taken literally, this clause might appear to require that the software development process be validated, because software deficiencies become apparent only after the product is in service. As a practical matter, software development processes are too diverse to be validated, so one must look for more subtle interpretations. Two are offered here.

For COTS software, for which *production* could mean replication and installation processes, the installed copy might be verifiable by direct comparison with the master. Validation would only be required for the installation program. Validation of the installation program would consist of verifying successful installs in the minimum and nominal configurations of supported target environments. The minimum target environment would include the minimum supported processor configuration, RAM, and boot disk. Verification of a successful install would include confirmation of correct file replication, correct directory structure, screen navigation, commands, and defined functions. The compliant organization performs these tests and evaluations for the COTS software it supplies.

Indirect verification methods should be validated before use. Examples of such methods include file size, parity check, check-sum, and cyclic redundancy. If the file size, parity, or check-sum are not as expected, then the copy is bad every time; but these methods can indicate that a bad copy is good under some conditions. For instance, two files with entirely different contents can be exactly the same size. For this reason, indirect verification methods should be combined to reduce the probability of false negatives.

In practice, most media copies are checked by direct comparison. Indirect methods are used when copies are sent by wire, so the question arises: "Should the process of distributing/producing software be validated by electronic transmission?" In theory, the answer is yes, but indirect verification methods have been used many decades for data transmission. The math is indisputable, the processes have become standardized, and the probability of failure is well known. A combination of error detection and correction methods should be selected to minimize the probability of accepting a bad copy. There is no benefit to be gained by repeating old research; however, if a new indirect verification method were developed using untested formulae, then it should be validated.

For custom software, production might include software design, development, testing, installation, deployment, and servicing activities. In this case, the software must be validated, and its validation must be integrated throughout the development, production, and servicing processes. Custom software validation has been covered in the discussions of subclauses 7.5.1 and 7.5.2.

Subclause 7.5.3   Identification and Traceability

Identification and traceability are crucial and difficult issues for software. It is hard to pin down version identities because of the complexity of the products and the flexibility allowed in software installation. In many cases, each installed instance of the same software version can differ from its siblings in significant ways, such as the omission of certain functions. Furthermore, software products are made up of hundreds or thousands of component routines, each with its own development history and version identification. The language of software version control is imprecise. There is no unambiguous definition of what constitutes a "version," nor any uniform taxonomy of changes. For these reasons and more, identification and traceability processes may be the most significant indicators of an organizational commitment to software quality. In short, traceability is always an appropriate requirement for software (see ISO 9001:2000 subclause 7.5.3, third paragraph).

For software, traceability is not simply the assignment and tracking of serial numbers or the identification of critical parts. Software traceability means that system requirements correlate to design features, code, and test cases. A requirement spawns design features and system test cases; design features spawn code and both unit and integration test cases; and code may spawn unit test cases and test code. Traceability can extend to so-called make files, which may include conditional instructions for creating executable files to accommodate variable factors such as different target environments. The property known as traceability is the ability to keep track of this web of relationships. It is important to keep track to test efficiently and intelligently and to enable full investigation of the effects of changes.

Traceability is a required quality to enable isolation and tracking of discovered problems and identification of areas impacted by modifications, per ISO 9000-3:1991 subclauses 5.3.7(b) and (c), respectively. Traceability is necessary to ensure unique and correct configuration of master copies for replication, per ISO 9000-3:1991 clauses 5.9.1 and 6.1.

The customary means for establishing requirement traceability has been the so-called traceability matrix, but it is recognized that requirement traceability is not conducive to a simple tabular matrix. Instead, it is a complex network of relationships in which one requirement may spawn several design features or one bit of code may be required to realize several design features. With respect to testing, a requirement may directly spawn one or more system-level tests and concurrently give rise to unit integration tests through related design features. Except for the very simplest software, traceability is beyond human abilities to manage. It is recommended that organizations acquire and use requirement traceability software to achieve the benefits of compliance with subclause 7.5.3. Such software often includes functions such as test generation, test optimization, and aids for reducing design complexity.

A crucial aspect of traceability is the tracking of software dependencies—that is, when one module or program depends on another to perform correctly. Both functional and data-linked dependencies must be tracked. In functional dependency—that is, a call/called-by relationship—one program or module calls another. In a data-linked dependency—that is, a using-data-in-common relationship—two or more programs or modules access and operate on the same data. In both types of dependency, the result or outcome depends on correct performance of all the related programs or modules. Failure to track software dependencies leads to a high risk of introducing errors in software development and maintenance.

There are some software tools for identifying functional dependencies. Often these are included with development software, such as compilers. Database engines and computer-aided software development and test programs may include functions for tracing data-linked dependencies. However it is done, traceability of dependencies is a fundamental requirement for software quality.

Traceability must become integral to the configuration management and maintenance processes. At the end of the day, the task of software configuration management per ISO 9000-3:1991 is shared by the supply organization and the customer, with the supply organization maintaining its configuration and current status records and the customer maintaining similar records for its instance of the software. This dual record keeping is not duplication of effort, because the customer may omit some of the functionality and updates that are available from the COTS supplier, and the custom software package is unique to the customer by definition. The customer organization bears the responsibility to maintain configuration records for its deployment, qualification, and implementation of COTS software packages and to ensure availability of the same sorts of records for custom software.

For custom software, contracts must address the sharing of configuration management tasks between customer and supplier organizations throughout development, installation, qualification, and maintenance. The supplier organization's configuration records must be available to the customer, and at all times, their combined records must reflect the current version and configuration of the installed software.

For both COTS and custom software, supplier organizations should keep their customers informed regarding current and planned configuration changes. The supplier organization must establish methods for complying with this requirement, but the method of compliance is left to the supplier's discretion.

7.5.4 Customer Property

For software, this subclause applies to the handling of intellectual property such as specifications, customer-developed software, and data. Customer-developed software and data may be regarded as intellectual property. In addition, customer-developed software might be regarded as a customer-supplied component, and customer data as customer-supplied ingredients. Customer-supplied software assets can include requirements documents, design documentation, source code, database queries, and database contents.

This subclause is expected to apply rarely to software. The most likely case is data transfer or migration from an old to a new system. On occasion, a customer supplies standard database queries.

When the subclause applies, the organizational requirement is to exercise care with customer property while it is under the organization's control. This includes the case when the customer's intellectual assets are stored in the supplier's systems and when the assets are stored in the customer's systems to which the supplier has access.

While the asset is under the supplier's control, the supplier organization is obligated to do the following:

- Ensure the continued integrity of the asset
- Provide protection against loss or damage of the asset and notification should loss or damage occur
- Maintain version and configuration control where applicable
- Maintain records regarding suitability for use of the asset
- Inform the customer of problems with the supplied asset

In addition, when customer-supplied assets are used, there should be contractual provisions regarding their support. Aside from the contractual matter of support, this requirement boils down to six processes:

- Identifying and segregating customer-supplied data and software
- Verifying and executing backup and recovery of customer-supplied data and software
- Qualifying customer-supplied software to ensure conformance to its requirements and compatibility with the supplied software
- Validating the transfer or migration of customer-supplied data into the supplier's storage
- Validating the transfer or migration of customer-supplied data into the finished system
- Keeping the customer informed regarding the status of its assets

7.5.5   Preservation of Product

For software, preservation of product is a collateral effect of subclauses 7.5.1 and 7.5.2, specifically version control, configuration management, and production control requirements. In many cases, these requirements are all that is necessary to ensure preservation of the product.

Some provisions of subclause 7.5.5 apply when software is delivered on physical media, as in the case of COTS software and configurable systems. In these cases, the supplying organization is required to do the following:

- Store loaded delivery media to minimize the chance of damage
- Package loaded delivery media to minimize the chance of damage during transit and receiving
- Put storage and handling instructions on the package labeling
- Put product identification and version on package labels, product manuals, and one or more display screens
- Provide minimum hardware requirements and installation directions

SUMMARY

Regarding control of production and service provision, ISO 9001:2000 requires little that is new to organizations that use ISO 9000-3:1991 as guidance. The principal difference one might notice is the stronger emphasis on process monitoring, measurement, and improvement than was evident in the 1994 edition of the standard.

Software engineering is still a relatively young discipline, and there are many controversial questions regarding the usefulness of some tasks and records required by this and other standards. This discussion has tried, in some cases, to provide reasonable suggestions and rationale regarding the purpose of tasks and the use of records that the standard mandates. In other cases, the software requirements of ISO 9001:2000 clause 7.5, are simply the processes one expects in the manufacture of any commercial product: for example, repeatable manufacturing, proper packaging and labeling, accurate product identification, and provision of warranty service.

Chapter 26

Production and Service Provision for Services

Diane M. Baguley
Beca Carter Hollings & Ferner, Auckland, New Zealand

INTRODUCTION

Service operations comprise the processes for provision of an established service. In terms of ISO 9001:2000 and ISO 9004:2000, this excludes the processes for determination of service requirements, customer communication, design and development, and purchasing. For some services, however, provision can be linked closely with other processes, particularly customer communication and design and development, and the processes may be best addressed together.

In practice therefore, organizations may elect to design their service provision processes according to one of the following scenarios:

- Defining provision processes for an established service where design and development has been completed prior to provision
- Defining common service processes (for example, job management) to support customer-specific service planning—for example, where customer communication, purchasing, and/or design and development occur parallel to service provision
- Integration of simple, low-risk design and development activities within service provision processes (see chapter 22)

One of the characteristics of a service is that, at least in part, it occurs at the interface with the customer. An important corollary of that is the need for flexibility in service provision to ensure that individual customer needs can be accommodated. For many services, there is at least one stage where personnel of the organization providing the service are dealing directly with a customer or customer organization. Those frontline staff therefore need to be empowered by service provision processes to adjust service delivery to meet the needs of each customer. Service quality begins and ends with people.

COMPLIANCE WITH ISO 9001

For compliance with ISO 9001, all service provision processes that impinge on the ability to meet specified requirements need to be planned and controlled. The processes must meet the quality objectives and requirements of the service. Where this cannot be confirmed by monitoring or measuring their output, the processes need to be validated at appropriate intervals so that the intended output is sustained. Control methods need to be implemented in a way that the quality of the service can be assured. This can include control of monitoring and measuring devices.

The key requirements for service provision are specified in ISO 9001:2000 clause 7.5, "Production and service provision." Prior to considering how those requirements apply, the organization needs to plan and establish service provision processes in accordance with clause 7.1, "Planning of product realization."

Defining Service Provision Processes

Service provision processes often are not readily apparent in service operations. Different process activities may be carried out in isolation from each other without a clear picture of their place in the overall service to the customer.

Decisions about how processes are defined and where divisions are made between one process and the next are in the hands of the organization. However, it is particularly important in service operations that activities within a single process are not artificially separated because of structural divisions within an organization. Two examples are given.

Understanding Service Provision Processes

Example 1: A team of inspection staff carries out inspection and measurement activities for evaluation of building condition for a portfolio of properties. The data they collect are entered into a database by data entry staff. The building condition information is processed within the database and reviewed by an engineer, who prepares a report for the owner of the properties. The report is used for planning of property maintenance, acquisition, and disposal. To the inspection staff, building condition assessment is one of a number of inspection and site supervision tasks. The data entry staff similarly see their work as one part of their data entry and clerical duties. These structural features of the organization may be needed to provide a matrix of resources for different services. Without changing the structure, the data collection, data entry, analysis, and reporting activities can be managed as a process so that all the activities and their control mechanisms can be focused on the building owner's needs.

Example 2: A hospital allocates specific responsibility for infection control, with the infection control team being responsible for formulating standards and guidance information for application throughout the hospital. The infection control team does not have direct management control over the day-to-day actions for infection control or the monitoring and measuring activities that are implemented. The information from such monitoring and measuring, however, needs to be accessible by the infection control team for feedback on the infection control process. The infection control team therefore needs ownership over the whole process, even though its management authority is limited.

Mechanisms of Control

Once processes have been identified and understood, the organization needs to determine and plan the mechanisms for control in compliance with ISO 9001:2000 clause 7.5.1. This clause needs to be understood in the context of the process-planning requirements of clause 7.1 and general requirements for the quality management system.

A number of factors are likely to be involved in the ability to control a process, including the following:

- Information about the characteristics of the product of the process, whether that is the final service, a constituent part of it, or the product of a stage of service provision
- The need for validation of any processes whose output cannot be confirmed by subsequent monitoring or measurement (clause 7.5.2)
- The required competence of personnel, and the need for training and qualification (see clause 6.2)
- The need for work instructions, together with any associated information such as guidelines and examples of service outputs (see clause 4.2.1)
- The requirements for equipment and related needs such as computer software (see clause 6.3)
- Provisions for monitoring and measuring the process (clause 8.2.3), including the control of any measuring equipment and monitoring devices (clause 7.6)
- The need for quality records (clause 4.2.4) to provide evidence of effective operation of the processes
- Mechanisms for taking and tracking actions to eliminate nonconformities and to analyze opportunities for improvement of the process (clauses 8.4 and 8.5)

The level of control required is often a matter of balance among these factors. In the service sector, the need to provide for flexibility at the customer interface often weights the mechanisms for control toward qualification and training of personnel rather than prescriptive details in work instructions.

Table 26.1 gives examples of services, the aspects that may be critical to them, and the prime methods of control that an organization could select.

Table 26.1   Examples of selecting process control methods.

Service Examples	Some Critical Issues	Examples of Methods of Control
Knowledge industries	Information Competence Time/cost	Information management Qualified personnel Project management
Banking	Data integrity Accuracy Prompt service	Data quality control Training and data quality control Training and service monitoring
Travel agency	Information Accuracy Personal service	Information update control Training and data quality control Training and service follow-up
Aged care	Personal service Competence Service interfaces	Training and service monitoring Qualified personnel Control of communication and records

Validation of Processes

ISO 9001:2000 clause 7.5.2 describes the requirements for validation of processes involved in service provision. Service provision processes need to be validated where the output cannot be verified by subsequent monitoring or measurement. Such processes used to be termed *special processes*, but that term can be misleading. People who carry out a particular process every day are unlikely to think of it as *special*.

A number of processes where a unique service is formed at the supplier-customer interface require validation, since the service cannot be verified prior to delivery. There are numerous examples in the healthcare sector, where validation often is carried out at a sector level through research and controlled testing of protocols. There are likely to be defined criteria for the validated service such as qualified personnel, approval of equipment, warnings about drug interaction, and so on.

With some services that are associated with production of tangible products the production process needs to be validated, such as road maintenance activities. Pavement-surfacing and line-marking processes need to be validated so that the resulting product will meet the maintenance requirements of the service. The equipment used needs to be retested and approved at appropriate intervals as a basis for revalidation. Equipment settings and control procedures need to be tested and approved.

Emergency services and contingency plans often need to be validated, since their effectiveness must be reliable at the time of operation. Firefighting techniques and safety procedures need to be practiced as a team. Security procedures and mechanisms—for example, alarms and grills used in the event of threatened bank robbery—depend on both physical and staff factors. Scheduled training exercises provide ongoing validation of the processes.

Identification and Traceability

Identification and traceability (ISO 9001:2000 clause 7.5.3) includes three requirements that sometimes cause confusion in relation to services:

- Where appropriate, identifying the service throughout product realization
- Identifying the status of the service with respect to monitoring and measuring
- Where traceability is a requirement, controlling and recording the unique identification of the service

Identification of the Service

A service often has constituent parts that are used or formed in realization processes, such as data, reports, and other deliverables such as, say, certificates or tickets. In many cases it is appropriate to identify these so that their relationship to the final service is apparent. A simple example is identification of documents by an order number or job number. The purpose of such identification is to ensure that the correct constituents are used in subsequent realization of the service—for example, that the correct data are used to prepare a report.

Many services do not need to be identified throughout their realization. Some are assembled at the point of service, such as, for example, a restaurant meal. Even if the chef knows "this steak is to be medium-rare," the steak is not identified as unique to the customer until it is on the plate for service.

Identification of Status of a Service

It is important that the status of a service or its constituent parts is clear in relation to monitoring or measurement requirements. For example, if data are collected and entered, what signifies that the data have been checked for completeness and accuracy before use?

Where checks are carried out on documents or data, approval may be identified by means such as a sign-off point. Many service-monitoring points are identified by date stamping and initialing—for example, bank transactions. In others, issuing a form or ticket signals completion of a monitoring step without the need for further identification of status—for example, the issuing of an airline boarding pass or a theater ticket. In others again, the person responsible for monitoring is responsible for release of that part of the service—for example, a chef placing cooked food on a plate or in a serving area. All of these methods can meet the requirements for identification of monitoring or measurement status.

Traceability

Traceability of some aspect of a service may be specified by a purchaser or, more commonly, may result from statutory or regulatory requirements. For example, in civil aviation, certification activities, and healthcare, the use of qualified personnel and/or approved methods of operation may need to be traceable to the delivery and use of a service. The means of traceability is through the use of appropriate quality records. These may be specific to each service or be collected in some form of database so that the information is readily available.

Traceability may be required by the organization itself—for example, to track authorization of accounting transactions. Traceability requirements also may apply to products used in association with services—for example, for compliance with food safety requirements.

Customer Property

Services often deal with customer property, whether physical property such as a car brought in for repair; intellectual property such as reports, data, or software provided by the customer as inputs to a service; or information such as personal data used in performing a service. The requirements for care of customer property are specified in ISO 9001:2000 clause 7.5.4. The property needs to be identified and protected while in the care of the organization. If there is damage or loss, that needs to be reported to the customer.

Confidentiality of customer information and intellectual property is a common issue in provision of services. It is important to protect customers from either inadvertent release of their information or exposure to other risks such as fraud. Control of such risks often depends heavily on training and organizational culture, not just physical protection systems.

Preservation of the Service Product

ISO 9001:2000 clause 7.5.5 covers preservation of product. While some aspects of services are commonly limited to the service transaction, there are many instances where preservation of a constituent part of a service is important. Photocopying documents is a simple example of a step where errors may occur during the processing of a service deliverable. Many important documents are handled and delivered to customers by mail or courier services—for example, travel documents, qualification certificates, and financial records. The documents therefore need to be protected during delivery.

In some cases, documents and data related to the service need to be stored for long periods by the service supplier, perhaps for decades, as in the case of customer records for a retirement savings scheme. There may be statutory or regulatory requirements for retention of other records, such as civil aviation and engineering records. The organization therefore needs to consider archiving and backup mechanisms for vital information.

Documentation of Service Provision

The level of documentation of service provision processes, as for all of ISO 9001:2000 clause 7, must be determined by the organization (clause 4.2.1). The purpose of the documentation needs to be assessed—for example, whether it will be used for day-to-day reference or mainly for training of personnel.

Documentation of service provision processes may use some or all of the following:

1. *Quality plans* (see clause 7.1 note) specifying service objectives, service realization processes, applicable procedures, quality control schedules, resources, and other key information. Quality plans commonly are used for certain types of contracts such as term maintenance contracts. The customer may specify submission of the quality plan.

2. *Process descriptions*, which may be simple flowcharts or more detailed work procedures addressing questions about why? who? what? and when?.

3. *Work instructions* concerning specific activities, detailing how work is to be done. These need to be simple and accessible if they are to be used on a day-to-day basis. Many work instructions may be little-used once people are familiar with the tasks, and their role may be principally for training. Others may be used for reference to provide guidance on less common activities.

4. *Software process management methods*, where control of the process is both documented and governed by software. Work instructions may be available within the software—for example, via drop-down menus or help functions.

5. *Guidance or training information* for occasional reference and/or training.

WHAT IS DIFFERENT FROM THE 1994 EDITION?

Tailoring of ISO 9001:2000

A major difference between 2000 and the 1994 versions is the need to tailor application of ISO 9001:2000 clause 7 rather than depend on the separate standards ISO 9001, ISO 9002, and ISO 9003 in the 1994 series. For the service sector, this probably has little impact in regard to the application of ISO 9001:2000 clause 7.5, since few organizations applying previous ISO 9000 series standards to services have considered it appropriate to exclude control of processes from their quality management systems.

However, the need to apply ISO 9001:2000 clause 7 to services may affect organizations previously supplying products under the requirements of ISO 9003:1994. Under ISO 9001:2000, services associated with the supply of goods need to be included in the quality management system if they affect the ability of an organization to provide the required product. This means that the service provision processes may need to be controlled in order to meet customer requirements. The intangible nature of the service product and the involvement of a customer at some point of the service transaction generally means that service processes as well as final product must be controlled.

Process Focus

ISO 9001:2000 clause 7.1 introduces an explicit requirement to determine, plan, and implement the processes necessary to meet customer requirements. This should generally be useful to the service sector. The requirement was implicit in the 1994 version of ISO 9001 and ISO 9002, at least for service provision processes, but was not highlighted as a necessary first step.

ISO 9001:2000 was designed with a focus on process rather than being based on a purchaser view of quality assurance. Clauses relevant to product and/or service operations have been brought together in clause 7.5—for example, traceability, customer property, delivery, and postdelivery services. Some requirements of clause 4.9 of the 1994 version are transferred to other parts of the 2000 version: for example, general requirements for all processes are transferred to clause 7.1, the requirement for a suitable working environment is transferred to clause 6.4, and the requirements for "special processes" are transferred to the separate clause 7.5.2.

The wording of clause 7.5 has been simplified, and 7.5.1 in particular has been made more applicable to service operations. To avoid confusion with service, the term *servicing* in the sense of after-sales service has been avoided, and the term *post-delivery activities* used in its place.

Documentation

The explicit requirement in the 1994 version for documented procedures, where their absence could adversely affect quality, is absent from the equivalent clause in the 2000 version. Organizations themselves are responsible for identifying where procedures and methods should be documented to ensure effective planning, operation, and control of its service provision processes (ISO 9001:2000 clauses 4.2.1 and 7.1). This is not a significant change of intent of the standard, but it puts the responsibility for determining documentation needs squarely on organizational management.

Process Validation

The term *validation* is introduced in ISO 9001:2000 clause 7.5.2 in relation to proving the adequacy of processes where the resulting output cannot be verified. The requirements for validating processes are similar to those in paragraph 3 of clause 4.9 of the 1994 version of ISO 9001 and ISO 9002 but are expanded and clarified.

Identification and Traceability

ISO 9001:2000 clause 7.5.3 covers identification and traceability in an abbreviated and simplified manner, covering clause 4.8 and 4.12 in the 1994 version. It adds a note that the means by which identification and traceability may be achieved is configuration management, but that term is not commonly used in the service sector.

Customer Property

The 1994 version clause 4.7 covering control of customer-supplied property is replaced by ISO 9001:2000 clause 7.5.4, "Customer property." As with other subdivisions of clause 7, the explicit requirement for documented procedures is removed. Clause 7.5.4 is substantially reworded, but the required actions in regard to customer property are not changed. The note to clause 7.5.4 points out that customer property may include intellectual property. This needs to be taken into account by service organizations if such an interpretation has not previously been observed.

Preservation of Product

Clause 7.5.5 of ISO 9001:2000, "Preservation of product," reduces the requirements of clause 4.15 of the 1994 version to two sentences. It has been made much less explicit so that it can be more readily applied to sectors other than hardware—in particular, the service sector.

BEYOND ISO 9001 COMPLIANCE

ISO 9004:2000 clause 7.5 outlines a number of aspects of service provision in which organizations may go beyond compliance with the requirements of ISO 9001:2000 to provide enhanced benefits to interested parties. This includes addressing both effectiveness and efficiency of support processes that, while not essential to compliance, influence wider outcomes of the services. Those wider outcomes may be internal—such as financial or people-related—or external—such as social and environmental impacts.

Benchmarking can be an important tool to use in seeking improvement of service processes. However, just as important for some service processes is investigation of innovative methods, particularly given the opportunities offered by information and communications technology.

There are many avenues for considering a more broadly based approach to the quality of service provision. This section introduces only a few.

Balancing Risk Control and Customer Satisfaction

Customer satisfaction is often a major driver of service improvement. For some services, however, customer satisfaction may be a poor guide to the processes that need to be targeted for improvement. Customer satisfaction, for example, may not be sensitive to serious hazards that have a low likelihood of occurrence. The organization may therefore need to balance the benefits of risk control against those of direct service improvement. The balance between risk control and customer satisfaction as drivers for improvement is one aspect of balancing the needs of different interested parties.

This can be illustrated by considering examples of public services. A utility company providing a municipal water supply is exposed to customer dissatisfaction not only from poor water taste or appearance but also from processes involving the customer such as meter reading and billing. However, water with good taste and appearance can be contaminated with potentially harmful agents. Water treatment may not eliminate all such risks. The utility needs to not only control the treatment mechanisms but also protect water sources from contamination. That is a much more significant risk to the customer than those aspects detected by the user. This needs to be taken into account in prioritizing areas for action.

On the other hand, a municipal bus company runs a service that is more readily judged by customers. There are some risks for which contingency planning should be considered, such as labor strikes and traffic disruption. However, in planning improvement activities the organization can choose to put priority on the customer interface and the customer experience.

Involvement of Customers

There can be many benefits from greater involvement of customers in the improvement of service provision processes. Customers often directly interact with the service supplier at some point of the process and therefore are likely to have considerable insight into the difference in service processes between an acceptable service and an excellent service.

Customer involvement in staff training may have enormous impact. This can be done at more than one level, involving both purchasers of services and direct users. For example, an organization providing corporate travel services may arrange sessions to gather feedback from both those with the authority to continue a preferred supplier arrangement and individual users of the service.

Where organizations supply services to other organizations, customer communication can be enhanced by establishing a "zipper" style of relationship, where relationships are maintained between people at appropriate levels of both the supplier and customer organizations. This means that customer needs and feedback information are obtained from a number of sources, perhaps including quite disparate views. It also means that if a key contact leaves either organization, only one part of the "zipper" needs to be repaired.

Staff Participation in Improvement

Many service operations rely heavily on the knowledge and attitude of staff performing activities at the customer interface. This means that an organization can benefit from placing a high priority on training and qualification of its staff. It also means potentially high rewards from direct participation of staff in improvement of the processes.

Staff participation can be combined with advanced uses of information and communications technology—for example, in the distribution of information to different geographical areas via an Internet or intranet Web site. It is enormously important that the needs of the users of the information are recognized and understood, so that the design of the Web site meets their needs for access to information while dealing with a customer inquiry.

Objectives for involvement of staff in improvement can be combined with training objectives. Many small service organizations that have developed quality management systems for compliance with earlier versions of ISO 9001 or ISO 9002 have had the experience of initial benefits that are not sustained over time. On reflection, the benefits appeared to have derived particularly from the involvement of staff in defining the processes in which they are involved. The staff appreciated the opportunity to describe and understand the processes, but the documented procedures they prepared turned out to be of less value to other staff than they expected. The corollary of this experience is that staff are likely to benefit from personal workshop experience of describing customer needs and the processes required to meet them. Therefore, such experiential workshops can be valuable (not only in small organizations) whether or not they are associated with a specific improvement initiative.

Application to Internal Processes

The principles of ISO 9004:2000 can be applied to all services within an organization, including management and support processes such as those involved in financial management, information management, human resource management, and administration.

The benefits of addressing internal service processes in this manner are many. For example:

- The service processes are defined and clear objectives are established, linking the processes to their purposes in the organization
- Procedures and work instructions can be developed to meet the needs of the staff carrying out the processes
- Monitoring and measurement of processes can provide information for benchmarking and improvement initiatives
- Staff training in quality management principles can be consistent throughout the organization, with improved understanding of the concept of both internal and external customers
- Internal audit and self-assessment techniques can be developed to meet overall organizational objectives

Chapter 27

Control of Monitoring and Measuring Devices

Dan Harper
Harper Quality Advisors, Portland, Oregon

INTRODUCTION

Clause 7.6 of ISO 9001:2000 states, "The organization shall determine the monitoring and measurement to be undertaken and the monitoring and measuring devices needed to provide evidence of conformity of product to determined requirements (see 7.2.1)." Further, subclause 7.2.1 clearly states that the product-related requirements that are to be determined include those specified by the customer, those necessary for the production and delivery of the product, and any needed to meet regulatory requirements.

Clause 7.6 does not describe a stand-alone system. It describes one element of the overall quality management process and provides tools to help control processes and to measure characteristics of a product or process. It is clear that the measuring and monitoring devices covered by 7.6 requirements are intended to prove conformity of product to requirements.

The focus of 7.6 is on basic control of monitoring and measuring devices. There is no stated requirement in this clause for procedures or work instructions—documented or otherwise—although it is clear that some records will have to be maintained.

The need for documented procedures and work instructions is driven by the complexity of the product and the processes needed to deliver that product. The necessary elements of process control are usually provided in the form of written instructions, which ensure consistency in the operation of processes. It is important to note that ISO 9001:2000 places the responsibility for determining the need for and scope of that documentation on the organization's management.

The importance of monitoring processes and product is clear since it is included in several of the requirements clauses, particularly in clause 7, "Product realization,"and clause 8, "Measurement, analysis and improvement." Each of these requirements must be examined in context with clause 7.6 for applicability of monitoring and measurement activities.

MONITORING AND MEASURING

One of the differences between ISO 9001:1994 clause 4.11 and ISO 9001:2000 is the specific inclusion of *monitoring* devices in 9001:2000. This raises the question: What are monitoring and measuring devices?

Consider a definition of the term *device:* a device can be a measuring instrument or combination of instruments, a tool, or something made or adapted for a particular purpose. According to the *Concise Oxford Dictionary (COD)*, a device could also be a plan or scheme. Using the latter definition, a quality plan, such as that mentioned in note 1 of clause 7.1 could be called a device. Procedures for the calibration, validation, or verification of a measuring instrument or for monitoring a process could also be considered devices.

It is important to understand the distinction between measuring and monitoring. According to *COD, monitoring* is observing and checking over a period of time. Monitoring may or may not provide a measurement value or result. However, monitoring should give an indication of status, or of a change in status. Moreover, a monitor can be a person or a piece of apparatus.

In contrast, *measuring* is determining a quantity or value of something compared with some standard or reference. *Measurement* is defined in the *International Vocabulary of Basic and General Terms in Metrology (VIM)* as a "set of operations having the object of determining a value of a quantity" (*VIM* 2.1). It is the process necessary to give an accurate statement regarding that value or quantity.

As an example, I once owned an automobile that, with the driver involved, was a good example of a complex monitoring, measuring, and warning system that would keep the driver informed of performance and operating conditions. It would also warn him or her if something was going out of normal operating limits.

This auto had the usual displays in the instrument cluster—speedometer, fuel gauge, odometer, warning lights if a door was open, and so on. It also had a "driver information center" that could—and would—display several types of data pertaining to the motor and how it was performing and many of the operating conditions at that particular time.

This display was not where the driver could conveniently see it. It was located between the driver's seat and the passenger's seat, in the console. When driving, the driver had to take his or her eyes off the road to see the display. Also, the measuring and monitoring going on was just that. The operator of the automobile had to take action when warned something was amiss.

There were sensors in the vehicle that would measure characteristics of the auto's operation, and monitor the status and change in status. The coolant temperature could be displayed in Celsius or Fahrenheit, to one degree; fuel left in the tank in gallons or liters. The automobile displayed fuel economy in miles per gallon or kilometers per liter, and the driving range based on consumption and amount of fuel left. There was also a warning light when the fuel remaining was down to 3 gallons or so.

When the motor was started, if all operations were within the predetermined normal operating range, a message came on that said, "monitored systems OK." That meant that the vehicle operating condition met requirements and was okay to drive.

If some characteristic in the monitored systems had reached the point where something needed attention, a message to "check information center" would be displayed in the instrument cluster—so the driver received a warning that something was amiss, and the information center would provide some data on the problem.

None of this measuring or monitoring would stop the car or take action to correct a problem. It was up to the driver or a shop technician to evaluate the data being displayed, make a decision, and take action.

Part of the automobile's system actually measured and reported data; another part evaluated those data and determined and reported if the operating conditions were okay and within requirements or not. All of this happened every time the ignition key was turned and the motor started.

Like all processes, it needed maintenance. If not properly set up and maintained, the monitoring and measuring processes could give you some bad information.

For example, the monitoring system was programmed to tell you to change the oil at 3000-mile intervals. However, when the oil was changed, the technician had to reset the system, or it continued to say "change oil soon" every time the engine was started.

There were other information displays dependant on correct setup and maintenance by a person. The clock was a 12-hour clock, but "A.M." or "P.M." was displayed only when setting the clock. Immediately after the auto was started, the display would show "good morning," "good afternoon," or "good evening." If the clock had not been set correctly, the greeting could be wrong.

All of this was of course computer controlled with embedded software. The data available through the monitoring and measuring system could and would tell the operator that the vehicle was functioning properly, or help prevent serious problems by warning that changes were occurring that could affect the usability of the vehicle—the product in this case.

That's what an operational monitoring and measuring process is there for—to provide evidence of conformity of product and process to specified requirements. A well-designed monitoring or measuring process with competent operators is essential.

That is what the monitoring and measurement requirements of clause 7.6 are all about.

MEETING THE REQUIREMENTS OF CLAUSE 7.6

Clause 7.6 of ISO 9001:2000 has most, but not all, of the requirements found in ISO 9001:1994 clause 4.11, "Control of inspection, measuring and test equipment." ISO 9001:2000 clause 7.6 does not add any new requirements for measuring equipment. The most noticeable changes in the transition from clause 4.11 in the 1994 version to clause 7.6 in 9001:2000 are as follows:

- The change from very prescriptive, checklist-type requirements
- The deletion of any mention of documented procedures
- The addition of "monitoring devices"

Clause 4.2.2 of the new standard, 9001:2000, clearly states that documented procedures established for the quality management system are required. The standard also clearly specifies that there must be evidence of conformity of product to specification. However, ISO 9001:2000 leaves it up to the organization to determine the specifics—the scope and detail—of the procedures and work instructions that are needed to provide the evidence of product conformity. ISO 9001:2000 also leaves it up to the organization to determine whether there is a need to provide documented procedures and work instructions.

An objective of clause 7.6 is to ensure that evidence of conformity of product to determined requirements can be provided when required. This same requirement can be found in the "general" clause 4.11.1 of 9001:1994. However, clause 7.6 covers only the equipment used to prove conformance of product to specified requirements.

To comply with 7.6, organizations must prove conformance and must ensure valid measurement results. To do this the organization must take the following steps.

Determine Monitoring and Measurement to Be Done to Demonstrate Conformance

These decisions should take place during the product planning process. The decisions about which monitoring and measurement will be done must be based on (1) what the customer requires and (2) where the best place in the product realization process would be to determine conformity (refer to 7.1).

For example, there may be a requirement that the product be made of a certain grade or type of material. The organization should confirm that the raw material meets specifications before any processing takes place. Options could include testing the incoming raw material before processing or purchasing certified material. For example, a machined item destined to be plated and polished would logically have the dimensions measured prior to the plating process.

If the product must be processed in a controlled environment where, for example, the air temperature, humidity, or other factors could affect the performance or processing of the product, then monitoring of those aspects of the facilities could be critical.

Determine the Monitoring and Measuring Devices Needed for the Task

These decisions should be part of the product planning process and are driven by the specifications of the material to be measured. The capability of the measuring process includes not only the correct measuring instrument but also anything that could contribute to measurement error, including the precision and accuracy of the measuring instrument, the experience and technique of the person making the measurement, and so on. If, for example, you must make a measurement to plus or minus 0.030 inch, you will require a measuring instrument that has a measurement capability with a greater accuracy than 0.030 inch.

ISO 9001:1994 included a requirement that the measurement uncertainty be known, and that this uncertainty be consistent with the required measurement capability of the measuring equipment. This requirement is not specified in the new standard, 9001:2000. However, estimation of measurement uncertainty cannot be avoided, since it is essential in the calibration of measuring equipment and documentation of the traceability of measurement result.

To Ensure Valid Measurement Results, Calibrate or Verify Measuring Equipment at Specified Intervals or Prior to Use

This requirement was also in 9001:1994, and the intent is that the measuring equipment be of a known accuracy. The terms *calibrate* and *verify* have specific, technical definitions (refer to the glossary at the end of this chapter).

Calibration is the process that establishes the accuracy of a measuring instrument. This is done by measuring standards of known value with the instrument to be calibrated and comparing the measurement result with the value of the standard. The calibration process may include the adjustment of the instrument to bring the indicated value closer to the known value of the standard. Calibration should always include the estimation of the uncertainty of the measurement result.

In some situations, all of a measuring equipment's measurement ranges or functions will not be used to prove conformity of the product. In these cases, only those ranges or functions used to demonstrate conformance to requirements require calibration. Selective calibration can significantly reduce overall calibration costs.

Verification is the confirmation that specified requirements have been met. Typically this would include examination of the calibration data, the intervals of calibration, and so on, and comparing the measuring instrument capability with the measurement requirement.

ISO 9001:1994 included a requirement that measuring equipment be used in a manner that ensured that the measurement uncertainty was known, and that it was consistent with the required measurement capability. This referred to determining how close the measurement result is to the true value of the item being measured. This requirement is not specifically called out in clause 7.6 of 9001:2000.

Calibrate Measuring Equipment against Standards Traceable to National or International Measurement Standards If They Exist. If Not, Record the Basis for Calibration

For calibration of measuring equipment, the key is that standards are available that are of known value, traceable as this requirement specifies to national or international standards, or calibrated using an industry-accepted basis for calibration. Many organizations maintain an in-house capability for some calibrations, with traceable standards and facilities adequate for the calibration process. However, a calibration lab can be an expensive operation to maintain, and the standards themselves must be periodically calibrated.

Traceability is established through an unbroken chain of comparisons of a measurement result, or value of a standard, back to a national or international standard in most cases. This is a formal process, and it requires documentation of calibration procedures or work instructions, records of measurements and conditions, and determination of measurement uncertainties.

If a standard for a calibration does not exist, then some agreement must be reached between the supplier and the customer on methods to be used in demonstrating conformity of product.

An excellent source of calibration services and one that has very real technical and economic benefits is a commercial laboratory that has been accredited for its technical competence. These laboratories have had their standards, procedures, processes, and the competence of their personnel examined against rigid requirements. Such a lab has demonstrated technical competence to perform specific calibrations with a specified uncertainty. For example, a lab may have a scope of accreditation to calibrate micrometers that have a measurement capability of 1 inch, with a specified uncertainty. The scope of the accreditation may also include the type of gage block or other device that is the standard used in the calibration.

The new standard ANSI/ISO/IEC 17025:2000, *General requirements for the competence of testing and calibration laboratories,* is the internationally accepted standard for accreditation of calibration and testing laboratories. This standard is a revision of ISO/IEC Guide 25, and it has been approved as an American national standard by the American Society for Quality, the American Society for Testing and Materials, and the NCSL International, a U.S.-based organization of calibration laboratories.

As the title indicates, it is a requirements document for the management of the technical activities of calibration and testing laboratories. It is very prescriptive and comprehensive in the stated requirements.

Adjust or Readjust As Necessary

How do you know when a measuring tool needs recalibration or adjustment? Typically, the equipment manufacturer will recommend a calibration interval for normal usage of the tool; however, that interval should be adjusted based on actual usage and on evaluation of the history of use, repair, calibration, and so on. Any time a measuring instrument has been damaged or abused or is suspected of giving erroneous measurements, it should be checked. If it will be returned to service, it should then be repaired (if necessary) and recalibrated.

One method to determine when recalibration or adjustment is needed is by use of a check standard. The check standard is a device of known value, similar in kind to the items being measured in the process. It is measured regularly with the measuring instrument, and the measurement data recorded and compared with the value of the check standard to detect any change in the measuring instrument. Use of check standards is described in ISO 10012-2, *Quality assurance for measuring equipment—Part 2: Guidelines for control of measurement processes.*

Identify the Measuring Equipment So the Calibration Status Can Be Determined

Any piece of measuring equipment that must be calibrated also needs to have a unique identification for control purposes. For many years, it was common practice to attach labels or tags to equipment showing the calibration status. ISO 9001:1994 required this tagging or labeling; however, ISO 9001:2000 does not. The requirement in clause 7.6 is only that measuring equipment be identified so that the calibration status can be determined. This means that identification can be by a unique serial number or special marking. If the measuring equipment is the only one of its kind in the organization, a brief statement of type and description could fulfill the requirement for unique identification.

However, labeling calibrated equipment is still an excellent practice. Labels or tags can clearly indicate the next due date for calibration and any limitations for use. Labels or tags serve as a reminder for usage and for due dates for checks or calibrations.

Safeguard against Adjustments That Would Invalidate the Measurement Result

For equipment that has an access to adjustments other than those normally used by the operator, it has been common practice to cover or close off the access with adhesive seals or labels. At best, this method only helps prevent inadvertent change of the adjustment or control. It will not prevent someone from deliberately gaining access.

Use of seals that show evidence of tampering, such as someone's attempt to remove the seal, will give a warning that the calibration of the instrument should be checked before continued use.

Protect against Damage and Deterioration During Handling, Maintenance, and Storage

The entirety of clause 7.6 is about making critical measurements—those needed to demonstrate conformity with requirements. Any measuring equipment used for critical measurements deserves special protection or consideration when being stored, when being moved, or during maintenance operations. This may necessitate special containers, carts, and/or storage shelves for the equipment—not only during transportation but also for storage. Personnel involved in the storage and handling of the equipment should have very clear instruction and guidance on the storage and handling of delicate measuring equipment.

Assess and Record the Validity of Previous Measurement Results When the Measuring Equipment Is Nonconforming, and Take Action on the Equipment and Any Product Affected.

There are instances when a piece of measuring equipment is found to be nonconforming. Nonconformance may be discovered at the scheduled calibration interval or through the use of a check standard or some other method. When equipment is found to be nonconforming, one must determine whether the equipment is sufficiently out of tolerance to have affected the capability to demonstrate product conformance to requirements.

One way to determine the severity of the problem is to examine the data taken at the last calibration and compare them with the data at the "as-found" check. Any data and records available pertaining to measurements taken of product should be examined for unusual variations in measurement values. In some cases, the same product characteristics might have been measured with more than one measuring instrument. In these cases the data from the other measuring instrument can be compared with the measurements taken by the nonconforming equipment. If an out-of-tolerance condition exists, then examination of any finished product that has not yet been shipped should be undertaken. If product that is suspected of being nonconforming has been shipped, notification of the customers should be considered.

It is important to (1) identify the cause of the nonconformity and (2) try to institute corrective action to eliminate the possibility of a reoccurrence.

Maintain Records of Calibration and Verification

Calibration records should include the description and unique identification of the measuring equipment being calibrated, the procedure used to calibrate the equipment, the reference standards and any other equipment used during calibration, and the actual data taken during the calibration. The date of the calibration and the name of the person performing the calibration should also be recorded. The measurement uncertainties should be determined and recorded.

In addition, where appropriate, the "as-received" data and the "after-calibration" data should be recorded.

Confirm Software Prior to Use, and Reconfirm As Necessary

Software used to monitor and measure specified requirements may be designed specifically for a particular measurement or unique application in a measuring or monitoring process. In other cases, the software may be designed to perform a general application such as data accumulation, generation of reports, and so on.

Confirmation of software requires testing the complete system configuration for the specific, intended use. This requires testing on the actual hardware platform (not on a duplicate), with the exact version of the operating system installed on which the software will run.

Overall confirmation still requires that the software be installed on and checked in the actual system and complete configuration being used for the monitoring and measurement. Functional testing of software in the actual system configuration and under actual measurement conditions is the best, and possibly the only way, to confirm that the application is fit for the specific purpose.

Software should be treated like hardware—each item must have a unique identification. Documentation must also include records of the initial testing of the software, subsequent testing, any problems encountered, software upgrades, and bug or deficiency patches. The records should also include information on the hardware being used, tests of that, and so on.

There are many commercial software products on the market that maintain calibration records, recall systems, calibration data, and estimation of uncertainties.

STANDARDS FOR MEASUREMENT PROCESSES AND CALIBRATION SYSTEMS

Several standards are currently on the market that can be helpful in improving processes. The appendixes in these standards discuss various methods to improve control and measurement processes in the calibration facilities and wherever measurements are made.

- ISO 10012-1:1992, *Quality assurance requirements for measuring equipment—Part 1: Metrological confirmation system for measuring equipment.* This standard, referenced for guidance in clause 7.6, describes a confirmation system for measuring equipment used to demonstrate compliance with specified requirements. It is prescriptive in format, but it lays out very clearly the essentials that go into confirming that measuring equipment is suitable for a specific application.

- *The companion standard,* ISO 10012-2:1997, *Quality assurance for measuring equipment—Part 2: Guidelines for control of measurement processes.* This standard applies to the measurement processes and provides guidance on the control of those processes.[1]
- ANSI/ASQC M1-1996, *American national standard for calibration systems.* This standard describes two approaches to ensuring the quality of calibration of measuring equipment.
- ANSI/ISO/IEC 17025:2000, *General requirements for the competence of testing and calibration laboratories.* This standard is the major revision of ISO/IEC Guide 25:1990. Although this standard is primarily directed to the management of calibration and testing laboratories, the information and guidance in several of its sections can be useful in managing measuring equipment and the measurement processes.

GLOSSARY

Accuracy of a measuring instrument: Ability of a measuring instrument to give responses close to a true value. *Note:* "Accuracy" is a qualitative concept. (*VIM* 5.21)

Accuracy of measurement: Closeness of the agreement between the result of a measurement and a true value of the measurand. *Note 1:* "Accuracy" is a qualitative concept. *Note 2:* The term *precision* should not be used for *accuracy.* (*VIM* 3.5)

Calibration: A set of operations that establish, under specified conditions, the relationship between values of quantities indicated by a measuring instrument or measuring system, or values represented by a material measure or a reference material, and the corresponding values realized by standards. (*VIM* 6.11)

Confirm: To establish the truth or correctness of; to state with assurance that something is true. (*COD*)

Conformity: Fulfillment of a requirement. (ISO 9000:2000 clause 3.6.1)

Device: A thing made or adapted for a particular purpose, especially a mechanical or electronic contrivance. Or a plan, scheme, or trick. (*COD*)

Measure: To ascertain the size, amount, or degree of something by comparison with a standard unit or with an object of known size. (*COD*)

Measuring equipment: Measuring instrument, software, measurement standard, reference material, or auxiliary apparatus or combination thereof necessary to realize a measurement process. (ISO 9000:2000 3.10.4)

Metrological confirmation: The set of operations required to ensure that measuring equipment conforms to the requirements for its intended use. *Note 1:* Metrological confirmation generally includes calibration or verification, any necessary adjustment or repair and subsequent recalibration, comparison with the metrological requirements for the intended use of the equipment, as well as any required sealing and labeling. *Note 2:* Metrological confirmation is not achieved until and unless the fitness of the measuring equipment for the intended use has been demonstrated and documented. *Note 3:* The requirements for the intended use include such considerations as range, resolution, maximum permissible errors, and so on. *Note 4:* Metrological confirmation requirements are usually distinct from and are not specified in product requirements. (ISO 9000:2000 clause 3.10.3)

Monitor: A person or device that monitors something. Also, to observe and check over a period of time. To maintain regular surveillance over something. *(COD)*

Precision: The quality, condition, or fact of being precise; (as modifier) marked by or designed for accuracy and exactness: *a precision instrument*; refinement in a measurement or specification, especially as represented by the number of digits given. (*COD*)

Traceability: A property of the result of a measurement or the value of a standard whereby it can be related to stated references, usually national or international standards, through an unbroken chain of comparisons all having stated uncertainties. (*VIM* 6.10)

Validation: Confirmation, through the provision of objective evidence, that the requirements for a specific intended use or application have been fulfilled. *Note 1:* The term *validated* is used to designate the corresponding status. *Note 2:* The use conditions for validation can be real or simulated. (ISO 9000:2000 clause 3.8.5)

Verification: Confirmation, through the provision of objective evidence, that specified requirements have been fulfilled. *Note 1:* The term *verified* is used to designate the corresponding status. *Note 2:* Confirmation can comprise activities such as:

- Performing alternative calculations
- Comparing a new design specification with a similar proven design specification
- Undertaking tests and demonstrations
- Reviewing documents prior to issue

(ISO 9000:2000 clause 3.8.4)

ENDNOTE

1. ISO/TC 176/ SC3/WG1 is currently preparing a new 10012 standard that combines parts 1 and 2 into one standard. Publication of the new standard is expected in 2002.

REFERENCES

ANSI/ASQC M1-1996, *American national standard for calibration systems.*
ANSI/ISO 14001-1996, *Environmental management systems—Specification with guidance for use.*
ANSI/ISO 14004-1996, *Environmental management systems—General guidelines on principles, systems and supporting techniques.*
ANSI/ISO/ASQ Q9000:2000, *Quality management systems—Fundamentals and vocabulary.*
ANSI/ISO/ASQ Q9001:2000, *Quality management systems—Requirements.*

ANSI/ISO/ASQ Q9004:2000, *Quality management systems—Guidelines for performance improvements.*

ANSI/ISO/ASQC Q9001:1994, *Quality systems—Model for quality assurance in design, development, production, installation and servicing.*

ANSI/ISO/IEC 17025:2000, *General requirements for the competence of testing and calibration laboratories.*

BIPM/IEC/IFCC/ISO/IUPAC/IUPAP/OIML:1993, *International vocabulary of basic and general terms in metrology (VIM).*

Concise Oxford Dictionary, 10th ed. Oxford University Press, 1999.

ISO 10012-1:1992, *Quality assurance requirements for measuring equipment—Part 1: Metrological confirmation system for measuring equipment.*

ISO 10012-2:1997, *Quality assurance for measuring equipment—Part 2: Guidelines for control of measurement processes.*

NCSL Recommended Practice RP-6:1999, *Calibration control systems for the biomedical and pharmaceutical industry.*

Section 7

Measurement, Analysis and Improvement

Introduction

John E. (Jack) West
Consultant, The Woodlands, Texas

Clause 8 of ISO 9001:2000 consolidates requirements related to monitoring and measurement, control of nonconforming product, analysis of data, and improvement. Control of nonconforming product was covered in section 6. The other topics in clause 8 are covered in this section.

GENERAL

Clause 8.1 of ISO 9001:2000 requires planning of the processes for monitoring, measurement, data analysis, and improvement. This means that these processes need to be planned in such a manner that the conformity of product can be demonstrated. It also means that the processes must ensure conformity and continual improvement of the effectiveness of the quality management system. This means that the organization needs to consider planning to enhance customer satisfaction and achieve improvements as well as to ensure conformity.

STATISTICAL TECHNIQUES

Clause 8.1 also requires "determination of applicable methods, including statistical techniques and the extent of their use." Statistical methods can be extremely important to the control and improvement of products and product realization processes. They also can have applicability in other processes of the quality management system. Harrison Wadsworth discusses the use of statistical techniques in chapter 28, "Statistical Procedures Useful for Implementation of ISO 9001:2000."

MONITORING AND MEASUREMENT

ISO 9001:2000 requires monitoring of customer satisfaction as well as appropriate monitoring and measurement of products and processes. Internal audits are also required as a means to monitor the quality management system. It is worthwhile to recognize the order of "monitoring and measurement." Monitoring usually provides less information than measuring. Monitoring may be considered a broader concept than measurement. Monitoring may involve general observation or it may include the use of specific measurements. The results of monitoring may indicate a need to gather more information through measuring. An organization might monitor or measure or do both for similar types of data:

- For customer satisfaction, methods must be developed and implemented to monitor customer perceptions of whether the organization has met customer requirements. Note that in this case only the work monitor is used. The requirement for monitoring of customer satisfaction is new. Chapter 29, "Measurement of Customer Satisfaction," by David M. Saunders, Charles A. Cianfrani, and Wayne G. Robertshaw discusses this important aspect of the quality management system.

- An internal audit program is required to determine whether the quality management system conforms to its own internal arrangements, meets the requirements of ISO 9001, and is effectively implemented. In chapter 30, "Internal Audit," John H. Stratton provides his insight into the auditing process.

- Products and processes also must be monitored and measured as appropriate to ensure conformity of product. These monitoring and measurement activities may be carried out differently depending on the product category. These topics are discussed by Jorgen Steen Petersen (chapter 31) for hardware, Diane M. Baguley (chapters 33 and 34) for service, and Frank Houston (chapter 32) for software.

CONTROL OF NONCONFORMING PRODUCT

The concepts related to control of nonconforming product are easy to understand and apply for hardware, processed materials, and even for software. Their application to the service sector requires greater depth of thinking. In chapter 35, "Clause 8.3: Control of Nonconforming Product," Lorri Hunt explains the requirements and gives examples of application for each product category.

ANALYSIS OF DATA

The improvement process is dependent upon the collection and use of data. The usefulness of the analysis depends upon understanding the analytical methods appropriate to the circumstances. Donald N. Ekvall provides insight into techniques for collection and analysis of appropriate data in chapter 36, "Process Analysis."

IMPROVEMENT

Clause 8.5 requires continual improvement of the effectiveness of the quality management system. This aligns with the requirement in clause 5.3 for the quality policy to include a commitment to such improvement. In chapter 37, "Improvement,"

Hitoshi Kume discusses the overall concept of improvement as well as corrective and preventive action.

The 1994 edition of ISO 9001 included many of the aforementioned requirements. The corrective and preventive action clauses of that standard, taken together, formed a requirement for improvement. But the improvement did not need to be part of a planned process to meet a required commitment in the quality policy, as is the case with ISO 9001:2000. The concept of corrective action has been well understood, but the idea of preventive action has generated much debate. Many organizations do not separate the concepts and use the same process for both corrective action and preventive action. Actually the concepts are quite different, and the techniques are different for each. While corrective action involves the solving of known problems, preventive action is intended to address finding potential causes of possible problems. In preventive action the organization is required to take preventive action to eliminate the "cause of potential nonconformities."

There are a number of ways to identify potential problems and to assess their potential impact. In chapter 37, Professor Kume discusses the situation where preventive action addresses core deficiencies in the quality management system. Organizations can look at preventive action in other ways, and the standard provides them the flexibility to define their own implementation methods. Some examples include the following:

- When nonconformities are identified in one part of the organization and causes are addressed by the corrective action system, some organizations look for similar situations in other areas. For example, if action is taken to correct the cause of a nonconformity in one product line, it may be desirable to determine if similar nonconformities are likely to occur in other lines. If so, preventive action may be appropriate for the other lines.

- Risk analysis or failure mode and effects analysis may be used to define potential problems and to assess their potential impacts.

- Analysis of data on process performance may identify process parameters that have a high probability of creating nonconformities.

- Management review may be used as a vehicle for discussing and evaluating areas for preventive actions.

Chapter 28

Statistical Procedures Useful for Implementation of ISO 9001:2000

Harrison Wadsworth
Professor emeritus, School of Industrial and Systems Engineering,
Georgia Institute of Technology, Atlanta, Georgia

INTRODUCTION

The use of statistical methods is helpful, if not required, for conformance to many requirements of ISO 9001:2000. This chapter identifies those requirements along with reasons for the use of statistical methods and briefly describes which techniques are useful. Details of the techniques may be found in other texts on statistical methods, although some discussion of how they may be used is included here.

The 1994 editions of the ISO 9000 series (9001, 9002, and 9003) contained a clause (4.20) titled "Statistical techniques." This clause required the identification of needs for statistical methods and the documentation of procedures that would be useful in implementing and controlling any needs identified. Since the clause did not specifically require users of the standard to identify some needs, many users merely stated that they had no need for statistics, even though they were using such things as control charts, sampling plans, or descriptive statistics. They found it easier to just ignore statistical methods when being audited.

The first thing one observes in ISO 9001:2000 is that there is no longer a clause titled "Statistical techniques." This does not mean that statistical methods are no longer required. The user should still identify needs for statistics, and auditors should be looking for their application. In fact, the only specific mention of statistics is in clause 8.1, which asks for processes, including statistical techniques, to demonstrate the product and the quality management system's conformance and effectiveness.

ISO 9000:2000 contains a clause (2.10) titled "Role of statistical techniques." This role consists of the following, according to the clause:

- Helping to understand variability
- Helping to solve and prevent problems
- Improving effectiveness of the quality system
- Assisting efficient decision making
- Promoting continual improvement

Clause 2.10 of ISO 9000:2000 indicates that all these activities involve the analysis of data. Statistical techniques enable this analysis to be accomplished in a more efficient manner even when the amount of available data is limited. The clause makes reference to the technical report ISO/TR 10017, which provides guidance for the use of statistical techniques in implementation of ISO 9001.

ISO 9004:2000 contains suggested statistical techniques for many of its clauses, which are the same as those of ISO 9001:2000. Although this standard is intended for those organizations that wish to go beyond the basic requirements of ISO 9001, the suggestions included will assist any organization in controlling and improving its quality system. In this chapter, reference to these suggestions will be included in the following discussion of specific clauses of ISO 9001:2000 that contain possibilities for the use of statistical techniques.

STATISTICAL TECHNIQUES USEFUL FOR CLAUSES OF ISO 9001:2000

4.1   General Requirements

Clause 4.1 requires top management to ensure that resources are available to operate all processes of the quality system. It also requires that the processes of the system be monitored and measured and that all processes be analyzed in order to establish a customer-oriented organization. Statistical techniques useful for this process include:

- Graphical techniques, including trend charts, Pareto charts, and line charts
- Control charts
- Sampling plans

5.1   Management Commitment

Clause 5.1 requires top management to commit to the development and implementation of an efficient management system along with its continual improvement. Statistical analyses are necessary to accomplish the activities necessary to create a customer focus for the organization.

5.4   Planning

Quality planning requires a statement of quality objectives and methods for achieving these objectives. To accomplish this, ISO 9004:2000 suggests several processes that are helpful and for which statistical techniques are useful. These include evaluation of product and process performance data, suggestions for opportunities for improvement, and related risk assessment studies.

5.6   Management Review

Periodic management reviews are required by ISO 9001. The purpose of such reviews is to ensure continued suitability, adequacy, and effectiveness of the quality system. The management reviews must include quantitative data. These data should include such statistical techniques as the following:

- Trend charts
- Pareto charts
- Process capability results
- Control chart results
- Gage R and R studies
- Benchmarking activities
- Marketplace evaluations
- Preventive action evaluations

6.2   Human Resources

The following statistical techniques are useful for the evaluation of competence, awareness, and training of personnel:

- Significance tests to determine the effectiveness of training, particularly if improvement in employee performance has occurred
- Design of experiments that will facilitate the determination of training needs
- Regression analyses to identify operator effects on quality characteristics

7.1   Planning of Product Realization

Clause 7.1 suggests the use of many statistical techniques for planning for product quality. The organization must determine its quality objectives, needs for documentation, requirements for verification of test activities and acceptance criteria, and required records. The following statistical techniques are useful in planning for high-quality products:

- Factorial designs needed to determine optimum product designs.
- Robust design methods, often called Taguchi procedures, that use the concept of signal-to-noise ratios. These procedures assist in the determination of optimum product designs in the presence of noise factors such as environmental factors. Quadratic loss functions are usually used to determine product tolerances. The experimental designs are usually in the form of orthogonal arrays.
- Reliability analyses that consider the time elements of quality—that is, the time to failure of the product. These concepts are very necessary elements of product and process design planning. A related technique is failure mode and effects analysis (FMEA). This useful process is used to identify potential failure modes and consider the seriousness of their occurrence and their likelihood. Actions that may be taken to lesson the frequency of their occurrence and their severity are identified.

- Statistical process control (SPC) procedures, including the use of control charts and other such techniques. Planning activities include the determination of processes that must be actively controlled and which SPC procedure should be used to accomplish this control.

- Acceptance sampling procedures provide a basis for evaluating incoming raw material and in-process and final product inspection to ensure that nonconforming product does not reach the customer. Acceptance sampling standards such as ISO 2859-1 and ISO 3951 or their American versions, ANSI/ASQ Z1.4 and ANSI/ASQ Z1.9, should be used for this purpose. The use of these or other equivalent standards is necessary to measure and control sampling risks.

- Regression analysis is a statistical procedure that enables the user to measure the effect of one quality characteristic on another. Using this approach, it is often possible to determine an easily measured quality characteristic that may be used to control another that is difficult to measure. This is especially useful in the case of "special characteristics" described elsewhere in this handbook.

- Process capability analysis provides a means to measure the capability of a process to meet its requirements. This type of analysis requires a measure of process variability and its comparison with its specification limits. The usual capability indexes are Cp and Cpk. Cp is the ratio of the tolerance limits, U – L, to the width of the process variability for a controlled process from a normal distribution, six standard deviations, or 6σ, where σ is the process standard deviation. Cpk is the minimum ratio of the difference between the process average and each specification limit divided by three standard deviations. That is, it is min $[(\mu - L)/3\sigma, (U - \mu)/3\sigma]$. Cp is a measure of the process capability without considering the centering of the process. Cpk considers the process average. Both are important measures of the process capability.

- Statistical tolerancing is used to design assemblies that are additive. It considers the fact that variances are additive but standard deviations are not. Thus, if the width of two parts are added, their total standard deviation is the square root of the sum of their variances.

- Simulation techniques that are used to evaluate possible process designs using Monte Carlo methods to simulate performance under various scenarios.

7.3   Design and Development

Many of the techniques just listed may also be used during the design and development stage. Some of these techniques are FMEA, simulation, statistical tolerancing, regression analysis, reliability analysis, and design of experiments, both robust and traditional design procedures. In fact, process design and planning should be considered a part of the product design and development process, and both should be conducted simultaneously.

7.4   Purchasing

Statistical techniques are an important part of the purchasing process. The standard requires the evaluation of suppliers. This may be done using acceptance sampling for receiving inspection. Reliability analysis should be used to evaluate the supplier's product. This includes life testing and environmental testing. In the case of long-lived items, accelerated testing procedures are available to determine the reliability of purchased parts. These may involve high-temperature or high-stress testing. To make use of these techniques, statistical procedures must be employed to relate the test results to actual expected operating conditions.

Other statistical techniques that should be used to evaluate purchased products include process capability analysis and statistical tests of significance. The latter may be used to determine whether the submitted product meets the specifications.

7.6   Control of Monitoring and Measuring Devices

To properly measure a product the appropriate devices must be selected. To do this the organization must understand the capabilities of each possible device. In addition the device must be properly calibrated. In some instances the calibration of the device may include a statistical analysis of the measurement results. This analysis may consist of measurements of the average and standard deviation and a comparison of these results with the requirements of the device.

The following statistical techniques are useful for this process:

- Calibration of gages as discussed above.

- Pareto analysis, in which the relative frequency of occurrence of various measurement requirements are indicated.

- Descriptive analysis—this may be needed to show the ability of the measurement devices to measure different stress conditions. These graphical techniques are especially suitable for showing the adequacy of a device to make the necessary measurements.

- Measurement analysis, usually consisting of determination of the precision of the devices. Trueness, meaning accuracy or bias of the device, is considered as is precision or agreement among measurements and random errors. Several causes of differences in measurements must be considered. These include the operator, the measuring equipment, the calibration, the environment, and the time between measurements. All of these must be considered and measured in order to evaluate a measuring device.

Two aspects of precision must be considered: repeatability and reproducibility. Repeatability is the case where all the factors mentioned in the previous paragraph are kept constant. That is, the same gage, the same parts, the same operator, and the same environmental conditions are used. The second aspect, reproducibility, is the same as repeatability except different operators are used. A study of these two aspects is called a gage R and R study. Typically several parts and two or three skilled operators are used. The operators measure the same parts in random order. The standard deviations of the measurements for each operator are calculated. The standard deviation of the measurements with the same operator is compared with the standard deviation using different operators. In this manner the percent of the total variation due to gage variability alone is determined. This is illustrated by means of a ratio called the gage R and R ratio.

8   Measurement, Analysis and Improvement

As noted earlier, the first subclause (8.1) in this clause is the only time the words *statistical techniques* are specifically mentioned in ISO 9001:2000. The purpose of this first subclause is to require the planning and implementation of appropriate monitoring and measuring processes. This includes the determination of applicable methods for the analysis of data, including statistical techniques.

The second subclause, 8.2, discusses monitoring and measuring, first with customer satisfaction, then with internal audits, and finally with the measurement of processes and products. The measurement of customer satisfaction is a difficult project for many organizations. ISO 9004:2000 can be used for guidance in this case. That standard suggests using customer surveys, feedback on product aspects, market needs, service delivery data, and information relative to competitors. Data that may be used to evaluate these things include customer complaints, direct communication with customers, surveys, focus groups, published reports of consumer organizations, and industry studies. The collection and analysis of whatever data are used to evaluate customer satisfaction requires the use of statistical techniques. Here are some of those techniques:

- Survey sampling, including development of survey questions and selecting the sample
- Market needs analysis
- Pareto charts to evaluate the relative frequency of customer complaints or suggestions
- Significance tests to evaluate competitor data and other results

Internal auditing may require the use of descriptive statistics to illustrate the audit results. It may also require statistical sampling techniques to determine audit locations. The audit process may also involve significance tests to evaluate actions taken to correct problems discovered by the audits.

Subclause 8.2.3 requires the monitoring and measuring of processes. All processes have required outputs, and statistical methods are useful to determine whether the processes are meeting those output requirements or whether they are even capable of meeting them.

Subclause 8.2.4 requires the monitoring and measurement of product. Its purpose is to ensure that all products conform to specifications. The monitoring occurs at appropriate stages in the production cycle. The monitoring may use control charts or other statistical means, such as line charts, or other graphical means. Statistical techniques that might be used to monitor processes and products include control charts, sampling process capability analysis, and graphical techniques. ISO 9004:2000 also recommends that an analysis of lifecycle costs be included in this evaluation of products and processes.

8.4   Analysis of Data

Clause 8.4 requires the collection and analysis of data so that decisions may be based on facts. The purpose of these data is to determine the suitability of the quality management system and its effectiveness. The data may also be used to evaluate the continual improvement of the system. The data are obtained from monitoring and measuring activities as well as other sources such as internal and external audits.

The data are to be analyzed to provide information for decision making relative to customer satisfaction and conformance to product and process requirements. The analysis also is used to review characteristics and trends for processes and products, and potential preventive actions. Another purpose of this analysis is to assist in the evaluation of all suppliers.

There are many statistical methods that may used to analyze the data. The appropriate technique depends on the data. Following are some of the statistical approaches:

- Determination of root causes of problems using such things as control charts, failure analysis, or graphical methods
- Design of experiments to determine reasons for the results that have been observed
- Regression and correlation analysis to determine the effects of certain characteristics on others
- Significance tests to determine if actions taken have resulted in process improvement
- Time series procedures to evaluate trends to differentiate between chance and real changes in the results

8.5   Improvement

This clause requires the organization to continually improve the effectiveness of the quality management system. The things that may be used to accomplish this requirement include reviews of the quality policy and objectives, audit results, proper analysis of data, management reviews, and corrective and preventive actions. Statistical methods useful for these evaluations include the following:

- Design of experiments, including robust designs, to determine parameter values that will result in improved processes and system operations.
- Regression and correlation analyses to study the effect of changes in one parameter on others.
- Failure mode and effects analysis (FMEA) to study potential problems and their effect on the product, even though they may not have ever occurred. This is one of the more important tools needed for the identification and understanding of preventive action projects.
- Descriptive statistics, which are useful in order to evaluate and justify continual improvement projects such as those needed in Six Sigma projects.
- Significance tests to determine if results are real or merely the effect of chance variation.

8.5.2   Corrective Action and 8.5.3   Preventive Action

The last two clauses of the ISO 9001:2000 standard address corrective and preventive action. Corrective action requires the organization to review all nonconformities to determine their root cause and to evaluate any need for action. The clause also calls for the implementation of any needed action and the recording and reviewing of all actions taken. These activities often are quite obvious, whereas preventive actions needed to guard against problems that have not occurred may be more difficult to determine even though the statistical methods for both may be the same.

The following statistical techniques have proved useful for corrective and preventive actions:

- Fault tree analysis that starts with a potential or real problem and works backward to the possible causes.

- Control charts and other SPC techniques. These enable the user to distinguish between chance or common causes and assignable or special causes of variation. The presence of an assignable cause is usually a signal that a corrective action is needed.

- Pareto charts that are used to distinguish among nonconformities to determine the most important or most frequently occurring. This assists the organization in setting priorities for working on corrective and preventive action projects.

- Significance tests that enable the organization to evaluate the effect of actions taken to correct or prevent nonconformities.

- Reliability analysis, including failure analysis, to determine the causes of failures and what may be done to increase the average life of the product.

- Time series analysis to study trends in the data. This study may be able to correct a process before any nonconforming items have been made.

- Cause-and-effect diagrams to assist in determining all processes that might be affecting the final product.

CONCLUSION

ISO/TC 69, Applications of Statistical Methods, has published many standards useful for the purpose of introducing statistical techniques into organizations wishing to conform to ISO 9001:2000. Some of these have been referenced earlier in this chapter.

A pertinent standard is ISO 11462-1, *Guidelines for implementation of statistical process control—Part 1: Elements of SPC*. This standard outlines the process of operating a system of statistical process control. It discusses the objectives and organization for SPC operations and the places where such techniques would be useful to the organization. It does not, however, introduce the theory and mathematics of SPC techniques. That is left to many texts on the use of statistics for the control of quality such as Wadsworth, Stephens, and Godfrey (2002) and Montgomery (2001). Where the techniques have been standardized, ISO/TC 69 has published them. Following is a list of some of the standards that will be helpful to the organization wishing to introduce statistical techniques:

ISO/TR 10017 (1998), *Guide to the application of statistical techniques for ISO 9001:1994.* This standard is being revised for the 2000 edition of ISO 9001. It is published by ISO/TC 176.

ISO 2602 (1980), *Statistical interpretation of test results—Estimation of the mean-confidence interval.*

ISO 2854 (1976), *Statistical interpretation of data—Techniques of estimation and test relating to means and variances.*

ISO 2859-0 (1995), *Sampling procedures for inspection by attributes—Part 0: Introduction to the ISO 2859 attribute sampling system.* This is also designated as ANSI/ASQC S2-1995.

ISO 2859-1 (1999), *Sampling procedures for inspection by attributes—Part 1: Sampling schemes indexed by acceptance quality limit (AQL) for lot-by-lot inspection.* This is also designated as ANSI/ASQC Z1.4-1993.

ISO 3207 (1975), *Statistical interpretation of data—Determination of statistical tolerance intervals.*

ISO 3301 (1975), *Statistical interpretation of data—Comparison of two means in the case of paired observations.*

ISO 3534-1 (1993), *Statistics—Vocabulary and symbols—Part 1: Probability and general statistical terms.* This standard is under revision and will be published in 2002. This standard is also designated as ANSI/ISO/ASQC A3534-1.

ISO 3534-2 (1993), *Statistics—Vocabulary and symbols—Part 2: Statistical quality control.* This standard is being revised (to be published in 2002) and will be titled *Applied statistics* rather than *Statistical quality control.* This standard is also designated as ANSI/ISO/ASQC A3534-2.

ISO 3534-3 (1999), *Statistics—Vocabulary and symbols—Part 3: Design of experiments.*

ISO 3951 (1989), *Sampling procedures and charts for inspection by variables for percent nonconforming.* This is also designated as ANSI/ASQC Z1.9-1993.

ISO 5725-1 (1994), *Accuracy (trueness and precision) of measurement methods and results—Part 1: General principles and definitions.*

ISO 5725-2 (1994), *Accuracy (trueness and precision) of measurement methods and results—Part 2: The basic method for determination of repeatability and reproducibility of a standard measurement method.*

ISO 7870 (1993), *Control charts—General guide and introduction.*

ISO 8258 (1991), *Shewhart control charts.*

ISO/TR 8550 (1994), *Guide for selection of an acceptance sampling system, scheme, or plan for inspection of discrete items in lots.*

ISO 9000 (2000), *Quality management systems—Fundamentals and vocabulary.* This standard is also designated as ANSI/ISO/ASQ Q9000-2000.

ISO 10725 (2000), *Acceptance sampling plans and procedures for the inspection of bulk materials.*

ISO 11648-1 (2001), *Statistical aspects of sampling from bulk material—Part 1: General introduction.*

ISO 11648-2 (2001), *Statistical aspects of sampling from bulk material—Part 2: Sampling of particulate materials.*

ISO 11462-1 (2001), *Guidelines for implementation of statistical process control (SPC)—Part 1: Elements of SPC.* This standard is also designated as BSR/ISO/ASQ S11462-1

All of these standards are useful for a complete understanding of the statistical methods needed for the implementation of ISO 9001:2000. Some, as indicated, have been adopted as American national standards and may be obtained from ASQ. In conclusion, it should be repeated that organizations wishing to comply with the ISO 9001:2000 standards will be expected to obtain and study many of the standards in the foregoing list.

REFERENCES

American Society for Quality. ANSI/ASQC Z1.4, *Sampling procedures and tables for inspection by attributes.* Milwaukee: American Society for Quality Control, 1993.
———. ANSI/ASQC Z1.9, *Sampling procedures and tables for inspection by variables for percent nonconforming.* Milwaukee: American Society for Quality Control, 1993.
International Organization for Standardization. *Sampling procedures and charts for inspection by variables for percent nonconforming.* Geneva, Switzerland: International Organization for Standardization, 1989.
———. *Guide to the application of statistical techniques for ISO 9001:1994.* Geneva, Switzerland: International Organization for Standardization, 1998.
———. *Sampling procedures for inspection by attributes—Part 1: Sampling schemes indexed by acceptance quality limit (AQL) for lot-by-lot inspection.* Geneva, Switzerland: International Organization for Standardization, 1999.
Montgomery, D. C. *Introduction to Statistical Quality Control.* 4th ed. New York: John Wiley & Sons, 2001.
Wadsworth, H. M., K. S. Stephens, and A. B. Godfrey. *Modern Methods for Quality Control and Improvement.* 2nd ed. New York: John Wiley & Sons, 2002.

Chapter 29

Measurement of Customer Satisfaction

David M. Saunders, Charles A. Cianfrani,
and Wayne G. Robertshaw
ARBOR and ISOize.com, Media, Pennsylvania

INTRODUCTION

"Adjust your product to the public, not the public to your product."

Dr. W. Edwards Deming pointed out in his famous lectures that the purpose of understanding customer wants, needs, and requirements should be to adjust *a product to the public* rather than to adjust *the public to a product.*[1] He suggested that marketing and sales departments all too frequently use their vast budgets to convince and persuade customers rather than to determine how to fulfill customer desires. The new ISO 9001:2000 standard places a significant emphasis on the measurement of customer satisfaction, thereby requiring that customer requirements be determined under controlled conditions. The authors believe that the marketing and sales departments, or others responsible for determining customer requirements, should now be subject to ISO discipline.

The logic of customer satisfaction measurement is simple. If you increase customer satisfaction, customers will repurchase, loyalty will increase, marketing costs will go down, margins will increase, and profits will rise. For instance, in the automobile industry, where loyalty rates typically are only 30 percent to 40 percent, the Toyota Lexus has a whopping 62 percent repurchase rate. It is reported that, although the Lexus accounts for only 2 percent of Toyota's sales, it delivers one-third of the profits.[2]

How Much Effort Is Your Company Applying to Satisfying Your Customers?

Although customer satisfaction has a powerful leverage on profits, many companies do not have a formalized system for collecting and utilizing customer information. Often the customer satisfaction measurement system is rudimentary, ad hoc, undocumented, uncontrolled, and underused.

In contrast, the same organization that has a rudimentary system for handling customer data may have an extremely sophisticated system for handling financial data. Usually there is an entire finance department; a required set of monthly, quarterly, and annual financial reports; a structured review process; a set of financially oriented decision-making criteria; and an entire "language" to understand and use financial data.

Modern organizations need good systems for both financial data *and* customer data. ISO 9001:2000 provides an opportunity to raise customer data to the level of usefulness previously found only in financial data.

8.2.1 CUSTOMER SATISFACTION

The new ISO 9001 standard addresses customer satisfaction as follows:

8.2.1 Customer satisfaction

As one of the measurements of the performance of the quality management system, the organization shall monitor information relating to customer perception as to whether the organization has met customer requirements. The methods for obtaining and using this information shall be determined.

Source: ANSI/ISO/ASQ Q9001-2000

What does this mean? Figure 29.1 shows that there may be many measures in a quality management system. Clause 8.2.1 requires that at least one of those measures be of customer perceptions.

The clause goes on to explain that customer perceptions are of "how well the organization meets requirements." ISO 9000:2000 defines *requirement* as "a need or expectation that is stated, generally implied, or obligatory." Part of the ISO discipline is to list requirements so that the organization can then establish a method for testing the degree to which customers perceive that requirements are met.

A suggested approach is to ask customers directly for their perceptions of the degree to which a product meets their needs. For example, "On a 10-point scale, with 10 being completely satisfied and 1 being very dissatisfied, how satisfied are you with this handbook's ability to meet your need for information on the new ISO quality management standard?" In the United States, the telephone interview is the method of choice (see Figure 29.2).

Finally, clause 8.2.1 says that the methods for obtaining and using this information shall be "determined." The clause does not go so far as to say that the methods shall be "documented." ISO 9000 does not define *determined*, but according to the Oxford English dictionary "determine" means control, resolve firmly, establish precisely. . . .

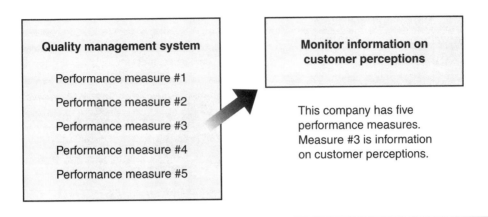

Figure 29.1 Measurement of customer perceptions.

Figure 29.2 Telephone interview for measurement of customer perceptions.

The intent is clear. Marketing and sales departments or others in the organization that are generally responsible for the study of customer perceptions, are now subject to the ISO discipline. As Figure 29.3 shows, marketing and sales are now required to show that they have determined their methods for obtaining and using customer data.

ISO 9000 (clause 3.1.4) continues to shed light on customer satisfaction with two relevant notes. Note 1 states, "Customer complaints are a common indicator of low customer satisfaction, but their absence does not necessarily imply high customer satisfaction." Experts in customer satisfaction have long known that the absence of complaints does not mean customers are pleased with your product; they just might not take the time to complain. Note 2 states, "Even when customer

Marketing Department

Figure 29.3   The marketing department has a key role in ISO 9001:2000.

requirements have been agreed with the customer and fulfilled, this does not necessarily ensure high customer satisfaction." Often satisfied customers will quickly switch when a better deal seems to come along.

Enhancements over the 1994 Edition

The 1994 edition of ISO 9000 had implicit but not explicit references to customer satisfaction. A frequently cited, but incorrect, criticism of the 1994 edition was that a firm could manufacture "concrete life preservers" and still achieve certification (see Figure 29.4). (Critics claimed that one could meet ISO requirements by ensuring that life preservers were made of high-quality concrete produced under controlled conditions!)

However, in fairness to the writers of the 1994 standard, the standard was explicit about the use of customer data on the front end in product design, even though it did not explicitly require studies of customer satisfaction for products delivered into the hands of customers. Clearly, the new edition of the standard ends the controversy and places the monitoring of customer perceptions in every organization's business plan.

This chapter covers three areas:

- Discussion of the customer satisfaction guidelines provided by ISO 9001:2000 and ISO 9004:2000

- A model for a customer satisfaction measurement system

- Discussion of various issues related to the study of customer perceptions

The chapter is written for quality professionals and ISO management representatives who need to know enough about customer satisfaction measurement to guide their organizations through ISO certification as well as for the marketing and sales professionals whose functions are now clearly included under the ISO discipline.

An incorrect, but largely held criticism of the 1994 ISO standard was the absurd idea that manufacturing concrete life preservers under controlled conditions was allowable.

Figure 29.4   An incorrect criticism of the 1994 standard.

USING ISO 9004 TO GO BEYOND 9001 COMPLIANCE

ISO 9004 provides guidelines (not requirements) for the measurement of customer satisfaction. Following the 9004 guidelines will bring your organization to an even higher quality level than following the 9001 requirements. ISO 9004 suggests that an organization establish, on a continual basis, a process to "collect, analyze, and use . . . many sources of customer-related information." Collection can be "active," as when the organization solicits information through surveys, focus groups, and interviews, or it can be "passive," as when customers volunteer complaints, suggestions, and advice.

ISO 9004 goes further than 9001 to suggest that organizations learn "to anticipate future needs." Customer research is a powerful tool to identify industry trends as well as the specific directions individual customers are pursuing. However, in the thirst for customer data, don't let valuable internal knowledge go untapped. In his lectures, Dr. Deming reminded us, "Did the customer ask for a lightbulb? No. Did the customer ask for the pneumatic tire? No." (Deming, at age 90, knowingly added, "First ones were not very good, I remember them well!"[3]) These innovations came from suppliers with profound customer knowledge—suppliers who knew far better than customers the nature of a specific problem, the capacity of a technology, and the power of a good idea.

However, the ultimate success of even internally-generated new products can be enhanced by customer research. Many companies have a "pipeline" of new product ideas or new technologies. Customer research can be used both to prioritize the commercialization of these products and to fine-tune their actual development in order to maximize their desirability in the marketplace.[4]

ISO 9004 makes the point that organizations should "define . . . the frequency of data-analysis reviews." As was mentioned earlier, most organizations have elaborate systems for the collection, analysis, and review of financial data but have little in place to regularly review customer data. A robust customer satisfaction measurement system should describe when, where, and how management should review customer data.

Going beyond the minimum ISO requirements into the ISO 9004 realm is well demonstrated by Xerox Business Services, winner of the 1998 Malcolm Baldrige National Quality Award. Table 29.1 shows Xerox's comprehensive approach to the measurement of customer satisfaction.[5]

Moving Forward in the New Millennium

Many companies already have clearly defined methods, procedures, and systems for obtaining customer feedback and are well on the way to compliance. To others, the requirements may be a rude awakening. For those who have never studied

Table 29.1 Xerox's approach to measurement of customer satisfaction.

#	Method	Description
1	Customer satisfaction measurement survey	• All customers are surveyed once per year • An independent third party administers a mail survey • A five-point scale is used for "overall satisfaction," "recommendation for renewal," and "recommendation for other organizations" • The question "Have you had a significant problem . . ." determines labeling as "vulnerable," which is flagged for immediate action
2	"Customer first" complaint-tracking system	• The tracking system uses a customer database • Closed-loop tracking of individual complaints takes place (resolution is required) • Best practices can be generated and shared across the company • The system has aggregation and charting capability
3	Customer listening posts	• Employees are stationed at customer sites • Complaints, comments, and suggestions go directly through the normal chain of command to the next level of management
4	Customer loyalty meetings	• Customer account managers (operations) and account executives (sales) regularly meet with customers • Information is carried back through the normal chain of command to the next level of management
5	Postinstallation survey	• A paper-and-pencil, through-the-mail survey is administered to all new customers and for all significant expansions • The theory is that "if they start out happy, it is easier to keep them happy" • Focus is on all aspects of the installation experience

their customers and/or have not documented their processes, the next section will provide a framework and a model for achieving compliance. Using this model, companies have successfully documented their processes, demonstrated their contribution to understanding customer satisfaction, and identified ways to increase satisfaction.

A PROVEN PROCESS MODEL FOR CUSTOMER SATISFACTION MEASUREMENT

This section describes a proven process model for defining, implementing, and documenting a customer satisfaction measurement system, also known as a "voice of the customer" measurement system. The adoption of this type of process will not only satisfy the requirements for ISO certification but will also provide meaningful information with which to make strategic and tactical business decisions.

Overall Process Model

The basic model can be described in the following four steps: plan your customer data system, gather customer data, understand the data, and deploy the data.[6] These steps can be shown as a cycle, similar to the Shewhart cycle (Plan, Do, Study, Act) for quality improvement, or in a flowchart (see Figure 29.5).[7]

We have often observed that organizations lack a basic, proactive plan for collecting and using customer data. They react to specific events rather than take the time to develop a comprehensive approach. Often the customer satisfaction measurement process is implemented piecemeal, as if on a "random walk." In one firm, the marketing group had an aggressive customer focus and had developed

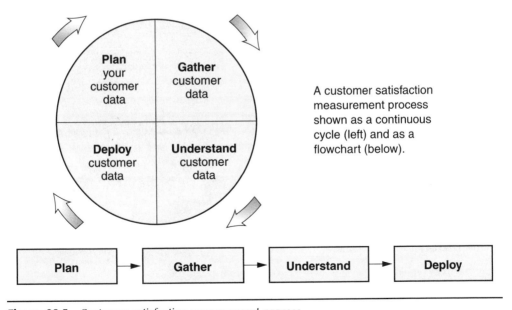

A customer satisfaction measurement process shown as a continuous cycle (left) and as a flowchart (below).

Figure 29.5 Customer satisfaction measurement process.

43 different methods to gather customer data. Each method grew from some well-intentioned effort, but there was little overall coordination among them, they generated substantial costs, and the use of the data was questionable.

Often organizations do not even have a comprehensive list of the data sources they use or have available. It is not unusual for part of an organization to use one customer data source, while another is completely ignorant of that source and is diligently using something else, frequently generating different priorities. Multiple sources of customer data can look like a jumbled puzzle and can cause all sorts of costly problems (see Figure 29.6).

To remedy this situation, establish a process to categorize and inventory the various data collection methods. Such an approach begins by establishing three primary categories for customer satisfaction data.[8] The first is *active,* in which the organization goes to the customer and asks deliberate questions or makes direct observations of customer behavior. The second is *receptive,* in which the customer comes to the organization with complaints or returns. The third is *indirect,* in which secondary sources are used, such as information published in *Consumer Reports* magazine. ISO 9004 suggests two categories of customer data, active and passive. The authors prefer to further split the passive into receptive and indirect (see Figure 29.7).

However, knowing and optimizing various sources of customer data is still not enough. For example, suppose an organization selects four data sources for measuring customer satisfaction. The four data sources are independent, each with its own plan, its own method of gathering data, its own tools for analysis, and even its own approach for deployment. Even though the company is using multiple sources of customer data, the sources are analyzed separately, which results in a significant degradation of value. In this example, the surveys might be analyzed by the marketing department, the focus groups studied by the sales department, the complaints analyzed by customer service, and the media handled by public relations. People are looking at the parts, but who sees the entire picture? (See Figure 29.8.)

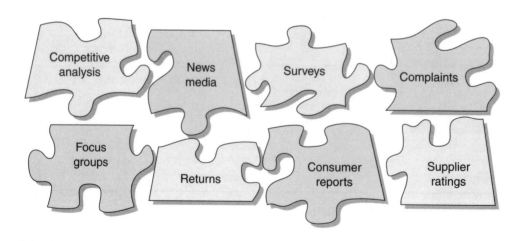

Figure 29.6 Multiple sources of customer data, but unorganized.

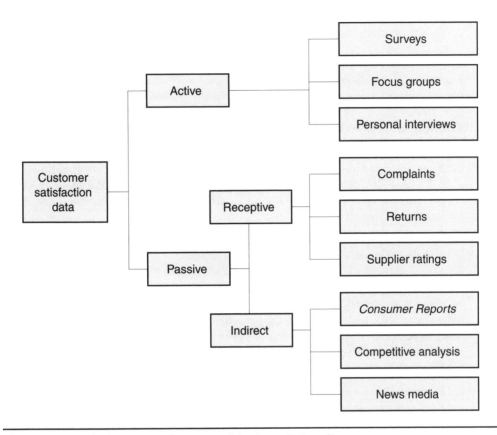

Figure 29.7 Multiple sources of customer data shown in tree diagram.

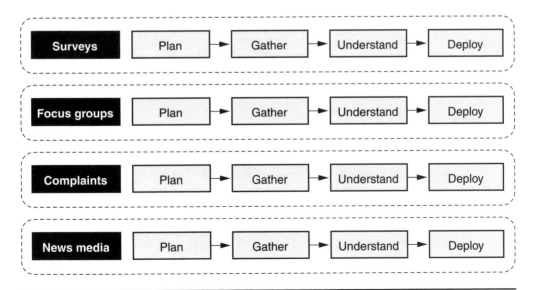

Figure 29.8 Each data source is analyzed separately, which often leads to confusion and misuse of data.

Many readers probably have systems similar to the one above—your company may be doing something, but it may not be defined, it may not be documented, and the elements may not be coordinated. A better approach, as shown in Figure 29.9, is to coordinate during the planning phase, analyze the data from all sources simultaneously, and then have a single unified deployment plan.

Determining a "Voice of the Customer" Measurement System

The last sentence of clause 8.2.1 says that the methods for obtaining and using customer information shall be determined. To accomplish this, the authors suggest the four-step planning process shown in Figure 29.10: first, create an inventory of current customer study methods; second, document these methods; third, evaluate the current methods; and fourth, use the evaluation to design a comprehensive approach.[9]

Step 1: Inventory Current Customer Study Methods

Simply, this means sitting down with a key group and making a comprehensive list of customer data sources that can be broken down into the categories of active, receptive, and indirect. We often assemble a cross-functional team, provide them with some training on how to recognize multiple data sources, and then have them brainstorm a list of currently used customer data sources. The team can then list these data sources on sticky notes and sort them into categories (see Figure 29.11).

Step 2: Document Current Customer Study Methods

As methods are listed, it soon becomes obvious that some are well known while others are obscure ("I didn't know we were doing that!"). For each method, a writer is assigned to describe the method using a simple template:

- What is the name of the method?
- Why do we collect these data?
- Who collects the data?
- Which customer segment is being studied?
- When are the data collected?
- How much do they cost to collect (not just in dollars but also in some estimate of time and organizational energy)?
- What is the value of the data?

Often just documenting the data collection method provides keen insight into organizational strengths and weaknesses. Once this list is generated, the next phase of the assessment can commence.

Step 3: Evaluate Current Customer Study Methods

During evaluation, an expert panel is established, criteria are determined, and a judgment is made about each data set. A summary tool, such as a cost-benefit quadrant, is used for determining the benefit and cost of each customer data source (see Figure 29.12).

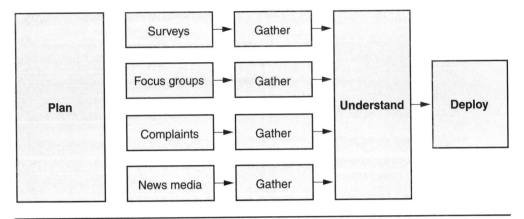

Figure 29.9 A "voice of the customer" system showing unified planning, holostic analysis, and coordinated action.

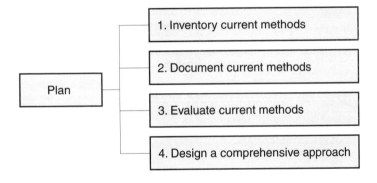

Figure 29.10 Determining methods for obtaining and using customer information.

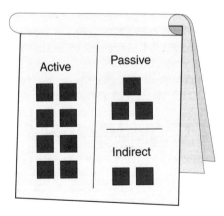

Figure 29.11 Sorting and organizing customer data sources.

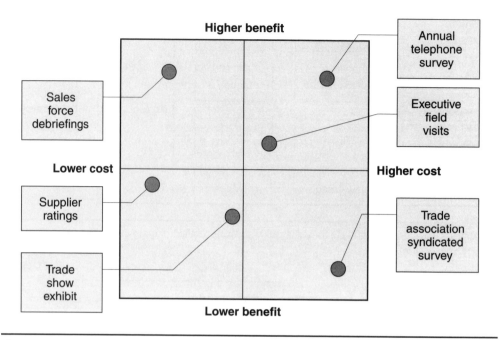

Figure 29.12   Quadrant displays relative cost and benefit of data source.

In this example, the trade association syndicated survey is of very high cost but of little perceived benefit, so it might be discarded, while the sales force debriefing that is low in cost but of high benefit would be encouraged. Using this type of analysis, the organization can determine which sources of customer data it wishes to enhance and which it wants to discard.

Step 4: Design a Comprehensive Approach

As each current data source is evaluated and either maintained or discarded, the opportunity exists to add additional methods that might round out a complete system. Consider all of your information needs and then add components to provide any missing information. For example, can your organization answer the following questions?

- How satisfied are our customers?
- Does satisfaction vary by segment?
- How has satisfaction changed over the past year?
- How is our performance rated on key attributes?
- What factors drive satisfaction with us?
- Is what my customers verbalize as important really what is important?
- What are our strengths and weaknesses?

- How are we viewed compared with our competitors?
- What improvements can we make to increase satisfaction?
- What improvements can we make to increase our perceived value?
- What is expected of us?
- What could we do to delight our customers?
- What percentage of our customers are loyal to us?

If your organization can answer these questions, it is on the path toward a customer satisfaction measurement system that will contribute to overall profitability.

Example of a Voice of the Customer System

Voluntary Hospitals of America (VHA), the Dallas-based healthcare alliance that serves 1,800 nonprofit hospitals, used a voice of the customer (VOC) system like the one shown in Figure 29.13. It commissioned annual telephone surveys to measure overall customer satisfaction; however, the telephone survey was just one source of customer data. They also conducted extensive focus groups with key customer segments to add rich detail. Interviews with regional field staff along with industrywide studies added market insights and technical points. Then, in intensive workshops, voice of the customer tables were prepared that combined the data from all sources, thereby structuring the understanding and deployment phases.[10] Voice of the customer tables can have many different variations. The authors use a four-column format that describes "what the customer said, what the customer meant, what it means to us, and what action we will take."

This section has described an easy-to-use model for developing a comprehensive customer satisfaction measurement system. The next section will discuss some of the issues faced in developing such a system for ISO compliance.

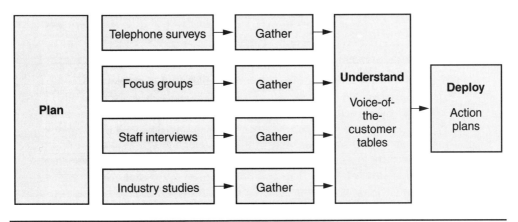

Figure 29.13 Comprehensive customer satisfaction measurement system using multiple sources of data.

SURVEY ISSUES RELATED TO PERCEPTION OF CUSTOMER SATISFACTION

Surveys are the most common component of formalized customer satisfaction measurement systems and also one of the best ways to "monitor customer perceptions as to whether the organization has met customer requirements" (clause 8.2.1). There are many issues involved in designing, conducting, and analyzing survey research. This section will serve as a basic introduction to some of the key issues:

- Qualitative versus quantitative research
- In-house versus third-party research
- Selection of scales
- Data collection method
- Sampling and nonresponse bias
- Statistical analysis methods

Issue 1: Qualitative versus Quantitative Research

Usually, customer research has two phases. The first is *qualitative,* in which the researcher conducts one-on-one interviews and focus groups to discover the underlying issues. Qualitative research is exploratory and is not statistically projectable to the total customer population. Qualitative data are subjective, are full of anecdotes and incidents, and are typically gathered to gain a sense of which product and/or service attributes are most important to include in the quantitative research (see Figure 29.14).

The next phase, the *quantitative* phase, is the actual survey. This portion of the research attempts to obtain a representative sample of customers (or, even better, a census), and the results are projectable to the population under study. Customer perceptions of product features or services are rated, thereby providing a numeric value for the importance, performance, expectations, and/or satisfaction with specific attributes. These data are typically analyzed using sophisticated multivariate statistical methods.

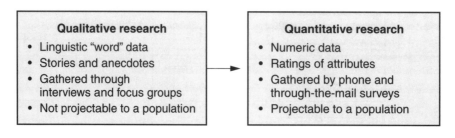

Usually qualitative research is conducted first to identify attributes, which can then be widely tested in the quantitative phase.

Figure 29.14   Qualitative research and quantitative research.

Issue 2: In-House versus Third-Party Research

As ISO-registered companies seek compliance with 9001:2000, they may ask themselves whether they should go out and buy the expertise of a market research company or build an internal customer research capability.

The market research industry is structured into two major components, full-service research firms and field services. In consultation with you, research firms design the overall customer study, develop the sampling plan, design the questionnaire, analyze the data, and report the findings. Often, the actual data collection is subcontracted to a field service. The field service operates the telephone center, is responsible for hiring and training the interviewers, and administers the actual survey. This allows those who collect the data to be independent from those who analyze the data.

The use of independent market research firms has many advantages. First, they have the experience to ensure that the study is implemented properly. Second, they train the field-service staff on the requirements of the particular study and then closely supervise and monitor the interviewers to ensure that the study is conducted properly. Third, they are objective; they tend not to carry the biases and opinions of internal management. Fourth, they are usually current on sophisticated research techniques and statistical analysis methods. (Market research firms often develop some type of proprietary analysis that can be purchased only from them.) Fifth, they may have extensive background in conducting research in either your industry or your type of customer segments so that they know the advantages and disadvantages of various approaches. Sixth, using them may be more cost-effective than hiring, training, and maintaining a permanent staff in-house.

The alternative is do-it-yourself "hands-on research." This approach has many advocates. On technical subjects, it is often helpful to have engineers, who have been given the proper training, talk directly to customers. Using internal staff ensures that nothing is missed because of technical language, and in some cases relationships can be strengthened through direct customer contact.[11] However, the design and analysis are usually less sophisticated.

Another aspect of the hands-on approach involves the use of direct observation of customer behavior instead of survey data. For instance, the managers of a hotel installed a video camera above the check-in desk. They noticed at what point customers seemed annoyed, defined as the time it took before they looked at their watches. They used direct observations to set service standards, rather than surveying customers about how they "feel" when waiting two minutes versus five minutes.[12]

Issue 3: Selection of Scales

Some companies agonize over the selection of the specific type of scale that will be used to measure and track satisfaction. Indeed, there are many options available, each with its own advantages and disadvantages. Most research organizations will suggest building an *index* of satisfaction. An index is composed of a number of correlated questions, each tapping a somewhat different dimension of satisfaction. Indices are more robust than any single question. For example, a car dealership might construct an index that comprises ratings of overall satisfaction with the dealership, satisfaction with the sales experience, satisfaction with the service experience, and likelihood to recommend the dealership to others.

In many cases, just one question is used as the ultimate criterion of satisfaction. Regardless of whether a single question or multiple questions are asked, it is still necessary to decide on the scale to be used. There are many ways to scale these questions. The question might be posed as follows:

"Overall, how satisfied are you with [the name of the company]? Would you say you are:
    [4] Very satisfied?
    [3] Somewhat satisfied?
    [2] Somewhat dissatisfied?
    [1] Very dissatisfied?"

This example shows a four-point scale that forces the customer to respond positively (the two top boxes) or negatively (the two bottom boxes). There is no "neutral" response. Other types of scales include a five-point scale that gives the customer the option of selecting a neutral middle ground ("neither satisfied nor dissatisfied"). Typically, however, satisfaction data tend to be positively skewed; that is, most customers (we hope!) tend to be at least somewhat satisfied. Therefore, four- and five-point scales often provide little room for variability. This can cause problems in attempting to analyze the data to explore ways to increase satisfaction. It also leaves little room to measure positive shifts over time after internal improvements have been made. Seven and 10-point scales offer more choices and greater sensitivity. For example, the question might be posed as follows:

"On a 10-point scale, where 10 means "completely satisfied" and 1 means "very dissatisfied," how satisfied are you with [the name of the company]?

Often, research specialists prefer to display data by "top-box" score rather than by merely showing the mean (average). Top-box scores can be more sensitive to shifts and are also easier to conceptualize. The top-box score tells you what percentage of your customers are satisfied. It is easier to conceptualize "80 percent were satisfied" than to conceptualize that "on average, customer satisfaction was 3.2 on a 4-point scale."

Another consideration in regard to numeric satisfaction scores is a growing literature that indicates that satisfaction is not enough. Often a satisfied customer will switch suppliers. Customer research experts are now asking "loyalty" questions in addition to, or even instead of, "satisfaction" questions. A loyalty question could be "Would you recommend this product to others?" or "Would you recommend that this service contract be renewed?"

Issue 4: Data Collection Methods

There are many ways to collect customer satisfaction data. Some of the more common data collection approaches include telephone, personal (face-to-face), mail, and Web surveys. Each method has advantages and disadvantages, but one method may be more suitable based on your own customer base.

In general, telephone interviews are the most effective. Customers can sit back and answer the questions; there is little effort required on their part. Also, the telephone interview offers a more personalized touch. Using the telephone allows the researcher to sequence the order of the questions so that the answers to some questions will not bias the answers to others. This is also true for face-to-face interviews, but the cost of using this approach on a national or international basis can be prohibitive.

Mail surveys and Web surveys require more effort on the part of the customer. It is often not possible to sequence the order of questioning, and exposing the whole survey to the respondent can daunt his or her motivation. However, these types of surveys can be quite cost-effective. The most serious problem, however, is the higher level of nonresponse. Generally a telephone survey is completed by many more of the targeted customers than are mail or Web surveys.

Issue 5: Sampling and Nonresponse Bias

A critical element of a quantitative survey is that the results obtained from a sampling of customers accurately represents the views of the total customer population. In some business-to-business categories, a company might have relatively few customers. In this case, the company might survey all of its customers and not need to select a sample. However, for those companies with a large base of customers, it is neither cost-effective nor necessary to attempt a census; only a sampling of customers is required.

Typically, the size of the sample is less important than the representativeness of the sample. Given a *random* sample of the population, the results from any size sample will be projectable to the population; what will vary is the *sensitivity* of the estimates. For example, a random sample of 100 customers might reflect the level of satisfaction in the population by plus or minus 10 percent, but a random sample of 2000 customers might reflect the level of satisfaction in the population by plus or minus two percent. The key is obtaining a random sample. Typically, the researcher will begin with an acceptable random sample; however, the response rate can undermine the projectability of the final results.

Response rate is a measure of the proportion of customers who agree to participate in a survey. Those who do not return a mailed questionnaire or who refuse to participate in a telephone interview are called "nonresponders." It is dangerous to assume that responders and nonresponders have the same beliefs, perceptions, and opinions. A large survey might claim a 95 percent confidence level, plus or minus four percent, but it might not mention that it only achieved a 10 percent response rate. A 10 percent response rate means that 90 percent of the customers did not respond! Assuming that the nonresponders hold the same beliefs as the responders can cause an organization to reach erroneous conclusions.

In one case, a large HMO found that it had an 82 percent satisfaction score using a mail survey (top two boxes on a five-point scale), but the mail survey resulted in a very low response rate. When a follow-up telephone survey was made of 100 nonresponders, the score went up substantially. This demonstrates that there can be substantial differences between the views of responders and nonresponders. (Possibly customers who have had a negative experience are more likely to take the time to fill in and mail back a questionnaire.) When one uses a telephone survey, which tends to have a higher response rate than mailed surveys, the impact of nonresponse bias can be mitigated.

Issue 6: Statistical Analysis Methods

Professional researchers apply a wide range of powerful statistical analyses to customer data. In addition, they can perform the appropriate tests of statistical significance to determine whether the results from different customer segments or from different measurement periods are, in fact, meaningfully different.

Some of the analyses that can be performed on the data include the following:

- *Factor analysis.* This type of analysis can be used to understand which attributes tend to be perceived similarly or tap into the same underlying dimension. It is also used to reduce a large number of questions down to a key subset of questions that will adequately represent a particular dimension.

- *Regression analysis.* This type of analysis can be used to understand which attributes best predict a particular outcome. For example, many researchers use regression to identify the implicit "drivers" of satisfaction.[13]

- *Structural equations.* These sophisticated models can be developed to understand the relative impact of various antecedent conditions or perceptions in a stepwise process on a particular outcome as well as their relative influences on one another. Because the theoretical model is specified in advance, the results are purported to predict a causal relationship.

- *Cluster analysis.* In many cases, companies segment their customers based on existing measures (such as sales region, sales volume, and so on). These are known as *a priori* segments. However, various statistical techniques can be applied to data sets to segment customers based on how they responded to various questions in the survey (such as customer needs, perceptions of the company's performance, demographics, and so on). The results identify the number of distinct customer segments, the size of each segment, and how the segments differ in terms of attitudes, perceptions, demographics, or purchasing behavior. These data can be used to highlight which segments are more or less satisfied with the company's products and to identify the unique requirements of each segment.

- *Conjoint analysis.* In general, conjoint analyses are used in new product development to understand the best possible configuration of product features. There are many types of conjoint designs and techniques, such as fully specified designs, discrete choice techniques, adaptive conjoint techniques, and so on. The results are used to simulate various marketplace scenarios. For example, computer simulations evaluate the relative efficacy of different new product concepts compared with each other, new product concepts compared with the existing product, and new product concepts compared with competitive products.

This section has covered some of the common issues faced when using customer data. As organizations become more skilled in their use of customer data and have more skill in integrating those data into their overall quality management system, the benefits of clause 8.2.1 will become more apparent.

SUMMARY

The power of ISO 9001:2000 clause 8.2.1 is in taking a vital area—customer satisfaction—and giving it the status and structure it rightly deserves. Many managers have been trained in finance, accounting, and economics and are therefore "financially focused." Being financially focused is easy because the unit of measure, the dollar, is simple to count. However, by following the ISO model, an organization has the opportunity to add "customer-focused management" to its repertoire, thereby retaining existing customers, attracting new customers, and adding to the bottom line.

ENDNOTES

1. W. J. Latzko and D. M. Saunders, *Four Days with Dr. Deming* (Reading, MA: Addison Wesley, 1995): 190.
2. F. F. Reichheld, *The Loyalty Effect* (Boston: Harvard Business School Press, 1996): 14.
3. Latzko and Saunders, 64.
4. W. G. Robertshaw, "Product Optimization to Maximize Customer Preferences" (presentation to the Delaware Section of the American Society for Quality Control, Wilmington, DE: April 1993).
5. Interviews with Sheila R. Marshall and Donna R. Truitt, Xerox Corporation, Baltimore, MD: June 7, 1999.
6. *Voice of the Customer Training Manual* (Media, PA: ARBOR, 1999).
7. Latzko and Saunders, 5.
8. The authors wish to thank Craig Cunningham for his many contributions to the ARBOR Voice of the Customer System.
9. Voice of the Customer Web-based training module, www.ISOize.com, and ARBOR, Media, PA: 2001.
10. The authors wish to thank Kim Alleman, John Fassnacht, and Sharla Jones of VHA for their help and support during this project.
11. J. K. Johansson and I. Nonaka, *Relentless: The Japanese Way of Marketing* (New York: Harper Business, 1996): 44.
12. Story told by participant at ARBOR Voice of the Customer workshop, March 1999.
13. W. G. Robertshaw and D. M. Saunders, "Quality of Design: The Customer Voice—Direct and Derived Measurement" (presentation to the annual conference of GOAL/QPC, Boston, MA: November 1988).

Chapter 30

Internal Audit

John H. Stratton

Management Systems Consultant, Eastman Kodak (Retired),
Rochester, New York

ESTABLISHING AND MAINTAINING AN AUDIT PROCESS FOR ISO 9001

Quality system audits are conducted for many purposes, with probably the least important reason being that they are required by the ISO 9001 standard. Audits have been used for countless generations to check up on the progress of a task or project, to determine if what a customer received was really what he or she wanted and paid for, to see whether products or production are meeting standards, and to establish confidence in functions or systems such as banking, financial services, and *quality*. Quality audits may be the newest example of audit application, having gained importance with the growth of industrialization and manufacturing.

Auditing of quality management systems gained some visibility, both good and bad, with the use of military standards, such as MIL 9858, and with regulated products, such as foods and drugs. The introduction of the ISO 9000 series in 1987 and the resulting popularity of the standards—with certification/registration growing—gave a completely new perspective to auditing of quality management systems.

For the first time, audits were to be done regularly by a company or organization itself in order to conform to the requirements of a standard. This meant that many people, from a wide variety of job functions within each organization implementing ISO 9000, needed to be trained, qualified, and assigned the responsibility of evaluating their conformance to requirements. Additionally, all those who sought certification/registration to one of the standards were audited by an outside organization, a registrar/certification body, at least yearly to attest to continuing and maintaining certificates.

This meant that in a relatively short period of time, organizations not only implemented a quality management system but also developed an understanding among many employees as to how that system should work. They then had those workers, who had acquired an appreciation for a quality system, evaluate part, or all, of their system—thus helping to improve that system through the corrective action process.

Consequently, the internal audit has become a key, even indispensable, part of the quality management process by highlighting whether the system is working the way it is intended and identifying specific areas where improvement is needed.

Why Do We Do Quality System Audits?

Several sound reasons for implementing an internal audit program are highlighted in the foregoing discussion. The key reasons reduce to a very few:

• *Audits are an effective management tool.* The internal audit is intended to be an integral part of the management process. Managers are expected to rely on the information provided by the audit process as one key measure of how their organization and its processes are operating. Actions are to be taken on the findings of an audit. Improvements are to be made. Those actions and the improvements are to be monitored by management as a part of their regular review. The cycle then repeats with the next audit and the opportunity to improve to ever-increasing levels.

• *The internal audit tracks the effectiveness of quality processes.* As audits are conducted and the findings recorded, they provide data as a part of the overall system measurement process. Audits completed on a schedule give part of the information needed to plot and track the performance of each process within the system. That measure of effectiveness can then be monitored by management, reported to the desired levels within the organization, and possibly reported to customers.

• *Contracts or regulations may require audits.* Many contracts negotiated between a supplier and a customer include audits as a condition of the agreement. Such audits often are done by the customer on the supplier and are sometimes called external, "second-party" audits. Other contracts, such as military contracts, may require external audits also, but they are sometimes conducted by an organization other than the direct customer. Those audits are called "third-party" audits. When products or services are regulated, an authority such as the government often requires audits. Such audits are usually completed by the authority itself or an external organization acting for the authority.

• *Audits are required by ISO 9001.* Last in the list is the fact that audits are required by ISO 9001. Although the primary driver for audits should be the inherent benefit from them, the requirement in the standard ensures that the activity will be completed if the organization is adhering to the standard. The audits specifically noted in the standard are the "internal audits" for self-evaluation. Added to this need for organizations certified, or registered, to the standard are the audits conducted by the registrar/certification body. Those audits provide additional, external information on the health and effectiveness of the quality management system.

What Will an ISO 9001:2000 Internal Audit Program Include?

The improved ISO 9001:2000 standard includes all the basic requirements for an internal audit program that are present in earlier versions of the standard. Those requirements are now clarified with an emphasis on the planning and implementation of the internal audit process, or "audit program" as it is called. Reference is made to the ISO 10011 guidance standard on quality systems auditing for more detailed information.

An effective internal audit program meeting the requirements of the standard will include the following:

• *Audits conducted at planned intervals.* We note that no specific interval is required, but the standard is commonly interpreted to mean that at least one complete audit of all ISO 9001 requirements is expected each year. Many organizations have found it beneficial to complete a full system audit more often, and it is common to find frequencies of two or three audit cycles done each year.

• *Audits evaluating conformance to ISO 9001 and any additional system requirements set by the organization and evaluating whether the system is being effectively implemented and maintained.* Evaluating whether the requirements of ISO 9001 are met is an expected purpose of the internal audit program. System requirements that go beyond the standard are becoming more frequent. Companies and organizations are adding the special requirements that originate from customers, government regulators, and even their own desires to achieve a status of "best in class." Those added requirements that are a part of the management system must be audited as part of the internal audit program.

Probably the most difficult objective to attain from the internal audit process is that of evaluating "effectiveness." Clarity has been added with the words of ISO 9000:2001, and uniformity is achieved with other management system standards, in that the implied effectiveness is that of the system implementation and its maintenance. So a clear purpose of the internal audit is to evaluate whether the quality management system is being appropriately applied within the organization and whether it is kept up-to-date.

• *Planning the audit program to achieve its purpose.* One of the words used more often in ISO 9001:2000 and with more emphasis is *plan* and its present tense, *planning*. This is applied to the internal audit program by clearly expecting it to be planned, and the planning responsibilities and requirements to be documented in a procedure. Several considerations are listed to be taken into account in the planning, such as status and importance of the system processes or product delivery (product realization) processes. Areas, departments, functions, and facilities are also to be considered in the planning, as well as results from previous audits.

As a result of this internal audit planning activity, specific audit program details must be defined. The audit criteria—that is, the policies, procedures, standards, and the like according to which the audit is conducted—are defined. The scope of the audit (the extent and boundaries) is to be defined along with the frequency of audits and audit methods or procedures. The auditor selection process and how auditors are assigned to audits must ensure objectivity and impartiality. A requirement of the standard is that auditors are not permitted to audit their own work.

• *Audits and an audit program that are coordinated and managed to achieve effective results.* Good internal audits and audit programs do not happen spontaneously. They are planned, resourced, coordinated, and managed to produce the results for which they are intended. The internal audit program meeting the requirements of ISO 9001:2000 typically has someone assigned the responsibility to manage the audits and to ensure that they are implemented. Those responsibilities and the responsibility to collect and report the results must be defined in a documented procedure.

The internal audit process will produce audit plans, records of findings, audit evidence, and other documents that need to be preserved for later use (that is, quality records). Those records must be effectively managed and controlled for an effective audit program and to meet the requirements of the standard.

What Will Happen As a Result of the Internal Audits That Are Conducted?

After each audit of an audit program is completed, the findings, including any nonconformities, must be acted upon. The management of the immediate area responsible for the finding must ensure that proper action is taken and taken in a timely fashion. The standard notes that two distinct types of action must be taken. The first is the short-term corrective action to fix the problem or nonconformity. But after that, the cause must be investigated and longer-term corrective action taken to ensure that the situation does not happen again.

As a follow-up, ISO 9001 requires that each action taken is verified to give even greater assurance that the results are, and will be, effective. Such follow-up activity may take many different forms and involve different people within the process or area. The internal auditors are often in the best position to lead and coordinate the follow-up, because they likely discovered the problem. They will know the circumstances and issues surrounding the nonconformity and often will have a better understanding of how to correct the problem in the system.

Of course, close involvement with the action taken to correct a nonconformity may affect the objectivity of that auditor or auditors. Typically, to avoid any possible bias, those auditors are not assigned to evaluate that process or area in the immediate future.

From the start of each audit activity of the internal audit program to the end of the corrective action and verification process, there is a need to track and report the results. The primary user of the internal audit information within the system is the individual or individuals representing top management. The audit results are a key source of input to the management review. Management should rely on the internal audit as the primary method of "taking the pulse" of the organization and its management system. Consequently, reports are typically generated publishing the findings of each audit, summarizing audit results over periods of time covered by the management review, and tracking summaries of audit results and verification of effective closeout.

Why Do Some Organizations and Some People Have Difficulty with Audits and the Process of Auditing?

Many of us have either an inherent or learned aversion to audits and auditing. We often attribute this feeling to the experiences related by those who have endured tax audits conducted by a taxing authority. Such audits seem to have only one purpose, that of identifying errors and failures to comply with the tax rules, and the result is financial penalties or even legal action. It is easy to see why a process whose primary goal is to uncover wrongdoings and then punish the auditee is perceived negatively.

Quality management system audits are, or should be, at the opposite end of the scale. The goal of the management system audit is to improve the system. The audit process focuses on the parts of the system and how they work together to give a desired result. People are only incidental to the system operation, although a necessary part of the system. People run the management system and make it work as it should. The focus of every quality management system audit is on the implemented system, and if problems or nonconformities are found, the root cause is most often a process or system issue. The people operating the system, then, are the last stop on the "audit trail" and should receive the least attention.

It is often helpful to visit some of the key reasons people fear audits, to look at each reason individually, and to note how internal auditors can help to diminish those fears. Here are some of the main fears people have of audits:

• *Audits are a threat to our usual way of doing things.* This feeling clearly results from the perceived punitive nature of audits. The most basic description of a punitive audit is that an auditor, with a club of authority, is coming to hit workers and change the way they behave. A quality management system audit should focus on the goal of improving a system. Improvement, then, is not a threat but an opportunity to make the system better and easier for everyone to work in.

Auditors can help people avoid this fear by stressing the goal of improvement at every opportunity. It can be briefly reinforced at each audit interview and certainly whenever a person being interviewed exhibits signs of fear. The auditor also has the responsibility to relate any problem or nonconformity found to the system cause and not the action of a person.

Managers, at all levels in the organization, can also help dispel this fear by creating an attitude and culture in the working environment that rewards improvement. The management style of "managing by walking around" has considerable merit and offers a prime opportunity to stress improvement and avoid trying to "catch people doing something wrong."

• *Auditors are prescriptive—they try to tell us how we should do our job.* To be effective, the internal auditor must be particularly conscious of how people react to auditors. Often the well-chosen internal auditor will have the experience and knowledge to be able to tell people how they should do their job. But the audit is not the time to take corrective action. That comes in a later phase. Internal auditors are to evaluate the process or system as it is operating at that time. Any recommendations for improvement should be offered at a later time.

An external auditor, or an auditor from another area, must also be conscious of people's fear. Someone from outside seldom has the knowledge to be an "expert" in a local operation. Even if such a person has expertise, a wise approach is to allow the local expert to demonstrate his or her knowledge, because one objective of the system audit is to determine how well the system has been implemented.

• *Audits are viewed as subjective, as being up to the whims of the auditor.* An audit should never be subjective; it is based on set "audit criteria." The audit criteria or references for the internal ISO 9001 audit are simply the procedures and policies of the organization, which in turn are based on the ISO standard. Auditors must not impose their own views on the organization, but rather should always look to the audit criteria for the requirements that need to be met.

It is quite easy to see how fear is propagated by auditors and auditing organizations. Many auditors use the phrases "I want to see . . ." and "I am looking for . . ." as they investigate the management system requirements. Phrases that would convey a more correct approach are "the standard [or your procedure] requires . . ." and "do you have evidence of meeting that requirement?"

• *Audits are judgmental, and auditors get to make the decisions.* This fear is closely related to the issue of subjectivity. Audits do require judgments and decisions to be made. The key to credible judgments is the direct reference to the audit criteria, the standard, or the policies and procedures. Judgments and decisions to be made in the internal audit may cover the complete range from very clear to vague and arguable.

Clear decisions are easily made because they reference clear audit criteria, and either the criteria are met or they are not. At the other end of the spectrum, the decision often is based on interpretation and often is seen differently by different people. The internal auditor should try to place himself or herself in the position of the auditee and see the issue from that perspective.

In any audit situation where a judgment and a decision needs to be made, an experienced auditor involves the auditee in the decision-making process. When the facts, or audit evidence, are reviewed against the requirement, both auditor and auditee often can agree on the decision, and so the judgment becomes one made jointly. Of course, in some cases agreement is not possible, and the auditor must make the final judgment as to whether the audit evidence warrants a finding. In those cases where the audit evidence is marginal, it is best to give the auditee the benefit of the doubt and risk an error. Remember that the goal of the internal audit is improvement, and if there is only a marginal reason to identify an improvement, it may not be a value-added activity.

AUDIT DIFFERENCES IN ISO 9001:2000

Several clarifications have been made in ISO 9001:2000 concerning the requirements and expectations of the internal audit process. An increased emphasis is also placed on the role of the internal audit in the entire quality management system. In addition to the somewhat subtle clarifications and increased emphasis, one finds significant improvements to the overall quality management system approach that can create major changes for the internal audit program.

Most of the clarifications and situations where an increased emphasis is placed on the internal audit have already been discussed. Here we note again those "big picture" changes in the new standard that affect auditors and the audit program, and we explain them further. The major improvements to the year 2000 standard that greatly affect the internal audit function are (1) the process approach to quality management systems; (2) the increased involvement of management in the operation and control of the system, including setting measurable objectives; and (3) the emphasis on continual improvement.

Auditors also should be aware of some "second-level" changes in the new standard that will cause some adjustment of the internal audit process. Those changes are (1) the use of "permissible exclusions" or defined "application" of the standard to the organization; (2) the increased emphasis on customer satisfaction in the standard; and (3) a lessening of clear requirements for documented procedures.

What Differences Will the Process Approach Bring About?

One of the major changes in the year 2000 standard is the focus on processes. One finds in several parts of the standard specific requirements to identify the needed processes, plan for those processes, implement them, and then measure and analyze the results of the processes for improvement. This represents a significant shift in thinking and application of traditional systems approaches to quality management. The improved approach and new way of thinking that is now forced upon us is to think of every part of our system as a process, a process with inputs, outputs, and linkages to many other processes within the system. For many people implementing the management system, this is a new way of viewing the quality system and of evaluating and auditing the system.

Many, if not most, internal audit programs implemented since the introduction of ISO 9001, 9002, and 9003, have audited systems in the same way they were designed and documented. The traditional 20 elements of ISO 9001 (or the fewer elements if 9002 or 9003), were audited element by element as each clause applied to the area being audited. This gave rise to internal audit program managers and coordinators dividing up the required elements over a 12-month year and then auditing two or three clauses each month. The result was to cover all elements of the standard over the year and thus audit the complete system.

With the ISO 9001:2000 focus on processes, that old approach will be difficult if not impossible and will certainly be less effective. Even if one counts the number of clauses, or more likely, the subclauses of the new standard and divides those 23 distinct clauses over a time period the approach will not be effective. A quality management system is a set of interrelated processes, and thus the internal audit of that system will be most effective if it audits those processes and their interactions over a brief period of time.

It is envisioned that the most effective way to audit a system conforming to ISO 9001:2000 will be to audit each area of the organization against the entire set of requirements instead of auditing only a single element of the standard, as is often the case with the 1994 version. This will mean that a larger organization with many departments, areas, or units may find it most effective to audit each unit within one short time period for all clauses in the standard. That approach will necessarily require careful audit planning and coordination and may require larger audit teams.

The smaller organization, with limited areas, functions, and units, may find it possible to audit several processes in one time period and cover the less interactive parts of the standard at a later time. Such an organization may, however, benefit in the same way as the larger organization if the entire quality management system is audited over a short span of time.

A second consideration of the process approach is that auditors are expected to have increased difficulty in auditing process by process. The process approach requires methods of auditing that are not common to all auditors. More preparation and an understanding of each process is required. A broader view of the organization and perspective of the interactions among the parts of the organization must be gained. It is likely to require more training and supervision of the internal audit teams.

What Will Greater Requirements for Top Management Involvement Mean to the Internal Audit Function?

In ISO 9001:2000, top management's role and involvement in the quality management system has been strengthened and clarified. Management that is accountable in each area of the organization now has a clear responsibility for quality policy and objectives, planning, resources, customer focus, communication, monitoring and measurement processes, analysis, and improvement. Where an organization is larger and more complex, top management has the task of effectively coordinating each area in such a way that all system management responsibilities are met.

The internal audit program now has an expanded task of evaluating whether its own management is meeting the requirements of ISO 9001:2000. The earlier versions of the standard stepped lightly in this sensitive area, with requirements of resource provision and policy implementation throughout all levels of the organization. Other requirements, such as policy development and management review, were clear-cut—either they were completed or not. The new standard requires a considerable amount of evaluation of management effectiveness. Will our internal auditors be up to that challenge?

Prior experience with the internal audit process has indicated no reluctance to cite management issues and nonconformities. The new emphasis on management involvement and responsibility is believed to go much further into this sensitive territory. Those responsible for an internal audit program play a key role in alleviating this potential problem. The internal audit program manager should have the clear authority to carry out an evaluation of management responsibility without fear of repercussion. With that relationship established and reinforced by top management, the internal auditors may then have any perceived sensitivities relieved.

How Will the Internal Audit Program Evaluate Continual Improvement?

The requirement for continual improvement is thought to be stressed more in ISO 9001:2000 than in earlier versions, with the expectation that the improvement process is working through several separate clauses in the standard. Continual improvement has not been a typical part of audit criteria in the past. The new standard has one long sentence describing the requirement in very broad terms, and the requirement is specifically mentioned 29 times throughout ISO 9001:2000 versus zero times in ISO 9001:1994. It is clear from the one sentence that improvement of the effectiveness of the quality management system is required, but other clauses allude to improvement of individual processes.

The internal audit process will need to compare improvements with the goals and objectives set by management as a part of, or resulting from, the quality policy. Only when those objectives are clear is a valid framework present for auditing to them. The usual criteria of progress on any and all common measures apply. Auditors should track how product and process measures align with stated objectives. (Are data being analyzed and used effectively? Is corrective and preventive action being taken to improve products and processes?) Such "audit trails" help to evaluate improvement as it relates to the clear goals and objectives set by the organization management.

The more sensitive case for internal auditors will be where goals and objectives are not clear or are not clearly measurable. In those instances, internal auditors may be able to ward off external audits to ISO 9001:2000 by highlighting the wisdom of establishing clear goals and objectives.

Will "Exclusions" in Application of the Standard Be a Part of the Internal Audit?

It has been well publicized that ISO 9001:2000 replaces the former three requirements standards where some elements of 9001:1994 were not appropriate. The vehicle for allowing such a change is the new clause under the scope of the standard (clause 1.2, "Application"), where its application is described. If parts of clause 7 do not apply and neither the customer nor any regulatory body require it, the requirement may be excluded due to "application." Any such exclusion must be justified and detailed in the quality manual.

Presumably, any appropriate exclusions will be justified and documented in the quality manual prior to an internal audit to the requirements of ISO 9001:2000. Even though the exclusion or exclusions have been made, it would be wise to thoroughly audit those requirements for the first complete internal audit to the new standard and then audit their maintenance thereafter. It will be helpful if the internal auditors are well versed in any exclusion and its justification. As the quality management system, products and processes, and the business climate change, the audit could well highlight the need to update one or more exclusions.

How Will the New Customer Satisfaction Requirements Affect the Internal Audit?

Greater emphasis on customer satisfaction is apparent in many of the requirements of ISO 9001:2000. But key requirements were present in the 1994 version, so the internal audit process should not find any new emphasis too difficult. One point of clarity in the new standard is to place the customer focus squarely in the hands of top management. Authority over parts of the management system dealing with the customer may rest with others, but the clear direction is for heavy involvement by top management.

Internal auditors auditing the customer focus requirements should probe whether methods of measuring customer satisfaction have been defined, whether data are now being collected and analyzed, whether customer feedback information is reported and analyzed in the management review, and whether action plans have been developed to improve customer satisfaction.

One new responsibility of which internal auditors need to be aware is the addition to the tasks of the management representative. The management representative is now tasked to ensure that awareness of customer requirements is promoted throughout the organization. Certainly the management representative does not need to fulfill the task personally, but must be certain that the requirement is implemented.

The new clause (8.2) on monitoring and measurement first focuses on measures of customer satisfaction within the quality system as the "perception" of whether the organization has met customer requirements. Auditors should recognize that perceptions are often difficult to evaluate. A key realization is that perceptions are "in the eyes of the beholder" and that perceptions of customer satisfaction may come from several sources—most directly from the customer itself, but often from trade or product journals, independent surveys, or even competitor information. Auditors should be open to any and all sources of perceived customer satisfaction.

What Do the Reductions in Required Documented Procedures Mean to the Internal Audit?

Another well-publicized change in ISO 9001:2000 is the reduction in the number of places where documented procedures are required. The stated intent of the reduction is to allow more flexibility in methods to achieve a workable process without having documented procedures. Some processes can be understood sufficiently through training or other means, and in such cases a documented procedure adds no value.

Internal auditors faced with processes where no documented procedure or work instruction exists should rely on investigating the process as expected by supervisors and then as done by several people who are routinely responsible for completing the task. If uniformity of method is critical to the process and observed in action, then training for the process is likely effective and detailed procedures may not be necessary. If uniform methods are not observed, then the impact of variation on the process must be investigated, and, possibly, documentation is required.

The internal auditors will need to be well aware of the six specifically required documented procedures and aware of the others where flexibility is intended. In all cases where documents are clearly needed to ensure effective planning, operation, and control of processes, then the documentation could include documented procedures. This will likely be one of the areas where judgment is required and the advice given earlier applies.

USING ISO 9004 AND INTERNAL AUDITS FOR PERFORMANCE IMPROVEMENTS

ISO 9001:2000 and ISO 9004:2000 were developed as a "consistent pair" purposely to help users align the text and requirements and to be able to use both standards to effectively improve operations. ISO 9004:2000 is geared for a system delivering performance improvements. It goes beyond the basic system requirements of 9001, adding the system enhancements that help us improve every aspect of performance.

The internal audit program put in place for ISO 9001:2000 can easily serve to improve systems intended for all types of performance improvement.

There are audit guidance standards that are a part of the ISO 9000 family that can help define how an internal audit program should function and how auditors should conduct audits.

Some organizations are going far beyond the quality management systems described in the ISO standards by implementing total quality management models and various quality award criteria. Can the internal audit program also meet those needs for auditing?

How Can the Internal Audit Program Facilitate Improvement?

The primary goal of the internal audit process is to find opportunities for improvement in the system and then foster the actions necessary for those improvements. A coordinated process, or program, has already been implemented to meet the requirements of 9001. That audit program is the foundation for auditing any manner of systems, processes, or requirements set out by the organization. An audit program implemented for ISO 9001 will work to audit all aspects of ISO 9004 with only a few additions.

The new ISO 9004:2000 was written with "auditability" in mind. It was observed that many organizations that wanted to go beyond the minimum requirements of ISO 9001:1994 had taken ISO 9004:1994 and implemented the principles as though they were requirements. They had converted the "shoulds" in 9004 to "shalls" and proceeded as though it were simply a higher-level standard.

The year 2000 revision paid close attention to the statements of principle and tried to make them in such a manner that an experienced audit team can evaluate them, if desired. So the process of going beyond ISO 9001:2000 is quite straightforward. Once the organization is ready and has decided to move beyond minimum requirements toward performance improvement, 9004 can be implemented as though it were a requirement standard. Each "should" is evaluated by the organization and converted to a "shall" if deemed appropriate. That revised standard then becomes the audit criteria against which internal audits are conducted.

If an internal audit program is to fulfill the objective of auditing to 9004, the most obvious need is to train auditors in the newly defined requirements. The auditors will need to understand clearly what the organization expects and, in some cases, how those expectations or requirements are to be met.

As we have noted, 9004 contains statements of principle, followed by several examples of ways to implement them. As many of the principles are converted to requirements, there will be considerably more flexibility and latitude in how the new requirements can be met. The organization may want to choose one or more of the options as its chosen method or methods of implementation. The internal audit program and the auditors that carry out audits will then have fewer and more "clear-cut" judgments to make as they audit.

This highlights a second difference or need the audit program designed for ISO 9004:2000 must meet. The number of judgments and the subjectivity of the audit process is greater as the requirements become less prescriptive. The auditors for 9004 will need to be comfortable auditing in a less well-defined situation. This may require more training and a thorough selection process to ensure that the auditors are capable of the task.

How Can the Auditing Standard ISO 10011 and Its Replacement, ISO 19011, Help the Internal Audit Process?

The ISO 9000 family has always included supporting standards and documents to help a user effectively implement the basic standards in the series. Unfortunately, those supporting standards have seemed to be a well-guarded secret, or at least a little-used resource. The year 2000 revision process has sought to reduce the number of standards in the family while drawing more attention to the more important documents in the series.

Auditing is thought to be crucial to the implementation of quality management systems and the ISO 9001:2000 and 9004:2000 standards. Because of that crucial role, the current audit standard, ISO 10011, *Guidelines for auditing quality systems*, is referenced in 9001 and 9004 and supported as a necessary document in the family. ISO 10011 was published by ISO in 1993 and adopted as an American national standard in 1994. Since that time, work has been done to develop a revised auditing standard incorporating the audit processes from quality system auditing and environmental system auditing into one standard. That new standard, ISO 19011, is nearing completion and should be published by the second half of 2002.

Both the current audit standard and its replacement contain worthwhile guidance for setting up and managing an internal audit program, conducting and reporting audits, and qualifying auditors as competent to conduct audits. Those who have used ISO 10011 and are familiar with its content will find that its guidance continues to be appropriate and may want to continue using the standard until it is withdrawn and replaced by ISO 19011. Those who have not used ISO 10011 are encouraged to get a copy of the new standard, ISO 19011, and use it for guidance as it progresses through the ISO process of final approval as the international standard for auditing quality management systems. ISO 19011 became available as a draft international standard in mid-2001.

The contents of the early drafts of ISO 19011 include guidance regarding the following important auditing issues:

- Audit terms and definitions
- Principles of auditing
- Managing an audit program
  - Audit program objectives and extent
  - Audit program responsibilities, resources, and procedures
  - Audit program implementation
  - Audit program records
  - Audit program monitoring and reviewing
- Audit activities
  - Initiating the audit
  - Document review
  - Preparing for the on-site audit activities
  - On-site audit activities
  - Reporting on the audit

- Audit completion
- Audit follow-up
- Competence of quality and/or environmental management system auditors
  - Knowledge and skills
  - Personal attributes
  - Education, work experience, audit training, and audit experience
  - Maintenance and improvement of knowledge and skills
  - Auditor evaluation process

What Are Some Examples of How Organizations Use Audits to Drive Improved Results?

Many large international companies have used audit processes to track performance and drive improvements in and among their major business units worldwide. Those audit processes have helped gain uniformity of practice and performance for both products and management systems. One such example was implemented in the manufacturing organization of Eastman Kodak Company in the mid-1980s. While employed as a quality systems consultant by the Manufacturing Quality Assurance Organization, this author designed the basis for an audit standard that was implemented throughout Kodak's worldwide manufacturing locations.

That manufacturing quality management system (MQMS) was drawn from published work done at Allis Chalmers Company and other companies that were, at the time, interested in driving improvement and uniformity of products and systems at their facilities. That MQMS incorporated 10 elements covering all the typical manufacturing quality system processes. It was implemented with teams of four to six auditors visiting a plant site and auditing every part of the manufacturing system over a week. Considerable progress was made by giving top management a uniform evaluation of each manufacturing unit within a relatively short time span and a "snapshot" of its quality operations.

The system was relatively short-lived, having been abandoned in 1987 or 1988 in favor of the new ISO 9000 series of standards, which were then showing good promise of acceptance. I credit that early experience with a quality management system as a large reason why, as we implemented systems based on ISO 9000, we quickly achieved about 120 registered systems worldwide without a single failure to gain recommendation for registration on the first audit.

Motorola implemented a similar quality management system in the 1980s and continued to use that process through at least the mid-1990s. That process had strong support from top management, and the results of the evaluation became a factor in each business manager's compensation for the year. The Motorola audit process could take two weeks at a site and went beyond minimum quality system requirements, reaching toward many of the criteria now in quality award programs.

Many other company programs were developed by using ISO 9000 as a base and adding some company-specific requirements. As progressive organizations implemented ISO 9001 and used it effectively, they began to realize that they needed new goals that would make them stretch even further. This need, in a large part, gave rise to the new version of the ISO standard, ISO 9001:2000, with new requirements that will make us stretch and add value to our organizations.

How Can TQM Audits and Quality Award Criteria Evaluations Supplement a Required Audit Program?

It was noted earlier that once an internal audit program is established and working to support the requirements of ISO 9001:2000, the largest part of the task is completed. That audit process can then be adapted and used to audit most any manner of other audit criteria. The modifications typically involve training and practice in the new requirements, with audit reporting and records as required by the new part of the program.

A common addition to an ISO 9000 internal audit program is quality award evaluations such as the Baldrige Award and the Canadian Quality Award. The award criteria for most awards are similar but have some fundamental differences from the traditional audit processes. In many award processes the comparison against the criteria is so different that distinctly different words are used to describe it. The award processes are called "assessments," "evaluations," or "reviews," while the term "audit" is applied where the audit criteria, or requirements, are clear and a direct comparison between a criterion and its application can be made.

As discussed earlier, some judgments must be made in an audit, and auditors strive to have those decisions be as clear as possible with the auditee most often involved in the decision. In an award evaluation process, less clear judgments are the norm. "Evaluation" teams are generally larger, and votes among their members or rating schemes are used to arrive at a score or tally in order to make a decision.

In a total quality management (TQM) or quality award evaluation, the criteria are less specific and less well-defined. The evaluation process usually has multiple phases with the first rounds being more like an audit, where it is determined if minimum criteria are met; then later evaluations rate how well the criteria are met until the "best" applicant is determined as the award winner.

Internal audit programs can easily adapt their processes to facilitate such evaluations. The individual auditors, or evaluators, will likely need to be much more thoroughly aware of the broad applications of quality management tools and techniques, be able to easily step back from a specific application and view the broader picture of its effectiveness for the entire organization, and be comfortable and adept at making judgments where needed.

In view of these differences and cautions, it may seem difficult or impossible to use an ISO 9001:2000 internal audit process to go beyond the basic criteria of those audits and add value in a TQM or quality award application. In fact, many audit programs have combined efforts from several levels in the organization to create an effective program for both needs. In several cases, organizations have augmented the ISO 9000 internal audit team with selected members of technical staff or managers who have a strong background and interest in quality. After appropriate training and awareness sessions, TQM and award evaluations are conducted with pairs of evaluators made up of one person from each background.

The ISO 9000 auditor brings the specific knowledge of that process while the person with a pure technical or business perspective brings that strength. Together these pairs of auditors give a balanced view and are able to identify many value-added opportunities for improvement.

SUMMARY

The internal auditor and all auditors using the year 2000 standard are faced with several important challenges to maintain effective evaluations of the management system and also to improve their audit skills as required by the new standard. Auditing interactive processes instead of auditing the specific requirements of an element of the standard is, in the opinion of this author, the greatest hurdle to overcome. Many internal auditors have been taught to audit one or two elements of the 1994 standard each month until the complete standard is finished. Unfortunately, this approach gives little experience analyzing interactive processes and framing audit questions or developing audit trails to effectively evaluate a system to the year 2000 standard.

Through training, coaching, and a dedication to improvement, most auditors can overcome past habits and become value-adding participants in the new ISO 9000 process. We are truly entering a time of transition with regard to both the new standard and internal auditing.

Chapter 31

Measurement for Hardware

Jørgen Steen Petersen
Radiometer Medical A/S, Copenhagen, Denmark

PLANNING FOR MEASUREMENT AND MONITORING

When planning for measurement and monitoring activities, it is necessary to include the determination of the need for and use of applicable methodologies and statistical techniques.

When performing a measurement, the result is often considered as the true value; however, there will always be an uncertainty on the result (see Figure 31.1). Many factors affect the measuring result.

Human Errors

The person who performs measurements may affect the measuring results. Education and training is an important factor. Examples are reading accuracy and the accuracy in performing the measuring process.

Measuring Method

The choice of measuring method is vital for the result of the measurement. When considering the choice of measuring method, it is important to choose a method that gives the necessary measuring accuracy and resolution for the particular measuring situation. Sometimes it becomes necessary to choose indirect measurements, because you are not able to measure the parameters you want to measure. In this situation you measure other parameters and derive the wanted measurement result by means of calculations on these parameters, knowing the physical relationship. A simple example of this is measuring the power dissipated in a known resistor by measuring the

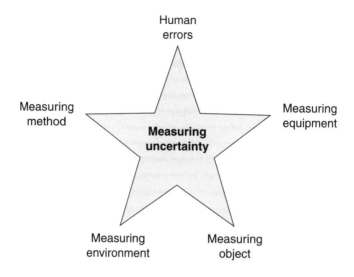

Figure 31.1   The measuring uncertainty star.

voltage across it. Sometimes the relationship between the measured values is not so straightforward as in this example, and you need to establish the relationship between the measured parameters and the measuring value you want.

A simple example is establishing the relationship between the temperature of a resistor and the power dissipated in it. Another example is measuring the air humidity with a hair hygrometer. You are here dependent on the relationship between the hair elongation as a function of the humidity.

The classical example of an indirect measurement is measuring the distance between two holes placed on a rectangular metal plate. One might choose to measure the distance between the holes as the difference between the distances from one edge of the plate and the holes, but one would have to consider the measuring accuracy (see Figure 31.2).

Sometimes a value can only be measured indirectly. An example is hardness. This can be measured as the indentation depth in the measuring object of a hard metal item of a defined shape pressed against the measuring object with a given force.

Measuring Equipment

When choosing measuring equipment, it is important to consider the requirement for measuring accuracy compared with the specifications of the measuring equipment. Figure 31.3 illustrates how measuring accuracy is dependent on precision and bias.

Precision indicates a relative degree of repeatability, that is, how closely the values within a series of replicate measurements agree with each other. Repeatability is the result of resolution and stability.

Bias is a measure of how closely the mean value in a series of replicate measurements approaches the true value. The mean value is that number attained by dividing the sum of the individual values in a series by the total number of individual values.

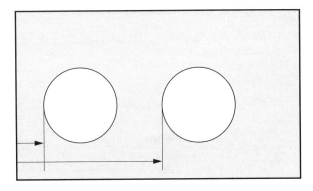

Figure 31.2   Measuring distance between two holes as the difference between distances from the edge.

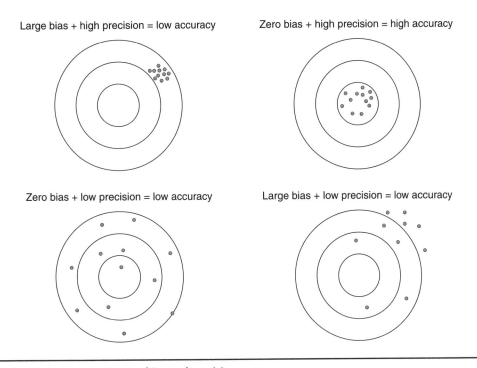

Figure 31.3   Accuracy versus bias and precision.

Accuracy is the measure of an instrument's capability to approach a true or absolute value. Accuracy is a function of precision and bias.

The following characteristics therefore have to be considered when choosing a measuring instrument:

- Stability/drift
- Repeatability
- Linearity

- Zero-point
- Hysteresis
- Resolution
- Calibration accuracy

Often the capability of measuring equipment with a digital readout is over-estimated because of the high resolution of the readout. It is therefore important to study the specification sheet of the instrument.

If the instrument to be used is not specified to a degree that makes it possible to estimate the precision and bias of the instrument, it might be necessary to make an investigation of these parameters, measuring a known measuring object with a series of measurements.

Measuring Environment

It is well known that the measuring environment might affect the measurement. The measuring object might change with the changing environment, and the measuring instrument might measure differently under different environmental conditions. Environmental parameters might be temperature, humidity, air pressure, light, electromagnetic fields, and radiation.

The parameter that most frequently has to be considered is temperature. Very often the temperature might affect the measuring accuracy of the measuring instruments as well as the measuring object. Almost all electronic measuring instruments are specified within a temperature range. Most measuring objects change shape or other physical parameters with temperature. Therefore, machined or molded parts should not be measured when they are still warm from the manufacturing process without temperature compensation.

Measuring Object

When measuring certain measuring objects, the results might be affected due to the measuring process. Mechanical measurements on elastic or soft objects, which apply a pressure on the measuring object, might deform the object. The best choice in this case would be to use optical measurements, which do not affect the measuring object. Other examples could be electronic instruments used for measuring high-impedance electronic circuits. These instruments could, depending on their specifications, load the circuits, and thus affect the measurements. To avoid this type of interaction between measuring objects and measuring instruments, the specifications of the measuring equipment must be studied carefully. They have to be considered for possible interaction with the measuring objects.

MEASUREMENT OF HARDWARE PRODUCTION PROCESSES

General

The reason for measuring and monitoring hardware realization processes is to ensure that the process capability is adequate for producing products that meet the customer requirements and that the process remains adequate during the product realization process.

If the process capability is not known, process capability studies should be carried out. This includes measurements of process output and process parameters.

If the result of the process is not verified by subsequent measurement or monitoring, the process must be validated before use. The validation should be based on the process capability studies and is proof that the process is adequate for producing the particular product. The validation requires measurements of process output and process parameters.

When producing products, the process should be monitored to ensure that the process remains under control. This includes measurements of process parameters and/or process output, depending on the conditions. Very often measurements of process parameters are a more efficient way to ensure product quality than measurements of products. Measurements of process parameters allow control of the process and in this way prevent failures rather than initiate corrective actions due to product failures.

Generally, when choosing the process, the more one knows about the process' capability to comply with the requirements, the less one has to measure and monitor. In other words, the higher the risk of producing defective products, the more it is necessary to measure and monitor the process. The ideal situation is that the process capability is much bigger than necessary for producing the products, and the process parameters and the raw materials are stable. In this case process measurements as well as product measurements seem unnecessary.

Process capability can be established by experience over time or by process capability studies.

Measuring process output on a sampling basis is important because it provides proof that the validation is still valid and that the product meets the acceptance criteria. The raw materials or process parameters, which are not considered, could have changed and have become important for the process output. Documented results of process output measurements can be used as the basis for release of products.

However, sometimes testing of process output is impossible, difficult, requires destructive testing, or is very costly. Examples are a welding process used for closing a bag containing a sterile product; a soldering under an integrated circuit that cannot be inspected visually; or a plastic molding process, where the result can only be verified by cutting the product into pieces. In these cases one has to rely on the process validation and the process remaining under control. It is therefore required that the process parameters, that during the validation have been found important for controlling the process, are measured and monitored in a way that ensures that the process is kept under control. This requirement is clearer in the ISO 9001:2000 version of the standard as it is spelled out that the measuring and monitoring of processes shall confirm the continuing ability of each process to satisfy its intended purpose.

MEASUREMENTS FOR PROCESS CONTROL

Process Capability

To plan for measuring and monitoring a process, it is necessary to know to what degree the process capability complies with the process requirements for producing the specified products. The process capability can be defined as the process' ability to produce the specified products uniformly under normal, well-defined, and controlled conditions. As a measure for process capability, two terms are usually used for a process having a normal (Gaussian) distribution (see Figure 31.4). The process variation index:

$$Cp = \frac{\text{Specification width}}{\text{Process width}} \text{ and}$$

Process capability index:

$$Cpk = \frac{\begin{array}{c}\text{(Specification width)} / 2 - \text{Shift of process}\\ \text{distribution average from nominal specification}\end{array}}{\text{(Process width)} / 2}$$

In Figure 31.4 the specification width is twice as wide as the process width; therefore, the Cp value is 2. As the average of the process distribution is displaced 1.5 δ from the nominal specification, the Cpk value becomes 1.5. Because the displacement of the process average reduces the safety margin of being within the specifications, the Cpk value is a better measure of the process capability than the Cp value.

To illustrate how important it is to center the process, see Figure 31.5 which shows that even a specification of 5 δ creates more than 200 parts per million (ppm) failures if the process center is displaced 1.5 δ, whereas if the process is centered, the failure rate is 0.6 ppm. Whenever possible it is convenient to specify the Cpk value required for the process output. This makes it possible to plan a row of

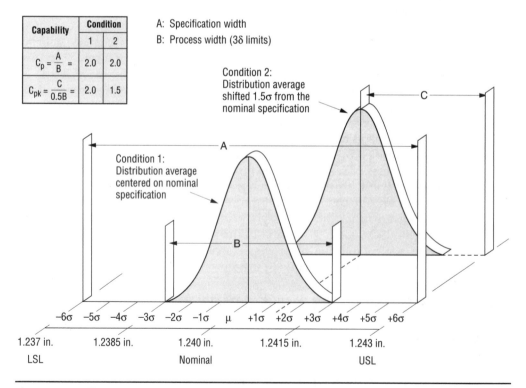

Figure 31.4   Illustration of Cp and Cpk concepts.

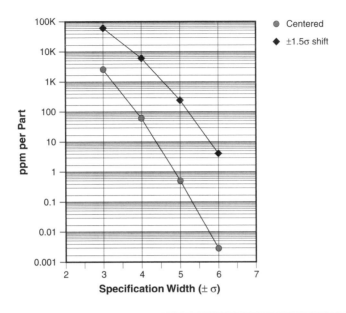

Figure 31.5 Defect levels for design margins from ±3 σ to ±6 σ when process is centered and shifted 1.5 σ.

Copyright, 1988, Motorola, Inc. Used with permission of Motorola University.

processes and to estimate the resulting output of this combination of processes. Using the Cpk values requires knowledge of the distribution of the processes. It is important to remember that the precondition for using the term is that the process has a normal distribution. Using the term for a process that has an output consisting of a number of distributions with different mean values, all distributed within the tolerance range, would give a wrong estimate of the process capability.

When planning measurements for process optimization and validation, the required measuring accuracy has to be big enough to give a good estimate of the Cpk value. The optimization of the process often requires designing a number of experiments in which the process parameters and eventually the raw materials vary within the normal range of variation of the process. A number of good tools for design of experiments and process analysis are given by Bhote (1991). During the optimization of the process, the critical output parameters of the product become known and the process capability can be estimated.

Process Control Measurements

When a process with an appropriate capability is chosen and operated, it is important to ensure that it remain under control. Process control gives no answer to the question of how the process can be improved if it appears to be out of control. This answer must be found by performing design of experiments that shows which knobs to turn to bring the process back on track.

Control charts have been used since World War II to ensure that a process is under control. The principle is that based on a number of samples, measured with a fixed frequency, in this case each hour, the mean value and range is calculated and plotted. Examples of control chart data and a control chart are shown in Figures 31.6 and 31.7.

Bushing Length
Specification .500" ± .002"

Sample #	8 am	9	10	11	12 pm	1	2	3	4	5	6	7 pm
1	.501"	.501"	.502"	.501"	.501"	.500"	.500"	.500"	.501"	.502"	.501"	.500"
2	.501"	.501"	.501"	.502"	.501"	.500"	.501"	.501"	.501"	.502"	.502"	.500"
3	.500"	.501"	.502"	.501"	.501"	.502"	.501"	.501"	.501"	.501"	.501"	.501"
4	.501"	.501"	.501"	.500"	.501"	.502"	.501"	.501"	.501"	.502"	.501"	.502"
5	.502"	.502"	.501"	.500"	.501"	.502"	.500"	.502"	.501"	.501"	.501"	.501
Sum of "X"s	2.505"	2.506"	2.507"	2.504"	2.505"	2.506"	2.505"	2.503"	2.505"	2.508"	2.506"	2.504"
$\bar{X}_1$	.501"	.5012"	.5014"	.5008"	.5010"	.5012"	.5010"	.5006"	.5010"	.5012"	.5016"	.5008"
R_1	.002"	.001"	.001"	.002"	.000"	.002"	.002"	.001"	.000"	.001"	.001"	.002

Sum of $\bar{X}_1$ = 6.0128

Sum of R_1 = .0115

$$\overline{\overline{X}} = \frac{\Sigma \bar{X}}{N} = \frac{6.0128}{12} = .50107$$

$$\bar{R} = \frac{\Sigma R}{N} = \frac{.015}{12} = .00125$$

Control limits:

For sample averages: $\overline{\overline{X}} \pm A_2\bar{R} = .50107 \pm (.58)(.00125)$

$$UCL = .50180$$
$$LCL = .50034$$

For range: $UCL = D_4\bar{R} = (2.11)(.00125) = .00264$
$$LCL = D_3\bar{R} = (0)(.00125) = 0$$

Figure 31.6   Control chart data.

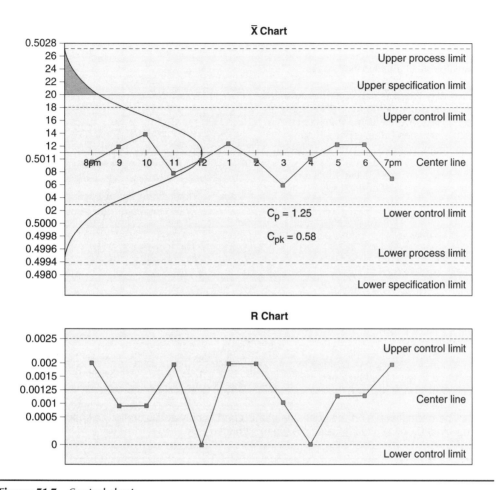

Figure 31.7 Control chart.
Copyright, 1987, Motorola, Inc. Used with permission from Motorola University.

The use of the control chart shows here that although all values are within control limits, five percent to seven percent of the items are likely to be defective.

During the last 10 years another tool for ensuring that a process is under control, precontrol, has been used frequently due to its simplicity and efficiency. The principle is illustrated in Figure 31.8.

The principles are as follows:

Rule 1. Divide the specification width by 4. The middle half becomes the *green zone,* and the areas between the specification limits and the green zone become the *yellow zones.* The area outside the specification limits becomes the *red zone.*

Rule 2. To determine if the process capability is adequate, measure a sample of five consecutive items. If the samples all are within the green zone, the process is ready to start. If only one of the items is outside the green zone, the process is not under control and an investigation has to be conducted to find the cause of variation.

Simple Precontrol Rules:

1. Draw two precontrol (p-c) lines in the middle half of specification width.

2. To qualify the process as ready to run (actually determining an instant *process capability*), five units in a row must be within p-c lines (green zone). If not, use diagnostic tools to reduce variation.

3. *In production*, sample two units consecutively and periodically.

Condition	Action
1. 2 units in green zone	Continue
2. 1 unit in green and 1 unit in yellow	Continue
3. 2 units in same yellow zone	Adjust
4. 2 units in opposite yellow zones	Stop*
5. 1 unit in red	Stop*

To resume production, 5 units in a row must be within the green zone.

4. *Frequency of sampling.* Divide the average time interval between adjacent stoppages by 6.

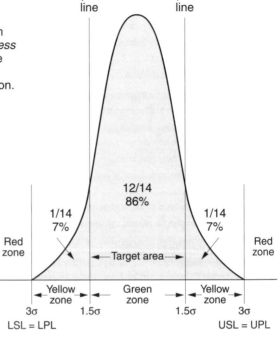

Note: The normal curve on the right side of this chart is only an illustration (a specialized case, with a C_p of 1) used to calculate the maximum σ risk.

Figure 31.8 Precontrol principles.
Copyright, 1987, Motorola, Inc. Used with permission of Motorola University.

Rule 3. Once the production process starts, measure two consecutive samples from the process periodically.

- If both items fall in the green zone, continue production.

- If one of the items is in the green zone and the other in one of the yellow zones, the process is still under control and can continue.

- If both items fall in the yellow zones, adjust the process if they are in the same zone. If they are in different yellow zones, stop the process and investigate the cause of variation. When the process has been stopped, repeat rule 2 until five consecutive samples measure in the green zone before resuming production.

- If even one of the items falls in the red zone, the process must be stopped and the reject cause investigated. When the process has been stopped, repeat rule 2 until five consecutive samples measure in the green zone before resuming production.

Rule 4. The frequency of sampling is six times the average frequency between stops or adjustments. When starting up the production, this frequency is estimated and adjusted during the production period. If the production is stopped for some reason (repair, lunch break, supply of new raw materials), the sampling frequency after the stop is:

$$6 \times \frac{1}{\text{stop period}}$$

That is if the stop has lasted 1 hour, the sampling frequency after the stop is a sample every 10 minutes.

When producing a very small series of items, it might not be possible to introduce process control because of time limitations. In these cases a 100 percent test strictly following the precontrol rules may be used.

If the requirement is an AQL value, sampling plans like ISO 3951 "Sampling procedures and charts for inspection by variables for percent nonconforming" might be used for monitoring variables and the appropriate part from ANSI/ASQ Z1.4, "Sampling Procedures and Tables for Inspection by Attributes" or ISO 2859, "Sampling procedures for inspection by attributes" for accepting or rejecting the production lot. It is important to follow the rules given in the standards for reduced and increased inspection.

In some cases the tolerance range is one-sided; that is, the requirement may be that burr size be less than X micron. In these cases, the tolerance range (from zero to the tolerance limit) is divided in two: the green zone closest to zero and the yellow zone closest to the tolerance limit. The precontrol rules are then the same as above (see Figure 31.9).

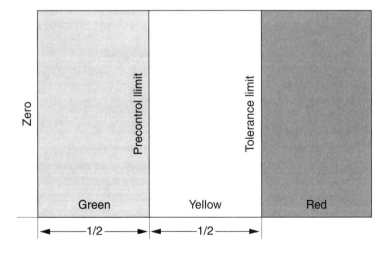

Figure 31.9 Precontrol rules for one-sided tolerance range.

INSPECTION PLANNING

Knowing the capability of the used processes, it is possible to plan the inspection of a row of processes and to estimate the resulting output.

When performing a test, the disturbing fact is that it will never become 100 percent effective but will leave the customers with a certain percentage of failures. The effectiveness of a testing process is dependent on a number of factors, which might be summarized in the following equation:

$$\text{Effectiveness (E)} = \text{Ability} \times \text{Correlation}$$

Where: ability is the ability of the test or inspection to identify good characteristics as good and bad characteristics as bad, and correlation is the ratio of the number of tested/inspected characteristics to the total number of characteristics required for use.

The ability varies with type of inspection/test and type of test object. A visual inspection might be effective in detecting unsoldered contacts where there is a physical contact that makes an electrical test inefficient. However a visual test is totally ineffective in detecting a nonfunctioning encapsulated part.

The correlation is often limited by purpose. Even when programming an automatic test, the programmer limits the tests to the most likely types to save test time. Besides this, the creativity of the test programmer might limit detection of likely failures.

By experience it is possible to estimate the test efficiency for a certain type of test and test object. With this knowledge we can estimate the following:

- Submitted defects
- Escaping defects

We will illustrate this with an example. Very often the test efficiency (e) is more difficult to estimate than the escaping defects and the observed defects (Motorola 1988). The escaping defects are often estimated on the basis of failures reported at later stages in production or by customers. The test efficiency can therefore be calculated as in the following example:

Given: Observed defects = 0.160 defects per unit (dpu)
Escaping defects = 0.040 dpu
Submitted defects = 0.160 + 0.040 = 0.200
$$\text{Test efficiency} = \frac{0.160}{0.200} = 0.8$$

Consider the example from production of electronic modules shown in Figure 31.10. In Figure 31.10 the assembly process contributes with 800 ppm failures (components turned wrong, components lost, etc.). For 1000 components this means that on average 80 percent of the boards fail due to assembly errors (dpu = 0.8). The visual inspection of the boards has an efficiency of 0.75, reducing the failure rate to 20 percent (dpu = 0.2). The soldering process contributes with 100 ppm, which with 10,000 soldering points means a dpu of 1.0, which together with the remaining assembly errors (dpu = 0.2) makes a dpu of 1.2. The visual soldering test that follows has an efficiency of 0.75, reducing the average failure rate to 30 percent (dpu = 0.3). The final test, an automatic functional test, has an efficiency

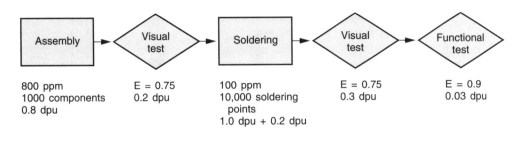

Figure 31.10 Inspection plan for electronic assembly and soldering.

of 0.9, reducing the failure rate to 3 percent (dpu = 0.03). If this final failure rate is not satisfactory, the most obvious solution is to try to reduce the soldering failure rate. If this is not possible, another solution is to improve the efficiency of the visual or functional test or, if this is not possible, to include an extra test before the functional test.

VISUAL INSPECTION

Sometimes the measuring process deals with items that need to look more or less like a certain standard. This is often the case when the purpose of the test is to verify the cosmetic quality of a product. When the measuring process is manual, this test is performed as a manual comparison of the item with bordering cases, like ideal, acceptable, and rejected.

When evaluating the cosmetic quality of a product, such as the quality of the paint on a part, it is important for the inspector to know how the part is used in the final product. Small painting defects may mean less if they are discovered after assembly when they are hidden by other parts. Because human evaluation of cosmetic errors can change for many reasons, it is necessary to ensure the ongoing competence of the humans who perform such evaluations on a regular basis. The inspector's assessments of a number of items as acceptable or rejected are compared with the assessment of the same items by a group of experienced people. Ideally, the inspector agrees with the average of the group. However, an acceptable situation could be an agreement of 90 percent, with equally many deviations for acceptable and rejected. Although not covered by clause 7.6(a) of ISO 9001:2000, this may be thought of as a "calibration" of the individuals involved.

If the inspector has a specific tendency to be more critical or less critical than the group, a "calibration" of the inspector is necessary. Figure 31.11 shows an example of an inspector who needed "calibration" at calibration numbers 4 and 5. Calibration number 6 shows that the inspector has adjusted the assessments.

Vision Systems

In a process control application the visual inspection process can become automated using a vision system with a television camera that creates a picture of the measuring object. The picture data is transferred to a computer that compares the shape of the measuring object with the programmed limits for the

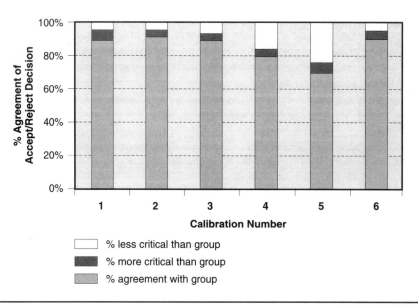

Figure 31.11 Competence of visual inspectors.

shape. It is very important that vision systems be validated for accepting good items and rejecting items not complying with the requirements.

EXAMPLES OF HOW TO USE PROCESS MEASUREMENTS SUCCESSFULLY

The following are examples of successful process measurements from different process technologies. Sometimes these examples go beyond the ISO 9001 requirements when profitable.

Plastic Molding

When planning design of experiments for plastic molding, it is important to show which parameters or characteristics of the product are the most critical (or the most difficult to produce) and which process parameters must be controlled to get the specified product. For multi-item molds, the exercise is also to find the most critical parts of the mold. Assuming that the process parameters are controlled, the process control measurements can concentrate on the most critical product measures. Using precontrol saves measuring cost and gives input for a good control of the process.

Remember the measuring uncertainty star. In particular, beware of measuring items right after the molding process, when they are still warm. Especially in foam molding processes, there is a risk of the part shrinking when the item becomes cold. It is therefore sometimes a good idea to compensate for known dimension changes when performing process control measurements.

Blown Plastic Products

Blown plastic products, such as plastic bottles, are often manufactured based on a plastic tube. As for the design experiments of a plastic molding process, show which parameters or characteristics of the product produced are the most critical (or most difficult to produce) and which process parameters need to be controlled to get the specified product. The weak point in this process is material distribution. The corners of the product often have less material than the rest of the product. To conduct the most useful process control measurements, therefore, weight the item and cut the corner of the item to measure material thickness. A common problem for this process is sink marks and surface shrinkage, problems that become important to control if the item is used in a process (such as welding or printing) that sets requirements for the surface or if such deviations are not acceptable for cosmetic reasons.

Extruded Plastic Tubes

In a process of producing plastic tubes with accurate dimensions, the first part of the production normally does not comply with the requirements and has to be scrapped. Therefore, bringing the process under control as quickly as possible is very important. Some manufacturers have established an automatic laser measuring system to measure the dimensions of two diagonals of the tube. The measurements are made by a computer that regulates the pulling speed of the tube so that the specified requirements are maintained. Such a system replaces other measurements of the product dimensions and reduces the start-up time for useful production.

Mechanical Assembly

Manual assembly processes are impossible to validate because humans are involved in the process. The failure rate of manual processes can never be reduced to the level of automated processes. The typical failure rate of a well-planned manual process exceeds 100 ppm. If very low failure rates are necessary, 100 percent inspection with automatic test equipment is a possibility. Test methods like vision control are sometimes useful tools in such cases. Another possibility for very low failure rates is process automation. However, automatic processes require higher component quality. Automatic assembly processes often require automatic testing and sorting because of component failures. If the failure rates of components are too high and reduce the yield of production too much, the only remedy is to investigate the component production processes using the aforementioned tools.

Electronic Assembly Processes

Monitoring electronic assembly processes may save a lot of money because corrective actions can be implemented promptly. Consider the assembly process illustrated in Figure 31.10. The process is used for producing a number of different printed circuit boards, some more difficult than others. Therefore, variations over time occur. Figure 31.12 shows the failure rate measured in ppm over a period. However, at a certain time the failure rate more than doubles.

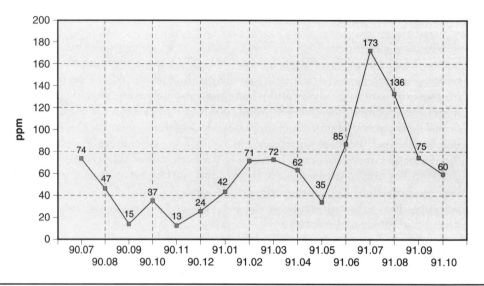

Figure 31.12   Failure rate for soldering process.

Failure investigations of the soldering process identified the problem to be a shipment of printed circuit boards with bad solderability. The shipment was rejected and the failure rate dropped again. The monitoring of the soldering process saved a lot of repair costs because the corrective action could be introduced earlier. Process monitoring gave an overview of the process used on a great number of different printed circuit board products.

"Special Processes"

Processes that cannot be verified (by such means as nondestructive testing) must be validated to ensure that process output complies with requirements. However, validation requires measurements. An example is the welding of a plastic bag that ensures the sterility of a medical device. Some regulatory requirements set the failure rate to a maximum of 1 ppm for ensuring sterility. Such a failure rate is impossible to verify directly by measurements. The following is one way to perform validation measurements:

- Find the process parameter that is most important for the failure rate and determine which setting of this parameter starts to create failures.
- Measure the failure rate. Now adjust the setting slightly to a more optimal value and measure the failure rate again.
- Assuming that there is a linear connection between the setting of the critical parameter and the failure rate, the limits for this parameter giving a failure rate of 1 ppm can be calculated.

As with many other indirect measurements, this is not very accurate and a safety margin must be added to ensure compliance with the requirements.

During the process operation, monitoring of the output must be done on a sampling basis. The purpose of monitoring is to see if the basis for the validation has changed. For example, raw material could undergo some changes that had not been identified before the process began. The measurements could involve the use of destructive testing, such as measuring breaking strength of the weld or exposing a closed bag to low external pressure.

MEASUREMENT OF HARDWARE PRODUCTS

General

Product measuring occurs at the end of the process when the risk of delivering products that do not conform with the requirements is too big. The reason for this situation could be that the process is not always able to produce the required quality. In principle, if a process always produces the specified product, product testing is unnecessary.

One situation in which product measuring could be necessary is when products are received from a supplier. The quality of the products could be unknown and it may be necessary to ensure before shipment that these products have the specified quality. The products are measured in incoming inspection and accepted or rejected.

Product measuring is also needed if products are produced with a process that is not validated and with an unknown or unsatisfactory capability.

Another situation requiring product measuring could be where the product has a complexity that requires a lot of processes, each having a high capability but together producing a final product with an unacceptable quality. In this case measurements of the products (modules or final products) are used to find products that are not conforming to the requirements and eventually can be repaired.

Product measurements during and/or after the process that are the basis for the release of the product must be documented. The product release must be carried out by an authorized person when all specified processes have been satisfactorily completed, unless otherwise approved by the customer. The release process has to be recorded.

How to Choose the Extent of Testing

Product measurements must ensure conformance with requirements. Often the requirements specify the failure rate.

For complicated, repairable products inspection planning, mentioned in the previous chapter, is a good tool to help choosing the extent of testing.

For simple products, like components, the failure rate often is specified as an AQL value using the attribute sampling rules and evaluation techniques in the appropriate part of the ISO 2859 series (See ISO 2859-1 "Sampling procedures for inspection by attributes—Part 0: Introduction to the ISO 2859" for a discussion on usage of this family), or other sampling plans, or a Cpk value, as mentioned in the previous chapter. The sampling plans are dependent on previous experience with the same product from the same supplier or process. The sampling plans specify acceptance criteria based on a known risk of accepting nonconforming shipments/lots or rejecting conforming shipments/lots. However, the AQL value is not as useful as the Cpk value for determining if a low failure rate is required.

Using measurements on a sampling basis to estimate the Cpk value is a more intelligent way to use the measurements than just to verify if the sample is inside or outside the tolerance range. However, the estimate based on samples from a shipment/lot mixed from several different populations with different mean values can lead to incorrect conclusions of the failure rate. Therefore, to avoid wrong decisions, it is necessary before using this method to know something about the manufacturing process.

The extent of testing is, of course, dependent on the consequences of failures. For requirements where failures may have fatal consequences, there are often legal or regulatory requirements requiring 100 percent testing before release of the products. Examples are compliance with the International Electrotechnical Commission (IEC) such as the IEC 61010:2001 series, "Safety requirement for electrical equipment for measurement, control, and laboratory use" or Underwriters Laboratories (UL) electrical safety requirements, the U.S. Food and Drug Administration Quality Systems Regulation (FDA QSR) requirements for medical devices (FDA QSR, 21 CFR Part 820), or the European Union medical device directive (EC Council Directive 93/42).

ISO 9001:2000 Requirements

The new ISO 9001 in general gives more freedom to plan where measurements are important as a basis for product release. Specific requirements for receiving inspection in-process testing, or final testing do not exist anymore. However, the measurements will be planned and implemented to an extent that ensures conformity and achieves improvement. This means that the weight of the measuring process will shift from accepting or rejecting products to controlling production processes. This strategy means more freedom and may lead to cost savings and improved product quality.

Examples of How to Use Product Measurements Successfully

The following are examples of successful product measurements from different process technologies. Sometimes these examples go beyond the ISO 9001 requirements when profitable.

Plastic Molding. A supplier of molded plastic components critical to an automatic assembly process validated the molding process and determined the most critical item in the multi-item mold. Precontrol process control was introduced, and the need for inspection was eliminated. Better quality and cost savings were the results.

Machined Metal Components. A factory supplying machined mechanical components performed measurements on the shop floor in accordance with the precontrol principle instead of inspecting the produced lot. The factory had previously used fixed tools like hole gages and external caliper gages to determine if the items were inside or outside the specifications. The personnel were familiar with these types of measurements. When introducing precontrol, an extra set of fixed-hand measuring tools was provided, allowing the operators to determine if the items were inside or outside the half tolerance range. The result was better quality due to better-centered processes and reduced scrap.

Electronic Assembly. In a factory for assembly of electronic printed circuit board modules, inspection planning was introduced (see previous chapter). When the failure budget was established, it was determined that it would be necessary to introduce an extra inspection to reduce the failure rate of the finished board to the required rate. It was also determined that the soldering process was the main contributor to failures. The failures were analyzed and a corrective action including a change of printed circuit board layout was introduced. The failure rate dropped, and the extra step of inspection was not necessary anymore. Results were cost savings and better quality.

REFERENCES

Bhote, K. R. *World Class Quality, Using Design of Experiments to Make It Happen.* New York: American Management Association, 1991.

Motorola, Inc. *Design for Manufacturability* no. 6. Schaumberg, IL: Motorola Training and Education Center, 1988.

Chapter 32

Measurement for Software Processes and Products

Frank Houston
EduQuest, Hyattstown, Maryland

PROCESS FAILURE AS A SOURCE OF ERROR

A software development group followed change control and review procedures, but it accumulated its changes over several weeks or months and presented them en masse. The review material generally consisted of two or three large ring binders, change records, and test results. Overwhelmed with this mass of paper in addition to other change requests, the change board had no chance to do a thorough independent review of each software item. Software defects that could have been found had each change been considered on its own went undetected.

This true story illustrates that having processes and procedures is not enough to ensure quality and that perceived goals often diverge from actual goals. In this example, the actual goal was to find errors, but the software development group perceived only a requirement to produce useless (to them) paperwork, so it did the minimum its procedures required (over and over again).

To solve software quality problems one needs technical tools and managed processes, but most of all one must win the hearts and minds of the software engineers and programmers. The idea of measurement frequently leads to an adversarial relationship between the measurers and the measured, making the task more difficult than need be. This is an unavoidable fact of human nature; but lacking a yardstick, one cannot assess progress objectively.

This chapter provides guidance for measurement of software processes and software objects in compliance with ISO 9001:2000 clauses 8.2.3 and 8.2.4. The guidance will include a process for deciding what to measure, techniques for measurement, and references to software process assessment literature.

THE GOAL–QUESTION–MEASUREMENT PARADIGM

Measurement should not be undertaken for its own sake. Only rarely can arbitrary measurements uncover fundamental problems. Measurement takes time, effort, and money, so one should begin a measurement program by determining the essential attributes of quality that one must measure. Then one should identify indicators and properties that correlate with or contribute to those attributes. Finally, one should decide whether the measurement effort can provide a worthwhile return.

The goal–question–measurement paradigm is a well-known method for determining what and how to measure. One first establishes goals for the organization, project, process, or product. Next, one formulates questions that help one monitor progress toward the goal. Finally, needing measurements to answer the questions, one devises and performs those measurements. In theory, one can assess progress toward the goals if one formulates a complete set of related questions having objective and measurable answers. Robert B. Grady (1992) discusses this methodology in *Practical Software Metrics for Project Management and Process Improvement*.

Quality means different things to different groups. On the one hand, a software project manager might think of attributes such as time to market, low incidence of defects, and low costs for development. On the other hand, customers might think of low purchase cost, ease of use, and low incidence of defects. Between the two, there is only one common element—low incidence of defects. Production and engineering groups also have distinct views of quality.

To establish consistent measures, one must first choose a viewpoint (such as project manager, programmer, customer, and so on) and then identify its related quality attributes and corresponding indicators. As a second order of refinement, one could identify the quality attributes and indicators that different viewpoints might share.

MEASUREMENT REQUIREMENTS AND GUIDANCE: SOFTWARE PROCESS AND SOFTWARE PRODUCT

Table 32.1 is a concordance table, that is, a table showing the relationships between the relevant clauses of ISO 9001:2000, ISO 9001:1994, and ISO 9000-3:1991. An examination of these references reveals very little guidance regarding process measurement in general, let alone software process measurement, and the references provide no explanation of how to measure the thing called software.

From the concordance table, one might deduce that process measurement will involve quality audits (ISO 9001:1994, 4.17) and statistical techniques (ISO 9001:1994, 4.20) and that the same will hold true for software measurement. The guidance of ISO 9000-3:1991 offers nothing further with respect to quality audits, but it indicates that one should measure the following:

- How well the development process is followed
- How effective the process is at keeping undetected defects to a minimum

ISO 9000-3:1991 further suggests that the important issues of process measurement are that the methods chosen should be useful for process control, have a direct effect on product quality, and be appropriate for the products produced.

Table 32.1 Concordance of ISO 9001:2000, ISO 9001:1994, and ISO 9000-3:1991.		
ISO 9001:2000	**ISO 9001:1994**	**ISO 9000-3:1991**
8.2.3	4.17	4.3
	4.20	6.4.2
8.2.4	4.10.2	6.7.3 and 6.8 all
	4.10.3	5.7.3, 5.7.4, and 5.8.2
	4.10.4	5.7.3(a), 5.8 all, 5.9.2, and 5.9.3(f)
	4.10.5	5.7.3 all, 5.8.1, 5.9.2, and 5.9.3(f)
	4.20.1	6.4.1
	4.20.2	

Regarding measurement of software, the references to clauses 4.10.2, 4.10.3, 4.10.4, and 4.10.5 of the 1994 edition are covered in the section on software production and servicing. Records of testing are necessary to enable measurement of conformance to software requirements and specifications. Chapter 25, "Production and Service Provision for Software," thoroughly covers the establishment and use of testing records, and the current chapter has little to add. The 2000 edition of ISO 9001 emphasizes measurement as a component of continuous improvement, so the concordance table refers to clauses 4.20.1 and 4.20.2 of the 1994 edition.

The latest edition of ISO 9001 requires one to identify measurable, quality-related properties of software and use those properties as indexes of improvement or indicators of potential problems. The guideline ISO 9000-3:1991 offers little guidance on software measurement beyond the tracking of defect statistics. The technology of software measurement has advanced considerably since 9000-3 was published, and one can now recommend some best practices for software measurement. This chapter examines software process measurement, then software measurement.

MEASURING PROCESS EFFECTIVENESS

Why is it necessary to measure software processes? Indeed, why should one try to measure any process? Because one must continually monitor and measure results in order to recognize continual improvement. Improving process effectiveness and efficiency are two primary goals of a business. The following discussion deals with efficiency because efficiency does not exist without effectiveness. A process that does not achieve its goals is inefficient by definition. The same techniques used to identify and analyze appropriate measurements of effectiveness can perform the same service for efficiency.

The measurement of effectiveness is the essence of validation, a word that comes from the root adjective "valid," meaning effective, effectual, or sound. Validation differs from verification, which derives from the root verb "verify,"

Table 32.2 Software process effectiveness goals.

Management View	Customer View	Technical View	Quality View
Minimize development effort and schedule	Minimize acquisition and upkeep costs	Minimize paperwork	Maximize process conformity
Maximize customer satisfaction	Timely delivery	Minimize defects	Minimize defects
Minimize defects	Maximize dependability	Optimize maintenance effort	Maximize maintainability
	Maximize usability	Maximize utility of process records	Aid product improvement
			Aid process improvement

meaning to show to be true by demonstration or evidence. At the end of the day, verification is the evaluation of truth while validation is the evaluation of effectiveness. To validate a process requires one to verify that the process has the quality of effectiveness, a quality that one must define. This requires one to consider the goals of the process, including fulfillment of defined customer requirements.

Table 32.2 illustrates the possible goals for a software process as seen from several different viewpoints. In his book, Robert Grady (1992) discusses the goals of management in depth. For purposes of this discussion, the listed goals of the quality viewpoint will be further defined with the aid of a definition tree as described in the next paragraph. The tree will include example questions and measurements.

A useful technique for establishing goals is the definition tree. The definition tree starts at the root with a goal. The first-generation descendents or branches are subgoals, or factors that describe more precisely the main goal. If the first-generation descendents are still too vague, a second generation must be added. This process goes on until the tree forms a list of questions and measurements that shows whether and to what degree the desired goal has been fulfilled.

Using this technique, one can formulate questions for evaluating software processes. In its most developed form, the definition tree might delineate the specific evidence to seek and who to interview.

Figure 32.1 shows a definition tree for the factors of the quality view of effectiveness as listed in Table 32.2. The illustrated tree suggests several questions and measurements related to the quality view of effectiveness.

This analysis is necessarily incomplete. One should consider other viewpoints, goals, and questions. Relevant questions may include the following:

- Do the processes save or cost time, money, or effort? Both short development and maintenance effects must be considered.
- Do the processes develop useful information?
- Do the processes yield complete and unambiguous records?

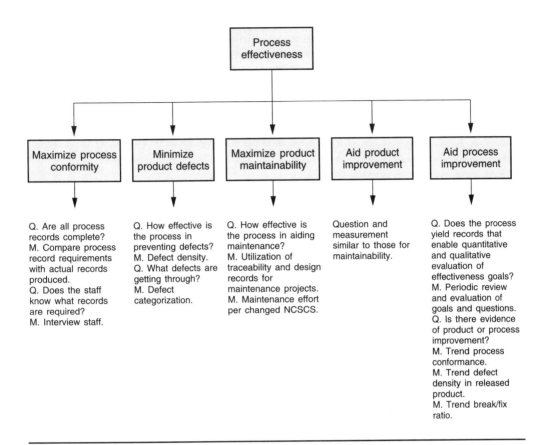

Figure 32.1   Definition tree.

- Do the processes yield records that an auditor can understand and trust?
- Do the processes establish objective acceptance criteria for work products?
- Do the processes produce consistent results—that is, are they in statistical control?
- Do the processes lend themselves to cause-and-effect analysis?

MEASURING CONFORMITY

Process conformity occupies an important niche in the analysis of process effectiveness. Nothing can be learned from or about a process to which nobody conforms. It is, therefore, essential that one monitor and measure how well the organization conforms to its established software processes. In the worst case, such monitoring can yield an unmistakable signal—that is, the process cannot be effective if nobody follows it.

The outputs of internal audits, including audits of active projects as required by ISO 9001:2000 subclause 8.2.2, are the logical inputs for assessing conformity to a process. This means software processes must produce records for the auditors and inspectors. These records must show what was done, when it was done, who did it, and what the outcome was.

Figure 32.1 shows two questions related to process conformity. To an auditor, these questions may be fundamental indicators of whether a process is followed; but it may be necessary to further define conformity. An auditor might need to ask more questions to learn the root causes of nonconformity, such as the following: "Are there written instructions for carrying out the process?" "Has the staff been trained, and is the training up-to-date?" and "What evidence demonstrates completion of a required record?" Clearly, the definition tree for process effectiveness should be expanded.

IDENTIFYING CANDIDATES FOR SOFTWARE PROCESS MEASUREMENT

A vital step in planning for measurement is to identify what processes are to be measured. The following processes could be considered as particularly relevant to software:

- Management support processes
  - Information management
  - Training of people
  - Finance-related activities
    - Allocation of time and resources
  - Infrastructure and service maintenance
    - Management review of process effectiveness and efficiency
  - Purchasing
  - Marketing
  - Risk assessment
- Product design and development processes
  - Planning
  - Requirements development
  - Requirements review
  - Customer communication
  - Design and development review
  - Design verification
  - Design validation
  - Requirements and dependency tracing
  - Control of design and development changes
  - Verification of purchased product
  - Supplier control
- Production and service provision processes
  - Control of production and service provision
  - Product/part identification and traceability
  - Preservation of product

- Control of monitoring and measuring devices
- Measurement, analysis, and improvement processes
  - Customer monitoring
  - Internal and external audits
  - Financial monitoring
  - Process monitoring and measurement
  - Product monitoring and measurement
  - Detection of nonconformities
  - Corrective action
  - Preventive action
  - Continual improvement

It is an extensive list, and one should not expect to manage all of it at once. The list provides a place to start to determine which processes to monitor and measure. It is recommended that the organization begin by measuring the product design and development group, followed by the production and servicing; management support; and measurement, analysis, and improvement groups in that order. The monitoring and measurement of product design and development processes should start with requirements development, followed by requirements/design/development review, traceability, and verification and validation. In the case of software, development review should include code review and test plan review. The remaining order of monitoring and measurement might depend on individual priorities within the organization.

MEASURING SOFTWARE WORK PRODUCTS

There is a fundamental reason for monitoring and measuring software processes and software. It is to identify and prevent from recurring the causes of software defects and the causes of failure to prevent, detect, or remove defects. The prior discussion dealt with analysis of processes including those intended for defect management. The topic now shifts to the measurement of software and indicators for tracking and predicting software defects.

Software defects can originate or occur in several areas. They include the following:

- Source code
- Documentation (for example, user manuals and help screens)
- Design (for example, program/data architecture)
- Specification (for example, functional requirements)
- Operator utilization
- Other sources (for example, errors in operating systems, "make" files, compilers, and so forth)

Use of the goal–question–metric method will eventually lead to a list of problem areas similar to this one. One then realizes that the bottom line of defect prevention and correction processes is the measurement of product defects.

One can devise ways to measure such attributes, but only after the software is in use. They are not predictive. One needs to identify properties of software designs and source code that correlate with some of the attributes listed enabling one to predict, identify, analyze, and resolve problems early in the development process. Academic and industrial researchers have identified some properties of design and code that correlate with development cost, maintenance cost, dependability, and ease of use. These indicators fall into the following general categories:

- Size
- Complexity
- Rate
- Clarity

SIZE AND COMPLEXITY

Complexity and size correlate so closely that one might regard them as slightly different views of the same property. The metrics and ways of depicting complexity, however, contain more information than program size. One can begin to measure complexity before one writes a line of code, and complexity analysis can be applied throughout the development process.

The size property applies to code and, to some extent, specifications. It is useful mainly as a first-order indication of likely problem areas and as a factor in estimating effort needed to review and test the code. Two manifestations of the property are commonly used: source lines of code (SLOC) and non-comment source code statements (NCSCS).

This property provides a rough indicator for comparing code modules with respect to the likelihood of discovering errors. This helps project management to allocate resources for review and testing activities.

A similar metric could be applied to fourth-generation languages such as Structured Query Language (SQL). It could also be used for so-called "macros" in spreadsheet and other software applications. Regardless of the type of code, the users must recognize that size metrics can provide only an order-of-magnitude estimate of the probability that errors will be found.

On the one hand, the size property has a big advantage—ease of measurement. On the other hand, complexity metrics often require manual analysis or specialized software tools, but complexity analysis often yields information that both management and developers can use.

One might start with four common indicators of design complexity:

- Number of requirements
- Cohesion or design strength
- Function points
- Design "weight"

Code complexity parameters initially might include the following:

- Fan out
- Fan in

- Cyclomatic complexity (McCabe)
- Depth of nesting

The following sections elaborate on the applicability and utility of complexity analysis.

INDICATORS OF DESIGN COMPLEXITY

Number of Requirements

The number of requirements is one indicator of basic design complexity. As the number of requirements increases, so do the opportunities for errors to occur and elude detection. A system with many user requirements and design requirements is likely to be more complex, harder to realize, and costlier to maintain than one with fewer requirements. As with program size, this metric is only a number. It provides no insight into why the design is complex, so it is most useful as a first-order "sanity check" for management.

One must not infer from the preceding discussion that one should continually drive down the number of requirements. If one attempts to shrink the number of requirements too much, one finds that they become trivial, vague, and impossible to measure.

One might apply a similar counting technique in object-oriented design and programming. In this case, one might start with two properties: number of object classes and number of objects in a class. Again, larger numbers might indicate a greater tendency toward errors, and the result should be taken as a first-order indicator of likely problem areas.

Cohesion, or Design Strength

Cohesion is the degree to which one limits the functionality of a module of code. The simplest method of classifying this property establishes three categories: single function or high strength, two functions or medium strength, and three or more functions or low strength (Card and Glass 1990). In Card and Glass's studies, there was a significant correlation between low module strength and number of detected errors. As a yardstick, this attribute is simple to apply. It provides a caution indicator for management, and it localizes the source of potential problems for system designers and programmers. It is applicable to old style procedural programming and might be adaptable to object-oriented programming. For more information, refer to the referenced article.

Function Points

Function point analysis is a scoring system sometimes used in project scheduling that provides a preliminary estimate of system size and complexity. It might also correlate with the amount of effort needed to test a system. Function points are calculated by counting certain characteristics of computer data systems and applying a complexity factor to each one. These characteristics include the following:

- Inputs
- Outputs

- Inquiries
- Master files
- Interfaces

Real-world examples of these characteristics include the following:

- Data entry screens
- Reports
- Database queries
- Database files
- Files shared with other systems

One applies a complexity factor to each characteristic and then adds the individual scores to calculate the function point score of a system. Like the number of requirements, the system score is more useful to managers than engineers and programmers. It provides little insight into design details, but the data gathered in calculating the characteristic scores might indicate areas that need improvement or simplification.

Although some experts question its utility, function point analysis has persistent champions, and the literature is extensive. Sources of function point information include Albrecht (1979), Albrecht and Gaffney (1983), and Symons (1988).

Design Weight

Design weight is a measure of complexity based on the architecture of a program, specifically the hierarchy of function calls. The property is a function of the flow of data and control and the predicted number of decisions based on the data structure on which a program module operates. One must have data flow diagrams and control flow graphs to analyze this property of a design, and the analysis and calculation are not as simple as other metrics. Design weight provides management with a high-level indicator, and it gives engineers or programmers some information useful for localizing and correcting problems. For further reading on design weight, refer to DeMarco (1982).

CODE COMPLEXITY METRICS

Analysts have used several indicators to evaluate the complexity of computer programs, code modules, procedures, and functions. Some of the methods appear simple and obvious, while others require significant effort or special software tools. Five metrics are discussed here because they have been used enough to establish statistical correlations with error rates, cost of testing, and cost of maintenance. The measurements are not hard to obtain, and software tools are available to do some of the required analyses.

Fan Out

Fan out is a count of program relationships. It can be determined from the software design and by analyzing source code. For third-generation languages it equals the number of code modules called by the module under analysis plus the number of common data structures to which it writes plus the number of parameters it returns. For system state designs, it might be regarded as the number of state transitions that originate in a given initial state. This measurement correlates directly with probability of discovering errors; therefore, it indicates the magnitude of effort needed for review, testing, and maintenance. It also may be inversely related to ease of use and reliability.

Another form of fan out might apply to object-oriented designs; that is, it would equal the number of relationships that are linked through a particular object. Used in this way, fan out can help estimate the impact on a database system when an object specification is changed.

The fan out metric might help project management to allocate resources and to predict the chances for successful deployment. The information analyzed to produce this metric can help designers and programmers locate potential problem areas, improve designs, and devise tests. In particular, fan out identifies the other modules, states, or objects that must be integrated together and tested with the one under analysis. It also indicates which modules, states, or objects may be affected by changes.

Fan In

Essentially the opposite of fan out, fan in is the number of software modules that directly call the module under analysis plus the number of common data structures from which it reads. In system state models, fan in might be regarded as the number of state transitions that terminate in the state under analysis.

Like fan out, the analysis that produces this metric also produces information useful for integration testing and assessing the effects of software changes. Fan in is an important parameter for utility code.

Cyclomatic Complexity and Essential Complexity

This metric emerged from attempts to count the number of logical paths in a program to estimate testing effort. To identify the paths, the code is modeled as a *directed graph* consisting of nodes and edges. In a directed graph, each node is depicted as a circle representing a statement, and each edge is depicted as a line representing a transition from one statement to another. Figure 32.2 is an example of a directed graph.

Cyclomatic complexity represents the number of independent paths through a segment of code. In Figure 32.2, the number is six. In early work, users of this metric arbitrarily designated 10 as the limit of complexity allowable without additional review. More recent work indicates that programming defect rates begin to increase significantly around a complexity of 14 (Grady 1992).

The cyclomatic complexity metric is a versatile quality indicator. It provides numeric feedback that correlates with probable error rates, and the graphic output enables engineers or programmers to analyze their code to identify potential problems and devise thorough tests. The method has two drawbacks. First, for anything but trivial code one must use a software tool for the analysis. Second, most, if not all, of the available tools are for third-generation languages such as C, C++, and Ada. Few tools, if any, are available for fourth-generation languages and application "macro" languages.

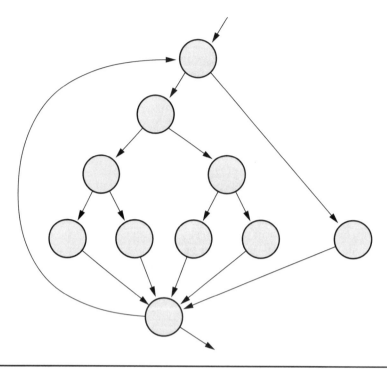

Figure 32.2   Example of a directed graph; cyclomatic complexity = 6.

Closely related to cyclomatic complexity, essential complexity uses a similar analysis. Where cyclomatic complexity counts every independent path, essential complexity allows one to count certain statement types as single paths when they actually generate multiple paths—for example, switch-case statements.

Depth of Nesting

Depth of nesting is related to design weight, cyclomatic complexity, and fan in/fan out. There may be decisions within decisions, loops within loops, and function calls within function calls. Depth of nesting is determined by counting the number of decision statements or subroutine/function calls stacked together within a section of code. The goal is to limit complexity by limiting the number of conditional statements, loops, and functions or subroutines that one may nest together. The underlying theory is that one makes programs easier to understand by limiting the number of parameters and conditions one must keep in mind while creating or analyzing a segment of code. This metric is usually associated with coding rules.

Defect Measurement

Defect measurement consists of counting, classifying, and normalizing the number of defects discovered in software work products. The concept may sound simple, but its application is not. There are no universal standards in this field.

Companies define defects, classify defects, and count code differently. Then there is the issue of how to treat defects in specifications, traceability files, and other documentation, which often are handled in diverse ways, even between segments of the same project. Still, the number of defects is a crucial factor in software quality. In fact, a prevalent theory of software quality measurement suggests that for each round of review or testing, the number of defects remaining in a program will be proportional to the number of defects found. At the end of the day, this theory predicts that a defect-free program is impossible.

Defect measurement and analysis is necessary to monitor a software quality process, but it is a treacherous field. The data are prone to interpretive errors, and they are easy to manipulate. Firm standards are crucial when two or more programs or projects are compared.

One thousand source lines of code (a KSLOC) in program A must be equivalent to a KSLOC in program B. Defect classifications and the definition of a defect must be absolutely clear. Program maintenance should be managed so that one can always identify corrective changes. One should never be allowed to correct a defect and then call the correction a program enhancement.

If one can establish such iron control, then one may have a valid basis for measuring the effectiveness of processes for preventing, detecting, and removing defects. These include design reviews, code reviews, and testing. Clean defect data allows one to identify when software reaches a state of control with respect to defect discovery. With such information, one can possibly improve future project estimates. A clean record of defect rates may enable one to spot second-order causes, such as process flaws. Clean, consistent defect data might be the most valuable asset a software quality engineer can have.

There are three rules for using defect data: normalize, normalize, and normalize. When comparing defect data, one must normalize for the specific programming language and tools by comparing statistics for like tools only. Then one must normalize for program size using exactly the same counting method for all programs or systems involved. One should treat error counting as a sampling process—that is, each error detection process represents a sampling of discovered errors. The normalized count represents the density of errors discovered in that sample. One does not assume that it represents the actual error density. When time is a factor, as in reliability measurements, one should normalize error discovery rates using the identical method of measuring operating time for each sample. Measuring program size has been discussed, and operating time is discussed with dependability measurements in the next section.

Today, most organizations count discovered errors and normalize them using either SLOC or NCSCS as the denominator. This technique is applied to both program modules and the final integrated programs. Normalizing for the sizes of executable programs, in bytes, might be a more consistent alternative. Again, consistency is the crucial factor.

The break/fix ratio is an important quality indicator for software correction processes. It is defined technically as the number of defects introduced divided by the number of defects corrected. In fact, only the denominator of this ratio can be known with any degree of accuracy. In practical application, one must 1) execute a defect detection process, 2) count the number of defects discovered, 3) perform corrective action for those defects, 4) again execute a defect detection process, and 5) count newly discovered defects. Each defect detection process represents a sample. The ratio of the second sample to the first approximates the break/fix ratio for that round. One might plot the trend of successive break/fix ratios as a factor in software stability and readiness for release.

This discussion has concentrated on static measurements of executable programs, complexity, size, and discovered defects. Databases and object-oriented programs present another challenge for static measurements. Such systems contain executable code to manage their data objects, but much of program performance depends on the suitability of the data architecture and the integrity of the data. Does one account for such factors in the normalization of error counts, and if so, how? As a first approximation, one might normalize error counts using the size of the database tables for a denominator. If so, then how does one measure size: by number of data fields or by the number of bytes of data the table holds? The measurement of database reliability and integrity remains a fruitful sphere of research for software quality engineering.

SOFTWARE DEPENDABILITY MEASUREMENT

The discussion of defects has concentrated on static characterization. Software dependability is an equally important indicator of software quality, and to measure dependability one must measure performance dynamically.

Software dependability has three performance components—reliability, maintainability, and maintenance support—all of which incorporate time-related measurements. Three important measurements are the occurrence of failures, restoration of operations, and rate of defect discovery.

Failures are not the same as defects. Indeed, a defect may cause a failure, but one might restore operation without correcting the defect. Defect discovery requires one to investigate and learn the cause of the failure. The main point is that the measurements under discussion are rate measurements, and all use time as the denominator.

Operating time can be measured in three ways. The easiest and most familiar is calendar time or real time, that is, time as kept by our clocks and watches. Another way to keep time is by system operating hours, that is, the so-called uptime of the system that runs the software in question. System operating hours typically are less than but nearly equal to calendar time. A third way to keep time is to measure processor time, that is, the time a computer spends actually running the software. This is typically a fraction of calendar time and system operating time, but it provides the truest indicator of software reliability if one can obtain it.

Historically, software reliability has always been a somewhat "soft" measurement, and the system advances of the past two decades have not helped. In the days of batch computing, the report of a program run included processor time; however, it is clear that the intricate computing environments common today have complicated the measurement of time for reliability calculations.

It is not clear how one measures the contribution of client and server to the processor time for a program or how one accounts for multiple client systems, the server, and the network in the measurement of calendar time.

Reliability is a measure of failure occurrence typically characterized in one of two ways: mean number of failures per unit of time or mean time between failures. In computing reliability, one should use the actual running time of the program. As discussed earlier, this time is most difficult to obtain in client–server environments; therefore, one must rely on calendar time as a tolerably good first-order approximation. At the end of the day, this approach is more understandable to most managers and users anyway. Reliability is a quantity that one may wish to track and trend using statistical techniques that will be discussed later.

As a first approximation of time for normalized rate calculations, one might use the sum of the number of clients, the number of servers, and one (to account for the network) and multiply it by the calendar time. One could then take steps to establish more realistic numbers if necessary to isolate problems.

Musa et al. (1987) describes a normalized time-based measurement he calls failure intensity. It is the number of failures detected per CPU-hour between sampling points. By tracking the trend of this quantity, one might predict when work products are ready for various development activities, especially code. (The gross total of detected errors is not very useful for tracking individual projects or products, but it might indicate that a process needs improvement.)

A second crucial indicator of software dependability is availability. Availability is the ratio of the time a system was available to the operating time for a defined period. This is a valuable indicator of system operation and maintenance trends, but it is not very useful for purveyors of commercial software packages, who are not involved in day-to-day operation and maintenance of their products.

Rate of defect discovery is an important quality measurement for all software development organizations. It is similar to Musa's failure intensity, but it deals only with failures that are traced to a confirmed defect. Its units are defects per unit of code per unit of time, where a unit of code may be SLOC, NCSCS, or executable byte, and the unit of time is calendar time elapsed since the previous sample. Trending this quantity may indicate changes in program usage or chronic failure to remove embedded defects that might require one to revisit the design and requirements of a system.

Many properties of system operation and maintenance are best tracked and normalized by time. This section has discussed a few. The crucial lesson is that the method of time measurement must be consistent from sample to sample. One should try more complicated time measurements only after one has exhausted the information available from a first approximation, that is, calendar time.

MEASUREMENT OF SOFTWARE AND THE TESTING PROCESS

Software testing has been discussed as part of product realization, but there is a measurement that should be included in this discussion, and that is test coverage. Test coverage may be defined in several ways. From the database view, there may be two components: the degree to which all available fields are used in testing and the degree to which a test exercises the functionality of a database implementation (for example, what percentage of screens, queries, and reports is used).

For procedural programs, the definition of test coverage includes logical control paths, calculations, variables, data structures, and so forth. Test coverage index is usually stated as a percentage. For instance, a test that covers three distinct paths of the possible six in Figure 32.2 has a path coverage index of 50 percent. If the same program has 10 calculations and only five are tested with multiple variables, then the coverage for calculations is 50 percent. In general, the closer one can get to 100 percent coverage, the better. It is possible to count coverage at different test levels into the overall test coverage of large complex programs.

There are database tools that aid in development and execution of tests, and some of these tools include a function for calculating test coverage. Tools for cyclomatic complexity measurement provide similar functions for third-generation programs.

USING STATISTICAL TECHNIQUES

Statistical techniques can be applied to any data obtained through process monitoring and auditing. One handy method is the histogram, which divides data into classes and graphs the number of items in each class. A histogram could be used to graph the number of software defects attributable to various processes, documents, or modules. Simple Pareto analysis might be applied to identify the most frequent source of error. A similar histogram-based method might use repair cost data to identify the most costly source of software defects.

Graphical analysis might be used to model "reliability growth" during software development. The reliability growth graph tracks the rate of defect discovery, that is, the number or density of defects found over a specified amount of time, which may be normalized to account for special conditions such as multiple instances of the software. This method is used to determine whether the software is "stable" (that is, that the rate of error discovery achieves a low and relatively constant level). At that point, the graph could be converted to a control chart to monitor the trend and stability of defect discovery over time. These methods could be applied to processes as well as software and used to establish control norms and measure process "health." For more information on applying defect and testing statistics to software, see Musa et al. (1987).

SOFTWARE MEASURERS BEWARE

Histograms and other statistical techniques are not valid if the data classifications overlap or are not applied consistently. This is a cardinal principle of statistical analysis. As valuable as statistical tools may be when used correctly, they can cause waste and damage if they are applied without careful planning and training. The software measurements discussed earlier are useful for comparison only, and they cannot be used to compare systems written in different languages. In the world of software measurement, there are no absolute references.

There is a cost associated with collecting and maintaining data, so one should not collect data without a good reason. There is a cost for erroneous conclusions, so one should be sure that one's data and analysis are both accurate and relevant. One should collect data only as long as there is a need for the results.

Simple histograms and graphical analysis techniques can point the way toward significant quality and cost improvements for software processes. The difficult work is to ask questions that yield statistical, or at least objective, answers.

DIFFERENCES FROM ISO 9001:1994

For software, the strong emphasis on process measurement and improvement is a departure from the last edition of the standard. ISO 9000-3:1991 offers very little help in this regard. Conformity to clause 8.2.3 is still being defined. No process is perfect, and one must measure and monitor processes as part of the continual improvement effort.

SUMMARY

In planning the measurement of software processes, one must consider the goal of the measurement and the factors that influence that goal.

Some important software process quality goals are the following:

- *Defining effective products.* Measure and trend trouble calls and complaints.
- *Error detection and prevention.* Measure trouble calls and complaints after release, debug, and rework during testing,
- *Maintenance of product integrity.* Compare change records to actual product baseline.
- *Efficiency of development and production.* Measure development hours, test hours, maintenance hours, and ratios of test to development and maintenance to development.
- *Continual improvement of software quality levels.* Measure trends in defects per unit of code.

Like software requirements, each of these goals must be defined in concrete (that is, observable or measurable) terms that suit the organization. Process improvement might happen without process measurement, but how would one know? Observation and measurement are, therefore, essential elements of any process improvement initiative.

One can measure the effectiveness and efficiency of software processes. This chapter has concentrated on effectiveness because an ineffective process does not accomplish its goals; therefore, it is inefficient by definition. Simple statistical techniques can be used to identify preliminary indications of problem areas, but statistics must be applied with careful forethought and planning. The strong emphasis of ISO 9001:2000 on monitoring and measurement might be regarded as a new requirement by software organizations, although the same principles were evident in the 1994 edition.

The goal of monitoring and measurement is to obtain useful information for correcting and improving both products and processes. Monitoring and measurement incur costs. If the monitoring and measurement of a given attribute does not yield useful data, then the monitoring should be changed so it does or else abandoned.

A process risk–benefit analysis is one way to establish priorities for measurement. For instance, an informal analysis of risk versus benefit may put processes for product design and development at a high priority because improvements there may represent the greatest potential to prevent errors. By reducing errors, one reduces the costs of a software product over its entire useful life (Grady 1992, 13–18).

REFERENCES

Albrecht, A. J. "Measuring Application Development Productivity." In *Proceedings of the Joint SHARE/GUIDE/IBM Application Development Symposium* (IBM, October 1979): 83–92.

Albrecht, A. J., and J. E. Gaffney Jr. "Software Function, Source Lines of Code, and Development Effort Prediction: A Software Science Validation." *IEEE Transactions on Software Engineering* SE-9, no. 6 (1983): 639–47.

Basili, V., and H. D. Rombach. "Tailoring the Software Process to Project Goals and Environments." In *IEEE Proceedings of the Ninth International Conference on Software Engineering.* Monterey, CA: IEEE (April 1987): 345–57.

Basili, V., and D. M. Weiss. "A Methodology for Collecting Valid Software Engineering Data." *IEEE Transactions on Software Engineering* SE-10, no. 6 (1984): 728–38.

Card, D., and Glass, J. *Measuring Software Design Quality.* Englewood Cliffs, NJ: Prentice-Hall, 1990.

Demarco, T. *Controlling Software Projects.* New York: Yourdon Press, 1982.

Grady, R. B. *Practical Software Metrics for Project Management and Process Improvement.* Englewood Cliffs, NJ: Prentice Hall, 1992.

Humphrey, W. S. *Managing the Software Process.* Addison-Wesley, 1989.

McDermid, J., ed. *Software Engineer's Reference Book.* Boca Raton, FL: CRC Press, 1993.

Musa, J. D., et al. *Software Reliability, Measurement, Prediction, Application.* New York: McGraw-Hill, 1987.

Symons, C. R. "Function Point Analysis: Difficulties and Improvements." *IEEE Transactions on Software Engineering* 14, no. 1 (1988): 2–11.

Chapter 33

Measurement for Services

Diane M. Baguley
Beca Carter Hollings & Ferner, Auckland, New Zealand

INTRODUCTION

Measuring the service product presents some particular challenges for two reasons. First, a service product is characterized by being intangible, though it may be associated with tangible product. Second, at least some part of service provision occurs at the interface with a customer. There is also an enormous variety of services, ranging from those that are standard products, such as an Internet retail operation, through to those designed and developed for individual users, such as consultancy services. No single approach to service measurement can address such a broad range of situations.

Most organizations find it extremely helpful to explore how service characteristics are evaluated in their particular sector. There are many different approaches. For example, sectors such as health, justice, and education that face particular challenges with regard to control of long-term outcomes are developing approaches to service measurement that differ considerably from those whose services focus on direct customer satisfaction.

In some instances, service measurement has become contentious because of conflicts between long- and short-term objectives, especially where short-term objectives are connected with performance measurement. Resolving such conflicts often requires organizations to revisit the underlying principles of service measurement.

This chapter deals with the principles of service monitoring and measurement, the expectations of compliance with ISO 9001:2000, and some opportunities offered by moving beyond compliance.

SERVICE MONITORING AND MEASUREMENT PRINCIPLES

ISO 9001:2000 and ISO 9004:2000 address monitoring as well as measurement for verification of the product. This inclusion of monitoring recognizes that some characteristics of products, in particular services, may be difficult or impossible to measure. Both monitoring and measurement of services therefore need to be considered.

The difficulties of measurement often lead to reliance on indirect methods of evaluating services, in particular evaluation of service processes (by monitoring, measurement, and audit) and customer satisfaction. See chapter 34 for a discussion of monitoring and measurement of service processes. While such methods can be appropriate, organizations need to ensure that they are not being used because of a lack of understanding of service characteristics or service measurement principles.

Service Characteristics

Services generally have some characteristics that can be measured (for example, agreed response or delivery time) and others that are more difficult to measure (for example, courtesy, friendliness, and helpfulness). The latter characteristics are frequently assumed—rather than defined—as service requirements, even though they may have a large influence on acceptability to the recipient of the service.

A further difficulty arises where defined service characteristics are not directly related to the intended result of the service. An example is the provision of corrections services such as prison confinement and probatory supervision. The goals of the services are complex, some short-term and some long-term. Longer-term outcomes such as rehabilitation and reduction of reoffending cannot be measured by direct assessment of service characteristics. Indeed, even short-term outcomes such as protection of the community and punishment of the offender can be only partly assessed. The organization responsible for such services can use output indicators, such as compliance (by the organization) with intended service levels and compliance (by the offender) with probation conditions. However, the linkage between these service characteristics and the intended outcome can be determined only by research. Further, the linkage may be statistically demonstrable but not valid for a particular situation or individual.

The linkage between the characteristics of a service and its intended outcome is a matter for design and development validation (and, in some cases, process validation). However, in practice, validation is an ongoing process for many organizations, particularly those providing health and social services. Validation of a method for effectiveness at the population level does not necessarily validate the service for an individual. There may even be a need for flexibility to allow frontline staff to allow deviation from the usual target characteristics in order to aim for the intended outcomes.

The organization therefore needs to keep service characteristics for monitoring and measurement under regular review:

- Have acceptance criteria been adequately defined? Do the criteria allow for individual customization where this is needed for an effective and efficient service?

- Are there other service characteristics that should be monitored or measured? These may include results of the service as well as its direct characteristics.

- Which acceptance criteria and other service characteristics need to be monitored or measured for an individual service? Which need to be evaluated for other purposes, such as design and development validation or process validation? How often and when should such evaluation take place?

Monitoring and measurement need to be practical and effective. Decisions about the treatment of service characteristics require understanding of the purposes of monitoring and measurement.

Purposes of Monitoring and Measurement

Service characteristics may be monitored or measured for one or more purposes.

Conformance with Requirements

The prime purpose of service monitoring and measurement is verification that service requirements are fulfilled. The effectiveness of such verification depends on service requirements being well defined. Service acceptance criteria need to be capable of being monitored or measured, while at the same time providing a balanced representation of customer and organizational needs.

Service monitoring or measurement can be closely connected with assessment of conformance with process requirements, especially where the customer is involved in a service process. A particular characteristic may be monitored both for control of the process and for assessing conformance with service standards.

Effectiveness of the Service Result

The effectiveness of a service can be influenced by variables outside the control of the supplier organization. These variables can include individual characteristics of the recipient of the service and effects of the environment in which the service is delivered.

In some instances of individual variation, the effectiveness of the service can be determined by the service recipient—for example, in the retail industry a customer can be offered a pair of shoes on the basis of their size, but the suitability of the shoes depends on individual customer variation and preferences.

In other cases, the supplying organization needs to assess the effectiveness of the result of the service. One example is in the supply of medical services, where individual variation can have a large impact on effectiveness. A particular treatment protocol may have an 80 percent probability of a successful outcome. Conformance with requirements is achieved by the planned treatment being provided in compliance with the protocol. However, the effectiveness of the result also needs to be assessed at the individual level.

Environmental influences may have an impact on service effectiveness. Services such as financial planning, marketing, and agricultural advisory support are provided on the basis of current information. The service provider may need to monitor the ongoing effectiveness of the services and make adjustments accordingly.

Improvement Objectives

Service characteristics may be monitored or measured to provide information for service improvement. Such initiatives may use information already collected for service verification purposes, or the organization may select additional characteristics for particular study.

Selection of Key Characteristics

An organization needs to decide which service characteristics should be measured. There may be many characteristics from which to choose. It may not be practical to verify all of them, especially the intangible qualities that should be expressed at the customer interface. In some cases, requirements for evidence of conformance are defined by customers (for example, a facilities maintenance contract may define acceptance criteria) or by industry codes of practice. Where such requirements are not defined, the selection of characteristics and the specification of monitoring and measurement activities are the responsibility of the provider organization.

Key characteristics for monitoring and measurement can be guided by both:

- Risks to the customer and organization—this may be to detect failures in the control of process characteristics or to control risks that are only expressed in the service product.

- Key attributes for customer satisfaction. The service provider can investigate which aspects of a service customers value the most. Special attention to these characteristics in monitoring and measurement can reinforce internal understanding of their importance, as well as assist in control of service quality.

Monitoring and Measurement Methods

Methods for evaluation of services range from simple monitoring of service delivery to the use of multiple indicators of service performance.

Monitoring by Inspection and Review

Some services can be monitored by inspection of service provision activities and checking of associated service documentation. This can take place at several stages of service delivery, taking account of authorities for service release—for example, the preparation of different components of a financial report.

Often staff responsible for direct service delivery (for example, in routine banking operations) are equipped with standards and/or are qualified by training to self-review the service. It is clearly important that unnecessary inspection processes are avoided to reduce complexity and delays in service delivery.

Examples of Monitoring

- Supervisory observation of direct service transactions, such as in retail operations

- Checking (self-checking or independent) of service documentation such as reports, certificates, or tickets

- Inspection of tangible results of completed service activities such as inspection of hotel room cleaning and preparation

- Inspection of status of tangible objects in relation to service provision, such as inspection of roads or buildings against agreed-upon maintenance standards

Qualitative and Semiquantitative Measurement

Intangible aspects of services can often be measured by qualitative methods (for example, rating a service characteristic as unsatisfactory, satisfactory, or excellent) or semiquantitative methods (for example, allocating numerical or dollar values to ratings).

Examples of Rating Methods in a Restaurant

1. *Rating customer service.* A restaurant may use an experienced person to rate several aspects of interaction between service staff and restaurant patrons on a scale of 1 to 5. The characteristics rated would depend on the key attributes expected by customers. They would depend on the nature of the restaurant—for example, accuracy of orders, friendliness, and cheerfulness may be rated in a family restaurant, whereas in a more formal environment, the focus may be on service skill and knowledge of wine and food.

2. *Rating defects in meal presentation.* A rating system for a restaurant meal may take account of minor defects in presentation (say, a rating of 1 or 2 for defects that a customer may not regard as important), serious issues of conformance (for example, a rating of 10 for missing or poorly prepared components), and critical issues of safety (for example, a rating of 50 for unsafe methods of preparation). The sum of defects across a certain sample size can provide useful information for guiding improvement.

The degree of subjectivity of rating measurement can be reduced by using clear descriptors applicable to the particular service at each level of the scale. Rating methods often work well for assessing trends of service quality and testing the effects of service improvements. However, the reliability of the measurement method may be inadequate for objectives such as assessing individual performance or comparing service quality between different locations.

Quantitative Measurement

Dimensional measurement is not applicable to service except where used in relation to tangible items associated with the service. Numerical measurement methods are widely used as indicators of service quality—for example, measurement of response time, completion time, and percentage clearance rate against service standards. These characteristics may be monitored for both process control and service measurement purposes. Graphical presentation of such data, such as in histograms or pie charts, can be extremely useful in conveying service performance information and trends.

In many cases, measurement of an indicator of a service characteristic is used, rather than direct measurement of the characteristic itself, because of the intangible nature of the characteristic.

Examples of Measurement

1. *Use of numerical data.* A social service organization may measure several characteristics in relation to customer requests and complaints, such as number of queries in particular categories, time to first response, and time to close out the issue. This information may be used both for control of the process (for example, staffing levels, information required by staff) and to track conformance with service standards.

2. *Use of indicators.* A university may measure indicators of research output such as papers, books and articles published, conference papers presented, and so on. These provide information on the output, but they are not comprehensive measures of research quality. One of the major concerns in such cases is ensuring balance between those characteristics that can be measured and those that cannot.

Multiple Indicators

Dealing with intangible aspects of services often involves analyzing several pieces of information to derive information on service performance. This can involve service characteristics plus other information, such as customer complaints and customer satisfaction measures.

Example of Multiple Indicators

An electricity retailer could find that although its measures for response rate, fault clearance time, and billing errors were showing evidence of service improvement, the number of customer complaints was rising. It might then use a customer survey and conclude that the probable reason for the rise in complaints was that customers had perceived that the retailer had become easier to contact and more responsive to customer complaints. This would confirm the assumptions made from the measurement of service characteristics.

COMPLIANCE WITH ISO 9001

An important focus of ISO 9001:2000 is on monitoring and measurement of product characteristics to verify that service requirements are fulfilled (clause 8.2.4). The full range of service requirements needs to be considered—those specified by the customer plus other characteristics necessary for intended use, required for statutory or regulatory reasons, or specified by the organization itself (clause 7.2.1). Data obtained from service measurement may be used for analysis as a basis for improvement (clauses 8.4 and 8.5).

Planning of Service Monitoring and Measurement

ISO 9001:2000 requires that an organization plan monitoring and measurement activities necessary to demonstrate conformity of the product (clause 8.1). This includes planning the use of statistical techniques, including sampling methods, where these are used.

Activities to demonstrate conformity of the service should be carried out at the appropriate stages of service processes. A travel service, for example, has a number of components, such as establishing the itinerary, making reservations, issuing travel documents, and collating these with support documentation for delivery to the customer. Completion of these components of the service needs to be monitored at appropriate points so that timely action can be taken if selected options are not available.

The organization needs to consider how to:

- Confirm that the service meets specified requirements prior to delivery (as far as this is practical)
- Confirm that the delivered service meets the requirements
- Where appropriate, confirm that the intended result is achieved (validation of a customized service)
- Obtain feedback on other service characteristics for purposes such as process control or improvement

Evidence of planning of service verification can be simply presented in working documents, such as forms or computer spreadsheets used in the course of service provision. Alternatively, acceptance criteria, monitoring responsibilities, and measurement methods can be described in work procedures or included in a quality plan for the service (or set of services). The level of documentation needs to reflect the complexity of service processes, the potential impact of failure, and the needs of staff using it. In some cases, customers, regulators, or their representatives can require organizations to supply service verification plans.

The appropriateness of the acceptance criteria, the characteristics selected to test conformity, and the plan for monitoring and measurement should be subject to review at suitable intervals. For ongoing services, this can be incorporated in the management review process.

Relationships between Service Processes

The selection of service characteristics and the identification of points for monitoring and measurement need to take account of how service processes for design and development, purchasing, and service provision relate to each other.

Some services are dependent on purchased (outsourced) products or services. The organization needs to ensure that the verification of outsourced components fits the needs of subsequent service verification.

Other services (for example, provision of policy advice by a government department) are controlled through design and development processes through to near completion of the service. Final inspection of the completed service deliverable could entail checking that the report is presented in the manner intended, including such requirements as number of copies, binding, and method for delivery.

Customers often have authority to accept or reject a service, sometimes at several points of development of an individualized service. However, customer acceptance of a service does not relieve an organization of the responsibility to confirm conformance with requirements. Customer acceptance or rejection is a decision point rather than a verification step. Nevertheless, in simple, low-risk services, direct customer response may be a very useful indicator of service performance.

Monitoring and Measurement Activities

Simple monitoring (observation, inspection, and review) of service characteristics against the relevant acceptance criteria can be sufficient for compliance with the product verification requirements of ISO 9001:2000. Frequently, particularly for service processes involving direct interface with customers, such monitoring comprises some combination of supervisory checks and self-verification by service staff. Working documents can be designed to facilitate verification—for example, to assist staff in checking that all items and information related to a service have been provided to a customer.

Methods may be needed to support a simple monitoring approach. A high dependence on staff understanding may necessitate some form of process validation, such as a requirement for completion of staff training in customer service. The adequacy of monitoring may be validated from time to time by sampling the service and evaluating by direct observation or by means such as the use of "phantom" customers.

Where customer feedback can be obtained relatively easily and directly as part of the service relationship, such as in hotel services, the information on customer satisfaction can be used to back up some aspects of service monitoring. Providing an easy avenue for customer feedback can in fact add value to the service. However, inviting feedback does not mean that monitoring can be transferred to the customer (it is not the hotel customer's job to find the blown light bulbs and the flat battery in the television remote control). Customer feedback also has a limited scope, since there are many service requirements (such as food hygiene) that cannot be determined by the user.

Some forms of monitoring can be conducted by software or system control mechanisms, rather than personal observation. Many databases, for instance, are designed to incorporate field controls that detect and disallow incorrect characters, over-length numbers, and so on. It can be important to remember that software monitoring methods are usually best designed as safety nets, rather than drivers of human activity. As in aviation, control instruments are good at detecting unexpected change. Pilots, on the other hand, are generally better at flying an aircraft than watching for unusual circumstances in the midst of tedious sameness.

Customers or regulatory bodies may specify measurement reporting requirements. Service measurement requirements, guidelines, and methods may be specified in national or international standards, industry codes of practice, and the like. Beyond this, the need for measurement of service characteristics (as well as monitoring) should be determined by the organization. However, an organization may be judged to be not in compliance with ISO 9001:2000 if there is evidence of service defects that could be detected, and hence controlled, through the use of measurement.

The growing use of information and communications technology means that some information can be collected with much less intrusion on service processes than was practical in the past. The practicality of measurement means that expectations have been raised that service will be measured as well as monitored.

Management review should consider the adequacy of the characteristics selected for measurement to determine if they meet measurement objectives. The measurement methods should also be subject to review for their suitability for the intended purpose.

Records of Service Monitoring and Measurement

Records of service monitoring and measurement need to be kept in accordance with ISO 9001:2000 clause 4.2.4. Customers or regulators may specify particular requirements for verification records, in some cases requiring them to be submitted for review. Where such records are submitted for review, the responsibility for confirming conformity remains with the service provider.

It is important to define the retention times for records of service conformity, taking account of the risks to both the customer (including user) and the service supplier. Some types of records, or liabilities that may require evidence of service conformity, are subject to statutory retention requirements.

WHAT IS DIFFERENT FROM THE 1994 EDITION?

The requirements for verification of the product through the stages of product realization are substantially reworded in ISO 9001:2000 compared with the 1994 version. For most requirements, the intent is not essentially changed, but some are more explicit. There are some added requirements for use of service monitoring and measurement for analysis and continual improvement.

ISO 9001:2000 introduces monitoring as an alternative to measurement of product characteristics, as it does for processes. This is a significant clarification of the intent of the 1994 version, which was often difficult to interpret in regard to "inspection and testing" of services, particularly for transactions that occur at the customer–supplier interface.

The 1994 version required inspection and testing to be carried out as required by the quality plan and/or documented procedures. ISO 9001:2000 requires planning of product monitoring and measurement (clauses 7.1 and 8.1), and then requires monitoring and measurement to be carried out in accordance with "planned arrangements" (clause 8.2.4). This reflects a more flexible approach in the 2000 version to the documentation of the output of planning. The need for documentation must be defined by the organization itself.

The wording of ISO 9001:2000 clause 8.2.4 is simpler and more generic than the equivalent requirements of the 1994 version. This more generic wording is helpful for application to service products. Clause 8.2.4 includes monitoring and measurement of both the final service and measurement of the service at appropriate stages of product realization. This is equivalent to ISO 9001:1994 clause 4.10.4 (final inspection and testing) and 4.10.3 (in-process inspection and testing). The requirements for inspection and test records in clause 4.10.5 of the 1994 version are also covered in this clause. However, the requirement in ISO 9001:1994 clause 4.10.3 for control of product release is transferred to clause 7.5.1 of ISO 9001:2000, as part of the product realization process.

ISO 9001:2000 is more explicit than the 1994 version in regard to analysis of information on product characteristics. It requires the planning and implementation of analysis processes, including the use of information derived from monitoring and measurement of product characteristics (clause 8.1). The requirement of the 1994 version for the organization to identify the need for statistical techniques is reworded and simplified in this clause. The analysis of data is one of the inputs to continual improvement (ISO 9001:2000 clause 8.5.1). This is an additional requirement.

BEYOND ISO 9001 COMPLIANCE

ISO 9004:2000 clause 8.1 gives general guidance on measurement, analysis, and improvement, some of which applies to service product monitoring and measurement. Clause 8.2.3 emphasizes two uses of measurement: first, to verify that the needs of all interested parties are met and, second, to improve realization processes.

Needs of Interested Parties

It can be useful to "unbundle" services in order to identify the service characteristics and effects of services that are important to the various interested parties. These can then be reviewed against the measures that are used to evaluate service effectiveness and efficiency. Further, involving representatives of the interested parties in the identification of needs may disclose priorities quite different from those used by the service provider in selecting service measures.

The needs of *purchasers, recipients,* and *users of a service* may need to be distinguished. A courier service, for example, supplies its services to both purchasing organizations and individuals. The users of the service include staff of purchasing organizations, purchasing individuals, and representatives of purchasers (delivery agencies, family members, and so on). The recipients of the services are the addressees of the courier articles. Each of these sets of people will evaluate the service according to its needs, both in relation to the core service (integrity, timeliness, and accuracy of delivery of items) and associated characteristics of the service (ease of purchasing, ease of access, friendliness and helpfulness of staff). In the case of such a service, an individual or group can also have several roles—as purchaser, user, and/or recipient—in different aspects of their lives.

Some services have considerable impact on members of the *public and community*. This may be through aspects of the use of the service, such as parking, access to points of service, and effects of traffic on the local community, as well as direct characteristics of the service.

The needs of *staff providing services* will influence practicalities of service measurement as well as aspects of the service itself. Staff are often very conscious of the impact of measurement on the relationship with a customer. They want to see that measurement adds value to the service transaction and that the recording of information does not deflect them from the service provided.

In some services, service *measurement information* needs to be supplied to *customers and/or regulatory bodies.* The design of measurement recording methods and formats can be adapted to meet these needs, so that data can be transmitted directly between the parties. Similarly, measurement information may be designed to be shared within *industry sector groups* for the purposes of benchmarking and improvement.

The *management, owners, and shareholders* of the organization may also have priorities for service evaluation. The efficiency as well as effectiveness of the service will be important. They may also place considerable weight on the relationship with other parties such as regulatory bodies and the community, taking account of future planning of organizational growth and diversification.

These different needs will have implications for the selection of service characteristics and the type of analysis that may be needed to make use of the information. This in turn will influence the location of points of measurement, the method of measurement, and the method of recording of measurement results.

Improvement Objectives

The priorities of interested parties assist in establishing priorities for improvement of both service measurement and the ways in which measurements are used. The use of service measurement in improvement can also be directed by opportunities, such as the availability of appropriate benchmarking information or initiatives.

The design of new or improved service processes presents an ideal opportunity for introducing innovative use of service measurement. With rapid advancement in the field of information and communications technology, service performance information can often be collected cheaply, and analysis of it can be rapidly fed back to the service team. It can be advantageous to enable flexibility in how the information is to be collected, processed, and presented, so that the team responsible for the service can experiment with types and uses of data.

Statistical methods can be used to identify and reduce unwanted variation in service characteristics. The use of statistical process control methods is somewhat limited in service provision by the need to supply individualized services. However, statistical methods often are used in the analysis of service data.

Measurement of service characteristics provides a means of demonstrating improvement of service performance. Hence, it can be one of the most satisfying activities, completing the circle with the identification of service requirements. Nevertheless, in service there are often characteristics that can only be evaluated indirectly. Organizations must be wary that they are not focusing on the measurable characteristics at the expense of those that are not measurable. Imagination can be the key to the effective use of service measurement.

Chapter 34

Measurement for Service Processes

Diane M. Baguley
Beca Carter Hollings & Ferner, Auckland, New Zealand

INTRODUCTION

Monitoring and measurement of service processes serves a three-pronged purpose: first, to meet customer requirements; second, to ensure that each process is (and remains) capable of satisfying its intended purpose; and third, to provide a basis for process improvement. These purposes need to be carefully considered when asking: "What should we measure?" and "What are suitable methods?"

Some people in service industries are wary of the emphasis of ISO 9001 and ISO 9004 on monitoring and measurement. A number fall into the trap of asking, "What *can* we measure?" rather than determining what information is important and how it can best be used. That attitude can result in measurement procedures involving considerable effort, without such effort being rewarded in terms of performance. The requirements for compliance with ISO 9001:2000 are, however, largely matters of good management practice. Beyond compliance, there are many opportunities for gains in both efficiency and effectiveness.

Service processes are not, of course, limited to the service sector. They may be associated with the supply of nonservice products. In that case, the need for monitoring or measuring service processes can easily be overlooked because they are regarded simply as "support processes." However, if they affect the organization's ability to meet customer requirements, they should be included in process monitoring and measurement.

COMPLIANCE WITH ISO 9001

Compliance with ISO 9001:2000 clause 8.2.3 requires the organization to "apply suitable methods for monitoring and, where applicable, measurement" of quality management system processes. This requirement includes those processes involved in service realization and thus applies to all service processes from identification of customer requirements to delivery of the service.

The use of the phrase "monitoring and, where applicable, measurement" in clause 8.2.3 recognizes that there are some situations where measurement is not practical and monitoring is the only option. Nevertheless, some form of measurement is widely applicable in evaluating service process characteristics. The use of measuring equipment, while uncommon in many areas of the service sector, is vital in some (for example, healthcare).

ISO 9000:2000 defines a product as the output of a process. The product that is the output of a service process is the service itself. Compliance with clause 8.2.4 of ISO 9001:2000 requires the service organization to measure these process outputs.

Purposes of Monitoring and Measurement

There are several purposes for monitoring and measurement of service processes under the requirements of ISO 9001:2000:

- To demonstrate the ability of the processes to achieve planned results (that is, to provide evidence that the processes planned under clause 7.1 are able to meet service requirements)

- To validate service provision processes where the resulting output cannot be verified by later monitoring or measurement (clause 7.5.2)

- To provide a basis for control of processes, signaling where action needs to be taken to ensure conformity of the service

- Where appropriate, to provide information on characteristics and trends that can be used for preventive action and process improvement (clauses 8.4 and 8.5)

Determining the Approach

For each process, the organization should determine the type of monitoring and measurement activity, its scope and frequency, the extent of data recording, and the documentation of methods required. This need not be daunting. Often the solutions are simple and, by the reduction in process problems and service errors, more than repay the effort involved.

The starting point is the planning of service processes (ISO 9001:2000 clause 7.1). Once the processes are defined, key stages for control can be established, and the need for monitoring and measurement can be determined. For an existing process, the organization can then review current practice against those needs.

Most organizations addressing compliance with ISO 9001 for the first time will find that they already use monitoring, and in some cases measurement, as a means of controlling their processes. However, these methods often have a number of deficiencies, such as variability when carried out by different people, failures when key personnel are absent, and inadequate records of monitoring activities. The chief underlying reason for such deficiencies is often that process standards and methods are inadequately defined.

Product and Process Characteristics

Both product and process characteristics may be used in monitoring and measuring service processes. Particularly in processes involving interface with the customer, there can be an overlap between monitoring or measuring the process and the service product. In other processes, there may be a clear distinction between process and product measures.

Example: Process and Product Characteristics in Process Monitoring

A customer seeks counter services at a bank to purchase foreign currency. The main service product comprises the supply of the requested currency at the correct exchange rate, accurate debiting against the nominated customer account, and supply of suitable transaction records. This product is quite distinct from the processes that enable the transaction to be carried out, such as the computer-based systems for transfer of monies between accounts and between banks, the mechanisms for determining exchange rates and loading them into the system, reconciliation processes, and financial audit. Those "behind-the-scenes" processes are subject to monitoring and control that is quite distinct from the product itself.

However, another aspect of customer needs, and hence also a part of the service product, is a reasonable waiting time in dealing with the request. The bank may determine that waiting time for a customer comprises a mixture of actual elapsed time and expectation of delay based on queue length. It therefore decides to set standards for maximum queue length and to monitor against those standards to provide signals for staffing levels on counters. In this case, queue length is used for monitoring and controlling the process, but it is also a measure of a characteristic of the service.

Is Supervision Adequate for Monitoring?

There are instances where good supervision practices provide adequate monitoring of service processes for the purposes of ISO 9001:2000, particularly where the processes are simple. Supervision also may be the prime form of monitoring where service processes are customized to meet unique customer needs and do not have routine characteristics. Day-to-day review and supervision are then important in monitoring that the processes are meeting the specific requirements.

Supervision can occur by direct observation, checking of work records, and review with staff whether processes are being carried out as planned. Supervisors also commonly have particular responsibilities within processes, such as approval of certain process steps and review of correction of nonconformities. These activities provide a "window" into the process through which deficiencies can be observed.

Records of supervisory activities can be kept as part of the process. Evidence of review of reports, monitoring of processes, and approval of resulting actions often can be recorded by simple methods such as the initialing and dating of key process documents. Both work instructions and training should convey the purpose and scope of such monitoring and hence the responsibility associated with sign-off steps.

In services involving coordination of a number of processes or activities, *job management* can be a more appropriate term than supervision. Job management techniques often are used for monitoring service realization where design and development is a major process. The job manager is given responsibility for coordinating the planning and implementation of the service processes. This may cover processes for identifying (or reviewing) customer requirements, design and development of the service, planning of service provision, and implementation of service delivery processes. The job manager has responsibility for monitoring the processes against time and activity schedules, planned monitoring and verification activities, and completion milestones.

Monitoring Process Characteristics

Where service processes are repetitive, or only slightly customized, the organization should consider what process characteristics need to be monitored and controlled. For many services that are initiated by customer request, the response and completion times can be key characteristics of service provision. For simple services, monitoring such time intervals and taking action on delays may be a basic component of process control. The information may be collected in a form that can be produced readily as reports for monitoring purposes but also collated for analysis if required for improvement initiatives.

Example: Wholesaler Service Processes

A small wholesaling company determined that its key service processes were customer account management, purchasing (including subcontracted delivery services), stock management (including supply planning), sales and orders, supply of goods, and managing returns, defects, and complaints. The products it supplied did not have defined shelf lives and were relatively easy to specify, handle, package, and deliver.

Order and delivery information was used to generate reports on time interval to supply, back orders, and stock levels. As well as review of those reports, day-to-day supervisory functions formed an important part of process monitoring. Particular attention was applied to interfaces between processes—for example, the flow of customer information on anticipated product usage to those responsible for setting stock reorder points.

Measurement of Service Processes

Process measures can be used to demonstrate the ability to meet process objectives, validate service provision processes, enable process control, and provide a basis for improvement. The nature and extent of measurements of service processes need to be determined by each organization on the basis of its objectives for process performance and improvement. Compliance with ISO 9001:2000 does not require the use of particular measures. It does require that measurement is consistent with service objectives.

Example: Call Center Operation

A call center operation in a municipal organization provided a 24-hour, seven-days-a-week service involving approximately 50 staff. The center established its objectives for call service performance and identified a number of measurements to assess the ability of the service delivery process to meet those objectives. Measurements and other records were collected and analyzed using a computer database linked to call center operations.

Data collected included the number of calls, time of calling, delay to reply, number of calls lost before reply, inquiry topic, duration of call, and percentage of calls resolved at first point of contact.

Statistical analysis of the information provided a basis for responsive planning. Process control signals were established for call-up of additional staff. Trend information was used for planning staff levels, establishing new topics to include in guidance information, and identifying areas for additional staff training.

Hazards of Monitoring and Measurement

There is a common dictum: "You get what you measure." Where indicators and measures are established as standards for service provision, it is frequently too easy for them to become the dominant target, to the detriment of other aspects of process performance.

Using the example of the call center operation, a target of, say, "80 percent of calls resolved at first point of contact" may be achieved at the expense of delay to reply and number of calls lost before reply. Therefore, it often is important to consider a range of indicators and measures so that the organization can control the overall performance of the process.

A further hazard is linking the achievement of target process indicators and measures to individual accountability. The interrelated nature of process operations means that achievement of individual targets can be at the expense of failure in other parts of the process or in other processes. If the incentives to perform are strong enough, achieving the desired results becomes the goal, rather than integrity of data.

Documentation of Monitoring and Measurement Methods

There is no explicit requirement in ISO 9001 clause 8.2.3 or 8.2.4 to document the monitoring and measurement methods. The requirement for documentation is covered under ISO 9001:2000 clauses 4.2.1(d), "documents needed by the organization to ensure effective planning, operation and control of its processes" and 7.1, "Planning of product realization." This puts the onus on the organization to determine the need for documentation and to prepare it where necessary. The requirement is flexible and allows innovative ways of controlling processes. For example, software systems may be used to control the sequence of activities, route documentation, and provide hold points for authorization.

WHAT IS DIFFERENT FROM THE 1994 EDITION?

ISO 9001:2000 formulates the requirement for monitoring and measurement of processes in a separate clause applicable to all quality management processes, including product realization processes (clause 7). This is much broader than the requirement for control of processes in the 1994 version.

Considering service realization, ISO 9001:2000 requires monitoring and measurement of all service processes including planning of product realization, customer-related processes, design and development, purchasing, and service provision. The 1994 version required process monitoring of service provision processes only.

In relation to service provision processes alone, the requirements of clause 8.2.3 do not represent a change from the intent of ISO 9001:1994 and ISO 9002:1994. Those standards required the organization to carry out such processes under controlled conditions including "monitoring and control of suitable process parameters" (clause 4.9). They also specified in-process inspection and testing "as required by the quality plan and/or documented procedures." The term *inspection* is often inappropriate for service delivery processes, so the generic wording of ISO 9001:2000 clause 8.2.3 should be welcomed by service sector users. The use of the phrase "monitoring and, where applicable, measurement" in ISO 9001:2000 recognizes that some processes are monitored but not measured.

The requirement for monitoring and measurement of service provision processes was not included in ISO 9003:1994. This is a significant difference from ISO 9001:2000 since under the provisions of clause 1.2, "Application," the requirements of clause 8.2.3 cannot be excluded. The effect of clause 8.2.3 can be reduced as a consequence of exclusions of sections of clause 7, but that cannot be done simply because the organization elects to do so. While this difference is unlikely to affect organizations in the service sector (which generally applied ISO 9001:1994 or ISO 9002:1994), it might affect some organizations providing services associated with nonservice products.

The requirement for documentation of process monitoring and measurement activities is made more flexible in ISO 9001:2000, through a subtle wording change in regard to planning. The 1994 version requires the output of planning to be "documented in a format to suit the supplier's method of operation," whereas the 2000 version requires the output of planning for product realization to be "in a form suitable to the organization's method of operations."

BEYOND ISO 9001 COMPLIANCE

Monitoring and measurement of processes is vitally important to organizations seeking to improve quality, productivity, and customer satisfaction, as well as for control of processes at their current level of performance. ISO 9004:2000 outlines how the organization should identify monitoring and measurement methods and use them to evaluate process performance. These methods may be suitable for use in process management in routine operation. In some cases they may be used solely for study of processes and guiding their improvement.

The Needs of Interested Parties

Efficient use of process monitoring and measurement depends on accurate targeting of process characteristics, taking account of the needs and expectations of all interested parties. It requires extensive understanding of the processes in question—for example, understanding what is critical in maintaining the capability of processes to meet intended needs, what may go wrong, and what information is already available about process performance.

The first question may be whether the processes under examination are well proven as capable of meeting all stakeholder needs, including the needs of the organization itself and interested parties other than those considered under ISO 9001:2000.

There are many examples where process measuring and monitoring may be extended to address such broader purposes. Measurement of service processes could be adequate for meeting user needs but not meet the organization's objectives for reducing waste of energy and consumables. There could be technological incompatibility issues preventing a desirable exchange of monitoring and measurement information with external organizations. Such broader purposes of process monitoring and measurement need to be evaluated and prioritized by the organization, in consultation with other parties where appropriate.

Benchmarking

Benchmarking is well established as a means of setting objectives, collecting information, and comparing performance of processes. In some instances there is ready access to benchmarking information because many organizations have an interest in a particular process. Call center operation is one example. In other cases it is difficult or impossible to obtain information from identical processes, but valid comparisons can be made with some aspects of similarly structured processes. The learning opportunity of sharing information within and between organizations should not be underestimated.

Chapter 35

Control of Nonconforming Product

Lorri Hunt
Honeywell, Federal Manufacturing and Technologies,
Kansas City, Missouri[1]

Although a company never plans to produce nonconforming product, let alone release it for use to the customer, companies must realize that it is a reality of doing business. The clause in ISO 9001:2000 regarding control of nonconforming product (clause 8.3) provides requirements for control of nonconforming product that is either created in your factory or provided by a supplier. It also applies to service companies, software, and processed materials.

In the past, the clause regarding control of nonconforming product used terminology that was easier to interpret for manufacturing companies than other industries. For that reason when the nonconforming product clause was revised, a concerted effort was made to make it more flexible for different types of business while not losing its applicability to manufacturing.

As a result, the standard might appear to some users at first glance to contain completely new requirements. In reality, the requirements are basically the same but use terminology that provides clarification or makes it easier to apply the requirements to all types of businesses.

To assist the user in the interpretation of this clause, this chapter provides a breakdown of each of the requirements in ISO 9001:2000 clause 8.3 and information about what in the standard has specifically changed or is new. The chapter also provides examples of how to apply the revised standard to different product types as well as guidance and methods that can be used to go beyond the requirements of ISO 9001 by using ISO 9004 to pursue organizational excellence.

CHANGES IN THE STANDARD

The requirements identified here are excerpted from ISO 9001:2000. New requirements and changes to ISO 9001:2000 are identified by comparing requirements with those from the ISO 9001:1994 version of the standard.

Requirement: *The organization shall ensure that product which does not conform to requirements is identified and controlled to prevent its unintended use or delivery.*

This requirement is not new, but it has been changed to no longer prescribe what the control should entail (that is, identification, documentation, evaluation, segregation). The 2000 version gives the organization the latitude to determine what methods should be implemented to control nonconforming product.

Requirement: *The controls and related responsibilities and authorities for dealing with nonconforming product shall be defined in a documented procedure.*

The requirement to define the controls and related responsibilities and authorities has also been incorporated into this clause, but again, it is not new to the standard. A procedure is still required for defining the controls and related responsibilities and authorities.

Requirement: *The organization shall deal with nonconforming product by one or more of the following:*

(a) taking action to eliminate the detected nonconformity

With the elimination of such terms as *reworked, rejected,* or *scrapped,* the terminology no longer has a manufacturing focus. The revised standard does not list methods for how to eliminate the detected nonconformity, which allows the organization to define the activities, simplifying implementation for nonmanufacturing companies.

(b) by authorizing its use, release or acceptance under concession by a relevant authority and, where applicable, by the customer

The revision takes a slightly different approach than did the 1994 edition, which emphasized that the customer or the customer's representative would grant the concession. Users will most likely see this change as an improvement because it provides the opportunity to identify who the relevant authority is for the company and potentially simplifies the concession process.

(c) taking action to preclude its original intended use or application

This requirement in its foundation is not new; it is a variation of the 1994 version, which allowed for "regrading for alternate applications." Even though the intent of the clause has always been to prevent unintended use or delivery, clarification has been added to the requirement to emphasize that the actions taken help ensure that the product is not used for its original purpose.

Requirement: *Records of the nature of the nonconformities and any subsequent actions taken, including concessions obtained, shall be maintained (see 4.2.4).*

The terminology of this requirement is new, but the revised standard does not require the maintenance of any new records for control of nonconforming product.

Requirement: *When nonconforming product is corrected it shall be subject to reverification to demonstrate conformity to the requirements.*

The change in this requirement is subtle—it uses what can be perceived as less prescriptive requirements. The 1994 edition required that the repaired or reworked product be reinspected in accordance with the quality plan and/or documented procedures. The change in terminology makes it easier to apply the requirement to nonmanufacturing companies. It also gives organizations the freedom to identify what will require reverification.

> Requirement: *When nonconforming product is detected after delivery or use has started, the organization shall take action appropriate to the effects, or potential effects, of the nonconformity.*

This requirement is new to the standard. The 1994 version did not require that an organization take action if the product had already been delivered and the customer had started use. However, many companies already have processes in place that require notification of the customer; thus they can build on existing processes to implement this requirement. The change in the standard is an improvement because the inability to provide objective evidence to an outside source that nonconforming product has not been used or released was perceived as a lack of control by the organization.

Because this requirement is new, it is important for an organization to identify and set thresholds at which the severity and the effects or potential effects of the nonconformity would warrant action. It is easy to determine appropriate actions for handling nonconformities after delivery when the potential effects relate to the public's safety, such as with toys that may cause harm to children playing with them, tainted food, or drug products that have been tampered with.

Determining appropriate action is not as easy when public safety may not be affected and the potential effects of the nonconforming product are perceived as not as severe. In a case where the product does not meet specifications but can still function, the actions required would not need to be as drastic. For instance, if a part is shipped to a customer but was not painted the right color, it is still functional. The organization needs to have a plan in place for what other action would be taken in this situation (for example, discount).

In the service world, the nonconformity is almost always identified after delivery. That is why it is more effective when a company has a plan of action that should be taken when a nonconformity is identified. For example, when a hotel guest has made reservations for a party of one and requested a room with a king size bed that is not available upon check-in, it can be determined that no actions need to be taken since another room with two double beds is available. On the other hand, if the reservation is made for two double beds for a family of four and only a room with a king size bed is available upon check-in, the hotel would need to take actions appropriate for the effects of the nonconformity. This might include an upgrade to a room at a higher rate or finding the hotel guests a room at a comparable rate at an alternative hotel.

APPLICATION OF ISO 9001:2000: CONTROL OF NONCONFORMING PRODUCT

Implementing a process that controls nonconforming product is never black and white. An organization needs to evaluate from where in the company potential nonconformities will come and determine what actions are going to be required in these instances.

Because it is generally easier for an organization to implement a system by reviewing companies with similar product lines, the following examples are provided.

Manufacturing

The process of applying the revised standard to the manufacturing environment will not change for many organizations. Because the clause has been revised to make its application to all product types easier, some of the prescriptive terms have been eliminated. That may in some cases make interpreting the standard more difficult for the organization that has implemented the 1994 version. With that in mind, the organization should consider terminology used in the 1994 version such as *segregation, rework, repair,* and *scrap* as good business practices and as approaches for implementing the revision.

When a manufacturer realizes a product is nonconforming, it must first identify the product according to documented procedures. Many companies use a system whereby the operator who identifies the nonconformity tags the product and places it in an area or on a shelf that will help preclude its use. When documenting the procedure for identification and control of the nonconforming product, the manufacturing company should remember that segregating the product might at times be impossible. In that situation, an organization needs to consider documenting a method in its procedures to use caution tape around the product, yellow lines taped on the floor, or a similar approach to identify the product as nonconforming.

Procedures should also document who in the organization has the authority to review and resolve what actions should be taken to disposition the product. Often in the manufacturing world the product or quality engineer or a product team determines what actions should be taken.

The relevant authority will determine the best course of action based on the type of nonconformity. An evaluation will be made as to whether the nonconformity warrants repair or rework based on potential costs, the nonconformity can be accepted by a relevant authority under concession, or it is more reasonable to no longer use the product for its original use and start over.

When a manufacturing organization determines that the more cost-effective solution is to scrap the product or slate it for an alternate use, it is important to maintain identification of the product to prevent its use or delivery to the customer. In the case where the relevant authority determines the product can be corrected, the product is subject to reverification to demonstrate that it is now conforming. This could be based on procedures, plans, or customer requirements. If the organization decides to use the product under concession without correcting the nonconformity, it becomes the responsibility of the organization to get the appropriate approvals.

When an organization discovers that the product has been delivered to the customer or is already in use, it needs to consider what actions should be taken based on the potential effects. The organization may choose to establish criteria under which notification is necessary or additional action is required. Those criteria should be based on what is appropriate for the product being produced and might include the following:

- Product is not operational
- Product is operational but does not meet customer specifications
- Safety concerns apply to the product's use

Any forms that document actions taken in investigating the nonconformity, any concessions granted, or final disposition on the status of the product should be recorded and maintained as quality records.

Service

The service industry always has been the most difficult of the four product categories in which to apply the requirements of the nonconforming product clause. The 1987 and 1994 versions of the ISO standard were focused on controlling nonconforming product from a hardware viewpoint. Therefore, during the ISO 9001:2000 revision process, a concerted effort was made to develop terminology to make it easier to apply the requirements of the nonconforming product clause to the service industry. This goal had not been reached at the Draft International Standard revision stage, and additional effort was made during the final revision process to further improve the text of the standard for application of the requirements to all product types.

However, in the final revision it is still at times difficult to differentiate between nonconforming product and corrective action for service organizations. This is due to the fact that in most instances the service has already been delivered at the point the nonconformity is identified. Since there is no nonconforming product to control, the focus is placed on whether corrective action should be conducted.

For this reason, the service organization should thoroughly analyze their business activities and determine the types of nonconformities that could potentially be identified. The organization should also consider whether these nonformities will be identified prior to or after delivery to determine if the activity is a nonconformity, a potential corrective action, or a recovery action. The examples below illustrate each of these scenarios.

The requirements of clause 8.3 can be applied to a service such as a hotel maid cleaning a room. If the hotel maid identifies something with the cleaning activities that would not meet the guest's requirements prior to the time the activity is completed, the task could be performed again to yield a satisfactory result. This provides an opportunity to eliminate the detected nonconformity prior to delivery.

In some cases, the hotel guest may not want to have their room cleaned for the day. The hotel guest might notify the front desk that they do not wish to have maid service or they may hang a sign on their door indicating "privacy please." Either of these situations would constitute a granted concession. The hotel guest accepts the fact they will not have maid service for the day.

The hotel can also avoid unintended delivery by keeping a list of rooms that have been cleaned and ensuring only those rooms which have been serviced are used to check in new guests. If the hotel would unintentionally deliver a room which had not been serviced, they would need to take action appropriate to the circumstances. They might be able to move the hotel guest to a new room or make adjustments to the current room. Such action is often referred to as "recovery" because the service organization is attempting to recover from a bad service situation. However, in this situation the nonconforming service has already been delivered and the action taken is neither "correction" nor "corrective action." Addressing the cause of the assignment of a room that has not been serviced would be considered corrective action.

Any actions taken would be subject to reverification. This could be completed by the maid's manager reviewing the additional service or the adjustments maid or the hotel manager checking the room prior to moving the hotel guest to another room to ensure it is satisfactory.

Another type of nonconformity in the service industry is where the nonconformity can be corrected, but it is not noted until after delivery. For example, a customer goes to a bank and the bank teller makes a mistake to the customer's account while completing the transaction. The nonconformity is not identified until some time after initial delivery when the customer receives the monthly bank statement. In this situation, the customer may have to exert a great deal of effort to prove the error existed. In this case, while the error may be corrected, the bank's investigation of the underlying circumstances to prevent recurrence would be considered corrective action.

A third type of nonconformity which could occur in the service industry is when the service is performed or promised, and it cannot be corrected. This is the situation that happens when an airline has overbooked a flight that is in the process of boarding. In many cases, the airline will offer tickets or other perks to passengers who agree to get off the plane and take a later flight. While these recovery actions are good business practices and help keep customers satisfied, they are not considered correction of the nonconformity or corrective actions.

In each of these scenarios, documented procedures should provide guidance to the relevant authority regarding options available for disposition of the nonconformity or in the case when delivery has already been made, appropriate corrective action.

Examples of records needed as objective evidence for clause 8.3 for the service industry might include:

- Checksheets that the hotel maid or their management might keep which indicate any nonconformities identified and actions taken with the hotel room
- Paperwork associated with making appropriate debits or credits to a customer's bank account after reconciliation
- Documents relating to the changes made to a traveler's airline reservations

Software

For our purposes here, software refers to computer programs, procedures, information, data, or records. As we live in the technology age, software has become a central part of doing business. We either purchase software or develop it in-house. When software is released, it generally is subjected to extensive testing, but it cannot be evaluated against every computer configuration or other software package that an organization might be running at the same time. For that reason, software can become nonconforming, and organizations should consider that possibility when developing their nonconforming product process in the quality management system.

Take, for instance, the company that has developed an in-house software training program that tracks the training history for each employee in the company. If after months of satisfactory performance, the system no longer functions properly, perhaps by not linking the training records to the employee who has completed the training, the system has become nonconforming.

The first step would be to identify and control the nonconforming software. That could be handled by adding a warning notice to the software when it is accessed or perhaps by eliminating access to the software altogether.

The relevant authority, generally the software system administrator, would then need to determine what action should be taken to eliminate the nonconformity. In most cases, the solution would be to correct the software so that it functions properly. If the software can be modified so that it operates to specification, it would then be subject to reverification. That would mean that after the software has been corrected, the company might process it through its software quality assurance program.

The relevant authority could also determine that the dysfunctional software feature is no longer required and a concession could be granted. If after evaluation it is determined that the software can no longer support the original requirements, action would need to be taken to ensure that it is no longer available for use and that it will not be used in the future.

Because the software was already in use and delivered, an evaluation would need to be made by the relevant authority regarding what action to take based on the circumstances. In that scenario, the system administrator might decide that the potential effects would require only that each employee review his or her training history to ensure its accuracy. The administrator also might call for backup of data that could be used to update the records.

Documentation to retain as quality records might include results from the software quality assurance testing, concessions granted by the customer, results of the investigation of the nonconformity, and actions taken.

Processed Materials

Another potentially nonconforming product is processed material. Processed materials can be in many different forms such as raw materials, liquids, solids, gases, sheets, and wires. Because some of these materials are not as widely used as others, this example will focus on material with shelf life, such as epoxy, paint, solder wire, O-rings, and batteries, and will also provide examples of applying the requirements to specific types of processed materials such as paint and motor oil. Options for dispositioning processed materials that are determined to be nonconforming include regrade, scrap, or rework.

Companies use shelf-life materials in a variety of ways. They may use them as part of the product they are building or they may be the product being provided. For example, a company might be responsible for stocking a ship—that will not return for three years—with supplies, including items that might have shelf life. When the shelf life of an item being used on a product assembly in a manufacturing company is found to have expired, the operator will identify the material as nonconforming. The relevant authority then, according to procedure, determines what actions are required to eliminate the nonconformity. The manufacturing company might have a procedure whereby the shelf life of products can be extended. That might be done by contacting the manufacturer of the material or by a qualified employee within the manufacturing company itself. The process constitutes the reverification that the material would be subject to.

For other types of processed materials, methods of eliminating the detected nonconformity might be to rework the product. For instance, an organization might find motor oil that is the wrong weight for a specific application. By blending the identified motor oil with that of a motor oil with a higher viscosity, the correct weight can be created and the nonconformity eliminated.

Alternatively, material with shelf life might be accepted with concession. This may not be common, but in some cases it may be acceptable to the customer. For instance, in the example of shelf-life material being stocked on a ship that will not return for three years, there may be some products with a shelf life of only 24 months. The customer in this case might grant a concession up front acknowledging the fact that the product will become nonconforming prior to the ship's return.

The shelf-life material might not be considered acceptable for its original use but could be regraded for another task such as development work. If a processed material such as paint is found not to meet specifications for application to a certain manufacturing product, it could be regraded for other uses in the organization including interior or exterior painting of the facility.

Finally, it might be determined that the shelf-life material cannot be used for any other use and should be scrapped. In these situations, the company needs to ensure that the controls put in place prevent the product from being used for its original purpose.

Quality records that should be maintained include documents that were used to extend shelf life, concessions granted by the relevant authority, and other documents that indicate the disposition of the product.

GOING BEYOND ISO 9001

Organizations that excel at the control of nonconforming product will go beyond the minimum requirements of ISO 9001 by looking at the requirements in ISO 9004 and implementing methods and tools that support them. Many times, simply designed systems are some of the best approaches to an effective nonconforming product process. Since there are many different methods by which to move beyond ISO 9001, an organization should consider what the potential return on investment is for implementing a process that exceeds the requirements. Following are examples of ways to extend an organization's quality management system past the requirements in the ISO 9001 standard at varying implementation costs.

One Nonconforming Product Control Process

Organizations that have taken the time to develop a single process for controlling nonconforming product find in many instances improved adherence to procedural requirements. When an organization has more than one system, employees who work in more than one department or switch from product line to product line can become confused by different processes. Sometimes customer or product requirements dictate different processes, but an organization should make this lack of standardization the exception and not the rule. When employees find it easier to follow procedures and understand the system, performance typically improves. Having employees follow one process for control of nonconforming product will help prevent the inadvertent use or delivery of product simply because they know, understand, and follow the process.

The costs of implementing a single nonconforming product process will depend on the complexity of the current system and the level of effort expected to consolidate multiple processes into one.

Visual Workplace

The visual workplace is a program many companies implement by labeling shelves, file cabinets, and work areas to help organize product, machinery, and data. It is always easy to spot a company that has implemented a visual workplace program because, even as a visitor to the area, you recognize good housekeeping habits and can see where things belong, including nonconforming product.

One way to implement the visual workplace to help prevent nonconforming product in a production area is by organizing tools and creating workstations for specific production tasks. Such workstations make only the tools for the particular task available for an employee to use, thereby reducing the risk of an employee using the improper tool, method, or approach.

In cases where the product is extremely large—such as a jeep or tank awaiting maintenance—the visual workplace may be used to identify vehicles parked in a certain direction as conforming and vehicles parked in the other direction as nonconforming. In other cases, where the nonconforming product is too large to physically store inside a building, it may be documented that the product is nonconforming until such time as it is moved inside the building and verified.

When employees are trained to use the visual workplace to organize their work areas, it not only helps control the nonconforming product once it has been identified but also can provide a system to assist in preventing nonconformities.

The visual workplace is another system that has minimal implementation costs but an opportunity for great returns.

Linking to the Corrective and Preventive Action System

Another method for going beyond the requirements of ISO 9001 is to link the nonconforming product system to the corrective and preventive action system. To avoid the need for a corrective action on each nonconformity, organizations identify thresholds at which a corrective action is needed. Some example thresholds are as follows:

- Nonconforming product is returned to an external supplier
- The nonconformity affects product already shipped to a customer
- Corrective action is requested by an external customer
- Corrective action is required by the product definition
- The nonconformity will result in more than $3000 of scrap

When none of the above criteria apply, a determination of need for corrective action can be made by evaluating the frequency of occurrence, effect on production, reliability, or when product or process improvements warrant the effort. By incorporating nonconformities that meet threshold levels into the organization's corrective and preventive action procedures, a mechanism is developed in the system that not only identifies nonconforming product but also works to prevent it from occurring in the future.

Because the organization already has implemented a corrective and preventive action system as a requirement of the ISO 9001 standard, there would be minimal costs associated with extending that system to nonconforming product. An organization could realize an increase in costs associated with processing corrective actions for nonconformities if thresholds were not identified.

Implementation of Electronic Systems and Retrieval of Data

More companies are beginning to exceed ISO 9001 requirements by implementing electronic systems that collect data on nonconforming product. The systems can be used to track the product and help ensure that it is not inadvertently delivered by noting the product's current status. Note that the electronic system should not replace the physical identification or segregation of the product but should be used to complement physical control. The electronic system also can be used to identify who has the responsibility and authority to determine what actions to take in dispositioning the product. In addition, it can monitor the nonconforming product to ensure that actions are taken to correct the nonconformity.

The key to a well-executed electronic system can be selecting a system that is easy to implement and manage and keeping the system simple. Since electronic systems have the ability to collect data, many have predetermined cause codes, occasionally reaching numbers in the 2000–3000 range. When a system has that many cause codes available, it may be difficult to see any trends because the cause codes may overlap in meaning, therefore making it difficult to analyze the data. In the past, one company that had an extensive list of cause codes found that typically only 30 or so were used with any frequency. When that company scaled down its cause code list, it was able to obtain metrics that provided trend information that could be used to improve performance.

In addition to discovering what caused the nonconformity, the electronic system can provide trend information that detects the following:

- An employee who has an increased or continuous number of nonconformities
- Trends with specific part numbers
- Increases in nonconformities on different shifts

Such metrics are not collected to attach blame to specific employees but to identify opportunities for improvement. It could be determined by analyzing the data that a specific employee is performing a job task for which he or she has not been trained, or the manager on the off-shift is not supervising the department. An organization can go even further beyond ISO 9001 requirements by presenting the data at management review and analyzing it along with other processes in the quality management system.

An electronic system is the most expensive of the examples provided here. A small organization might not be able to justify the expense of implementing an electronic system. It might, however, be able to develop something on a smaller scale specifically designed for its company. A larger company would need to evaluate the benefits of implementing an electronic system to determine its cost-effectiveness.

Application of Process Improvement Tools

Given that it is difficult to apply the nonconforming product clause to the service industry, it can be assumed that in that setting it is even more difficult to go beyond the requirements of the standard. However, tools exist in the business world that can be used to help improve processes in all business areas. Tools such as failure mode and effects analysis (FMEA) and process mapping can be applied to processes to identify potential nonconformities.

When a company maps its processes and then analyzes them using a tool such as FMEA, it focuses on potential problems and nonconformities that could occur. For the purposes of this discussion, this would be the inadvertent use or delivery of product. Using FMEA, the organization determines what actions it can take to mitigate or eliminate the nonconformity. This gives the organization an opportunity to improve its control over the possibility of inadvertent delivery.

If a service company wants to go beyond ISO 9001 requirements, it might evaluate using preventive tools since such tools often identify solutions that can be implemented quickly if a nonconformity is identified.

The costs associated with using tools such as FMEA and process mapping could be minimal depending on the amount of training needed to train employees to apply the tools.

Mistake-Proofing

Mistake-proofing falls into the toolbox, but it also is used in conjunction with the corrective and preventive action system.

Mistake-proofing is a process that provides a structure for designing a failure mode out of a product or process. Examples of mistake-proofing can be seen in everyday life. If you encounter any of the following, you are using a system that has been designed by a company to prevent a nonconformity:

- The beep on an ATM to notify the user to retrieve his or her card
- The kill switch on a lawnmower
- The inability to lock car doors when the lights are still on

Companies also use mistake-proofing to prevent potential nonconformities in the work environment:

- An X-ray lab adds a sensor and light on its film processor. The sensor detects the progress of the sheet through the processor and signals when the next sheet can be safely inserted without the sheets overlapping inside the machine and causing a nonconforming X-ray.
- Hybrid microcircuit fixtures are designed to hold the microcircuit through the production process to eliminate handling damage. The fixture has guide pins to locate the board and slots to hold the cable for attachment and ensure the right cable is in the correct location. The unit stays on the fixture throughout component mounting, solder reflow, cable attach, lidding, and testing.[2]

Again, after initial training, the costs of using mistake-proofing to go beyond ISO 9001 requirements would be minimal.

SUMMARY

As long as deadlines for production schedules change, operators are interrupted from their job tasks, and service employees make mistakes on the job, there will be nonconforming product. Perhaps that is the reason so many companies believe clause 8.3 is difficult to implement. However, because there always will be nonconforming product, it is important for companies to understand their processes, simplify them wherever possible, and work to document procedures.

Companies will then be in position not only to comply with the ISO 9001 standard but to begin to look at those methods that are not requirements but that can help them improve their business and go beyond ISO 9001 in pursuit of organizational excellence.

ENDNOTES

1. Operated for the U.S. Department of Energy under contract number DE-AC04-76DP00613.
2. This section draws on information from the Honeywell Federal Manufacturing and Technologies Cause Analysis and Mistake-Proofing Workshop.

Chapter 36

Process Analysis

Donald N. Ekvall
Management Systems Analysis, Lansdale, Pennsylvania

Analysis, or the separation of a whole into its component parts, has been the central theme of scientific and engineering endeavor and development for the past several hundred years. Process analysis focuses this strategy on the process in order to determine key features of process performance. From this activity we can determine the degree to which our processes are meeting expected standards, and expectations, and take appropriate action to correct, control, or improve the process outcome.

The forms of analysis are as many as the forms of processes—chemical, mathematical, statistical, physical, to state just a few. The methodology is also vast, and is described in handbooks, texts, and the papers of the scientific community; it will not be repeated in this chapter. Generally, it deals with determining central value, variability, stratification, and percent ingredient consistency of key process performance indicators. The purpose of this chapter is to help the handbook user determine what should be analyzed and the key strategies that guide the process analysis.

With ISO 9001:2000, and its recognition that "all work is a process," understanding and managing processes becomes a key focus of management responsibility. Universally, managers need to understand process structure and to be able to identify the best direction for effective and efficient process improvement. The need to upgrade and manage processes is at the core of global competition. Analytical strategies and tools developed in this chapter apply to both administrative services and production processes and to all product types. ISO 9000 is concerned with the long-term, continual improvement of the process. At times the tools used in process management are the same ones used in other improvement programs, but just as a saw can be used to make a cabinet or build a house, the goal is different.

WHAT TO ANALYZE

The Concept of Dominance, or What to Measure and Analyze

All processes involve numerous variables that affect the resulting performance.[1] These variables are not equally important; they follow the Pareto principle of the vital few and the trivial many. Often one variable is so completely decisive to the outcome of the process that it "dominates"—it is more important than all the other variables combined. This dominance of one variable (or a very few) is widespread, and many planners have instinctively made use of it. For example, in service work "people" are the dominant ingredient, and hence training and education are critical factors in consistently good process performance. In punch press processes it is the die that is dominant; hence skilled toolmaking is required for consistently good process performance. As a result, management of the process must be built around these facts. In too many cases the dominance is there but not acted upon because the business has not established a measurement system or standard to ensure that it receives the attention it deserves (that is, measurement, analysis, and action).

Following are some examples of process dominance:

Setup-dominant. A setup-dominant process is one that has been engineered to so high a degree of detail that it provides an essentially uniform product during the operation of the process, and the results are always the same. In such cases if the original "setup" is correct all of the work is correct, but if it is not then the entire job is wrong. Operation of such processes should concentrate on:

- Creating a highly reproducible process with little or no time-to-time variation
- Providing the process planner or operator with the means for self-control
- Ensuring that the process is correct in the first place by such actions as trial runs, preproduction, program testing, and having reproducible metrics

Machine Dominant. The machine-dominant process, though reproducible, undergoes continuing change over time (for example, depletion of reagents, tool wear, heat buildup, and so on) of such magnitude that nonconformance is inevitable in time. To deal with this continuing change, provisions must be made for periodic check and adjustment (for example, inspection and control charts in manufacturing; internal audits and corrective action for administrative and service systems).

Operator Dominant. In this category is the vast array of processes that are not fully engineered and for which the engineered residue is the major source of nonconformance. For such processes, the attention and skill of the "operators" (or managers) is decisive. Hence the processes are classified as operator dominant. Nonconformances from operator-dominant processes are commonly, but in error, classified as "operator controllable" when in fact they are caused by system-related weaknesses. We will see more of this when we discuss the "five yes method." The remedies the process manager can apply include training and evaluation, internal audits, foolproofing the process, and discovering the knack and skill factors during test trials of the process.

Material Dominant. In material-dominant processes, the purchased material (or externally supplied data) possesses qualities that are collectively so vital that they

Table 36.1 Process dominance.

Setup Dominant	Machine Dominant	Operator Dominant	Material Dominant
Typical processes			
Programming Computer operations Punch Press Molding Printing Faxing Educating Training	Screw Machine Packaging Volume filling Weight filling Payroll preparation Computer reports	Order filling Hand soldering Training classes Adjusting Repairing Service provision Budgeting Planning	Forecasting Mechanical assembly Food preparation Electronic assembly Report preparation
Typical control and management actions			
Preproduction Process testing Precontrol First-piece inspection Debugging Internal audit Periodic verification Inspection	Computer control Periodic inspection Control charting Process controllers Report audit	Training Education Operator scoring Process charting Process inspection	Vendor selection procedures Vendor rating Third-party certifications Internal controls Acceptance verification Annual on-site site audit

are the main factor in determining the ultimate performance of the process. The process manager has an important role in the decisions that shape the supplier relationships so that they blend into the process, and thereby the extent of the internal safeguards to protect against process failures from this source. Technical or economic limitations may prevent complete elimination of this source of failure and detection. Monitoring and audit systems are frequently put in place to provide early detection, which can reduce failure impact.

There are, of course, other categories of dominance, and some combination forms as well. However, the four categories listed are the most common and can be used to illustrate the concept.

Deciding what features dominate a process is key to successful process management. It is not possible to optimize a process for all of the features, nor is that economic. It is important to recognize the dominant factors of the process and to deal with them effectively. See Table 36.1.

PROCESS ANALYSIS STRATEGIES

There is a small group of strategies that call for and guide effective process analysis. They are simple but powerful. One of the best is a set of rules popularized by Robert Reid, which he called Reid's Rules. This set of three rules applied to any process will guide one to the types of analysis needed and help one achieve the process objectives sought by ISO 9000.

1. *No process without meaningful measurement and recording.* This rule requires us to determine the dominant process features to measure, determine how often to measure, determine the quantity of data to be collected, determine the adequacy of

the measurement system (that is, repeatability and reproducibility), and provide a useful recording system. (If it wasn't recorded, it didn't happen.)

This rule establishes the requirement for meaningful process metrics—meaningful in that the metrics correlate with customer-expected process performance. The metrics must be reproducible regardless of the individual making the measurement and repeatable (that is, the individual making the measurement will get similar readings when the measurement is repeated).

2. *No recording without analysis.* This rule requires us to predetermine analytical methodology, the stratification and analysis process we intend to use, and apply it to the collected process information. Typically we determine process target value, process variability, and relative event frequency for comparison with established process parameters or past process performance. This rule requires management knowledge of the performance, variability, and capability of the process. This knowledge sets the stage for the appropriate action. The direction of process improvement may be ever smaller process variability, a predetermined movement in the process target, or a reduced frequency of events known as "things gone wrong." In a typical process analysis a process capability index (Cp) for dominant features may be determined as follows:

$$Cp = \frac{\text{process performance tolerance width}}{6 \text{ standard deviations}}$$

A usable process will have a Cp of greater than 1.33. Today many organizations use a standard of Cp of 2 or more to achieve an easily managed process.[2]

3. *No analysis without action—correction, control, or improvement.* This rule requires us to establish process performance standards and apply pre-set actions that guide the eventual process improvement. It requires that the process manager act on the basis of the analyzed data in a manner appropriate to predetermined process rules. These rules could be derived from the control chart techniques or system operating instructions.

A second strategy, known as the "five yes method," is suggested to locate the probable cause of process problems for follow-on management action. The method is suggested for use by process operators/managers to determine that all of the conditions of a controllable process exist or to determine the most probable area of process problems should the process not perform to expectations. For adequate processes the answer to the following five questions is always "yes." The questions may be asked to confirm an adequate process or to search for the root cause of process-generated nonconformance. The questions must be asked in the sequence shown. In my experience I have never come across a process with problems that did not have a "no" answer to one or more of these questions. This is a great problem identifier.

THE FIVE YES QUESTIONS

The following questions are asked at the place where the process is operating, observing people who ordinarily do the work. When a "no" answer is obtained it is necessary for management to take a corrective action.

1. *Does the operator know what is expected?* If the answer is yes, follow on with these confirming questions: How was the operator selected? How was the

operator trained? Are adequate work instructions available to the operator? Does the operator's prior experience record confirm adequate process knowledge? When the answer is "no" management must rectify the situation to be able to obtain a "yes" answer.

2. *Does the operator have adequate resources, including time?* If the answer is yes, follow on with these confirming questions: Do records support process capability? Do maintenance records support a continued reduction of process downtime? Do experienced operators routinely complete assigned tasks in standard times allowed?

3. *Does the operator have the means to know how well he or she is performing?* If the answer is yes, follow on with these confirming questions: Does the operator have access to adequate measurement equipment and standards? Is he or she trained in proper use of measuring equipment? Are measurement repeatability and reproducibility analysis performed on a regular basis?

4. *Does the operator have the ability to adjust the process when it is not conforming?* If the answer is yes, follow on with these confirming questions: Are operators trained and qualified to make process adjustments? Can process adjustments be made in small enough increments to easily adjust the process target? Is adequate adjustment tooling available to qualified operators?

5. *Does the operator have the ability to stop and get help?* If the answer is yes, follow on with these confirming questions: Do operators have regular and easy access to supervisors? Can operators ask for process information without fear of reprisal?

PROCESS IMPROVEMENT STRATEGIES AND METHOD

The following eight sequential steps describe a workable methodology to support the continuous improvement goal for all processes in an enterprise. Some useful analytical tools are suggested.

1. *Draw a pictorial representation of the process to understand the key variables and process interactions.* This could be a simple flow diagram, a completion of a "work as a process" chart, or a process map. At times, more than one of these may be used at the same time to help understand how the process works.
   - Analytical methods:
     - Flowcharting (simple is better)
     - Process mapping

2. *Determine the adequacy of the measurement system.* One of the key sources of excess process variation is the measurement system. The General Motors *Statistical Process Control Handbook* provides a simple and effective method for determining measurement system adequacy. It involves two or more operators measuring the same five items, taking the ranges of the measurements, and using a conversion factor to change average range into a percent of tolerance statistic. Good measurement systems will have a measurement uncertainty of 10 percent or less of the tolerance width.

- Analytical method:
  - Repeatability and reproducibility analysis (General Motors *Statistical Process Control Handbook* short method is adequate most of the time).

3. *Ask the "five yes" questions and resolve any "no" answers.* When you get all "yes" answers you are in good shape, but when one or more of the answers is "no," management must act to resolve the problem area.

4. *Determine the process capability.*
  - Analytical method:
    - Normal probability paper (better than computer computation)

5. *Determine the appropriate process monitoring and/or measuring approaches.* There are numerous methods, tools, and techniques available. The methods used are dependent on the process to be controlled. The pictorial representation of the process developed in step 1 typically indicates where to monitor and measure.

6. *Determine the appropriate process improvement mode (that is, incremental, redesign or radical change, reengineering).*

7. *Continually apply the selected process improvement mode.*

8. *Repeat, starting at the first step.*

"People do what you review." This silly little ditty is the most enduring strategy for process control and improvement. We all know that a key element of process performance is a regular measurement, monitoring, and analysis process. Our experience is that when processes are not reviewed, subtle and continuous changes occur that degrade the outcome performance. Whether it is observation, inspection, or a process audit, process review produces data that need to be evaluated by some predetermined analytical process.

SUMMARY

Using the simple techniques described, along with the many analytical tools available to the quality professional or to whoever is addressing the process control and improvement, all processes can be effectively analyzed and improved. The magnitude of the improvement is limited only by the capabilities of those performing the analysis and the availability of human and capital resources.

ENDNOTES

1. D. N. Ekvall and J. M. Juran, *Quality Control Handbook*, 3rd ed., section 9 (New York: McGraw-Hill, 1974).
2. Ekvall and Juran.

Chapter 37

Improvement

Hitoshi Kume
Chuo University, Tokyo, Japan

THE PDCA LOOP

Possible reductions in quality losses are limited by a lack of awareness that losses exist and a failure to realize that these losses can be reduced economically through systematic, methodical, and continuous activities. The first thing needed to improve quality is a precise grasp of existing losses. Quality improvement can begin only after quality losses have been accurately recognized, the desire to reduce them has arisen, and people have acknowledged their responsibility for doing so.

Systematic control and improvement activities follow a set cycle composed of planning, implementing, checking, and taking corrective action. They start with the formulation of a plan; the plan is then implemented, and the results are checked. If the results do not turn out as predicted, the original plan is modified, the new plan is implemented, its results are checked, and further corrective action is taken as needed. Control and improvement can be simply described as a repetition of planning, doing, checking, and acting (PDCA). Faithfully following the PDCA loop leads to reliable execution of work. The concept was originally proposed by Walter Shewhart and became central to the teachings of W. Edwards Deming. Since improvement occurs and achievement levels rise as a result of this process, J. M. Juran redefined the concept as a spiral.

A large part of work is a repetition of something done before. Even tasks regarded as completely new contain many elements identical or similar to things previously done. Quality improvement consists mainly of carefully and systematically examining the methods by which such repetitive work is performed, checking the results obtained, and correcting any deficiencies discovered.

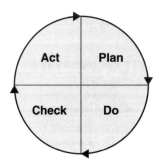

Figure 37.1 The PDCA loop.

Figure 37.1 illustrates the quality improvement process, showing that work consists of a repetition of planning, doing, checking, and acting (PDCA). Usually, corrective action is taken on the basis of the results of the original work, but the next round of corrective action in the subsequent PDCA loop based on the results of the first should also be taken to provide continual improvement.

Planning

Of the four elements of the PDCA loop, planning should be treated as the most important. This is not to say that the other elements are immaterial as long as plans are satisfactory; but plans do determine the other elements. If the plans are inadequate, all subsequent activities are ineffective. When original plans are well established, less corrective action is needed and activities become more efficient.

Planning Procedures

Improvement consists of bridging the gap between the ideal situation and the actual situation, and effective improvement activities require an accurate perception of both of these. With this point in mind, plans should be formulated according to the following procedure:

- Analyze the status quo and recognize problems
- Set targets
- Note any restrictions and limitations that must be considered
- Look for practicable improvement methods
- Decide on a plan of action
- Specify methods for checking and evaluating the results

Developing Plans

The problems that must be solved when trying to effect improvements usually consist of many different elements. To solve these problems through systematic activities, organization leaders must formulate and develop improvement plans. Such plans are developed through the following actions:

- Clarifying the basic activities needed to effect improvement
- Breaking these down in accordance with the organizational structure

- Distributing the subelements of the basic activities among the various departments of the organization

- Specifying how to evaluate the success of each department in achieving its objectives

The most senior person in the organization should set the quality objectives and decide on the task allocation and the methods of evaluation through discussions with each department. Similarly, the head of each department must then draw up and develop plans designed to achieve the objectives assigned to the department. The plans are cascaded down through the organization in this way and are suitably developed at each level of the organizational hierarchy until they no longer need to be broken down further. The final step is then to decide on the people responsible for putting these activities into effect, the resources required, and the schedules to be followed. The developed plans are documented thoroughly to ensure that they are communicated accurately.

Care must be taken when creating plans. The following guidelines should be helpful:

- During planning, resources restrictions (that is, people, money, materials, and equipment) and time constraints must be clarified. Methods must be found to meet objectives under these restrictions. If possible, these restrictions and constraints may be relaxed. After all relevant proposals have been considered, the best method is finalized as an action plan.

- Procedures must be devised for checking and evaluating whether the plans are effective and whether or not they are being followed and incorporated into the original plans.

- Information must be constantly collected, organized, and fully used during the planning process.

- Resources are not inexhaustible, and it is impossible to do everything. The planning process must therefore determine what *must* be done and what it would be *nice* to do.

- A good balance between goals and resources must be achieved. It is counterproductive to set pointlessly high targets.

- Effective information systems must be implemented to communicate the aims of the plans to every part of the organization.

- Material resources are generally limited, but human abilities are not. Improvement is always possible; therefore, people's abilities should be constantly developed.

Doing

To ensure that the plans are properly implemented, the following steps are necessary:

- Ensure that the department responsible for carrying out the plans is fully apprised of the need for doing so

- Ensure that the plans are communicated adequately to the department in charge of implementing them

- Provide any education and training required for implementing the plans
- Provide the necessary resources at the necessary times

Checking

When the results of implementing the plans are checked and evaluated, the following two aspects should be evaluated separately:

- Whether the plans were followed
- Whether the plans themselves were adequate

If targets are not being met, it is essential to determine why. Failure to attain targets is due to failing to follow plans, inadequacies in the plans themselves, or a combination of both. It is essential to discover which, because entirely different corrective actions will be required in each case.

When the cause lies in failure to follow the plans, this may be due to any of the following factors:

- Lack of awareness of the need for improvement
- Inadequate communication and understanding of the plans
- Insufficient education and training
- Leadership and coordination problems during implementation
- Insufficient resources

When the cause lies in inadequate plans, this may be due to any of the following factors:

- Mistakes in understanding the existing situation
- Wrong selection of techniques because of insufficient information and knowledge at the planning stage
- Inaccurate estimates of the effect of implementing the plans
- Incorrect calculation of the person's ability to put the plans into effect

Acting

When taking corrective action, it is essential to draw a clear distinction between eliminating a phenomenon or symptom and eliminating its cause. As mentioned earlier, much work is repetitive. In repetitive work, eliminating a symptom does not solve the underlying problem; it is merely a means of putting off its solution to a later date.

With improvement activities, the causes of failure to achieve the objectives should be accurately identified and the plans should be modified to enable the activities to be carried out more effectively. Likewise, when failure to achieve targets is due to inadequate planning, simply revising plans is not enough; the quality of the planning process must be improved by finding out why such poor plans were made and taking suitable preventive action. Quality improvement activities should be reviewed on a half-year or yearly basis to ensure that they are reliable and appropriate.

IMPROVEMENT AND STANDARDIZATION

In ISO Guide 2:1996, standardization is defined as an "activity of establishing, with regard to actual or potential problems, provisions for common and repeated use, aimed at the achievement of the optimum degree of order in a given context." In this definition, the key concept is "optimum degree of order," but standardization has a more positive meaning. Standards should be used not only to establish order but also to attain quality and work efficiency. Standardization forms a basis for improving the level of work. This aspect is frequently overlooked in the efforts of standardization. The late D. Marquardt, who was the leader of the American delegation to ISO/TC 176, said that a standard is the end point of one improvement and also the starting point for the next improvement.

If the results of activities are unsatisfactory, it is necessary to trace the cause in order to prevent recurrence. From the viewpoint of standardization, there are three main causes of failure:

- Standards have not been set
- Standards were set but were inadequate
- Standards were set but were not obeyed

In some cases, the required outcome of a process is clear, the method to obtain it can be readily understood by viewing the outcome, and the method can be implemented easily. In most cases, the process is too complex for these conditions to apply, and there is little hope of realizing the intended result unless a proper working method is established and the workers trained. Standardization of methods, providing education and training, and making sure that the work is done in accordance with the standardized methods is essential to prevent unsatisfactory results.

The results of work should always be checked, and if they are unsatisfactory, the following should be asked:

- Has a standard been established?
- Is the standard being observed?
- Is the standard adequate for the purpose?

An appropriate corrective action should be taken if the answer to at least one of these questions is no. The effort constitutes a loop of standardizing, doing, checking, and acting (SDCA), as shown in Figure 37.2.

Even when work is done according to a standard, troubles occur when the standard is not adequate. Investigating and eliminating the cause of the trouble can establish a better standard. An organization's technology is supported by its engineers and by its technical standards. An organization's knowledge and skills are accumulated in the form of standards. An organization's performance is supported by its people and its standards. These internal standards can be in many forms, such as technical specifications, drawings, company standards, and documented procedures. If individual failures end with only the rework of defects or if the action taken is only preserved as an experience of the personnel concerned, the organization cannot achieve advancement. Improvement takes place and performance levels rise when standards are revised as a result of failures.

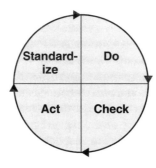

Figure 37.2 The SDCA loop.

Organizational activities that are not standardized cannot last. Unwritten methods are forgotten when persons move on. Even if good methods are developed, they cannot be thoroughly implemented and simply vanish unless established in written form.

Daily management activities consist of maintenance and improvement. Maintenance involves setting standards and working in accordance with them, and improvement involves setting targets above the present level and working to achieve those targets. To convert a prevailing situation into a more desirable one, existing standards must be altered.

To run an organization effectively requires conducting maintenance and improvement in a well-balanced manner. All organizational activities are based on standards. Neglecting standards lowers efficiency. Far from producing improvement, such neglect actually decreases the effectiveness of the organization. Progress and development are not held back by solid maintenance of the status quo. The elements of progress and development are always contained within the existing situation, and rigorous maintenance of the status quo highlights what needs to be improved and allows improvement activities to effectively progress. When a new situation is created as a result of improvements, activities designed to maintain the new situation begin, and the next round of improvement starts. Although the status quo is maintained, this does not imply the status quo is static. It is continually changing, and accurately identifying those changes creates a driving force for improvement. Although standardization and improvement seem to be contradictory, they are closely related. Standards are the results of improvement and the starting point for the next round of improvements (see Figure 37.3).

CORRECTION, CORRECTIVE ACTION, AND PREVENTIVE ACTION

If the present status is unsatisfactory, there are two ways to correct it: take action for what has occurred and take action regarding the cause. Action taken for what has happened in order to make unsatisfactory results of work acceptable is generally called correction. Rework and repair are examples of correction. Several examples of action taken for what went wrong are shown in Table 37.1.

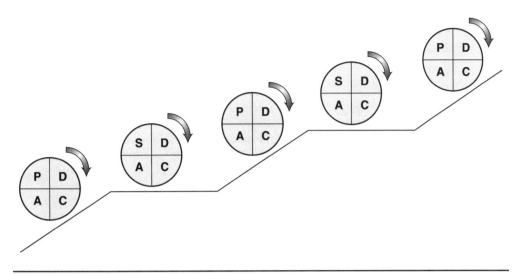

Figure 37.3 Maintenance and improvement.

Table 37.1 Examples of action taken for what has occurred.

State of Affairs	Action
Fire	Firefighting
Dental caries	Extraction of decayed teeth
Defective products	Reworked after shipping
Products in a lot rejected by sampling inspection	All products screened and only conforming products shipped
Customer complaints	Replaced with good products
Failures	Repair
Delay in production	Make up the delay by working overtime
Mistaken delivery	Redelivery
Omission of signature	Signature given

Some activities are performed only once, but many of them are repeated. In such repeated activities, action taken to achieve the desired result does not lead to resolving problems, because similar problems may occur so long as the cause exists. Putting out a fire is a typical example of taking action for what has occurred. Firefighting is necessary, but one should go beyond that. If the fire resulted from an overloaded electrical outlet, efforts should be made to decrease the level of electrical load for each outlet. If one continues to overload a single electrical outlet, a fire is sure to break out again. Action taken for the result of what has occurred merely postpones solving problems to the future. Improvements are obtained by eliminating the cause of defects. That is, improvements stem from actions aimed at processes. Preventing the recurrence of problems is achieved by clarifying their cause, revising work methods and standards to eliminate that cause, and training workers to use the new methods and standards.

ISO 9001 requires organizations to take two types of action to prevent problems from recurring: corrective action and preventive action. In the example of tooth decay, if the elder of two brothers has a bad tooth and has it pulled, this is correction. And if he starts to brush his teeth every day to prevent further dental decay, this is corrective action. If the younger of the two, who has not suffered a toothache yet, emulates his brother and starts to brush his teeth every day, he has taken preventive action.

Reworking defective products is correction. If it is found that an operator made a mistake when doing the job and he or she is retrained to prevent its recurrence, corrective action has been taken. Reviewing training methods for newly employed operators and preventing new operators having a similar job from making the same kind of mistake in the future are forms of preventive action. Repairing defects is correction. If the cause of a defect lies in inadequate drawings, their revision is a corrective action. Further actions to prevent issuing unsatisfactory drawings by improving design review systems and testing methods of prototype products are preventive actions.

Catching up with work that has fallen behind schedule by doing overtime is a way of treating the result but not the cause. If the cause of the delay is equipment failure, then maintenance methods of the failed equipment must be improved and further preventive steps should be taken to minimize the effect of similar breakdowns of other equipment in the factory.

The characteristics of correction, corrective action, and preventive action are shown in Table 37.2.

AN EXAMPLE

Improvements can range from small-step continual improvement to strategic breakthrough improvement projects. The following is an example of a breakthrough improvement project carried out in an American and Japanese joint venture that manufactures and markets electronic measuring instruments. For a while after its foundation, the company had enjoyed steady growth. However, because of a rapid increase in wages and technological progress, the company's profit ratios were

Table 37.2 Correction, corrective action, and preventive action.

Action	Target of Action	Examples
Correction ~~Patch~~	Results of work	Rework or repair of products
Corrective action	Cause of defects in design, processes, and so on	Design change, process change
Preventive action	Deficiency in quality system	Revision of quality system elements and procedures

Developmental action   Researching and implementing new + better processes   Process reengineering

beginning to decline, product quality had become unstable, and productivity had stopped increasing. To break out of this situation, a new production manager was appointed to reduce production cost. Believing that the painstaking elimination of all forms of waste was needed, he started examining the production processes.

Production was organized so that work could be done as much as possible in batches, and lots were made as large as possible with the idea of improving production efficiency. To achieve this, the necessary parts were also issued from the stores in large batches, and the workers had a large number of shelves beside them to accommodate these parts together with work in hand. It was noticeable that parts and work in hand were held up for a long time between processes. In addition, inspections were carried out after each process, and a particularly striking feature was that each process had its own reworking process. The production personnel were working as hard as they could in the cramped spaces left among all the in-process inventory.

To begin eliminating wasted space, unnecessary inspections, and rework, the new production manager discussed them at a production department meeting and set out a policy of process quality improvement. However, in the discussion about what should be done before starting specific activities, the following opinions were expressed:

- "The specified inspections are done conscientiously, and we can't imagine there can be any problems with product quality."
- "Considering the fact that a lot of the equipment we are using is old, we are managing very well."
- "We are told to base our comments on data, but we are so busy that we don't have time to collect any."

In other words, the discussion got no further than everyone trying to shift the blame for the problem onto someone else, while claiming that they themselves were doing their best. In order to break this deadlock, the production manager invited an outside consultant to give some specific advice on how to carry out production quality improvement. At the first quality control consulting seminar, he asked the production people to tell him the current state of quality control in their sections. Naturally, they presented their reports with plenty of confidence, each in their own way. However, they were surprised when the consultant told them the following:

- Products were being made by inspection, adjustment, and rework. The causes of defects remained undetected.
- There were no quality data. The organization was making products somehow or other and sending them on to the next process in the same vague way.
- Work was not standardized. The level of standardization was so low that some of them asked what standardization was. Where standards existed, they were taken from those of the parent company, and there was no local ownership.

After hearing these points, the production staff realized that the idea of quality control they had previously held was rather incomplete and quite different from quality control in the consultant's sense. On investigating the poor quality of each process and attending the second quality control consulting seminar, they were again surprised to be told that, while the fraction defective for their company's automatic soldering process for printed circuit boards (PCBs) was 0.4 percent, ordinary outside manufacturers measured the same fraction defective in parts per million [ppm; the fraction defective of soldering = (the number of solder defects / the total number of holes on a PCB) $\times 10^6$]. Many people in the organization had not even heard of a unit called ppm, and they were shocked into appreciating the size of the gap between their quality control and that generally accepted in industry. These seminars made the production manager feel keenly that his people were like ostriches with their heads in the sand when it came to quality control. He began to doubt whether their improvement activities could really bring them up to the level of the outside world. Nevertheless, he decided to start improvement activities in earnest.

Improvement Activity I—Analysis and Standardization

The example organization started improvement activities of the soldering processes for the following reasons:

- The automatic soldering fraction defective in ordinary companies is measured in ppm, while theirs is 0.4 percent (4,000 ppm)—a huge difference. (A fraction defective of 0.4 percent means an average of two defects per PCB.)
- The quality of PCB assembly is the key to the quality of the product (75 percent of the parts determining the electrical performance of a product are mounted on PCBs).

Work Observation

Before improvement activities were started, a four-member project team, headed by the production manager, was formed and members of the team collected current production-line data and carried out observations on the shop floor. Among other things, they found the following:

- There were differences in the way different operators collected defect data.
- Some PCBs required no reworking at all, while others required extensive reworking.
- Operators were changing the equipment settings; that is, the settings were not clearly defined.

The team therefore reorganized and unified the previously vague inspection standards to provide a uniform standard for data collection.

Identifying the Current Situation

To identify the problems occurring on the shop floor more promptly and accurately, the project team members themselves went to the shop floor each day and collected data while working. The data for one month were collated, and the figures for each type of defect were plotted on a Pareto chart (see Figure 37.4), which shows that bridging, floating parts, and nonwetting accounted for 86.1 percent of the total number of defects.

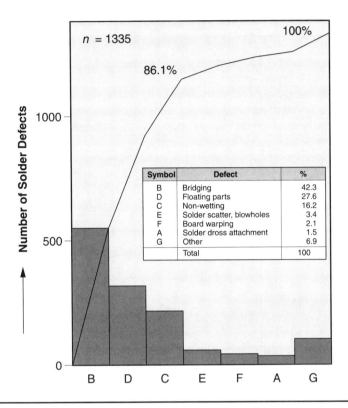

Symbol	Defect	%
B	Bridging	42.3
D	Floating parts	27.6
C	Non-wetting	16.2
E	Solder scatter, blowholes	3.4
F	Board warping	2.1
A	Solder dross attachment	1.5
G	Other	6.9
	Total	100

Figure 37.4 Pareto chart for solder defects.

Identifying Problems and Countermeasures

As part of the project, brainstorming sessions were held based on the team's experience on the shop floor to pinpoint the causes of the solder defects. Countermeasures were then put into effect. At this stage, the countermeasures consisted of setting uniform operating conditions, revising equipment maintenance and control standards and making sure they were put into effect, and clearing up the various separate defect causes and eliminating them one by one.

Improvement activities were promoted in this way to deal with the various defects involving a diversity of technical problems. As this was done, the details of problems involving the workers became clear. For example, workers sometimes mounted the wrong part or forgot to mount a particular part on a board. This kind of operating problem was taken up for improvement activity by quality control circles.

Identifying Results

Improving the quality of the automatic soldering process had the direct effect of cutting down on solder defects and the resulting rework (see Figure 37.5). Naturally, the number of problems with the PCBs arising in the subsequent product testing process also decreased greatly along with the number of man-hours required to deal with these problems. Another effect of the improved quality was that the inspectors in the automatic soldering process ended up inspecting only

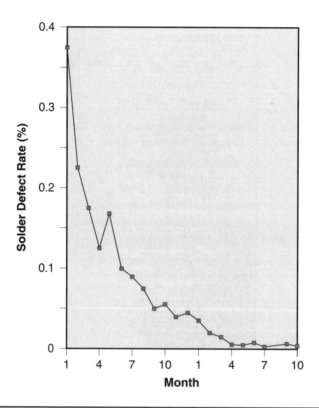

Figure 37.5   Trend in fraction defectives of soldering.

defect-free products, and it became clear that they were wasting their time. Inspections by inspectors were therefore abandoned and autonomous inspections (inspections by the workers themselves) were introduced. The concept of having the workers check their own work and take responsibility for sending only defect-free products to the next process was thoroughly established.

In this way, the fraction defective was reduced from the percentage level to the ppm level—an achievement considered almost impossible before improvement activities were started. As a result of these wide-ranging improvements, wasteful processes such as reworking, inspection, and troubleshooting were eliminated; the idea that "rework is a part of the process" disappeared; and the problem worrying the organization—high production costs—was solved. In addition, the number of defective PCBs held up in the process decreased sharply, making the process flow more smoothly and consequently increasing production capacity dramatically.

Improvement Activity II—Elimination of Overproduction

The production manager now decided that the time was ripe to aim at "eliminating wasteful overproduction" and decided to switch from large-lot to small-lot production. This kind of change to the operating setup naturally meant

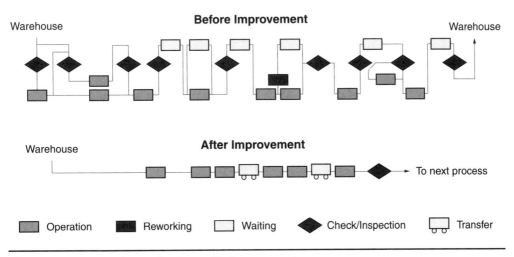

Figure 37.6 Process innovation by quality improvement.

changes to the working habits of every worker, whether directly or indirectly involved in production. To put these changes into effect, the production section manager concerned with the project made efforts to train not only the shop-floor workers but also those who were supposed to be providing support to the shop floor—those indirectly involved in production. By switching to small-lot production in this way, stagnation in the production line, process inventory, and stocks of completed products were all reduced.

It also became possible to cope with increased production at that time without increasing the working space. Before these changes, the company had planned to build a new plant to cope with the lack of working space, but this plan was canceled as a result of the improvements. The resulting process simplification can be seen in Figure 37.6. This made a big contribution to the significant cost reductions achieved. The fraction defective of the existing process dropped steadily in this way, helping greatly to reduce costs and stock levels.

Quality Improvement at the Source

To deal with the huge number of problems occurring on the shop floor, the project team had intended on making them the focus of improvement activities. The team members now noticed that they had not been providing proper feedback for improvement at the design stage—the original source of the problems. They strongly felt the need to start improvement activities at the design stage of a new product, not merely to deal with the defects occurring after it was put into production on the shop floor.

They therefore summarized the results they had obtained through their improvement activities until then and used them to revise the production engineering standards. They also promoted the application of these standards from the design stage to produce quality improvement at the source. This resulted in a decrease in the number of defects during start-up.

Overall Results

1. The fraction defective, previously at the percentage level, could finally be kept at 3 ppm.

2. Reworking and in-process inspections were abolished, and reworking and other problems arising during the product testing process after the following assembly stage also decreased. The number of man-hours decreased by 42 percent (the number of workers went from 22 to 14)

3. Small-lot production became firmly established. In-process waiting decreased, and a production system that produced only what was needed when it was needed was established.

4. Production lead time (from PCB fabrication to shipping of product) was reduced from 20 weeks to 6 weeks.

5. The flow of production became uniform, and missed delivery dates were eliminated. (The percentage of missed delivery dates dropped from 30 percent to zero.)

6. Previously, two workers had been required to monitor the automatic soldering process for abnormalities. The stabilization of the process and a rearrangement of the equipment enabled the number of workers monitoring the process to be reduced to one.

Another noteworthy effect was that, as the improvements progressed, the workers became more and more positive and tackled their work with greater and greater enthusiasm.

What Did the Organization Learn?

Here is a summary of what people learned as a result of these quality improvement activities:

1. The production manager and staff need an attitude that allows them to focus on finding out where the poor quality of their own work shows up in what the shop-floor workers do, and putting things right.

2. Operating errors are not necessarily operator errors; more often, they arise from poor standards or training and are the responsibility of the manager and staff.

3. Processes must be understood and their capability measured so that the ability exists to adjust and improve them.

4. If these matters are not dealt with conscientiously and in a detailed manner, quality defects will turn into unnecessary operations, such as reworking. Working lead-time is then required to compensate for this.

5. If this lead-time is accepted, the quality problems will not appear on the surface. They soon take the form of costs, and the waste has become rationalized.

THE ROLE OF STATISTICAL METHODS IN QUALITY IMPROVEMENT

Most quality problems are caused by inaccurate work or an erroneous grasp of facts. The causes of problems arising from incorrect work are often easy to pinpoint, and appropriate countermeasures can be readily applied. However, the causes of problems because of misunderstood facts are usually more difficult to discover and often more deep-rooted. Wrong judgments arise when facts are not correctly identified and knowledge is based on inaccurate or mistaken information; this was illustrated by the examples given earlier in this chapter.

Human beings think in terms of concepts and express those concepts verbally. However, a single concept is multifaceted and cannot possibly be described with a single word. For example, the word *house* indicates a building in which people live, but it covers a large number of different types dwellings, ranging from huge mansions to rabbit hutches. A builder cannot satisfy a customer's wishes if simply told to build a house, because there is a big difference between the house imagined by the builder and that envisioned by the customer. Some people may leave things entirely up to the builder, but they are highly unlikely to be satisfied with the result. A single word actually represents huge variety and diversity. What is more, what a word represents depends on the person using the word, and it is rare for both speaker and listener to be talking about exactly the same thing. Language is inherently imprecise, and it is extremely difficult to communicate information accurately with words alone. Formulas, drawings, and numerical data are used to compensate for the imprecision of language, and as a way of expressing facts by means of numerical data, the statistical method is part of this.

One example is surface damage to a product. The phrase *surface defects* covers a wide variety of phenomena, such as dents, chips, scuffs, and scratches, all of which have different causes. The actual situation relating to such defects can only be clarified by collecting and collating data on which parts of the product they affect, when they occur, how often they occur, and other factors. When defects are stratified and classified in this way and their individual frequencies of occurrence are determined, their causes come to light. If this kind of analysis is not performed and all the different types of defects are bundled together as a single problem under the same heading—surface defects—each person will have a different idea of what the word means, and any action taken will be inappropriate.

The statistical method is based on expressing phenomena in numerical terms, classifying them, stratifying them, and observing their frequency of occurrence. Doing so enables us to identify a situation precisely and communicate information about it accurately. The following things can be said about the statistical method:

- It gives more importance to concrete facts than abstract concepts
- It expresses phenomena in terms of numerical data linked to specific observational procedures rather than in terms of sensory or conceptual language
- It accepts that observations are always performed only on part of a situation and that the results contain errors and fluctuations
- When a definite tendency is observed among large numbers of observations, it accepts this as reliable information for the time being

One of the fundamental tenets of quality improvement is to base thinking and action on facts. Quality problems are generally affected by a plethora of complexly interrelated factors. Statistical techniques are indispensable tools for accurately identifying facts, and this is their primary role in quality improvement.

HOW TO USE ISO 9004 FOR IMPROVEMENT

ISO 9004:2000 clause 8.5, "Improvement," describes necessary items for continual improvement. The improvements can range from small-step continual improvement to strategic breakthrough improvement projects. In any cases, the use of the PDCA and SDCA loops is a basic principle for improvement.

As previously discussed, there should be clear understanding on the difference among correction, corrective action, and preventive action. The improvements are only realized when corrective and preventive actions occur. And to ensure the effect of these actions, standardization or permanent fix for these actions and training to ensure implementation of the new standards should follow. The level of performance of an organization is closely related to the standards they use. This section describes the key issues that determine the level of performance of the organization from the viewpoint of standardization. These issues should be considered carefully in the application of ISO 9004.

The Three Elements That Decide the Performance of Quality Activities

The ISO 9000 standards specify the what of quality management but not the how. In other words, they say what must be done to manage quality but not how to do it. This attitude is basically correct for standards, such as the ISO standards, that are widely used all over the world. However, although this is what defines the scope of quality management, it does not define its level. As mentioned before, in activities based on standards, the following three points are the key questions to ask about a particular item under consideration:

- Has a standard been established? (What)
- Is that standard appropriate for the purpose? (How)
- Is the standard being observed? (Conformance)

The what specifies the breadth or scope of the activities, while the how specifies their depth. For example, ISO 9001:2000 clause 5.3, "Quality policy," states, "Top management *shall ensure that the quality policy is . . . communicated and understood within the organization.*" But how exactly is a company supposed to achieve this? To ensure the realization of its quality policy, a company could adopt cross-functional management, policy management, quality control circles, and top management quality diagnosis, which form the bedrock of Japanese-style total quality management. On the other hand, some companies being audited for ISO 9001 merely print their quality policy on little cards and make their employees carry these cards in their breast pockets to demonstrate to auditors that the employees are familiar with the policy.

Although most automobile parts manufacturers go no farther than processing customer quality complaints and claims as their way of capturing market quality information, one manufacturer practices the activity known as initial flow control or start-up management. This consists of having their quality staff make systematic visits to automobile dealers for several months after a new model has been launched onto the market in an attempt to uncover any quality problems and take prompt corrective action. Auto parts manufacturers usually only deal with their direct customers—the manufacturers of the finished automobiles—and have no contact with the end users of their products—the vehicle drivers. This means that market quality information reaches them via the automobile manufacturers, and except in special emergencies, they only receive it a considerable time after quality problems have actually occurred. However, believing it essential to act rapidly to correct new-product teething problems, this company has its quality people visit sales outlets to gather quality information in addition to collecting it through the usual channels.

Communicating top management's quality policy and capturing market quality information are both elements of quality management, and the scope of an organization's quality management is determined by which elements it decides to include within it. However, the fact that a company's quality management activities are broad in scope does not necessarily mean that they are at a high performance.

Another element that determines the performance of an organization's quality management is its degree of conformance to the relevant standards. However excellent a set of standards it may have prepared, an organization cannot be said to be managing quality well if it is not following those standards. We can only say that the performance of an organization's quality management is high if it has a good set of standards that are being followed properly. The automobile parts manufacturer mentioned earlier stipulates that customers' delivery deadline requirements are to be strictly observed. One winter, the roads were paralyzed by heavy snowfalls, and it was impossible to deliver some heater core parts on time by the usual truck delivery. The company avoided a late delivery by having all the employees involved in making these parts load them into rucksacks and take them directly to the customer by bullet train.

The performance of an organization's quality system is determined by the appropriateness of the quality management elements included in its quality system, their methods of implementation, and the thoroughness with which they are implemented.

The What and How of Quality Management

Although we describe the what and how of quality management as if they were different things, we do so to sort out the issues relating to the performance of a company's quality management. In reality, the what and how are not separate entities; they simply denote different stages of an activity. ISO 9001 specifies how quality should be assured by listing items as the requirements of a quality system. However, to actually apply this standard, it is necessary to further specify how each of these items is to be implemented. At this stage, these items become the what of assuring quality, and we have, in turn, to specify how these whats should be carried out. But even doing this does not tell us what must ultimately be done. Whenever something is to be done, how it will be done is determined by breaking it down progressively into its elements and selecting what is to be done at each stage. The chain of whats selected when breaking down the activity in this way determines how the activity will be done.

As mentioned earlier, the ISO 9000 standards are regarded as specifying the what of quality management but not the how. Nevertheless, the how of quality management is in fact specified in these standards, although it consists of those elements belonging to the top stage of quality management. In practice, the how must be further broken down, but the standards do not specify how to do so. Since the way in which this is done will depend on factors such as type, size, and technical capability of the industry and the cultural background of the organization involved, it is reasonable not to involve the ISO standards too deeply in the how question. In real-life quality management, however, the how is often more important than the what. For example, ISO 9004:2000 clause 8.5.4, "Continual improvement of the organization," gives the necessary elements to continue improvement activities briefly. These elements are to the point, but the user of the standard who wants to make the most of it must complement the guidance by breaking down the standard's guidelines into the series of hows that are appropriate to the organization. This may make ISO 9004 appear to be incomplete, but this incompleteness gives users of the standard flexibility in the way they use it. The effectiveness of the standard will depend largely on the way it is used. ISO 9004 is formulated in general terms, and therefore its effectiveness depends on how the guidance in the standard is deployed to deal with various situations.

REFERENCES

Kume, H., *Management by Quality*. Tokyo: 3A Corporation, 1995.
———. The Scope and Depth of Quality Standards. *Proceedings of Annual Quality Congress of ASQ*. 1999.
ISO Guide 2, *Standardization and related activities—General vocabulary*, 1996.
Shibata, K., and Kume, H. *Production Reform through Quality Improvement*. Kenshu 108, 1988.

Section 8

Applying the ISO 9000 Family in Organizations

Introduction

John E. (Jack) West
Consultant, The Woodlands, Texas

Organizations of all types are using the ISO 9000 family as key input to the development and maintenance of their quality management systems. The reasons for applying the family vary from organization to organization. This section explores concepts related to applying ISO 9001 and ISO 9004.

APPLYING ISO 9001 TO DEVELOP A BASIC QMS AND DEMONSTRATE ITS COMPLIANCE

The most common use of the ISO 9000 family has been its use in developing basic quality management systems.

• The concept of meeting customer requirements is central to the ISO 9000 family. In chapter 38, "Using ISO 9000 to Achieve Customer Requirements," Leslie S. Schnoll discusses the use of the ISO 9000 family to achieve customer requirements.

• The three requirement standards of the 1994 series have also formed the basis for third-party certification of the quality systems of more than 400,000 organizations worldwide. This type of usage can be expected to grow further with the introduction of ISO 9001:2000. But certification is not the only means to demonstrate compliance with the requirement standard. In chapter 39, "Certification and Conformity Assessment," Dale Misczynski discusses three basic methods for demonstrating conformity: self-declaration of conformity, certification by a customer, and third-party certification (or registration). He also discusses the third-party system, explains the role of accreditation bodies, and provides guidance on selecting a registrar.

• Understanding the new ISO 9000:2000 series is important for both implementers and for auditors. In chapter 41, "Understanding ISO 9000:2000: The Role of the International Standardized Testing Organization A.G.," Dr. Nigel H. Croft describes the International Standardized Testing Organization, which has been established to test individuals' understanding of the new standards. This testing process will not guarantee the competence of individuals but will provide confidence that those passing the test understand the new standards.

• The role of the International Accreditation Forum (IAF) is important to the integrity of the third-party certification system. Noel Matthews discusses the role of the IAF in chapter 40, "The International Accreditation Forum."

APPLYING ISO 9004 TO ACHIEVE EXCELLENCE

ISO 9004:2000 is an excellent tool for organizations to use in developing quality management systems focused on performance improvements. Juhani Y. Anttila and Malcom Bird discuss the use of ISO 9004:2000 in chapter 42, "Using ISO 9004 to Achieve Excellence."

GETTING HELP AND APPLYING THE FAMILY IN SMALL AND MEDIUM-SIZE ENTERPRISES

Many organizations that use the ISO 9000 family are small or medium-size enterprises. In chapter 43, "Small Businesses," Herbert C. Monnich provides insight for small businesses. Often, small organizations need help with implementation and cannot afford expensive consulting fees. There are programs available to help. In chapter 44, "Use of Consortia and the NIST MEP Network," Morgan Hall discusses the use of consortia and special programs that can provide such help.

APPLICATIONS IN GLOBAL TRADE AND EMERGING ECONOMIES

There is also a growing use of the ISO 9000 family in emerging economies. Armando Espinosa discusses this in chapter 45, "ISO 9000 and International Trade—ISO in Emerging Economies."

INTEGRATED MANAGEMENT SYSTEMS

With the approval of ISO 14001 in 1996, the need emerged for organizations to integrate a number of the processes for quality and environmental management. James W. Highlands discusses the use of ISO 9001 and 14001 together in chapter 46, "Using ISO 9000 and ISO 14000 Together."

Chapter 38

Using ISO 9000 to Achieve Customer Requirements

Leslie S. Schnoll
Gliatech, Cleveland, Ohio

The year 2000 revisions of the ISO 9000 series of quality standards, namely, changes in terminology and a complete reorganization of the structure of the standards, will pose a few additional requirements for organizations. Chapter 8 discusses the major changes that have been made to ISO 9001 and their impact on organizations. While the intent and expectations of these changes are to enhance customer satisfaction, there will still be a learning curve to gain complete understanding of the reasons for the enhancements. For those who have not yet initiated a program of compliance, these provisions will not constitute a problem.

BACKGROUND

The revisions to the standards were made as a result of extensive, worldwide surveys to better understand the needs of all user groups of the standards, including the customers of the organizations who develop and implement quality systems in compliance with those standards. These revisions take into account previous experience with quality management systems and emerging insights into generic management systems. Hopefully, the revisions will result in a better alignment of organizations' quality management systems with the needs of the organizations and their customers.

It is important to remember that we are in a constant race for quality; however, this race has no finish line because the requirements and expectations of customers are constantly changing. The ISO 9000 standards do, however, provide us three tools with which to compete: the quality policy provides the map and the rules for the journey, quality management is the driver, and the quality system is the vehicle to get us there.

The standards provide a generic, rational approach that is consistent with the evolution of the concept of quality. In the 1970s, quality was defined as "conformance to requirements." This meant that if our company had a set of sales specifications (that we ourselves determined) and we were able to consistently meet those specifications, we had a quality product or provided a quality service. Using an example of an automobile, if our vehicle (let's call it "ISO-vette") came off the production line on schedule and met the specifications set by the engineers (and advertised in our sales showrooms), we had a quality product.

In the 1980s, quality evolved to the point where it was defined as "conforming to the customer's requirements." This meant that not only did our product have to meet our own specifications, but if we accepted an order from a customer who had additional requirements, we had to meet those as well to claim that we had provided a quality product or service. Using the same example, let's assume that we manufacture our ISO-vette in only six colors: green, blue, silver, red, black, and white. Let's also assume that the production time from placement of an order to delivery of the vehicle is three weeks for a standard product; anything that can be considered as made-to-order will take longer. However, we have a potential customer who really likes our product but wants a custom color (let's say neon orange) and needs it in three weeks to surprise his wife on her birthday. Our sales manager really would like to make this sale and promises that the neon orange ISO-vette will be delivered on the required date. The sales manager has committed our company to meet some additional (customer) requirements. We can now provide a quality product only if the ISO-vette that meets the specifications set by our engineers can be delivered *ahead of schedule* (since we have to provide something out of the ordinary in the same time period as our routine product) and in a *brand-new* color.

The 1990s brought the concept of quality to new heights, where it was defined as being "fit for use." Now, not only does it have to meet our own specifications and all customer specifications that we have accepted, *but it must actually work in the intended application* to be considered a quality product or service. In our example, if the ISO-vette is a roadster and our customer intends to use it to haul his 30-foot yacht to the lake on weekends, we may have a problem. The roadster may not work in the intended application (hauling a heavy load) and would not be considered a quality product. We have not been informed of all the facts by the customer since our process of reviewing customer needs and expectations was not at the level that it should have been. In the eyes of the customer, we have provided him with a product that will not work for him, and therefore it is not a quality product.

The year 2000 standards are based on the concept that quality involves "satisfaction of needs and expectations." These needs and expectations of our customers are generally either stated or implied. The stated needs (for example, neon orange with a delivery date of three weeks) are considered requirements. The implied needs, which are not often communicated (for example, hauling a 30-foot yacht), are the expectations. One perception that appears to be universal is that a majority of organizations in the world will be happy if they can simply meet the customer's requirements; they care very little, if at all, about the customer's expectations. The complementary perception is that fewer organizations, considered to be "world-class" at what they do, have taken the philosophy of customer satisfaction to heart

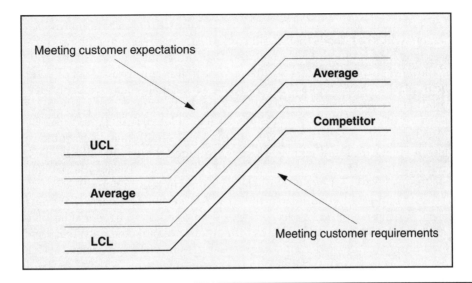

Figure 38.1 World-class quality vision.

and are as concerned with the customer's expectations as they are with the customer's requirements. If we view these two types of companies in a control chart format (see Figure 38.1), we have defined our "vision of quality."

This control chart depicts the philosophy of meeting the customer's requirements as being synonymous with the lower control limit and meeting the customer's expectations as being analogous with the upper control limit. Due to the concept of variability, we typically operate between the two control limits.

With most processes, we want to remain within the control limits—having too many points on one side of the average, falling below the lower control limits (LCL), or falling above the upper control limit (UCL) means that we are not in statistical control. However, in this scenario, to be world-class and meet customer expectations, we want to consistently hit the upper control limit (or at the very least be above average). Many of our competitors will be satisfied in meeting the customer's requirements; this is an opportunity for us to excel. The ISO 9000 standards will assist us in meeting our goals.

Now that we have set the stage for quality and the need for customer satisfaction, let's look at accomplishing this goal from two standpoints: from the viewpoint of those organizations who are not yet compliant with the 1994 revisions of the ISO 9000 series standards and from the viewpoint of those organizations that are currently compliant but want to "upgrade" to the 2000 revisions of the ISO 9000 series standards.

FOR THE "BEGINNER," OR STARTING AFRESH

For those organizations that are not yet compliant, there is the benefit of not having to "reorganize" a system; however, they face the process of having to initially define and implement one. A critical piece of the puzzle is subscribing to the philosophy that the basis of the ISO 9000 series standards is demonstrating *for the customer* the manner in which the organization manages quality. This activity is the heart of the customer–supplier interface, where the organization provides its customers with confidence that it will consistently provide a quality product or service. It is also important to remember that the evidence needed to provide this confidence does not require additional effort, it is simply a subset of what should be in place to provide the organization's own management with confidence in its products, services, and systems (see Figure 38.2).

The ISO 9000:2000 series (ISO 9000:2000, ISO 9001:2000, and ISO 9004:2000) has been developed to clarify the international quality management system philosophy. ISO 9001 and ISO 9004 were developed jointly, with the same sequence and structure, to form a consistent pair of standards. ISO 9000 was developed parallel to ISO 9001 and ISO 9004 to ensure coherent terminology.

It is important to remember the basis for the standards and that they must be used in conjunction with each other to obtain the most benefit. The revised ISO 9001 clearly defines and addresses the quality management system *requirements* for an organization to demonstrate its ability to meet customer needs. The revised ISO 9004 is intended to go beyond the requirements in ISO 9001 to the development of a comprehensive quality management system designed to address the needs of concerned parties. This standard serves as the basis for *performance improvement*. Chapter 4 discusses the consistent pair and the purposes of ISO 9001 and ISO 9004. The revised ISO 9000 is designed to provide the fundamentals for quality management systems and to *define* the terms used in the process. For a complete discussion of the role of ISO 9000:2000 see chapter 3.

The year 2000 standards are based on eight quality management principles (further described in chapter 5) that reflect the management practices developed

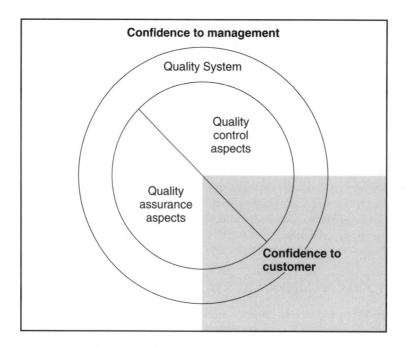

Figure 38.2   Relationship of concepts.

and endorsed by international quality experts. These eight principles are customer focus, leadership, involvement of people, process approach, system approach to management, continual improvement, factual approach to decision making, and mutually beneficial supplier relationships. Principles two through eight have a direct impact on the primary principle, resulting in customer satisfaction.

Keeping the three documents (and their respective roles) in mind, personnel in the organization seeking compliance to the ISO 9001 international quality management system standard should begin by *reading all three standards.* It is not in the best interests of anyone to develop a goal to "become registered" without fully understanding what will be involved in achieving compliance and registration. *Compliance* with ISO 9001 should be an easy decision—the requirements are based on common sense and should serve as the minimum for doing business. In fact, any organization seeking to remain competitive should develop a program to ensure compliance. It does not matter if the organization decides to pursue the next steps to registration; compliance will have a positive impact on satisfying the customer. Whether or not the organization should become *registered* is a business decision and is the final 5 percent of the process. Will there be value added by registration (also known as certification) to the standard? If the answer is yes, then the decision is probably a simple one to make. See chapter 39 for a discussion on demonstrating compliance with ISO 9001.

A review of ISO 9000 will provide the reader with a general overview of quality management systems and the terms used in those systems on an international basis. Clause 2, "Fundamentals for quality management systems" is an excellent place to learn about the basis of quality management: the rationale, approach, focuses, management roles, objectives, evaluation of the system, and improvement processes. It is critical that the organization and its personnel responsible for leading the compliance effort are familiar and comfortable with the concepts discussed in this section of ISO 9000. A review of the terms in clause 3, "Concepts, terms, and definitions" may add a bit more insight, but could also be confusing; readers may be well advised to avoid spending too much time reviewing the terminology until after they have more hands-on experience.

ISO 9001 should be the next document reviewed. As stated under the scope of the standard, ISO 9001 "specifies requirements for a quality management system where an organization needs to demonstrate its capability to consistently provide product that meets customer requirements." The requirements are expected to achieve customer satisfaction through "the effective application of the system, including processes for continual improvement of the system and the assurance of conformity to customer and applicable regulatory requirements."

The requirements defined in ISO 9001 are found in five clauses (4 through 8). While clause 7.2, "Customer-related processes" and clause 8.2.1, "Monitoring and measurement of customer satisfaction" deal *directly* with meeting the requirements and expectations of customers, the remainder of the requirements set in motion a process to ensure that there is a *system* to do so. The standard also allows an organization to exclude those activities (required in clause 7) that are not applicable to the organization.

Finally, the ISO 9004 standard should be reviewed. It is important to note that it is designed to be used *in conjunction with* ISO 9001. ISO 9004 goes beyond the requirements of ISO 9001 to provide guidance on all aspects of a quality management system and to improve the organization's overall performance. In fact, the document can be used to evaluate the maturity of the organization's quality system as performance is enhanced. In other words, ISO 9004 can be used by the organization that wishes to go from meeting a minimum set of requirements (defined in ISO 9001) to becoming a "world-class" organization that is benchmarked and sets the standards for the industry in which it participates.

Once the three documents are reviewed and at least a rudimentary understanding obtained by the personnel who will be responsible for implementation, evidence of executive management support and commitment *must* be obtained. See chapter 1 for additional discussion. In any organization, there are typically several causes of problems, including the following:

- Lack of top management support
- Lack of organization
- Lack of a disciplined approach
- Lack of training
- Lack of resources
- Lack of time

With the exception of the first item, the causes are in no priority order. However, it is imperative that top management support and commitment be in place and visible to the entire organization; without that support, *any* activity will ultimately fail.

Assuming the organization (and the personnel "chosen" to lead the implementation of the quality system) has obtained the needed support, an action plan must be developed. This plan is required whether or not the organization ultimately decides that it would like its quality system to be registered by a third party (registrar). The plan should include the steps shown in Table 38.1.

Many "novice" organizations seeking to develop and implement a quality management system for the first time have a tendency to require activities that make the system a bureaucratic avalanche of paperwork without adding any value to the system or to the organization. Unless something is a legal requirement or specifically mandated by a standard, contract, or other requirement, an organization would be well advised to think through the activity before that activity is implemented.

To picture this, let's look at a quality system matrix with two parameters: the existence of a system (yes or no) and use of common sense in the organization (yes or no). The matrix would be depicted as follows:

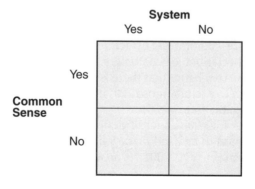

Table 38.1 Quality system implementation.

Action Step	Responsibility
Appoint an implementation team/team leader to coordinate activities for development of a quality management system.	Executive management (including management representative)
Obtain functional and operational support.	Implementation team/team leader; executive management
Identify critical materials and components.	Implementation team; functional and operational units
Identify critical process control instruments and other equipment requiring calibration.	Implementation team; functional and operational units
Select registrar.*	Management representative; implementation team
Develop the organizational quality manual.	Implementation team; functional and operational units
Define requirements; document current procedures and modify them to conform to the quality standard requirements.	Implementation team; functional and operational units
Perform internal audits.	Trained internal quality auditors and/or qualified consultants
Define actions to write, approve, and implement documentation (manuals, procedures, and so on).	Implementation team; functional and operational units
Set target date for compliance.	Executive management; implementation team
Schedule assessment by registrar.*	Management representative

*For organizations that will seek to register their quality systems.

In one of the worst-case scenarios, known as "mindless chaos," there is no system, and absolutely no one in the organization has (or uses) any common sense:

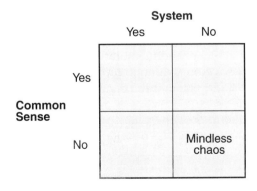

This is, unfortunately, the status of many organizations around the world. In this scenario, nothing is documented, no one is trained (there may be no one capable of being trained!), and the basic thought processes needed to identify and address issues are just not present.

In the next scenario, known as "creative chaos," there is still no system, but at least one person in the organization possesses—and uses—his or her common sense:

System

		Yes	No
Common Sense	Yes		Creative chaos
	No		Mindless chaos

The drawback to this type of organization is that whenever a problem occurs, the organization and its personnel have to "reinvent the wheel" because no one has documented the corrective action used when the problem last occurred. A great deal of time and effort is wasted in organizations that operate in this quadrant.

In the third scenario, known as "mindless bureaucracy," the organization is in at least as poor a position as if it were in the state of mindless chaos:

System

		Yes	No
Common Sense	Yes		Creative chaos
	No	Mindless bureaucracy	Mindless chaos

In this case, a system is in place, but no one has given any thought to how it may impact the operation. For example, the manager who developed this system may require that *every* document be authorized by 15 people, when only one may be sufficient. To make matters worse, if this policy were allowed to remain, it would mean that letters and memoranda would also need to be approved when, if common sense were used, no approvals would be necessary. In this quadrant, activities do not add value to the organization; they are actually counterproductive and expensive.

In the final scenario, known as the "quality management system (QMS) zone," a system is in place, and it was developed by personnel using their common sense:

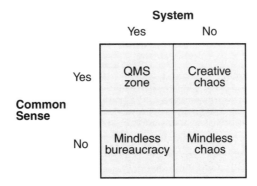

In this quadrant, which is where organizations want to be, an effective system is in place that meets all applicable requirements, is appropriate, and adds value to the organization.

In our quest for documenting and implementing an effective quality management system, the next step entails developing an implementation plan that is reasonable and realistic. An often-asked question is "How long will it take me to be compliant with the standard?" The answer is: "It depends." If an organization can barely spell "quality," let alone have a system, it could take five years or more. In a highly regulated industry (for example, medical device or nuclear) where systems are already in place, the organization could be ready in less than a year. The "average" organization, if there were one, would require 15 to 18 months. The process is not simple and requires good time and project management skills. A generic plan and its associated timing are found in Table 38.2. For those organizations that desire to have their quality systems registered, activities associated with that goal are included in the plan.

Once the quality management system (located in the "quality zone") is in place and has been implemented, the organization should experience several benefits. However, it is important that the organization establish measures to assess the performance of its quality management system and, more importantly, monitor the system to ensure that it is adequate, meets the needs of the organization (and its customers), and adds value to the business. Some of the more common paybacks of an effective quality management system include these:

• *Enhanced partnering relationships between organizations and customers.* The trend in the relationship between customers and those organizations providing them with products and services has been one of "partnering." All organizations are seeking ways to work together and work smarter at the same time. This philosophy will result in customer loyalty and reduced costs/increased profits for all involved.

• *Implementation of a prevention attitude in the organization.* This benefit is attributable to the basis of quality costs, which are divided into the costs of appraisal, prevention, internal failure, and external failure. For the past two decades the quality evolution has been toward enhancing prevention activities. A quality management system should be based on prevention activities that will ultimately result in cost containment by reducing total cost of quality.

Table 38.2 Implementation planning.	
Activity	**Timing (Weeks)**
Obtain management support/commitment.	1–3
Assign a management representative and deputy.	3–5
Perform initial system preassessment audit.	8–9
Identify areas for improvement.	10–15
Develop strategic quality plan and objectives.	12–18
Present internal seminars and workshops.	14–16
Hold review/progress meetings.	14–52
Develop quality manual (level 1 document).	14–20
Develop procedures (level 2 documents).	16–30
Provide internal auditor training.	16–17
Develop work instructions (level 3 documents).	18–50
Develop forms, tags, and labels (level 4 documents).	20–50
Implement quality system.	20–52
Establish measures of system performance.	20–24
Select registrar.	21–35
Perform internal audits.	21–50
Implement corrective actions.	22–60
Management review of quality system.	22–60
Perform second system preassessment audit.	40–41
Evaluate/perform corrective actions to quality manual.	41–50
Measure and evaluate system performance; take any corrective actions needed to ensure adequacy and value-added activities.	45–66
Submit quality manual and application to registrar.	51–52
Registrar preassessment and corrective action.	60–66
Have third-party assessment.	66–68

- *Establishment and maintenance of clear, well-documented procedures.* This goes back to our system matrix. The organization's system should be documented to allow for consistency, training, and objectivity. The key point is to document the quality system so that it makes sense, reduces or eliminates bureaucracy, and adds value.

- *Availability of adequate training.* Training of *all* personnel, including management personnel, in the organization is critical. We cannot expect an employee to properly perform his or her job unless appropriate training has been provided.

Most regulations require personnel to be trained in the regulation; ISO 9001:2000 requires personnel to be trained to the standard to the extent that it affects their jobs. One reason unions are generally supportive of quality systems such as that in the ISO 9000 series is that much of the training for which they had to bargain in the past is ensured by compliance to the requirements of the standard.

• *Greater emphasis to focus on the needs of the customer.* This is what the standards are all about—customer satisfaction and meeting or exceeding customers' requirements and expectations. This concept is so important that a new requirement for measurement of customer satisfaction has been added to the year 2000 revisions.

• *Enhancement of ability to compete in global markets.* Everything else being equal, the organization that has an effective quality management system (registered or not) will have an advantage over its competitors who do not. Customers are looking for assurance that the products and services that they purchase are consistent and meet their requirements. A system compliant with the requirements of the ISO 9001 standard will provide an added thrust for an organization's ability to increase business.

• *Reduction in the number of costly and time-consuming customer audits.* This benefit applies both to organizations and to their customers. Audits are expensive on both sides of the fence. If a customer has confidence in the organization from which it purchases based on a quality system compliant with an accepted international standard, it will be more likely to reduce or eliminate audits of those organizations.

• *Reduction of costly and time-consuming customer incoming inspection and testing.* This takes the previous benefit one step further. If the customer has confidence in its supplier, it may elect to reduce or eliminate incoming inspection or testing activities. This is a saving that goes directly to the bottom line while decreasing the cost of quality.

For those organizations that decide to register their quality management systems, there are a couple of additional potential benefits:

• *Enhanced marketability through the use of a recognizable logo and inclusion in a registered suppliers' listing.* Once an organization is registered to the ISO 9001 standard, it is permitted to use the logos of its registrar and accrediting organizations on virtually everything (within the constraints of the rules provided by the registrar) except its product. This means that an organization can publicize its registration on its letterhead, business cards, and brochures. It can paint the information on the side of its buildings or fly a flag pronouncing its achievement. This is a relatively inexpensive way to market the fact that the organization's documented quality system is recognized around the world. In addition, most registrars also periodically publish a listing of those organizations that they have registered. This is another *free* source of marketing.

• *Assessment by an independent third party, indicating compliance with a set of internationally accepted unbiased criteria.* Having an independent third party assess an organization's quality management system to an internationally accepted set of requirements shows that the organization is not just *blowing its own horn*. A positive recommendation by the registrar provides objective evidence that an effective, compliant system has been implemented.

Finally, those organizations attempting to obtain compliance and/or registration for the first time should recognize that there are a variety of ways to accomplish the same end, some of which are better than others. This advice can be put into a list of *dos* and *don'ts*. The list can be extensive; however, here are some of the more important considerations:

- Do obtain top management support and commitment before proceeding with a program to develop and implement a quality management system
- Do use common sense when developing the system, attempting to add value
- Do not create a bureaucracy that provides no benefit
- Do not correlate the number of pages or weight of the documents with the quality of information or the system
- Do use a team approach during development and implementation
- Do ensure that personnel receive the training required to perform their jobs and to implement the system
- Do develop the system internally
- Do not select a consultant based on price alone
- Do ensure that the consultant selected is experienced and familiar with your industry
- Do not expect (or allow) the consultant to develop the quality system for the organization
- Do begin to perform internal quality audits as soon as possible
- Do make certain top management is always aware of progress, issues, and roadblocks
- Do not rush to complete the system
- Do not develop the system only because a customer asks for it
- Do develop the system because of the value it adds and the potential for continuous improvement

FOR THE EXPERIENCED: TRANSITIONING TO ISO 9001:2000

For organizations that are already compliant with/registered to the ISO 9001:1994 or ISO 9002:1994 standard, much of the learning curve has already been satisfied. The philosophies embodied in the international quality management system standards should, by this time, be second nature. The potential pitfalls and problems associated with compliance have already been experienced, and many of the potential benefits have been realized. With the emphasis on the business process structure of the revised standards, the comfort of the 20-clause standard that many organizations have dealt with for over a decade is now a thing of the past.

Chapter 8 discusses the major changes from ISO 9001:1994 to ISO 9001:2000 and discusses the impact of these changes. The significant changes in the year 2000 revisions of ISO 9001 and ISO 9004 include the following:

- The year 2000 revisions are a *radical* change to the structure of the 1994 revision of ISO 9001. While the new ISO 9001 retains the essence of the original 20 requirements, they have been *repositioned* into five main sections: quality management system requirements; management responsibility; resource management; product and/or service realization; and measurement, analysis, and improvement.

- The ISO 9004 standard has been revised so that the format and language are consistent with ISO 9001. ISO 9004:2000 has also been updated to accommodate modern management practices and includes a guideline to self-assessment.

- The consistency between ISO 9001:2000 and ISO 9004:2000 and the more logical sequence of requirements and guidelines, are necessary to help users cope with the standards' new process orientation.

- An enhanced requirement of *continual improvement* has been introduced into ISO 9001.

- A provision for *exclusions* of requirements for product realization has been introduced in ISO 9001 as a way to accommodate the wide spectrum of organizations, industries, and activities.

- A new requirement for evaluation of customer satisfaction has been introduced in ISO 9001, providing key information for continual improvement.

- Attention has been placed on the need to provide and make available the necessary resources, which now include elements such as information, communication, infrastructure, and work environment.

- Terminology changes have been introduced, notably, *organizatio*n replaces *supplier*, and *supplier* replaces *subcontractor*.

This chapter does not describe the current ISO 9001 requirements and the details for compliance with those requirements. However, it is important for a currently compliant or registered organization to develop a plan to ensure that it meets the requirements of the year 2000 standards. It is also important to remember that it was not the intent of Technical Committee 176 to generate business for consultants and an organization's employees by requiring that current documented quality systems be rewritten to follow the format of the revised standards. The quality system should be used for the *organization*, not the external auditor. If an organization and its management feel that it would be in the best interests of and add value to the organization, they may elect to rewrite their documents (primarily the quality manual). However, there is no requirement to do so!

One recommended action plan for the organization that wishes to *upgrade* and ensure compliance with ISO 9001:2000 appears in Table 38.3.

This entire process should take less than six months, plenty of time to meet any transition period requirements.

There is one final activity that needs to be stressed, that is, focusing (or refocusing) the system on the customer. Companies have seemingly forgotten about the customer in their quest to build bigger and better programs and systems that they used to boast about the quality of their products and services. In many cases,

Table 38.3 Upgrade planning.
Activity
Confirm management support/commitment.
Confirm the management representative and deputy.
Select/confirm an upgrade/implementation team to be responsible to lead the process.
Review and understand the requirements in the ISO 9001:2000 standard. In addition, review the ISO 9000:2000 and ISO 9004:2000 standards (see discussion in the preceding section for the novice organization).
Provide appropriate training to all employees of the organization by qualified personnel.
Prepare a listing of all requirements in the ISO 9001:2000 standard.
Cross-reference the revised requirements to the current documents and determine where elements need to be strengthened and/or (re)written (gap analysis).
Use this book to compare the requirements of ISO 9001:1994 and ISO 9001:2000. This will enable the organization to match subclause to subclause. Pay particular attention to use of the term "shall," indicating a mandatory activity or requirement.
Close the gaps identified by documenting the appropriate activities, policies, and procedures needed for compliance (in particular the new requirements).
Establish measures of system performance.
Perform internal audits.
Identify areas for improvement.
Develop strategic quality plan and objectives.
Hold review/progress meetings.
Implement revised quality system.
Perform internal audits to revised quality management system.
Implement corrective actions.
Have management review revised quality system.
Evaluate/perform corrective actions to quality manual and other documentation.
Measure and evaluate system performance; take any corrective actions needed to ensure adequacy and value.

the data that they referenced did not come from the entities that should have been the primary focus of the survey, the customer.

There are several new or enhanced requirements in ISO 9001:1994:

- Customer focus (clause 5.2), where executive management is required to ensure that the requirements of their customers are identified and met. Companies are encouraged to add this topic to the agendas of their management review meetings.

- Customer communication (clause 7.2.3), where the organization determines and implements effective systems for communicating with their customers. Topics include, at a minimum, product information, contract review and amendments, and customer feedback (including customer complaints).
- Monitoring and measurement of customer satisfaction (clause 8.2.1), including customer perception of the organization's ability to meet their needs.

There is excellent guidance in ISO 9004:2000 that provides companies with potential methods to go beyond just compliance with the requirements. Activities such as market research, review of competitor product and information, complaint trending and analysis (and timely response to the customer), customer satisfaction surveys, and benchmarking studies will not only provide an organization with objective information relative to their level of customer satisfaction, it will also enhance the communications and relationships with those customers and aid in the development of partnerships.

The *experienced* organization will have had up to 13 years managing its quality system to the ISO 9000 series standards. Hopefully, the system has matured and improved along the way, providing for a relatively simple transition to compliance with the year 2000 standards. As mentioned previously, the most difficult roadblock will be "forgetting" about the 20-clause structure and becoming familiar with the new configuration.

Once an organization has transitioned to compliance, it would be appropriate for it to adopt the philosophy of the ISO 9004:2000 standard, that is, to advance to world class, creating an environment and structure that enables it to satisfy customer requirements and expectations by going above the upper control limit of the world-class quality vision.

In either scenario (starting afresh or upgrading), the project should be aggressively managed and tracked. A variety of tools exists to assist the implementation team in this effort. There are several commercially available software systems that manage projects and allow users to use calendars, Pert charts, and Gantt charts to keep the assignment on schedule. Such software also allows users to manage tasks and resources to achieve their goals. In a large or complex organization, tools such as project management software are extremely useful, if not essential.

From a continuous improvement standpoint, corrective action software can be extremely useful. A variety of reports can be generated from these systems and can be beneficial in management review and communications. With the added requirements of measurement of customer satisfaction, these same systems can be used to manage complaints and the results of surveys.

Organizations that have embraced the quality management principles embodied in the ISO 9000 series standards have made considerable investments. Those investments will result in increased profits, lower cost of quality, and enhanced customer satisfaction. The recommendations made in this chapter are presented as guidance and should not be construed as the only way to accomplish compliance. The information provided in the rest of this text will serve as further assistance to the reader.

SUMMARY

The original intent of the ISO 9000 series standards, even going back to the original documents published in 1987, was to focus on the needs of the customer. Unfortunately, this philosophy was lost in the rush of companies wishing to be the *first on the block* to achieve registration. The organization's quality system saw the benefits from ISO 9000, but the customer slowly faded into the sunset while their suppliers pontificated to each other about whose system was best. The quality of documents improved, but the quality did not necessarily follow.

The 1994 revisions to the standards did not resolve the lack of customer focus; they merely clarified wording in the original standard. Documents continued to proliferate; customer confidence in their suppliers and their supplier's products and services did not.

The year 2000 standards go a long way to increasing focus on the customer. ISO 9001:2000 clearly identifies requirements for *customer focus* and *customer-related processes*. A startling new concept for *customer communication* defines the common sense activity of talking with your customers; the requirement for monitoring and measurement of customer satisfaction provides the company with feedback to enhance their customer responsiveness, product quality, and level of service. In all cases, ISO 9004:2000 provides additional guidance and accepted practices to achieve these requirements.

We've been talking about focusing on the customer for about 14 years—now we're really doing it!

Chapter 39

Certification and Conformity Assessment

Dale Misczynski
President and CEO, The Isoagile Group, Austin, Texas

WHAT IS CONFORMITY ASSESSMENT?

Conformity assessment is a process by which an organization has its products, processes, or systems evaluated against specified requirements. In the context of this book, ISO 9001:2000 comprises the "specified requirements," and "systems" comprise the organization's quality management system. Thus, our focus is on conformity assessment of an organization's quality management system against the requirements of ISO 9001:2000.

WHEN AND WHY IS CONFORMITY ASSESSMENT IMPORTANT?

Customer Requirements

There are many reasons that an organization may wish to demonstrate that its quality management systems conform to ISO 9001:2000. First and perhaps most importantly, the customer may require that the organization demonstrate conformity to the standard. Many customers, in their quest to ensure that they receive products and services of a known quality level, stipulate that their suppliers must implement and operate their quality systems in a specified manner. ISO 9000 serves as a common framework to achieve that requirement.

Some industry sectors have found a need to develop quality system standards that are unique to their industries. This was done because the requirements of ISO 9001 are of a minimal nature and are not stringent enough for these industries. These industry, or sector-specific, variants are built on the framework of ISO 9001 and are driven and owned by industry groups. For example, the Automotive Industry Action Group "owns" QS-9000, the automotive industry quality system standard. With the possible exception of Japanese automotive manufacturers, the automotive industry worldwide requires that its suppliers demonstrate conformity to QS-9000 or to its derivative, TS 16949. See chapter 48 for a discussion of the automotive industry quality system standards. Another example is Quality Excellence for Suppliers of Telecommunications (The QuEST Forum), which has developed a standard specifically for telecommunications equipment manufacturers. The large telecommunications service providers, such as the regional Bell operating companies, require suppliers to demonstrate conformity to TL 9000. See chapter 60. A similar movement is apparent in the aerospace industry with AS 9000. The Aerospace Industries Association is the key driver of this standard.

An interesting problem that is emerging, is that some manufacturers are suppliers to two or more of these industry segments that require specialized quality system certifications. The conformity assessment industry has not responded with a solution to combine the multiple assessments.

Thus, customers have an important influence in a company's need to demonstrate conformity to ISO 9000. In the majority of circumstances, the customer will drive the need to comply to the standard as well as the means used to demonstrate compliance.

Government Regulation

If a company trades internationally, the need for demonstrating conformity to ISO 9000 increases. Within the European Community (EC), there are a series of product directives that define the requirements for specific product categories. The product directives cover a wide spectrum of products and define the EC quality and performance requirements for the products covered. A partial list of the product directives is included in Table 39.1. A complete list is available at http://www.newapproach.org/directiveList.asp.

The directives cover the product families that have requirements for quality assurance conformity assessment. In other words, the directives cover what must be considered by candidates for conformity assessment. The European Council Resolution of 1989 on the global approach to certification and testing states the following guiding principles for EC policy on conformity assessment:

- EC legislation develops a consistent approach by devising modules for the various phases of conformity assessment procedures and by setting criteria for the use of these procedures, for the designation of bodies operating these procedures, and for the use of the CE marking.
- The use of European standards relating to quality assurance (EN ISO 9000 series) and to the requirements to be fulfilled by conformity assessment bodies operating quality assurance (EN 45000 series) is generalized.
- Establishing accreditation systems and the use of intercomparison techniques are promoted in member states and at the EC level.

Table 39.1 The product directives promulgated by the European Community cover a wide range of product areas. Approximately 15 percent of products will be covered by one or more of the directives.

Construction products	Machine safety
Electrical appliances	Motor vehicles
Electrical equipment	Roadworthiness
EM compatibility	Emissions
Explosive atmosphere	Safety belts, etc.
Machine controls	Measuring instruments
Telecom terminals	Medical devices
CRTs—emissions	Personal protective equipment
Electrical lifts	Pressure vessels
Furniture—flammability	Safety signs
Gas appliances	Toys
General product safety	Tractors
House appliances—noise	Weighing systems
Hydraulic diggers—noise	Workplace equipment

Conformity assessment is based on:

- Manufacturers' internal design and production control activities.

- Many products covered by the directives have specific technical requirements. These may be in the area of interface, emissions, safety, or biohazards. Testing to determine conformance is usually called "type approval" and may be accomplished by a third party or the manufacturer's internal processes, or a combination of both.

- Third-party type or design examination combined with third-party approval of product or production quality assurance systems, or third-party product verification.

- Third-party unit verification of design and production.

- Third-party approval of full quality assurance systems.

There are several important thoughts to be gleaned from these guidelines. First, the EC does *not* require that the quality assurance system of a manufacturer doing business in Europe be certified; manufacturers can demonstrate conformity using alternative routes or modules. Second, the EC promotes accreditation and third-party conformity assessment. Thus, while the EC can take the position that certification is voluntary, it is much easier to have the quality assurance system certified than to pursue any of the alternative routes.

For a detailed explanation of the European requirements, the reader should obtain a copy of *Guide to the Implementation of Directives Based upon the New Approach and the Global Approach*. This excellent treatise on the subject is available at no cost on the EC Web site and may be downloaded as an Acrobat file. The URL is http://europa.eu.int/comm/enterprise/newapproach/legislation.htm. Within the United States, companies operating in the medical area have specific quality systems requirements that can be partially fulfilled by demonstrating conformity to ISO 9000. The Food and Drug Administration (FDA) has revised the good manufacturing practice (CGMP) requirements for medical devices and incorporated them into a quality system regulation standard. The quality system standard includes requirements related to the methods used in, and the facilities and controls used for, designing, manufacturing, packaging, labeling, storing, installing, and servicing medical devices intended for human use. This action is necessary to add preproduction design controls and to achieve consistency with quality system requirements standards worldwide.

The FDA requirements are complex and demand very careful attention because of the legal liabilities associated with nonconformity. Companies operating in this area should obtain professional advice on the best approach.

Marketing Advantage

Some companies may choose to demonstrate their conformity to ISO 9000 as a way to differentiate themselves from their competitors. They may wish to advertise that they operate "in compliance to the international standard for quality assurance: ISO 9001." There are many ways of communicating the message. In some areas of business this message might make a difference. When the supplier has a well-known brand, the customer probably bases a buying decision more on the brand than on the statement of the type of quality assurance system.

There are some very specific directions in the way that a company can use its ISO 9000 certification for market promotion. It is important to understand that the company's quality system is certified, not its products or services. Thus, one could say that the products come from an ISO 9000–certified factory, but you can't say that the products themselves are ISO 9000 certified. ISO has an excellent guide titled *Publicizing Your ISO 9000 or ISO 14000 Certification*, which is available as a free download from its Web site, www.iso.ch, and gives clear direction in terms of what is allowable and what is not.

If one company advertises conformity to the quality system standard, others will follow. When the majority of companies competing within a specific market segment can demonstrate conformity to the quality system standard, there is little differentiation over that factor. Hence, it does not significantly alter the customers buying decision. From a marketing perspective, building the value of the brand is critical. It is uncertain, particularly in the consumer sector, if certification contributes to that value.

A Tool for Improvement

The application of ISO 9000 may serve as the basis for improvement within a company. If a company has little or no quality assurance system, the design of a quality system based on ISO 9001:2000 would be a step along a journey of improvement. In this context the improvements in process development, process documentation, and management review are helpful and can contribute to an overall improvement in company activities. Demonstrating conformity to the standard is one step that the company should take to understand the progress that it has achieved in that journey. That is, normally this demonstration requires some sort of audit against the standard. The audit findings serve to identify gaps in the current process as measured against the requirements of the standard, and these gaps, in turn, can serve to drive actions for improvement.

WHAT ARE THE METHODS TO DEMONSTRATE CONFORMITY?

There are several different methods that an organization can use to demonstrate conformity to a standard, such as ISO 9001:2000. The organization needs to make a choice depending on its motivation. Many factors may enter into this decision, such as relationships with customers, maturity of the quality system, and the regulatory environment in which the organization desires to operate.

The three different methods of demonstrating conformity are first party, second party, and third party.

- First Party: the organization declares its conformity to the requirements. This is called "Suppliers Declaration of Conformity" (SDoC).

- Second Party: a customer conducts an audit of the organization and indicates the organization is in conformity to the requirements. The customer may choose to share the results with other customers.

- Third Party: the organization hires a qualified independent firm to assess the organization's conformity against the requirements. Upon finding the organization to be in conformity, the third party can issue a certificate stating that the organization is in conformity with the requirements.

Each of these has a legitimate place in business, and none will fulfill the market requirements 100 percent of the time. Thus, most companies will find that they will have to understand the relationships among the three formats and use the proper format depending on the circumstances. Figure 39.1 illustrates the relationship between the three methods.

First-Party Method

In many cases, the company can use the Suppliers Declaration of Conformity (SDoC) to demonstrate conformity to ISO 9001:2000, or any standard for that matter. ISO/IEC Guide 22:1996, *General criteria for supplier's declaration of conformity*, sets forth the proper application of SDoC. This method represents the most cost-effective method for a company to demonstrate conformity with a standard. It is widely used to demonstrate conformity to product standards, particularly in the information technology area. One has only to leaf through a manual supplied with a personal computer or peripheral to see a Compliance Information Statement or Declaration of Conformity Statement—statements that the manufacturer has taken the proper steps to ensure that the products they are supplying comply to the indicated standards. These statements are applicable to safety, interface, emission, and other standards.

Recently, the Information Technology Industry Council, a U.S. industry trade group, has undertaken an extensive campaign to educate regulators, customers, and consumers on the benefits of SDoCs. Clearly, wider use of this technique can offer some cost reduction for the manufacturer and bring innovative products to the market at a faster pace. This idea is starting to gain market acceptance.

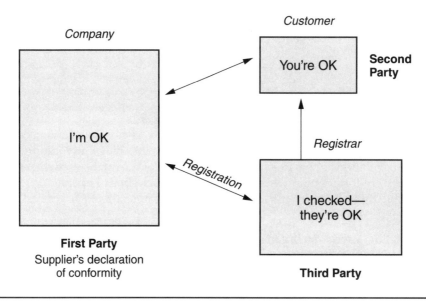

Figure 39.1 There are three different, although interrelated, methods of demonstrating conformity to a standard.

In the automotive area, every car that is sold in the United States has a sticker, usually on the window, that indicates that the vehicle complies with all applicable EPA and DOT requirements. This is another example of an SDoC; the automobile manufacturer is declaring that the relevant requirements have been met.

It must be understood that there are also some potential liabilities in using an SDoC. Usually, an executive of the company must sign an SDoC. Should litigation arise over some failure in the product or service covered by the declaration, the individual signing the declaration could potentially be liable for civil or criminal penalties. However, similar conditions exist in the other two methods. In the case of the third-party method, where a company is certified by a registrar, the company still bears the full responsibility for its actions. The registrar usually avoids any legal responsibility and requires the company to indemnify the registrar from damages.

There are those who contend, in fact, that is one of the strengths of the SDoC. Having a senior executive of the company attest to the company's demonstration of conformity might have more strength than a certificate signed by a third party who declines any liability in the process.

There is one major misunderstanding concerning the SDoC. It is not "self-certification." There is no legitimate place for self-certification at this time. Certification implies that a third party confirms that the company has demonstrated conformity to a standard. In the case of the SDoC, the manufacturer "declares" that the requirements of the standard have been met. The term self-certification has been widely misused and misunderstood.

Second-Party Method

In many cases there is a contractual requirement that a supplier operate a quality assurance system in accordance with certain requirements. Commonly, that is ISO 9001 or one of its derivatives. The customer may retain the right to verify that the supplier does, in fact, have a quality assurance system that meets the requirements. Many times the customer may send an audit team to verify that the system is in place and is operating correctly. This is called a second-party demonstration of conformity. The customer checks to determine that the system is in conformity.

Many proponents of third-party certification have indicated that having a third party certify that the quality system is in conformity to the standard eliminates the need for customers to audit their suppliers. That is partially true. In fact, most companies find that the relative frequency of quality system audits does decline but not disappear completely. Customers, for whom the supplier represents a critical link, sometimes find it very difficult to depend on a third-party auditor, especially if the supplier is a mission-critical element. A customer's auditor will normally have greater expertise in those areas that are critical to their requirements.

Some companies treat customer audits as bothersome and wastes of time. In some cases that might be true. However, the audits could also be a major tool in relationship building between the supplier and customers. There are several steps that should be undertaken to foster that relationship.

First, you and the customer should have a clear understanding of the requirements. Set the customer's and your expectations carefully. Make sure that you can meet, or exceed, the expectations. Identify the areas where you exceed the requirements so that they can be highlighted to the customer. Also, make sure that you understand the gaps, the deficiencies, in your processes. If they can't be remedied in time for the customer audit, it usually makes sense to identify them up front to the customer's auditor.

Second, be prepared. Make sure that you are in a position to respond to all the requirements. A little preparation will go a long way in terms of making the audit visit run smoothly and positively.

Third, communicate with the customer audit team during the audit process. That will tend to eliminate surprises on both sides. If you treat this as a learning experience on both sides, the audit process will run much smoother.

Fourth, in the closing meeting, come to clearly defined agreements as to how you will react to each of the findings. Do not leave things open-ended. This is the best time to set expectations, both internally and with the customer, as to your response and actions.

Finally, use the entire process as a step in building the relationship with your customer. The customer is spending money to audit your process. You should take that as a signal that they want to conduct business with you. You should also understand that they are trying to help you improve as a supplier.

All things considered, a customer audit of your quality system is a win–win situation for all concerned, you and the customer. A third-party audit can never replace that relationship-building potential.

Third-Party Method

What's a third party? Basically, a third party is someone a company hires to verify, through a structured assessment process, that the company is operating in accordance with a particular standard, in this case, ISO 9001:2000 or one of its derivatives. The organization that conducts the assessment to determine conformity is normally called a registrar in the United States; in Europe and other parts of the world, it is called a certifier. Sometimes the terms *registration body* or *certification body* are used. They all perform the same function around the world, irrespective of their name.

The industry of conformity assessment, composed of certifiers/registrars and accreditors has become a major industry in the last 30 years. It's important to understand the difference between registration and accreditation, because they are different and yet people get them confused.

ACCREDITATION

Accreditation is the process used to determine if an individual or organization is competent to perform a particular function. On the other hand, registration or certification is a procedure by which a third party gives formal written assurance that an organization's products, processes, or services conform to certain specified requirements. There are fundamental differences between the two.

The word *accredit* is an interesting word, with the same root as *credible*, or believable. An accredited institution, therefore, is one that can be believed. It has earned the approval of those who know it.

Accreditation means the following:

This organization is fulfilling its stated purpose with integrity and excellence.

Universities are accredited to teach certain curriculum. For example, the Accreditation Council for Graduate Medical Education might accredit a university that has a medical curriculum. That means that the Accreditation Council for Graduate Medical Education has determined that, following its procedures, the particular university will receive formal written recognition that it is qualified to conduct an educational program in the particular field of medicine for which it has been accredited. People can also be accredited.

In the context of ISO 9000, the registrar is accredited to perform assessments of companies against the ISO 9001 standard. Then, based on the outcome of the assessment, the registrar is allowed to give written formal recognition that the company meets the requirements of ISO 9001. This recognition is in the form of a certificate containing the name of the registrar, the lead assessor, and the accreditation body. It must be noted that some registrars are not accredited.

In the United States, the National Accreditation Program is operated by the Registrar Accreditation Board (RAB), which was established in 1989 by the American Society for Quality (ASQ). Its original mission was to provide accreditation services for ISO 9000 quality management systems (QMS) registrars. The new organization was structured as an independent legal entity. RAB is governed and operated independently from ASQ. When RAB was first created, it immediately sought to strengthen the U.S. system for registrar accreditation by pursuing a formal relationship with the American National Standards Institute (ANSI). In 1991 ANSI and RAB joined forces to establish the American National Accreditation Program for Registrars of Quality Systems.

The next year RAB introduced QMS course-provider accreditation and auditor certification programs that were separate from the joint program with ANSI. Then in 1996, with the release of new ISO 14000 Environmental Management Systems (EMS) standards, the ANSI–RAB National Accreditation Program (NAP) was formed, replacing the original joint program. The NAP covers the accreditation of QMS and EMS registrars as well as accreditation of providers of QMS and EMS auditor training courses. Certification programs for both EMS and QMS auditors are operated solely by RAB, separate from the NAP. RAB policy is established by the RAB board of directors and, for those programs operated with ANSI, by a Joint Oversight Board populated equally by representatives of each organization.

RAB, headquartered in Milwaukee, Wisconsin, is a not-for-profit organization that is financially self-supported and governed by a 15-member board of directors. Members of the board represent both quality and environmental stakeholders and include technical experts, business executives, industry representatives, and employees of registrar organizations.

RAB has accredited over 50 organizations to conduct conformity assessment against the ISO 9000 standards. There are many different types of registrars, and their fields of expertise are defined by the scope of their accreditation. That is, registrars must demonstrate competence in the particular areas for which they seek accreditation. There are 40 major areas, or scope categories, for which registrars might seek accreditation. Table 39.2 lists the categories.

It costs money for registrars to add scopes to their accreditations. Hence, they are only going to have scopes if they have viable business opportunities in those business areas. They will have to undergo ongoing surveillance audits to ensure that they are complying with competency requirements.

REGISTRATION

A registrar is a third-party company contracted to evaluate if an organization's quality management system complies with the requirements of the ISO 9000 standards and issue a registration certificate. There are several important differences between registration bodies, or registrars, and accreditation bodies, or accreditors. First, the accreditation body is a not-for-profit organization. Within the area of quality systems accreditation, all national accreditation bodies are in that category. On the other hand, registration bodies, or registrars, are profit-making companies. Second, there is typically a single accreditation body within a country. There is no limit on the number of registrars that may choose to pursue business opportunities within a country, irrespective of whether they are accredited by that country's accreditation body.

For example, there are presently 52 registrars accredited by RAB to perform quality system assessments and award certificates. There are another nine applicants in the queue. At the same time, there are some registrars who are operating within the United States who are accredited by accreditation bodies from other countries. There are also registrars who have no accreditation or are accredited by an independent accreditation body; in these cases certification costs may be lower,

Table 39.2 There are 40 different business areas in which a registrar may be accredited to conduct business. In the process of selecting a registrar, the organization must make certain that the registrar is accredited in the business area within which the organization operates.

Scope Category	Scope Description	Scope Category	Scope Description
01	Agriculture, hunting, forestry, and fishing	20	Shipbuilding
		21	Aerospace
02	Mining and quarrying	22	Other Transport Equipment
03	Food products, beverages, and tobacco		
		23	Manufacturing Not Elsewhere Classified
04	Textiles and Textile Products		
05	Leather and leather products	24	Recycling
		25	Electricity Supply
06	Wood and wood products	26	Gas Supply
07	Pulp, Paper, and Paper Products	27	Water Supply
08	Publishing	28	Construction
09	Printing	29	Wholesale and Retail Trade; Motor Vehicle Repair, Motorcycles, Personal and Household Goods
10	Coke and Refined Petroleum Products		
11	Nuclear Fuel	30	Hotels and Restaurants
12	Chemicals, Chemical Products, and Fibers	31	Transport, Storage, and Communications
13	Pharmaceuticals	32	Financial Intermediation, Real Estate, Renting
14	Rubber and Plastic Products		
15	Nonmetallic Mineral Products	33	Information Technology
		34	Engineering Services
16	Concrete, Cement, Lime, Plaster, and so on	35	Other Services
		36	Public Administration
17	Basic Metals and Fabricated Metal Products	37	Education
18	Machinery and Equipment	38	Health and Social Work
		39	Other Social Services
19	Electrical and Optical Equipment	40	Medical Devices

but the probability of the certification being useful for international trade purposes is lessened. That is, other accreditation bodies that are members of the International Accreditation Forum's Multi Lateral Agreement Group would not recognize the accreditation.

SELECTION OF A REGISTRAR

So, how does one select a registrar? Candidly, much of the selection process has to do with chemistry. In the end it is not easy to change registrars, so you should be comfortable with the relationship that will exist between the registrar and your organization.

Let's start with something basic. Why are you seeking registration?

- Is registration seen as a tool for improvement? Do you expect that the process of driving for the certificate will cause improvement and rigor within your organization?

- Do your customers require that your quality system pass a test that you must demonstrate through the process of registration? Is this a marketing tool? Are your competitors registered and you must follow suit?

- Are regulatory requirements forcing you to become registered?

- Will the process of registration enhance your control over the organization? Does it give you a stick to influence the direction of the organization?

Each of these, or variants, are frequently cited as the reason for registration. Whatever the purpose, it's important that you know exactly why you are going through the process because to some degree the reasons for registration, both verbalized and unsaid, will guide you in choosing a registrar.

The next factor to consider is the intended scope of your registration. In this context the scope means, just as it did for accreditation, the business area within which you will conduct business. In the United States scopes are easily defined by the Standard Industry Classification (SIC) codes, which are used for economic analysis by the United States government. Every economic activity fits into one SIC code.

The scope, or SIC code, of your business unit to be registered must align with the accreditation scope of your selected registrar. That is, if your business manufactures plastic hoses, you must make sure that the registrars you are considering have been accredited to scope category 14, plastic or rubber products. It is important that the registrar you select be accredited in the scope in which you conduct business. Registrars do not cover every category so make certain your registrar covers your scope. It is also important to understand that registrars tend to specialize. It is not wise to deal with a registrar that does not specialize in your area of scope.

The next factor to consider is the geographic extent of your business. If the main reason for registration is to export to Europe, it might be in your best interests to work with a registrar who has experience operating in that environment. There are many registrars who have their roots in Europe. Many of these are very broadly based and do business on a global scale. They will have experience in the various requirements of CE marking and the EC directives.

For example, if your firm manufactures telecommunications that connects to the public switched network and you wish to export to the European market, the odds are that you must comply with the telecommunications directive. In the case of directive compliance, dealing with a registrar who is also a "notified body" under that directive can be an advantage. Some of the European registrars operating in North America such as KEMA and BABT are also "notified bodies" for one or more of the various European directives. They would bring a higher level of expertise to the encounter.

What about geographical coverage? Several registrars have global operations. If you have sites in several countries, then this would be a consideration. In general, you should try to focus your registration business with one registrar rather then to have different registrars in each country. Maximize your purchasing power!

As part of the process, ask the registrar for references. You must recognize that they will always give you "good" references. That's OK, as long as you understand that situation. Once you have interviewed the "good references," go to one of the publicly available databases that list registered companies and select companies who have been registered by the candidate. It makes sense to try to select companies that are about your size and complexity. Contact their quality managers and then learn the "true" story about the registrar.

All these factors should be taken into account in your decision-making process. Is the chemistry of the situation becoming clear?

Each registrar should be able to give you a proposal that includes schedule, costs, and terms and conditions.

Does the schedule fit your plans? How flexible is the registrar? Normally, the schedule is driven by the availability of auditors. Lack of flexibility can imply that the registrar is understaffed. That is not a good indicator for the future, because you will want a degree of flexibility in scheduling.

The overall costs are a function of several issues:

- Audit day rate and travel policy
- Preassessment
- Assessment
- Number of audit days

Let's look at all five issues. The first is the basic cost of an auditor's day. Currently, that rate can vary between $900 and $1500 per day. The experience of the auditors, the flexibility of the registrar, and overall market conditions will impact price. Audit days are a commodity. The registrar's travel policy is linked with the day rate. In most cases, you should not be charged for travel time although you should expect to pay direct out-of-pocket travel expenses. Normal policies are that domestic air travel is coach class and transoceanic is business class. If your company has a travel policy make sure that the registrar's policy does not provide greater cost exposure. Further, make sure that you understand the expense documentation that the registrar will provide. You might want to make the travel arrangements so that you have better control over the costs.

The bigger your purchase, the lower the price, all other factors being equal. The audit day rate is negotiable.

By this point, you should understand the costs associated with the registration process, the schedule, the registrar's reputation and competencies, and the time, in auditor days, that will be required. Several different evaluation matrices have been developed to evaluate the trade-offs. The RAB Web site (http://www.rabnet.com) has some excellent thoughts on the issue. In the end, you must feel comfortable.

Once you've made the decision, the next step is contract discussions and award. Every registrar has a "standard contract." Few favor the client. You don't have to accept all the terms and conditions of the standard contract. If you have an attorney, have her or him review the proposed contract. You might be better off to have the attorney take the lead in terms of the negotiation of the terms and conditions. A lot of registrars will state that certain clauses are "required by RAB." That is usually not true. RAB dictates very few of the contractual requirements the registrar imposes on the client.

THE PROCESS

Once you have made the decision to seek registration, there is a series of steps that you must follow. The steps may be different for your organization than they are for other organizations, but in the end you will have traveled a similar journey.

First is the decision. The decision to move ahead with registration must have with it a commitment from the senior leadership of the organization. It's very much like the ham-and-eggs metaphor. The leadership must be like the pig, committed.

Second, someone at a fairly senior level must be responsible for and accountable to getting the job done. The responsible person needs the resources, people, money, and time to get the job done. Remember that the cost of the registrar is just one element of the cost equation. There will be many things that must occur within the organization—training, documentation, process mapping—all of which require time and money to accomplish. Experience indicates that it is better to move at a fast pace then a slow pace. You should consider that this effort will improve the organization.

Third, a schedule needs to be developed. Your selected registrar should work with you in developing the schedule because the registrar needs to have auditors available at the planned times.

A communication plan must be developed that "tells the story" to the organization. The process of ISO 9000 registration will involve almost all parts of the organization. The people within the organization need to understand the objective, the plan to get there, their roles, and the expected outcome. That will help to get all pulling in the same direction.

You will begin the "makeready" phase. Usually a gap analysis is conducted to identify the gaps between the present and the standard. An internally staffed audit team does this best. Using an internal team is less threatening, increases the level of ownership, and builds expertise. The gap analysis must examine the organization's procedures, its processes, and the operations to determine their conformity to the requirements embodied within the standard.

Once the gaps have been identified and the processes and procedures developed that meet the clause-by-clause requirements, the essence of a system emerges. The system must be implemented, refined, audited, and improved. It is an adaptive process.

The overall registration process can take anywhere from several weeks to a year or more. The time required is driven by many factors, with the readiness of the organization being the prime factor. Other factors that will modulate the time requirements are the size of the organization, the scope of the registration, and the number, size, and diversity of the sites being registered.

During the process the registrar will analyze many issues. The organization's administrative, design, production, distribution, and support processes will be assessed. The organization's quality systems documentation will be scrutinized. Careful attention will be paid to the personnel training records, minutes, and results of management reviews. The reported findings of internal audits will be reviewed and considered with the appropriate corrective action reports.

Preassessment

A preassessment is an option offered by registrars to help your organization determine its readiness for the registration audit. Other terms for *preassessment* are *preaudit* and *trial audit*. Preassessments offer the opportunity for a "no risk of failure" audit and the experience of a third-party audit. It will normally be tailored to the requirements of the organization.

During a preassessment, the registrar's audit team evaluates all applicable quality system elements for approach, implementation, and amount of evidence available. Audit findings are limited to weak implementation or failure to address an element or requirement. These are described in a written preassessment report; formal nonconformity reports may or may not be issued. Clearly, the nonconformities must be cleared before the "real" assessment. To prevent the perception of consulting or advice giving, the accreditation body limits the number and frequency of preassessments.

In general, organizations that are immature with respect to the ISO 9000 process can benefit from going through the preassessment experience. The amount of audit days to conduct the preassessment is a function of the size, complexity, and scope of the organization.

The Assessment Process

The registration process itself will drive the next variable—the number of audit days involved in the process. It is accomplished through a series of document reviews and facility visits and audits. The registrar's auditors look at an organization's procedures, processes, and operations to determine their conformity to the requirements (elements) of the applicable quality system standard.

The registrar looks at a variety of issues, including but not limited to the applicant organization's administrative, design, and production processes; quality system documentation; personnel training records; management reviews; and internal audit processes.

Number of Audit Days

The IAF provides guidance for the registrar as to the amount of days that should be used to conduct an assessment at an organization.

Table 39.3 shows the framework for the number of days. It is not absolute, despite what some registrars claim. That is, the registrar has a degree of flexibility to increase or decrease the number based on justifiable circumstances. Factors that can affect the number of audit days, for example, are the amount of similarity among departments or sites and the degree of complexity of the processes.

The latest table (yes, it changes) and the supporting commentary are available from the RAB Web site (http://www.rabnet.com/content/qr_crit1.htm) or from the International Accreditation Forum (IAF) Web site (http://www.iaf.nu/).

Table 39.3 The Registrar Accreditation Board provides accredited registrars with guidance on the number of audit days they should use to conduct the initial assessment as well as reassessments.

Number of Employees at Certified Entity	Initial Assessment (Auditor Days)		Annual Surveillance Visits (Auditor Days)		Reassessment Visits (Auditor Days)	
	Total	On-Site Minimum	Total	On-Site Minimum	Total	On-Site Minimum
Less than 5	2.0	1.0	1.0	0.5	1.5	1.0
5–9	2.5	1.5	1.0	0.5	1.5	1.0
10–19	3.0	2.0	1.0	1.0	2.0	1.0
20–29	4.0	2.5	1.5	1.0	3.0	2.0
30–59	6.0	4.5	2.0	1.0	4.0	2.5
60–100	7.0	5.0	2.0	1.5	4.0	3.0
100–250	8.0	6.0	2.5	2.0	5.0	3.0
250–500	10.0	7.0	3.0	2.0	6.0	4.5
500–1000	12.0	9.0	4.0	3.0	8.0	5.5
1000–2000	15.0	12.0	5.0	4.0	10.0	6.5
2000–4000	18.0	14.0	6.0	5.0	12.0	8.0
4000–8000	21.0	17.0	7.0	5.0	14.0	9.0

Why is this important? Just like the other variables, the number of auditor days is negotiable. You need to understand the variables, the constraints, and the degrees of freedom as you negotiate your individual situation. Once you have understood the variables, you stand a better chance of developing a contract that is more balanced, that tilts to your side, that increases the potential value to your company.

Nonconformities

As the registrar's auditors proceed through the assessment, they will probably identify areas where your system, its processes, procedures, or the way you have implemented them do not comply with the clauses of the standard. These findings are called nonconformities. It is important to note that there are several degrees of nonconformities. Typically, these are minor and major nonconformities and possibly observations.

An observation is not a violation of the criteria but typically identifies that there may be a better way to monitor a process or document a procedure. It's not a problem but rather a potential for improvement, a way to avoid future problems.

A minor nonconformity is one that when taken by itself doesn't indicate a systemic problem with the quality management system. It is typically an isolated or random incident. An example would be that the most current version of a document is not available at an operator's station. The updated version exists, but a copy of it is not available for the operator's use. The operator is using an outdated procedure. Other examples are a form that may not have a document control number on it and an internal audit that has an overdue corrective action request.

A major nonconformity occurs when one of the criteria of the standard is not addressed or has not been addressed adequately. Typically, these occur when an organization has not addressed all the requirements of a specific element or criterion. These also occur when an organization has put a process or procedure in place but has not implemented it or cannot yet demonstrate effective implementation. A major nonconformity is a "hold point" that prevents the issuance of a certificate.

A major nonconformity can also occur if a significant number of minor nonconformities in a given activity, or against a given element, point to a systemic failure. For example, a minor nonconformity in document control may not in itself constitute a significant problem. But several (the audit team leader judges what is a significant number) problems with document control point to a systemic problem with document control and would constitute a major nonconformity.

Receiving Approval

Finally, the assessments have been completed, nonconformities have been cleared, and the registrar's representatives advise you that they will recommend your organization for a Certificate of Approval. That means that you have passed the test. Congratulations on step one. And that's all it is, a step.

Awarding the Certificate

A lot of people in the organization have worked very hard to pass this test. It's time for recognition, reward, and celebration. It's also time to communicate your success. Organizations thrive and grow stronger on recognition and success.

Normally, a senior official of the registrar is invited to the company facility to present the certificate to the executive of the organization. The team that actually did all the work is usually invited to the event. Press may be invited depending on the circumstances. Photographs should be taken.

A press release should be prepared to communicate the certification to the media. Many times, a communication is sent to customers. If the registration was customer driven, then this step is critical and must be accomplished with some fanfare. You should consider having key customer representatives participate in the award ceremony.

The achievement should be communicated widely within the company. Registration is not something that can be achieved by just a handful. Everyone in the company is affected in some way.

A copy of the certificate should be digitized and placed on the company's external Web site. This provides customers with evidence of the accomplishment and avoids having to pay the registrar's extra charge for copies of the certificate. It also makes things very easy for the salespeople.

Earlier we discussed the rules of displaying or promoting the certification. This is a good time to start the rollout of various promotional materials.

Surveillance

The accomplishment of receiving the certificate was a step along the path of improvement. The next step is maintaining certification. This is done through a series of surveillance assessments. There is a high degree of variability among registrars as to how this is approached.

The registration must be periodically renewed. The process basically consists of ongoing surveillance audits at six- to 12-month intervals. Some accredited registrars require a complete reassessment every three years and issue a new certificate stating an additional three-year period of registration that is contiguous with the previous period. Surveillance frequency may be extended to every 12 months in this case. The surveillance audit may not cover every element, or clause, of the standard on each visit. The auditor does not necessarily inform you which part of the standard will be assessed.

Other accredited registrars do not perform a complete reassessment on-site at the end of a three-year period. Instead, the effectiveness of the quality management system is determined by previous surveillance audits and the organization's responses to corrective action. In this situation, the registrar performs surveillance audits at six-month intervals "continuously." A registration issued under this arrangement most often will not have an expiration date, implying that the registration is valid unless revoked.

Some registrars offer either option to their clients. This is a topic that needs to be covered during the original contract negotiations with the registrar. Depending on the size and structure of the organization, there are cost implications to the decision.

Two variables involved in surveillance are the periodicity of the audits and the population of the site. The IAF has developed guidance for registrars to use. Registrars differ on the periodicity, the time intervals between surveillance audits, and the audit days per site. The RAB procedures require the surveillance audit at least on an annual basis. The registrar may have a procedure that requires surveillance audits at six-month intervals. That exceeds the international and RAB requirements.

The population at the site will influence the number of audit days required per surveillance audit. Just as RAB has provided a guidance table for the original certification audit, they have also developed guidance for the surveillance visits. The suggested number of days is contained in Table 39.3. Just as there are variables in the use of the table for the certification assessment, there are similar variables in the case of the surveillance visits. One variable is the demographics at the site. That is, a site that has 10 percent of the population in management and administration with 90 percent in production could be treated differently than a site that has 30 percent in design, 30 percent in administration and management, and 40 percent in manufacturing. The former should require fewer audit days.

CHANGING REGISTRARS

Earlier I had indicated that the "chemistry" of the situation would play an important role in your selection of a registrar. Unfortunately, sometimes the chemistry goes wrong. Maybe the registrar's people changed, maybe your organizational culture changed, maybe you made a mistake. In any case a situation may develop that causes you to want to change registrars. What do you need to consider?

First, you need to consider the real reason that you want to change registrars. Is the present registrar too "tough"? What makes you think that a new registrar will be any different? If you researched the registrars correctly during the selection process, the "toughness" should not have been a surprise. Have the people changed? If you find yourself dealing with an auditor that is incompatible with your organization, discuss the situation with the management of the registrar. You have a right to have people serve your requirements who are compatible with your environment.

When faced with these kinds of issues, it's usually best to try to work them out with your present registrar rather than try to change. Each registrar is required to have a documented complaint process. Have you escalated your problems as high in the chain as is practical? Still no solution? Then change might be the only solution. However, change will cost money.

There are several factors to consider. Are you moving from an accredited registrar to another accredited registrar? Especially if both are accredited by the same accreditation body, that should be fairly easy to determine. The new registrar will want to review your latest audit reports, nonconformity findings, corrective actions, and other information. In some cases they may want to do a site audit. They may issue a new certificate at that point. In other cases they may want to do several audits. It depends. They are really trying to determine the quality of the audit work done by the original auditors, the compliance of your system, and the condition of the noncompliances. If the situation is clean, the certificate should be forthcoming.

Suppose your original registrar is not accredited by a national accreditation body but a national body does accredit the new one. That situation will always be more costly because the new registrar has almost no acceptable evidence on which to build confidence. They may have to start from the beginning with a complete document review and then redo the entire process. That is one of the pitfalls of selecting a nonaccredited registrar.

Be careful of timing! That is, if you are in a market that requires a certificate to conduct business, you must be very careful you don't find yourself in a situation where the "old" registrar has cancelled the certificate and the "new" registrar hasn't issued a certificate. That would have significant business implications.

At this point the IAF is drafting guidance to registrars in terms of the methodology to be followed when clients change registrars. Currently none exists, so each registrar follows their own procedures.

MULTISITE REGISTRATIONS

A sizable number of registered companies have multiple certificates. A company with four locations could have four certificates, one for each site, or it could have one certificate covering all four sites. In general, the latter situation is the least expensive approach because of the way registrars are allowed to handle organizations that have multiple sites.

Let's take a macro view of the rules. A multisite organization is defined as an organization having an identified central function at which certain activities are planned, controlled, or managed and a network of local offices or branches (sites) where such activities are fully or partially carried out. The organization does not have to be under one legal entity, such as franchises. But the central office must have the authority to implement corrective action within each site.

The organization's quality assurance system must be centrally administered under a centrally controlled plan and be subject to central management review. All the relevant sites (including the central administration function) must be subject to the organization's internal audit program and must have been audited in accordance with that program prior to the certification/registration body starting its assessment.

It must be demonstrated that the central office of the organization has established a quality management system in accordance with the standard and that the whole organization meets the requirements of the standard. This includes consideration of relevant regulations.

The organization should have the ability to collect and analyze data from all sites, including the central office, and it should have the authority and ability to initiate organizational change if required. The products or services provided by all sites have to be substantially of the same kind and have to be produced fundamentally according to the same methods and procedures.

Having an organization with multiple sites that fits the definition and requirements for multisite registration has two very important implications. First, the original certification assessment may be possible using a sampling plan. Second, sampling plans may be applicable for the surveillance audits as well. What does that mean? Costs are reduced through the proper application of sampling plans.

SAMPLING PLANS

Many organizations seeking certification or already certified have multiple sites. The common way of handing this situation is to certify each site. Thus audit days are determined by the population at each site multiplied by the total number of sites. That is typically the most expensive approach. It is possible to approach the situation somewhat differently through the application of sampling.

Sampling plans can reduce the number of days for certification audits and surveillance audits without materially reducing the integrity of the audit results. Sampling has a strong basis in statistics and is a very useful method when the number of sites grows. One of the largest certified organizations in the world is Federal Express Corporation. Did the registrar visit every one of the 15,000 FedEx sites? No, a sampling plan was developed, reviewed with the RAB, and then implemented. The first step is to determine whether or not the organization meets the criteria for the registrar to use a sampling plan.

The IAF Guidance for Multisite Methods provides a macro view of the organizational requirements:

Where a supplier is operating through a number of geographically separate facilities, all of which:

- *are part of the same entity,*
- *are performing similar activities,*
- *are under common management control,*
- *use the same Quality Systems and procedures,*

the assessment of activities at these separate facilities can be on a sample basis, ensuring, however, that all geographically separate facilities are assessed at least once in a certain period. In these circumstances, the certification/registration relates to the entity as a whole and not to any individual facility. The supplier shall/should demonstrate an effective internal audit and review procedure covering all such facilities and/or locations at appropriate intervals.

The fact that the organization meets all these criteria does not in itself mean a sampling methodology can be applied. The IAF guidance documents also require the registrar to have procedures to restrict site sampling where site sampling is not appropriate to gain sufficient confidence in the effectiveness of the quality system under assessment. Such restrictions should be defined by the certification/registration body with respect to:

- Scope sectors or activities (that is, based on the assessment of risks or complexity associated with that sector or activity)
- Size of sites eligible for multisite assessment
- Variations in the local implementation of the quality system, such as the need for frequent recourse to the use of quality plans within the quality system to address different activities or different contractual or regulatory systems
- Use of temporary sites that operate under the quality management system of the organization

Given the criteria that define the requirements for the organization and the registrar, the difference between using a sampling plan and not using one can be significant, as shown in Table 39.4. Let's consider an example. The Smith Leather Company has 10 factories with approximately 1000 employees at each. If each site had a separate certificate, the normal process would require 120 audit days for the initial assessment of the 10 sites. Surveillance audits would require 40 audit days a year. Using the RAB sampling methodology, the initial assessment would require 60 audit days. The ongoing surveillance audits would require 16 audit days per year. If we assume that the auditor day rate is $1200 per day, not including any travel expenses, the savings at the initial certification assessment is $72,000. The ongoing annual savings for surveillance visits is approximately $28,000 per year.

The proper use of sampling plans can result in significant savings to the organization. But they must be approached with caution and require a carefully developed approach for the registration architecture. Further, this places another criteria in the registrar selection process. Not all registrars are capable of handling a sampling approach.

What happens if the organization is already registered using the site-by-site approach and desires to move to a sampling environment? This presents a very difficult situation because the registrar will typically see a significant reduction in annual revenues and will not be eager to move in this direction. The organization may have to consider steps as drastic as changing registrars. However, the end result can be very beneficial to the organization.

There are several different sampling plans available. The RAB has a version that registrars it has accredited may use. The example cited earlier used the criteria

Table 39.4 The use of sampling can significantly reduce the number of audit days for the initial assessment as well as the surveillance audits

Number of Sites	Sample Size for Initial Audit and Triennial Audit	Sample Size for Six-Month Surveillances*	Comments
1–3	100%	50%	Each site must be audited once per year
4–7	3	3	**
8–11	5	4	**
12–19	40% (minimum 6)	5	**
20–29	30% (minimum 8)	6	**
30–39	25% (minimum 9)	7	**
40–99	20% (minimum 10)	10% (minimum 8)	**
100–199	15% (minimum 21)	9% (minimum 10)	**
200–399	10% (minimum 31)	8% (minimum 19)	**
400–699	7% (minimum 40)	7% (minimum 33)	**
700–999	6% (minimum 50)	6% (minimum 33)	**
More than 1000	5% (minimum 60)	5% (minimum 60)	**

from the RAB method. Some of the European accreditation bodies, such as RvA of the Netherlands, use a plan that basically allows for a 30 percent audit rate during the surveillance process and requires every site to be visited at least once during the three-year certification cycle. The IAF has recently completed work on a sampling plan that uses the "square root" method. In this method the number of sites visited each year is equal to the square root of the total number of sites. Since this method was approved, all accreditation bodies are expected to adopt it eventually.

To summarize, sampling plans offer a significant cost advantage to an organization. However, not every organization can meet the requirements to use sampling plans. The registrar must have specific procedures in place to implement a sampling plan and, depending on the situation, may not be motivated to move in this direction.

ALTERNATIVE METHODS

In the 1990s, as experience with the process of quality system certification grew, it become apparent to many companies and to some registrars that not all quality systems were created equal—that quality systems built on a "quality" culture far exceeded the requirements of the standard. There was a certain maturity to these types of organizations that had nothing to do with the age of the organization. The quality culture started from the top of the company and permeated every employee. Companies of this genre typically gain little value from the classical certification process and ongoing surveillance audits.

Out of this environment grew a type of certification process, called alternative methods, that looked at an organization's quality system with a different perspective. The perspective had to ensure that the company was compliant to the standard, but it approached it differently.

A company with a mature quality system tends to have a very well established internal audit process that is significantly more rigorous than that of the registrar. It tends to be broader in scope; that is, it covers more processes and procedures, and it covers them in greater depth and intensity than the registrar.

In 1998 the IAF recognized a need to respond to the requirements of this type of company in a way that would bring added value and not just additional cost while at the same time ensuring the creditability of the conformity assessment process. An IAF position paper was published that established criteria for accreditation bodies to follow in the application of alternative methods. The document is titled "Alternative Method for Maintaining ISO 9001/2/3 Certification/Registration" (document number IAF 98-020, which you can download from the IAF Web site at http://www.iaf.nu). It sets forth criteria and methods that organizations with mature quality systems can use to increase the value of the certification process. Working Group I of the IAF is currently investigating the revision of that document based on the learning to date.

THE CONFORMITY ASSESSMENT INDUSTRY

The global conformity assessment industry is a well-organized set of relationships between governments, nongovernment organizations, profit-making concerns, and clients. It is a multibillion-dollar-a-year industry that touches each of us in many ways. As an organization considers certification, it is important to understand the processes and the players.

The major steps in the conformity assessment "value chain" are the following:

- ISO/TC 176
- ISO Conformity Assessment Committee (CASCO)
- IAF
- Accreditation bodies
- Certifiers/registrars
- Certified organizations

Let's look a minute at each, their makeup, and their direction.

ISO/TC 176

Technical Committee 176 of the International Organization for Standardization is the owner of the ISO 9000 family of standards. This committee drafts the standards, the requirements, against which organizations wishing to be certified are assessed. The committee stipulates which standards are "requirements" and which are "guidance." "Requirements" *may* be used for certification; "guidance" *may not* be used for certification.

CASCO

The ISO Conformity Assessment Committee is an important player in this process. It defines its charter as follows:

- To study means of assessing the conformity of products, processes, services and management systems to appropriate standards or other technical specifications
- To prepare international guides and international standards relating to the practice of testing, inspection, and certification of products, processes, and services, and to the assessment of management systems, testing laboratories, inspection bodies, certification bodies, accreditation bodies, and their operation and acceptance
- To promote mutual recognition and acceptance of national and regional conformity assessment systems, and the appropriate use of international standards for testing, inspection, certification, assessment, and related purposes

In other words, ISO/TC 176 prepares the requirements, and CASCO tells how they will be assessed. The CASCO guides and standards set the criteria for operation of accreditation bodies as well as certification/registration bodies. In the context of conformity assessment of ISO 9000, there are three CASCO guides that are of interest:

- ISO/IEC Guide 22: 1996, *General criteria for supplier's declaration of conformity*
- ISO/IEC Guide 61, *General requirements for assessment and accreditation of certification/registration bodies*
- ISO/IEC Guide 62, *General requirements for bodies operating assessment and certification/registration of suppliers' quality systems*

Guides 61 and 62 define the process and procedural requirements for the accreditation body and certification bodies, respectively. These guides may be purchased from ISO, ANSI, or one of the many companies that resell ISI/IEC standards and guides.

International Accreditation Forum

The IAF is the world association of conformity assessment accreditation bodies and other bodies interested in conformity assessment. Its primary function is to develop a worldwide program of conformity assessment to promote the elimination of nontariff barriers to trade. For additional discussion of the role of IAF see chapter 40.

IAF membership includes accreditation bodies from nations in all parts of the world, industry representatives, and accredited certification/registration bodies in an international organization that seeks to encourage development of a single worldwide system of mutual recognition of conformity assessment certificates. The organization's objectives include facilitating trade and commerce, in accordance with World Trade Organization policies, by establishing a Multilateral Mutual Recognition Agreement (MLA) based on the equivalence of accreditation programs operated by accreditation body members, verified through peer review among those accreditation body members.

IAF works to find the most effective way of achieving a single system that allows companies with an accredited conformity assessment certificate in one part of the world to have that certificate recognized everywhere else in the world. It aims to facilitate world trade by working to remove technical barriers that may flow from demands for specific certification and/or registration of management systems, products, services, personnel, and other programs of conformity assessment. They promote the international acceptance of accreditations granted by its MLA signatory accreditation body members, based on the equivalence of their accreditation programs.

Accreditation is increasingly being used by regulators and the market as an impartial, independent, and transparent means of assessing the competence of conformity assessment bodies. IAF provides the technical basis for the worldwide recognition of the competence of the bodies accredited by its members, realizing the concept "tested or certified once—accepted everywhere."

All members of IAF are committed to adopting policies and procedures in their own operations to facilitate trade, in conformity with the World Trade Organization's Agreement on Technical Barriers to Trade.

Both accreditation body and certification/registration body members are committed to basing their own conformity assessment procedures on standards or guides developed by ISO/CASCO and adopted in accordance with ISO/IEC rules. When members of IAF provide a conformity assessment service to meet market needs, but ISO/IEC standards or guides developed by ISO/CASCO and adopted in accordance with ISO/IEC rules are not available for that service, the members commit themselves to ensuring that the standards they use are developed in accordance with the principles in articles 5 and 6 on conformity assessment (consensus-driven open process) of the World Trade Organization's Agreement on Technical Barriers to Trade.

The accreditation programs of members of the MLA are based on relevant ISO/IEC guides. To ensure that the various programs are operated in an equivalent way, IAF issues guidance to the application of the various ISO/IEC guides. The IAF guidance documents are based on the experience of accreditation bodies in applying the ISO/IEC guides in practice and represent agreement among IAF members on best practice in the application of those guides. Accreditation bodies that are members of the MLA are required to adopt the IAF guidance as part of their general rules of operation.

IAF also publishes guidance for the use of accreditation bodies when accrediting certification/registration bodies to ensure that they also operate their programs in a consistent and equivalent manner. IAF guidance documents are not intended to establish, interpret, subtract from, or add to the requirements of any ISO/IEC guide but simply to ensure consistent application of those guides.

Several IAF guidance documents are of interest in this discussion:

- IAF Guidance on ISO/IEC Guide 61:1996—General requirements for assessment and accreditation of certification/registration bodies.
- IAF Guidance on the Application of ISO/IEC Guide 62:1996—General requirements for bodies operating assessment and certification/registration of suppliers' quality systems.
- IAF Guidance on Certification/Registration of Organizations Operating Multiple Sites—Guidance for certification/registration bodies certifying organizations that operate through many sites using the same management system. The document is a supplement to the IAF Guidance to the Application of ISO/IEC Guide 62.
- An Alternative Method of Maintaining ISO 9001/2/3 Certification/Registration—A contribution to the exploration of modified methods of maintaining accredited certification/registration that may be more economical to suppliers. The document is published for the guidance of organizations that wish to use this innovative method of maintaining certification/registration once the capability of the organization has been demonstrated to the satisfaction of the certification/registration body. This document will shortly be superceded by an Annex to the IAF Guidance to ISO/IEC Guide 62.

All IAF documents are available free of charge at the IAF Web site (http://www.iaf.nu).

Accreditation Bodies

Almost every developed economy in the world has a national accreditation body. In some countries, China for example, there are several. The majority of the accreditation bodies are members of the IAF. The IAF Web site has direct links to each member accreditation body.

Registration/Certification Bodies

Many organizations provide quality system certification/registration services. You can locate a list at the RAB Web site (http://www.rabnet.com), the Quality System Update (QSU) Web site (http://www.books.mcgraw-hill.com/qsu/registrars.html), and the Quality Digest Web site (http://www.qualitydigest.com).

Chapter 40

The International Accreditation Forum

Noel Matthews
Secretary, International Accreditation Forum, Canberra, Australia

Accreditation reduces risk for the users of conformity assessment certificates by assuring them that the body that issued the certificate is competent to do the work needed and to make the decisions necessary to issue a credible certificate. Accreditation bodies regularly assess and reassess the bodies they accredit to ensure that the body complies with the relevant international standards and that its management and staff are appropriately qualified and resourced for the work they do.

The International Accreditation Forum (IAF) is the authoritative world body for the accreditation of conformity assessment bodies that issue certificates of conformity for management systems, products, personnel, inspection, and similar conformity programs. IAF was incorporated as an international organization in September 1998.

The membership of IAF includes conformity assessment accreditation bodies (including developing accreditation bodies), associations of accredited certification/registration bodies, and industry/user associations from all parts of the world. The membership of IAF as of June 2001 included 36 accreditation body members, three regional groups of accreditation bodies (the European Cooperation for Accreditation [EA], the Interamerican Accreditation Cooperation [IAAC], the Pacific Accreditation Cooperation [PAC]), and nine association members (associations of accredited certification/registration bodies and industry/user associations). A further six applications for membership are currently under consideration.

IAF began as a forum of national accreditation bodies for management system certification/registration. By the mid-1990s it was clear that developments in globalization and world trade were requiring the accreditation body members of IAF to assist in the elimination of nontechnical barriers to world trade by ensuring that conformity certificates issued in one economy would be recognized in other economies to which goods and services were exported.

Figure 40.1 shows the IAF charter, which will guide IAF's development over the next few years. IAF has adopted strategic policies and basic plans intended to place the organization in the vanguard of the changing world environment for conformity assessment. Members are currently (mid-2001) considering a revision of the IAF bylaws and a revised memorandum of understanding (MoU), which will update the rules for membership to meet future needs.

IAF's objectives include the facilitation of world trade, achieving and maintaining the confidence of stakeholders and users, and reducing the costs of trade by achieving acceptance of certificates anywhere in the world. IAF works closely with industry and a wide range of international and national organizations and governments to support the development of standards for worldwide conformity assessment, to better understand and respond to the needs of industry and government, and to provide confidence to governmental and industry users in the outcomes of accredited conformity assessment.

The International Accreditation Forum, Inc. (IAF) is an international association of organizations that have agreed to work together on a worldwide basis to achieve common trade facilitation objectives. We are a major world forum for developing the principles and practices for the conduct of conformity assessment that will deliver the confidence needed for market acceptance. We act through the accreditation of those bodies that certify or register management systems, products and/or personnel. We promote the worldwide acceptance of certificates of conformity issued by certification and/or registration bodies accredited by an accreditation body member of IAF, and seek to add value for all stakeholders through what we do, and through our programs.

We bring together, on a worldwide basis, partner accreditation bodies and representatives of stakeholder groups that seek to facilitate global trade through the acceptance of accredited certificates of conformity.

We develop and/or approve/recognize the appropriate processes and practices for the conduct of conformity assessment worldwide, and ensure their universal application by recognized IAF member accreditation bodies and their accredited certification and/or registration bodies.

We consult widely with stakeholders in developing our programs, and we work to deliver the best possible standard of conformity assessment in order to provide our stakeholders with a value-added outcome.

We influence world trade through linking, and working, with other key international organizations and industry groups.

Figure 40.1 The IAF charter.

The IAF Multilateral Recognition Arrangement (MLA) provides a mechanism for worldwide industry and government acceptance of certificates of conformity, issued by bodies accredited by IAF MLA signatories. The MLA has reduced costs to industry and customers by allowing accreditation certificates issued in one economy to be accepted across national borders. The objective of the MLA is to eliminate requirements for multiple certification, leading to *certified once, accepted everywhere.*

Accreditation bodies that are admitted to the MLA (29 as of June 2001) must undergo a thorough peer review that requires them to prove to the other members of the MLA that the bodies they accredit have been subjected to a high standard of assessment, which guarantees that the accreditation certificates they issue meet the high standards expected by IAF. The peer assessment also looks to ensure that the procedures they follow and the qualifications and resources available to their staff meet the high standards required. Members of the MLA are regularly reassessed to ensure that they maintain the high standards expected of them.

IAF issues *guidance* to its members regarding the application of international standards, designed to ensure that all accreditation body members operate to the same high standards, and require the bodies they accredit also to operate to uniformly high standards. The equivalence of accreditation certificates issued in various economies throughout the world adds real value to industry and consumers through facilitation of global trade, improved consistency and reliability of product and service delivery worldwide, and confidence at lower cost.

IAF has issued a *procedure for identification of MLA status*, which is intended to ensure that members of the IAF MLA and regional MLAs are able to claim membership in the MLA in a consistent fashion and thus allow certification/ registration bodies accredited by them to claim worldwide recognition for the certificates they issue, based on the accreditation body's membership in the IAF MLA. IAF expects that this approach will help organizations take advantage of a single certification by using that certification anywhere in the world to demonstrate its compliance with standards, and so address one of the concerns of industry to reduce demands for multiple assessments across national boundaries.

IAF is working to further develop IAF guidance on the recognition of certificates issued by certification/registration bodies accredited by members of the IAF MLA. The aim is to implement fully the goal of the MLA to allow suppliers to achieve one certification/registration recognized worldwide and provide the option to select and change certification/registration bodies freely, without repetition of assessment activities, and to reduce duplicated accreditation assessments between MLA partners.

IAF has agreed jointly with ISO/TC 176 and the ISO Committee on Conformity Assessment (ISO/CASCO) to transition arrangements for the implementation of the ISO 9001:2000 standard. The agreed-upon arrangements for the introduction of the new standard should assist industry, suppliers, customers, and both accreditation bodies and certification/registration bodies to achieve a smooth and low-cost transition to the new standard. Following a joint review with ISO/TC 176 and ISO/CASCO of the best way to implement the ISO 9001:2000 standard, IAF issued guidance on the application of that standard intended to ensure smooth and effective movement by certified companies to the requirements of the standard.

IAF continually develops new and revised guidance on the application of ISO and IEC (International Electrotechnical Commission) standards and guides as the needs of industry and customers dictate. The objective of the IAF guidance is to ensure that members of the IAF MLA conduct their operations consistently in ways that allow their accreditations to be accepted as equivalent to the accreditations issued by all other members of the MLA. IAF has adopted significant changes to its guidance for the application of ISO/IEC Guides 61 and 62 in the last year and will be proposing further amendments later in 2001.

IAF recognizes that the world demand for conformity assessment in areas other than quality management systems (QMSs) is growing. In 2001, IAF will extend the coverage of its MLA to environmental management systems and products. It is already working on extension of its work to other areas such as food safety, personnel certification, and medical and pharmaceutical management. IAF is working with the aeronautical and telecommunications industries with the objective of meeting the specific needs of those industries and extending the benefits of the IAF worldwide program to those industries. IAF stands ready to work with any industry sector that sees the need for a worldwide conformity assessment program to reduce risk, reduce costs, and facilitate international trade.

IAF will extend coverage of its MLA, which now encompasses ISO 9001/2/3 certification/registrations, to include ISO 14001 certification/registrations and product certification accreditation toward the end of 2001.

IAF is working to find a way for industry-specific conformity assessment programs to be brought into the existing worldwide system of conformity assessment. IAF has stated that it is prepared and willing to provide support and cooperation to relevant bodies to ensure and maintain the consistency of such emerging programs with the existing worldwide accepted system. In that regard IAF is now working with a number of specific industry groups with the intention that IAF accreditation programs to meet the needs of those industries will be available in the near future.

IAF stands ready to work with producers, marketers, and customers in any industry that seeks to facilitate reliable, safe, and value-for-money world trade of its products. The advantage to the industry is that the existing IAF infrastructure, and processes with established credibility can be quickly and easily mobilized by the industry at minimum cost with maximum returns to the industry in terms of world acceptance of certificates issued.

IAF has liaison arrangements with other international organizations including ISO, ISO/TC176, ISO/CASCO, the International Auditor and Training Certification Association (IATCA), and the International Laboratory Accreditation Cooperation (ILAC). The objective of these relationships is to develop closer working relationships with those bodies. The liaison relationships give reciprocally the same status to those organizations. These reciprocal arrangements are developed to maintain closer communication between IAF and the various other bodies.

IAF works closely with similar bodies that work in other areas, particularly ILAC, with which it shares many members in common. High-level meetings between the senior executives of both bodies are now held regularly. Both bodies are interested in harmonized and globally consistent accreditation and conformity assessment and cooperate to that end. The common objective is to remove any duplicated works between them and to reduce any redundant costs incurred by accreditation bodies and conformity assessment bodies, ultimately borne by industries. A joint working party with the task of developing harmonized procedure documents has started work.

IAF is moving toward closer relationships with IATCA, recognizing that the effectiveness of conformity assessment depends to a large extent on the skills and competence of the auditors and evaluators.

In all these activities the primary aims are to reduce costs, facilitate world trade, and enhance the status and the effectiveness of the conformity assessment programs of all members and their stakeholders. IAF is most conscious that in a fast-moving and highly competitive international environment, IAF and its members need to constantly review practices and policies to ensure that their services meet the needs of their stakeholders in the most cost-effective manner, and that the credibility of and confidence in their programs is enhanced to the ultimate benefit of customers throughout the world.

More information about IAF is available at the IAF Web site (http://www.iaf.nu) or by contacting the secretary via e-mail at iafsecr@email.com.

Chapter 41

Understanding ISO 9000:2000: The Role of the International Standardized Testing Organization A.G.

Nigel H. Croft
Chairman, International Standardized Testing Organization A.G.,
Zug, Switzerland

INTRODUCTION

The ISO 9000:2000 family of standards represents a significant improvement over the 1994 versions of the standards, and, if implemented in an appropriate manner in organizations, should facilitate the development of an effective, process-oriented quality management system. If the focus of the 1994 versions of the standards was perceived to be *developing documented procedures, and providing evidence in the form of records*, then the focus of the year 2000 standards is *understanding and managing processes, and providing evidence in the form of results.* For this to happen, however, it is of fundamental importance that those individuals who are involved in the development, implementation, and evaluation of an ISO 9000–based quality management system understand not only the requirements of ISO 9001:2000, but also the underlying eight quality management principles, the concepts and terminology used in the standards (as defined in ISO 9000:2000), and the guidelines for performance improvement provided by ISO 9004:2000, which allow an organization to look beyond registration and to use the quality management system to its best advantage.

The International Standardized Testing Organization A.G. (ISTO) is a commercially-run organization based in Zug, Switzerland. ISTO provides a global examination and certification service to individuals who wish to demonstrate their understanding of the ISO 9000 family of standards. It fully supports and embraces the international standards published by the International Organization for Standardization (ISO), a worldwide federation of national standards bodies based in Geneva, Switzerland, but no formal links between the two organizations exist or should be implied.

This chapter provides information regarding the ISTO ISO 9000 examinations and discusses some of the more common misconceptions regarding the standards, based on examination results.

THE ISTO TEST OF UNDERSTANDING OF ISO 9000:2000

Background

ISO 9001:2000 (*Quality management systems—Requirements*), ISO 14001:1996 (*Environmental management systems requirements*), and the joint *Environmental/quality management auditing* standard, ISO 19001, have shifted the traditional focus away from "training" of personnel to a competence-based requirement. The way in which competence is achieved may or may not include the need for training. This concept was further reinforced by the requirements specified in the International Accreditation Forum/ISO-CASCO/ISO/TC 176 policy for the transition to ISO 9001:2000, where it was noted that certification body auditors and other relevant personnel must be able to demonstrate:

> . . . *knowledge and understanding of:*
>
> - *the eight Quality Management Principles on which the revised standards are based;*
> - *the requirements of ISO 9001:2000; and*
> - *the concepts and terminology of ISO 9000:2000.*

No specific training requirements were mandated in this policy for individuals to be able to achieve the necessary knowledge and understanding, although auditor recognition schemes such as those operated by the Registrar Accreditation Board (RAB), the International Register of Certificated Auditors (IRCA), the Japanese Registration of Certified Auditors (JRCA), and the International Auditor and Training Certification Association (IATCA) have established their own training requirements.

With this trend toward the demonstration of *understanding*, coupled with an ever-increasing number of self-proclaimed *experts* on ISO 9000, the need became apparent for a single, internationally recognized examination that could be used to demonstrate an individual's understanding of the ISO 9000 standards. The publication of ISO 9000:2000 in December 2000 only added new urgency in this respect, since its correct utilization necessitates a radical change in *mind-set* for many quality practitioners.

The ISTO Test of Understanding of ISO 9000:2000 is not intended to be a compulsory examination for the qualification of internal or external auditors or of personnel responsible for implementing the standards. It does, however, provide individuals with the opportunity to demonstrate their understanding of the ISO 9000:2000 standards, which may be desirable in the following circumstances:

- For quality professionals to demonstrate to their employers that they are able to take full advantage of the improvements offered by the ISO 9000:2000 standards

- As one of the criteria for the qualification of internal auditors
- As one of the criteria for the qualification of external auditors
- For consultants to demonstrate their knowledge of ISO 9000:2000 to potential clients
- For job candidates to demonstrate their knowledge of ISO 9000:2000 to potential employers

Within this context, the ISTO examinations facilitate the following:

- *A focus on* understanding, *rather than on training.* It is recognized that some individuals who have accompanied or participated actively in the development of the ISO 9000:2000 standards or in the practical application of the standards may be able to demonstrate their understanding without undergoing any training at all. At the other end of the spectrum, some may spend significant amounts of time attending training courses and still not fully understand the standards.

- *The possibility for professionals to demonstrate their understanding of international standards, with the ISTO certificate as objective evidence.* This can provide confidence to senior managers that key personnel involved in implementing the organization's quality management system truly understand the underlying principles and will be less likely to generate unnecessary bureaucracy.

- *The demonstration of an individual's* competence, *with the understanding of the standard as an important component.* It must be clear that the ISTO examinations themselves do not demonstrate competence, but they do demonstrate that the individual possesses the necessary *knowledge* of the standards, which serves as a basis for achieving competence. It is appropriate to remember that the definition of *competence* given in ISO 9000:2000 is the ability to *apply* knowledge and skills. (Emphasis added.)

- *The opportunity for individuals to acquire knowledge by home study or distance learning.* Many individuals prefer to learn in the comfort of their own home, via the Internet, or by group or individual study, rather than by taking a specific training course. Because the ISTO examinations concentrate on evaluating the *results* of the learning process, the way in which the knowledge is acquired becomes less important.

- *A basis for the responsible dissemination of knowledge by training organizations.* Many professional and competent organizations around the world provide accurate and practical training regarding the ISO 9000 standards. Unfortunately, however, there are also less scrupulous organizations who are more intent on selling the training itself than on transmitting accurate and practical information and achieving the desired results for the students.

- *The opportunity for professionals to acquire additional qualifications, as part of their continuing professional development.*

- *Selection and/or qualification of staff by employers.*

- *Greater credibility for the standards themselves, by ensuring that professionals using them are cognizant of their intent.*

Examination Syllabus

The ISTO examination aims at testing individuals' understanding not only of the requirements of ISO 9001:2000 but also of the underlying concepts, terminology, and principles on which the standard is based, and the opportunities provided by following the guidance of ISO 9004:2000. It has been designed specifically to ensure that successful candidates are aware of the practical realities of implementing an ISO 9000–based quality management system and have the knowledge to do this in a pragmatic, results-oriented, and nonbureaucratic way.

The body of knowledge for the ISTO Test of Understanding of ISO 9000:2000 was developed and subjected to consensus among recognized international experts from the following backgrounds:

- Quality managers from organizations currently registered to ISO 9001:2000 (including service organizations)
- Management representatives from organizations making the transition to or implementing ISO 9001:2000
- Experts from ISO/TC 176/SC1 and SC2 involved in the development of the ISO 9000:2000 standards
- Delegation leaders from ISO/TC 176 member bodies and liaison members
- Convener and experts from the official ISO/TC 176/WG19 interpretations group
- National standards bodies
- Managers from professional quality institutions
- International registrars
- Consultants
- Accreditation bodies

Geographically, representatives were drawn from these countries:

- United States
- United Kingdom
- Brazil
- Canada
- Germany
- Egypt
- Hong Kong SAR
- Japan
- France
- Mexico
- Colombia

Full details of the body of knowledge for the ISTO Test of Understanding of ISO 9000 may be found on the ISTO Web site (www.isto.ch), but in broad terms, the syllabus for the examination includes the following:

- The *eight quality management principles* on which the ISO 9000:2000 series of standards is based. (Note: this not only includes topics covered by ISO 9000:2000 and ISO 9004:2000 but also includes topics from the *Quality Management Principles* brochure).

- The *fundamentals* of a quality management system, as described in ISO 9000:2000.

- The *terminology* used in ISO 9001:2000 and ISO 9004:2000, as defined in ISO 9000:2000. Candidates are also advised to familiarize themselves with the ISO/TC 176 *Guide to the terminology used in ISO 9001:2000 and ISO 9004:2000* (document ISO/TC 176/SC2/N526R, provided as Appendix L on the accompanying CD).*

- The requirements of ISO 9001:2000, as applicable to each of the generic product categories defined in ISO 9000:2000 clause 3.4.2, and for different kinds of organizations.

- The role of ISO 9004:2000 guidance in helping organizations go beyond ISO 9001:2000 requirements toward performance improvement.

- The application of ISO 9001:2000 requirements within an organization (ISO 9001:2000 clause 1.2). See also ISO/TC 176's *Guidance on ISO 9001:2000 clause 1.2 "Application"* (document ISO/TC 176/SC2/N524R2, provided as Appendix I on the accompanying CD).*

- An understanding of the principles of a *process approach* to quality management systems. Candidates are recommended to consult the ISO/TC 176 guidance document on the process approach to quality management systems (document ISO/TC 176/SC2/N544R, provided as Appendix J on the accompanying CD).*

- An understanding of the type and amount of documentation required by ISO 9001:2000, and the interpretation of these requirements to different kinds of organizations. See also ISO/TC 176's *Guidance on the documentation requirements of ISO 9001:2000* (document ISO/TC 176/SC2/N525R, provided as Appendix K on the accompanying CD).*

Examination Details

The ISTO Test of Understanding of ISO 9000:2000 is a three-hour examination, comprising:

- Thirty multiple-choice questions
- Thirty true/false questions requiring a test of logic
- Thirty questions based on practical cases of implementation of a quality management system
- An essay question

A sample examination paper may be found on the ISTO Web site.

---

* Signifies a document that may be downloaded free of charge from the ISO Online Web site (www.iso.ch). This is the only official Web site of the International Organization for Standardization.

DIFFICULTIES IN UNDERSTANDING THE ISO 9000:2000 STANDARDS

Based on data extracted from an analysis of the initial ISTO examinations conducted around the world in the first half of 2001, the following topics from the body of knowledge were the ones with which candidates consistently experienced the greatest difficulty, and where a number of conceptual errors exist (or in some cases persist from the 1994 versions of the standards).

Lack of Clear Understanding of ISO 9001:2000 Documentation Requirements

Traditional Focus on Procedures Rather Than Processes. Many of the answers provided in the examinations make it clear that candidates and their organizations are still *document driven* rather than *process driven*. Readers are encouraged to consult the ISO/TC 176 guidance documents ISO/TC 176/SC2/N525R (*Guidance on the documentation requirements of ISO 9001:2000*) and N544R (*Guidance on the process approach to quality management systems*) for further clarification.

Tendency to Overestimate the Documentation Requirements of ISO 9001:2000. Over the years, it has been common to hear such criticisms as "Our organization has a lot of documents, because ISO 9000 requires them." In fact, ISO 9001:2000 actually has very few explicit requirements for documented procedures. The onus is on the organization to decide where such procedures are needed in order to manage its processes and to achieve the planned results. Thus, ISO 9001:2000 has no requirement for a document called a "quality plan," although depending on the nature of the product provided and the size, type, and culture of the organization, some organizations may find it convenient to develop specific quality plans in order to control their processes. Likewise, ISO 9001:2000 does not require a documented procedure for the management review process. Most organizations find it convenient to determine the frequency, participation, topics to be discussed, and responsibilities for the management review process in a written procedure, but that is their option. If they can demonstrate that they are carrying out the management review process without the need for a documented procedure (in some small businesses, for example), then that should be acceptable.

Lack of Understanding of the Definition of Procedure. ISO 9000:2000 clause 3.4.5 defines *procedure* as a "specified way to carry out an activity or a process" and notes that "procedures can be documented or not." This gives organizations the opportunity to reduce the burden of documentation, while at the same time retaining control of their processes. This may be particularly useful in some small organizations or for managing less critical processes in larger, more complex organizations. The decision for a procedure to be documented or not can usually be validated over time by analyzing the results achieved, and by using the "plan–do–check–act" cycle.

Confusion over Confirmation of Order Where the Customer Provides No Documented Statement of Requirements (ISO 9001:2000 clause 7.2.2). There is no requirement in ISO 9001:2000 for the organization to provide its customers with a *written* confirmation for each order. Indeed, this would be impractical for many situations. Some examples of verbal order confirmations are given in chapter 19 of this handbook.

Document Control Requirement for the Quality Policy. There is no requirement in ISO 9001:2000 for the quality policy to be included in the organization's quality manual. Although many organizations may have traditionally chosen to include the policy in their quality manual, a *stand-alone* quality policy that meets all the requirements of ISO 9001:2000 and is controlled in accordance with ISO 9001:2000 clause 4.2.3 would be equally acceptable.

Confusion over *Objective Evidence* versus *Records*. Once again, there is a tendency for both organizations and auditors to be overbureaucratic in their approach to records. ISO 9001:2000 defines very clearly where records are specifically required. In other circumstances where records are not specifically required, if the organization wishes to claim conformity to ISO 9001:2000, it must still provide objective evidence that it is meeting the requirements of the standard. In some cases, it may be convenient to provide this evidence in the form of records, whilst in others, this would only add to the bureaucracy.

Confusion over *Processes*

Product Realization Processes versus Quality Management System Processes. Many candidates for the examination do not understand that clause 4.1 of ISO 9001:2000 refers to all the processes needed for the organization's *quality management system* and not only to the product realization processes. The quality management system processes include, for example, the management review *process*, the internal auditing *process*, and the document control *process*, among others.

Need for Validation of Processes. The requirement in ISO 9001:2000 clause 7.5.2 relates only to production and service provision processes where the resulting output cannot be verified by subsequent monitoring or measurement.

Confusion Regarding ISO 9001:2000 Clause 7.1 (Planning of Product Realization)

Planning of Product Realization Processes versus Product Design and Development. Clause 7.1 of ISO 9001:2000 relates to the planning and development of the *processes* needed for product realization. Note 2 of clause 7.1 adds that the organization *may* also apply the requirements given in clause 7.3 (Design and development) to the development of product realization processes, but this is not normally something that is compulsory unless it forms a part of the customer's contractual requirements or is required by statutory or regulatory bodies.

Concept of a Quality Plan. ISO 9000:2000 clause 3.7.5 defines a "quality plan" as a "document specifying which procedures and associated resources shall be applied by whom and when to a specific project, product, process or contract." However, ISO 9001:2000 includes no specific requirement for the organization to prepare such a quality plan, but simply states that the "output of the planning shall be in a form suitable for the organization's method of operations." For some organizations, it may be necessary, or convenient, to document this output in the form of a discrete quality plan for each project, product, process, or contract, whilst for others, the output of the planning could be distributed over a number of other quality management system documents. In some cases (small or very small organizations, for example), the output of the planning may not need to be documented at all.

Problems in Understanding the Application and Requirements of ISO 9001:2000 Clause 7.3 (Design and Development)

Some of the following problems are not specific to the new ISO 9000:2000 standards; they have also been previously recognized in the 1994 versions of the standards.

Definition of Design and Development. Traditionally, different geographical regions and/or industry sectors may have very different common usage of the terms *design* and *development*, none of which coincide with the ISO 9000:2000 definition. ISO 9000:2000 clause 3.4.4 defines *design and development* as "the set of processes that transforms requirements into specified characteristics or into the specification of a product, process or system." This is the only definition that is valid for ISO 9001:2000.

Many organizations are wary of the term *design and development*, which for them conjures up images of research and development departments or the design of sophisticated hardware products, and they will go to great lengths to justify the exclusion of clause 7.3 from their quality management system. In many cases, the organization's products (*which might be services*) may be very simple but are still covered by clause 7.3 of ISO 9001:2000. It is important to remember that *simple products may only require a very simple design and development process*. It is perfectly feasible for an organization to meet all the requirements of ISO 9001:2000 clause 7.3 with minimal documentation, and in a way that will benefit the organization itself, by ensuring that the product will meet all customer, statutory, and regulatory requirements, as well as the organization's own objectives.

Application of ISO 9001:2000 Requirements for Design and Development. Clause 7.3 of ISO 9001:2000 requires the organization to "plan and control the design and development *of product*." (Emphasis added.) By applying the definition given in ISO 9000:2000 clause 3.4.4, we can see that this means the organization must plan and control the "set of processes that transforms requirements for the product into specified characteristics for the product."

Lack of Understanding of ISO 9001:2000 Requirements for Calibration of Measuring Equipment

Lack of Understanding of the Concept of Monitoring versus Measuring. Clause 7.6 of ISO 9001:2000 refers to the control of *monitoring* and *measuring* devices. The standard dictionary definition given in the ISO/TC 176 guidance document ISO/TC 176/SC2/N526R (*Guidance on the terminology used in ISO 9001:2000 and*

ISO 9004:2000) defines *monitor* as "observe, supervise, keep under review; *measure or test at intervals*, especially for the purpose of regulation or control." (Emphasis added.) The same guidance document provides the dictionary definition of *measure* as "ascertain or determine a spatial magnitude or quantity by the application of some object of known size or capacity or by comparison with some fixed unit." In many cases, processes may be monitored simply by *observing, supervising*, or *keeping the process under review*, without actually making any measurements. This is the case, for example, when calls to a hotel reservation service are "monitored for quality assurance purposes," or when a remote or dangerous/dirty process is monitored by video cameras. Nothing is actually being *measured*.

What Equipment Needs to be Calibrated? Calibration is required only for *measuring equipment* where necessary for valid results of measurements to demonstrate conformity of product to determined requirements. This certainly includes any measuring devices used in testing *product* conformity, but it may also include those used to measure *process characteristics* in situations where the resulting output (product) cannot be verified by subsequent monitoring or measurement.

Confusion over Correction, Corrective Action, and Preventive Action

General Lack of Understanding of the Differences between These Terms and Their Application in ISO 9001:2000. This is not a new problem associated with ISO 9001:2000, but something that has persisted over the years. The definitions given in ISO 9000:2000 clauses 3.6.6, 3.6.5, and 3.6.4 respectively are very clear:

- *Correction* is the action taken to eliminate a detected nonconformity. This may involve reworking or regrading the product.
- *Corrective action* is the action to eliminate the *cause* of a detected nonconformity or other undesirable situation.
- *Preventive action* is the action to eliminate the cause of a *potential* nonconformity or other undesirable potential situation.

Too often, organizations consider *rework* to be *corrective action*. It is not.
Action taken to avoid nonconformities from occurring *again* is corrective action, *not* preventive action.
True preventive action normally results from a sound understanding of the organization's processes and the analysis of *trends* or *future plans*.

A General Lack of Awareness of the Guidance Presented in ISO 9004:2000

- Requirements versus guidelines
  - ISO 9004:2000 contains only guidance for performance improvement; there are no requirements in this standard.
- Lack of familiarity with self-assessment model (ISO 9004:2000 Annex A)
- Lack of familiarity with improvement methodologies (ISO 9004:2000 Annex B)

Miscellaneous

Who Can Authorize a Concession for the Use of Nonconforming Product? A common misconception is that only the customer can authorize a concession for nonconforming product. While this is generally true for any product that does not conform to *customer* requirements, circumstances such as the following can occur:

- The concession may be authorized internally within the organization if the nonconformity relates to an internal requirement that does not affect the ability of the product to meet customer or applicable statutory and/or regulatory requirements. An example could be a product being outside the engineering department's machining tolerance but still able to meet all customer and statutory/regulatory requirements. In this case, it may be appropriate for the engineering department to authorize a concession.

- In cases where the requirement that is not being fulfilled is a regulatory or a statutory requirement, then even the customer cannot authorize a concession.

Release of Product. ISO 9001:2000 clause 3.6.13 defines *release* as "permission to proceed to the next stage of a process"; it does not only relate to final release.

Customer Property. It is not always well understood that customer property not only includes tangible products supplied to the organization, such as a car that goes into the shop for servicing, but also can include intellectual property, or other intangible products, such as confidential information (credit card numbers, for example).

Interested candidates in other countries should consult the ISTO Web site (www.isto.ch) for further details.

CONCLUSIONS

It is hoped that the results presented in this chapter will allow individuals and training bodies to focus their attention on the areas of knowledge where deficiencies have been noted. By promoting a better and common understanding of the new ISO 9001:2000 family of standards, ISTO aims to encourage organizations to demand professionals (including quality managers, facilitators, consultants, and internal and external auditors) who can provide value-adding, nonbureaucratic services. This in turn will help organizations take full advantage of the greater flexibility of ISO 9001:2000 (particularly in terms of the documentation requirements) to develop and improve quality management systems that focus on achieving *results* as a natural consequence of *well-managed processes* and not simply on generating unnecessary and unwelcome documentation.

REFERENCES

ANSI/ISO/ASQ Q9000-2000, *Quality management systems—Fundamentals and vocabulary.* Provided as Appendix F on the accompanying CD.

ANSI/ISO/ASQ Q9001-2000, *Quality management systems—Requirements.* Provided as Appendix G on the accompanying CD.

ANSI/ISO/ASQ Q9004-2000, *Quality management systems—Guidelines for performance improvements.* Provided as Appendix H on the accompanying CD.

International Organization for Standardization. ISO/TC 176/SC2/N525R, *ISO 9000:2000 introduction and support package—Guidance on the documentation requirements of ISO 9001:2000.* Geneva, Switzerland: International Organization for Standardization, 2001. Provided as Appendix K on the accompanying CD.

———. ISO/TC 176/SC2/N544R, *ISO 9000:2000 introduction and support package—Guidance on the process approach to quality management systems.* Geneva, Switzerland: International Organization for Standardization, 2001. Provided as Appendix J on the accompanying CD.

———. ISO/TC 176/SC2/N526R, *ISO 9000:2000 introduction and support package—Guidance on the terminology used in ISO 9001:2000 and ISO 9004:2000.* Geneva, Switzerland: International Organization for Standardization, 2001. Provided as Appendix L on the accompanying CD.

Chapter 42

Using ISO 9004 to Achieve Excellence

Organizational Improvement through ISO 9004:2000—the Thinking Person's Quality Management System Standard

Malcolm Bird
GKN, Birmingham, England

Juhani Y. Anttila
Sonera Corporation, Helsinki, Finland

INTRODUCTION

If you use the ISO 9000 family to gain certification solely to satisfy a customer requirement, then read no further—this chapter is not for you. You will already be aware of the requirements of ISO 9001:2000 through the other chapters of this book. Less known is the fact that ISO 9004:2000 has advanced from what most people perceived as guidance for the use of the ISO 9001 standard. The team that produced the 9004:2000 standard did so with the understanding that while being part of the harmonized pair of standards, 9004:2000 would provide a model for quality management beyond compliance and that an organization using the standard could add value to all its interested parties.

The ISO 9004:2000 standard is entitled "Quality management systems—Guidelines for performance improvement," and while it enhances the use of its partner, ISO 9001:2000, it also stands alone, and is intended for use by organizations that want to improve. In a wider context, ISO 9004:2000 can be seen as a means to facilitate the maturation of an organization as it progresses from product compliance toward performance excellence as considered by the excellence models of the Malcolm Baldrige National Quality Award and the European Foundation for Quality Management.

In this overview, we consider the concepts and ideas behind the new document and discuss the thinking that led to this international standard based on improvement. The requirements specified in ISO 9001 are concerned with effectiveness of a quality management system and the achievement of customer satisfaction.

ISO 9004 emphasizes both effectiveness *and* efficiency, and the performance of the *whole* organization with regard to all interested parties.

WHAT IS ISO 9004:2000 ABOUT?

The scope of ISO 9004:2000 clearly states that it contains guidance and recommendations and is not intended for certification. What it is intended for is to provide guidance for organizations that wish to improve, recommendations on approaches that might be adopted, and suggestions for issues to consider. In what is a fundamental difference from ISO 9001:2000, it seeks to achieve efficiency as well as effectiveness in the deployment of the quality management system (QMS). It deals with the satisfaction of needs and expectations of more than the customer. It embraces the wants and needs of all interested parties—for example, suppliers, employees, shareholders, and the community, as well as customers.

Where compliance raises the issue of corrective action, improvement is focused on going further. A basic principle must be accepted—corrective action is not the same as improvement; the former is compliance with specified requirements, the latter is using the specified requirements as a foundation on which to improve.

The standard also contains two annexes, in the form of guides for two specific approaches. The first consists of guidelines for self-assessment, a means to assess progress over time. Here we should consider the difference between audit and assessment, two of the most confused terms in modern quality management. An *audit* is a methodology for obtaining evidence against specified criteria. An audit is also used for compliance and certification to verify compliance with defined requirements. *Assessment* is based on factual judgment. It is a fundamental tool in the measurement of progress. There are many assessment tools available in relation to quality and organization performance; the annex in ISO 9004:2000 provides a simple model for how to assess performance. Like the rest of this standard, it provides guidance but requires thought in its application.

The second annex reinforces the theme of 9004:2000; it contains a process for continual improvement. It recognizes that improvement can be planned and may consist of big-step or "breakthrough" improvement—a cure for cancer, the splitting of the atom, the reorganization of a factory, and the introduction of a new computer system are breakthrough improvements. It also identifies the value of small-step improvements, conducted within existing processes. Breakthrough improvements are normally undertaken by specified teams outside of normal routine, while small-step improvements are achieved by people improving the way in which they perform everyday work. Both need to be planned and monitored. While the annexes are at the end of the standard, one may consider that they represent a starting point.

The nature of improvement and assessment should certainly be understood before applying recommendations contained in the standard. If change is to be effective and positive, one must have measures. The moment we review an activity, change will inevitably result. The measurement of this change, over time, can be monitored through assessment. Whether an organization is based on process management or any other management strategy, immediate benefit can be gained through the deployment of a process for continual improvement and assessment of that improvement over time.

THE PROCESS APPROACH

ISO 9001:2000 and 9004:2000, commonly called the "consistent pair," are based on "the process approach." This is addressed in detail in the content— specifically in ISO 9001:2000 clause 4, "Quality management system," and clause 7, "Product realization." The introduction to ISO 9004:2000 (in clause 0.2) states that "the application of a system of processes within an organization, together with the identification and interactions and managing of these processes can be referred to as 'the process approach.'" If this is a concept the reader is familiar with, then continue. If not, then pause, and consider what constitutes a process. Further discussion of the process approach can be found in chapter 2 and Appendix J (as provided on the accompanying CD).

The ISO 9000:2000 standard defines a process as "a set of interrelated or interacting activities which transforms inputs into outputs." This is supported by clarification that "inputs to one process are commonly outputs of another," and that "processes in an organization are generally planned and carried out under controlled conditions."

The standard adopts the premise that any organization consists of a collection of processes. These are divided into realization processes, which add value and represent the purpose or scope of the organization, and support processes, which are necessary for the organization to function but do not in themselves directly add value to the products or the organization. The networks of interacting activities that underpin both realization and support processes are collectively known as subprocesses. In addition to realization processes there are in all organizations management processes (for example, a strategic planning process).

This immediately provides for a differentiation by managers. Improvement of an organization's performance may be achieved through investment in realization processes to increase added value or by the planned reduction or replacement of support processes that are costs to the organization without adding direct value. If the organization is robust, both may be addressed in parallel; the key is to recognize that improvement must be specific to process and activity, not generic to the whole organization. A cost-reduction exercise applied to the whole organization could have a positive impact on support processes but inhibit realization processes and therefore the ability to add value or achieve the purpose of the organization.

Representation of an organization in the form of processes can be done, for example, in the form of a matrix chart, overlaying the more normal function structure on a process map, demonstrating that key functions have an impact on several processes, with different outputs.

THE QUALITY MANAGEMENT PRINCIPLES

The foundation of ISO 9001:2000 and ISO 9004:2000 is the eight quality principles that are integrated into all elements of the standards.

The principles are published in full as an ISO brochure that is available online. The principles are also summarized in ISO 9004:2000 (see clause 4.3) and are discussed in chapter 5. They represent the essential issues that face any organization in conducting activities in a way that promotes improvement. The principles also can be used to guide the behavior of people in the organization.

MANAGEMENT SYSTEMS

An issue that faces organizations today, and one that faced the drafting team for ISO 9004:2000, is that of addressing several different management systems, only one of which is the QMS. The ISO 9000 family of standards is clearly focused on QMSs. ISO 9004 provides guidance both for integration with other existing management systems and for applying the principles within as a management system for the organization. The QMS can also provide the framework for all aspects of management.

The overlap between management systems is something to be considered at the earliest opportunity to avoid waste and duplication. In the consideration of needs and expectations of all parties with an interest in the organization, management systems may already exist for environmental management, the health and safety of employees, and the management of commercial and operational risk, among others.

Elements of any system include the need for policy, procedures, and work instructions to ensure consistency of activities and processes; an audit to ensure compliance; and management review of results. In addition, as detailed in the process approach, the planning of processes including inputs, outputs, and interlinked activities is a common element of all management systems.

The ISO 9004:2000 standard addresses these issues in considerable detail, offering suggestions and recommendations regarding issues to consider in the planning of a quality management system—or any other management system.

ISSUES TO BE CONSIDERED

While the harmonized approach is evident through common clause headings in ISO 9001 and ISO 9004, a section in each of the main clauses in ISO 9004 marks a significant difference. "Issues to be considered" was inserted by the drafting team as a discrete section in order to address concepts and issues to provoke thought by the user.

These issues include discussion and explanation as well as general guidance, which progresses beyond ISO 9001:2000 and would not align well with that standard.

The issues detailed address the reality of how an organization works in all respects—performance of the organization rather than performance of the organization's QMS.

HARMONIZED BUT DIFFERENT

There are specific differences between the requirements standard—ISO 9001— and the improvement objectives standard—ISO 9004. Some of these differences are in the form of emphasis, others as additional information.

6.2   People

In the requirements standard, the corresponding section is entitled "Human resources." As a system requirement, people are clearly a resource to be matched to the requirements of processes in terms of skills and knowledge. On the other hand, when considered in the broader context of ISO 9004:2000, people are more than mere resources to be managed.

For an organization to improve the recognition of people as individuals and the coordination of talents, the motivation of people to work together toward a common aim and innovate cannot be understated. *Empowerment* is a word widely used in relation to people taking responsibility for their input to the organization.

In this standard, the emphasis on empowerment recognizes that abdication of responsibility by management is not empowerment. The focus of the standard's recommendations and guidance is for management to recognize people as individuals and provide a framework for their innovation that supports the objectives of the organization. Empowerment is a reality only when channeled into useful effort, and this does require a framework of rules and guidance, but one that permits freedom of thought. Reward and recognition is an essential element of such a system—to stimulate commitment and involvement of people.

6.5 Information

Clause 6.5, "Information," does not exist in the requirements standard. It recognizes that the accumulation of data as evidence of conformance takes on a different meaning in an organization concerned with efficiency and improvement. The recognition of data as information useful to the organization, its conversion to knowledge, and the application of that knowledge to add value is a fundamental realization process that may be created in any organization. It is generally accepted that the speed at which information is managed has become a new source of competitive advantage in competitive markets.

6.6 Suppliers and Partnerships

While clause 7, "Product realization," in both ISO 9001 and 9004 addresses the issue of the processes associated with purchasing material, the inclusion of clause 6.6, "Suppliers and partnerships," under "Resources" reflects the view that true partnership with suppliers, with a sharing of success and failure and profit and loss, is a significant resource to the organization, without which improvement potential will be limited.

6.7 Natural Resources

The statement in 9004:2000 in relation to natural resources focuses on the lack of control that an organization has over naturally occurring resources, and therefore the mitigation of risk arising from this lack of control. Considered in relation to the requirements of ISO 14001, and the issue of sustainability of natural resources in general, then the protection and maintenance of these resources is a positive method by which the risks may be negated.

6.8 Financial Resources

This clause is considered in the 9004 standard in the context of adequate financial resources being necessary for the efficient operation of the QMS.

Discussion throughout the development of the new standards focused on the possible understandings by users of material on financial resources in either of the standards. In the context of ISO 9004:2000, recognition is given to the need for adequate financial resources to operate any business process, and to the fact that the efficient operation of a process would be hindered by lack of financial resources. This builds on the principles already stated in relation to realization compared with support processes, where if finance is focused on cost control, the potential for adding value through realization processes will be impaired.

In commercial organizations, management reporting normally emphasizes financial terms, and the inclusion of other QMS performance data will in similar terms enhance management involvement. Equally, in noncommercial organizations, the ability to translate quality performance into financial terms provides a common language for budgeting and planning.

PROCESSES AND ORGANIZATIONS

Any organization may be described in process terms, and the conventions of process management recognize certain generic processes as common to all organizations.

A significant proportion of the ISO 9004:2000 standard is devoted to clause 7, "Product realization," which appears disproportionate when compared with ISO 9001:2000. The logic behind this is that the QMS requirements for any process are generic and readily defined. ISO 9004:2000 contains significant guidance, which is not appropriate to repeat here—but the underlying principles may help understanding.

First, let us consider the application of these generic processes to an organization. Currently, organizations state the scope of their quality management systems in relation to products they provide. Under the definitions given in ISO 9000:2000, products are the output of processes. These outputs are achieved by conversion of inputs, through activities that add value. This means that the true scope of an organization relates to its operation of realization processes, in order to achieve products.

Similar processes exist in all organizations, and the assignment of *realization* or *support* to describe them is a management responsibility that is fundamental to the organization. An example to illustrate this might relate to a manufacturing organization where "design of product" and "manufacture of product" are clearly realization processes, yet "management of financial resources" is a support process.

An area for consideration is certainly the issue of design responsibility. The requirement standard, based on compliance and the achievement of customer satisfaction through product conformance, provides for exclusions related to issues of design control when they are not relevant as requirements.

ISO 9004:2000 recognizes the reality that any organization has a design responsibility, not in relation to product, but to top management and its responsibility for the design of the business processes of the organization. We have already identified that product conformance is the province of ISO 9001, and in the context of satisfaction of all interested parties and organization performance, every organization has a design responsibility. This responsibility relates to the design of the organization itself in the form of its processes. As with product design, all the elements of a lifecycle can be applied, including design intent, risk analysis, and mitigation and performance evaluation.

The 9004:2000 standard provides guidance on the generic elements of all processes before addressing what are currently recognized as the intrinsic processes of any organization:

- Design and development of products and processes
- Purchasing of materials
- Production and service operations
- Control processes

CONTROL AND IMPROVEMENT

The content of ISO 9004:2000 related to measurement, data management, and improvement has a common theme. Measurement should always have a purpose.

The application of QMSs to organizations is often associated with significant effort put toward data collection and related measurement. The image of quality management in many organizations is instinctively that of measurement and inspection of product.

Today, modern quality management relates to the quality management of processes with planned objectives and measured performance. The issue of product quality is only one element of the QMS, normally addressed in the realization processes.

Measurement therefore provides data, and those data should have a stated purpose—a purpose that is either related to validation and verification or is a basis for action, either corrective or improvement-oriented in nature. Typically data also subsequently become part of quality records.

There is a maxim that says *do not change without measuring, and do not measure without change*. An inefficiency in many organizations is *overmeasurement*. This can arise from the ease with which data can be gathered and a lack of clarity on how the organization will use the data. In some organizations managers may also use data to represent what they believe—or even wish—the situation to be. This may be compounded further by the lack of a process for disposition of the data, resulting in storage of redundant information.

The solution is detailed in other parts of 9004:2000. The analysis of the processes of the organization will cause an evaluation of all activities, in terms of purpose and efficiency as well as their potential for adding value.

A simple check is to ask, "Who is the customer for this process?" and "By what measures will it be satisfied?" If the answers are not apparent, the need for the process will be questioned in terms of purpose. Analysis of the steps in the process provides a focus for efficiency of the process and, ultimately, of the organization. Finally, if the process and the associated activities do not add value and are not a customer or regulatory requirement, then management will inevitably question the need for their existence. The measurement requirements that remain can then be matched to the extensive advice and guidance in clause 8 of ISO 9004:2000, in order to undertake them efficiently and to gain value for them through planning for improvement.

MEASUREMENT OF SATISFACTION

The achievement of satisfaction of all interested parties, including customers, provides the focus for organization performance, and therefore improvement. ISO 9004:2000 suggests that resources need to be balanced in terms of satisfying needs and expectations of interested parties.

Whereas the principles of customer satisfaction are simple to measure using quantitative data, this becomes more subjective in relation to other interested parties.

The standard's suggestions for people in the organization relate to surveys of opinions and assessment of individual performance. The measures for owners and shareholders generally relate to (financial) value. In this respect, both the absolute value as well as benchmarking to other similar organizations provide a source of measurement. Suppliers and partners should consider opinion surveys. For society at large, the data to be monitored should relate to the defined objectives of the organization and its relationship to the local community. (See also chapter 29, "Measurement of Customer Satisfaction.")

It should be recognized that the true value of any satisfaction measure is related to trends over time. The subjectivity of some satisfaction measures renders them no less important than hard measures for items such as product-reject rate or delivery performance. For an organization to understand its overall performance, planning to gather data becomes essential as well as systematic review with resulting corrective or improvement actions.

WHAT ALTERNATIVE IS THERE?

If an organization does not use ISO 9004:2000, what alternative is there? The drafters of ISO 9004 gave consideration to what materials already exist for management systems that relate to the performance of organizations. The notion of ISO 9004 as a guide to the requirements standard was not acceptable, and that document was produced more as a way forward, an advance beyond base-level requirements for organizations that were open to the idea of improvement. Hence its title, *Guidelines for performance improvement*. It is useful to those businesses that want to improve, rather than to organizations where modern quality management is already established and the quality management system has become a self-sustaining tool providing value for the organization. The latter organizations have thus already realized ISO 9004 guidelines in their own way. However, the standard may give them some ideas as well.

Not all contents of the document will be appropriate for every organization; the recommendations and guidance are broad and designed to provide choice. This is a standard to read, think about, and from which to select clauses that complement your organization. This is not a document with a money-back guarantee—blindly following all the advice provided will not in itself lead to excellence!

ONE WAY FORWARD

While it is not appropriate to detail a *correct* approach to using the 9004 standard, one way forward would be to start with annex A and define an assessment tool for the organization to measure where it is today. This could be followed by applying annex B to define the resources and methods necessary to achieve improvement within the organization.

In this way, the organization would have a baseline against which future change could be measured and an improvement process that would deliver value. The management of the organization will have taken a step—perhaps its first—in the application of process methodology.

Once those actions occur, the next step could be to identify or confirm the realization processes of the organization and the associated process steps, activities, and resources. The identification of the *customer* for each process and suitable measures for the customer's satisfaction will provide insight to both the process efficiency and the interfaces to other realization processes.

The next step could be to extend this into a process map for the organization, which would include the support processes required for operation of the realization processes and thus the entire organization.

This process map provides a view of what is happening in the organization, and management can compare this with what they planned to happen (management review). The *rules* for consistent operation of the processes are the management system.

The *final* step is to return to annex A and perform the self-assessment once again, comparing the new results with the initial results to measure progress and improvement. In this way the process starts over again—and continual improvement driven by customer satisfaction will be the result.

KEY POINTS TO REMEMBER

If you have persevered to this point, you will benefit from applying ISO 9004:2000. You clearly have the desire to establish improvement in your organization. To aid your review of the document, Table 42.1 represents important points in the standard together with comments linked to the preceding discussion.

Table 42.1 Key ISO 9004:2000 clauses.

ISO 9004:2000 Clause	Comment
0.2 The process approach	Considers any organization to be a collection of processes, normally planned by management. The QMS provides a means for structured control of the processes. Processes are either "realization," which deliver the purpose of the organization and add value, or "support," where they exist only as part of the organization infrastructure.
4.3 Use of quality management principles	Eight principles are integrated into the document: • Customer focus • Leadership • Involvement of people • Process approach • System approach to management • Continual improvement • Factual approach to decision making • Mutually beneficial supplier relationships
X.1.2 Issues to be considered	Subclause in each of clauses 5 through 8 unique to this document to identify issues that exceed ISO 9001 and application of concepts and ideas.

continued

Table 42.1   Key ISO 9004:2000 clauses *(continued)*.

ISO 9004:2000 Clause	Comment
5.2 Needs and expectations of interested parties	Any organization should consider the needs of customers and other interested parties to be both efficient and effective. The interested parties include: • Customers and end users • People in the organization • Owners/investors • Suppliers and partners • Society
6.2 People	Clause that recognizes that to progress beyond specified requirements, an organization must realize that people are individuals rather than a human resource on a par with materials, finance, and so on.
6.5 Information 6.6 Suppliers and partnerships 6.7 Natural resources 6.8 Financial resources	Additional clauses not included in ISO 9001 representing issues that must be considered in the QMS related to organization performance.
7 Product realization	Main section related to what a business "process" is, with guidance on construction and operation. Provides guidance on top-level processes intrinsic to any organization: • Processes related to interested parties • Design and development of products and processes • Purchasing materials • Production and service operations
Measurement and monitoring of: 8.2.2 Processes 8.2.3 Product 8.2.4 Satisfaction	Guidance on need for measurement, methods, and application of data to improve performance of the organization.
Annex A Guidelines for self-assessment	Generic principles to be applied as a guide on how to approach self-assessment as a time-based tool to assess progress within or of the organization.
Annex B Process for continual improvement	Generic process that can be used in any organization either integrated with the process approach or independently that provides for structured improvement at two levels in the organization.

Chapter 43

Small Businesses

Herbert C. Monnich Jr.
Herbert Monnich and Associates, Humble, Texas

T he size of the small business is both a help and a hindrance in the application of ISO 9001:2000.[1] Small businesses typically have a shallow organizational structure and very little bureaucracy. This enables them to have a simple operating system. On the other hand, this lack of formality sometimes causes small businesses to lose the gains from corrective actions, process improvements, and other positive actions that are usually documented in larger businesses.

ISO 9001:2000 enables a small business to implement an effective and efficient quality system tailored to its specific business. With a few basic exceptions, the business can determine the records and documents required. The standard allows it to establish its own policies, goals, and plans. The techniques of ISO 9001:2000 help the small business manage information and decision loops to improve the efficiency, effectiveness, and profitability of the organization.

This chapter describes how all small businesses can use the standard and guides such organizations through the standard's clauses. The chapter:

- Identifies the key differences between the 2000 and 1994 versions of 9001 that small businesses should be aware of
- Identifies the clauses that most small businesses can easily and effectively implement
- Identifies the clauses that small businesses will have to pay careful attention to in their implementation of ISO 9001:2000
- Directs the small business to guidance in ISO 9004:2000 that is especially meaningful to small businesses

IMPORTANT ENHANCEMENTS IN ISO 9001:2000 FOR SMALL BUSINESS

The new, enhanced requirements of the standard generally make the implementation of an effective quality management system easier for the small business because they are less prescriptive and allow the small business to take advantage of its small, close, simple, unbureaucratic organization.

There are five new elements of the standard that small businesses should be especially aware of:

• **Clause 1.2 Application.** Businesses may consider elements or subelements of clause 7 of the standard for exclusion when the requirement therein cannot be applied because of the nature of the organization and its product. This means that organizations that do design work but don't want to cover it in their quality system cannot say that they are compliant with the standard. They are not allowed to become ISO 9001 registered as a result of this change in requirements.

• **Clause 5.2 Customer focus.** Top management has the ultimate responsibility for ensuring that customers are satisfied. This includes making sure that customer requirements are determined and met. This concept is not new to most small businesses. The top management of small businesses is usually extremely close to the customer. This is true because of the shallow organizational structure of small businesses. As a result, most small businesses can easily implement this requirement.

• **Clause 7.2.1 Determination of requirements related to the product.** Three new requirements have been added to the process of determining the customer's needs: (1) requirements not stated by the customer but necessary for the specified or known intended use; (2) statutory and regulatory requirements related to the product; and (3) additional requirements determined by the organization. Item 2 could cause some problems for small businesses because they may need to develop a system for determining statutory and regulatory requirements from around the world.

• **Clause 7.2.3 Customer communication.** Organizations must now have effective arrangements for communication with customers in all areas from determining product needs through production and delivery to positive and negative customer feedback. This is another area where small businesses have the edge because of their shallow organizational structure and open communication system.

• **Clause 8.2.1 Customer satisfaction.** The concept of customer satisfaction is seen throughout the standard. This clause emphasizes the concept by requiring the organization to monitor the customer's *perception* of whether the organization has met the customer's requirements.

There are also eight enhanced requirements of the standard of which small businesses should be aware:

• **Clause 4.1 General requirements.** There is more emphasis on the need for continual improvement. In addition, the steps for implementing a quality management system are listed.

- **Clause 4.2.1 General.** The minimum documentation requirements of the quality management system are identified as: (1) documents and documented procedures required by the organization to ensure the effective planning, operation, and control of processes; (2) documented statements of a quality policy and quality objectives; (3) a quality manual; and (4) documented procedures and records required by the standard. This is one of the more important changes for small businesses. The earlier versions of the standard prescribed which documents, records, and documented procedures an organization had to have. The 2000 version leaves most of this up to the small business and further states that the documentation of a system will differ because of the size of the organization, types of activities performed, complexities of processes and their interactions, and competence of personnel. Many small businesses perform simple activities using simple, basic processes with competent personnel. This allows for less documentation but still a very effective quality system.

- **Clause 4.2.2 Quality manual.** The standard now clearly states what the content of the quality manual will be.

- **Clause 5.1 Management commitment.** More emphasis is placed on top management commitment, especially communicating to the organization the importance of meeting customer as well as statutory and regulatory requirements, establishing the quality policy, ensuring that the quality objectives are established, and ensuring the availability of resources.

- **Clause 8.1 General.** The standard requires that monitoring, measurement, analysis, and improvement processes needed to demonstrate conformity of the product, ensure conformity of the quality management system, and continually improve the effectiveness of the quality management system be planned and implemented, including the determination and use of applicable methods and statistical techniques.

- **Clause 8.2.2 Internal audit.** The standard states that selection of auditors and conduct of audits must ensure objectivity and impartiality of the audits. It no longer restricts who the auditors may be.

- **Clause 8.4 Analysis of data.** The standard focuses on the analysis of applicable data as one means of determining where continual improvement can be made in the quality management system, especially in the areas of customer satisfaction, conformance to product requirements, characteristics and trends of processes and products (including opportunities for preventive actions), and suppliers.

- **Clause 8.5.1 Continual improvement.** The standard requires that the organization must continually improve the effectiveness of the quality management system through the use of the quality policy, quality objectives, audit results, analysis of data, corrective and preventive actions, and management review.

SMALL BUSINESS GUIDANCE

The following discussion notes the important requirements of the clauses of ISO 9001:2000 to which small businesses must pay particular attention when implementing the standard.

4 Quality management system

4.1 General Requirements

When a small business chooses to implement ISO 9000:2000, it has an excellent opportunity to improve its efficiency, effectiveness, and profitability. Implementing the standard offers an opportunity to review and improve the organization's processes. Every organization that I have seen implement a quality management system has found dead-end processes that are no longer necessary and endless-loop processes where information is needlessly cycled before moving to its final destination.

Clause 4.1, in connection with clauses 5.4, "Quality Planning," 7.1, "Planning of product realization," and 8.1, "Measurement, analysis and improvement—general," forms the backbone of a quality management system. *All businesses, especially small businesses, should use the excellent opportunity given by these clauses to thoroughly evaluate and improve their quality management system and increase their profitability.* Clause 4.1 requires you to identify the processes you need for operating your quality management system and then manage those processes. The other clauses require you to plan your management system, product realization, and measurement processes. First, you identify what you need; then you plan what you are going to do and measure how well you have done it.

Probably the best way to identify your processes is to start at the top of your organization and determine what your basic processes are. These *macroprocesses* can include the following:

- *Administration.* How are you going to administer all of your processes and get feedback from customers and your employees?
- *Product planning.* What service or services are your business going to provide?
- *Product design.* Is there a product design function that designs a physical product such as a vase, lawnmower, packaged vacation cruise, or sandwich?
- *Marketing.* How are you going to let people know you are in business?
- *Sales.* How do you know what the customer wants?
- *Accounting.* How will you get paid and pay for supplies?
- *Product realization.* How will you make the product?

You need to identify these macroprocesses—their inputs, outputs, and interrelations. Break down each macroprocess into its subprocesses to the extent you need to identify the important processes and interrelationships. An excellent source for mapping work processes is *Mapping Work Processes*, 1994 by Dianne Galloway (ASQ Quality Press). Older, successful companies have generally but not necessarily done a good job of identifying their processes and process interrelationships. All companies need to study and try to improve their processes while they are implementing or updating their quality management system.

Processes need to be managed. They can be effectively managed or poorly managed. Just leaving the processes alone (ignoring them) is a form of management, albeit a poor form. Actively managing processes by evaluating their performance and correcting them as necessary is a much better idea.

This identification and management effort is easier for small businesses because their structure is shallow and streamlined.

Processes that may affect product conformity that are outsourced must be controlled by the organization. Such outsourced processes must be identified in the quality management system. Examples of such processes are training when employee administration is outsourced and subcontracted manufacturing processes.

4.2 Documentation Requirements

Note 2 in this clause of the standard highlights the important benefit of this latest revision of ISO 9000 by pointing out that "the extent of the quality management system documentation can differ form one organization to another due to: a) the size of organization and type of activities, b) the complexity of the processes and their interactions, and c) the competence of personnel." The extent of the quality management system documentation for a small business can be minimal because of the business's small size, relatively narrow range of activities, simple processes with basic interactions, and generally extremely competent personnel. These minimal documentation requirements are still very important and are discussed later under applicable areas of the standard.

4.2.2 Quality Manual

The quality manual has to state the scope and describe the processes and interactions of the quality management system. The scope must identify the details and justification for any elements or subelements of the standard that are excluded.

Process mapping can be used in addition to explanations when the manual is written. Small businesses should seriously consider including their documented procedures as part of their quality manual, thereby simplifying the documentation structure. These documented procedures must be referenced in the manual if they are not included. Given their size, uncomplicated processes, and competent employees it is entirely possible for small businesses to end up with only the six documented procedures required by the standard.

4.2.3 Control of Documents

The document control needs of small businesses are similar to but simpler than those of any other business. Most small company documents are approved by one function and receive a limited distribution. However, given their informal nature, small businesses need to make sure that they prevent the use of obsolete documents, including those of external origin. This is one of the subelements of the standard that requires a documented procedure.

4.2.4 Control of Records

Clause 4.2.4 is another of the standard's subelements that requires a documented procedure. A formalized approach can accomplish this task easily. Go to ISO 9000:2000 and determine what the term *record* covers. Make a list of all covered records. Prepare a matrix of the records using identification, protection, retrieval, retention time, and disposition as column headings. List the individual records in the identification column, and fill out the matrix.

5   Management Responsibility

5.1   Management Commitment

The success of a quality management system depends upon top management commitment and involvement. Small companies have an advantage over larger companies because the top managers see and work with most of their employees on a regular basis. Top management must show their commitment both in words and deeds by explaining that commitment in meetings, backing it up in day-to-day activities, and not counteracting it by negative actions.

5.2   Customer Focus

Top management must make sure that the organization is focused on the customer. Clause 7.2.1, "Determination of requirements related to the product," expands on this requirement by pointing out that the organization must determine the specific requirements stated by the customer, requirements necessary for the product's intended use, and statutory and regulatory requirements related to the product.

In large organizations, it is sometimes necessary to establish somewhat complex documentation and reporting structures to make sure that customer comments reach intermediate and top management reliably, consistently, and in a reasonable time frame. However, top management of most small companies has the advantage of being very close to the customer and often receives the input directly from the customer. The product requirements are handled through the sales or contract process. Regulatory and legal requirements relative to the business are usually, but not always, known, as was explained earlier. Customer concerns are handled directly by management.

Some measures of customer satisfaction are number of customer complaints, severity of customer complaints, customers' opinion of the organization, positive and negative customer feedback, ability to retain old customers, and ability to obtain new customers.

The business can use a customer contact log or journal to follow trends in customer comments. Customer contact report forms can be used if there are many functions that work with the customer.

5.3   Quality Policy

Quality policy is an area where being small can be a hindrance. Some small businesses may find it difficult to take time to sit down and develop a quality policy and quality plans. They may feel that they have been in business for a long time and are doing fine. This philosophy will not work. The quality policy must be developed with thought. It is the centerpiece of the quality system. It must be appropriate to why the organization exists.

Top management needs to discuss what the quality policy of the organization really is. Management should involve all functions in these discussions. Some of the questions quality policy developers may want to ask themselves are as follows: What needs are being met by the organization? What goods and services are and will be provided? Who are the stakeholders (customers, employees, community)? What beliefs and values form the organization's culture? And, Where is the organization headed?

Everyone in the organization should understand what the quality policy is and what it means. If they do not understand the organization's quality philosophy, they will not know how to fit into the organization's quality culture. The quality policy is generally documented at the beginning of the quality manual.

ISO 9004:2000, *Quality management systems—Guidelines for performance improvements,* is a document that small businesses should refer to for ideas on improving business performance. It is written parallel to ISO 9001:2000 and gives small businesses ideas for expanding their quality system from minimal compliance to a tool for increasing profitability. The quality policy and planning elements (5.3 and 5.4) of ISO 9004:2000 are notably helpful.

Annex A of ISO 9004:2000 is a guideline for self-assessment. It can be used by small business management to develop fact-based guidance to optimally direct improvement resources. It is also useful for measuring progress against objectives. The ISO 9004 self-assessment approach can "be applied to the entire quality management system, or to a part of the quality management system, or to any process, be applied to the entire organization or part of the organization, be completed quickly with internal resources, be completed by a multi-discipline team, or by one person in the organization who is supported by top management, form an input to a more comprehensive management system self-assessment process, identify and facilitate the prioritization of opportunities for improvement, and facilitate maturing of the quality management system towards world-class performance."

This approach permits an organization to rank itself against the major clauses of ISO 9001:2000 and the additional ISO 9004:2000 clauses using a five-point scale. The scale ranges from 1 for no formal system to 5 for best in class. The annex provides typical questions that the organization can ask itself for each element.

5.4 Planning

5.4.1 *Quality Objectives and 5.4.2 Quality Management System Planning*

Quality planning must be addressed before we talk about quality objectives. We addressed identifying and managing the processes of your organization in the discussion of clause 4.1. Quality management system planning stresses that you need to plan how you are going to understand and manage you processes. What are the correct who, what, when, where, and why of your processes? From where do they get their input, and where does the output go?

Next, you can start looking at the quality objectives of your organization. How are you going to plan your system to meet the objectives? What are the objectives? How do you develop your objectives?

The first step in establishing quality objectives is to determine what the primary measurements are. They must be quantifiable and should be indicators of success or failure.

Primary measurements for quality objectives must be based on the quality policy. The function managers of an organization should be included in the planning of the measurements of the quality program. The measurements should be kept to a minimum and should be representative of a wide range of the organization's interests in order to gain acceptance by all functions involved. Concepts to consider when establishing measurements are as follows: What are the inputs and the sources of data? How are the data to be analyzed? What are the units of measurement? What will the outputs be? And, How frequently will the results be reported? Objectives should be tied to one of the primary measurements. For instance, a service industry objective might relate to customer service responsiveness with waiting time, satisfactory completion of service, and friendliness of the service representatives included in the basic objective and measurement. Objectives must be compatible throughout the organization. Increased production in an operation that is not a bottleneck operation might help a manufacturing function improve its efficiency but would not necessarily improve the effectiveness of the organization.

5.5 Responsibility, Authority and Communication

5.5.1 Responsibility and Authority
The authority and responsibilities of all the functions must be known. Responsibilities and authorities can be established by job or function descriptions when documentation is necessary. Organization charts are helpful in showing the interrelationships between functions. The same results can be attained informally as long as everyone knows the responsibilities and authorities and the organization maintains consistency. Individuals may wear many hats in a smaller organization without causing any problems.

5.5.2 Management Representative
The responsibility and authority for the quality management program needs to be centrally controlled. The standard requires that the organization put this responsibility and authority in the hands of a *management representative*. Experience has shown that in small businesses the management representative is usually the person in charge of the facility or someone who reports directly to the person in charge.

5.5.3 Internal Communication
Small businesses have an advantage over large businesses in internal communication. There is frequent interaction in most small businesses. This naturally promotes communication.

5.6 Management Review

5.6.1 General, 5.6.2 Review Input, and 5.6.3 Review Output
Because of their close structure and open communication, small businesses may tend to try to skip management review meetings. However, management reviews of the quality management system are necessary—they are the end and the beginning of the control loop. This is where past results are evaluated and plans are made. How, then, can management reviews become a valuable tool? Some small businesses have made the review extremely effective by combining it with regular staff meetings. A review of most staff meeting agendas and quality management system reviews shows many overlapping areas of concern. Items covered in management reviews include the following:

- *Follow-up items from previous management reviews.* Management must determine whether the action items have been completed and whether the actions have been verified as effective.

- *Customer feedback.* This shows how well the business is meeting customers' product requirements and where problems may be occurring in marketing, sales, delivery, customer service, and other customer-related processes.

- *Internal audits.* These show where the quality management system is working and where it needs to be improved.

- *The frequency, magnitude, success in implementation, time required for implementation, and other measures of the preventative and corrective actions.* These show where needed modifications or improvements are needed in the quality management system.

- *Process performance data and product conformity data obtained from major production and quality records and from nonconformance reports.* These serve to highlight where product realization processes need improvement.

All of the concepts above are reactions to something that has occurred. The organization should develop additional ideas to improve the quality management system.

Small businesses should use the management review as an opportunity to stand back from the everyday operations and take a comprehensive look at their organization.

ISO 9004:2000 provides guidance on management review input concepts and review outputs that offer opportunities to enhance efficiency.

6   Resource Management

6.1   Provision of Resources

"Resources" are all the resources needed for the entire quality management system, not just the resources necessary to produce a product. They include resources necessary to design, develop, and manage the quality management system; manage resources; provide for product realization; and measure, analyze, and improve the quality management system. Such resources include personnel, supplies, materials, equipment, facilities, and time. They include temporary and permanent personnel; both purchased and leased equipment and facilities; and, in most cases, subcontracted services.

6.2   Human Resources

6.2.1   General

Personnel performing work affecting product quality must be competent in terms of appropriate education, training, skills, and experience. Virtually any job within any business will have a possible effect on quality.

6.2.2   Competence, Awareness and Training

In large organizations competence requirements are documented many times by the use of job descriptions, which define job skills; proficiency requirements; or similar documents for personnel requirements. Such detail is generally not necessary for small organizations. In fact, it may be unnecessarily bureaucratic. Simple techniques used by some small businesses are a brief table of minimum skill, training, and education requirements or a brief paragraph explaining these requirements. These documents are usually only one to two pages in length for the entire organization. Even these techniques are not necessary for small businesses where management is in routine contact with the entire workforce. In such cases, management knows what the position requirements are.

Once the organization has determined what competencies are necessary, it needs to provide the training or take other actions to satisfy these needs. The competency requirements are then compared with the actual competencies of the employees. A training plan for the organization can be developed from these data. Training can be performed in-house or at external facilities such as seminars, institutions providing adult education, or similar facilities.

The effectiveness of training needs to be evaluated immediately after it is given and later to determine how well the training was understood and retained. This evaluation may be formal or informal.

Records of education, training, skills, and experience need to be maintained.

6.3 Infrastructure

Infrastructure consists of everything that an organization needs to produce and deliver the product or service. The only thing that it does not include is personnel. Infrastructure includes buildings, workspace, utilities, process equipment, supporting services such as building and equipment services, transportation and related equipment and facilities, and communications systems.

Most small businesses should not have to establish special systems for handling infrastructure. Usually small businesses work with the existing facilities, equipment, and support services. When small businesses make any significant changes to their infrastructure they go through an evaluation process that is unique to the anticipated change. The planning behind such changes usually involves most of the management of the organization.

6.4 Work Environment

The work environment is the set of conditions under which work is performed and includes physical, social, psychological, and environmental factors (such as temperature, recognition schemes, ergonomics, and atmospheric composition).

This requirement includes the concepts of clean rooms for electronic assembly operations, air-conditioning for some warehouse and manufacturing operations, special atmospheres for unique heat-treating operations, and ergonomic workstations for employees performing repetitive operations. The small business can handle the requirements of this clause similar to the way that it can handle the requirements for infrastructure.

7 Product Realization

7.1 Planning of Realization

This planning element ties in with clause 4.1, "Quality management system—general requirements," in understanding and managing the processes of your organization. The planning of realization is an area where most small businesses excel since this is their specialized area of expertise. Meeting requirements of this product realization element should not be difficult for most small businesses. In many cases, the product or service is well established. The quality objectives and requirements of the product are well known. New or additional processes or documents are usually not needed. The resources specific to the product have already been established, and no additional resources are usually necessary. Verification, validation, monitoring, inspection, and test activities are in place. The criteria for product acceptance have also been established.

In some cases, additional records may be needed to provide the evidence that the process and products fulfill the requirements in the specifications.

The product realization processes can be described concisely in the quality manual for simple products and services. It should not be necessary to include extensive details in the procedures. Repetitive product processes can be described in the quality manual, augmented when necessary by procedures and work instructions.

The challenge to the small business is to make the product realization processes more effective. The business needs to look for all opportunities for improvement when the current processes, procedures, documents, and records are reviewed during the implementation of ISO 9001:2000.

ISO 9004:2000 provides extensive guidance on the product realization element. An overall review of the concept and an extensive discussion of the issues to be considered in product realization are found in ISO 9004:2000 clauses 7.1.1 and 7.1.2. ISO 9004:2000 clause 7.1.3.1 identifies some of the basic and support processes that can be considered for a quality management system. ISO 9004:2000 clause 7.1.3.2 addresses process input and outputs including input concepts to consider and topics for review of process performance. Remember, ISO 9004:2000 is a guidance document. The ideas and guidance therein are not requirements for a quality management program.

7.2   Customer-Related Processes

7.2.1   *Determination of Requirements Related to the Product*
Customer product requirements are usually relatively easy to obtain for routine, off-the-shelf items and catalog products. Customer requirements are also easy to obtain for services such as those provided by service businesses. Records related to these requirements are usually either paper forms or computer data programs and files. In both cases data control can be maintained by requiring certain blanks in the forms to be filled out or requiring data to be entered into specific data fields.

Requirements that are not stated by the customer but necessary for the use of the product, such as a requirement dealing with the shape of a hammer handle, need to be determined. The supplier is also responsible for determining the statutory and regulatory requirements related to the product or service, since the supplier is supposed to be the expert. Most suppliers include requirements of their own that improve the desirability of the product or that make the product easier to produce.

Such product requirement processes are usually effectively operating in small businesses and need only to be documented as necessary.

7.2.2   *Review of Requirements Related to the Product*
Experience has shown that clerical personnel perform this review for simple or repetitive products. The review usually includes at least one member of top management when the product is complex or large.

7.2.3   *Customer Communication*
Most small businesses have an advantage in this area. Usually the people in a small organization are close to the customer. Feedback given to any employee gets

to top management rather quickly. Many times top management receives customer complaints and positive comments directly from the customer.

Small businesses can document customer feedback easily with log or journal entries. The logs and journals are used to review customer feedback during management reviews.

ISO 9004:2000 clause 7.2 offers ideas on expanding communication to interested parties other than the customer.

7.3 Design and Development

Small businesses may want to review the guidance in ISO 9004:2000 clause 7.3 on design concepts.

Many small businesses will have a relatively simple design process, and therefore the design planning will be minimal. Frequently the designer in a small business will have design responsibility as one of many tasks. Interfaces involved are minimal.

7.3.2 Design and Development Inputs

A journal or perhaps a single sheet of paper in a product design file can be used to record the design requirements for product when design efforts are minimal.

7.3.3 Design and Development Outputs

Existing businesses performing design usually have their design output documented in some manner. The approval process is usually in place.

7.3.4 Design and Development Review

Design reviews in small businesses need to include all affected functions, including the customer when necessary. Design reviews can be conducted in a meeting, or the various functions involved can review the design output individually. Design review records may consist of meeting minutes, journal entries, or notes in a design file.

7.3.5 Design and Development Verification

Most small businesses compare a new design with a similar, proven design or use alternative calculations or methodologies, perform qualification tests, or review the design documents before release. Their choice of technique is based on what has proven successful in their line of business.

7.3.6 Design and Development Validation

As with verification, most small businesses have determined what form of design validation is successful for them.

7.3.7 Control of Design and Development Changes

Most successful small businesses have a design change and review process in place that includes the maintenance of records. However, many small businesses must watch out for a problem. There's a tendency to forget documentation because of the ease of informal communication. As a result, there is lack of communication and the change is not implemented.

7.4 Purchasing

Purchasing is an area ripe for improving profitability. One of the quality management concepts is partnering with suppliers, essentially making them an integral part of the organization.

7.4.1   Purchasing Process

Supplier records and evaluations may be documented in a journal or log. Problems with nonconforming or defective product, off-schedule delivery, and quality system problems are some of the primary evaluation criteria used by businesses. Some businesses find that an approved supplier list backed up by supplier data is a useful technique.

7.4.2   Purchasing Information

Information about the desired product or service must be communicated to the supplier. The format this takes may be as simple as the identification of a catalog number or as complicated as a 60-page contract that describes the product in extreme detail including design, fit, form, function, and performance requirements. It may also include elements such as requirements for qualification of personnel and/or equipment or supplier quality management system requirements. Purchase requirements must be reviewed for adequacy before they are submitted to the supplier. This may amount to signing or initialing a purchase order for a simple product. But for complex products or services, it may mean using a multistage purchasing document package review process.

7.4.3   Verification of Purchased Product

Several techniques are used to verify product including certifying suppliers and their ability to meet purchase requirements, inspecting 100 percent or a sample of the product upon its receipt, and verifying the product at the supplier's facility. Small businesses use a combination of these verification techniques.

This is an area ripe for profit improvement. Here are two examples:

- Large reductions in return of noncomplying raw metal plate, bars, shapes, and forgings in numerous small companies by the disqualification of suppliers without effective quality or traceability programs

- The use of a rigorous equipment performance qualification program at the supplier's facility to ensure the receipt of effective machine tools

7.5   Production and Service Provision

7.5.1   Control of Production and Service Provision

Production and/or service provision control systems should be evaluated. Are the product characteristics adequately described? Are work instructions available if and where they are necessary? Have the processes for the release, delivery, and postdelivery activities been implemented?

7.5.2   Validation of Processes for Production and Service Provision

Most small businesses that use processes to produce product and provide services have already established their systems for process, equipment, and personnel qualification and validation.

Lack of process validation can cause problems. One organization did not discover a chemical incompatibility between a base material and a new coating substance until it was put into production. This incompatibility reduced the strength of the base product to close to the minimum limit. Extensive research had to be performed to find a coating that would eliminate the strength problem and still allow the final product to meet requirements.

7.5.3   Identification and Traceability

Again, most small businesses have effective identification and traceability systems in place. If this is your situation, just briefly describe your system for product identification in your quality manual. If traceability is a requirement, briefly describe your traceability system. If you already have documented procedures, refer to them in your quality manual.

7.5.4   Customer Property

Most small businesses, especially those in the service industry, already have systems in place that meet the requirements for handling customer property.

7.5.5   Preservation of Product

Most small businesses have adequate systems in place to handle the preservation of their product.

7.6   Control of Measuring and Monitoring Devices

Most small businesses have good calibration programs. However, small businesses frequently only check their measuring devices against one or two standards instead of performing a thorough calibration. As an example, if a machine shop only checks a 0-to-1-inch micrometer at 0 and 1 inches, the shop will not know if the thread is worn somewhere else in the actual working range, such as at 0.627 inches. Likewise, the shop won't know the accuracy of the barrel if it is only checked at 0.025-inch increments. Therefore, it is better to check several increments around the barrel and several positions along the full range of the travel.

ISO 10012-1, *Quality assurance requirements for measuring equipment—Part 1: Metrological confirmation system for measuring equipment*, and ISO 10012-2, *Quality assurance for measuring equipment—Part 2: Guidelines for control of measurement processes*, are good references for the establishment of a measurement control program. This is definitely not a requirement, but it should help a small business establish a calibration program that will help the organization improve. Both of these documents are being updated, combined, and revised. The new standard will reflect current measurement concepts and the structure and concepts of ISO 9001:2000.

One 20-person machining organization was able to cut prospective calibration costs by more than 80 percent by establishing a simple but comprehensive gage utilization and calibration program.

8   Measurement, Analysis and Improvement

8.1   General

This section of ISO 9001:2000 is possibly the most important section for the small business. This is because it shows how to use measuring and monitoring to improve the effectiveness of the organization. The information attained through measuring and monitoring is used by management in management reviews and otherwise to guide future operations of the organization.

Small businesses need to concentrate on this area. Small businesses are less likely to have an effective measuring and monitoring program because their organization is often informal and their measurements are subjective.

ISO 9001:2000 strongly promotes the use of statistics. ISO/TC 176 developed ISO/TR 10017:1999, *Guidance on statistical techniques for ISO 9001:1994,* which can help identify the various techniques businesses can use for various elements of a quality management system. Although it was written for the 1994 edition of the standard, it is a useful guidance tool for an ISO 9001:2000 quality management system.

ISO/TC 69 has developed ISO 11462-1, *Guidelines for implementation of statistical process control (SPC)—Part 1: Elements of SPC*. That document can help a small business design an SPC program for any type of organization, not just high-volume manufacturers.

Virtually every small business, especially ones with informal operating systems, should review clause 8 of ISO 9004:2000 for ideas on how to implement the measuring, analysis, and improvement aspects of their quality management system.

8.2 Monitoring and Measurement

8.2.1 Customer Satisfaction

Customer satisfaction is one of the primary reasons for having a quality management system, and it is a prime focus of ISO 9000:2000. This, as was explained earlier, is an element of the quality management system that should be relatively easy for most small businesses to comply with because the upper-level management of such businesses is usually extremely close to the customer base.

Management should consider maintaining logs or journals of customer comments. This material can then be reviewed and analyzed for trends and for possible areas for improvement. The standard requires the use of this customer input in management reviews.

8.2.2 Internal Audit

Internal auditing is an extremely effective tool for the management of small companies. Many times management in small organizations tends to rely on its feel of the processes and how well they are working. A formal internal audit system will yield concrete information on the true status of the organization and will improve operations.

8.2.3 Monitoring and Measurement of Processes

Most small businesses, especially those that have been in business for a long time, have identified their important process parameters and process measurements. This is true for the critical measurements of their products, their product realization processes, and their management processes.

However, many new small businesses have not identified their important process parameters. They should look at any successful fast-food chain to help them understand how to identify important process parameters. The chain has developed the specifications for making a product such as French-fried potatoes. Equipment has been designed that contains the correct amount of shortening, heats it to the correct temperature, holds the correct amount of potatoes cut to the correct size, and has a timer to let workers know when to remove the fries. As a result, a customer can obtain a consistent product at any of the restaurants in the chain. The chain has also developed other processes for the managers to use such as a process to determine the amount of food to start processing at any time based on sales volume.

Examine your processes. Are there areas where confusion is occurring? Can you identify areas that you feel may cause problems? Are there areas where you feel your workers don't quite understand what they are doing or why they are doing it? Such areas are good candidates for establishing process controls and measurements.

A good after-the-fact technique to identify important process characteristics is to examine sales, complaint, customer comment, production, and inspection records looking for areas where problems or losses are occurring. Study these problems and the parameters that contribute to them, and make use of statistical techniques.

You must determine the specifications, numerical limits, or signal points to operate the process once the important parameters have been identified.

8.2.4   Monitoring and Measurement of Product

Most successful small businesses already have systems in place that enable them to deliver conforming product to their customers.

8.3   Control of Nonconforming Product

The technique used to control nonconforming product depends on the product and organization. Successful systems have just used notes on production reports, logs, or notes made by the appropriate personnel. The primary needs are that the material is controlled and that the data are available for analysis of the quality system's effectiveness.

An in-depth analysis of one organization's nonconformance reports showed that losses were about 20 percent of sales (over 100 percent of profits). Half of these losses were due to errors made by sales personnel on sales orders. The problem was corrected by modifying the sales order process and increasing contract review activities.

8.4   Analysis of Data

Collected data are provided directly to top management in small companies. The top managers then conduct the analysis of the data as part of the management review. Data-planning, data-gathering, and data analysis techniques for smaller organizations do not have to be as complex as they do for large organizations. However, since this is an extremely important part of the quality management system, the management team needs to examine this element and plan the analysis processes.

8.5   Improvement

A quality management system needs to be continually improved because that means improved profitability. Data analysis is used to find areas for improvement. A classic example of data analysis involved a bank with branches in the city's business district and in the suburbs. The management felt that their clients wanted to get their business done as fast as possible and established programs to successfully implement the program. They were able to trim waiting times in half. However, one branch received a significant increase in customer complaints. Analysis of the complaints showed that the branch with increased complaints was near an old, established neighborhood that had residents with a high median age. These older customers preferred more personalized service and were not concerned about the waiting time.

A second example involved a manufacturing firm that was threading large-diameter customer pipe. The product specifications called out the threaded areas specifications and specified a minimum wall thickness. About 20 percent of the product was being rejected for wall thickness slightly below minimum. A study of the data showed that the raw pipe wall thickness was centered close to the minimum wall thickness. (The pipe was sold by the foot, but the material cost for the manufacture of the pipe was by the pound. The steel mill had good process controls and could manufacture the product within specifications while running the wall thickness on the minimum side.) The threading company's product design engineering had specified the finished wall thickness based on the nominal wall thickness. The finished wall thickness specification was changed to a dimension based on the minimum wall thickness. The rejection of pipe for thin wall thickness was eliminated.

Corrective action, then, is used when problems occur, and preventive action is used to make sure that similar problems do not occur in other areas. Corrective action, preventive action, data analysis, and audit results are then used in management reviews. The quality policy and objectives should also be examined for modification and improvement.

8.5.2 Corrective Action

Corrective action is a problem area for many small businesses. Because many small organizations have a shallow structure, corrections to problems are made on the fly. As a result, they do not get documented. This can cause small organizations to "reinvent the wheel" by continually making the same correction without finding the root cause of the problem or even identifying the fact that there is a root cause.

Large companies usually have specialized forms and complex procedures to identify areas for corrective action and to follow those corrective actions through completion and validation.

Small companies can use logs or journals to document problem areas as they occur. One company makes copies of the repair person's customer contact form. A copy of the form is made when a customer makes a significant positive or negative comment. This file of comments is then reviewed periodically to categorize them and identify areas of concern. These areas of concern are prioritized, and the important ones are selected for improvement. Areas of increased favorable comments are also evaluated to see whether techniques can be identified to improve other areas of the business.

Corrective and preventive action systems should be as simple as possible.

8.5.3 Preventive Action

Like corrective action, preventive action is a problem area for many small businesses, again due to their shallow structure. That structure can cause small organizations to miss opportunities to identify actions that can be applied to other product lines or other areas of the quality system.

A technique called failure mode effect and criticality analysis (FMECA) was developed as a reliability technique to reduce the likelihood of failure of complex systems such as the early missile systems and the U.S. space program. This technique is a handy one for small businesses that are about to expand with new equipment, buy new tooling, or start up a new process. The first step is to determine all the possible ways that failure could occur. This can be done by individuals or a group. All possible failures are documented. None are thrown out at this time. The next step is to evaluate the probability of failure. Is failure almost certain or is it extremely unlikely? The possible causes are then grouped by their probability of occurrence. The next step is to determine the criticality of a failure. Will a failure cause death or just a slight inconvenience for the customer? The small business can then implement preventive actions to minimize risks as much as possible.

CONCLUSION

This chapter has discussed how to implement a small business quality management system or update one to ISO 9001:2000. Remember the major elements of the quality management system. Identify the processes and their interrelationships. Plan the major processes, including the management processes, product realization processes, and measurement processes. Establish quality objectives and measure yourself against those objectives and the requirements of clause 4.1, which are the general requirements for your quality management system.

ENDNOTE

1. Material for this chapter was taken from *ISO 9001:2000 for Small and Medium Sized Businesses* by Herbert C. Monnich Jr. (Milwaukee: ASQ Quality Press, 2001).

Chapter 44

Use of Consortia and the NIST MEP Network

Morgan Hall
University of Maryland Center for Quality and Productivity,
Baltimore, Maryland

M any small companies have experienced sticker shock for consulting services as they face strict customer requirements for ISO 9000 registration.
Expert consultants charge fees of $1200 per day and up. Typically, a
small firm requires 10 to 20 days of consulting/training support during their
implementation. This can add up to an often unaffordable cost for a firm to obtain
ISO 9000 registration as a market requirement and often an entry point to doing
business. Consortium programs—generally administered and often subsidized by
universities, NIST-sponsored assistance centers, and other public organizations—
are vehicles to substantially reduce the costs of implementation support. By sharing an expert resource with other companies involved in implementation,
significant cost savings can be realized. An additional benefit is that people are
able to work together with their counterparts from other companies to design procedures and develop a quality management system (QMS). The generic nature of
processes such as purchasing, training, contract review, and others often allows
one company to share its quality methodology with another. This is useful considering that small manufacturing companies experience less employee turnover,
so many employees rise through the ranks to middle and upper management
without having worked elsewhere.

Implementing ISO 9000 in a consortium requires a strong management commitment to the implementation and its required resources. Often a lack of such a
commitment leads to an overly lengthy deployment of the QMS and, much worse,
disconnection from the true objectives of the company. Many small business owners and managers perceive ISO 9000 as a necessary evil required by customers. As

a result, full responsibility is handed over to a middle manager who lacks the organizational foresight, creativity, and/or authority to effectively deploy an organizationwide QMS. To be successful in a consortium (or individual) implementation of ISO 9000, upper management must play an active and participatory role, especially in the early stages. Upper managers cannot "toss it over the wall" to a quality or plant manager. Instead, they must embrace quality management as an effective management system along with financial, sales, environmental, human resource, and other management systems.

There are two basic approaches to ISO 9000 consortia: large-group fixed programs and small-group hybrid programs.

LARGE-GROUP FIXED CONSORTIUM PROGRAMS

This approach provides the most substantial cost savings but has displayed a relatively low level of success. Anywhere from 10 to 25 companies form a consortium with a fixed (normally one-year) time frame. Their common goal is to achieve ISO 9000 registration in a one- to two-year time frame. A fixed program is presented at monthly training sessions to management representatives from the participating firms. Trainees are provided with training materials to use on-site at their companies to further train employees in ISO 9000 and to assist in the deployment of the QMS. To augment the group training, consultants visit each company two to three times during the implementation to provide individualized support. These programs follow a set curriculum that requires each company to stay in lockstep with the other participating companies. They are also led toward synchronizing their efforts by addressing each clause of the standard at the same time and in a similar fashion. Documentation templates are often provided to facilitate the process.

This approach can be effective, to a point, and can enable a company to obtain ISO 9000 registration in the defined time frame. The QMS will not be as effective as it can be, however, due to the lack of individual attention a consultant and management representative can give to the uniqueness of the organization's business culture and environment. A supportive management understanding, commitment, and involvement in the process from day one should augment the "train the trainer" approach. Care must be taken to implement a system that is consistent with the culture and organizational goals. It must be designed and perceived as a value-added process that justifies the resources allocated to it. This requires teamwork between the ISO 9000 management representative, the implementation team, and upper management. Additional activities and meetings must be scheduled beyond the formal training sessions provided by the consortium. The management representative must be a true leader with the authority to manage the QMS and its implementation process. He or she must also have training skills and the skills required to manage meetings. It must be clear that the management representative is not implementing QMS alone but acting as guide and coach for the rest of the organization.

It must be noted that the true and total cost of implementing ISO 9000 and obtaining registration includes the costs of consultants and trainers, the cost of the registrar, and internal labor costs. The internal labor costs of this approach tend to be high due to the duplicity of training. In addition, management representatives who are provided materials and are trained to train are often not the most effective trainers. Unfortunately, many organizations, realizing this, minimize internal training of the workforce. A QMS system is implemented but, due to lack of buy-in and other factors, is often ineffective and burdensome.

SMALL-GROUP HYBRID CONSORTIUM PROGRAMS

Halfway between going it alone and working one-on-one with a consultant/trainer in a fixed consortium approach are hybrid consortia. These programs are designed for smaller consortia consisting of four to six companies. Member organizations receive their ISO 9000 training as a group during the program's inception. Because the hybrid consortium is smaller, more people (two to four) from the organization attend training sessions. This enables upper management to get involved early in the program and develop the same understanding of QMS as the management representative. The all-important implementation team comes together early and uses the power of teamwork to kick off the implementation with an added impetus. These up-front training sessions for the implementation teams encompass two to three days. Economy of scale is still realized for the training. Although costs do range higher than with a fixed consortium, there are still savings over hiring a consultant/trainer on an individual basis.

After completion of group training, each participating organization continues its ISO 9000 implementation at its own pace and in its own sequence. The consultant/trainer provides on-site support for the duration of the program. The amount and nature of this support varies, depending on the schedule, needs, and resource availability of each company. The support requirement can be determined in two ways: It can be estimated based on the results of a preassessment, or it can be determined internally after the training portion by the implementation team. The individualized support does escalate the out-of-pocket costs but can go a long way toward reducing time and internal resource requirements. This approach also provides greater assurance that the QMS will align with organizational goals, thereby adding value and ensuring effective deployment and upper-management support.

FUNDING ISO 9000 CONSORTIA

Many state governments provide funding for ISO 9000 implementation. In some instances, the funding is earmarked for workforce training. There is a fine line between ISO 9000 training and consulting. In some cases, it has been necessary to catalogue all implementation support as training, though its true value is derived from the experience and guidance provided by the consultant. Private corporations have supported consortium programs for their vendors, thereby enhancing the quality of their own supply chain.

NIST MEP CENTER SUPPORT

Nationally, the Manufacturing Extension Partnership (MEP) network of the National Institute of Standards and Technology (NIST) provides the effective link among government funding and support; ISO 9000 training, consulting, and auditing services; and the needs of small to mid-sized manufacturing companies. The following is a statement of MEP's goals posted on their Web site (www.mep.nist.gov/index2.html):

> MEP is a nationwide network of not-for-profit centers in over 400 locations nationwide, whose sole purpose is to provide small to medium sized manufacturers with the help they need to succeed. The centers, serving all 50 states, the District of Columbia and Puerto Rico, are linked together through the Department of Commerce's National Institute of Standards and Technology. That makes it possible for even the smallest firms to tap into the expertise of knowledgeable manufacturing and business specialists all over the U.S.

There are many advantages for a company to turn to their local MEP Center for ISO 9000 support. The MEP agenda reaches far beyond quality management. The group seeks to establish long-term relationships with manufacturing companies and provide support in a number of areas, including quality, business management, human resources, market development, materials engineering, plant layout, product development, environmental studies, financial planning, information systems, and e-commerce.

SOME EXAMPLES OF MEP QUALITY PROGRAMS

California Manufacturing Technology Center (CMTC)

CMTC is the largest MEP in the system with more than 170 people. In the quality group, there are 17 full-time people, 15 of which are full-time consultants working on quality-related projects. These consultants are stationed in offices in the Southern California area. CMTC has offices in Inland Empire, San Diego, Los Angeles, Orange County (Anaheim), Ventura/Santa Barbara, Fresno, and Burbank.

CMTC products are quality systems implementations, which include ISO 9000:1994, ISO 9000:2000, aerospace (AS 9000 and AS 9100), automotive (QS 9000 and ISO 16949), calibration (ISO 17025, ANSI/NCSL Z540), food processing (HACCP and GMP), medical devices (QSR), pharmaceuticals (GMP), and telecommunications (TL 9000). They also work in the areas of auditing (internal and gap), software quality assurance, total quality management (TQM), Six Sigma, ISO 14000 environmental assistance, and safety assistance.

CMTC also provides services in product assurance, such as statistical process control, reliability, and CE marking.

CMTC's partners are the centers for applied competitive technologies in the local colleges who do a lot of the training on-site for their clients. They do educational training programs (ETPs), which are funded by the portion of manufacturers' state tax money designated for employee training.

Maryland ISO Consortium Program

Through a Maryland consortium program, groups of 15 to 20 participating companies are brought to the point of readiness for certification and registration of their individual QMSs by third-party registrars if they choose to do so. Nearly 300 organizations have participated in the Maryland ISO program. Organizations completing the Maryland consortium represent approximately 20 percent of the ISO certifications in the state.

The consortium approach is particularly applicable to organizations wishing to become registered but unwilling or unable to commit large financial resources for outside assistance in this effort.

As a prerequisite to joining an ISO consortium, top management from prospective member companies must attend a preconsortium meeting. The purpose of this meeting is to give these managers the information they need to decide if consortium membership has value for their companies and if they are willing to commit the necessary time and resources to the process.

Once formed, the consortium follows a generic plan based on the implementation of a quality assurance system conforming to the ISO 9001 model. The plan takes approximately 18 months and consists of over 90 benchmark events, the majority of which are internal company activities. Seventeen of these events are focused group meetings, each covering a particular aspect of ISO registration. An additional seven meetings are held for company top management. These meetings, which are focused on management's role, are intended to keep top management informed and engaged. Training at all sessions is provided by staff from the University of Maryland Center for Quality and Productivity (UMCQP) staff, representatives of ISO registered companies, and/or registrars.

The consortium normally meets once every four to six weeks according to a time schedule based on the generic plan. Each meeting consists of a brief program status update, appropriate scheduled training, and the sharing of experiences. Time is also available for the discussion of problems and solutions. The structured part of the meeting normally lasts four hours. In addition to the meetings, UMCQP staff also provide on-site guidance to each member organization.

Participating companies are asked to commit to the development and implementation of an ISO-9000 QMS; appoint a person to participate in the consortium activities and meetings and to coordinate the development and implementation of the company's plan; involve all company management and the workforce in the effort; provide the necessary resources; and keep the company's implementation appropriately synchronized with the other companies in the consortium.

Funding for the program is provided by the Maryland Department of Business and Economic Development (DBED). Technical guidance and program management are provided by UMCQP.

Chapter 45

ISO 9000 and International Trade— ISO in Emerging Economies

Armando Espinosa
President, Latin American Institute for Quality (INLAC), Mexico City

BACKGROUND

Latin American industry emerged after World War II, when large companies sprung up mainly in the siderurgical, iron, and steel industries and oil sectors in countries such as Brazil, Argentina, and Mexico. In the 1940s, quality was based on the fulfillment of the products' technical reference standards. Normally, American standards were used, such as those of the American Society for Testing and Materials (ASTM), the American Petroleum Institute (API), the American Society of Mechanical Engineers (ASME), the Tubular Exchange Manufacturers' Association (TEMA), Underwriters Laboratories (UL), and the American National Standards Institute (ANSI), among others. Certain national organizations of emerging countries based their performance on their own standards, adapting and translating those previously mentioned. Whatever technical standard was used, quality was focused on the fulfillment of the referenced standards through inspection at the final stage of the process. In addition, large buyers created and gave specific importance to the inspection departments. They also established management processes that supported the engineering area by selecting the appropriate standards for a specific material or product, in accordance with its use and operation. These organizations verified, in the suppliers' plants, that the goods requested, once manufactured, would be within the tolerances set forth by the corresponding standards.

During the 1950s to the 1980s, the growth of the industries of emerging countries focused on the internal market, creating customs tariffs protection and supports to projects for import substitutions. This caused the growth of large companies, and promoted and developed small and medium companies but without the knowledge of a true quality culture based on managerial indicators. The costs of this lack of quality were secondary, covered up under the policy of high production volumes to handle the growing demands of clients.

It is important to mention that in these economies, the ISO product standards were practically not used, and there was an erroneously understood policy of national sovereignty. This could be contrasted with the European tendency, which after World War II created international organizations as discussion forums to resolve controversies, reinforce cooperation among countries, and to avoid conflicts.

Thus, during the 1940s, the following world entities were created:

- United Nations (UN)
- International Organization for Standardization (ISO)
- General Agreement on Tariffs and Trade (GATT)
- World Trade Organization (WTO)
- International Telecommunications Link (ITL)

Within the world trade scenario and the notion of sovereignty, many countries, at their own initiative, became members of the WTO. By doing so, they accepted the Code of Good Practice for the Preparation, Adoption, and Application of Standards, which is a part of the WTO exhibit entitled Agreement on Technical Barriers to Trade (TBT), with the understanding that these agreements prevail over all regional or national agreements. The TBT attempts to avoid or eliminate technical nontariff barriers to trade. The countries that adopt this covenant agree to:

- Give national nondiscriminatory treatment to import products
- Avoid unnecessary trade obstacles by using international standards

With this evolution, which has minimized the substitution of import projects, any country's attempt to defend the national markets by means of standards and regulations, such as barriers for products or services, is unpractical. There are reciprocity laws that can be exercised between those countries that consider themselves affected by these barriers.

While the purpose of international standardization is to facilitate open trade, it is important to mention that the international standardization process is established to promote the participation of all interested nations to ensure a balance of representation from around the world. The process involves experts from industry, traders, consultants, and service-rendering organizations in certain forums to discuss and defend their points of view during the development of these international standards. This responsibility cannot be the exclusive work of governments. Companies that will use the standards need to participate with their knowledge of technology, production, inspection, and the satisfaction of their clients. It is only by including such users that international standards can be validated.

More and more countries, such as Argentina, Brazil, and Mexico, are working together, their groups of experts in the technical committees participating in the discussion of changes to the basic globalization tool for the next millennium of international standardization. One cannot conceive that countries, such as those of Latin America, Africa, and some Asian countries, would not consider the scientific and technological information represented by more than 10,000 technological international standards ISO/IEC has published to date. Yet these emerging economies do not commonly use these standards. This enormous combined reserve of information may and should be used in countries under development.

Countries in Europe, North America, and Asia gain many benefits from this information. They also benefit from having active member bodies of ISO and IEC, such as ANSI from the United States, the Standards Council of Canada (SCC), the European regional standards body (CEN), the British Standards Institution (BSI) and the Japanese Standards Institute, to mention a few of the most frequent participating organizations. These organizations adopt existing ISO standards, participate in various technical committees, and propose new standards to convert them to ISO standards. Their coordination favors trade exchange to the benefit of their countries and their companies.

In summary:

- Trade globalization is irreversible
- There are international agreements on good practices for the drafting, adoption, and application of standards that do not constitute technical barriers to international trade
- Countries with emerging economies should be encouraged to participate in the ISO technical committees
- There is a combined reserve of more than 10,000 existing ISO standards, with limited use by countries under development

NEED FOR ISO 9000 IN THE INTERNATIONAL TRADE AREA AS A FACILITATOR OF INTERNATIONAL TRADE

The discussion in the previous section relates mostly to product standards and other standards of a technical nature, such as testing methods. Standards have also become important in the field of quality management systems. In some emerging countries, attempts have been made to change the policy for appraising quality to substitute quality assurance for production inspection.

In the mid-1980s, an attempt was made to promote quality assurance systems through standards, such as the Canadian Standards Association's Z-299 series and the American Petroleum Institute's API Q1. These standards did not gain wide acceptance because emerging countries would consider them regional standards.

The need to establish a normalized quality system arose in the 1980s, specifically due to problems satisfying the quality criteria set forth by clients, in addition to the referenced technical standards of products. This occurred within the context of growing market internationalization and the inclination of large companies to make quality the central axis of their productivity and competition strategy.

This market internationalization gave rise to the need for uniform quality of not only the product but also the process as a whole, starting with the suppliers of raw materials and ending with delivery and service to clients. Thus, when an Asian supplier provides a product to a Latin American company, the specific quality criteria under which it delivers its product must in all cases comply with a certain uniformity, based on a standard that supplements the technical standard of the product in question. In this context, uniform criteria, based on internationally accepted principles, are required. At the same time, the criteria must be sufficiently flexible to be adapted to the large range of production situations, from agriculture to service rendering.

The ISO 9000 standards, accepted throughout the world, constitute a series that basically ensures that organizations have a system to manage achievement of quality. This could lead us to believe that when a product or service is acquired from an ISO 9000–certified company, we will, in most cases, receive the expected quality. But we must remember that certification of management systems to standards like ISO 9001 is completely different from certification of products to specific technical product standards. ISO 9000 certification means there is a system in place to manage quality, not that products meet a specified technical requirement.

In a global context, the ISO 9000 standards and associated certification can provide needed confidence to support international trade activities. In this respect, for example, trade agreements such as the North American Free Trade Agreement executed by Mexico, Canada, and the United States have facilitated trade operations. It is important to mention that initially these standards were not easy to comply with due to economic and cultural differences among the participating countries. It was somewhat like a minor league baseball team being suddenly informed that the following year it would compete in the major leagues. The minor league team would undoubtedly suffer loses during its first few seasons until it adapted to a field of greater competition, but eventually the team would increase its competitive capabilities.

It is important to note that standards such as ISO 9000 facilitate complying with the internalization objectives. In addition, these standards represent a letter of introduction for companies that wish to export. While export may be a possibility without such a letter of introduction, certification certainly can help.

It is important to highlight the value of the documentation required by these standards. In the long and medium term, the quality management system and its documentation should be set up so that they increase the internal quality levels of organizations, to improve profits while allowing for integration of domestic and international production chains. An important facilitator of this longer-range improvement is the common language established by the standards. Another aspect that should be noted is that by holding an ISO 9000 certificate, a company can avoid the various evaluations and audits required by each client to which the company supplies products or services.

Certain countries have integrated into regional organizations such as the Latin American Confederation of Technical Standards (COPANT); MERCOSUR, which has provided the grounding for regional trade agreements; and the Latin American Quality Assurance Institute (INLAC), a Liaison A organization to ISO/TC 176.

Spanish-speaking countries represent more than 600 million consumers. This is the reason why initiatives have been submitted for Spanish to be considered as an official language for the ISO 9000 standards, in addition to English, French, and Russian. At an ISO/TC 176 committee meeting held in San Francisco in September

1999, a work group headed by the technical ministry of COPANT, based in Argentina, was formed to perform Spanish translations. COPANT will be assisted by Spain and with the support of the INLAC. The concept is that, at the same time the ISO 9000:2000 standards are published in the official languages (English, French, and Russian), they will also be available in a single official Spanish-language version.

It should also be noted that the ISO 9000 standards series has definitely been a facilitator for international trade relationships and a basic tool in the execution of free trade agreements.

One problem experienced by companies that trade internationally was that other countries receiving products did not acknowledge the certification performed by domestic organizations. These domestic certification organizations were not recognized in the other countries. This problem will be reduced through the policies, regulations, and mutual recognition agreements of the International Accreditation Forum (IAF) for ISO 9000 quality management systems certification and the International Laboratory Accreditation Cooperation (ILAC) for laboratory accreditation.

The purpose of IAF is to group the accredited bodies of the evaluation organizations pursuant to each country. Last year, the IAF decided to establish a board comprising accreditation organizations and interested parties, applying the principle of representation of all interests, without any being dominant. The board's immediate goal is to achieve improvements to multilateral agreements so they may be deeper than just general acknowledgments. The advantage of this approach is that an accreditation certificate issued by any of the members of the IAF will be accepted by all the others.

With respect to ILAC in the field of laboratory accreditation, both for product calibration and certification, it has the same goals as the IAF. The active members of ILAC belong to four large regional blocks: Asia/Pacific, through the Asian/Pacific Laboratories Accreditation Cooperation (APLAC); the European Community through the European Cooperation for Accreditation; the U.S. through National Cooperation for Laboratory Accreditation (NACLA); and ILAC. An ILAC technical committee established a work group to implement a new ISO/IEC 17025 standard for accreditation of laboratories. Mutual recognition of certification is possible only if evaluation personnel are competent and professional in evaluating conformity.

Another international organization with the goal of establishing, by consensus, the criteria for the qualification, recording, and maintenance of auditors is the International Auditor and Training Certification Association (IATCA). The objectives of IATCA are to:

- Support the most extended acceptance of certificates, pursuant to a supplier's quality system that would lead to world acceptance of a sole certificate
- Establish international acceptance of auditors' equivalence certificates and approval of training courses
- Eliminate the need of multiple auditors' certifications and approval of training courses

To support these goals, two projects are being developed based on ISO/CASCO ISO/IEC 17025 guidelines and general criteria for the operation of personnel certification organizations.

The implementation and certification of quality systems in developing countries has been restricted by certain cultural aspects. In addition, at the start of ISO 9000 (1987), countries such as the United States and Japan, because of their solid standards for specific products, did not fully accept the ISO 9000 standards. However, when they realized that these standards were a world language that facilitated trading, they decided to promote them, rapidly increasing the number of certified companies based on a well-founded quality culture.

In emerging countries, this process has been slower, and regional organizations like INLAC have undertaken orientation campaigns, focusing on the new generation through a project named Child Induction to Quality. During INLAC's last three world forums (held in 1999 at León, Guanajuato, Mexico, in 2000 at Veracruz, Mexico, and in 2001 at Mexico City, Mexico), seminars were conducted for children 10 to 12 years old.

The certification process must have credibility. The ISO 9000 certification of companies in certain Latin American countries was achieved by a group of persons who were made responsible for the preparation of manuals and procedures. However, with respect to follow-up audits, we note that the involvement did not extend to top executives or operating areas.

THERE IS MUCH TO BE DONE

At the end of 1999, there were well over 300,000 certified companies in the world. It is noteworthy that only about 5 percent of these are from emerging countries. So much remains to be done, but based on trade agreements under discussion, this percentage will increase significantly in coming years. It is expected that certifications from emerging countries could increase by approximately 30 percent during the next five years because currently there is a common language of quality—ISO 9000. "The true quality is not in the things made by man, but in the man who does the things."

Chapter 46

Using ISO 9000 and ISO 14000 Together

James W. Highlands
President, Management Systems Analysis, Limerick, Pennsylvania

The ISO 14000 series of standards for environmental management systems (EMSs) encompasses a broad range of environmental management tools, including a specifications document and documents on environmental auditing, environmental performance evaluation, environmental labeling, and lifecycle assessment. Published in September 1996, ISO 14001, *Environmental management systems specification with guidance for use on EMSs*, is the centerpiece of the series.

Similar to ISO 9001 in that it may be used for third-party registration purposes, ISO 14001 provides the needed elements to develop and implement an environmental management system (EMS). Supporting this standard is ISO 14004, which provides additional guidance and suggestions for the implementation of an ISO 14001 system.

The numbering of this standard and its similarity to the more familiar ISO 9000 series is no accident. ISO 9001 was one of the primary source documents used during the drafting of ISO 14001. This was to provide greater ease of use for the thousands of companies that already conform to the quality requirements, as well as to gain economic efficiency by integrating EMS and quality management system (QMS) programs.

Consequently, the two standards are very compatible as they exist in their current form. While there are no counterparts to ISO 9002 or 9003, ISO 14001 is considered generally compatible with the requirements of ISO 9001, and indeed the standard shares several common elements with its quality counterpart. There are no counterparts to ISO 9002 and 9003, however, since few implementation differences exist among organizations that perform design activities and those that do not in the context of ISO 14001. All elements of the standard apply to every organization. The standard is flexible enough to address any differences that do exist.

While the quality and environmental requirements standards are compatible, there are differences with respect to the intent of guidance documents like ISO 14004 and ISO 9004. ISO 9004 is intended as optional guidance for organizations wishing to implement higher-performing quality management systems beyond the minimum requirements contained in ISO 9001. It was created to assist organizations on their journey to excellence. In contrast, ISO 14004 simply provides additional guidance to users implementing ISO 14001. The clause numbering and subject matter are identical to that of the requirements document. It provides guidance and helpful hints. One might consider ISO 14004 to be a toolbox or perhaps a substitute for your favorite consultant. It was not meant to provide additional requirements.

As a voluntary private-sector consensus standard, ISO 14001 has many possible uses. Some organizations adopt the standard for internal purposes or to demonstrate conformance to external parties, whether they be contractual requirements or legal mandates. As with ISO 9001, this standard does not mandate third-party registration. It merely provides a meaningful framework to achieve consistent and reliable management of the environmental dimensions of the organization. That framework shifts the emphasis from end-of-pipe controls to process management and from staff function monopoly to line and employee involvement and responsibility for environmental outcomes. This is the same shift that occurs with the implementation of ISO 9001 as companies look beyond final inspection and testing to focus on both economic and process efficiency. Consequently, the similarities that exist between the two standards are not surprising since the fundamental principles are the same.

From the user's point of view, the two systems are easily integrated. The principal difference is that ISO 9001 deals primarily with customers and meeting their requirements, ultimately to achieve customer satisfaction through product quality, while ISO 14001 deals with the organization's broader relationship to the environment. Consequently, ISO 14001 deals with the society or community in which we live, along with legal requirements and regulations.

Indeed, organizations would be best served to have a single management system encompassing environment, quality, health and safety, human resources, and even accounting. Because of the inherent compatibility of the two ISO standards, this is readily achievable, at least in the case of quality and the environment.

It may be useful to comment briefly on recent discussions and proposals concerning the integration and compatibility between the two series of standards. While there is virtually unanimous agreement that there are no incompatibilities between the standards, various parties (for example, registrars, course providers, and users) have asked for greater alignment between ISO 14001 and 9001, and for an outright merger of auditing documents ISO 10011 on the quality side with ISO 14010, 14011, and 14012 on the environmental side. In fact, the Technical Management Board (TMB) of ISO, which oversees the organization's many technical committees, mandated in 1998 that TC 207 and TC 176, the technical committees responsible for the 14000 and 9000 series, respectively, begin to work cooperatively to achieve these ends. Normally, ISO technical committees work out such issues at a much lower level.

From the U.S. point of view, there is nothing wrong with achieving greater alignment if that can be done. We also believe that a merger of the auditing documents is theoretically possible and desirable, however, we do have some concerns:

1. The variances in 14001 and 9001 reflect the fact that these standards are designed to achieve different ends. ISO 14001 addresses the environmental aspects of the organization through a hierarchical infusion of awareness, commitments, training, controls, and employee competencies. These begin at the top with management commitment and allocation of resources and then filter down to the various "levels and functions" through training and communications. The goal is to saturate the entire organization with greater environmental awareness and with specific abilities, objectives, and control strategies particularized at each level and function. ISO 9001, on the other hand, addresses the quality aspects of the organization by focusing primarily on the consistency of horizontal processes. The product output of any enterprise is the result of a series of horizontally connected processes. The quality of the product is dependent on the integrity of each process and the connection between them. The system's focus in ISO 9001 is therefore horizontal integrity, whereas in 14001 success is achieved by hierarchical penetration of the environmental ethic and the resources and competencies necessary to achieve objectives and targets. The U.S. concern is that this difference between ISO 14001 and ISO 9001 is only vaguely understood and that calls for greater alignment understate the need for maintaining existing differences.

2. A separate concern of the United States is that various countries are still angling for a universal standard on "generic management." Since they have been rebuffed on numerous occasions by TMB, they have sought to use the ISO 14001/9001 alignment issue as a way to promote their idea for a generic standard. Some parties promote their goal by merging ISO 14001 and ISO 9001 into such a standard. From the U.S. perspective, this undermines the usefulness of both ISO 14001 and ISO 9001—not only because the standards have different objectives, but also because the communities they serve (for example, customers, general public, and regulators) would no longer be certain that their own needs were being met by organizations implementing such generic systems. The United States will continue to oppose the merger of the specification documents ISO 14001 and ISO 9001.

This brings us to the third-party registration and/or certification process. Independent registration of an organization's ISO 9001 system by an accredited body has been available in the United States for nearly 10 years. Upon publication of ISO 14001, the Registrar Accreditation Board, in concert with the American National Standards Institute, launched the National Accreditation Program for the registration of ISO 14001 EMSs. While there are some unique legal and regulatory issues with respect to ISO 14001 registration, companies should find this process to be entirely compatible with their existing ISO 9001 or 9002 registration process. The process of selecting an environmental registrar, contracting with them, and undergoing the registration audit, including corrective action, is almost identical to that employed in quality system registration. The major difference in the two is the legal compliance aspect of ISO 14001. Commitment to compliance with applicable laws and regulations is required. It is effected through the identification of significant environmental aspects, through the setting of objectives and targets, and through monitoring compliance status. Some organizations interview registrars on this issue prior to signing a contract. Executives want to know exactly what actions auditors will take in the event they stumble upon a compliance violation. Organizations need to give careful thought to such compliance issues during the development of an EMS.

Other than the issue noted above regarding regulatory compliance, registration to ISO 9001 and ISO 14001 are indeed very similar. In fact, in most cases organizations may use their same ISO 9001 registrar for ISO 14001. Currently, many firms offer a single registration audit option that covers both standards. The issue that needs to be considered here is the scope of the EMS as opposed to the scope of the QMS. Some organizations establish different scopes for the two systems. Consequently, registration audits may need to be conducted separately. For example, an organization might attain ISO 9001 registration throughout all of its operations but may elect to implement ISO 14001 at one division or site. While there are certain financial benefits to be gained from a single-audit approach, organizations must give careful thought to this strategy. Failure in one audit could easily result in failure of the entire system, extending to both the quality and the environmental areas of the organization.

As mentioned previously, both requirements documents share a number of common requirements. The various elements of the two standards can be divided into three categories: common elements, similar elements, and dissimilar elements. Common elements are those elements within either system for which one common procedure may be used to satisfy the requirements of both standards. Similar elements are those elements that result in a similar process or procedure; however, the content may be different for either system. Dissimilar elements are those that are unique to ISO 14001, requiring a new process or procedure. It should be noted that even among the dissimilar elements, companies are likely to find that processes and procedures that exist currently within their ISO 9001 systems may be useful for their EMS. For example, while ISO 14001 does not address design activities, an organization's ISO 9001 design control system may provide information on environmental aspects as required by ISO 14001.

COMMON ELEMENTS

ISO 9001 users already have many of the processes and procedures required by ISO 14001. The content of the resulting records may change, but one procedure might be used to meet both standards. Organizations are free to duplicate procedures and still conform to the requirements of either standard. Some of these common elements include document control; nonconformance and corrective and preventive actions; monitoring and measurement (calibration); EMS records; EMS training, awareness, and competence; and process control to some extent.

Several elements share nearly identical controls and may be accommodated through minor changes to existing QMS procedures. Others depend on the nature of the business and the resulting EMS. For example, both systems have document control requirements. Companies that already have the resources to develop and implement a document control system would probably be wasting resources to create a separate system for ISO 14001. Accommodating ISO 14001 procedures as they are developed requires little more effort than adding them to the existing system. While there may be differences in the authority to review and approve procedures for your EMS documents, the system that controls their distribution, recall, and revision is likely to be identical. The only real reason to maintain separate systems is to soothe the personalities in your organization. Sharing a document control system is likely to bring the greatest return on investment with respect to leveraging your QMS investment. Developing an effective document control system is one of the most significant obstacles for many organizations seeking to implement a quality management system. Why suffer twice?

The other obvious shared element is the maintenance and control of records. ISO 9000 and 14001 both require companies to develop a record retention system providing for the identification and maintenance of records for a specified time. This includes provisions for legibility, retrievability, and prevention of deterioration. Possibly the only difference within ISO 14001 is the specific reference to records for training, the results of environmental audits, and management reviews. ISO 14001 explicitly identifies these records for inclusion in the record system. Organizations with an existing record system are likely to discover that meeting the requirements of ISO 14001 requires little more than expanding the matrix, or list of records, to include EMS records.

One cautionary note, however, is that many national regulatory schemes, such as the Code of Federal Regulations, contain lists of records that must be maintained for compliance. Many EMSs also have associated confidentiality issues that may or may not be present on the quality side. Consequently, you may want to have a discussion with executive management concerning the maintenance of records before proceeding too far. It is probably also a good idea to verify that your record system complies with existing regulations (in the United States, Title 40 of the Code of Federal Regulations) if you plan to use it for your EMS. Any system not in compliance will be a fairly easy target for third-party and regulatory auditors. In any case, a good ISO 9001 or 9002 record system will require only minor changes for use with ISO 14001.

ISO 14001 has a requirement for *nonconformance and corrective and preventive actions*, requiring companies to investigate nonconformances and take action to mitigate their impact. This includes corrective and preventive actions to eliminate actual or potential causes. Actions taken here should be commensurate with the environmental impact encountered. Sound familiar? If you have an ISO 9000 system, it should sound familiar, since a very similar requirement already exists within ISO 9001 and 9002. While an ISO 9001 or 9002 nonconformance system for the control and disposition of nonconforming product is unique to materials or product manufactured, your existing corrective and preventive action system may easily be adjusted to accommodate this requirement in your EMS. Both systems are targeted toward the identification and elimination of root causes: actual or potential nonconformance in the system. As such, a few minor modifications (largely dealing with terminology) could be made to an existing corrective/preventive action procedure to accommodate EMS requirements. Beyond a possible name change of the procedure and resulting forms to accommodate your EMS, the most profound change might be in identifying who has authority to review and approve (or complete) the actions taken. Within an EMS, personnel with that authority may be different from personnel with similar authority under the QMS. This is often easily resolved by adding a decision point at the beginning of the process regarding applicability, EMS versus QMS, with the appropriate definition of authority to review and close. Consequently, an existing ISO 9000–based corrective and preventive action procedure may easily be adjusted to accommodate ISO 14001 requirements. For those organizations where quality and environmental management personnel are the same, even the change and authority may not be necessary. While this takes a little more thought and effort than document control or records, the savings from using your existing system is still excellent.

The EMS training, awareness, and competence requirement in ISO 14001 is similar to training requirements in ISO 9001 or 9002 in that companies must identify training needs, along with a process to meet those needs, of personnel whose activity affects environmental aspects. A few minor revisions to an ISO 9000–approved training program could easily accommodate this activity for environmental issues. Many organizations that develop ISO 9001 or 9002 training programs create a matrix or list of training subjects or procedures for each job title and/or individual. To meet ISO 14001, these organizations may need to make only a simple revision to include environmental procedures and issues, thereafter providing the necessary training to appropriate personnel. This is also true for competence. As used in ISO 14001, personnel whose activity may have a significant environmental impact are required to be competent on the basis of education and training experience. Again, this should be familiar, since a similar requirement also exists within ISO 9001 and 9002 for personnel performing specific assigned tasks. While this is likely to result in new procedures dealing with competence (qualification), the existing procedures can provide a ready format for development.

ISO 14001 includes a unique requirement to make employees and members of the organization aware of the EMS, the benefits of conformance to the system, and the potential consequences of nonconformance. This requirement covers all personnel within an organization and may also cover subcontractors performing certain on-site activities. While the existing system for maintaining training records within ISO 9001 may easily accommodate the records of awareness training, a system of awareness training would have to be created. A similar ISO 9000 requirement exists for communicating the quality policy throughout the organization, and the existing process could be a starting point for developing EMS awareness training.

Another subject easily addressed within an existing ISO 9001 or 9002 system is calibration. Within ISO 14001, the accuracy of monitoring equipment, including records, must be maintained. This requirement is included in the monitoring and measurements section. Most, if not all, ISO 9001 or 9002 quality systems contain some form of calibration program. These systems are usually rather extensive, as metrology has matured in the quality field. Addressing this requirement in your EMS may require little more than including your monitoring equipment under the existing calibration system, which would provide more than enough control to assure its accuracy, stability, and traceability to national or international standards. Of the common requirements in both standards, this is probably the simplest to integrate. Since the requirements for calibration are not very extensive in ISO 14001, having a developed system for ISO 9001 or 9002 will be of great value.

Beyond these elements, companies are likely to see a strong interaction between process control of ISO 9001 or 9002 and operational controls within ISO

14001. ISO 9001 requires companies to have procedures or work instructions to control critical activities within processing, production, or manufacturing processes, while ISO 14001 requires that organizations identify those operations with significant environmental aspects and implement procedures to control these processes to achieve environmental objectives and targets. It is likely that an existing ISO 9001 or 9002 organization will identify the operations under ISO 14001 that are currently controlled by existing work instructions or procedures. Consequently, some of the operational controls needed for ISO 14001 might require little more than revisions to existing work instructions or procedures to control the environmental aspect of the operation. An example of this would be an organization that performs welding and has identified welding gas as a significant environmental aspect in its EMS. Under ISO 9001, it would have to put in place a procedure to control welding activities to assure the quality of the weld. The same organization identifying weld gas as a significant environmental aspect of its EMS would have a related procedure or work instruction. In this case, minor revisions may be needed to the existing weld procedure or work instruction to ensure that it not only will produce a quality weld but also will be consistent with the objectives and targets set within the organization's EMS. How prevalent these cases are will depend largely on the environmental aspects identified in the organization.

It should be noted that this example of existing process and operational controls may be limited to certain activities. The scope of an EMS tends to be much broader than a QMS, including facilities operation, maintenance, and transportation, along with other non-production-related activities. Once an organization implementing ISO 14001 has identified its significant environmental aspects and related operations, it will be able to easily identify existing operations controlled by procedures. The amount of resources saved here will, of course, also depend on the identification process.

Also within the requirements of operational control in ISO 14001 is a requirement to establish and maintain procedures related to significant environmental aspects of goods and services. This includes communicating relevant procedures and requirements to suppliers and contractors. In short, wherever an organization has identified a significant environmental aspect and determines that it comes from a supplier, it must, at a minimum, communicate its own procedures and requirements to the supplier of the material or product containing the significant environmental aspect. This might easily be accomplished through a minor modification to an existing ISO 9001 procurement control system. Organizations should be able to alter their procurement procedure to address applicable environmental requirements of the organization. The usefulness of an existing QMS procurement procedure will be difficult to assess until the implementing organization has identified its significant environmental aspects.

Any number of existing ISO 9001 and 9002 procedures might be useful depending on the significant environmental aspects identified by the organization. These could include receipt inspection of materials containing significant environmental aspects. Many organizations use common storage areas for both raw materials for production and items such as cleaning fluids (VOCs) and lubricants. In these cases, a minor alteration in the existing storage procedure could easily be used to address requirements in ISO 14001. The list here includes handling procedures, shipping procedures, and preservation procedures. One can even conceive of variations on design control procedures that would take into account significant environmental aspects. Once again, the usefulness of specific procedures in developing and implementing an ISO 14001–based EMS hinges on the significant environmental aspects. For example, the usefulness of an existing QMS procedure would depend on whether the organization is dealing with spent nuclear fuels, toxic waste, or recycled paper.

SIMILAR ELEMENTS

Some elements of ISO 14001 share similar intent with ISO 9001 and 9002. While the concept of these elements is often the same in both standards, differences may result in the use of different procedures, documents, or records. In some cases, however, the ISO 14001 process could be similar to the ISO 9000 process when dealing with issues that are similar to those encountered by the quality system.

The first of these in ISO 14001 is environmental management systems policy. While content is different for an EMS, including specific commitments to compliance with laws and other requirements to which an organization subscribes and to prevention of pollution, the concept here is essentially the same as that of quality policy. Policies are the stated intent of management, including goals for the EMS. Similar to ISO 9001 or 9002, ISO 14001 requires that an organization's EMS policy be communicated to all personnel throughout the facility. Many organizations that implement ISO 9001 or 9002 find the policy and its communication to personnel to be a challenging activity. Organizations have already wrestled with creative ways to convey the quality policy, whether it be through banners, posters, slogans, customized hard hats, or jackets. You may want to review the process used and the problems encountered when communicating your organization's quality policy to determine which methods will be most effective for conveying your EMS policy.

ISO 14001 also contains a requirement for the establishment of an environmental management program for achieving the organization's objectives and targets. This includes the designation of responsibility for achieving objectives and targets at each relevant function and level of the organization and the time frame in which they are to be achieved. While this appears to be a unique requirement, it is very much along the lines of clause 4.2 in ISO 9001 and 9002 that also requires the establishment of a program to meet the requirements of the standards. Within ISO 14001, this program may be documented in paper or electronic form and must address the core elements of the standard. For many organizations, this is likely to be little more than the documentation of an environmental management manual that gives a brief description of the system and how it addresses the requirements of the standard. Organizations must decide whether to have a separate or combined manual for QMS and EMS activities.

There are several possibilities here. You may want to simply expand your existing quality manual to be a quality and environmental manual. The revision of an existing quality manual to address the unique elements of 14001 requires only the addition of a few chapters and adjustments to terminology. Or you may prefer to have separate manuals, with each referencing a common set of procedures, wherever practical. A third possibility is to have two entirely separate manuals with very few common procedures. Companies that have implemented ISO 14001 have tried each of these methods. For most organizations, the discussion of combined or separate manuals usually comes down to one of legal compliance and openness and availability of information. Environmental professionals have espoused each of these strategies, using rationales that range from sensitivity over legal compliance to efficient use of resources. Once again, this is largely a decision for top management. There are certainly synergies between the EMS and QMS systems that could yield significant benefits, such as improvements in efficiency and significant reduction of resources. However, each organization is likely to have a different opinion on the risk or liability encountered by combining the two systems, as weighed against potential benefits.

Another similar requirement in ISO 14001 is that of structure and responsibility. This includes the definition, documentation, and communication of roles and responsibilities within the EMS to assure its effectiveness. In this section, we also find top management's responsibility for appointing a management representative to ensure that the EMS is established, implemented, and maintained in accordance with the requirements of the standard, plus reporting on its performance. Once again, this should be familiar. It's the same process your organization would have already gone through to implement an ISO 9001 or 9002 system. As before, the lessons learned from QMS implementation should be useful in building your ISO 14001 system.

ISO 14001 has a requirement for the monitoring and measurement of key characteristics of operations and activities that can have a significant impact on the environment. This includes recording and tracking of performance, relevant operational controls, and conformance to the organization's objectives and targets. As before, the usefulness of existing QMS procedures to meet this requirement will depend largely on the significant environmental aspects identified. Where the operations related to the EMS intersect with existing ISO 9001 or 9002 monitoring controls for the production process or inspection and test, existing procedures may be easily adapted to address this requirement. Procedures such as in-process inspection, receipt inspection, or inspection of storage areas might be adapted to include significant environmental aspects. This will depend largely on the significant environmental aspects identified by the organization. While some of these aspects may be part of the organization's production, inspection, and test processes, some are likely to be related to nonproduction issues. Operations such as facility maintenance, heating, air-conditioning, transportation, and management of land resources will likely fall outside the scope of an existing ISO 9001 or 9002 system and require new procedures.

Both standards also require internal audits to assure conformance. An existing ISO 9001 or 9002 internal audit system would provide a good framework for developing an environmental auditing system to meet ISO 14001. There are organizations that have merged both processes into one coherent internal audit of the entire system for both quality and environment. This, of course, requires the training and qualification of environmental auditors with appropriate education and background. It may allow for the use of existing quality auditors to audit common management systems requirements. However, organizations should be aware that the knowledge and training needed to perform an adequate environmental audit may differ greatly from that required of quality auditors.

The result of both processes is the documentation of audit results and their communication to management, including the identification of nonconformances and the corrective actions taken. It should be noted, however, that there is one fundamental difference between quality and environmental auditing. Within ISO 9001 or 9002, the internal auditor evaluates the adequacy and effectiveness of the system. Typically, this is contained in a report that may include such references as "opportunities for improvement or comments" as practiced by quality professionals for more than 30 years. ISO 14001 auditors, on the other hand, merely document the results of the audit and forward them to top management for evaluation of the adequacy and effectiveness of the system. An underlying concern here is the legal considerations with respect to environmental auditing and information disclosure. There is also a fundamental difference in beliefs. Environmental professionals see this job of evaluating the adequacy and effectiveness of the organization as the responsibility of top management, not auditors. This may be an approach that quality professionals should seriously consider. The type of Monday-morning quarterbacking that surfaces on internal quality audits often undermines the credibility of the auditors. Qualified professionals, with more experience and education than many internal auditors, should have the responsibility of making recommendations.

Finally, we come to the issue of management review. Both standards require a periodic management review performed by top management to evaluate the adequacy and the effectiveness of the system. Each must be performed on a periodic basis and must be documented. However, there is one noteworthy difference with respect to ISO 14001 in that it contains objectives and targets and a requirement for continual improvement. Consequently, the management review process must address areas that may not normally be included in an ISO 9001 or 9002 management review. An organization may elect to expand the scope of its QMS review to include the EMS in a single review of the integrated systems. As before, this will be largely dependent on the individual organization, on environmental aspects identified, and on the level of integration desired. In any case, an organization can use its existing ISO 9001 or 9002 management review process as a model to construct an EMS management review process.

UNIQUE ELEMENTS

As previously discussed in this section, there are some unique requirements of ISO 14001 that will not be addressed in an existing ISO 9001 or 9002 system. These requirements reflect the difference in perspective between the two disciplines. Quality systems are driven by customer requirements, while environmental management systems are driven by the significant environmental aspects identified and may be profoundly influenced by laws, regulations, and interested parties. Consequently, the following topics may represent additional chapters within an integrated management system manual of an organization.

The first truly unique requirement in ISO 14001 is environmental aspects. ISO 14001 requires a procedure for the identification of environmental aspects related to the organization's activities, products, and services, including a determination of which are significant based on impact. These significant environmental aspects act as the driver for the resulting management system in much the same way that customer requirements are a driver of the QMS. It is likely that there will be strong interactions in this identification process with many of the existing processes required by ISO 9001, such as design control or contract review. However, ISO 14001 requires a new procedure to define the process of environmental aspect identification and determination of significance. You may want to reference existing procedures as sources of information or control. Adding an environmental review to your design, contract review, or purchasing procedures may provide excellent controls in your system.

Having identified your significant environmental aspects, the next step in the ISO 14001 process is to have access to laws and regulations that specifically relate to your environmental aspects. Once again, this is a new requirement that is not specifically addressed within ISO 9001 or 9002. It should be noted, however, that the QS-9000 automotive standard already requires compliance to environmental laws and regulations. An organization with a QS-9000 system may have an existing process in place to provide for this identification process. It should also be noted that organizations operating in the highly regulated business community of North America are likely to have systems in place that may provide access to laws and regulations. Companies such as medical device manufacturers, for example, may already have systems in place.

ISO 14001 requires that you establish environmental objectives and targets. These objectives and targets are analogous to customer requirements within ISO 9001 or 9002, with objectives on a slightly higher level than targets. They establish the requirements that the system seeks to achieve. Objectives and targets also provide needed links between performance and policy, which, it could be argued, is a missing element of ISO 9001 and 9002. While ISO 9001 and 9002 refer to objectives in the policy requirements, few organizations have set quantifiable objectives. As a result, the policy becomes much more measurable by including a set of higher-level requirements that support and are consistent with policy. As such, these tend to be uniquely different from anything in the existing ISO 9001 or 9002 requirements.

ISO 14001 also requires that you monitor and measure your compliance with laws and regulations. This may be covered partially by compliance auditing. Such monitoring systems are not normally included in typical quality systems, with the possible exception of process controls. And while an organization may have similar systems in place, as previously discussed, this requirement is unique to ISO 14001. As before, those organizations that operate QS-9000 systems may find that some of these systems and procedures already meet the requirements of the standard. Additionally, organizations that have had active EMSs will find that they have existing monitoring and measuring systems in place for compliance-based environmental aspects.

The final unique element in ISO 14001 is that of environmental emergency preparedness and response. The standard requires an emergency response and preparedness procedure that must be tested where practical. While organizations with a rigorous compliance system may have existing procedures already in place, there is little within ISO 9001 or 9002 that is useful in this respect.

In summary, organizations with existing ISO 9001 or 9002 systems are likely to find tools already in place that address many of the ISO 14001 requirements. The development and implementation time to achieve ISO 14001 conformance should be significantly shortened based on their experience and existing quality systems. Full integration of the two systems could result in significant savings of time and money. One of the biggest obstacles, however, may involve getting quality and environmental personnel to exchange information.

ISO 9001:2000

The new revision of ISO 9001 will improve the compatibility and consequently the integration of EMS and QMS for users of both standards. In drafting the new revision one of the primary considerations has been the compatibility issue. While the consensus has been that there is no incompatibility the new revision goes a long way toward improving common use of terms and concepts. This should greatly improve the understanding and use of the standard in both management systems.

Documentation

The ISO 14001 standard contains a more flexible system of documentation. Documented procedures are only explicitly mandated in three areas: operational control and measurement and monitoring of both its operations and activities and compliance to laws and regulation. ISO 9001:2000 has greatly improved its flexibility in this area and thus compatibility. Documented procedures are only explicitly required in six areas: control of documents, control of quality records, internal audit, control of nonconformity, corrective action, and preventive action. This additional flexibility allows the implementing organization to customize the system to meet their needs similar to ISO 14001. Larger organizations or those with more complex processes may require additional documented procedures while others may be able to effectively implement a QMS without unnecessary documentation.

Top Management

In the ISO 9001 and 9002 world there has always been a discussion of who is "management with executive responsibility for quality." Is this the CEO or the Q.A. Manager? ISO 14001 resolved some of this confusion by use of the phrase "top management." This meant that the scope of the system, a plant, a division, a corporation, determined who was responsible in the EMS. The 2000 revision of 9001 now incorporates the use of the phrase "top management." With this change the compatibility of the two standards is improved simply from the point of view that both standards are now referring to the same individual when the scope of both systems is identical.

Organization

ISO 9001:2000 now uses the term "organizations" which encompasses a much broader group of users similar to ISO 14001. In the 1994 edition of ISO 9001 and 9002 the term supplier was used to refer to the contractual relationship between a customer and supplier for use in two-party contractual relationships. With the registration of schools and even a city it was obvious that the standard had exceeded the boundaries of two-party contracts and was being employed by a much broader audience. Ultimately this will mean that an organization can refer to itself using the same term to meet both standards. This is also consistent with the shift from "stakeholders" to "interested parties" in ISO 9001:2000. Since ISO 14001 has always recognized this broader group, the change is entirely compatible with the existing standard and EMS systems.

Objectives

From its beginning ISO 14001 has used measurable objectives and targets as a method of making the EMS system measurable. In practice these objectives and target have served to express the policy in terms that allow a organization to measure their progress toward a stated goal. While this concept was always implicit in the ISO 9001 and 9002 standards, the 2000 revision makes it explicit requiring organizations to set quality objectives. As a result, similar systems of setting, measuring, and evaluating stated objectives may be used for both EMS and QMS.

Communications

Another unique requirement of ISO 14001 was communications, both internal and external. Originally this was incorporated into the standard as a form of a reporting requirement, stating an organization needed a procedure for receiving, documenting, and responding to relevant external communication, including consideration of communications on its significant environmental aspects. ISO 9001:2000 now includes requirements for both internal communications and communication with customers. While the latter may not integrate well with existing systems, the former, internal communication, should. The internal communications process used for organizations' ISO 9001 systems could easily be the same for ISO 14001. Similar to document control, it is difficult to conceive of an organization using two separate processes in either system.

Continual Improvement

Since the original publication of ISO 9001 and 9002, standards writers have intended the system improve. It was always believed that this was implicit in the standard since the management representative was reporting for the purpose of improvement. Within ISO 14001 this concept was made explicit requiring a commitment to continual improvement in the policy and objectives. ISO 9001:2000 now includes those explicit requirements as a basic concept throughout the standard. While this point of increased compatibility may not improve the integration of the two systems it does provide for a commonality in processes that could be employed by a single user. In short having developed a process for measuring, analyzing, and improving in one system could form a model for the other.

Training

Training is one of the common processes. While an existing training procedure could have been used to meet the ISO 14001 requirements there was always one piece missing, awareness training. Since its inception ISO 14001 has contained requirements that employees and members of the organization receive awareness training regarding the EMS. This requirement has now been included in ISO 9001:2000. The new training requirement states: "the organization shall ensure that its personnel are aware of the relevance and importance of their activities and how they contribute to the achievement of the quality objectives." This new requirement is entirely consistent with the ISO 14001 requirements.

There is however one new requirement here that may need to be taken up in an organization's integrated EMS based on the new ISO 9001:2000 requirements. This is the subject of measuring the effectiveness of training. While this requirement has always been in the QS-9000 requirements for the automotive sector, it now appears in the new ISO 9001. At present ISO 9001:2000 states, "evaluate the effectiveness of the actions taken," to meet competency needs. Those actions include training. This is a new concept for ISO 14001 and may need to be addressed in the upcoming revision.

Laws and Regulations

Finally laws and regulations need to be considered as they pertain to a company's management systems. Obviously a significant part of any organization's EMS is affected by the laws and regulations where they operate. As such, the concept of compliance threads its way throughout ISO 14001. Organizations that adopted and used 14001 have been required to have access to laws and regulations as they relate to their EMS. This requirement has been unique to 14001 due to the subject matter. While there are laws and regulations that can apply to the design, production, and quality of certain industries, they are product-unique. As a result, ISO 9001:2000 deals with this situation in a product-unique manner through communications in management commitment, customer requirements, and design.

In summary, organizations with existing ISO 9001 or 9002 systems or the new ISO 9001:2000 are likely to find tools that address many of the ISO 14001 requirements already in place. The development and implementation time to achieve ISO 14001 conformance should be significantly shortened based on their experience and existing quality systems. Full integration of the two systems could result in significant savings of time and money. One of the biggest obstacles, however, may involve getting quality and environmental personnel to exchange information.

As of June 2000, ISO TC 207/SC1, the committee responsible for maintaining ISO 14001, started their next revision cycle. While there has been a resolution not to include new requirements in this revision, one of the issues to be addressed is compatibility. Consequently the process of improving compatibility to eliminate any undue hardship for users of both standards continues.

Section 9

Applications

Introduction

John E. (Jack) West
Consultant, The Woodlands, Texas

M any organizations have adopted the ISO 9000 family as the model for their quality management systems. There are a number of ways to look at the population of ISO 9000 users:

- Some industrial sectors have chosen to use ISO 9001 as a basis of quality management systems for their suppliers. Some use ISO 9001 or ISO 9002 without defining industry-particular requirements. Some, such as the aerospace, automotive, and telecommunications industries, have prepared sector-specific documents based on ISO 9001 but with very detailed sector-particular requirements.

- Some industrial sectors have adopted ISO 9001 or ISO 9002 as a basis for their own operational quality management systems. The chemical and paper industries are examples.

- Some individual organizations have chosen ISO 9000 even though they have no customer requirements to do so. Those organizations may feel that they gain a competitive advantage by having systems that comply with one of the ISO 9000 family standards.

- Some industrial sectors, such as medical devices, have seen ISO 9001 adopted as a means to meet regulatory requirements.

Section 9 of this handbook provides a number of application examples from a variety of industries.

Chapter 47

AS9100 Technical Content

Eugene M. Barker
The Boeing Company, Commercial Airplanes Group
Seattle, Washington

INTRODUCTION

At the heart of the SAE AS9100 standard are the additions and supplements to ISO 9001 that ensure that requirements unique to the aerospace industry are included when implementing an ISO-based quality system within the industry. Such requirements have historically been addressed by robust aerospace quality systems. It is the consensus of the industry experts who wrote AS9100 that the additions are essential to ensure product, process, and service safety and quality.

The discussion that follows addresses the thinking behind the inclusion of the clarifications in AS9100. The specific requirements are available by reading the standard. The author has refrained from supplying information about how to implement the standard. This is consistent with its developers, who refrained from including any *how-tos* in the standard. It was the belief of those authors and is the belief of this author that how-to information stifles continuous improvement. It also ignores the fact that quality systems must be designed to meet the specific needs of the user. The more advanced best practices today are at best only the foundation for even better methods tomorrow and on into the future. As quality professionals learn more about managing the quality system as a holistic entity, the development of practices will continue to span a larger number of functions and processes within the business, making the application of specific approaches across the industry even less feasible. So while the minimum *whats* that must be addressed by the system can be listed, the determination of how to address accomplishing those requirements is left to the individual implementers.

The requirements of the standard are complementary to contractual and applicable law and regulatory requirements. Those implementing a quality system compliant with AS9100 must make sure that the additional requirements of their customers; regulatory agencies such as the FAA and the JAA; and local, state, and national laws are also included. Such additional requirements shall be included or referenced in the documentation of the quality system.

KEY CHARACTERISTICS

At several places in AS9100, direction is given for the management of key characteristics. *Key characteristics* are features of a material, part, or process whose variation has a significant influence on the fit, performance, service life, or manufacturablity of the product. Typically the key characteristics are identified by the customer on the design drawing, in the process specification, or in the purchase order. The customer also may require the organization to identify key characteristics. Once identified, the process or processes that influence the variation of these characteristics must be determined. Those processes must be managed using statistical techniques to minimize their variation. When successful, the resultant product conforms very closely to its nominal requirements.

Whether or not key characteristics are identified, the organization is responsible for ensuring that *all* product features conform to specified requirements.

MANAGEMENT RESPONSIBILITY

Consistent with ISO 9001, the organization is not required to have a separate quality organization. The quality activities may be managed by other functional organizations. This supports activities that place the responsibility for quality with those functions actually performing the work, thereby increasing the ownership of quality.

The organization must appoint a management representative; he or she must be a member of management and have the organizational freedom and authority to resolve matters pertaining to quality. Regardless of where in the organization the management representative reports, he or she must have sufficient visibility and support to have the final say on issues that affect quality.

DELEGATED RESPONSIBILITY FOR QUALITY

The organization may delegate the responsibility for performing quality assurance activities to those individuals within the organization who perform the work that is to be verified. For example, this allows production operators to verify the quality of the work that they perform, for buyers to ensure that the quality of their purchase orders are adequate prior to release, and for software developers to ensure the quality of their own product. When delegation is used as a method of ensuring product or process quality, the organization shall have procedures that define the specific tasks that are delegated, the extent of the delegated responsibility, and the training necessary for those performing the delegated verification tasks.

Delegation places the responsibility for quality with those doing the work. Not only must they ensure that they have completed the work but they must also ensure that it meets the quality requirements. Properly implemented, this approach increases product quality by eliminating the reliance upon inspection to sort good from bad. It also is more efficient because it provides the people doing the work with instant feedback on their performance, allowing them to adjust the process if required to produce error-free product.

PROCEDURE AVAILABILITY

The organization shall ensure that the quality system procedures necessary for performing work are readily available to those performing the work. These procedures shall also be readily available to customers and regulatory authority representatives.

Well-documented work instructions and procedures that define business processes are essential to communicate the consistent methods by which work is to be performed. Consistency is what ensures repeatable quality. The documents must be written at a level suited to those using the procedures, in a language that they readily understand. They should be readily available to ensure that they are frequently consulted as work is performed. They should be used when training new employees as well. When process audits are conducted by both internal employees and customer and regulatory personnel, they serve as a basic element of both adequacy and compliance verification.

QUALITY PLANNING

Several additional areas for consideration are included in AS9100. Consistent with ISO 9001, these are not mandated requirements but rather activities that should be given careful consideration when planning the quality activities to be performed:

• The method to be used to capture variable measurements when designing, manufacturing, and using tooling should be determined when the tools are being designed. As the industry transitions to the use of in-process controls, the ability to capture variable rather than attribute data becomes increasingly important. That capability must be considered when tooling is designed.

• The organization's selection and management of its suppliers has a major influence on the final quality of the delivered product. That process must be deliberately managed and should include the process for identification of suppliers, the method(s) to be used to ensure product quality, the method for measuring supplier performance, and the process for providing feedback to suppliers on their performance.

• The method of managing key characteristics through the development of control plans should be considered. The identification of key characteristics provides an excellent means of communicating those few features of each part that would benefit from variation reduction. The identification is most economical during the initial design activity; therefore the decisions regarding the extent of use of key characteristics should be made during the initial planning activity.

• Supporting and maintaining the product after delivery may require substantial preplanning to ensure that the proper materials are available, processes defined, and services available. Aerospace products typically have very long lives and therefore require extensive maintenance and support over their lifecycle. This planning begins during the design, when maintainability must be an integral design consideration, and extends throughout the procurement and manufacturing processes. It continues long after the delivery of a quality product to the customer and frequently plays a pivotal role in maintaining a high level of customer satisfaction.

CONFIGURATION MANAGEMENT

The management of the configuration of the product during its entire lifecycle is essential to ensure safety and quality. This process must be established and documented. The system developer is encouraged to consult ISO 10007 for guidance in the establishment of the configuration management system.

Product complexity and serviceability are just two of many factors that must be addressed during the configuration management process. Because it touches the entire product lifecycle, the configuration management system must be addressed as a set of integrated processes.

CONTRACT/TENDER REVIEW

It is important that the organization carefully review all contracts and tenders *prior* to their execution to ensure that the organization has the capability to perform the work requested. This review should ensure, in addition to all the other specific areas mentioned in ISO 9001, that the organization understands any risks associated with any new technology or short delivery times requested by the customer. As the industry becomes increasingly sophisticated, the quality risks associated with the development and application of new technology necessitate greater attention. Customers expect shorter and shorter cycle times. This requires more attention to improvement of the enabling processes to ensure delivery with first-time quality.

As the expectations of customers change, they are reflected in revisions to the initial contract or tender. Those revisions must be reviewed with the same systematic thoroughness as the initial review to ensure that the organization maintains the ability to satisfy its customers' expectations.

DESIGN CONTROL

The quality of the delivered product is never any better than its design. This truism mandates that significant attention be devoted during the design process to ensuring that the product meets the customer's expectations. Almost universally within the aerospace industry, extensive efforts are directed to ensure the quality of the design, and then subsequent activities are directed to verify exact conformance to that design.

The design process defined in ISO 9001 is essentially the same as that employed for more than 40 years in the aerospace industry for hardware and software. AS9100 adds requirements that have been found to provide the high level of safety and quality that is a hallmark of the industry. These practices should be used by all organizations in the industry that are involved in design activities. The organization responsible for approving the design and related data shall be clearly defined. Where all or part of the design or development activities is subcontracted, those activities shall be controlled to the same extent. Those performing the subcontracted actions must understand their responsibilities and have implemented documented processes to ensure a quality design.

Design and Development Planning

A well-developed plan is essential if the design and development process is to be effectively accomplished. Elements of the design process should be defined, the individual responsible specified, the resources required identified, the performance conditions quantified, and any risks identified with risk mitigation plans developed. The application of project or program management techniques and tools is strongly encouraged to ensure the on-time delivery of a high-quality, economically producible product.

Most aerospace products must be designed to operate for a long period with extremely high reliability and to be easily serviced. Parameters of the design that affect safety, reliability, and maintainability shall be identified. Verification and validation activities to ensure that those parameters have been achieved shall be defined and accomplished. Consideration shall be given to customer and regulatory authority requirements.

Design Input

The design input process shall establish the functional requirements for the hardware or software being developed. Those requirements will be used during the design output process to verify that the design meets its intent. More important, they ensure that those performing the design activity adequately understand all the expectations of the design. When design and development planning is required, each element of the design shall have specific input data, and those elements and their requirements shall be reviewed at a systems level to ensure consistency. This process provides an excellent opportunity for the application of systems engineering methodologies.

Design Output

ISO 9001 provides a number of specific expectations from the design output process. Because of the safety and serviceability aspects of aerospace products the organization is also expected to ensure that the data necessary to support the product during its entire lifecycle is verified prior to the release of the design. These include, but are not limited to, drawings, part lists, and specifications; a listing of the drawings, part lists, and specifications necessary to define the configuration and design features of the product; and the information on material, processes, type of manufacturing, and assembly of the product necessary to ensure the conformity of the product. This data package should be complete enough to allow the product to be produced and serviced without any intervention by the design personnel.

Design Review

Formal design reviews have long been recognized as a valuable tool to ensure the adequacy of the design, both during the design process and at its conclusion. They afford the opportunity for representatives from other functions, such as manufac-turing, quality, and product support, as well as technical design experts from elsewhere within engineering other than those that created the design, to system-atically review the design against the design input criteria. During these reviews consideration should be given to ensure that the expectations of the specific stage of the design have been fully achieved. If that is not the case, then the formal recov-ery plans or modifications to design input requirements should be reviewed. Prior to the design advancing to its next stage, those mitigating actions should be accom-plished. This systematic review process ensures that design deficiencies are identi-fied as soon as possible to allow contingency plans to be economically implemented with a minimum impact on the scheduled product release.

Design Verification and Design Validation

Design verification and design validation are essential processes to ensure that the output from the design process meets the design input requirements. The require-ments in ISO 9001 for conducting verification and validation of aerospace prod-ucts are adequate when properly implemented. Implementation may require very sophisticated testing, and those tests must be planned including the establishment of acceptance criteria. Independent verification of the test process is encouraged, and this verification must be documented.

Following the completion of the verification and validation testing, the test data that demonstrate that the product conforms with design input and specifica-tion requirements shall be reviewed to ensure that the desired design output has been accomplished. Those data and the resultant review become a quality record.

The planning, control, review, and documentation of verification and valida-tion tests are essential to ensure that adequate testing has been conducted to ensure that the design accomplishes the desired results. The decisions on what type of testing is required and what characteristics of the design are being verified by each test should be documented. The data to be recorded and the acceptance criteria should also be documented. Where the sequence of testing is of importance, that sequence shall be included within the test plan. The plan shall also identify all resources required, including equipment, materials, facilities, personnel, energy sources, and the associated costs.

Test procedures shall be written for each test. They can use existing proce-dures and documented processes. At a minimum the procedures shall describe the equipment to be used in conducting the test, the test setup, the test methods, the acceptance criteria, qualifications of the personnel performing the test, and the data to be recorded.

Prior to beginning the test the configuration of the item being tested shall be verified to validate that it conforms to the required item to be tested. This action is essential to ensure that the configuration of the item is known.

During the test, evidence should be provided to validate that the test plan and procedures were met. That can be accomplished by using checklists, taking photo-graphs of or videotaping the test setup, obtaining independent verification of the test practices, and a number of other validation approaches. It is important that the method of verification be agreed to before the test begins. This is especially impor-tant when customer or regulatory agencies will rely on the test results. Failure to accomplish this action may result in having to conduct the test a second time.

At the conclusion of the test, verification must be provided that all acceptance criteria have been met. This may be as simple as the review of a few items of the test results. In the case of sophisticated system tests, independent experts may be engaged to review a comprehensive set of test data to independently validate the satisfactory accomplishment of the test program. Again, this process should be documented prior to the initiation of the tests to preclude any disagreement at the conclusion of the tests. Any deviation from the test process and anticipated test results must be documented and dispositioned.

Design Changes

In many cases the customer may require that some or all design changes be submitted for approval prior to incorporation. Similar requirements may exist from regulatory or other government agencies. This notification is necessary to ensure that the changes do not affect the performance of a higher-level product.

Typically in the aerospace industry design changes are classified as either class 1 or class 2. Class 1 changes are those that affect safety, fit, form, function, interchangeability, maintainability, or reliability. Class 2 changes are those that affect none of the above. In some cases the customer may allow the organization to make class 2 changes without notification. The organization must understand its responsibilities for communicating design changes to customers and/or regulatory agencies. This process must be documented.

Document and Data Approval and Issue

The aerospace industry is relying more and more upon digital data to communicate design, production, and inspection requirements, both internally and with suppliers and customers. The day of two-dimensional drawings is coming to a close. Digital data provide several advantages in that the product can be produced directly from this data definition without the intervention of master models and tooling. Because most of the product configuration relies on aerodynamic shapes, typically called "loft data," these shapes require definition in three dimensions. Prior to the use of digitized data, that necessitated complex translation during both the production and inspection processes. The achievement of zero-fit interfaces between mating parts was more art than science, frequently requiring a very high skill level. Digital data have moved that function from the mechanic to the computer operator.

The process for controlling the development, release, distribution, and updating of the data must be documented. It must provide for adequate safeguards to ensure the integrity of the data being used to produce and verify the product. Configuration management is an essential element of this process.

Document Change Incorporation

Changes to the design are made to address new customer requirements, to incorporate new technologies, and to incorporate producibility enhancements. Each of these changes is accompanied by an effectivity that specifies the anticipated implementation of the change. The organization is responsible for maintaining a process that ensures the correct incorporation and documentation of such changes. This process must cover drawings, standards, specifications, planning, and purchase orders. When changes are requested by a customer, the process shall ensure that those requests are reviewed in a timely manner and properly dispositioned. The process shall ensure that a change is communicated both internally and to the organization's suppliers if the change affects purchased product. The organization shall ensure that changes that require customer or regulatory agency approval are properly coordinated prior to release.

PURCHASING

The organization shall maintain a process to control the quality of the products and services procured from suppliers. The organization is responsible for the quality of all products and services purchased from suppliers. That includes the quality of products and services procured from sources designated by the customer.

Evaluation of Suppliers

In addition to the responsibilities for evaluating suppliers as specified in ISO 9001, the organization shall also ensure that it and its suppliers use customer-approved special-processing sources when such sources are required in the process specification or purchase order. Special processes are those processes the output from which cannot be readily identified using ordinary inspection techniques. Such special processes include heat treatment, plating, painting, and nondestructive inspection to name just a few. Each customer will designate those processes that it deems to be special processes and will provide a list of organizations authorized to perform them. The organization then selects the source that it intends to use. As was said earlier, the organization must ensure the quality of the product or service received from these sources.

Organizations must have in place a process for approving the quality systems of their suppliers. That process must include the individual or organization responsible for performing the reviews and granting the approvals. That same individual must have the authority to disapprove suppliers, and that authority must be documented.

Once a supplier has been approved, a process must exist that periodically reviews the supplier's performance. The requirements for this review must be documented and records maintained of the reviews. If the organization relies upon the performance of the supplier to adjust its level of control, then the criteria for that adjustment must be documented. Frequently the organization will adjust the frequency and type of controls based upon the supplier's performance. When that method of supplier control is used, the criteria must be documented.

Unfortunately, on occasion, steps must be taken to deal with the supplier whose performance fails to meet the organization's expectations. The initial steps focus on corrective action in which the supplier is required to explain what caused the nonconformance and what actions were taken to correct the existing situation and to preclude additional occurrences of the same situation. When several similar instances occur, the supplier may be asked to determine if a systemic situation exists and if so to implement actions to solve this more systemic problem. A good supplier will automatically review every request for corrective action to determine if the true root cause is a systemic issue. The ultimate weapon that the organization has in dealing with a supplier that does not meet expectations is to cease doing work with that supplier. This process and the criteria that precipitate its initiation should be documented.

The organization must maintain a list of all approved suppliers. The list should include the scope of each approval and may need to designate the type of work each supplier is approved to perform. The procedure should mandate the use of this list when selecting suppliers.

Purchasing Data

The purchase order shall clearly specify whether design, test, examination, inspection, or customer acceptance data are required from suppliers. The purchase order shall also specify that the organization, the organization's customers, and regulatory authorities shall have access to the supplier's facilities and all applicable quality records. That requirement is essential to ensure that customers at every level have the ability to monitor the performance of the entire supplier chain.

When test specimens are required to support design approval, inspection, investigation, or auditing, the requirement shall include the production method, quantity, storage conditions, and other parameters essential to the integrity of the samples.

The method to be used by the supplier in notifying the organization when nonconforming product or processes or other anomalies occur shall be included in the purchasing data. Similar methods shall be specified for notification of changes to processes, process approvals, and process definition. The intent is to ensure that a document process exists that facilitates the supplier's ability to communicate with the organization.

The specific requirements of a purchase order that the supplier must flow down to his suppliers shall be identified. They include the requirements to flow down key characteristics when the supplier's supplier has the responsibility for managing the variability of those characteristics.

Verification of Purchased Product

The organization has a number of methods available for controlling the quality of the products and services it obtains from its suppliers. Selection of the appropriate method or methods and their use is the responsibility of the organization. The alternate approaches used by an organization shall be documented, and the method of selecting the appropriate technique explained. AS9100 allows a broad number of methods ranging from the traditional inspection of products at receipt to the more sophisticated methods of delegation of verification to the supplier. If delegation is used, the organization shall define the requirements for delegation and maintain a list of those organizations to which product acceptance has been delegated.

Product Identification and Traceability

Because many aerospace products must perform for a significant period of time and because some are used in very critical applications, the identification of the product and its traceability are issues of concern to the industry. The industry has developed sophisticated approaches for specifying and managing those requirements. When such processes are required, the organization shall maintain documentation. The standard specifies specific situations that may be required:

- If the product requires identification throughout its lifecycle, the identification method must be robust enough to survive the product usage. The method of identification shall not negatively affect the performance or safety of the product. Typically the specific method and location of identification is denoted in the engineering drawing or supporting process specification.

- If the product requires traceability of all parts produced either from the same raw material source or during the same manufacturing processes, then a system must exist by which to know the existence of each part and its final destination. That system must be dynamic enough to allow the fielded product to be moved to alternate sources.

- It may be required to know the specific parts contained in an assembly and then the assembly's location in the next higher assembly. If the assembly has components that can be changed, a process must exist for knowing the ongoing status of the assembly and its contents.

- In a number of instances, what is important is a sequential record of the production processes used to produce the product, the equipment and tooling used, the personnel involved, and the results of inspections and tests.

Inherent in the identification and traceability requirements is the need to know the configuration of the product. That information is frequently consulted to identify any differences between the actual configuration and the desired configuration.

All of the above requirements related to traceability necessitate quality records that are subject to the requirements of clause 4.2.4 of ISO 9001:2000.

PROCESS CONTROL

The aerospace industry has relied on process control methodology to control product quality since the inception of the industry. Recently that methodology has been expanded to include its use to achieve variability reduction and to provide an alternative to product inspection. The requirements of the process control provisions of ISO 9001 have been substantially expanded to address the methods used in the industry.

The environment in which the product is produced can have a significant impact on its quality. Control of temperature, humidity, lighting, and cleanliness may be essential to achieve the level of quality necessitated by the industry. When those variables can be a factor, they must be controlled.

If the purchase order or internal requirements require the monitoring and control of key characteristics, the quality system shall document the control processes used. The objective of those processes is to minimize variation of the characteristics through management of the process characteristics that influence the key characteristics.

During the manufacturing process, it is important that the supplier account for all items introduced into the production stream. If a batch of 20 pieces is started, then at the completion of the batch the status of all 20 parts should be known. Along the way the batch may have been broken into two smaller batches to allow a few parts to be expedited to meet an immediate need for spare parts. This is commonly referred to as "splitting the order." Parts may have been rerouted to allow a nonconformance to be reworked or repaired, and a few items may have been scrapped. Whatever the case, the organization must be able to account for every piece. The process needs to be robust enough to survive an after-the-fact audit, which means that the paper trail must be easily established.

The production work instructions typically provide that those doing the work should indicate who performed the work and when. The provisions are made for those verifying the quality of the work performed. It is assumed that the work must be performed in the planned sequence unless otherwise noted. At the work's completion, the work instructions shall be reviewed to ensure that all manufacturing and inspection operations have been performed or that specific authorization exists for deviating from that practice.

In the aerospace industry, foreign objects (FOs) can threaten the safe operating performance of the product. The history of aviation is blemished by instances of flashlights, mirrors, loose parts, tools, rags, and other items that are not part of the designed configuration (foreign objects) becoming jammed in a control cable, control rod, or control surface or shorting out an electrical system. The best way to preclude FOs is to prevent their interjection into the aircraft and to continuously review the product to identify and remove any FOs. Approaches include tool identification and accountability; clean-as-you-go programs that remove all FOs (including drill chips, tooling, loose parts, and so on) at the end of every shift; and distinctive marking of flashlights, tools, and protective items to make them visible. Many more approaches have been found acceptable. Specific detection processes should be planned to be executed prior to the closing up of areas and the installation of parts and insulation that may cover up an FO. The process for FO control depends on the item being produced and its propensity for containing FOs. Assistance in developing effective FO programs is available from industry associations and from the prime manufacturers.

Processes can be influenced by a number of factors. For example, the humidity level of compressed air can affect the operation of pneumatic tools, and the chemical composition of water may contaminate a cleaning process. Chemical products used for cleaning, if not properly controlled, may leave vapor residue on adjacent surfaces. The consistency of electrical power can cause fluctuations in test results and variation in plating and soldering processes. The impact of changes in the quality of utilities and supplies must be understood and controlled to the extent necessary to preclude changes in the quality of the affected product.

Production Documentation

The production documentation shall include all the data necessary to consistently produce the product or perform the process. These may include drawings, part lists, and process flowcharts including inspection operations. The production work instructions and inspection documents shall be clearly identified and linked to the appropriate configuration of product being produced. Typical types of production work instructions include manufacturing plans, travelers, routers, work orders, and process cards. When specific tooling is required, it shall be identified in the work instructions. That includes the programs to operate numerical controlled (NC) machines.

Specific categories of documents requiring control are those associated with tools designed to produce a specific part or series of parts. Such special tooling shall have its design documented. The instructions for producing the tooling and verifying its conformance also shall be controlled, as well as records maintained of its use and maintenance.

Control of Production Process Changes

When it becomes necessary to change a production process, the changes must be documented. Design changes, producibility enhancements, process improvements, variation in sources of raw material, and a number of other factors may necessitate changes. The reason for the change shall be documented.

The production change process shall identify those authorized to make changes to production processes. If customer approval is required, that shall be identified and the method for notifying the customer explained.

Any changes to processes, production equipment, tools, and programs that may affect product quality shall be documented. The procedures for implementing such changes shall be available. Every change to the production process shall be assessed to confirm that the desired effect has been achieved without adverse effects to product quality. That process shall include changes made by employee teams.

Control of Production Equipment, Tools, and NC Machine Programs

Documented procedures shall exist for validating, prior to use, production equipment, tools, and programs used for NC machines. Such procedures also shall include the maintenance and periodic inspection of those items. The validation process shall include verification of the first article produced to the design data or specification. The method for storage of this equipment and the periodic review to ensure that the equipment does not deteriorate during storage shall be documented. Records of the preceding shall be maintained.

Control of Work Occasionally Performed Outside the Organization's Facilities

In the industry it occasionally becomes necessary to divert work normally performed at the organization's facility to a supplier. Such diversion may be called for because of a breakdown of a specific piece of production equipment, the performance of preventive maintenance, an unplanned demand in excess of production capacity, or a need for a single item to meet a spares requirement, to mention but a few reasons. In such cases the supplier is typically provided with the organization's work instructions. The procedures for having such work performed shall be documented, including the selection of the source for the work and the method of validating that the work has been correctly completed.

Special Processes

A number of processes performed in the aerospace industry do not lend themselves to having their results verified after the fact by inspection and testing. They include plating, heat treatment, chemical processing, and nondestructive inspections. Such processes are typically managed by using qualified operators in conjunction with in-process monitoring and control of process parameters. When production operations require the use of special processes, those processes shall be clearly identified and qualified prior to use. The organization shall ensure that applicable controls are in place as defined by the process specification. Specific attention shall be paid to process changes. The organization shall identify the specific process parameters in the process that will be controlled during production and identify the data that will be recorded.

INSPECTION AND TESTING

The documented procedures for inspection and test activities shall specify the resources and methods to be implemented as well as the method of recording the results. The identification of authorized personnel, including any limitations to that authorization, and the associated training and qualification shall also be documented.

The organization shall perform the maintenance and control of the inspection documentation. That documentation may be part of the manufacturing work instructions or other manufacturing documentation. The documentation shall include acceptance and rejection criteria, where in the manufacturing sequence the verification activity is to be performed, and how the results of the inspection are to be documented. The inspection instruments to be used shall be identified either in the specific work instructions or by use of a supplementary standard. When special inspection equipment is required, the documents associated with that equipment's design, production, validation, control, maintenance, and use shall be controlled.

If the organization subcontracts inspection or test activities to another organization, the organization shall control the performance of that supplier consistent with the requirements of AS9100, clause 4.6, "Purchasing." Although the organization can delegate the performance of the work to another organization, the organization remains responsible for the quality of the work performed.

Receiving Inspection and Testing—Certification Test Reports

The use of certified test reports is relied upon in the industry as one method of accepting material. If the organization chooses to use this method, it shall ensure that the data in the test reports are acceptable to the applicable specifications. This step is necessary to ensure that the material tested complies with the details of the specifications, which may be different from the more generic requirements of the basic material. The organization shall also periodically validate the test reports. Two methods, among several, to validate are having the material tested using an independent source and witnessing the supplier's inspection and test process. The process used by the organization shall be documented.

Inspection and Test Records

The specification, acceptance test plan, or purchase order may require the organization to record actual test data. The process for performing that work shall be documented.

If the organization is required to demonstrate product qualification, the organization shall ensure that the quality records provide evidence that the product meets the defined requirements. That is most easily accomplished by completely listing all qualifications, including the acceptance criteria, and then recording the actual qualification results adjacent to those criteria. Care must be exercised in the performance of qualification testing to ensure that the product tested is conforming and that the test processes and procedures are carefully and completely followed. Qualification testing can be an expensive and time-consuming activity, and every effort should be made to allow successful completion on the initial submittal.

First Article Inspection

The aerospace industry relies on a detailed inspection and test of an early production article to provide objective evidence that the manufacturing process can yield a conforming product. Different customers interpret the term *first article* differently, and the organization should ascertain from its customer whether the article must be the first item produced, the first item that conforms to the requirements, or a representative item produced early in the production run.

The organization shall document its process for the inspection, verification, and documentation of the first article. The results of the verification shall include a list of the design criteria and any allowed tolerances and the actual results of the inspections and tests. Some customers may require the recording of additional information including the type of equipment used to perform the inspection or test, the identity of the person performing the inspection or test, and the atmospheric conditions during the inspection or test. The results are considered quality records.

When the production process is changed or the configuration revised, the organization shall perform a partial or complete first article inspection, depending on the extent of the change.

CONTROL OF INSPECTION, MEASURING, AND TEST EQUIPMENT

The definition of what constitutes inspection, measuring, and test equipment in the aerospace industry is very broad. It includes all devices used to determine that the product conforms to the engineering design. Because assembly equipment is frequently used to demonstrate that the product conforms, that equipment, when used for demonstration of conformance, is included within the definition. Computer-driven plotters are used to make full-size transparencies of the product, and these are then used to verify that the product conforms to the template. The plotters are defined as inspection test equipment unless a separate inspection operation is performed on the template to validate its conformity. These are but two examples that demonstrate the breadth of the aerospace definition.

Simply stated, all equipment used by an organization to validate that materials, products, processes, or other inspection, measuring, or test equipment conforms to stated requirements is defined as inspection, measuring, and test equipment and must be controlled and managed per the requirement of AS9011, clause 4.11. This definition includes test hardware, test software, automated test equipment (ATE), and personally owned equipment used for product acceptance. In larger companies personally owned equipment is being replaced with company-supplied tools to reduce the costs associated with maintaining and calibrating equipment from multiple manufacturers.

The responsibilities for the control of inspection, measuring, and test equipment, including its calibration, shall be defined. This shall include personally owned tools and customer-furnished tools. A list of all such equipment shall be maintained. The process for notifying organizations and personnel that measuring devices require calibration and the method of effecting this recall shall be defined. That process should preclude the use of equipment that requires calibration being used to perform inspections and tests.

When a piece of equipment is found to be out of calibration to the extent that it can potentially affect the results of its use, the supplier shall disposition any product that may be nonconforming. This requirement has existed for a long time in the industry. It still provides challenges in its application. When a piece of equipment is found to be outside its calibrated limits, an analysis should be performed to determine whether the nonconformance of the equipment has any impact on the product accepted by the equipment. If the quality of the product can be compromised because of the equipment, then the product must be dispositioned, typically using a process similar to that used to process other nonconforming material.

INSPECTION AND TEST STATUS

The aerospace industry customarily uses stamps, electronic signatures, and passwords, commonly referred to as *acceptance authority media,* to identify the acceptance of product and the associated records. When acceptance authority media are used, the organization shall establish a process for their control. Typically that includes the configuration of the media, the method of issuance and tracking, and a listing of the personnel that are assigned the media.

Persons who are authorized to verify, certify, and release product must be identified. This includes all personnel who have been delegated those responsibilities.

CONTROL OF NONCONFORMING PRODUCT

Product or processes that fail to conform to engineering data (drawings and specifications) or approved manufacturing work instructions must be identified, controlled, dispositioned, and subsequently verified. This includes process nonconformities that may result in product nonconformity and product returned by a customer until further verification demonstrates that the product is conforming. The organization may be required to notify customers, regulatory authorities, suppliers, and distributors, as well as internal personnel when nonconformity is discovered. The procedures shall describe the process for notification.

Typically organizations in the aerospace industry have used a two-person process for the disposition of nonconforming product. While it is called a material review board, it is rare for this board to ever meet. Rather the process is for the engineering member of the board to disposition the product and the quality member of the board to concur with the disposition. Recently a few companies have begun to use a single-party disposition in which those authorized to disposition the product do so without any verification from quality. That process, operating with adequate oversight controls, is yielding very high quality dispositions with shorter span times and lower costs. The disposition process also may require approval from the customer before the disposition can be implemented. All personnel authorized to disposition nonconforming material shall be approved, and the approval process shall be documented.

Types of dispositions typically used in the industry include the following:

- *Use as is.* In this case the nonconformance is accepted.
- *Rework.* The nonconforming condition can be returned to drawing condition. A typical example is enlarging an undersize hole.
- *Repair.* Additional work is performed that makes the condition acceptable but does not return it to drawing condition. Installing a bushing in an oversize hole is an example. While the part remains functional, the initial engineering documentation does not authorize the bushing.
- *Scrap.* The part is not suitable for use. The part must be physically rendered unusable for its intended purpose. Prior to that, the part must be conspicuously and permanently marked or positively controlled to preclude its inadvertent use.
- *Regrade.* The product has its identification changed to preclude the use of the product for its original use. All inspection and test reports and certifications shall reflect this reidentification.

Material Review Authority

In the aerospace industry all *use-as-is* and *repair* dispositions require the approval of the customer if the product is produced to the customer's design or the nonconformity results in a departure from contract requirements. Organization-designed product that is controlled via a customer specification may be dispositioned as *use as is* or *repair* by the organization, providing the nonconformity does not result in a departure from the contract requirements. Care should be taken to ensure that the customer has not taken further restrictions in the contract.

Notification

When the organization becomes aware of a nonconformity that may affect delivered product, it shall notify the customer in a timely manner. Notification shall include a clear description of the nonconformance, which includes as necessary the parts affected, customer and/or organization part numbers, quantity, and date of delivery. If continuing airworthiness actions are required, they must be noted and clearly communicated. The organization, working with the customer, shall determine whether the airworthiness authorities should be notified and, if so, by whom.

CORRECTIVE AND PREVENTIVE ACTION

An effective quality system includes a robust process to eliminate the causes of actual or potential nonconformities. That system shall verify that the actions taken have been effective in eliminating the root cause of the nonconformance. This type of process is typically referred to as *closed loop*.

Corrective Action

The organization shall ensure that the requirement to maintain an effective corrective and preventive action system is flowed down to all suppliers. The organization shall document the process for responding to situations where corrective actions are not timely or are ineffective.

HANDLING, STORAGE, PACKAGING, PRESERVATION, AND DELIVERY

The organization's procedures for handling, storage, packaging, preservation, and delivery of product shall specifically cover, where applicable, the following:

- The method of cleaning and preserving products during the production process and at its conclusion
- The method for prevention, detection, and removal of FOs as discussed in AS9100 clause 4.9.1 on process control
- The method of handling sensitive products including such products as those that are sensitive to damage by electrostatic discharge
- The method of marking and labeling the product and its packaging, including safety warnings
- The methods for ensuring that life-limited items are properly rotated when in storage and that out-of-life parts are neither included in assemblies nor delivered
- The methods used to identify and manage hazardous materials

The above processes can have a negative impact on product quality if not properly managed. Care shall be given to ensure that all affected employees understand and execute their responsibilities.

The documents required at product delivery are specified in the contract, purchase order, or referenced specifications. The organization shall ensure that those documents are available at time of delivery and that they are protected from loss or deterioration.

CONTROL OF QUALITY RECORDS

All quality records related to product that will be used on commercial aircraft shall be available for review by the regulatory authorities. Additional requirements for reviews by customers and other government agencies may be specified in the contract or purchase order. An orderly records storage and retention system can facilitate this process and will cast a favorable light on the organization 's business.

INTERNAL QUALITY AUDITS

The internal audit process in conjunction with an effective set of internal and external performance measures will provide an adequate picture of the health of the quality system. Personnel performing the audits should be trained organizationally independent from the immediate area being audited. Effective audits will look at several of the quality system elements concurrently. This higher-level, systems approach is important to continuously verify that the elements are properly integrated.

The audits shall ensure that the quality system design complies with the requirements of SAE AS9100 and that the operation of the system complies with the quality manual and implementing procedures. A clear flow down of the requirements of AS9100 to the organization's quality manual and to the working-level procedures shall be demonstrated. Detailed procedures for conducting the audits shall be developed. The establishment of checklists and process flow charts is encouraged to facilitate the audit process. It is important to remember that these are only tools and should not be used to the exclusion of an objective, top-down review process. The effectiveness of the audit process should be evaluated periodically to ensure that audit results are consistent with the input received from customer satisfaction data and internal escape information.

Personnel performing the audits must be trained. It is strongly encouraged that this training be consistent with the guidance provided in ISO 10011.

TRAINING

Adequate training is essential in the implementation of an effective quality system. The amount of training required is determined, in part, by the decisions made regarding the extent and detail of the implementing procedures and work instructions. Organizations choosing to provide detailed instructions will need to do less in-depth training. Those that choose to maintain only high-level procedures and production processes must ensure that those using these documents understand the actions necessary to successfully implement the desired practices.

It is important that all personnel understand the organization's approach to implementing the quality system. They must be aware of the procedures and instructions that are relevant to performing their work, know how to access those documents, and be aware of the process for requesting changes. They also must understand that no deviation can be made from the procedures or work instructions without formal revision of those documents.

SERVICING

As previously emphasized, products in the aerospace industry are frequently designed to operate for 30 to 40 years. That means that periodic maintenance must be performed and that some of this maintenance is extensive. Technical documentation is required to support the maintenance function. Such information must be formally released, controlled, and updated in a manner that ensures that those using the information are aware of the revisions. When the owner or operator of the equipment must perform repairs that are outside the scope of the published documentation, a formal process must exist for the approval, control, and use of this repair scheme. To the extent that the organization is involved in performing service activities at a customer's facility, the procedures for performing that work and verifying its quality must be documented in the quality system.

Information received from the field regarding the performance of the product is an important indicator of the effectiveness of the quality system and should be used during the management review. It also provides valuable information to those designing and producing the product regarding areas for improvement. Customer satisfaction is essential to retaining existing customers and growing business. The systematic use of in-service data can enhance that relationship. The quality system also must document the process used when problems are identified after delivery. This shall include the method used to investigate and report the incident. The process also shall document how corrective actions are taken to eliminate the root cause, the methods of implementing the resultant changes required, and the associated reporting activities. This should include a process for advising other customers when a similar problem might exist on a product provided by the organization and, when appropriate, the method used to notify the regulatory agencies.

STATISTICAL TECHNIQUES

The proper use of statistical techniques can provide an effective method for ensuring product quality and for developing product and process improvements. The effective use of statistical techniques can span the entire product lifecycle. Many of the engineering disciplines rely heavily on statistical methodology when performing safety, reliability, and maintainability projections. The test laboratories may make extensive use of experimental design to determine the optional product configuration or process parameters.

Within manufacturing, statistical techniques are essential to achieving process control and variability reduction. They are used in establishing key product and process characteristics, in conducting gauge repeatability studies, in taking process performance measurements and computing the resultant capability, and in establishing statistical process control methodology. Design of experiments is being used to analyze and improve process performance.

Sampling inspection has a long history in the aerospace industry. Understanding the underlying theory behind these methods is essential to their proper application. In the industry it is generally agreed that when sampling inspection is used for product acceptance the plan must preclude the acceptance of known defectives. This means that only sampling plans that have "accept on zero, reject on one" acceptance criteria shall be used. The customer may require that the sampling plan be submitted for approval.

The application of statistical methodology to the understanding and analysis of field data may yield significant results. This can include the use of failure mode and effects analysis to determine the underlying cause of lower-than-expected reliability. Product performance data can be analyzed and compared with reliability and availability projections to determine if the product is performing in the anticipated manner.

At the quality system level, statistical techniques may be beneficial in analyzing the performance of the quality system and identifying areas for improvement. Recently emerging simulation technology may assist in this effort. As in all areas of the quality system implementation, it is essential that those using statistical techniques be adequately trained.

CONCLUSION

The author has attempted to address most of the additions to ISO 9001 contained in AS9100. It is hoped that the reader will have gained a better understanding of the intent behind the inclusion of those additions and thereby will be better able to implement the standard. The final decisions regarding the meaning and interpretation of the standard rest with the organization and its customer.

Chapter 48

Automotive Industry Applications

R. Dan Reid
General Motors Corporation, Detroit, Michigan

The ISO 9001 standard and the third-party certification portion of the ISO conformity assessment process have become a basis for international automotive industry supplier quality efforts. QS-9000, developed by Chrysler, Ford, and General Motors (GM) in 1994, was the first industry sector document to incorporate the full text of ISO 9001 "as is" and add additional requirements. However, a number of other sectors have now followed the same path. In this chapter, we (a) provide the history of QS-9000, as well as of some of the similar documents; (b) discuss the ISO automotive pilot project that led to the issuance of the first ISO technical specification (TS); and (c) review the requirements in these documents that are in addition to the ISO 9001 requirements.

HISTORY: IN THE BEGINNING . . .

With the advent of the industrial age in the United States, the distance between customers and suppliers increased. No longer would it be feasible for the customer to deal directly with the supplier, such as in the agricultural age when the farmer conducted business at the local general store. At that time, if quality was poor, the end customer could resolve the issue face-to-face with the supplier. When the industrial age hit, the population grew and new companies were formed and fitted into material supply chains. It became difficult for companies to hear the "voice of the customer." As an interim step, companies worked to a "specification." As specifications multiplied, there was no standard for the terminology. As a result, multiple terms carried the same meaning; and some terms had multiple meanings. Over time, it became clear that standardization was needed. Countries began writing national standards; trade associations began writing industry standards; and companies began writing their own supplier quality standards. Many of these had their own documentation requirements. Many also had their own rating schemes. The following are just a few of the standards companies faced by 1987, when the ISO 9000 family was introduced:

- 1963: MIL-Q 9858A (U.S. military)
- 1965: GM's General Quality Standard (GQS)
- 1969: AQAP Defense Standards (NATO)
- 1971: ANSI N45-2 (United States)
- 1973: DEF STANS (U.K. Ministry of Defense)
- 1975: CSA Z299 (Canada)
- 1975: AS 1821/22/23 (Australia)
- 1979: BS 5750
- 1979: ANSI/ASQC Z 1.15 (United States—generic)
- 1981: Ford Q101 (global automotive)
- 1983: Chrysler's Supplier Quality Assurance
- 1987: GM's Targets for Excellence (TFE) (North American automotive)

THE U.S. INITIATIVE

Chrysler, Ford, and General Motors (the Big Three) had made a significant contribution to this proliferation, as their three supplier quality standards at the time totaled almost 1000 pages of prescriptive requirements. Each used second-party audits of its suppliers, many of which supplied two or all three. However, those second-party approaches used different processes, and each company had a different perspective, with some unique areas of emphasis. Each process linked to additional tiers of company-specific reference manuals and additional requirements that added complexity for shared suppliers. Further, while the intent of each was nearly identical, the content was not standardized.

In this context, some companies dedicated full-time employees to each customer account just to understand the varying quality requirements. For tier-two suppliers, the situation was worse. They were subject to numerous unique tier-one supplier quality standards that incorporated their customer (for example, Ford, GM) requirements with their own. Typically the tier-two supplier has fewer resources to deal with the variation than the tier-one supplier has.

THE FIRST DAY: AND LEADERSHIP SAID . . .

In June 1988, the American Society for Quality Control (at that time) Automotive Division hosted a summer workshop with the purchasing vice presidents from Chrysler, Ford, and GM addressing the subject of supplier and original equipment manufacturer (OEM) relationships. The suppliers in attendance made clear that the multiple quality standards and reference manuals used in the industry were driving a significant amount of non-value-added cost. Cost reduction was a subject that the OEM vice presidents proposed to address.

As a result, they formed a small OEM task force under the auspices of ASQC. The task force was chartered to standardize reference manuals, reporting formats, and/or terminology. The original task force objectives included elimination of supplier confusion and redundancy concerning the three OEMs' assessment systems reporting, reduction of supplier/OEM assessment system transaction costs, and concentration on specific projects with definable cost benefits. The vice presidents:

- Designated the task force as the prime agency for accomplishing the objectives
- Appointed Bruce Pince, a representative of ASQC Automotive Division, as task force facilitato
- Documented their support by issuing internal memos and a joint letter to the supply chain
- Suggested teaming with ASQC and suppliers to augment their OEM resources
- Approved the formation and membership of a task force Supplier Advisory Council to define and prioritize projects

At that time, there were no quality manuals in use with more than one company logo on the cover. Expectations were small. Nothing in the task force charter addressed development of a common quality system standard. In fact, one of the vice presidents at that time told the task force that there would be no such document in his lifetime. In reality, that took another six years.

THE SECOND DAY: CREATION OF THE PLAN

The original task force was formed by recruiting OEM quality and purchasing resources. Having no precedent for its work, the group struggled in the early days, and the size of the group limited its effectiveness. Concerns about antitrust and resources resulted in the formation of an alliance with the Automotive Industry Action Group (AIAG), a nonprofit automotive trade association. AIAG provided a "neutral" meeting ground for task force activities and administrative support. Initial meetings were marked by very general group discussion.

The task force established a plan of action identifying potential projects—for example, measurement system analysis (MSA), statistical process control (SPC), and production part approval process (PPAP). Each OEM had its own manual for many of these. The potential task was to combine them into one, where the cost-benefit analysis led to project approval. To facilitate progress, the task force agreed to use for each approved project the OEM "best practice" manual as defined by the Supplier Advisory Council. The task force Supplier Advisory Council, which consisted of representatives from a combination of small, medium, and large companies of varied commodities, was convened to provide the cost-benefit analysis that resulted in a prioritization of the potential projects and to select the base OEM manual for each project. OEM "buy-in" was then obtained to begin project work.

At the time, Lotus 1-2-3 and Freelance were state-of-the-art software packages, and the fastest personal computers had the 286 chip.

THE THIRD DAY: THE FIRST FRUITS

The first key task force deliverable was the first-ever valid combined OEM supplier list. This was facilitated and maintained by AIAG. Each OEM provided its supplier list, which AIAG merged into a single list after purging duplications. The list was kept confidential by AIAG, used only to send out joint communications by the vice presidents, as well as to distribute the eventual task force deliverables. Somewhat surprising was the low number of supplier locations shared by all three OEMs, which confirmed that the OEMs still used dedicated suppliers at the manufacturing level to a large extent.

Wanting to avoid the usual non-value-added dynamic that characterizes a new group, the task force issued a sanctioning document to each approved project team defining the project team membership—including a project leader, the expected deliverable, and the due date. This enabled project teams get a "fast start." The project teams' memberships were supplemented by subject matter experts as necessary. The task force typically defined the deliverable in terms of a "draft" document, which it would circulate inside the OEMs for comment and approval. Project team progress was monitored by the task force. Roles and responsibilities for project identification, resourcing, funding, approval, communications, and distribution were documented in a task force project process model, an early form of RASIC chart.

At the end of the task force's first year, the project team working on PPAP delivered a common warrant form—one sheet of paper. Not to be discouraged, work continued.

THE FOURTH DAY: GO FORTH AND MULTIPLY

The first common manual produced by the OEMs was the Measurement Systems Analysis reference manual released in October 1990. That manual, based on GM's *Gage R&R* manual, was the first quality manual in the U.S. automotive industry to bear the logos of Chrysler, Ford, and General Motors. As the manual was nearing completion, the issue of distribution cost had to be addressed. The OEMs contributed about $90,000 collectively, with each one's contribution based on the number of supplier locations it had as a percent of the total. This money was used by AIAG to fund the initial printing of manuals and to mail one copy free of charge to each supplier on the OEM list. Subsequent sales of the MSA manual were used to fund the printing and distribution of the second and subsequent manuals in the series. Pricing of the manuals was established to cover costs, not generate profit, but enough profits were made to fund the next project. In this manner, the task force activities since then have been self-funding. This initial seed money continues to be the only out-of-pocket cost to the OEMs to date for task force activities and deliverables.

In 1992, the common Fundamental SPC reference manual, based on the Ford manual, was released. This manual had wider application in the industry than its predecessor, MSA; however, the supplier community enthusiastically received both manuals.

Throughout the years, the task force sustained a mutually beneficial relationship with the ASQ Automotive Division, which provided technical review and comment on drafts of each project. The ASQ national and international contacts also were used for mutual benefit.

Having produced something of perceived "value" to the supplier community, the task force was asked by the Supplier Advisory Council to significantly increase the standardization activities. The highest priority continued to be a common quality standard, but the time for that had not yet come.

The task force doubled the number of approved projects at that time, launching teams to work on advanced product quality planning, control plans, potential failure mode and effects analysis (FMEA), problem reporting and resolution, and a key characteristics designation system.

NEW VISION

Up until that time (1992), the task force had operated under a "tactical," or project-by-project, approach. By May 1992, the task force had defined a recommended long-term vision and path forward to migrate first to a more "strategic" approach, calling for integration of quality and existing OEM business requirements into common standards, and then move to a "systems" approach, defined as integration of the OEM auditing processes and use of third parties. The ultimate vision at that time was for the eventual use of "voluntary" standards by the supplier based on generic descriptive requirements, perhaps based on ISO standards and/or the Malcolm Baldrige National Quality Award criteria. GM's Targets for Excellence requirements at the time defined expectations of the supplier in quality, cost, delivery, technology, and leadership, while the Chrysler and Ford manuals were limited to quality only. OEM approval of the task force vision would take six more months.

The common PPAP and FMEA manuals were released together in February 1993. PPAP became the first common requirements manual of the OEMs. These were followed in June 1994 by release of the Advanced Product Quality Planning (APQP) and Control Plan reference manual. Originally the content was developed by separate project teams, but since the control plan is the primary deliverable of the APQP process, it was combined into one manual for supplier use. Efforts to reach OEM agreement on common deliverables for problem reporting and resolution and key characteristics were unsuccessful.

THE FIFTH DAY: QS-9000/QSA

By mid-1992, two of the original OEM vice presidents had been replaced. At Ford, Clint Lauer was replaced by Norm Ehlers, who took the position that a common supplier quality standard for the Big Three should be developed within a year. Inaki Lopez had replaced Don Pais at GM and had redirected most supplier quality resources from doing TFE assessments to conducting his "PICOS" workshops with tremendous value-added results.

On November 4, 1992, the purchasing vice presidents met and approved the task force recommendation to begin work on a common automotive industry quality standard. The earlier success of the reference manuals and PPAP provided confidence that agreement could be reached because the content of the common manuals was included as major parts of the quality system requirements. Significant portions of the work had already been accomplished.

In preparation for this approval, the task force conducted a comparison of its three supplier quality standards: Chrysler's Supplier Quality Assurance, Ford's Q101, and GM's Targets for Excellence. The comparison included the content of ISO 9001:1987. The amount of correlation between the OEM content and the ISO 9001 content was estimated, as well as the significance of the difference, if any. This clearly identified the work that lay ahead and gave an estimate of the difficulty in achieving success.

There were two elements of the process to be agreed upon: (1) the standard, to define the requirements; and (2) the process for determining compliance to the requirements. As 1992 was drawing to a close, in the United States there were rumors that companies would need to have an ISO 9000 certification to do business in Europe going forward. As a result of this and the analysis of the ISO 9001:1987 text, the decision was reached to use the ISO 9001 text as a base. The common view was that nothing in ISO 9001 was objectionable but that the OEM quality manuals at that time went much further in providing the customer with confidence of supplier quality. The task force recommendation to migrate to the use of third-party certification was also agreed to, given that the OEM resources were being redirected for activities that were more value-added (for example, APQP, PPAP, waste elimination workshops, and so on).

The initial design of the common quality standard comprised three parts, with options for two more parts:

- Part one: ISO 9001
- Part two: supplemental requirements to ISO 9001, bringing the ISO 9001 content up to current standards in the U.S. automotive industry
- Part three: additional requirements not addressed by ISO 9001 content (for example, manufacturing capabilities)
- Part four (potential): company-specific requirements
- Part five (potential): supplier-specific requirements

The initial work plan approved by the vice presidents specified a completion date of July 1993. As the work progressed, the task force had dialogue with a number of organizations including the AIAG Heavy Truck Group, which eventually adopted QS-9000, the American Association of Laboratory Accreditation, the Electronic Components Certification Board, the National Electronic Component Quality Assessment System, the Steel Industry Supplier Audit Process, and the International Organization for Standardization. It became clear during the drafting of the document that the ISO 9001 text would be revised, with the 1994 revision due out shortly.

The Chrysler, Ford, and GM Quality System Requirements (QS-9000) and the Quality System Assessment (QSA) manuals were released in August 1994. The delay from the planned release date was due to several factors: (1) the timing of the release of the ISO 9001:1994 revision, which was six months past the ISO/TC 176 forecasted release date; (2) OEM buy-in of the new standard and the third-party process; (3) the time necessary to secure agreements with national accreditation bodies for the automotive certification scheme; and (4) the time to build training capacity and qualify certification bodies and third-party auditors in the QS-9000 certification scheme.

The response to QS-9000 was overwhelming. AIAG's resources were insufficient for the volume of transactions that were requested. It had to install a new phone system, expand its facilities, and hire additional staff from the office to the order-fulfillment process. Questions directed to the task force regarding QS-9000 content or interpretation were too numerous to disposition individually. The task force quickly convened an ad hoc group of third-party stakeholders to address the questions and develop standard responses. That group, which became known as the International Auto Sector Group, began publishing binding "QS-9000 Sanctioned Interpretations" for QS-9000 content and application in an attempt to reduce variation in the process.

Additional dialogue began with the Independent Association of Accredited Registrars and various internal OEM stakeholders such as the tooling, equipment, semiconductor, and international purchasing and quality colleagues. Interest among the OEMs in adopting QS-9000 globally was high from the beginning. To accommodate the international rollout, the second edition of QS-9000 was released in February 1995. That edition was the first version deployed by the OEMs worldwide. This required the translation of the requirements, the certification scheme information, and the training materials into a number of languages including German, Spanish, French, Italian, Japanese, Chinese, and Portuguese.

A number of process controls were implemented in the QS-9000 certification scheme in order to minimize variation in the process in addition to the sanctioned QS-9000 interpretations. These were documented in the requirements listed in QS-9000, Appendixes B, G, and H (and Appendix I in the third edition of QS-9000).

BENEFITS

QS-9000 was quite a success for the industry. Supplier surveys were conducted in 1997 and 1998 by AIAG and ASQ to document the costs and benefits of QS-9000 certification. The 1997 survey, with 613 respondents, indicated that the average cost to obtain QS-9000 certification was US$118,100. That included costs for preparation ($36,900), consultants ($26,000), certification body ($18,300), and software ($5,100). Of these the certification body, which represented 15 percent of the total reported cost, was the only out-of-pocket nondiscretionary cost driven by requiring QS-9000 certification. The average reported benefit was $304,300— a 2.6:1 payback for the total reported cost, or a 16.6:1 payback for the cost of the certification body. Improved process or quality improvement was reported by 76 percent of the respondents. Better understanding of jobs and tasks was reported by 75 percent. Reported reduction in parts per million (ppm) defect rates was also significant. Fifty-four percent of the respondents reported an average improvement in ppm of 46 percent from preregistration levels. Other benefits reported included fewer parts returned, reduced cost of nonconformance, and improved delivery performance.

In the 1998 survey, the cost-benefit findings were consistent with those of the 1997 survey. The average cost was reported to be US$120,000. That included preparation ($79,000), consultants ($8,100), certification body ($20,000), training ($6,100), and software ($3,000). The cost-benefit relationship was asked for in a different manner than in the 1997 survey. Suppliers were asked what their annual sales were and how much savings as a percent of total sales resulted from QS-9000 certification. The 207 respondents to the 1998 survey had average annual sales of US$130 million. They reported as the benefit of QS-9000 six percent of sales, which was almost $8 million on average.

It is hard to imagine another initiative at the time that could have yielded that amount of quality improvement and cost reduction, especially given the scarce amount of OEM resources devoted to the development and launch of QS-9000 worldwide. The OEM leadership viewed the work as largely complete with the publishing of the manual, but much work remained in terms of building the third-party infrastructure to support the QS-9000 certification scheme and in further harmonization efforts.

SUCCESS FACTORS

The development, implementation, and success of QS-9000 as the first ISO 9001–based industry sector document with a tailored third-party certification scheme can be attributed to some key success factors, many of which were employed by other sectors as they followed with their own document and certification process.

The charter of the task force by the vice presidents was key. There was OEM sanction from the highest levels for the work, even when expectations for success were small. This is another testament to the importance of leadership to the success of a project. When a project has support from the top down, the potential for success is great. The OEM vice presidents were industrial statesmen working for the North American industry's common good. They provided true leadership in establishing a vision—narrow at first—and appropriate boundaries. They helped break down internal barriers to success and made themselves available to the task force on a regular basis to monitor and guide the work. A critical turning point came when one vice president, who said there would never be a common quality standard in his lifetime, was replaced by a vice president who took the position that it should be done in the next year.

The task force membership and design were also key to success. The members—Russ Jacobs (Chrysler), Radley Smith (Ford), and R. Dan Reid (GM)—were technically competent and managerially astute, with expertise in both quality and procurement. Jacobs was the director for supplier quality at Chrysler. Rad Smith was the primary author of Ford's Q101 standard, a predecessor of QS-9000. And Dan Reid, an ASQ-certified quality engineer, managed GM's Targets for Excellence program and was the overseer of the TFE revision in 1987. Bruce Pince, as task force coordinator appointed by the vice presidents, was an independent second party who brought high-level stakeholder interface to the project. Pince, often a mediator, brought vision and constancy of purpose to the work. The reputation of the task force individually and collectively gave the work credibility, which positively contributed to the eventual OEM buy-in and supplier acceptance. The task force developed and "sold" the vision with personal commitment to "making it happen" using a practical and action-oriented approach.

The task force was designed to be small, to focus on win–win results, and to be self-funding. This lean, focused approach provided an environment where sufficient "airtime" was available for all to contribute to discussion and then reach consensus. It also facilitated the frequent meetings that were necessary by minimizing the number of schedules that had to be coordinated to arrange for each meeting. The suppliers also provided the initial motivation to begin the work, invaluable counsel, technical expertise, and resources as strategic allies for the eventual projects. Acknowledgments of those contributions were published in each of the common manuals.

A third key success factor was the emergence of ISO 9000. Introduced in 1987, it was not well deployed in the United States until after the launch of QS-9000. However, when the task force began the design work for the common quality standard, there were significant rumors that ISO 9000 certification would soon be a requirement for companies wanting to do business in Europe. The Big Three at the time were becoming more global in their supplier quality and procurement approaches, so the decision was made to use ISO 9001 as the base text after discussions with the leading national accreditation bodies and a large number of certification bodies from North America and Europe.

The task force conducted a survey of those third-party stakeholders, which identified early the shortcomings of the existing ISO conformity assessment process that it would need to address in order for the existing third-party process to be used by the automotive industry as a replacement for its second-party auditing processes. Qualification processes were established for accreditation bodies, certification bodies, and third-party auditors for the QS-9000 certification scheme. Additional rules were implemented to reduce the variation in the certification process. Specific QS-9000 training sanctioned by the OEMs was developed for suppliers, certification bodies, and internal OEM stakeholders to support the international launch of the process.

Finally, the support of ASQ and later AIAG in the process was valuable in providing at the start a neutral ground for the OEMs to come together to work, and later to provide the administrative support required (for example, administration of training and distribution of manuals).

Without these success factors coming together at an opportune time, there would likely have been no common automotive quality standard. In fact, since the vice presidents have handed off their involvement in the harmonization work, there has been a gradual proliferation among OEMs of supplier quality standards, particularly in the area of APQP. That trend may continue unchecked for a number of years until the proliferation again prompts suppliers to voice their concern to the OEMs and demand action.

LESSONS LEARNED

This effort resulted in some "lessons learned" that others could benefit from. They include the following:

- Get support and sanction for the work at the highest levels in organizations.
- Use a small, focused core team, with technical competency and credibility required.
- The challenge is not primarily technical, but cultural.
- Be business-oriented and use market drivers to prompt action.
- Have a vision for the common good; then avoid optimization at the company level.
- Be ethically correct, with constancy of purpose and consistency in process.
- Overcome resistance at the highest organizational levels.
- Be patient and persevere.

THE SIXTH DAY: ISO/TS 16949

In May 1995, during a QS-9000 rollout meeting for suppliers and certification bodies in Europe, representatives of the European automotive OEMs approached the task force to point out that parallel efforts already had been undertaken in Europe. In fact, there were already three automotive supplier quality requirements manuals in Europe: VDA 6.1 in Germany, AVSQ in Italy, and EAQF in France. The German VDA 6.1 was based loosely on ISO 9004:1994, while the others were based on ISO 9001:1994. As a result of that discussion, it was agreed that for the benefit of the shared supply base, additional harmonization should be pursued. A meeting was scheduled for September to continue the discussion.

In Italy, Fiat Auto, IVECO, and 16 primary suppliers representing some 85 suppliers in total had worked on the Italian automotive standard, AVSQ. In France, Renault and PSA, which consists of Peugeot and Citroen, teamed with FIEV, the French automotive supplier association, and four primary suppliers representing some 300 suppliers in total to publish the French standard, EAQF. In Germany, it was Adam Opel, Audi, BMW, Daimler Benz, Ford Werke, and VW who worked with their automotive trade association, VDA, and 18 primary suppliers representing some 500 total suppliers in the development of the German automotive standard, VDA 6.1, one of a number of common manuals in the VDA 6 family of quality documents. VDA 6.1 has been translated into several languages and has been deployed internationally, as has QS-9000.

Extensive efforts were undertaken early in the process to identify where the content of the documents was similar and where it differed. Much of that effort involved translation of the documents into English, the only language common to the group. When the content of these manuals and QS-9000 was compared, the manuals were found to be remarkably similar. There were some differences in content, but more so in areas of emphasis and in the amount of guidance included with the requirements. The German VDA 6.1 provided a significant amount of guidance in implementation of its system compared with the others.

The more significant differences were in the methods of determining conformance to the requirements. The European approaches were based on second-party (customer/supplier) audits, with a general agreement for reciprocal recognition of each other's audits.

Subsequent meetings of the U.S. and European OEMs were scheduled, and the group became known as the International Automotive Task Force (IATF).

The initial project for the harmonization of the automotive sector manuals was known as the Advanced Quality System, or AQS-2000. The plan for AQS-2000 was to exclude the ISO 9000 standards verbatim and use instead a paraphrase of the ISO 9001:1994 requirements with the additional automotive requirements. Those requirements would then be organized around the planned outline for the ISO 9000:2000 family.

ISO Technical Committee 176

The international launch of QS-9000 was also being noted by ISO member bodies and ISO Technical Committee 176 (ISO/TC 176). In November 1995, ISO/TC 176 chair Reg Shaughnessy contacted the task force as a follow-up to a TC 176 resolution passed in the ISO/TC 176 plenary meeting in Durban. At that annual meeting, TC 176 resolved to undertake efforts to try to avoid proliferation of sector-specific standards such as QS-9000 by investigating collaborative efforts with the automotive group with an aim of convincing this group to adopt the use of ISO 9001. This was consistent with the ISO directives at the time concerning sector-specific requirements. There were several additional meetings and numerous communications before the next ISO/TC 176 plenary in Tel Aviv in November 1996 to explore the possibilities of collaborative efforts. It was soon apparent to all that the ISO 9001:1994 text alone was insufficient for use by the automotive industry, so efforts were then focused on how best to accommodate the industry's needs going forward.

At the November 1996 ISO/TC 176 plenary, a resolution was adopted to ensure that the generic quality management needs of the automotive industry would be addressed in the future revision of the ISO 9000 family. A number of alternatives regarding how that might work were discussed, but the prevailing thought was to use another type of document in the ISO portfolio, a technical report, to house the additional requirements. Additional meetings between IATF and TC 176 leadership led to the recognition of IATF as a liaison member to ISO/TC 176 under a new category of liaison for "industry consortia," which was identified as "liaison D."

The ISO/TC 176 plan was then for the automotive industry to participate in the ISO 9000:2000 revision process already under way to see if enough additional content could be added to make the next version of ISO 9001 fit for automotive industry use without supplement. Eight IATF members became engaged in the various activities of TC 176 and its subcommittees. However, that participation came about too late. The year 2000 design specifications for the revision were complete by then, so much of the significant content brought forward by the automotive group was rejected on the basis that it was outside the design specification or not applicable to other product sectors.

In discussion with the other sectors involved with ISO/TC 176 (for example, medical devices, aerospace, telecommunications), it became apparent that the technical committee would have to find a way to accommodate the automotive sector specifics outside ISO 9000 but within the ISO portfolio of documents, or the automotive group would continue to publish its own supplier requirements.

The other sectors preferred that ISO 9001 contain only the minimum requirements for quality assurance, and they also preferred publishing their own sector-specific requirements.

In consultation with ISO/TC 176, it became clear that the best path forward was through a "pilot" project with the automotive group so that ISO could gain some experience in how to address sector-specific requirements going forward in conjunction with a revision to the ISO directives. At the November 1997 ISO/TC 176 plenary meeting in Rio de Janeiro, another resolution was adopted, which approved the pilot to go forward according to the plan jointly developed by TC 176 and IATF. The plan called for the development of a technical report as the vehicle for the automotive requirements. It also targeted a decision to be made by the end of the first quarter of 1998 with regard to which version of ISO 9001 to use: the 1994 text, which would allow the project to begin immediately, or the 2000 text, which would require a delay in beginning the project but would include the Japanese OEMs in the project. The work group would consist of subject matter experts (SMEs) from TC 176 Subcommittees 1, 2, and 3 and IATF if the short-term option was chosen, or IATF and representatives from the Japanese Automotive Manufacturer's Association (JAMA) if the long-term option was selected. The SMEs on the work group would ensure consistency with ISO protocols for terminology, standards, and auditing.

The issue of the Japanese OEM involvement was raised a year earlier by TC 176. In discussion with JAMA, the committee indicated its preference to have one or two representatives join the ISO pilot project when the work began on integrating the new ISO 9001:2000 text. Hence, if the short-term approach were selected, it could go forward rapidly based on the IATF work already done at that time.

The Japanese OEM affiliates in the United Kingdom had considered adopting QS-9000 some years earlier as part of the U.K. automotive trade association, the Society of Motor Manufacturers and Traders (SMMT). SMMT stopped short of endorsement and use of QS-9000 over some terminology differences at that time. The Japanese OEMs had indicated that QS-9000 was not particularly objectionable to them, but rather that their process was "different." In fact, Toyota's North American operation issued a supplier quality manual several years ago referring suppliers to use techniques from the Big Three reference manuals (for example, FMEA, MSA). A key difference was that the Japanese OEMs allocated a significantly higher number of resources to supplier quality than did the U.S. Big Three or the European OEMs. Given these resources, the Japanese OEMs worked much closer with their supply base, both in the initial sourcing and in problem resolution when required. The U.S. and European OEMs did not have sufficient resources allocated to accommodate this type of approach, so they relied more on the use of standards, second-party activities (for example, PPAP, APQP), and third-party certification to provide information on suppliers and drive supplier quality.

By the end of the first quarter of 1998, IATF had made significant progress on development of a common supplier quality standard. Work that had begun on AQS-2000 was converted into the ISO technical report format. As the pilot project began, IATF agreed to pursue the short-term option for the pilot using the ISO 9001:1994 text. It also agreed to use the third edition of QS-9000 as the baseline document to work from due in part to its similarity in format to the ISO technical report.

The draft document was balloted by ISO/TC 176 in the third quarter of 1998, and was approved for release. During the ballot, the ISO Central Secretariat indicated that there was a new document type in the ISO portfolio, a technical specification (TS), available if IATF wanted to use that category rather than the existing technical report category. This was supported, and in November 1998, ISO/TS 16949 was released as the first ISO TS.

IATF announced, also in 1998, that ISO/TS 16949 would be an "optional" document for automotive suppliers. A supplier with numerous automotive customers requiring third-party certification to their own requirements document can now choose a certification to ISO/TS 16949, which will satisfy those customers when the relevant customer-specific requirements are included in the registration scope by a recognized certification body. A current listing of the recognized certification bodies for ISO/TS 16949 is available from the International Automotive Oversight Board at 248-799-3939.

A new feature incorporated into the IATF-recognized certification scheme for TS 16949 is the selection and contracting of approved certification bodies by IATF oversight bodies in the United States and Europe. This contract gives IATF members a mechanism to use to revoke the TS 16949 qualification of certification bodies whose performance proves unacceptable. Examples of such performance could be failure to abide by IATF rules for the TS 16949 certification scheme or maintaining the certification of companies who chronically ship poor-quality product to their customers.

LESSONS LEARNED

There are some additional lessons that can be learned from the development of ISO/TS 16949. They include the following:

- Get industry procurement representatives involved early in the development of ISO "new work items" to represent the voice of the customer in the process.

- Make proactive efforts to dialogue early, and at all relevant stages of the process, with the relevant third-party stakeholders (for example, CASCO, IAF) to build consensus.

- Secure adequate resources to support the work, and develop a work plan taking into account the support activities that may be required (for example, translation, database development, training development, internal and external communications).

- Develop efforts across industry sectors. This could likely yield adoption of more common terminology (at a minimum) and/or common documents (best-case scenario) to benefit the shared supply base, particularly at the tier-two and below levels.

THE SEVENTH DAY: REST

Unlike the biblical creation story, the work of standardization does not lend itself to a cessation of activity. The challenge ahead is for industry organizations to find a way to value the work so that their procurement and/or supplier quality representatives can participate in the process from the beginning to the end of projects. There are already numerous standards bodies, certification bodies, consultants, and a growing number of industry supplier representatives involved in the international standards–developing arena. However, without the balance of the voice of the customer, including the major purchasers in industry, there will likely continue to be company-specific supplier requirements and second-party audits that add cost to suppliers and customers alike.

It also is important that, going forward, ISO continues to reengineer itself to provide standards faster to market and to provide more integrity in the conformity assessment process to build customer confidence in the process.

AUTOMOTIVE-SPECIFIC REQUIREMENTS

In the remainder of the chapter, we will review the more significant of the automotive industry requirements that are used in addition to ISO 9001. Since the European and U.S. OEM requirements are now harmonized in ISO/TS 16949, we will use that document as the source for the discussion. However, it should be noted that these requirements also are contained in one or more of the following: QS-9000, VDA 6.1, AVSQ, and EAQF. The list of automotive requirements that follows is not exhaustive but rather a summary of those that are most significant.

The goal of TS 16949 is worth noting. It calls for developing fundamental quality systems that provide for continuous improvement and emphasize defect prevention and the reduction of variation and waste in the supply chain. It is debatable whether the ISO 9001:1994 standard provides for continuous improvement. Clearly it has no direct reference to continuous improvement; however, some argue that the cycle of internal audit, corrective/preventive action, and management review provides for continuous improvement. In drafting the ISO 9001:2000 text, representatives from the regulated sectors insisted that continuous improvement, or continual improvement as it is now referred to, cannot be included in the ISO 9001 standard, which they say should include only the minimum requirements for quality assurance, as contrasted with quality management. They argue that continual improvement of product cannot be mandated, because if for some reason it could not be demonstrated, that could result in some adverse legal action. In the automotive arena, continuous improvement has been a requirement since the mid-1980s. This is discussed in more detail later. The concept of continual improvement in the ISO 9001:2000 text is aimed exclusively at improvement of the quality system and excludes the product or the process.

The goal of TS 16949 also emphasizes defect prevention, as opposed to defect detection. The ISO 9001:1994 text has been criticized for too much reliance on inspection and testing, which is defect detection. The best opportunity to positively influence the cost and quality of the product is up front in the design and development phase. The automotive industry requires the use of appropriate tools in the planning phase to prevent defects.

The final component of the TS 16949 goal is the reduction of variation and waste to benefit the supply chain. For many years, it was thought that any part characteristic that was within the allowable tolerance range was equally acceptable, and that any outside the tolerance were equally unacceptable. The current thinking in the automotive industry is that reduction of variation around some optimal target, or nominal, will produce better quality at lower cost to society—that is, the closer to nominal the characteristic is, the better. The concept of waste has been understood in the automotive industry in a new way for the last decade. Waste is present in every organization. It can take many forms—too much inventory, overproduction, rework/scrap, material movement, non-value-added processing time, waiting, or motions. Waste can be attacked within organizations but also across a product supply chain. See chapter 23 on purchasing for more discussion.

TS 16949 also assumes that there will be additional requirements for the quality system as it contains those pertaining to the fundamental quality system. This differs from ISO 9001:1994 in that the automotive industry design for the fundamental quality system addresses quality management, not just quality assurance. In fact, a properly designed and implemented TS 16949 quality management system should result in best-in-class quality and customer satisfaction.

TS 16949 defines "sites" and "remote locations" to address the support functions represented. Many organizations to date have been certified to ISO 9002, even though they manufacture or assemble a product that is designed by their organization but in another facility. The fact that this is allowed by the ISO conformity assessment process is one of the shortcomings of the third-party system. The issue of design responsibility is dealt with simply by the automotive sector: either the customer or the supplier ultimately is design responsible. If it is not the customer, then it is the supplier, regardless of whether the design is done by or at the manufacturing site or by a subcontractor. This means that to satisfy the automotive OEMs' requirements for third-party certification, the scope of the supplier's certification must include ISO 9001 unless the customer is design responsible for all the product supplied. To allow otherwise is to risk customer confidence in the process.

One of the key generic quality management system requirements included by the automotive industry is customer satisfaction. The supplier must have a process for determining customer satisfaction that specifies the frequency of the determination and provisions to ensure objectivity and validity. Indicators are required for monitoring trends in both customer satisfaction and customer dissatisfaction, and the supplier must have objective data to document compliance. It is recognized that satisfaction and dissatisfaction are not opposite ends of the same continuum but rather are separate continuums; thus both are to be tracked in the automotive industry. Further, the concept *customer* addresses both internal and external customers of the organization. The supplier is to determine both current and future expectations of the customer.

Continuous improvement is another of the key generic quality management system requirements used by the automotive industry. In the new ISO 9000 family, the term *continual improvement* is used for the same concept. Continuous improvement in quality, service, cost, and technology has to be provided for in the supplier's quality policy. Many quality policies in place today that are acceptable for ISO 9000 certification will not be in compliance with this expectation. The supplier is obligated to identify and implement appropriate quality and productivity improvement projects. Further, the supplier must use appropriate measures and methods for continuous improvement. Specific examples include the use of control charts, PPM analysis, value analysis, and mistake-proofing. To comply with this requirement, improvement must extend to product characteristics and process parameters with the highest priority or those that are most important to the customer. They can be identified in the quality planning or product approval process.

The automotive industry also requires the supplier to use a formal, comprehensive business plan with both long- and short-term goals. Given the trend of suppliers going bankrupt combined with the OEM's migration to lean manufacturing, the customer needs to be able to rely on continuity of supply from its suppliers. Typically, a business plan includes the following types of information: market issues; cost and operational performance objectives; growth projections; capital investment plans; research and development plans; product/project plans with funding, health, safety, and environmental issues. The business plan must be based on analysis of competitive products and, where available, on benchmarking inside and outside the automotive industry and the supplier's product commodity. Methods to track, update, revise, and review the business plan have to be documented.

The supplier must assign responsibility to appropriate individuals to represent the voice of the customer internally in addressing quality requirements. This includes selecting key product, or special, characteristics; setting objectives; product design or development; and improvement actions.

The supplier's management review process has to include all elements of the quality management system and its performance. Another shortcoming of the existing third-party process is that some wording in the ISO 9001:1994 text has been interpreted by some certification bodies to mean that all elements of the quality system do not have to be included in management review.

In current ISO 9000 practice, the performance of the system has been completely "divorced" from the concept of the quality system capability. A disclaimer is typical when discussing ISO 9000 certification. It goes something like this: "ISO 9000 certification does not guarantee product quality, only that the system has the capability to produce good quality." The automotive industry has addressed this by mandating that the quality management system must be effective in meeting quality objectives specified in the quality policy and the business plan and result in customer satisfaction. Failure to do so is evidence of a nonconformance according to ISO/TS 16949. This requirement for quality system performance is the only new requirement introduced in TS 16949. The intent is that suppliers that chronically ship poor quality to a customer should not continue to be certified. This is contrasted with "sporadic" problems that may arise. The quality management system should be designed with provisions to identify and contain at the supplier's facility any nonconformances that may occur in its product realization or production processes. Ideally the product realization and production processes should be designed and mistake-proofed to preclude the manufacture, or the passing through the process, of any defect.

The supplier is expected to use mistake-proofing methodology for the planning of processes, facilities, tooling, and equipment. This also is identified as one of the continuous improvement tools to be used. Mistake-proofing also must be used in the corrective/preventive action process to an appropriate degree. Given the emphasis that is to be placed on defect prevention in the quality management system, there is considerable work that still can be done in the supply chain with implementation of mistake-proofing methods to achieve substantial quality and cost improvements.

While the ISO 9001:1994 text introduced quality planning, it stopped far short of the content required by the automotive industry. The new ISO 9001:2000 text de-emphasizes the need for use of quality plans, while the auto industry requires that they be used. Quality plans must include customer requirements and references to appropriate technical specifications. In TS 16949 the scope of "product realization" extends from the quality planning phase through product and/or process design and production part approval. Manufacturing and delivery of product is outside the scope, although in the new ISO 9001:2000 text, product realization includes those phases.

The supplier must have a product realization or project management process in order to deliver products on time and to customer expectations for quality, cost, and delivery. Measurements must be taken at appropriate stages as well as review of product/project status. The supplier must use a multidisciplinary approach in the planning phase for items such as development of key product characteristics, failure mode and effects analysis, and control plans. This is another significant difference from the ISO 9001:1994 text. The automotive industry requires the use of tools including feasibility studies, FMEAs, control plans, quality plans, and operator (or job) instructions. Guidance in the use of these tools, as well as the topic of advanced quality planning, is provided in separate reference manuals by the automotive industry for supplier use. Those manuals are listed in the TS 16949 bibliography. The automotive industry uses a prescriptive list of requirements for the job instructions with the intent of providing support for the employee at his or her workstation. By using well-developed job instructions, organizations are finding out that they can make use of self-directed work teams and minimize supervisory overhead. The instructions can be used for jobs including rework, inspection, and assembly. Automotive suppliers also have to use job instructions for tool setups, which must be verified whenever a setup is performed.

The identification, marking, and control of key product, or special, characteristics is also required. Such characteristics have to be shown on the control plan, and for those identified by the customer as key, the customer's symbology must be used. The control plan is considered to be the primary output of the advanced product quality planning phase. There are a number of prescriptive content requirements for control plans listed in ISO/TS 16949, Appendix B. They fall into the following categories: general, product control, process control, methods, and reaction plans or corrective action. The requirement that a reaction plan is to be developed for each control plan characteristic during the planning phase is important to the quality management system's ability to identify and contain defects prior to shipment to the customer. The intent is for a plan of action to be specified ahead of time, so if something unusual occurs, the operator will have appropriate and well-thought-out guidance readily available at the workstation. This should occur because the control plan information is a key input in developing the process flowcharts and operator or job instructions.

Another key generic quality management system requirement of the automotive industry is the control of process design. ISO 9001:1994 and 2000 address product design and development, but completely ignore process design and development. The subject has been given significant treatment in the automotive OEM reference manuals and now in TS 16949. In the latter, the process design inputs have to be identified, documented, and reviewed; then process design output has to be verified against the input requirements and recorded.

For many years, the automotive industry has mandated some form of production part qualification or approval for suppliers prior to shipment for production. That used to consist of the submission of a number of sample parts for customer inspection, but it has evolved into a product and process approval with various documents and records required in addition to sample parts. Each customer has such a process for its suppliers, and compliance with the appropriate process is now a quality management system requirement for both the supplier and its suppliers, or subcontractors, as they are referred to in ISO 9001:1994.

Automotive suppliers also have to provide appropriate technical resources for tool and gage design and fabrication. Further, they must have a system for tooling management and planned total preventive maintenance, including a system for tracking and follow-up of any subcontracted work. The preventive maintenance system must use predictive maintenance methods and provide for the availability of spare parts for key process equipment.

The supplier also is obligated to perform some type of subcontractor development with the goal of having subcontractor compliance to the automotive OEM requirements. This is key to achieving the real benefits of the OEM harmonization activities. The problem this addresses was not so much that the OEMs had different supplier quality requirements. The problem occurred when OEMs mandated that the supplier deploy OEM requirements to subcontractors. That meant that the tier-two supplier, or subcontractor, could be faced with multiplied thousands of varieties of (tier-one) supplier quality manuals—all attempting to include their OEM requirements in with their own. Thus, to optimize the harmonization activity, it is critical that the suppliers use the same fundamental quality system requirements as do the OEMs. There will always be some company-specific requirements to add to those, but if the base requirements are common, significant benefits will accrue across the supply chain. There is no similar requirement for subcontractor development in ISO 9001.

To verify purchased product, suppliers must use one or more of a number of methods for incoming material: (a) evaluation of statistical data, (b) receiving inspection, (c) second- or third-party assessments with records of acceptable quality performance, or (d) part evaluation by an accredited laboratory. In-house supplier laboratories used for inspection, testing, or calibration are to be compliant with ISO 17025, and any commercial laboratories so used have to be ISO 17025 accredited.

The automotive industry has traditionally required specific practices for measurement system analysis (MSA). Customer OEM reference manuals are available for guidance in using the appropriate methodologies. In order to understand what the data are telling the user, it is critical to know the level of measurement uncertainty, or error, due to the measurement system itself. Appropriate methods, which may include bias, linearity, stability, repeatability, and reproducibility, must be used with the OEM guidelines for acceptance criteria. Records of calibration, including any employee-owned gages used in the system, must be maintained with specified information. These MSA requirements go beyond the ISO 9001:1994 text, and far beyond the new ISO 9001 text, which reduced the number of control of measuring and test equipment requirements.

Several automotive requirements pertain to the delivery of product to the customer. The supplier has to implement systems to support 100 percent on-time delivery and that includes a systematic approach to monitoring its adherence to lead-time requirements. There must be an order-driven production scheduling activity supported by an information system that provides information at key stages of the process. Further, the supplier must have an electronic system for receipt of customer-planning information and schedules, as well as for the transmission of advanced shipping notices to the customer.

Chapter 49

Impact of ISO 9000 on the Chemical and Process Industries

Ann W. Phillips
Omni Tech International, Huntsville, Alabama

Robert W. Belfit
Omni Tech International, Midland, Michigan

The chemical industry transforms natural raw material from earth, water, and air into valuable products for consumers and the world's industries. These valuable products are raw materials for other industries (that is, agriculture, pharmaceutical businesses, and a wide variety of individual customer needs). The U.S. chemical industry produces 70,000 products accounting for 25 percent of the world total, which is a $1.5 trillion global industry. Ranking next are Germany, Japan, and China. The U.S. chemical industry exports about $400 billion and has historically had a $15–20 billion positive trade balance.[1]

The chemical industry is itself the largest single-sector purchaser of its own chemical products, amounting to 28 percent of the volume in 1998. The 70,000 products have been classified by the U.S. Census Bureau into several categories (see Figure 49.1).

In the period of the 1950s through the 1980s, a number of discussions were held pertinent to product specification and testing procedures for products, whether sold to their own market sector or elsewhere. During this time the American Society for Testing and Materials (ASTM) became very active in promoting product specifications and testing procedures. Many specifications and procedures were developed via the round-robin technique. Problems of inconsistency appeared to be resolved, but in reality most laboratories did not have the necessary basic equipment except those participating in the specification developments and test-method procedures. Nevertheless, progress was made toward agreement on specification and test methods; accuracy and repeatability became

1997 NAICS Chemical Products Categories

3241	Petroleum and coal products
3251	Basic chemical products
3252	Resin, synthetic rubber, artificial and synthetic fibers, and filament products
3253	Pesticides, fertilizer, and other agricultural chemical products
3254	Pharmaceutical and medicine products
3255	Paint, coatings, and adhesive products
3256	Soap, cleaning compounds, and toilet preparation products
3259	Other chemical products
3261	Plastic products
3262	Rubber products
3271	Clay and refractory products
3272	Glass and glass products
3273	Cement and concrete products
3274	Lime and gypsum products
3279	Other nonmetallic mineral products

Figure 49.1   Chemical products categories.

common phrases in the industry. But customers and producers continue to have significant differences about the quality of goods.

For the chemical industry, universal or country standards and practices did not exist. Balances were not generally calibrated. Conditions of testing for specific items varied from one laboratory to another. Results consequently varied. Invoice resolution became a big issue—often extending over months because of disagreement on testing, specifications, and volumes supplied.

Although there seemed to be some uncertainty in the chemical business related to product composition (specifications and testing procedures) as well as quantity of goods delivered to the customer, the chemical industry grew relatively fast and is critical to every country in the world. Every industrial country has a capable and valuable chemical industry to support and contribute to other industries' success.

APPLICATION OF THE ISO 9000 SERIES TO THE CHEMICAL AND PROCESS INDUSTRIES

In 1985 representatives from 12 companies began a series of meetings to draft a document eventually entitled *Quality Assurance for the Chemical and Process Industries—A Manual of Good Practices.*[2] There was a need for the document, as evidenced by the preceding discussion. The manual was published in 1987 by the ASQC Quality Press and is the result of the efforts of the Chemical and Process Industries Division of the American Society for Quality. The recommendations found in this publication are the basis for the interpretations for the industry.

In 1987, ISO Technical Committee 176 issued the ISO 9000 series of standards. Many elements of the chemical industry eagerly pursued and began to be registered to these standards partly through the initial guidance presented in the *Manual of Good Practices*. The rate of growth of U.S. registration is shown in Figures 49.2 and 49.3.

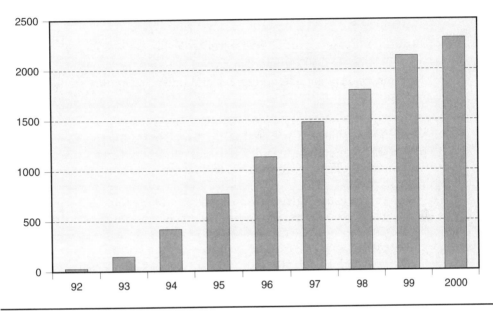

Figure 49.2   U.S. chemical industry registration totals, ISO 9000 systems.

Source: Paul Scicchitano, executive director, *Quality Systems Update*, Private Communication QSU Publishing Company, Fairfax, VA. Used with permission.

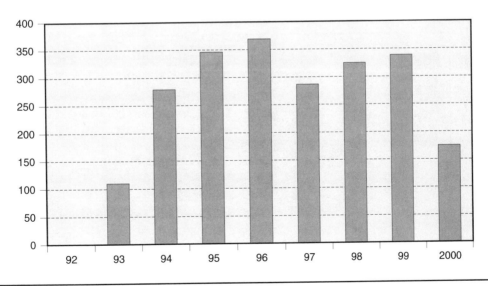

Figure 49.3   U.S. chemical industry additional registrations per year, ISO 9000 systems.

Source: Calculated from the data of Figure 2.

But the application of the ISO 9000 standards in the chemical and process industries (CPI) was initially difficult. The chemical industry differs from the mechanical industries in many ways:

- Raw materials are often natural materials of varying composition.
- The technology of sampling presents complex challenges because of the varying nature of the intermediates: fine powders, bulk units, liquids, gases, pipeline delivery, and solids of varying types.
- Chemical processes occur at the molecular level, and results are often based on secondary information.
- Measurements are complex processes and must be carefully standardized and controlled.

From the registration data, it appeared that chemical companies with significant overseas markets but few nationalized production facilities were among the first to obtain ISO registration in order to protect those markets. Chemical companies with multiple offshore production facilities were not as aggressive initially to obtain registration.

The chemical industry registrations as a percent of the total ISO registrations in the United States reached a peak in 1994 and have plateaued in recent years (see Figure 49.4). Other business sectors have since become more active in registrations (see Figure 49.5).

In 1992 the ASQ Chemical and Process Industries Division published *ANSI/ASQC Q90/ISO 9000 Guideline for Use by the Chemical and Process Industries*.[3] In 1996, a second edition was issued to reflect the 1994 revision to ISO 9001.[4] The first and second editions of the "*Guideline*" were based on the 20 standard requirements of the ISO 9001:1994 standard. Each requirement is interpreted, and guidance is provided for the chemical industry. As with the ISO 9001 standard itself, new ground is not broken, but rather the tried and proven quality practices are explained through the guidance sections presented with each element. The guideline was

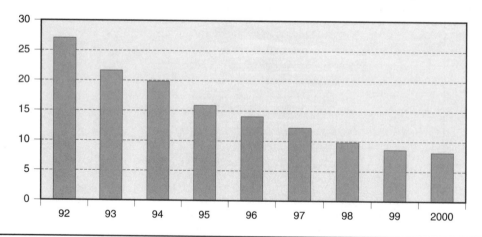

Figure 49.4 U.S. chemical industry registrations as a percent of total registrations per year, ISO 9000 systems.

Source: Calculated from the data of Figure 2 plus Figure 5.

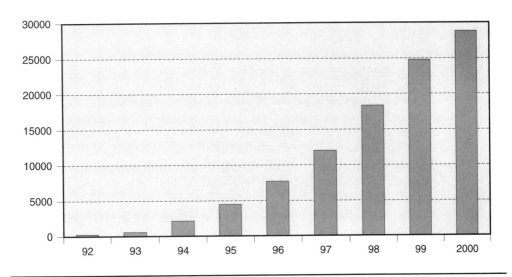

Figure 49.5 Total U.S. registrations, ISO 9000 systems.

Source: Paul Scicchitano, executive director, *Quality Systems Update*, Private Communication QSU Publishing Company, Fairfax, VA. Used with permission.

largely based on the *Manual of Good Practices*. A third edition of the guideline is in preparation based on ISO 9001:2000.

The application of ISO 9000 systems in the chemical industry has resulted in needed attention to critical processes. Design and development control (clause 7.3)[5] is a particularly important requirement for the chemical industry. Chemical reactivity is an area needing unique attention. Process and product hazards, material safety data sheets, local requirements, regulatory requirements, and waste disposal procedures create other needs. Guidance relative to this documentation is given throughout the *ASQ Guideline for Use by the Chemical and Process Industries*.

Application of the ISO 9001 requirements has also increased discipline in CPI purchasing processes. Raw materials must be expressed in terms of chemical compositions with targeted values and limits, physical forms, size distribution, and limits of molecular sizes. Emphasis is placed on performance characteristics, sampling and test methods, packaging, labeling, and transportation. Many of these items are covered by federal regulations (that is, there are at least 16 major federal health, safety, and environmental laws regulating the chemical and related industries). These regulations must be understood and met. Dependence on the supplier's quality system is paramount to ensure proper process control.

ISO 9001:2000 requires product identification and traceability (clause 7.5.3) throughout the manufacturing, handling, and delivery processes. The traceability system should be documented and maintained from raw materials to the finished product. Particles or molecules are impossible to label, but batch analysis and/or continuous monitoring via sensors or other devices as the raw material or intermediate is added from a pipeline or tank to a reactor will suffice. Reactor rates, volumes, flow rates, and results from online analyzers may also be recorded for traceability.

In the chemical process industry the term "product realization" (clause 7.5) often refers to a system of sensors, analyzers, and controller feedback loops. In a broader sense process control applies to all the components of manufacturing operations including packaging, shipping, testing, and labeling.

Customer-related processes (clause 7.2) have emphasized the importance of clear communication between the supplier and the customer on such topics as inspection and testing, measuring accuracy and precision, documentation such as material safety data sheets, certificates of analysis, government regulations, special unloading requirements, preservation of quality, and the cleanliness and practical usage of shared or multiple uses of pipeline or multiuse vessels.

Frequently in chemical industry developmental projects, process and product specifications may have to be established after full-scale production has been attained. In any case design consideration must include the items required to meet the customer's needs—usually thoroughly handled in the contract review.

Customer property (clause 7.5.4) in the CPI may include proprietary information, tolling operations, incorporation of customer-provided materials into production, or customer-provided equipment, labels, or packaging materials. Suppliers must treat customer-supplied product as any other raw material for the process. In tolling operations, multiple products are frequently manufactured in common facilities. Procedures to avoid cross-contamination must be instituted.

The application of ISO 9001 has also contributed, in part, to more disciplined inspection and testing (clause 8.2.4). In the early days of the chemical industry, much of the product testing was very dependent on the skills and consistent laboratory performance of the tester or operator. To a limited extent, this is still true today. However, testing technology has advanced sufficiently. The performance of the testing through automation and installation of sensors and process control devices results in more consistency and greater customer satisfaction.

In addressing the calibration of measurement devices (clause 7.6), the CPI industry uses laboratory equipment as well as online analyzers and research instruments, which may have different standardization procedures. Analyst changes, reagent changes, equipment repair, equipment location changes, and equipment replacement may all affect standardization methodologies. While mechanical systems may require instrument calibration weekly or monthly, some CPI instruments may require daily or more frequent calibration to verify conformance to the required accuracy and precision. Internal reference materials often must be developed, as National Institute of Standard Technology (NIST) standards are rarely available for the chemical industry.

Packaging, storage, and handling (clause 7.5.5) also present special challenges to the chemical industry. Containers may include caverns, tank cars, tank trucks, barges, hopper cars, boxcars, tote bins, piles, and warehouses. Consideration must be given to dated materials, construction material, pressure ratings, temperature, humidity, corrosion, previous usage, loading and unloading facilities, recyclable packages, or vessels.

Some containers (such as rail cars, trucks, barges, pipelines, and other bulk containers) require special labeling or use of placards. Some storage facilities must be blanketed with special gases. If the atmosphere is devoid of oxygen or contains flammables, other special precautions are needed. To prevent cross-contamination, pipeline banking may be necessary. Loading and unloading equipment lines, conveyors, and packages must be procedurally controlled to avoid contamination. Environmental storage may be specially defined for certain products. Multiuse equipment must have effective and sure proof procedures to avoid environmental exposure and contamination.

Handling products in the CPI frequently involves many transfers of bulk or package products from raw material through the intermediates to production of a final product. This requires proper labeling, appropriate packaging, and vessels, pipelines, and vehicles meeting federal regulations. In many cases dedicated equipment is required. Unexpected interruptions need to be recorded to ensure that environmental problems are not created and that unsatisfactory environmental degradation of the product is not incurred.

In each unique application to the chemical industry, special consideration must be given to discrete details because many materials or intermediates may present toxic potential, flammability concerns, and environmental concerns. The complexity of the industry in terms of selling products to other chemical producers or to entirely different customers requires effective communication based on a common language.

How can communication between a supplier and customer be effective? The answer is through a common language—which means the language of ISO 9001.

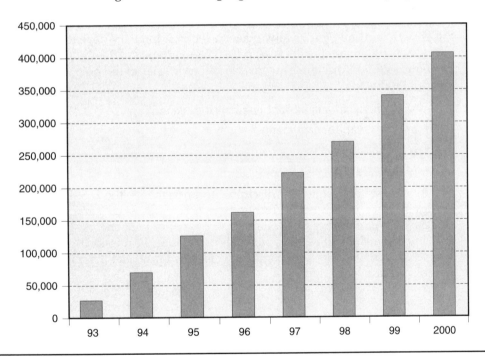

Figure 49.6 Global ISO 9000 registrations.
Source: *Quality Sytsems Update*, July 2000, pages 1–5 and data from the year 2000 from Paul Scicchitano, Executive Director, *Quality Systems Update*, Private Communication, QSU Publishing Company, Fairfax, VA. Used with permission.

In the United States alone, there are nearly 30,000 registrations, and about 8 percent of those represent the chemical industry. A single or corporate registration often covers multiple plants or multiple businesses. Worldwide ISO 9000 registrations are now at over 400,000 (see Figure 49.6). Today the chemical market is the globe; the language of ISO 9001 effectively permits freedom of product movement anywhere in the world based on the understanding of the ISO 9001 quality management system. Other factors still must be considered but are becoming more focused as a result of the ISO 9001 commonality.

FUTURE USE AND IMPACT OF ISO 9000 SYSTEMS ON THE CHEMICAL AND PROCESS INDUSTRIES

Technology Vision 2020: The U.S. Chemical Industry states that the U.S. chemical industry:

- Leads the world in technology development, manufacturing, and profitability
- Promotes sustainability by investing in technology that protects the environment and stimulates industrial growth while balancing economic needs with financial constraints[6]

The participants in the development of *Technology Vision 2020* concluded that the growth and competitive advantage of the U.S. industry depends on the individual and collaborative efforts of industry, government, and academe.

Four technical disciplines were selected as crucial to the progress of the U.S. chemical industry:

- New chemical science and engineering technology
- Supply chain management
- Information systems
- Manufacturing and operations

To achieve the technology discipline improvements, the U.S. Department of Energy's Office of Industrial Technology (OIT) has asked corporate consortia along with academic experts to submit proposals for joint chemical research projects[7] in partnership with government laboratories. OIT's mission is to put funding into research that shows commercial development potential that might otherwise never be done.

An example of futuristic research currently being carried out academically is the Freidel Crafts Alkylations in near supercritical water without the use of aluminum chloride.[8] What's the value? There could be a reduction of by-product waste of 3 pounds of salt per pound of product.

Once again, what is the value of ISO 9000 systems to this type of effort? ISO 9001 provides the common language in terms of communications: rigorous statement of project needs, validated technology testing, design control, product realization, and system audits for improvement and other obvious values providing the needed scientific innovation for the chemical industry in 2020.

That future will be influenced by several factors:

- The publication of ISO 9001:2000
- The trend toward integrating management systems for quality, environmental, safety, and health
- The impact of the automotive industry

IMPACT OF ISO 9001:2000 ON THE CPI

In December 2000 the International Organization for Standardization (ISO) published the highly anticipated revisions to the ISO 9000 family of documents.

ISO 9001:2000 requires that companies go beyond clearly defining customer requirements and developing systems to meet those requirements. ISO 9001:2000 moves from the "say what you do, do what you say" mentality to effectively managing processes in the organization. It places more emphasis on developing systems to measure and analyze appropriate data to facilitate continual improvement. The primary internal sources of data will continue to be process and product monitoring as well as internal quality audits, but a formal system to determine and track customer satisfaction levels has been added as a primary source of external data.

ISO 9001:2000 also emphasizes follow-up activities for measurements taken throughout the organization: from developmental product verification and validation results to process and product monitoring. The standard clearly emphasizes taking appropriate actions based on data generated.

Requirements for employee training—critical to the CPI—are also expanded in ISO 9001:2000. Competency requirements for employees who have an impact on product quality must be defined, and training must be provided to meet those needs. The effectiveness of training must be evaluated as well.

In addition, ISO 9004:2000 was published in December 2000. ISO 9001 and ISO 9004 were written to be a "consistent pair" of standards, with similar structures, making it easier to build on the 9001 requirements and move the quality management system to a higher level. Whereas ISO 9001:2000 focuses on the effectiveness of the quality management system at meeting customer requirements, ISO 9004:2000 is more comparable to quality excellence models such as the Malcolm Baldrige National Quality Award. ISO 9004:2000 provides the CPI with an excellent model to continually improve the performance and efficiency of its overall business systems.

INTEGRATION OF MANAGEMENT SYSTEMS

Though ISO 9001:2000 does not require integration of the quality management system with environmental, safety, and health systems, it does encourage such (see clause 0.4 in ISO 9001:2000). The standard was revised, in part, to facilitate its integration with ISO 14001. Specific verbiage from ISO 14001 has even been incorporated into the ISO 9001:2000 document.

In this era of mergers and cost cutting, integrating quality and environmental management systems is becoming more and more popular in the CPI as a means of keeping costs in control. CPI organizations that are already certified to ISO 9001 or ISO 9002 are building on their current systems to implement the requirements of ISO 14001, thus reducing the time and resources needed to

Integration Point	ISO 14001:1996 Reference	ISO 9001:2000 Reference
Policy	4.2	5.3
Objectives	4.3.3	5.4.1
Defined responsibilities and authorities	4.4.1	5.5.1
Training	4.4.2	6.2.2
Document control	4.4.5	4.2.3
Operations control	4.4.6	7.5.1
Control of measuring and monitoring devices	4.5.1	7.6
Handling and investigating nonconformances	4.5.2	8.3
Corrective and preventive actions	4.5.2	8.5.2/8.5.3
Control of records	4.5.3	4.2.4
Internal audits	4.5.4	8.2.2
Management review	4.6	5.6

Figure 49.7   Integration points—ISO 9001 and ISO 14001.

establish an effective environmental management system. Some CPI companies are generating additional cost savings by folding ISO 9001, ISO 14001, responsible care, and process safety management (PSM) into one common management system. Baker Petrolite has such a system, which not only has resulted in significant cost savings, but has created a common focus for employees, customers, stock holders, and the community.

An additional incentive to integrate quality and environmental management systems has come from the automotive industry. In September 1999 Ford and GM issued a mandate that tier-1 suppliers comply with ISO 14001. Ford requires that at least one manufacturing site in each company be certified by December 31, 2001, with the remaining sites to be certified by 1 July 2003. GM requires that each tier-1 site be at least self-certified by 31 December 2002. Because tier-1 suppliers are currently required to comply with QS-9000, CPI companies are looking to integrate the implementation of ISO 14001 into their current systems.

Specific integration points between ISO 9001 and ISO 14001 are defined in Figure 49.7.

IMPACT OF THE AUTOMOTIVE INDUSTRY

The future of automotive standards lies in the fate of ISO/TS 16949, *Quality Systems—Automotive Suppliers—Particular Requirements for the Application of ISO*

9001:1994. ISO/TS 16949 is an international automotive quality system document published by ISO. It harmonizes supplier quality standards of U.S. (QS-9000), German (VDA 6.1), French, and Italian automotive manufacturers. Its goal is to create a single set of requirements and a single third-party registration system that will meet the needs of the global automotive industry.

Whereas the Big Three have no immediate plans to revise QS-9000, ISO/TS 16949 is scheduled to be revised in 2002 to incorporate the requirements of ISO 9001:2000. Provided that the revised ISO/TS 16949 is well received by the automotive industry, it may replace QS-9000, VDA 6.1, and other automotive quality system requirements.

The transition from QS-9000 to ISO/TS 16949 should have minimal impact on the chemical industry. The structure of the current draft document mirrors that of ISO 9001:2000 with additions that are somewhat similar to those in QS-9000, third edition.

The much-anticipated revision of the production part approval process (PPAP) document was published in November 1999. The impact on the CPI will be significant. The revised document provides for a bulk material approval process that is more applicable to the chemical industry.

SUMMARY

The ISO 9000 management system has been broadly accepted in the chemical and process industries globally because it provides a common language and documented procedures. Other important factors related to use of The ISO 9000 family in this industry include:

- Guidance and interpretation have been provided by the ASQ's Chemical and Process Industries Division publications *Quality Assurance for the Chemical and Process Industries—A Manual of Good Practices* and the first and second editions of *ISO-9000 Guidelines for the Chemical and Process Industries*

- Unique problems addressed are the nature of raw materials and complex reactions of unusual intermediates at the molecular level requiring discrete measurements

- ISO 9000 provides a mechanism to comply with worldwide regulations

- Corporate and site registrations may obscure actual implementation of ISO 9000 systems

- The chemical and process industries will continue to grow, but the technology will change, resulting in less energy consumption and fewer by-products and waste

- Integration of management systems covering environment, safety, health, and cost control will become more common than is evident today and be based on the ISO 9000 system

- Supply chain management whereby the total chemical process from raw material through the transfer of the chemical products to the customer and beyond offers great economic return and is best achieved by an integrated ISO 9000 system

ENDNOTES

1. *U.S. Chemical Industry Statistical Handbook* (Arlington, VA: Chemical Manufacturer Association, 1999).
2. *Quality Assurance for the Chemical and Process Industries—A Manual of Good Practices* (Milwaukee, WI: ASQC, Chemical and Process Industries Division, 1987).
3. *ANSI/ASQC Q90 ISO 9000 Guideline for Use by the Chemical and Process Industries* (Milwaukee, WI: ASQC, Chemical and Process Industries Division, 1992).
4. *ISO 9000 Guidelines for the Chemical and Process Industries,* 2nd ed. (Milwaukee, WI: ASQC, Chemical and Process Industries Division, 1996).
5. Though each of the referenced requirements have been included in earlier revisions of ISO 9001, the references given are applicable to ISO 9001:2000.
6. *Technology Vision 2020: The U.S. Chemical Industry* (Washington, DC: American Chemical Society, 1996).
7. *Chemical and Engineering News* (9 August 1999): 10.
8. *Chemical and Engineering News* (3 January 2000): 26.

Chapter 50

Department of Defense, NASA, and Other Government Applications

Dale K. Gordon

Director, Quality and Business Improvement, Defense North America,
Rolls-Royce, Indianapolis, Indiana

The adoption of the ISO 9000 standards by governments around the world should be of little surprise to those familiar with the evolution of the standards. The creation of ISO 9000 is a well-told tale that actually had its genesis when the U.S. Department of Defense (DoD) created MIL-Q-9858 and its subsequent "A" revision of 10 December 1963. The military specification *Quality Program Requirements* was widely hailed as the model for a quality program requirement that looked at all aspects of the business and systems, not just the end result. Over time MIL-Q-9858A "morphed" into other similar standards such as AQAP-1 or NATO-1 for procurements by governments worldwide.

While MIL-Q-9858A was a mainstay of almost all the aerospace companies in the late 1950s and early 1960s, these requirements also were evident at the beginning of the U.S. space program. Since the space program was largely an offshoot of the military's missile program efforts, the quality program came with it. While separate requirements had emerged through the creation of the Federal Aviation Administration in the late '50s, there existed a loose coalition of commercial and military quality system requirements for a period of time. These requirements began to diverge as the commercial aviation market developed. This prompted some major aerospace manufacturers to actually separate their military and commercial businesses into different sites that had distinctly different quality systems. The rationale behind this was simple. The commercial markets were more cost sensitive and more open to innovations in quality control and assurance, while the military market was still contract driven and not as cost sensitive (hence less prone to change). Added on top of this was the rapid development of the space program with its military beginnings and its evolution into a government agency, the National Aeronautics and Space Administration (NASA). NASA subsequently developed its own quality management system requirements document called NHB 5300.4(1D-2).

The proliferation of quality management system requirements came to a head in the late 1980s as a strange thing happened worldwide. Peace broke out in many parts of the world, and many countries wanted to cash in on the "peace dividend." This had the effect of shrinking defense budgets as a percentage of domestic national product. This was coupled with a loss of public support for moon landings, forcing a reduction of space agency budgets to fund more societal programs. The military industrial complex had to survive on smaller defense department budgets and adopt cost-effective manufacturing procedures and systems. Many major defense contractors had to shift reliance to commercial sales for profits and growth. About this same time (1987) ISO 9001 appeared on the scene and was readily adopted on the commercial side of the business as meeting many of the basic needs for a standard covering quality management system requirements for the same types of procurements that were covered by the MIL-standard type procurements.

As the military, NASA, and other parts of U.S. government began to look for cost savings, one of the first and more logical steps was the elimination of contract-specific specifications. The first such step, which was easiest to accomplish, was the adoption of a single process for quality assurance. In the early '90s the DoD head of acquisition directed this single process initiative (or SPI) when he called for procurement officers to drop as many contract-specific requirements as possible and adopt commercial practices instead. To find a replacement model they turned to Europe. Europe had already begun this process, as the ISO 9000 standards were being enacted as a way to level the commerce activity amongst the European Community (EC) nations. When it comes to military equipment, the United States was one of Europe's largest trading partners, and it saw the use of the ISO 9000 standards as a likely alternative to the MIL-Q-9858A-driven contracts.

About the time ISO 9001:1987 was being revised into the 1994 version, the U.S. military began to shift its requirements. A letter was issued on 8 March 1993 from the offices of the assistant secretaries of the Army, Air Force, and Navy, which read as follows:

> *Activities in quality assurance have seen . . . numerous changes. Our offices are working with the office of the Secretary of Defense in evaluating standards for quality programs and inspection systems. Until we get these efforts finalized, you are authorized as an interim measure to use the . . . ISO 9000 series and the . . . ANSI/ASQC Q90 quality system series. . . .*
>
> *As this is interim guidance, we suggest prudent use of these standards. If you elect to use these non-Government, commercial standards, supplement their application with other standards and contract requirements as needed, and tailor them where it makes sense.*

This essentially opened the floodgates. Because government contracts were negotiable items, any chance to delete a MIL-specification item was seen as cost saving to industry. Another aspect that made the ISO 9000 series of standards appealing was the integration of the supply base. While the number of companies doing business with the military was decreasing, the products being supplied grew in complexity. The need for cost containment/reduction was highly prevalent, an increasing amount of the manufacturers' work was being contracted out, and the manufacturers were looking for simple, cost-effective tools to control quality.

A follow-on letter dated 2 April 1993 from the U.S. assistant secretary of defense gave further guidance on the use of the ISO standards. Basically the letter opted for a go-slow policy on use and adoption of the ISO 9000 series standards, and it closed with these sentiments:

> *The ramifications of ISO adoption are broad and important. The new USD(A) must be afforded the opportunity to review and approve the DoD position. We want to move ahead with plans to upgrade our quality standards, however, we want this to be done in a coordinated and well planned out manner. It is OSD's desire to continue with the plan outlined in the DASD(PR) memorandum of January 15, 1993, to move forward swiftly to develop the necessary policy, guidance, and training strategy necessary to improve the DoD quality program.*

The net effect was that ISO 9000 standards were readily adopted in U.S. DoD contracting where items were being procured from commercial applications. The standards were also being applied where the companies doing both commercial and military work substituted ISO 9000 for MIL-Q-9858A. Those companies doing work only for the DoD remained in a MIL-Q-9858A backwater until the government procurement organizations and the Defense Contract Management Command (DCMC now DCMA) got themselves up to speed on how to audit, monitor, and understand the ISO 9000 standards. This was finally realized in the late 1990s. However, there are still U.S. DoD contracts today that call for either MIL-Q-9858A or the lesser MIL-I-45208A inspection system requirements even though the DoD officially canceled both.

By the end of the 20th century, defense departments worldwide had come to the conclusion that the ISO 9000 series of standards was acceptable as a minimum requirement for most procurements and where required was adequate with supplementation. This was documented in the U.S. federal acquisition regulation (FAR) 46.202-4, which allows for the use of higher-level quality standards such as the ISO 9000 standard series in solicitations and contracts for complex or critical items or when the technical requirements of the contract require:

1. Control of such things as work operations, in-process controls, and inspections.

2. Attention to such factors as organization, planning, work instructions, documentation control, and advanced metrology.

NASA went even further and issued Policy Directive (NPD) 8703.3, *NASA Quality Management System Policy (ISO 9000)*, which establishes the NASA policy to contractually require, where appropriate and beneficial to NASA, supplier compliance with the appropriate standard contained in the current version of the ISO 9000 standard series or the ANSI/ASQ Q9000 series.

ISO 9001:2000 DILEMMA

Now that we have all the major players in government on the same page, we have added a new problem to the mix. We have improved and revised the ISO 9000 standard to the year 2000 revision. This is of concern because the U.S. Government works on contracts, FARs, and other slow-to-change regulations.

Most of the contractual language given to companies relative to contracts (many of which may extend for years into the future) references ISO 9001:1994(E).

Most companies have represented the change to the new revision of ISO 9001:2000 as a "no-cost change." But there is much hesitance to make this change until the new revision is well understood by the contracting officers and the DCMA specialist that are responsible for contract oversight. To ease the transition the principal undersecretary of defense stated the following in a memorandum dated 19 March 2001:

> *This memorandum authorizes a streamlined process and consistent approach for the DoD on Defense contracts to simplify transition from the 1994 edition of ANSI/ISO/ASQ 9001, 9002, or 9003 to the 9001:2000, Quality Management Systems—Requirements, version, when elected by a contractor. Contracting officers shall authorize contractors and their subcontractors to implement ISO 9001:2000 in place of 1994 ISO 9001, 9002 or 9003, subject to no change in price, fee, cost or contractual product or service requirements. As applicable, DoD activities should encourage contractors to notify management councils or administrative contracting officers of their transition strategy.*

NASA so far has been out front on this issue and has offered guidance to its procurement personnel. NASA's R. Scott Thompson (Director, Contract Management Division) has said that "the associate administrator of management systems has advised that the transition to ISO 9001:2000 by December 2003 transition date is required under NASA contracts where compliance with and/or certification to the ISO 9000 series of standards has been stipulated in the contract." He further stated, "This change is being implemented, subject to no change in price, fee, cost or contractual product or service requirements. This is consistent with the guidance that the principal deputy undersecretary of defense issued in a letter dated March 19, 2001."

The DoD, however, has left it up to contracting officers to deal with the manner and method of change at this point in time. Once a contract has been issued, the contract change process can be a costly and laborious affair. Some industry groups are proposing that the government adopt the following position: *A quality management system in compliance with ISO 9001:2000 meets or exceeds the requirements of ISO 9001:1994, and no contractual change for this transition is required.*

This statement follows the basic premise that ISO 9001:2000 is an enhancement/improvement over the current contract requirements and that any company that demonstrates that it is meeting the new ISO 9001:2000 requirements is actually meeting or exceeding what the customer required to begin with.

CONCLUSION

Where do we go from here? Seemingly all regulatory and procurement areas of the government have accepted that ISO 9001 quality management systems requirements are beneficial to industry and commerce at large. The change to ISO 9001:2000 is seen as transparent by the consumer, if not the producer. Several government agencies are even going so far as to require or suggest ISO 9001 certification (Food and Drug Administration) or even supplementation (AS9100 in the case of the FAA), and there is more to come as we begin the 21st century.

Chapter 51

Education

F. Craig Johnson

American Society for Quality, Education Division Chair, Professor Emeritus
of Educational Research, Florida State University, Tallahassee, Florida

INTRODUCTION

This chapter discusses the need for and application of quality management systems in education. The chapter was developed by answering six questions:

- What is the nature of the education sector?
- Who are the customers and the stakeholders?
- What are the traditional methods used in education to ensure quality, accredit schools, and to certify teachers?
- What is the need for overall quality management in education?
- What are the key success factors that make good education programs work?
- What changes in accreditation are likely to affect the future use of ISO 9000 in education?

Partial answers to these questions were found in public records. Additional expert opinion was contributed by e-mail from following members of the ASQ Education Division:

Linda Quinn, Chair, Northwest Association of Schools and Colleges

Dana Egerczky

Carol Sager, Consultant, Sager Educational Enterprises

M. Eugene Hall, Professor, Southern Illinois University

Robert Bowen, Consultant, Lancaster Public School District

Rick Utz, Principal, Liberty Center High School

Walter DiMantova, Director, Centers for Corporate Eastern Michigan University

Frank Caplan, President, Quality Sciences Consultants

Chester Francke, President, Quality Systems International

William Golomski, President, W. A. Golomski and Associates

EDUCATION AS A SECTOR

Size

The National Center for Educational Statistics predicts that 70 million students will be enrolled in U.S. education institutions by the year 2008. Fifty-five million will be enrolled in public and private elementary and secondary schools, which is a 20 percent increase in 25 years. The remaining 15 million students will be enrolled in colleges and universities, which is a 12 percent increase in 25 years. The annual expenditure for this education is predicted to rise from $300 billion in 1984 to more than half a trillion dollars by the year 2008.

Complexity

Most statistical data for education is divided into schools (kindergarten through high school) and colleges (community colleges and universities) to reflect the major differences between their charters, organizational structure, and legal status. National statistical summaries often present a blizzard of data that obscures the complexity of education. A clearer view of its complexity emerges from case studies of one school district or of one university where the interaction among variables can be seen. To illustrate the complexity, several variables (rounded numbers) have been selected from one Florida public school district and one Florida university.

Florida's Orange County Public School District is the sixth largest in the state. It has a total annual budget of $1 billion; 20,000 part- and full-time employees; 125,000 students; 125 buildings; 800 buses that transport 54,000 people 75,000 miles each school day; and 100,000 meals served every school day.

The Florida State University ranks among the 25 largest public universities in the country. It has an operating budget of half a billion dollars; 10,000 employees; 30,000 students; a 500-acre campus; 16 colleges; 100 academic fields of study; and freshmen entering with SAT scores between 1040 and 1240 for the middle quartiles.

Data for other schools, colleges, and universities can be found on the Internet at http://nces.ed.gov/

Even though the education sector is large and complex, few people in education think of themselves as workers in an industry sector. The education sector is owned and operated independently by 50 states to preserve the culture of each state and by private institutions to serve their interests. Most boards of directors are either appointed by elected officials or elected by community members. This local control of education was established early in the country's history and local issues continue to dominate today.

CUSTOMERS AND STAKEHOLDERS

While it is clear that the primary beneficiary of education is the student, it is not as clear that students are typical customers. Typically, most students are too young to be legally responsible, are legally required to be students, and are provided with an education at no cost to them. Education institutions that spend a great deal of time deciding "Who is the customer of education?" can delay progress of initiating a quality system in education. Progress has been made when customers were defined for specific transactions occurring within a given timeframe. For example, when a teacher is presenting new material to a class, the students are the customers. Later, when the student is preparing homework for the teacher, the teacher is the customer. Thus different transactions have different customers.

Further progress has been made when people who have an interest in education are defined as *stakeholders*. These stakeholders might include parents, community members, local employers, school board members, and government officials. Since it is possible for one individual to be included in all of these stakeholders groups, satisfying each stakeholder's individual, and often conflicting, concerns is almost impossible. Data can, however, be collected on "clusters of stakeholders' concerns." For example, in Florida, when stakeholders' dissatisfaction with their public schools was studied (Johnson and Grant 1996), it was found that stakeholders' dissatisfaction clustered around four factors. Stakeholders express dissatisfaction unless they found:

- Safe schools with someone in charge
- Communication with the school that could be easily understood
- Proper and decent treatment when visiting the school
- Qualified people doing appropriate things

These four "clusters of stakeholders' concerns," and other clusters can be used to evaluate and improve a school's management system.

ACCREDITATION

The fifty states are divided into six geographic regions and use private associations to oversee, review, and accredit degree-granting institutions that voluntarily join the association and pay dues. The accreditation associations for these six regions are:

MSA—Middle States Association
NASC—Northwest Association of Schools and Colleges
NCA—North Central Association of Colleges and Schools
NEASC—New England Association of Schools and Colleges
SACS—Southern Association of Colleges and Schools
WASC—Western Association of Schools and Colleges

Regionally accredited schools and colleges recognize degrees and credits earned at accredited schools and colleges of all regions.

For additional information on accreditation, see www.geteducated.com .
Some personal opinions of experts in regional accreditation of schools follow.
Linda Quinn, current chair of NASC, describes the quality assurance these
associations provide public schools as follows:

The primary mission of the school is to facilitate student learning. Therein lies the
value of the school as a public asset. However, this value is relative, not absolute.
The relative value of the school is based upon:

1. *the current performance level of the school's students; and*

2. *the public's confidence the elements within the school system will*
   produce more value (e.g., more students meeting standards at a high
   level) in the future.

The obligation of each school is to establish, develop, maintain, and improve
the value of his or her school.

As a public asset, a school has higher value when the public has confidence
in the process by which estimates and evaluations are made. Public confidence is
increased when:

1. *accepted state, national and/or international standards are used in making*
   value estimates;

2. *public school education operates as a system and the system's value is*
   estimated; and

3. *the estimation process is open with results available for public review.*

Today there are many states that are developing accountability systems that
have as their desired outcome improved student performance through improved
school performance. Some states have established standards for student perform-
ance. These standards delineate what the students should know and should be
able to do. State Accountability Task Forces have determined how many students
should be able to know and do these things, at what levels, and by what dates. The
focus of all of this work is on the improvement of student learning.

Regional School Accreditation Associations have established standards for
school quality (ten "opportunities to learn"), a process for improving school per-
formance (the "School Improvement Process"), requirements for evidence of the
school's performance, and checks for consistency with state and locally determined
goals. In addition to traditional input measures like number of books, teachers, and
course offerings, schools must also be able to demonstrate results in terms of stu-
dent learning. Despite this new emphasis on student learning, however, the pri-
mary focus of the accreditation of schools is still on the improvement of schools.

Taken separately, we do not think those state education reforms and regional
accreditation improvements will get us all the way to where we need to go—at
least not on the most expeditious route.

The International Organization for Standardization (ISO) has established
standards for quality assurance within the organization that, we believe, can
effectively address the shortcomings of the current accreditation system. The ISO
standards do not identify specific targets for student performance or for school
performance. State standards and regional accreditation standards do this.
Rather, ISO standards help minimize conditions that negatively affect student

learning. They provide specific strategies for assuring the integrity of the school's improvement process. They offer specific strategies for thinking of schools as a system (as opposed to a collection of individuals) for dealing with data. The focus is on continuous improvement. (E-mail from Linda Quinn dated June 2001)

Dana Egreczky addresses the need for professional accountability in the teaching profession to assure stakeholders of quality in education:

The chief roadblock in moving education toward a quality system is the difficulty in defining and the disconnect among three critical components: standards for performance, outcomes measures related to standards, and teacher accountability. While many states have instituted "world class standards" (New Jersey is one of those states), the statewide assessment that measures student performance (outcome measures) against those standards has been rejected by the teachers. The teachers' union, the most powerful lobbying group in the state, is currently trying to whine away the miserable student performance documented by the test, saying the teachers didn't know enough about the test beforehand and didn't have enough time to prepare the students (the dog ate their homework, I guess.) This in turn has called into question the credibility of the standards, which the teachers themselves created under the auspices of the DOE. As an ex-teacher, I find the situation personally embarrassing.

This leads to the core of the issue—when is a student performing adequately (when has a teacher done the job)? Since so many students don't perform well in traditional classroom environments, does this mean the teacher is not doing the job? If the teacher changes the classroom environment, will the administration/parents support the change? What is good teaching and learning? Is it reading, 'riting, and 'rithmetic, or is it in-depth critical thinking learned through rigorous and relevant curriculum? These issues have never been defined because education spends less on research than any other industry in the country. (E-mail from Dana Egreczky June 2001)

There is some movement among these accrediting associations to accept ISO 9000 registration in place of traditional self-study. The exact number of registered institutions changes daily.

Certified schools/colleges in North America are listed under Standard Industrial Classification (SIC) Code 82, Educational Services. The following examples of registered institutions are provided here to illustrate the variety among institutions.

- Elementary and Secondary Schools
  - Lancaster School District, Pennsylvania
  - Liberty Center High School, Ohio
- Colleges and Universities
  - Holland College in Canada
  - Eastern Michigan University—Centers for Corporate Training
  - Georgia Technical Institute
- Community Colleges
  - The Metropolitan Community College Business and Technology Center, Missouri

NEED FOR A QUALITY MANAGEMENT SYSTEM

Carol Sager expresses the need for a quality management system in the following e-mail:

> *Having a formalized quality management system in place based on ISO standards provides a common language, which can unite constituencies and show them how their needs can be stated and met in ways that serve the entire educational community. A formalized quality management system also provides consistency from year to year that frees up more time for school leaders to spend on education. ISO especially provides a necessary link between business and education. Required documentation that is built into the system clearly shows progress made and corrective action taken. What better report card could parents, students, the press, and other constituencies want?* (E-mail from Carol Sager dated 18 June 2001)

The growing interest of the business community in quality management systems for our schools is illustrated in the following *Business Wire* item:

> *The traditionally business-driven market of quality certification enters a new era of thinking as service industries seek out third-party registrars for quality management. Applying the ISO framework for quality and consistency in service organizations is very forward thinking. For schools to implement and maintain an internationally recognized and proven management system to create consistent teaching, policies, curriculum development or administration for educators across the board is a tremendous concept.*

M. Eugene Hall, a professor of education at Southern Illinois University, in an e-mail said the following about this growing community interest in quality management for education:

> *We have always had standards in Education, some have been followed and some have been ignored, many have changed over time. My sense after many years in industry, the military, and in vocational/technical education is that our focus should be on quality. Just as in competency-based education as we prepare objectives, we are urged to place the emphasis on the student and what the student does (outcome) as opposed to what the teacher does (process). If we focus on quality of the outcome, the process (designing and following standards) will flow more naturally. I will never forget my first week of teaching in the public school system. It was a first year mechanical drawing class (back in the days of the "T" square and slide rule). A student finished his work, a simple block drawing, brought it to me and asked, "is this good enough?" After a ten-minute lecture on quality the student repeated his question and then remarked, "I don't care about quality, I just want to finish this thing and get a grade." This was back in 1961, and I see very little change in students at the secondary level, and this attitude is certainly the prevailing one at our University. Quality is an attitude, not an externally imposed "standard." Yes one will need to enforce standards at a very early age (or stage if one is dealing with adults in industry). However, unless quality in internal, unless quality drives the individual (and the individual efforts) all the external standards created will not lead to quality, and quality must be the goal. What is the future of ISO 9000 standards? Unless integrated*

into a self-directed/motivated quality system, they will continue to be "compliance models" and not "commitment models." As such they will serve, as they do now, as a good basis for developing a quality system, and when major business and industries have moved beyond the "basics," they will be of little value. (E-mail from M. Eugene Hall dated June 2001)

KEY SUCCESS FACTORS

The following six general key factors of improving organizational effectiveness have evolved from experience with successful registration of education institutions to ISO 9001.

1. *Top management.* Top management took on a continuing obligation to support ISO registration over an extended time provided there was reasonable assurance of success in progress reports.

2. *Critical improvement.* Top management received reports on successful process improvement using quality tools and techniques. Some examples of critical improvements in education are:
   - Raising students' average national test score from the 50th to the 90th percentile
   - Reducing teachers' waiting time for supplies from six weeks to 24 hours
   - Eliminating a two-week shutdown for warehouse inventory
   - All high school biochemistry students answering all weekly test items correctly

3. *Scalability.* Critical improvements were used to improve related processes when scalability was built into the critical improvement.

4. *Premeasurement.* Measurements of critical improvements that were taken before the improvements were implemented provided more good news for top management.

5. *Periodic measurement.* Performing measurements during the intervention created additional opportunities for corrective and preventive actions.

6. *Distributed effort.* The design time spent on critical improvements was more effective when users were involved in the design phase, implementation was codeveloped with users, and users promoted the application to related processes.

Three Education Division members, with major responsibility for preparing public school districts and universities for ISO 9000 registration, sent the following e-mail accounts.

Bob Bowen was the quality consultant for the Lancaster Public School District, which was certified to ISO 9001 in February of 1999. He reported on the stakeholders' support of certification as follows:

Community response has been mixed. The business community is overwhelmingly positive. The Lancaster Alliance, consisting of top CEOs, has consistently supported

ISO implementation. The media has consistently been positive about quality system initiatives. The general public is divided, but expressed no specific problems. The non-working public is generally unfamiliar with ISO 9000 and, therefore, often noncommittal on ISO 9000 activities. The working public that is familiar with quality system disciplines is strongly positive. Electronic media has not aggressively reported ISO 9000, due to the general complexity of the topic and quality system jargon. Independent observers and philanthropic foundations are overwhelmingly positive. (Source: *Frequently Asked Questions about ISO 9000 in Education,* Bowen International [1998] sent in an e-mail)

Rick Utz, superintendent of the Liberty Center High School describes its ISO 9000 registration as follows:

We named the students our customers, and our products the curriculum and its delivery. Our district discovered that we run really well. But we lacked a way to document that fact. ISO 9000 helped us to do that. We rarely get an honest evaluation from a third party with no vested interest. The series of internal audits involved in the registration process helped us to identify gaps and address them throughout the process. Liberty Center Schools used this process as a part of a continuous improvement plan for ensuring the quality of our teaching. The district funded the registration process with a $50,000 school-to-work community block grant. The district used CRS Inc. as registrars.

Walter DiMantova is the director of the Centers for Corporate Training (CCT) at Eastern Michigan University. His responsibility is to develop mutually beneficial relationships between the university and businesses. He has found the following:

The concepts of quality management and the values of higher education often seem to come from different organizational galaxies. Treating students as "customers" and faculty as "suppliers" challenges centuries-old roles and definitions. Adding international quality standards developed for manufacturers to the more familiar accreditation standards looks like, as one university president put it, "business infecting the academy." There is suspicion and distrust when acronyms better suited to The X Files *enter the conversation between the quality manager and the higher education administrator.*

Yet, in February of 1999, the Centers for Corporate Training at Eastern Michigan University registered to ISO 9002, becoming one of first organizations within public higher education in North America to do so.

The benefits of ISO registration efforts to this higher education organization have been enormous. The insights gained are hopefully valuable to those dedicated to making quality management the norm, and not the exception, in our colleges and universities.

The Centers for Corporate Training (or CCT) is one of the largest university-based corporate training operations in the country. Each year, we provide training and consulting to over 15,000 people, primarily from the Big Three automobile manufacturers and their tier-one and tier-two suppliers.

Unlike most higher education training centers, Eastern Michigan University faculty accounts for a minority of trainers; most of our associates are experts from the private sector. We are financially self-supporting and operate much like any other business. Our role is, however, to answer one of the four primary missions of the University: to partner with the business community through corporate training, consulting, and applied research.

Our close connections to business and industry, our in-house ISO expertise and our relative distance from the mainstream of university administration all contributed to the success of our ISO efforts.

Walter DiMantova in an e-mail suggested three motivational factors for seeking ISO certification:

1. *Our customers demanded it. It was increasingly obvious that the same standards applied to suppliers of products would eventually be applied to suppliers of services (including training). Our goal was to reach ISO before it became an explicit requirement of our clients.*

2. *We needed to practice what we preached. Our Center for Quality, part of the CCT, provided ISO and quality-related training to thousands of people a year. It was no longer acceptable to provide training on a standard we did not ourselves meet.*

3. *It would help the organization meet customer needs. This was perhaps the most important reason of all. ISO was another way to stay competitive and continuously improve what we provide. Our ISO efforts have reduced customer complaints, increased the quality of our programs and products and lead to the solution of some long-standing problems. ISO became a tool to a reach a higher goal—namely, customer satisfaction.*

The process of creating a customer-focused quality system was, more than anything else, a learning experience for the fifteen staff directly involved. There were many lessons learned on the road to ISO:

Involve everyone. *Developing a functioning and effective quality system needs the energy, intelligence, and insights of every member of the organization.*

Banish organizational levels. *"Top-down" and "bottom-up" no longer make sense; quality management is truly practiced when hierarchy no longer restricts the flow and exchange of great ideas and best practices. In the case of the CCT, everyone—including management, staff and students—worked together towards a common goal. Key roles (such as Management Representative and Internal Auditor) were the responsibility of union-represented professional and clerical staff.*

Don't tell, ask. *Recognize early on that the people who do the job know the job best. Asking them to develop procedures and work instructions is the most efficient and accurate way to create a working quality system.*

Expect delays. *Regardless of what some consultants may say, reaching ISO is not a sixty-day effort. Our initial estimate said "nine months"; it took us fifteen. Was this time wasted? Absolutely not. It was the time we needed to make a system that would work long after our initial registration audit.*

Audit, audit, audit. *Recurring internal audits kept us all aware of the fundamental ISO tenant: "say what you do and do what you say." Our two internal auditors were as important to our success as the external auditor provided from our registrar.*

Pay attention. *ISO requires a close look at everything you do. Lofty mission statements and quality policies are not enough to make a quality system worthy of ISO work. Careful examination of what you actually do in your office (or your classroom) is the first step towards building a viable quality system.*

Think "system, system, system." *ISO is a closely-knit standard of mutually dependent elements. No one element can dominate the others; attention must be paid to each requirement and, even more importantly, the complex interrelationships between these requirements.*

Fit the standard to your organization. *Many times, we needed to interpret the standard to meet the requirements of a training organization quite unlike, say, a maker of bolts. The translation of ISO to education is an evolving field. We decided to be a part of that evolution by actively questioning what the standard said and by translating it into practices and instructions that did not undermine our commitment to education and the sharing of knowledge.*

Get outside help. *In the case of the CCT, we relied on our in-house trainers to act as facilitators and consultants. They added invaluable insights; as knowledgeable outside observers, they could ask pointed questions and objectively evaluate how far we'd come (and how far we needed to go).*

Certification is just the beginning. Being registered to ISO 9000 is just the beginning. Instead of focusing on a piece of paper, we focused on creating the best quality system we could—and trusting that this would certainly be enough for registration. It was. The next step after certification is recertification—passing the annual mandatory audits.

What does this mean for higher education?

Whether ISO standards can be used to complement current accreditation standards remains an unanswered question as much for K–12 public schools as for four-year post-secondary institutions.

ISO is much more than a set of rules. Making real use of the standard to improve teaching and learning will require some fundamental changes in language, attitudes, and concepts before there can be widespread application in the higher education world.

Rapid changes in technology and in the global economy means that educational institutions at all levels must be ready to change how they work. In the past, educators have stressed continuity—the preservation of practices whose effectiveness is unmeasured. ISO is one of many potential steps toward a new measure of educational progress: continuous improvement. (Source: E-mail from Walter DiMantova dated June 2001)

Several quality professionals have worked extensively with education to implement quality management systems. Their views on success factors follow.

Frank Caplan, president of Quality Sciences Consultants and founder of the National Educational Quality Initiative (now a technical committee of ASQ's Education Division) says the following:

The top officials in many schools, school districts, and postsecondary institutions have accepted the concept that there is a role for quality management in education. However, most administrators seem to have convinced themselves that this role pertains only to support activities such as food service, transportation, and janitorial services. Applying it to all processes in the school system has only recently become a concept adopted by just a few such organizations.

The need for the overall approach becomes apparent when one begins to understand that virtually all processes are interdependent and, for the greatest impact on the organization's ability to meet its objectives, must be mutually intersupportive. Given that realization, the top administrators then recognize that the quality of all processes must be managed. This inevitably includes the instructional and personnel processes as well as the support activities. To accomplish that requires that the involved personnel must be thoroughly trained in the quality management principles and practices.

When these concepts are then learned by all faculty, staff, and students (rather than by just a few), it becomes practicable to establish effective multi-functional teams to adapt and apply them to all the organization's processes. The management function then becomes one of support and coordination to ensure that the process changes prove effective, that the desirable interactions of the processes with each other are planned for and accomplished, and that the undesirable interactions are prevented.

The aggregate of all the necessary changes, when the processes are fully aligned with each other and the school's vision, then results in a manageable system. Only through such a systematic approach to the operations of the school can it produce the desired exceptional benefits for the school's customers, personnel, and all other stakeholders. (E-mail dated 18 June 2001)

Chester Francke, a quality systems consultant, said in an e-mail:

While many don't like to compare industry sectors with education, sometimes such an analysis can be helpful. A look at the challenges facing education in comparison to the challenges facing industry can, perhaps, be useful. For example, industry and education both grapple with complacency, brought on by the belief that the best don't have to work as hard to maintain their standing. There are few providers for the many users and virtual monopolies could control the market. The tendency toward customer and stakeholder insensitivity can create a loss of focus on the products and services provided and performance suffers.

Given these similarities, it seems reasonable in education to concentrate on quality concepts, principles, and techniques as a different way of looking at techniques for meeting management's responsibilities. Perhaps the single most pervasive principle is customer and stakeholder focus. This requires studying and responding to the needs, preferences, desires, and expectations of all current and potential customers and stakeholders. In education, it means that educators must first identify their customers and stakeholders (student, the parent, school board members, employers, and the community). This is not easy for any sector. Managers need to find ways of identifying their customers and stakeholders, what they need, and what they expect from an education. It is also important to identify the transactions in which the school, the customer, and the stakeholders are involved. These relationships differ for a given individual depending on the time and events of the transaction.

Management needs to understand education as a system beyond the campus. The concept of schools as a system is not well developed, yet the importance of system knowledge is beyond debate.

Planning, operating, and measuring the results of an education institution is very different than such activities for education. In industry, a standard is established for quality, the product is produced to that standard, the product is monitored and performance tested to ensure that the standard was met. As long as standards were being met management's responsibility was being met. Educators began to learn that even those who graduated were not always meeting the needs and expectations of customers and stakeholders. Standards were rapidly changing. The quality model requires that continuous improvement uses such techniques as benchmarking and self-assessment.

Quality management is a broad topic, and only a few concepts and examples are given here. The quality management approach has been effective in business, industry, education, government, and other organizations throughout the world. Management responsibilities can be met by the application of quality management principles, concepts, and practices. (E-mail dated June 2001)

William Golomski, international consultant in many fields of quality since 1949, including in education starting in the 1950s, has been a member of a public school board and on the advisory committees of many universities throughout the world. He examines the critical role of monitoring and measurement in the following comment:

The distinction between monitoring and measuring is only a part of the story in auditing for ISO 9001. I usually think of observing a process and making qualitative and/or quantitative measures. My next step is whether or not to record them, and which decision approach to use. This converts data into information. But, in some cases today, the decision is made for my own use, or is decision support for others, or is automatic decision-making as is embedded in some process controllers.

During the last twenty years we have gone a step further in converting information into knowledge, and now see books and papers on knowledge management. Finally, in the last few years we have gone beyond, and are now talking about the transformation of knowledge into wisdom. The field of marketing is ahead of the other functions on those four stages.

The people in quality who like to quote Kelvin on measurement have missed these linkages. Much of higher education has been on the latter two transformations. The measurement part has been more qualitative than quantitative, because we have been aiming for knowledge and wisdom. Deming tried his hand at a part of this in his musings on profound knowledge. ISO completely misses the point. (E-mail 9 July 1999)

FUTURE USE OF ISO 9000 IN EDUCATION

To a large extent the future use of ISO 9000 in education depends on the future of education. If there are realistic demands for accountability and an increased demand for systems for managing education, the educators will find willing hands among the business community. The driver will very likely relate to the demand for a new kind of worker and new ways of delivering education to individuals.

The future of the education sector is no less difficult to predict than any other sector. Sector leaders rely on experts like Peter Drucker to help them see into that future. Peter Drucker wrote the following about the future of education in *The Atlantic Monthly*, November 1994:

> *By the end of this century knowledge workers will make up a third or more of the workforce in the United States—as large a proportion as manufacturing workers ever made up, except in wartime. The majority of them will be paid at least as well as, or better than, manufacturing workers ever were. And the new jobs offer much greater opportunities. But—and this is a big but—the great majority of the new jobs require qualifications the industrial worker does not possess and is poorly equipped to acquire. They require a good deal of formal education and the ability to acquire and to apply theoretical and analytical knowledge. They require a different approach to work and a different mind-set. Above all, they require a habit of continuous learning. Displaced industrial workers thus cannot simply move into knowledge work or services the way displaced farmers and domestic workers moved into industrial work. At the very least they have to change their basic attitudes, values, and beliefs. In the closing decades of this century the industrial workforce has shrunk faster and further in the United States than in any other developed country—while industrial production has grown faster than in any other developed country except Japan.* ("The Age of Social Transformation," originally published in *The Atlantic Monthly*, November 1994. http://www.theatlantic.com/politics/ecbig/soctrans.htm)

Assuming Peter Drucker is correct, the question then becomes one of means for educating this new kind of worker. Perhaps we need to turn to technology to help solve this problem.

One of the new technologies is distance learning. Distance learning is any learning that takes place with the instructor and student geographically remote from each other. Distance learning may occur by surface mail, video, interactive or cable TV, satellite broadcast, or any number of Internet technologies such as message boards, chat rooms, and desktop video or computer conferencing. These remote locations with easy access by the general public raise questions of the authenticity of the information provided. The traditional accreditation safeguard needs to be reviewed and perhaps revised to protect customers from fraud. The quality implications for distance learning were reported in the *Chronicle of Higher Education* of 6 August 1999 and are reproduced by permission.

The first-ever accreditation of a "virtual" institution, Jones International University, has become a flash point in the debate over accrediting standards for online higher education. How could a for-profit university, whose only classrooms are in cyberspace, meet the same measures of quality as traditional bricks-and-mortar institutions?

The Jones decision in March was, to some faculty members, a slap in the face of traditional accrediting standards. And the questions it raises have put accreditors and policy makers in a quandary: Should they treat the new, electronic institutions the same way they have treated traditional colleges? Or should they develop new approaches? If so, what should those approaches be? Does anyone understand online education well enough to decide? Right now, accreditation experts say, the questions far outnumber the answers.

"This is going to be a serious issue for the next five years," said David A. Longanecker, former assistant secretary for postsecondary education at the U.S.

Department of Education, who is now executive director of the Western Interstate Commission on Higher Education. "It's leading us to a very different concept of quality assurance than we've traditionally had—but I'm not sure what that is."

Technology-intensive changes in higher education have convinced some administrators and accreditors—Mr. Longanecker among them—that new models for college and university accreditation are needed. "Our concern is that the old forms of accreditation really aren't appropriate for the new delivery mechanisms," he says.

But critics of the Jones accreditation see it as evidence that accrediting agencies have moved away from reliable standards and are more willing to approve what Christine Maitland, higher-education coordinator for the National Education Association, says "are really experiments" in higher education. The director of the agency that accredited Jones International, however, thinks otherwise. The current controversy may be short-lived, says Steven D. Crow, executive director of the North Central Association of Colleges and Schools. He thinks that the Jones case is exceptional—that their virtual institutions will operate as extensions of traditional colleges or universities, rather than as accredited, degree-granting institutions themselves. In fact, he says, traditional universities and for-profit businesses are likely partners in distance-education marriages—especially if they involve companies with large amounts of capital to invest "in good curricular design and course work."

Already, accreditation officials say the sheer number of colleges and universities offering some form of distance education is making their work more challenging, as the programs attract a larger share of students—and of accreditors' attention. "It's the magnitude that is the issue," says Sandra Elman, executive director of the Commission on Colleges of the Northwest Association of Schools and Colleges. "Distance education has been going on for years, but not to the degree, and not in all kinds of institutions, that it is now."

Among the regional agencies, North Central is by far "the most aggressive and open-minded about distance learning," says Michael P. Lambert, executive director of the Distance Education and Training Council, which accredits distance-education programs. "I find its attitude refreshing, somewhat different, more entrepreneurial."

In conducting recent institutional evaluations, including the one for Jones, North Central has relied in part on guidelines for "good practices in telecommunicated learning," similar to those developed by the Western accrediting agency, says Mr. Crow.

The only unusual aspects of the Jones accreditation, he says, were the procedures used to review the curriculum and conduct interviews—many of which the evaluation team held online. For about two years, members of the team reviewed library resources, administration, and finances—"the standard stuff," he says.

Even so, educators who question the decision to accredit Jones say they suspect that the institutions received waivers on some requirements—a suspicion that university officials deny. "I can tell you right now, we didn't," says Pamela S. Pease, president of Jones International, which is based in Englewood, Colorado.

Winning accreditation was a key business objective of the university, which began operating in 1995. In March, when it received accreditation, it was offering two degree programs—one graduate, one undergraduate—in business communications, and enrolled 74 students (*The Chronicle,* March 19). "Frankly, we knew we really couldn't scale up our marketing without first securing accreditation," Ms. Pease says.

Ms. Elman, of the Northwest commission, thinks there has been far too much second-guessing of North Central's decision. She says the public should interpret the accreditation of a virtual university for what it is: "Jones International meets the same standards for accreditation as does any other institution accredited by North Central—that's what it means, and that's what happened."

But some faculty-union leaders argue that, at the very least, North Central should have made a better case for its decision. The agency "has perfectly nice criteria, but certainly, at this point, they've not done a good job of explaining how those criteria applied in the Jones case, and how the institution was able to meet them," says Lawrence Gold, higher-education director for the American Federation of Teachers. Accreditation "is quality assurance"—and in the Jones case, he says, the assurance is lacking. Members of the teachers' federation plan to spend part of this year taking a new look at all aspects of higher education, he adds. "We're going to start by going back to basics," thinking about what a student really needs from a college education, "and whether e-mail is as effective as personal interchange. Or, if it isn't as effective, it is okay enough?"

According to Mr. Gold, state legislators bear much of the responsibility for decisions that lead more and more students to take college courses over the Internet.

The same legislators who are "not interested in providing more facilities, not interested in beefing up video-conferencing programs, not especially interested in teacher salaries, and certainly not interested in replacing adjuncts with full-time faculty members," he says, "are in fact very interested in spending a ton of money on something we don't know a whole lot about."

Faculty members represented by the American Association of University Professors are also critical of the Jones accreditation. Two weeks after North Central announced its decision, the AAUP sent a four-page letter to Mr. Crow, the agency's executive director, asking that it "give further consideration" to the accrediting standards and procedures used in the Jones case.

The Jones decision still rankles the author of that letter, James E. Perley, chairman of the AAUP's Committee on Accreditation and a professor of biology at the College of Wooster. He is dismayed by the growing acceptance of virtual universities as candidates for accreditation, and he fears that such online institutions will destroy the tradition of higher education as a community of scholars defining "what and who we are."

Denise Tanguay, another member of the AAUP's accreditation committee, says students gain significant benefits from a university's investment in libraries and other research facilities. "Accrediting bodies are not requiring virtual universities to share some of those research costs that other universities have," says Ms. Tanguay, a professor of management and industrial relations in the business school at Eastern Michigan University. But Mr. Lambert, of the distance-education council, says such negative reactions to the Jones accreditation result from faculty members' suspicion that online learning will mean "an erosion of faculty freedoms."

Professors "had a good thing for a long time," he says, but now they should recognize the potential of information technology—especially the Internet—to deliver higher education to many nontraditional students. As a means of providing postsecondary education, the technology is "completely convenient and delivered when, where, and how the consumer wants it."

He notes that distance education has been "legitimized" by prestigious institutions like Duke, Harvard, and Stanford Universities, which are offering courses online. "I was a professor, too," he says, "and I enjoyed the heck out of having the kids' faces light up—there's nothing like it." But changes in faculty members' roles are inevitable, he argues. Within five years, he says, most college teachers will be involved in distance learning—"and it will be old hat."

Mr. Crow thinks that adult students, who typically need "packages of learning," or courseware modules, will find distance education well suited to their needs. But Jones International will need more than the commission's *Good Housekeeping* "seal of approval" in today's highly competitive higher-education market, he adds. "For Jones, the issue is going to be whether it finds a market, and whether the market believes that what it is getting from Jones is quality education."

To some observers, Mr. Crow's statement sounds like *caveat emptor*—precisely the warning that accrediting agencies were created to eliminate. David F. Noble, a professor of history at York University, in Toronto, says the Jones case is the inevitable result of "a uniquely lax system of regulation" of higher education in the United States.

According to Mr. Noble, a critic of what he calls "the commoditization of higher education," all the fuss about Jones and its virtual cousins simply "diverts attention from how much our established institutions resemble them." He sees nothing new in the current controversy over the legitimacy of online education. "For-profit companies are muscling in on the established territory of the universities, and so the universities have to attack them—and emulate them."

The same thing happened in the 1890s, he says, when businesses opened to provide correspondence courses for engineers, draftsmen, and others in new industries. "The universities attacked the correspondence firms, and at the same time set up their own correspondence courses."

In recent months, accreditation-reform efforts have gained substantial financial backing, with grants from private foundations providing millions of dollars to test new models for evaluating the quality of traditional and online universities alike. For the most part, though, the proposed changes don't refer specifically to questions posed by online programs.

Working with a $1.5-million grant from the Pew Charitable Trusts, North Central will offer an optional "quality improvement" program of accreditation next year as an alternative to its traditional reviews. Under the new option, colleges and universities—virtual or otherwise—would analyze their institutional processes and devise long-range plans for improving them, says Stephen D. Spangehl, director of the association's Academic Quality Improvement Project.

Grants of $1.6 million from Pew and $400,000 from the James Irvine Foundation have helped the Western Association of Schools and Colleges to experiment with new models of accreditation for higher education, whether traditional or virtual. Western says it wants to deploy smaller teams on shorter visits to assess institutions' overall "educational effectiveness."

One accrediting body intent on examining online programs specifically is the American Academy for Liberal Education, which is seeking to establish its own standards for the quality of liberal-arts programs delivered online.

"Everyone's in a state of crisis" about quality, says George Lucas, executive director of the two-year-old agency, which is based in Washington and accredits undergraduate liberal-arts programs nationwide. Are liberal-arts programs delivered over the Internet "a rip-off, or a second-rate experience?" he asks. "Those are unanswered questions we want to work on."

More than a few educators believe that the traditional standards of accreditation have served higher education well. One strength of those standards, which look at an institution's full-time faculty, degree programs, research libraries, shared governance, and other matters, is that they are flexible—or, some say, even elastic.

"We've been able to make them work, and that's a tribute to the accreditors and the institutions working with them," says Judith S. Eaton, president of the Council of Higher Education Accreditation, in Washington, a non-profit research center for higher education. The debate over accrediting online programs, she adds, "is energizing the profession."

"Do we need new standards? Will the old standards work?" Ms. Eaton asks. "These are the kind of questions we're working with the different accrediting organizations to answer."

REFERENCES

American National Standards Institute (ANSI). ANSI/ASQC Z1.11:1996, *Quality assurance standards—Guidelines for the application of ANSI/ISO/ASQC Q9001 and Q9002 to education training institutions.* Milwaukee, WI, 1996.

Malcolm Baldrige National Quality Award. *Education criteria for performance excellence.* Gaithersburg, MD, 1998.

International Organization for Standardization (ISO). ISO 10015, *Quality management—Guidelines for training.* Geneva, Switzerland, 2001.

E-mail Contributors and <E-mail Address>

Robert Bowen, President, R. Bowen International <RBIINC@aol.com>
Frank Caplan, President, Quality Sciences Consultants <frankcaplan@cco.net>
Walter DiMantova, Director, Centers for Corporate Eastern Michigan University <walter.dimantova@emich.edu>
Dana Egreczky <dana@njchamber.com >
Chester Francke, President, Quality Systems International <CAFrancke@aol.com>
William Golomski, President, W. A. Golomski and Associates <wgolomski@itol.com>
M. Eugene Hall, Professor, Southern Illinois University <ghall@siu.edu>
Linda Quinn, Chair, Northwest Association of Schools and Colleges <lquinn@puyallup.k12.wa.us>
Carol Sager, Consultant, Sager Educational Enterprises <cs@CarolSager.com>
    Carol Sager, Sager Educational Enterprises, The Critical Linkages II Newsletter, 21 Wallis Rd. Chestnut Hill, MA 02467-3110, www.CarolSager.com
Rick Utz, Principal, Liberty Center High School <rlutz@henry-net.com>

Newspapers

Houston—(Business Wire)—Dec. 30, 1998

Olsen, F. " 'Virtual' Institutions Challenge Accreditors to Devise New Ways of Measuring Quality" *Chronicle of Higher Education.* 6 August 1999 Section: Information Technology, Page: A29. http://chronicle.com

Magazines and Journals

Drucker, P. "The Age of Social Transformation." *The Atlantic Monthly*, November 1994. http://www.theatlantic.com/politics/ecbig/soctrans.htm

Johnson, F. C. and G. Smith, "What Parents Say and What Schools Hear" *Quality Engineering*, 1995–96: 405–09.

Chapter 52

Fiber Box Industry

Steve Tokarz
Packaging Corporation of America, Lake Forest, Illinois

Pat Buzek
AOQC Moody International, Houston, Texas

The fiber box industry supplies corrugated shipping and point-of-sale containers and point-of-purchase displays for American businesses. Corrugated containers have proven to be one of the more versatile and effective means of packaging, displaying, and transporting products. Industry shipments in 1998 were 396 billion square feet of packaging, which generated revenues of $20.3 billion. Roughly 80 percent of corrugated packaging is used for nondurable goods, with food and beverage representing 39 percent of the industry's shipments.

The industry is highly fragmented and competitive. It comprises integrated companies and independent companies, which represent 75 percent and 25 percent of shipments, respectively. Integrated companies are larger and have papermaking operations as well as converting operations that manufacture the corrugated packaging. Examples of integrated companies are Smurfit-Stone, Weyerhaeuser, Georgia Pacific, and Packaging Corporation of America. Independents, on the other hand, are smaller; they have one to several converting operations, and a few have some papermaking operations—typically smaller recycled paper mills. Examples of independent companies are Ideal Box and Graphics, Pride Container, Advance Packaging, and Colorado Container.

Industry manufacturing operations include paper mills, corrugator plants, and sheet plants. The paper mills make containerboard, the paper that is used to manufacture the corrugated packaging; containerboard can be kraft paper, which contains a high content of virgin fiber to recycled paper, which is itself made of 100 percent recycled paper fiber. In 1998, 30 million tons of containerboard were produced.

Kraft paper mills are large, capital-intensive operations with a few hundred to several hundred employees. Paper mills are "continuous processes," in that once they are producing product, it is very expensive to stop the process. A paper mill may have one or more paper machines. Each paper machine usually is set up to manufacture a specified range of papers with specific specifications for basis weight per thousand square feet, strength, smoothness, and so on.

Corrugator plants process the containerboard into the combined corrugated sheets that make up the two outer facings of paper and the fluted interior paper. Most all plants with corrugators also have converting equipment that converts the corrugated sheets into finished boxes and displays. Some plants that have corrugators alone produce corrugated sheets for converting operations that do not have corrugating capabilities. Corrugator plants will generally have about 75 to 150 employees.

Sheet plants have only converting equipment and buy corrugated sheets that have already been combined. Sheet plants may be small and employ 10 to 20 people or they may be quite large, employing more than a hundred people. In 1998, there were 1472 fiber box plants in operation: 612 corrugators and 860 sheet plants. By far, the corrugator plants generate the lion's share of shipments, 86 percent. Corrugator and sheet plants are job shop operations. They print, score, slot, die-cut, and/or join the containers or displays as specified for each individual item. Each order for containers is different in some respect from all other orders (color, print, size, style, etc.). A typical plant may have a few hundred customers and manufacture thousands of different corrugated products. As a consequence, it is a business that depends on mastering details.

Prior to the development of the ISO quality standards, quality systems in paper mills, corrugator plants, and sheet plants varied greatly. They ranged from no discernible quality system to partially documented systems with little integration with other operating processes. The quality level and effectiveness of the plant was very dependent on the experience and continuity of the workforce. If a plant had a very low employee turnover rate, it could function satisfactorily because people were experienced, knew their jobs, and knew the nuances of what individual customers wanted. The opposite was true for plants that had high employee turnover rates. The absence of documented and standardized processes allowed for critical details to get lost. New employees did not fully know their jobs and, just as important, did not know the customers' expectations and requirements.

During the late 1980s and early 1990s, the fiber box industry was in a situation common to most industries. To maintain a competitive position and survive financially, the industry had to resort to aggressive cost cutting and downsizing in all aspects of the business. The cost cutting resulted in the elimination of many technical and managerial support personnel who had been key to sustaining business operations. Executives of the large integrated companies realized that success in sustaining customer loyalty in an industry whose products were being characterized as "commodities" would require a different approach to business. Reliance on internal technical expertise and operator "experience" to ensure that products met customer requirements had been only marginally successful in the 1970s and 1980s. However, the business climate of the 1990s was changing.

Quality and service were becoming more important, and demands from U.S. customers were increasing. Also, U.S. companies were participating more in the global economy. In order to continue to support their customers, industry companies would not only have to be more global in meeting packaging needs but would have to provide globally recognized quality packaging. The issuance of international standards for the management of quality was at first perceived as a solution to the issue of having "global products." Fiber box managers thought—as did managers in the chemical and steel industries, which also had what were considered "commodity" products—that being certified to an international standard would provide the assurance that their products met requirements. They felt such status would give them the competitive advantage not only to stay in business but to prosper in the aggressive environment of the 1990s. At the same time, the more quality conscious customers were prodding, and in some cases requiring, their packaging suppliers to install documented quality systems. Those more sophisticated customers had installed quality systems and had witnessed the benefits.

The directives and the resources were given to mills and corrugator plants to implement systems in their operations that could be certified by an established third-party registration body. Generally, the direction embraced by the industry was based not on an understanding of the principles found in the ISO 9001 and 9002 standards but on the perceived benefit of meeting the requirements of an internationally recognized standard and being able to market that achievement to current and prospective customers. As a result, early system implementations focused on meeting each individual requirement of the standard and not on the incorporation of the principles across the scope of the business.

Compounding that problem was the relative inexperience of the consulting and registration communities in developing and assessing quality management systems. The consultants and auditors from the registrars were very experienced in the technical intricacies of certain businesses, since they typically had more than 10 years of industry experience. They were not necessarily skilled in the interrelation of processes to ensure an effective operation that is suitable within the scope of the business. What occurred as a result of the interactions with the consultants and the third-party auditors was the implementation of procedures that were certifiable under the registrars' rules but lacked the capability to provide ongoing benefits to the paper mills and to the converting plants.

The systems were implemented as ISO systems and included only the parts of their operation that were needed in order to be certified. Safety was most often excluded, usually at the direction of the consultant, because having it within the system made it an area that could be audited, and the third-party auditor might identify nonconformities. The basis for deciding what to include became ease of achieving conformance rather than benefit to the business. For the large multi-plant companies, which were having each plant certified separately, the nonconformities were closely watched and were addressed through additional documentation at each subsequent facility. Very rarely in this sequence was there a challenge to the third-party auditor's determination of nonconformity; and very rarely was there a challenge to the consultant's claim that the third-party auditor would find the documentation or the contents of the record to be nonconforming.

Systems were implemented and maintained to avoid nonconformities, not to ensure the success of each and every process in meeting the requirements of both internal and external customers. The separate parts of the system were kept separate as a means of attaining and sustaining certification. The "technical experts" from the consulting and registration communities had managed to misdirect the fiber box industry, as they were doing to other industries as well. The principles embodied in the requirements of ISO 9001 and 9002 were valid frameworks for running a prosperous business that could consistently achieve customer satisfaction. However, the interpretations by the outside groups detracted from the benefits that could have been attained.

Notwithstanding the lack of understanding and misdirection, companies in the fiber box industry did benefit from the development of documented quality systems. Just as in companies from other industries, fiber box managers often were elated with the results achieved through the initial implementation. The process of having to define and document policies and procedures had provided a much-needed evaluation of what was actually occurring in each of the plants' operations. By incorporating the policies and procedures described in the standard, they were achieving a level of control and communication that had been missing in their pre-ISO days. Almost every plant saw some positive changes in its performance results.

Packaging Corporation of America (PCA) became involved with ISO at its plant in Ashland, Ohio, in 1993. At the direction of one of its larger customers, the Ashland plant began development of a documented quality system. The Ashland plant's success prompted PCA management to establish a business-wide goal to install ISO-registered quality systems in all of its 38 corrugator plants. In 1996, 20 PCA plants were ISO registered or very close to that point. The remaining 18 plants lagged well behind, either just starting the process or not having begun at all.

The performance of the two groups were compared. This was done by analyzing change in performance on three key business measures:

- Operating profit
- Paper yield (effective use of material and minimization of waste)
- Product-related returns and allowances as a percentage of sales (a measure of product quality to the customer)

PCA compared performance during the first five months of 1994 with performance during the first five months of 1996. It should be noted that during 1994, 1995 and 1996, all plants were also engaged in implementing a newly created Manufacturing Excellence Program. That program provided tools and best practices for various manufacturing operations and functions. It actually complemented ISO quality system development because it provided the plants with proven practices that could be integrated into their new procedures.

Figure 52.1 shows operating profit box plots for groups 1 and 2 for each of the time periods:

Group 1 = plants that were ISO registered or soon to be ($n = 20$)

Group 2 = plants that hadn't started or had just started developing their quality systems ($n = 18$)

The 1994 operating profit base for group 1 was a little higher than the base for group 2. Both groups improved operating profit; however, the median operating profit for group 1 increased 35 percent more than group 2. It is also interesting to note that the degree of operating profit variation among group 1 plants was significantly less than for group 2 in 1996.

Figure 52.2 shows paper yield box plots for both groups. Again the 1994 starting point for group 1 was higher than for group 2. The medians of both groups improved by the same number of points of paper yield. Again, the 1996 box plots show much more variation among group 2 plants than among group 1.

Figure 52.3 shows returns and allowance box plots for both groups. The 1994 starting point for group 1 was again a little higher than that of group 2. The median for group 1 improved more than twice than did that of group 2 over the two years.

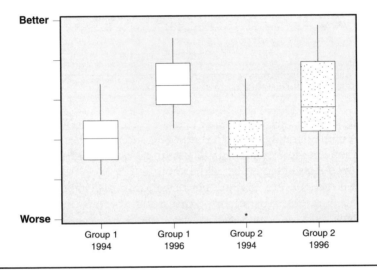

Figure 52.1   Operating profits.

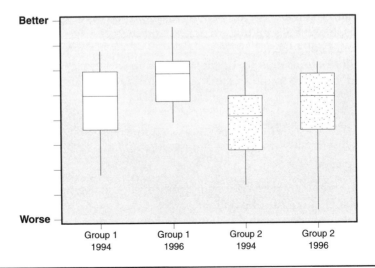

Figure 52.2   Paper yield.

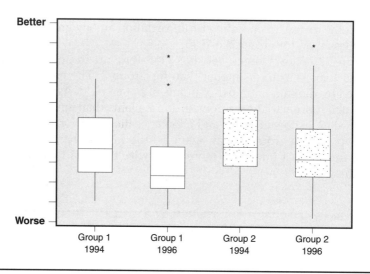

Figure 52.3 Returns and allowances.

PCA management at both the corporate and plant levels believe that the effective implementation of ISO quality systems does improve plant performance. They view documented systems like knots tied in a rope that one must climb. The system allows one to "lock in" performance improvements and not slide back down the rope, which is often the case when there is no mechanism to sustain improvements. Much anecdotal support for ISO is found among PCA's general managers, production managers, sales managers, supervisors, and so on. For example, when a long-skeptical production manager was asked by a corporate visitor if ISO had helped his plant he said, "Look around, and tell me what you see." (They were standing by the copy machine in the customer service department of a corrugator plant.) The visitor said, "I don't see anything." "That's the point," responded the production manager. "Before ISO my supervisors would be in here all the time checking on specifications and orders and making copies of load tags. Now that's all under control, and they can stay out in the plant where they should be!"

Feedback from those in the fiber box industry suggests that the following elements of ISO were found of most benefit during initial implementation:

- Management review
- Contract review
- Internal audit
- Corrective action

These elements help define and control essential functions and the management of large amounts of detail.

What is now occurring in many plants in the industry is the recognition that the initial performance improvements realized when ISO was first installed are not continuing. In part, that is attributable to a focus on the administration of the system instead of its effectiveness. That has increased the bureaucracy and administrative burden involved with the system, and ISO is becoming more of a "cost" than a competitive advantage. Document and data control administration is constantly taxing the operations because the documentation and data become more voluminous with each interaction with a consultant or a third-party auditor. What has developed is an expansive use of words and phrases that are intended to avoid nonconformity to an issue already identified or that might possibly be identified. That has resulted in policies and procedures that contain words and phrases that do not clearly define an activity but provide justification for an activity that might be executed several different ways or not at all. Such terminology as "at the discretion of" and "when necessary" are frequent culprits. The extensive use of explanations for the auditors, not for the employees, makes the document much bulkier than it needs to be to ensure system effectiveness. Therefore, changes to any document require additional workload in an environment where the eight-hour day is no longer a reality.

This phenomenon is pushing many plants to look at computerized read-only access of their system. As a result, employees have ready access to documents and data, but usually the degree of difficulty in scrolling through a procedure or work instruction provides an incentive for doing tasks by memory. The very principle that dominates the contents of the standard is being bypassed in order to alleviate the administrative burden that has crept into far too many systems.

One company in the industry that has successfully implemented ISO and has continued to benefit from it is Deline Box Company in Denver, Colorado. Registering in 1993, Deline Box was one of the first in the industry to attain ISO 9001 certification. Its involvement with ISO was prompted by one of its large, sophisticated customers that had itself gone through the process. Jim Deline, president, said that if it was that important to his customer, it was important to take a hard look at it. Deline quickly saw that it was an "ideal blueprint to run a small business."

The company worked very hard on process control to install procedures to help it do things right the first time and eliminate errors. It realized significant benefits in ensuring the integrity of information (for example, order entry, manufacturing specifications, and so on). Another area in which the company realized substantial improvement was maintenance; currently, scheduled maintenance accounts for 97 percent of maintenance time versus three percent for breakdowns, an enviable achievement. Furthermore, Jim Deline states that ISO is a "wonderful way to take the pressure off of the boss." Deline continues, "Before ISO it was up to the boss to follow through to ensure things were fixed and corrected. Now it's in the system, which ensures that it's acted upon. If not acted upon, problems stay there like smelly fish!" Deline Box has made effective use of corrective and preventive action to remove root causes and avoid potential problems. Also, the company uses internal audits to its advantage as it has become "very good at finding its own faults."

Deline management have not been shy about using ISO to their continuing benefit. They have included "other operational areas" in their system. Those include safety, housekeeping, customer complaints, productivity, and a suggestion system. If it's important to the business, they willingly include it in their system; they do not constrain their system to limit the scope of external audits for fear of getting a nonconformity. Continual improvement and getting better is the driving force. Deline Box gets results. The company received a coveted quality award from a major U.S. company for having achieved a 230 parts per million defect performance. (That is not defects per million opportunity, but rather 230 defective boxes!)

The revisions to the ISO 9001 standard coming about in the year 2000 will affect quality systems presently in place in the industry. The more notable changes from the 1994 version are summarized here:

• *The adoption of one standard with criteria for reduction in scope rather than having three standards.* For the paper mills, the ISO 9002 standard was selected as the model because the products were most often based on similar industrywide specifications. For the converting organizations, the ISO 9001 standard was most often used as the model for the quality system, as the products were designed and produced for specific customer applications. There are, however, many converting plants that have not subscribed to the design control section of the 1994 version. Those currently 9002-based organizations will need to review their "responsibility to provide product and/or service which meets customer requirements." They will need to determine if that can be accomplished without control of design and development outputs that define acceptance criteria and characteristics for a specific product that meets customer needs and expectations. With many of the products being based on industrywide construction formats, the scope of what can be excluded from the quality management system, and its definition in the quality manual, will require an examination of the nature of what specifically is being offered to customers.

The papermaking organizations also will be affected when they introduce any new products that have been reformulated to "improve" some property that enables either more efficient manufacturing or converting or reduces product costs. With the addition of edge crush as a basis for carton certification, new products were developed such as high-performance papers. While the principles of design control were applied, procedural control within the scope of the quality management system was not utilized. The 2000 version requires that that type of process be included since it affects "the organization's ability to provide conforming products."

• *An expanded description of the objectives of quality.* Although quality objectives were described in the other supporting standards of the ISO 9000 family, to reflect the scope of these important measurements, the ISO 9001:1994 left it open for the organization to avoid the use of measurable objectives. Thus quality objectives were most often not defined and applied throughout the business. The 2000 version fills the void by specifically requiring definition at each function and level in the organization. This should provide the focal point for the operation to plan and progress within the limited resource environment that has become a way of life for this industry and still achieve customer confidence.

• *An expanded definition of the management review process.* Management review most often has been relegated to a meeting with minutes being maintained for a record. Management groups have focused on the status of the system—such as completion of such processes as internal quality audits and corrective actions—and on covering other miscellaneous subjects such as the quality policy, the results of external audits, and any related business objectives from corporate management. The importance of the word *continuing* was not put into the context of planning and the issuance of an action plan. The 2000 version not only kept the word *continuing* that was in the 1994 version but added the description of what was meant by defining a requirement: "The review shall evaluate the need for changes to the organization's quality management system." The 2000 version also changed the definition of the output of the management review process. The intent is to describe the actions to "ensure continuing suitability and effectiveness." The wording was changed from "records of such reviews will be maintained," which had generated a meeting minutes approach. The 2000 standard requires that "results of management reviews shall be recorded." This will ensure that the *decisions* are put in writing and minimize the importance of just having meeting minutes.

• *The introduction of the concept of continual improvement as a defined part of the quality policy.* Because continual improvement involves a process that uses statistical tools to evaluate process capability and stability, it does not have widespread application in the fiber box industry. Most activities defined by the quality management system have been developed to address meeting customer requirements and not to break through to new levels of reduced variation. Although the paper mills have automated inspection systems that do generate considerable data points for each reel of paper, and in some cases, each roll, the decisions relating to those data are usually determinations of conformity/nonconformity. The converting operations have not used automated inspection systems for boxes and displays and also evaluate their products primarily based on conformity/nonconformity. Process control techniques are used extensively but not statistical process control. The commitment to continual improvement required by the 2000 standard will require the quality management systems developed in the industry to change. It will take the industry an additional step beyond the corrective and preventive action processes that are slowly overcoming the correction-only mode that prevailed during the 1970s and 1980s.

• *An expanded requirement for defined and documented interrelation of personnel who manage, perform, and verify work affecting quality.* This section in the 2000 version focuses on the process for internal communications between the various levels and functions. This principle has been incorporated into the existing procedures for the industry but not necessarily in a formal, structured approach that ensures that all essential activities involving internal communications are defined and documented.

• *An expanded definition of special processes.* The 2000 version drops the term *special* and replaces it with "where the resulting output cannot be readily or economically verified by subsequent monitoring, inspection and/or testing." This brings a new scope to fiber box industry processes as most of the products are not 100 percent inspected, nor is that feasible within typical operating margins. As such, the defined processes are based on a combination of process control techniques and product sampling. The validation-of-processes section of the 2000 standard defines requirements that will certainly benefit each segment of the industry: there is a revalidation step that will keep process capability current for management decisions relating to customer feedback. In many situations, the definition in the 1994 version led to a statement by management that there were no special processes since all parameters could be verified. The 2000 version emphasizes the full scope of the intended system control to address all processes where the resulting output is not 100 percent verified, but rather is sampled for decisions regarding conformity.

- *A specific requirement for measurement and monitoring of customer satisfaction.* The fiber box industry has definitely recognized and carried out measurements of customer satisfaction. The methods usually are not defined in the quality system and therefore will need to be formalized.

- *A specific requirement for measurement and monitoring of processes.* The measurement and monitoring of processes will be tied to continual improvement; so here significant changes will be needed. And because the activity in this area typically relies on some type of statistical technique, an additional area of training will be required for management in order to select and apply those techniques that provide suitable results without inefficient expenditure of administrative resources. Using statistical techniques for the sake of statistical techniques is not practical in the limited-resource environment of the industry.

In summary, ISO implementation in the fiber box industry has had a beneficial impact. Primarily, it provided a quality template that was flexible enough to meet the needs of individual operations; and the documented systems that were developed introduced consistency and control. In addition, early-on ISO registration provided a degree of competitive advantage over companies that were not registered; however, with the proliferation of registrations over the past few years, registration has become a baseline rather than an advantage.

Beyond the basic benefits enumerated in this chapter, the industry has not successfully used the standard to its full potential and benefit. Concerned more about avoiding nonconformance than building effectiveness, plant management, with few exceptions, have not incorporated other essential elements into their systems. Rather, they have introduced greater amounts of administration to avoid audit findings.

The standard as revised in 2000 should help move the industry to modify and expand its systems to generate greater benefit. The goal is to view one's system as a living system that changes to ensure continual improvement of the business.

Chapter 53

Food and the Use of Hazard Analysis Critical Control Points

John G. Surak

Clemson University, Clemson, South Carolina

H azard analysis critical control points (HACCP) is a product safety system that was developed and has evolved in the commercial food-processing industry. This industry is still the primary user of the system. Therefore, to understand HACCP, one should understand the basics of food processing and food-processing regulations.[1]

FOOD PRODUCTION AND FOOD REGULATIONS

Food is critical to sustaining human life. In addition, food can also add to a person's physiological and spiritual well-being. However, the same food can easily be mishandled and cause sickness, injury, or death. As a result, food processors have developed systems to ensure the safe production of food, and nations have developed laws and regulations to govern the production and distribution of food. In the United States, food is regulated by two federal agencies: the Food Safety Inspection Service (FSIS), an agency in the United States Department of Agriculture (USDA), and the Food and Drug Administration (FDA), an agency in the Department of Health and Human Services (Surak 1999). The FSIS regulates the production of meat products (beef, pork, lamb) and poultry products (chicken, turkey), while the FDA regulates the production of food products that do not contain meat or poultry. These regulations are designed to ensure that food is wholesome, safe, and properly labeled.

In recent years, the food-processing industry, and subsequently, food-processing regulations, have been moving away from the dependence on end-product inspection, adopting proactive methods to ensure the safety and quality of foods. The food-processing industry, FDA, and FSIS have standardized on using HACCP as a system to ensure food safety.

HISTORY OF HACCP IN THE UNITED STATES

HACCP was developed in the early days of the space program. NASA wanted assurance that the foods taken on board a space flight would not cause food-borne disease. As a result of this requirement, the Pillsbury Company and the U.S. Army Natick Research Laboratories developed a process that would ensure the production of a safe food supply. The process was named hazard analysis critical control points, or HACCP. The original concept of HACCP was based on three principles (Stevenson and Bernard 1999):

1. Identification of hazards.
2. Determination of critical control points to control any identified hazard.
3. Establishment of a monitoring system.

Pillsbury first presented the concept in 1971 at the National Conference on Food Protection.

Food-processing companies started to apply these principles beyond producing food for the space program. One example was the development of procedures to ensure the microbiological safety of canned food. The efforts resulted in the publication of Low Acid Canned Food Regulations in 1974.

In 1985, the National Research Council (NRC) of the National Academy of Science published several articles recommending that all food-processing companies adopt HACCP as a means to ensure the safety of food produced in the United States (NRC 1985a, 1985b). In general, the NRC report was well received by the industry. However, the report elicited unfavorable responses in the following two areas (Stevenson and Bernard 1999):

1. If HACCP were widely adopted by the food-processing industry, it would have to be incorporated into regulations.
2. The regulatory adoption of HACCP would give regulators greater access to processors' records.

The NRC report also recommended the formation of an expert advisory committee on food safety that would report to the secretaries of agriculture, defense, and health and human services. This committee was formed in 1988 and named the National Advisory Committee on the Microbiological Criteria for Foods (NACMCF). As part of this process, the number of principles was expanded from three to seven, thus changing HACCP from an "FMEA" for food to a systematic system to manage food safety. In 1988, the NACMCF published its first HACCP document, which was revised in 1992 and 1997.

In recent years, there has been a movement to make HACCP mandatory for all food-processing industries. This requirement has been driven, in part, by the customers of the food-processing industry and, in part, by the incorporation of the seven principles of HACCP into food-processing regulations. The FSIS has mandated the implementation of HACCP in all federally regulated meat and poultry processing establishments. The FDA has mandated the implementation of HACCP in the seafood industry and the fruit and vegetable juice industry. The FDA also incorporated HACCP into the Food Code, a compendium of model food safety guidelines for the food service industry. The code is used by more that 3000 state and local agencies that regulate food safety in restaurants, grocery stores, nursing homes, and other institutional and retail settings.

INTERNATIONALIZATION OF HACCP

The incorporation of HACCP into food-processing regulations is not just a U.S. phenomenon. Many nations have also adopted and evolved the concept of HACCP to ensure safety of the food supply. Most notable are the activities in Canada, where Agriculture and AgriFood Canada is credited with the addition of the defining concept of prerequisite programs to HACCP.

In addition, during the late 1980s and early 1990s, the Codex Alimentarius Commission (Figure 53.1) started the process of developing HACCP into an international standard. In 1993, Codex published *Guidelines for the Application of the HACCP System* (ALINNORM 93/13A, Appendix II). Later, Codex incorporated HACCP into an appendix of the *Recommended International Code of Practice— General Principles of Food Hygiene* [CAC/RCP 1-1969, Rev. 3 (1997)] (Codex 2001).

The Uruguay Round of Multinational Trade Negotiations gave special recognition in the Agreement on the Application of Sanitary and Phytosanitary Measures (SPS) to Codex standards, including the Codex standards for HACCP. The SPS measures outline the basic rules for food safety as well as animal and plant health standards (WTO 2001). As part of the agreement, nations that are members of the World Trade Organization (WTO) are to harmonize their national measures with international standards. The agreement specifically identified the Codex Alimentarius Commission as the international standards organization that sets international food safety standards.

PRINCIPLES OF HACCP

HACCP in its current form is composed of prerequisite programs, preliminary steps, and seven principles (FD&C 2002). The prerequisite programs are not part of the HACCP system and are typically managed as separate programs but are necessary for HACCP to work. These parts are linked to form a food safety management system shown as the "House of Food Safety" in Figure 53.2.

Prerequisite Programs

HACCP is built on a foundation of prerequisite areas (Figure 53.2). These programs are not a classified part of the HACCP system. The prerequisite programs are designed to ensure that the food is wholesome and does not contain objectionable contaminates. HACCP is designed to control significant life- or health-threatening food hazards.

One difference between prerequisite programs and the HACCP system is that prerequisite programs control a number of general processes, and a momentary failure in a prerequisite program will usually not create a safety hazard in a food product. In contrast, HACCP is designed to control specific steps in a process. A failure of a critical control point (CCP) can potentially cause a biological, physical, or chemical hazard in the food product.[2]

What Is Codex?

The Codex Alimentarius Commission (Codex) was established in 1962 as an intergovernment agency of United Nations under the Food and Agriculture Organization (FAO) and the World Health Organization. Codex is headquartered in Rome, Italy. The secretary of the Codex is a senior officer in the FAO.

Currently, Codex comprises 158 member nations. In the development of standards, Codex uses the same principle as ISO—one country, one vote. A major difference between Codex and ISO is the structure. The voting members of Codex are the national agencies, departments, or ministries that regulate the production of food rather than the national standards organization.

In addition to governmental agencies, Codex solicits input to standards through 46 intergovernmental agencies (IGOs), and 142 nongovernmental organizations (NGOs). Examples of IGOs are the Southern Common Market European Commission (MERCOSUR), the European Commission, and the World Trade Organization (WTO). Examples of NGOs are the International Bottled Water Association (IBWA), the International Commission on Microbiological Specifications for Foods (ICMSF), the Institute of Food Technologists (IFT), the International Life Sciences Institute (ILSI), and the International Organization for Standardization (ISO). These agencies are nonvoting members.

The responsibilities for representing the United States' position to Codex falls under the USDA, the FDA, and the Environmental Protection Agency. The U.S. Codex office is located in the Food Safety Inspection Service of the USDA. This office is responsible for developing the official U.S. position to Codex. FSIS holds public meetings and solicits comments from industry, regulatory agencies, academia, and consumer groups. Notices of the public meetings and comment periods are published in the Federal Register.

Codex is responsible for the development of the Codex Alimentarius, or food law. Codex Alimentarius is a set of international standards that govern all food principles, whether the foods are raw, semiprocessed, or processed. The standards contain requirements to ensure sound, wholesome, and safe food. In addition, the standards also ensure that food is free from adulteration and properly labeled. Since its conception, Codex has developed over 230 food standards, developed 185 codes of hygiene and technical practices, published 25 guidelines for contaminants, established over 2500 limits for pesticide residues, evaluated the safety of over 750 food additives, and evaluated over 150 veterinary drug residues. Included in these standards is the international definition for HACCP.

Figure 53.1 What is Codex?
Source: Codex 2001.

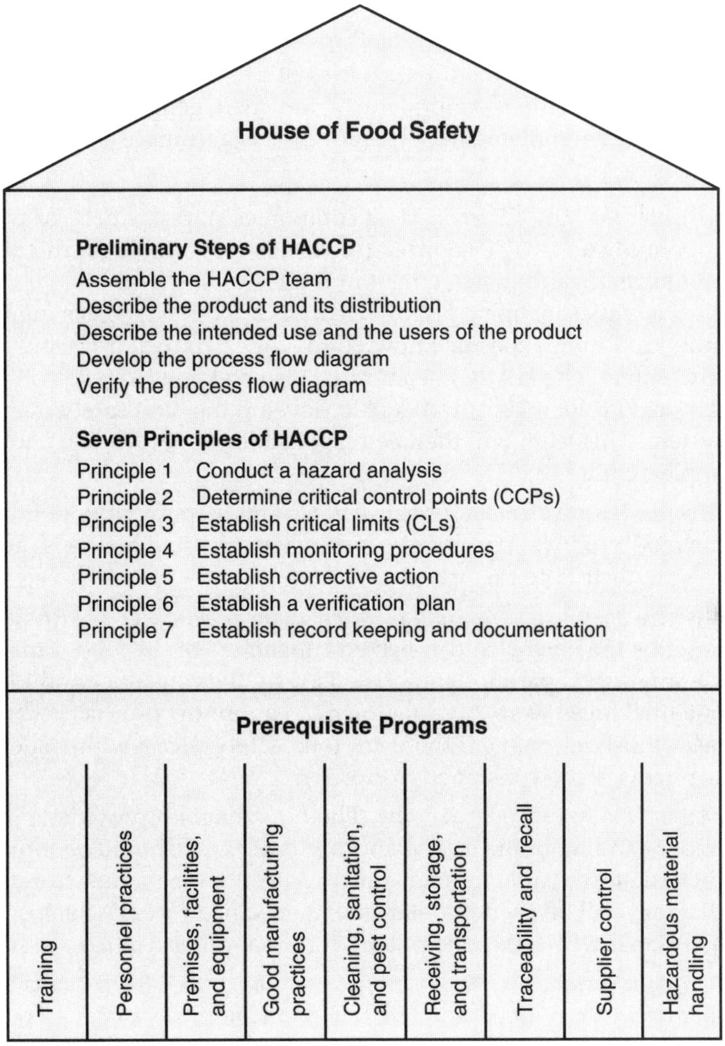

Figure 53.2 The house of food safety.
Adapted from FD&C 2002.

The prerequisite programs are designed to ensure the control of operating conditions within the food-processing operation, thus creating an environment for the safe production of food. The actual number of prerequisite areas vary from author to author. However, these areas must be properly designed, maintained, monitored, and document. This has two positive effects on the HACCP plan:

- The prerequisite programs allow for simplifying the HACCP plan by possibly reducing the number of CCPs
- The prerequisite programs help ensure the integrity of the HACCP plan

Preliminary Steps

HACCP starts with implementing a series of preliminary steps. Implementation of HACCP requires the commitment of top management and begins with the development of an implementation plan. This is accomplished by taking the following steps:

- *Assemble the HACCP team.* Most companies start this process by appointing a HACCP coordinator who is responsible for the development, organization, and management of the HACCP system.
  Next a cross-functional HACCP team is appointed, consisting of individuals with specific knowledge of the product, processes, and food safety. The HACCP team must also be knowledgeable in applying the seven principles of HACCP to develop the food safety management system. This team will then be responsible for developing and implementing the HACCP plan.

- *Describe the product and its distribution.* This step involves defining in detail the food product, ingredients, formula, processing methods, and system used to distribute the product.

- *Describe the intended use and the users of the product.* The team needs to describe the normal and expected consumers of the food. This is done by identifying preparation methods used by the consumer and identifying potential areas were the consumer can abuse the product. In addition, the team must determine if there are food safety issues within specific segments of the consumer groups.

- *Develop the process flow diagram.* The flow diagram provides a clear understanding of the manufacturing process. It should be limited to the process steps that are under direct control of the manufacturer. The flow diagram will be used to determine if specific processing steps will be associated with either the potential formation or control of a hazard.

- *Verify the accuracy of the process flow diagram.* Once the process flow diagram is developed, the HACCP team should perform an onsite review to ensure that the flow diagram is complete and accurate.

After completion of the preliminary steps, the HACCP team can develop the HACCP plan by applying the seven principles of HACCP.

Seven Principles of HACCP

Principle 1: Conduct a Hazard Analysis

Hazard analysis is a multistep process and consists of hazard identification and hazard evaluation. It is used to determine which potential biological, chemical, or physical hazards may be present in a specific food product. In addition, it also must focus on determining which hazards are significant to consumers. This process allows the HACCP team to determine the severity of the hazard and the probability that the hazard will occur. Upon completion, a list of hazards will be identified that must be controlled in the HACCP plan.

Principle 2: Determine the CCPs

The second step is to determine the CCPs. Each hazard that was identified during the hazard analysis must be controlled by one or more CCPs. As part of the process to determine if a control step is a CP or CCP, agencies such as NACMCF and Codex have developed decision trees (FD&C 2002). One major question a new HACCP team may ask is: How many CCPs are necessary to control the process? The team should strive to minimize the number of CCPs to achieve the food safety objectives. If too few CCPs are selected, then the company may not have adequate control of the process. If too many CCPs are selected, the HACCP system may be overburdened in an attempt to control nonfood safety hazards at the same intensity as it controls food safety hazards (NFPA Stevenson and Bernard, 1999).

Principle 3: Establish Critical Limits

Critical limits (CL) can be defined as "a maximum and/or minimum value to which a biological, chemical, or physical parameter must be controlled at a CCP to prevent, eliminate, or reduce to an acceptable level the occurrence of a food safety hazard" (NACMCF 1997, page 4). Therefore, critical limits define what constitutes an acceptable or unacceptable process parameter. Critical limits are set based on scientific principles that must be followed to ensure control of a hazard. Operational limits need to be set tighter than the critical limits. To ensure a process is capable, the operational limits must take into account both the critical limits and process variation.

Principle 4: Establish Monitoring Procedures

Monitoring involves collecting, recording, and analysis of process data. It has several functions in the food-processing operation. The first function is to ensure that a critical limit has not been exceeded. When this happens, the processor can be assured that the food does not contain a hazard. Next, monitoring allows the processor to determine if there is a trend indicating a potential loss of control of the process. The processor can thus take appropriate actions before a process deviation occurs. If a process deviation occurs, monitoring allows the processor to isolate the portion of a lot that may contain a hazard, for either further analysis or proper disposition. Finally, monitoring provides documentation that is an essential part of the verification process.

Principle 5: Establish Corrective Action

Problems or deviations will occur in many manufacturing processes.[3] When a deviation occurs, the company must take corrective action. The FDA and USDA have stated that a corrective actions elicits the following responses: (1) Identify and eliminate the cause of the deviation; (2) respond to the CCP to bring the process back into control; (3) take measures to prevent the reoccurrence of the problem; (4) take actions to ensure that no unsafe or adulterated food enters commerce; (5) determine whether the HACCP plan must be modified to prevent reoccurrence of the deviation; and (6) document the corrective action. Corrective actions must be addressed in the HACCP plan. At a minimum, the HACCP plan should specify who is responsible for the corrective action, what must be done when the problem or deviation occurs, and what records must be maintained when the action is taken (NACMCF 1997).

Principle 6: Establish a Verification Plan

Verification is used to answer the following three questions:[4]

1. Is the HACCP plan working?

2. Is the HACCP plan valid? This question is answered by using a science-based review of the rationale used to develop the HACCP plan.

3. Is the HACCP plan relevant for the operation?

Verification is further subdivided into two parts: verification of compliance and validation.[5] There are two major types of validation:

1. Initial validation, which is done after the completion of the HACCP plan. The objective is to ensure that the plan is valid in controlling biological, chemical, and physical hazards and that the plan can be implemented as written.

2. Revalidation, which is done after changes are made to a process that could affect the hazard analysis or the HACCP plan. FSIS and FDA require that revalidation be done at a minimum of once in 12 months. The objective is to determine if the HACCP plan is current and effective. Compliance verification is done on a periodic basis to determine if the HACCP system complies with the HACCP plan. These activities include ongoing verification of the HACCP activities to ensure that the HACCP plan is functioning effectively and a comprehensive review of the HACCP plan.

Principle 7: Establish Record Keeping and Documentation Procedures

Records provide evidence that the plan was carried out as intended. The NACMCF recommends that the following types of records be generated and maintained (NACMCF 1997):

- Summary of the hazard analysis, including the rationale for determining hazards and control measures

- The HACCP plan, including:
  - A list of the HACCP team and assigned responsibilities
  - A description of the food, its distribution, and its intended use and consumer
  - A verified flow diagram

- HACCP plan summary table, including:
  - Steps in the process that are CCPs, including hazard(s) of concern and critical limits
  - Monitoring, including activity, procedure, and frequency
  - Corrective actions, including activity, procedure, and frequency
  - Verification procedures and schedule, including activity, procedure, and frequency
  - Record keeping procedures, including activity, procedure, and frequency

- Documentation that supports the HACCP plan, such as validation of records use and consumer information

- Records to support daily operational results

APPLICATION

HACCP is becoming the recognized method to develop a food safety management system in the United States and other countries. This has been accomplished through both voluntary and regulatory compliance. Larger food-processing companies in the United States have done more to voluntarily implement HACCP than have smaller food-processing firms. Part of this voluntary compliance has been achieved by customers in the supply chain when they require their suppliers to implement HACCP. Since the mid-1990s, U.S. regulatory agencies have started the process to incorporate HACCP into food-processing regulations. Currently, FSIS requires that federally regulated meat and poultry processing establishments have an approved HACCP plan. In addition, the FDA has implemented HACCP rules in the seafood industry and in the fruit and vegetable juice industry. Differences exist between the NACMCF definition of HACCP and the regulatory definition of HACCP. These differences are in part attributed to the need for regulatory agencies to develop a HACCP system that can be implemented by all sizes of food processors and can be audited for regulatory compliance. The federal regulations define the minimum aspects of the application of HACCP in the food-processing industry.

Regulatory agencies have developed models for the implementation of HACCP. These models are very conservative and were intended for training purposes. The most effective HACCP systems are those that were custom developed for specific food-processing operations.

President Clinton initiated a national food safety strategic plan (United States Department of Agriculture 2001). Part of this strategy uses the concept of food safety from farm to table. HACCP plays an important role in achieving this strategy. The strategy includes the implementation of good agricultural practices on the farm to further reduce food safety risks in the U.S. food supply. In addition, it takes the principles of HACCP to the table, both in the home and the food service establishments. In response to this need, the National Restaurant Association developed the ServeSafe program to teach food service employees the correct methods to handle food, reducing the risk of food-borne disease.

COMPARISON OF HACCP TO ISO

A precise comparison between HACCP and ISO 9001 is difficult because the two standards have different scopes, forms, and applications. The difference in forms can be attributed to the histories of the standards and differences between the international organizations that are managing the standards. HACCP evolved in the commercial food-processing industry in the United States. The U.S. food-processing industry separates food quality issues from food safety issues. This is done because of the regulatory environment. The FDA and FSIS rules do not regulate the quality of the food; they focus on ensuring that the public has safe, wholesome, and properly labeled food. Consequently, agency officials have limited authority when conducting regulatory activities, including audits. For example, the FDA has limited authority in reviewing processing records in a commercial food-processing company. Most quality records cannot be reviewed without a search warrant. Thus, most food-processing companies typically implement separate systems for managing product quality issues and food safety issues. In addition, food safety is currently managed with a zero-tolerance attitude. Either the food is safe, or the food is not safe.

The following compares HACCP with ISO 9001. Comparisons of HACCP will be made to the ISO 9001:2000 process model. There has been a lot of discussion that HACCP is not a complete food safety management system. The objective of this section is to compare the requirements of HACCP and ISO 9001:2000 to show that HACCP is a complete food safety management system. There are some differences between the two standards, however, these differences can be attributed to the fact that two different standards organizations developed the standards, and that the standards have different scopes. (See chapter 2 for a discussion of the process approach of ISO 9001.) The U.S. definition of HACCP was used for this comparison (NACMCF 1997).

- *Process based.* HACCP has used a process-based model since the publication of the 1988 standard.

- *Continual improvement.* HACCP requires food-processing companies to reevaluate and determine if the current food safety management system is adequate. Input into the review includes evaluating the scientific literature for emerging food safety concerns and determining if similar products are linked to food-borne disease outbreaks.

- *Management responsibility.* HACCP requires top management commitment. In addition, a HACCP coordinator is appointed to oversee the development and maintenance of the food safety management system. The HACCP plan is developed by a cross-functional team. The HACCP plan and HACCP activities must be documented.

- *Resource management.* The HACCP team must be provided with the appropriate training and resources to develop and implement the HACCP plan. Personnel working in a HACCP environment must have the appropriate training and education. The company must maintain the proper environment (prerequisite areas) for the safe production of food.

- *Product realization.* The HACCP standard describes a systematic and defined method to develop the HACCP plan. This plan must be implemented and validated. Corrective actions must be taken when a problem or deviation occurs. At a minimum, the corrective action procedure must define the following: what must be done to the product that has been affected by the deviation, what actions must be taken to prevent unsafe or adulterated product from entering into commerce, and what actions must be taken to prevent reoccurrence of the deviation. HACCP stresses process monitoring and control of processes rather than reliance on end-product inspection.

- *Monitoring and analysis.* HACCP requires the determination of CCPs and critical limits. Critical limits must be monitored to determine if a process parameter has been exceeded, causing a process deviation. In addition, the critical-limit data should be monitored to determine if adverse trends are occurring, so action can be taken before a process deviation occurs. Period verification must be conducted to ensure that the plan is being followed. An annual validation must be conducted to ensure adequacy of the food safety management system. The need for calibration is defined as part of the validation activities.

• *Link to the customer.* During the development of the HACCP plan, the HACCP team must describe the food, its intended use, and the distribution system. In addition, the team needs to determine if any customer group has special sensitivities to a potential food hazard.

HACCP and ISO 9001 have different emphases, resulting from their different evolutions and the applications of the standards. The differences are most notable in the 2000 version of ISO 9001, which has a process approach and a strong management component, control of records, and a calibration requirement. HACCP focuses on a system to manage food safety. Thus, HACCP includes a strong method to identify hazards that are specific for the food and processing conditions and a method to control the process. In addition, HACCP has a strong component on process verification. Verification ensures that the HACCP plan is both current and effective to keep pace with the rapidly evolving knowledge of biological hazards. Microorganisms that were once thought to be innocuous are being identified as pathogens. When this occurs, HACCP plans must be revalidated to ensure the safety of the food supply chain.

FUTURE OF HACCP

HACCP is constantly evolving. Codex is incorporating the concept of risk analysis/management to a greater degree into HACCP and is developing the concept of food safety objectives, or FSOs (Codex 2001). The objective is to move away from the concept that food is either safe or not safe toward the concept that there is a need to reduce or minimize the risk to an acceptable level. This goal can be achieved using the following process:

• *Risk assessment.* Risk assessment involves defining the parameters and the scope of the problem. Next, the hazard must be identified. The potential hazards must be qualitatively characterized and assessed quantitatively to obtain a dose response value. The impact of the hazard on human health can then be determined.

• *Risk characterization.* Risk characterization provides an estimate of the adverse effect likely to occur in the target population.

• *Risk management.* Risk management defines safe food-handling procedures, process controls, and standards and criteria for the food product. This then allows for the development of food safety objectives (FSOs), which are performance criteria that link assessment and effective measures to the control of identified risk

• *Risk communication.* Risk communication involves reporting the results of the hazard analysis and assessment to the public. The information is communicated to either the target population or target group that is at risk from the hazard.

FSOs will be a key link in the WTO issue of ensuring the equivalence of regulatory food safety programs between nations involved in international trade. FSOs become the required outcome to ensure that the food is safe. It also communicates the level of control necessary to achieve an acceptable level of protection.

In addition, HACCP may be transforming from a food safety management system to a product safety management system. The Center for Radiological Health (FDA 2001) of the FDA is conducting a study to determine the advantages of using HACCP principles for (1) premarket submissions, product, and process review; (2) identifying and correcting product and process problems for devices currently on the market; and (3) streamlining inspections.

SUMMARY

There is a greater consumer awareness of food safety. In addition, the global marketplace has brought new challenges to ensure that food does not contain biological, chemical, or physical hazards. As a result of these issues, many food-processing companies are implementing HACCP as a method to ensure the production and distribution of a safe food product. In response to marketplace demands, the Codex Alimentarius Commission defined HACCP as the international standard for a food safety management system. HACCP has a proven record as a food safety management system that food processors can use to decrease the risk of producing food that can cause a food-borne disease outbreak. HACCP may be changing from a food safety management system to a product safety management system. Currently, the FDA is conducting a pilot study to determine the effectiveness of using HACCP to improve the quality and safety of medical devices. One can readily see the complementary nature of HAACP and ISO 9001:2000 and how ISO processes are an essential dimension of the prerequisite programs that are the foundation of the House of Food Safety.

ENDNOTES

1. An in-depth discussion of HACCP is presented in Food, Drug, and Cosmetic Division of the American Society for Quality (FD&C), *Certified Quality Auditors HACCP Handbook* (Milwaukee: ASQ Quality Press, 2001).
2. A critical control point (CCP) is defined as any step at which control can be applied to prevent the occurence of or reduce the occurence of a biological, chemical, or physical hazard to an acceptable level. In contrast, a control point (CP) is any step where a biological, chemical, or physical factor can be controlled.
3. A deviation is the failure to meet a critical limit.
4. Verification is defined as "those activities, other than monitoring, that determine the validity of the HACCP plan and that the system is operating according to the plan" (NACMCF 1997).
5. Validation is defined as that element of verification focused on collecting and evaluating scientific and technical information to determine if the HACCP plan, when properly implemented, will effectively control the hazards (NACMCF 1997).

REFERENCES

Codex Alimentarius Commission (Codex). Rome, Italy, 2001. www.codexalimentarius.net.
Food and Drug Administration (FDA). *Hazard Analysis Critical Control Points: A Study for Medical Device Manufacturing.* Washington, DC, 2001. www.fda.gov/cdrh/gmp/feasibilitystud.html.
Food, Drug, and Cosmetic Division of the American Society for Quality (FD&C). *Certified Quality Auditors' HACCP Handbook.* Milwaukee: ASQ Quality Press, 2001.
National Advisory Committee on the Microbiological Criteria for Foods (NACMCF). *Guidelines for the Application of HACCP Principles.* U.S. Food and Drug Administration. 14 August 1997.

National Research Council (NRC). *An Evaluation of the Role of Microbiological Criteria for Food and Food Ingredients.* Washington, DC: National Academy Press, 1985a.

National Research Council (NRC). *Meat and Poultry Inspection.* Washington, DC: National Academy Press, 1985b.

Stevenson, K. E., and D. T. Bernard. *HACCP: A Systematic Approach to Food Safety.* 3rd ed. Washington, DC: Food Processors Institute, 1999.

Surak, J. G. "Quality and Commercial Food Processing." *Quality Progress* 32, no. 2 (1999): 25.

United States Department of Agriculture. *Gateway to Food Safety Information.* Washington, DC, 2001. www.foodsafety.gov.

World Trade Organization (WTO). Brussels, Belgium, 2001. www.wto.org.

Chapter 54

ISO 9001:2000 and Healthcare

M. M. "Mickey" Christensen
TQM Systems, Baton Rouge, Louisiana

ISO 9000 has been around since 1987, but only since about 1996 has it received any serious attention by healthcare personnel in the United States. In recent years, however, more people in healthcare have recognized the value-added aspects that ISO 9000 provided to the manufacturing sector. A few healthcare "mavericks" ventured out and implemented a system compliant to ISO 9000 with the anticipation that it would help them improve efficiency and effectiveness in the provision of care. The critics had a number of concerns about how ISO 9000 would work in healthcare. Most of the wording in the 1994 version of the standard appeared to be oriented more to manufacturing than to service functions. In ISO 9001:2000 the wording has been changed to be more applicable to service functions. As discussed later, terminology has been one of the bridges to cross during implementation of the standard.

GENERIC VERSUS PRESCRIPTIVE CRITERIA

One concern was that the ISO 9000:1994 standards were too generic and did not have specific requirements for healthcare. Other types of accreditations or certifications commonly used in healthcare are prescriptive and primarily focus on the clinical tasks performed in the organization. ISO 9001:2000 is still generic and allows the organization to define the processes and procedures used, but it focuses on the whole process and not just tasks. ISO 9001:2000 defines process as "any activity that receives inputs and converts them to outputs." It further states that the output from one process often will directly form the input to the next or linked process.

ISO 9001:2000 specifies not how the process is actually performed but how it is identified and managed within the organization and the *interactions* between the significant processes. They should be monitored and managed to meet customer and regulatory requirements. Continuous improvement of the management system is also a requirement.

Some of the prescriptive criteria of other accreditation and/or certification agencies tend to be very specific to healthcare and in some cases specific to the discipline involved in clinical functions. This can be a good source of information about industry standard ways, methods, or protocols of providing a service or patient care. When prescriptive criteria are implemented, some people may say "I'll do what I am told, nothing more and nothing less." But for most providers, their desire to provide excellent care will win out.

ISO 9001 Is Complementary to Other Systems

ISO 9001:2000 is very complementary to other systems. Considering the pressures that healthcare organizations are under to implement "systems," it is no wonder they are struggling to determine what it is that governments, payers, patients, doctors, communities, accrediting and/or certifying agencies, and investors want. In the United States, a compliance system is necessary. Federal agencies want safety and environmental compliance. Payers want quality control on billing and coding, as evidenced by the fraud and abuse issues raised by the federal government. Doctors want efficient and effective support services to assist them in providing care. The community wants providers to be able to handle any situation that occurs. As one hospital CEO stated, "The patient would like a system that does not cause pain, is free (or at a minimum cost), does not inconvenience them, and will help them live forever." Where do healthcare organizations turn for a "one size fits all" system? Compromises have to be made for some of the expectations, as with any system. Not all patients will leave feeling better than they did when they came in, and not all procedures performed will be painless or free. Safety and environmental issues may never get to zero incidents. ISO 9001:2000 allows for building a management system that allows other influences to become part of the system. A number of hospitals are accredited by a healthcare organization and are also certified to ISO 9002:1994. ISO 9001:2000 is a basic quality management system, and other quality tools and criteria can be referenced or adopted as part of the system. Criteria established by the Joint Commission on Accreditation of Healthcare Organizations (JCAHO) or the American Osteopathic Association (AOA) mesh well with ISO 9001:2000. An organization could also build on ISO 9001:2000 by using the Malcolm Baldrige National Quality Award criteria or ISO 9004:2000. A new ISO document designated an Industry Workshop Agreement (IWA) was approved by the International Organization for Standardization. A document recently approved for publication, IWA-1, is based on ISO 9004:2000 and has healthcare wording and examples added. This document is a guide for process improvement and is not for third-party certification, nor is it intended as a guide to implement ISO 9001:2000. Meeting accrediting agency criteria, as well as regulatory criteria, can be incorporated in the ISO 9001:2000–compliant system. The office of inspector general of the U.S. government has published a model set of compliance criteria. The American Health

Lawyers Association has also published a model compliance manual. Both these criteria models fit like a glove with an ISO 9001:2000 system.

BASIC QUALITY MANAGEMENT SYSTEM

One issue that comes up as organizations investigate ISO 9000 is that it is a basic quality management system and not a total system. Most people would not argue that point. However, the ISO 9000 system allows the incorporation and institutionalization of almost any other quality tool or criteria. Organizations that just use some of the quality tools without an infrastructure risk losing the gains in time. As they say in thermodynamics, entropy is when energy evolves to the lowest level. This happens to management systems, too. They evolve to the lowest level unless managed well. Institutionalizing any change that improves the system is a must for retaining the gain. ISO 9001:2000 provides that structure to build on at whatever rate the organization chooses.

Many healthcare organizations that have pursued compliance to ISO 9001:1994 or ISO 9002:1994 have taken from four to 18 months to implement the changes to their organizations. The rate at which they implement the ISO 9000 system depends on resources and other incentives, such as contractual reasons. The benefits usually begin to show up in a few months as the overall quality management system comes together. Some of the benefits are listed in the following section.

BENEFITS TO HEALTHCARE ORGANIZATIONS

The following are benefits that healthcare organizations certified to ISO 9000 have mentioned.

Fewer Problems with Vendors and Supplies

One hospital's food service was having problems with vegetables that were not fresh being delivered at their busy time before lunch. By monitoring this vendor, presenting the data to the vendor's management, and requesting corrective action, the problem was solved. Savings resulted from fewer returns, people freed up during busy time, and fresher vegetables being delivered.

A hospital pharmacy was having late deliveries from a wholesale drug supplier. Collecting data and presenting this to the supplier along with a request to correct the problem was the first step. After several attempts to get satisfactory deliveries, the pharmacy changed vendors. The new vendor provided more service for the same cost and made almost no late deliveries. Costs decreased because "hot-shot" drug deliveries from other suppliers were no longer needed to cover late orders. Also, the pharmacy was able to order online, giving them access to the supplier's inventory and immediate notice if they had to make alternate selections to get on-time deliveries.

Another hospital has documented significant savings each year by working with vendors to correct problems so they don't happen again. When problems do reoccur, vendors are quicker to respond to and solve them. As a result, the hospital has reduced the time its staff spends dealing with problems, has saved money by not having to rush replacement shipments, and has decreased its inventory somewhat because it is assured of timely deliveries. Savings were also documented when the materials management personnel reviewed how many dollars were tied up in different types of sutures. The doctors were asked by administration if they could agree on a smaller number of sutures. The doctors agreed, and a number of sutures were taken off the inventory list.

Better Control of All Documentation, Especially Forms and Checklists

Many forms are originated by employees who have good intentions. These forms take on a life of their own and multiply. Sometimes no one knows who generated the form or if it was ever approved for use in the organization. Changes to forms are made and different versions start appearing. At some point, employees don't always know which one is correct. By controlling all documentation, organizations have found that employees have the right information to do their jobs correctly the first time. The result is less wasted resources by employees looking for information, doing tasks incorrectly, and then having to redo them, or just not getting the jobs done. Savings have occurred from reducing the number of forms and checklists through control. Departments have very similar but different forms for collecting the same information. By combining, condensing, merging, or discarding forms, they have seen a reduction in numbers and inventory.

Regularly Updated Policies and Procedures

Before ISO 9000 implementation, many policy and procedures would get reviewed every few years and were then put back on the shelf. With the ISO 9000 system requiring internal audits of the system and the registrar certification agency coming in for surveillance audits at least once a year, the policy and procedures are kept up-to-date. They are used for training new (to the job or organization) employees because they are current. Also, many redundant policies and procedures have been combined, so the total number has decreased. This also provides more consistency across departments, especially when personnel are moved to handle fluctuating workloads. The benefits have been reduced supply costs, less wasted time, more consistent outcomes and results from work processes, and fewer adverse events because of better familiarity with the procedures, forms, and checklists.

Improved Problem Solving through Corrective and/or Preventive Actions

In an ISO 9000–compliant system, someone must check a corrective action for effectiveness in solving the problem and management must review the results. Consequently, information is shared across department boundaries. This process has reduced the resources wasted on recurring problems and/or has prevented problems in other departments. This is the closure step in the typical PDCA (plan, do, check, act) cycle mentioned in various books on quality management systems.

Better Communication with Patients

Through better communication early in the healthcare process, some problems have been eliminated because the patient has a better understanding of what is going to happen. Also, getting more information from the patient during the assessment or evaluation has led to better diagnoses. Many patients do not include herbs, food supplements, and over-the-counter drugs in their responses to the question "What medications are you taking?" They tend to think prescription medications. By changing the nurse's assessment form in one hospital, nurses are now asking questions to cover most of the things patients might be allergic to or substances they may be taking.

Uniform Procedures

An issue came up in one hospital when it was discovered there were multiple procedures for starting an IV. Almost every department had their own version. None was wrong, just different. When nurses were moved to accommodate high patient populations in different wards, they had to follow different procedures. Confusion and the potential for adverse outcomes were possible. Reducing this to one procedure hospitalwide minimized the confusion. Document control with authoritative review prior to use helped identify similar situations.

Improved Control and Calibration of Measuring Equipment

Inspection, test, and measurement equipment in hospitals have varying degrees of preventive maintenance (PM) and calibrations (or calibration checks). When calibrations are done, it often is not clear that the calibration devices are traceable to a national or international standard. One hospital that was certified to ISO 9002 in 1999 discovered 4072 devices were used for inspection, test, or measurement. Of these, 3259 were identified as being used for clinical reasons and should have been calibrated to verify results. At that time, only 436 were under a PM and calibration program. They found 783 devices that had to have new procedures created for the PM and calibration. The rest had procedures, but they were not being followed when it came to scheduling the PM and calibration. Records were not always there to verify the PM or calibration was done. In a similar situation in another health center, the calibration of blood pressure manometers was checked against a certified manometer. Of 32 devices checked, 6 had problems so serious that they could not be calibrated. The remaining ones were checked at various pressures. The average reading was 153 mmhg (millimeters of mercury) (high = 158, low = 148) when the certified reading was 150 mmhg. When the certified unit was reading 101 mmhg, the average was 106 mmhg. When eight doctors and nurses measured the same pressure with the same device, the variance was 15 mmhg. The benefits from this total exercise were better maintained devices that are more trustworthy because they give more consistent readings, better diagnoses, and better outcomes.

Improved Relationships among Departments

During the implementation of ISO 9001:2000, the organization will have to take a process approach to managing the system. This approach starts at a higher level than the task approach. The patient sees the process from admitting to discharge. From that perspective, departmental interfacing gets more attention and the work flows much better after reviewing and documenting the process. Monitoring the process for effectiveness then identifies discrepancies or nonconformities. ISO 9001 requires prompt corrective action that is effective in solving problems. Hand-offs of patients, supplies, paperwork, data, lab specimens, and so on then occur with fewer mistakes.

Frequently Asked Questions

Does ISO 9000 certification carry deemed status with the U.S. Government payer HCFA (Health Care Finance Administration)? No, it does not have deemed status, but most if not all state health agencies have deemed status. *Deemed status* is simply defined as HCFA acceptance of a survey or audit that determines compliance with their conditions of participation. If an organization meets HCFA's conditions of participation, it is eligible to receive payment for Medicare services. ISO 9000 is not healthcare specific, so it is hard to envision deemed status as part of an ISO 9001 audit result.

I provide a service and this standard talks about product, so how does this fit what I do? The answer to this question is simple and requires looking at the definition of *product* in ISO 9000. ISO 9000 defines *product* as the result of a process, and *process* is defined as set of interrelated activities that transform inputs into outputs. A note provided with the definition of *product* states that there are four generic product categories—services, software, hardware, and processed materials—and many products comprise elements of more than one generic category. Another note states "Service is the result of at least one activity necessarily performed at the interface between the supplier and the customer and is generally intangible." These activities could include the delivery of information in the context of knowledge transmission, creation of ambience for the customer, or an activity performed on customer supplied intangible product.

How do you deal with nonemployee personnel (credentialed and privileged professionals) performing services in your organization for the patient? Many doctors and other privileged professionals are not employees of a hospital but are an integral part in the provision of care. These people are considered both customers and vendors. They are customers because the hospital wants to encourage these professionals to practice at the facility. At the same time, these professionals are vendors providing services for the hospital. The determination is transaction or activity sensitive as to which way the arrow is pointing, toward the customer or vendor.

ISO 9000'S SHORT HEALTHCARE HISTORY

The history of ISO 9000 with U.S. healthcare is not very long. In 1987, right after the standard was first published, I got involved with manufacturing plants seeking certification. This was driven by the European Economic Community (now the European Union) settling on ISO 9000 as an acceptable quality standard for goods crossing country boundaries. Since I worked for an international manufacturing company, we were asked by customers to comply with ISO 9000 criteria. Not much effort was focused on service functions, much less healthcare services.

Then, as customers were beginning to understand what the benefits of ISO 9000 were, some service organizations were beginning to get certified.

In 1992 the first review and revisions of the standard were begun, and two years later the 1994 version of ISO 9001 was published. In 1997 the second review and revisions were begun. Due to some major format changes to the standard, it took until December of 2000 to publish the current version of the ISO 9000.

CERTIFICATION "FIRSTS"

The first healthcare facility providing care to patients that was certified in the United States was the Cleveland Center for Joint Reconstruction in Cleveland, Ohio, which received ISO 9001:1994 certification in May 1995. The Difco Laboratories of Livonia, Michigan, was certified in March 1994 and is listed here as the first healthcare organization certified in the United States. However, the Cleveland clinic is recognized as the first facility that provides care directly to patients to be certified.

The first acute care hospital certified in the United States was American Legion Hospital located in Crowley, Louisiana. It was certified to ISO 9002:1994 in February 1996.

OTHER CERTIFICATIONS

Two physician practices were certified to ISO 9001 in October 1996: Drs. Mark Figgie and Richard Laskin, orthopedic surgeons in New York City. The dental practice of Dr. Robin Conway was certified to ISO 9002 in Toronto, Canada, in May 1997.

The Occupational Medicine and Environmental Health Services for the National Aeronautics and Space Administration/Lyndon B. Johnson Space Center in Houston, Texas, was certified to ISO 9002 in December 1997. NASA views certification as a positive step for vendors and has certified its own facilities.

The second and third acute care hospitals certified were Pulaski Community Hospital in Pulaski, Virginia, certified to ISO 9002 in April 1998; and Lane Memorial Hospital in Zachary, Louisiana, certified in May 1999.

Wayne Regional Orthopaedics in Sodus, New York, was certified in December 1998.

The Henry Ford Health System, Department of Occupational Health and Industrial Rehabilitation in Detroit, Michigan, was certified to ISO 9002 in July 1999.

Two more hospitals were certified to ISO 9002-1994: Memorial Medical Center in Ludington, Michigan, and St. Charles Medical Center in Bend, Oregon. Then in December 2000, the largest hospital system to date in the United States, Freeman Health System of Joplin, Missouri, was certified to ISO 9002:1994.

There are currently (as of the end of the fourth quarter 2000 publication of the registry) 45 organizations listed under the Standard Industry Classification for healthcare organizations in North America. There are several others that may have been certified and not published yet. There are also about five or six other hospitals that are preparing for certification. A number of others have made contact to investigate the use of ISO 9000.

STORY OF THE FIRST ACUTE CARE HOSPITAL

Having had the pleasure of consulting with American Legion Hospital, I can give some account of its story. The certification was influenced by a friend of the CEO who had his manufacturing company certified about a year earlier than the hospital. The owner of the manufacturing company told the CEO of the hospital he should look into ISO 9000 because it had helped his company.

Reasons for Certification

The CEO of the hospital had discontinued their accreditation with one of the accrediting agencies about two years before and decided he needed some form of third-party review to verify that the hospital was still providing quality care to the community. On the recommendation of his friend, he investigated ISO 9000. After some investigation, he made the decision to get certified to ISO 9002:1994. Once the decision was made, he wanted to be certified in four months. That is a very tight time frame to get the job done, but he and his staff were committed and made it. I do not recommend that tight a time line. A year is more proper for hospitals that are running lean to begin with under current economic conditions.

The system implemented has proven to be good for the hospital. They have documented that in one year, after they were certified, they saved over $100,000 in the purchasing function alone. This was done in a hospital of about 130 beds. Recently the local newspaper ran an article stating that this small, rural hospital has more full time equivalent (FTE) people per adjusted discharge and is less expensive than hospitals of similar size in the Gulf Coast region of the Volunteer Hospital Association. This hospital also has a nosocomial infection rate that is about five percent of the national average.

Things That Worked

The following worked well at American Legion Hospital:

- Management was committed to make it happen and provided the resources
- Employees "bought in" very quickly because they saw it as a way to help them
- Individuals doing the work helped write the procedures
- Middle management was trained to understand ISO 9002 requirements
- A simple "crosswalk" to relate healthcare examples and ISO 9002 criteria was developed
- The registrar was willing to learn and work extra time since this was a first for them

Things That Did Not Work Well

The following did not work too well at American Legion Hospital:

- Time was too tight and a fair amount of overtime was used
- Documentation control was difficult to establish quickly

- An interpretation for ISO 9002 in hospitals was not available
- Developing what the "product" was and who was the customer was difficult
- Understanding the "work process" versus task concept took time to understand
- There were not any examples to follow in this country
- Consultant and staff not speaking the same language (terminology, see below) was a barrier

TERMINOLOGY

As mentioned above, the terminology of healthcare was a barrier to implementing ISO 9002:1994 standard. The word *product* elicited comments like, "We don't make widgets, we provide service." Developing a simple crosswalk helped when the staff was struggling with reviewing and revising policies and procedures. As the consultant, I had trouble communicating with the staff at times because I came from a manufacturing background and am an engineer by training. To help me out, the staff gave me the following crosswalk to healthcare terminology. I want to share it with you because it helped me out tremendously.

Artery—The study of paintings

Barium—What you do when CPR fails

Cesarean section—A district in Rome

Colic—A sheep dog

Coma—Punctuation mark

Congenital—Friendly

Dilate—To live longer

G.I. series—Baseball game between soldiers

Medical staff—Doctors cane

Morbid—Higher offer

Nitrate—Lower than the day rate

Outpatient—Person who has fainted

Protein—In favor of young people

Secretion—Hiding everything

Serology—The study of English Knights

Tumor—An extra pair

Tablet—A small table

Urine—The opposite of "your out"

Varicose veins—Veins too close together

X-rays—Sunlight for adults only

CURRENT SITUATION

Interest in ISO 9000 in Healthcare

Currently, there is considerable interest in ISO 9000 by international healthcare personnel. For example, Australia and New Zealand have a national standard: AS/NZS 3905.14:1998, *Quality system guidelines, part 14, Guide to AS/NZS ISO 9001, 9002 and 9003 for health services.* Several other countries have also adopted this standard, which was written around the 1994 version of ISO 9001, 9002, and 9003. It appears this document will be updated to ISO 9001:2000.

Documents Relating to ISO 9000 in Healthcare

Not to slight any organization but in the interest of space only a few examples of other documents relating to ISO 9000 in healthcare are presented here. The National Committee for Clinical Laboratory Standards published GP26-P, built on the model provided by ISO for quality standards in business and industry. The National Standards Authority of Ireland published its ISO 9000 Quality for Health Services application of ISO 9002 in a hospital environment.

Additional ISO 9000 interest is identified through some of the following early stage efforts from around the world. Interest in ISO 9000 in healthcare is expressed in a 24 March 2000 letter to a number of healthcare organizations from a member of the European Co-operation for Accreditation (EA). The letter states EA's intention to start a process to develop an internationally accepted application document based on ISO 9000 for the healthcare sector. EA invited members to a meeting on 11 September 2000, where future work and meetings were also planned. Interest in providing assistance for the use of ISO 9000 in healthcare is evidenced by a working group, in cooperation with the Swiss accreditation body (SAS), who drafted a document that could be used as a basis and an aid to interpreting the international standards ISO 9001 and ISO 9002 for bodies providing healthcare. This document is undergoing review as part of the development. Another document in development for the use of ISO 9000 in healthcare is identified in a report by "The Working Party Quality Care in Hospitals, The Subcommittee of Co-ordination" of HOPE, which is the standing committee of the hospitals of the European Union. HOPE is actively pursuing raising the awareness of the use of ISO 9000 in healthcare organizations.

Many other documents have been written or are in development. Some coordination of these should be undertaken by an international organization to minimize confusion about the way ISO 9000 is implemented in healthcare.

INSTITUTE OF MEDICINE IMPACTS

In late 1999 the U.S. Institute of Medicine (IOM) published a document, titled "To Err Is Human, Building a Safer Health System," that has stirred up activities in many arenas. Bills are being submitted to Congress to deal with medical errors, and several organizations are studying methods to reduce medical errors. In addition, the American Society for Quality, Health Care Division and the Society for Healthcare Epidemiology of America have formed a special interest group to propose solutions for reducing medical errors. Payers are looking harder at the outcomes and results and attempting to correlate costs and errors, and administrators and owners of healthcare organizations are reviewing their policies and procedures more closely. Whether the data in the IOM document are valid or not, many people are reacting.

The IOM published a second document, "Crossing the Quality Chasm, A New Health System for the 21st Century," in March 2001, recommending six aims for improving the healthcare system. The six aims for improvement as mentioned in the report are: *safe*, avoiding injuries; *effective*, providing services based on scientific knowledge; *patient-centered*, providing care that respects and is responsive to patient's needs; *timely*, reducing waits and delays; *efficient*, avoiding wasted resources; and *equitable*, providing care that does not vary in quality. Any activities related to this report are still in the development stage.

Industry Interest

In reaction to the IOM documents, along with escalating costs, some of the largest payers for healthcare are investigating how the quality, efficiency, and effectiveness of healthcare can be improved. The Automotive Industry Action Group (AIAG), for example, is concerned about the well-being of its employees and the cost of providing healthcare benefits. If errors do occur as often as the first IOM document implies, one large automobile manufacturer probably loses several employees a week due to errors. This is of real concern to AIAG, and in the interest of preserving employees, it cowrote IWA-1, the previously mentioned document designed to help healthcare organizations improve their quality management systems.

WHAT IS THE FUTURE?

As shown by the documents mentioned above, there is a lot of international interest in improving healthcare and reducing errors. Many organizations around the world consider ISO 9000 to be a tool to help them accomplish that goal and are actively working on ways to aid its implementation. Several conferences have been devoted solely to ISO 9000 in healthcare or at least have had a track devoted to the subject. This will probably be the situation for some time, because people want to learn more about ISO 9000 in healthcare. Plans are already in the works for several conferences in the United States, where healthcare quality management is the focus.

ONE PERSON'S OPINION

Where will this go? One person's opinion is that this interest in ISO 9000 will go on for a number of years until it becomes old hat and something new and exciting comes along. People in healthcare know there are areas that need improving (just like any other business) and have been awakened to pursue changes with vigor. The U.S. Navy has certified its Bureau of Medicine and Surgery to ISO 9001:1994. The navy plans to certify more of its healthcare facilities as time and resources allow and has started the process with one of its hospitals. This could lead to all military healthcare facilities getting certified in time.

If payers begin investigating the quality, efficiency, and effectiveness of healthcare, they will keep the pressure on healthcare to continually improve. Healthcare has provided good care in many cases currently and in the past, but there is always room for improvement. As one administrator opined, we were in the habit of using healthcare standards as a way to compare ourselves. It was not a surprise that almost always the results were favorable to us. As we looked outside to compare ourselves to others, we questioned whether our standards measured much of anything that was relevant to quality management.

Interest is growing, both in the United States and internationally, to find a system that allows organizations to continue to function but still forces management and personnel to review and improve what they are doing. ISO 9000 does that, and in fact it is one of the criteria to be met.

Chapter 55

Medical Devices

Leslie S. Schnoll
Gliatech, Cleveland, Ohio

For more than 20 years, good manufacturing practice (GMP) regulations for medical devices have been based on a quality systems approach for assuring regulatory agencies that medical devices were manufactured in compliance with their approved designs. These regulations were left to the discretion of the applicable national regulatory agency [for example, the U.S. Food and Drug Administration (FDA)] and, as a rule, bore no resemblance to regulations in other countries. In the United States, the Medical Device Amendments of 1976 revised and extended the device requirements of the 1938 Federal Food, Drug, and Cosmetic Act. As a result of these changes, the FDA acquired significant new authority to ensure safe and effective devices. This activity resulted in the promulgation of the current GMP regulations (21 CFR 820). The Federal Food, Drug, and Cosmetic Act was subsequently amended by the Safe Medical Devices Act of 1990 and the Medical Device Amendments of 1992. These amendments enhanced pre- and postmarket controls and provided for additional regulatory authority. Added authority was given to the FDA to incorporate design control requirements with the GMP regulations.

Medical devices include several thousand healthcare products, from simple articles (such as thermometers, tongue depressors, and heating pads) to complex lifesaving equipment (such as heart pacemakers and kidney dialysis machines). Under the Federal Food, Drug, and Cosmetic Act, a *device* is defined as "any healthcare product that does not achieve its principle intended purposes by chemical action in or on the body or by being metabolized." The term *devices* also includes components, parts, or accessories of devices; diagnostic aids such as reagents, antibiotic sensitivity discs, and test kits for in vitro diagnosis of disease (for example, diabetes); and other conditions (for example, pregnancy).

THE QUALITY SYSTEM REGULATION (21 CFR 820)

The original medical device GMP regulations were drastically revised in 1996 and renamed the Quality System Regulation. The revision was modeled after the 1994 revision of the ISO 9001 international standard, *Quality systems, Model for quality assurance in design, development, production, installation, and servicing*. ISO 9001:1994 was not adopted verbatim because of copyright issues and the agency's belief that the quality management system standard was insufficient to adequately protect public health. In its revision of GMP regulations, the FDA "strengthened" several areas with which they had concerns and gave the agency access, for the first time, to design information—an area long considered to be the cause of product recalls due to inadequate design and development activities.

Entire books have been written on the specifics of the various regulatory requirements, including the Quality System Regulation. Readers who are interested in obtaining more detailed information on regulations and regulatory compliance should refer to one of many publications on the subject (for example, *The Regulatory Compliance Almanac: A Guide to Good Manufacturing, Clinical, and Laboratory Practices*, written by Les Schnoll). Kim Trautman of the FDA has also compiled an excellent book (*The FDA and Worldwide Quality System Requirements Guidebook for Medical Devices*) that deals specifically with the medical device regulations and their mapping to the ISO 9001:1994 elements. Figure 55.1 shows a brief summary of the structure of the regulation:

As mentioned previously, the FDA did not adopt ISO 9001:1994 verbatim because the agency did not feel that the international quality standard sufficiently defined several requirements critical to regulating medical devices. The specific "additions" made to enhance the quality system regulation are described in the following sections. The requirement is listed under the ISO 9001:1994 elements, and the applicable section of 21 CFR 820 is identified in parentheses:

4.2   Quality System

- The organization has established and maintains a quality system that is appropriate for the specific medical device(s) designed or manufactured (820.5).

4.4   Design Control

- Procedures have been developed and implemented to ensure that the device design is correctly translated into production specifications (820.30).
- Design history files have been established and are being maintained for each type of device and contain or reference the records necessary to demonstrate that the design was developed in accordance with the approved design plan (820.30).

4.5   Document and Data Control

- There are procedures for making changes to documents. Such changes are approved and documented by a designated individual and include the approval date and the date the change becomes effective (820.40).

Part 820 Quality System Regulation
(April 1, 2001, Revision)

Subpart A—General Provisions
820.1 Scope
820.3 Definitions
820.5 Quality system

Subpart B—Quality System Requirements
820.20 Management responsibility
820.22 Quality audit
820.25 Personnel

Subpart C—Design Controls
820.30 Design controls

Subpart D—Document Controls
820.40 Document controls

Subpart E—Purchasing Controls
820.50 Purchasing controls

Subpart F—Identification and Traceability
820.60 Identification
820.65 Traceability

Subpart G—Production and Process Controls
820.70 Production and process controls
820.72 Inspection, measuring, and test equipment
820.75 Process validation

Subpart H—Acceptance Activities
820.80 Receiving, in-process, and finished device acceptance
820.86 Acceptance status

Subpart I—Nonconforming Product
820.90 Nonconforming product

Subpart J—Corrective and Preventive Action
820.100 Corrective and preventive action

Subpart K—Labeling and Packaging Control
820.120 Device labeling
820.130 Device packaging

Subpart L—Handling, Storage, Distribution, and Installation
820.140 Handling
820.150 Storage
820.160 Distribution
820.170 Installation

Figure 55.1 Part 820 quality system regulation.

Subpart M—Records
820.180   General requirements
820.181   Device master record
820.184   Device history record
820.186   Quality system record
820.198   Complaint files

Subpart N—Servicing
820.200   Servicing

Subpart O—Statistical Techniques
820.250   Statistical techniques

Figure 55.1   Part 820 quality system regulation *(continued)*.

4.8   Product Identification and Traceability

- Labels and labeling are stored and maintained in a manner that provides proper identification and that is designed to prevent mix-ups (820.120).

4.9   Process Control

- The principles and practices specified by the FDA in its *Guideline on General Principles of Process Validation* (May 1987) are being addressed (820.75).

- Written cleaning procedures and schedules are adequate to meet manufacturing process specifications (820.70).

- There are procedures designed to prevent contamination of equipment, components, or finished devices by rodenticides, insecticides, fungicides, fumigants, hazardous substances, and other cleaning and sanitizing substances. Adherence to such procedures is documented (820.70).

- Where eating, drinking, and smoking by personnel could have an adverse effect on a device's fitness for use, such practices are limited to designated areas (820.70).

- Sewage, trash, by-products, chemical effluents, and other refuse are disposed of in a timely, safe, and sanitary manner (820.70).

- Equipment used in the manufacturing process is appropriately designed, constructed, placed, and installed to facilitate maintenance, adjustment, and cleaning (820.70).

- Manufacturing materials are subsequently removed from the device or limited to a specified amount that does not adversely affect the device's fitness for use (820.70).

- There are written procedures describing any processing controls necessary to ensure conformance to specifications (820.70).

- Any approved change in the manufacturing process is communicated to appropriate personnel in a timely manner (820.70).

- Written manufacturing specifications and processing procedures are established, implemented, and controlled to ensure that the device conforms to its original design or any approved changes in that design (820.70).

- Labels are designed, printed, and applied to remain legible during the customary conditions of processing, storage, handling, distribution, and use (820.120).

- Prior to the implementation of any labeling or packaging operation, there is an inspection of the area where the operation is to occur by a designated individual to ensure that devices and labeling materials from prior operations do not remain in the labeling or packaging area (820.120).

- Any prior devices and labeling materials found in the area are destroyed, disposed of, or returned to storage prior to the onset of a new or different labeling or packaging operation (820.120).

- When automated data processing is used for manufacturing or quality assurance purposes, there are documented procedures designed to prevent inaccurate data input, output, and programming errors (820.70).

4.10 Inspection and Testing

- Labels and other labeling are not released to inventory until a designated individual has proofread samples of the labeling for accuracy (820.120).

- Labeling materials issued for devices are examined for identity and accuracy (820.120).

4.13 Control of Nonconforming Product

- The requirements of the Medical Device Reporting legislation (Title 21 of the U.S. Code of Federal Regulations, Part 803) are being met (820.198).

- Any complaint involving the possible failure of a device to meet any of its performance specifications is reviewed, evaluated, and investigated (820.198).

- Any complaint pertaining to injury, death, or any hazard to safety is immediately reviewed, evaluated, and investigated by a designated individual and is maintained in a separate portion of the complaint files (820.198).

4.15 Handling, Storage, Packaging, Preservation, and Delivery

- Distribution records include or refer to the location of the following:
  - The name and address of the initial consignee
  - The identification and quantity of devices shipped
  - The date shipped
  - Any control numbers used

4.16   Control of Quality Records

- Records are retained for a period of time equivalent to the design and expected life of the device but not less than two years from the date of release for commercial distribution (820.180).
- The device master record includes or refers to the location of the following information (820.181):
  - Device specifications, including appropriate drawings, composition, formulation, and component specifications
  - Production process specifications, including the appropriate equipment specifications, production methods, production procedures, and production environmental specifications
  - Quality assurance procedures and specifications, including quality assurance checks and equipment
  - Packaging and labeling specifications, including appropriate methods and processes used
  - Installation, maintenance, and servicing procedures and methods
- A Device History Record is maintained to demonstrate that the device is manufactured in accordance with the Device Master Record (820.184).
- The Device History Record includes or refers to the location of the dates of the following information (820.184):
  - The dates of manufacture
  - The quantity manufactured
  - The quantity released for distribution
  - The acceptance records, which demonstrate that the device is manufactured in accordance with the Device Master Record
  - The primary identification label and labeling used for each production unit
  - Any device identification and control numbers used
- A quality system record is maintained and includes or refers to the location of procedures and documentation of activities that are not specific to a particular type of device (820.186).
- Complaint files are maintained and include or refer to the location of the following (820.198):
  - The name of the device
  - The date of receipt of the complaint
  - Any device identification and control numbers used
  - Name, address, and phone number of complainant
  - Nature and details of complaint
  - The dates and results of the investigation
  - Any corrective actions taken
  - Response to complainant

4.18   Training

- Employees are made aware of device defects that may occur from the improper performance of their specific jobs (820.25).
- Personnel performing verification activities are made aware of defects and errors likely to be encountered as part of their functions (820.25).

4.19   Servicing

- Service reports are analyzed by appropriate statistical methodology (820.200).
- If a service report indicates a reportable incident, the incident is reported in compliance with the requirements of 21 CFR 803 (820.200).

INSPECTIONS AND ENFORCEMENT

The FDA is using several methods to inspect medical device manufacturers, including the following:

- *Inspections by the "old" method.* This involves a complete inspection in accordance with the full requirements of the GMP regulations.
- *Inspections using the quality system inspection technique (QSIT):* The result of a reengineering effort within the FDA, the QSIT was implemented in 1999 to develop an inspection program that covered the quality system regulation and should result in more focused and efficient inspections. The QSIT should help FDA investigators focus on key manufacturing and quality areas at the manufacturer during inspections to determine their state of compliance with the Quality System Regulation. This effort should lead to increased compliance with the Quality System Regulation and, therefore, improved medical device product quality. Several aspects of this program were derived from the Global Harmonization Task Force's document titled *Guidelines for Regulatory Auditing of Quality Systems of Medical Device Manufacturers.* The QSIT method consists of seven interwoven subsystems:
  - Management
  - Corrective and preventive action
  - Design controls
  - Production and process controls
  - Material controls
  - Equipment and facility controls
  - Records, documents, and change controls

More information is given in the official FDA publication, *Guide to Inspections of Quality Systems* (August 1999).

- *Inspections using the pilot hazard analysis and critical control points (HACCP) program.* The result of another reengineering program, the HACCP is a systematic approach to the identification, evaluation, and control of hazards. It has achieved international recognition as a management tool for developing a rational and scientifically based system to minimize impact from manufacturing processes on product safety and performance (that is, risk management). Key elements of an HACCP system consist of the following:

- Identification of all potential hazards to safety and performance and corresponding preventive measures necessary for their control, for both the *product* and the *process*
- Identification and effective control of these hazards at critical steps during the manufacturing process, called critical control points
- Documentation that this control is maintained on a continuing basis

The main advantage offered by an HACCP system is that defects compromising the safety and performance of medical devices can be identified more quickly at specific points in the manufacturing process. This means corrective actions can be taken sooner. By contrast, traditional control systems rely more on the government and industry to conduct infrequent inspections and end-product testing to identify defects. The HACCP process contains seven principles:

- Conducting hazard analysis
- Determining critical control points
- Establishing critical limits
- Monitoring critical control points
- Establishing corrective actions
- Establishing verification procedures
- Establishing record keeping and documentation procedures

Regardless of the inspection method used by the investigator, the FDA has several options available to bring the manufacturer of a medical device into compliance with the quality system regulation (as well as other regulations). These include, in increasing order of severity:

- *FDA-initiated or voluntary recalls.* A recall is a regulatory action that enables the FDA to remove a hazardous, potentially hazardous, or misbranded product from the marketplace. A recall is also used to convey additional information to the user concerning the safe use of the product. Either the FDA or the manufacturer can initiate a recall.

- *Civil monetary penalties.* Section 303(f) of the Safe Medical Device Act authorizes the FDA, after an appropriate hearing to assess noncompliance with the Medical Device Reporting legislation, to impose a civil monetary penalty for a violation of the Federal Food, Drug, and Cosmetic Act. The monetary penalty cannot exceed $15,000 for each violation or $1,000,000 for all violations adjudicated in a single proceeding. In determining the amount of the civil penalty, the FDA will take into account the nature, circumstances, extent, and gravity of the violations; the violator's ability to pay; the effect on the violator's ability to continue to do business; and any history of prior violations.

- *Warning letters.* The FDA may issue written communications to a manufacturer, indicating that the manufacturer will incur more severe sanctions if the violations described in the letter are not corrected within a specified period. Warning letters are issued to cause prompt correction of violations that pose a hazard to health or that involve economic deception.

• *Seizure.* A seizure is a court action against a specific quantity of product that enables the FDA to remove the product from commercial channels. After seizure, no one can tamper with the product without the permission of the court. The court usually gives the manufacturer of the seized merchandise 30 days to decide on a course of action. If the manufacturer wishes to take no action, the court recommends disposal of the products.

If the manufacturer decides to contest the government's charges, the court schedules the case for trial. The manufacturer also has the option to request the permission of the court to bring the product into compliance with all applicable laws and is required to provide a bond (security deposit) to ensure that they will perform the actions ordered by the court. The manufacturer must also pay for any FDA supervision of activities to bring the product into compliance.

• *Citation.* A citation is a formal warning to a manufacturer of the FDA's intent to prosecute the manufacturer if violations of the Food, Drug, and Cosmetic Act are not corrected promptly. A citation provides the manufacturer an opportunity to convince the FDA not to prosecute.

• *Injunction.* An injunction is a civil action filed by the FDA against an individual or a company. Usually, the FDA will file an injunction to stop a company from continuing to manufacture, package, or distribute products that are in violation of the law.

• *Prosecution.* Prosecution is a criminal action filed by the FDA against a company or an individual, involving alleged violation of the law. There have been several landmark U.S. Supreme Court decisions that verify the authority of the FDA to successfully prosecute for violations of the Food, Drug, and Cosmetic Act.

As an added "bonus," if a manufacturer or its employees knowingly make false statements or knowingly falsify any records or reports requested or required by the FDA, the manufacturer is subject to prosecution by the Department of Justice under Section 18 of the United States Code.

TECHNICAL COMMITTEE 210

The ISO Technical Committee 210 (ISO/TC 210) is charged with developing quality management systems for medical devices. The committee comprises representatives from more than 30 countries and is currently chaired by the United Kingdom Medical Devices Agency. Official representatives include industry and regulatory agencies that serve as national experts.

The committee is structured into three working groups (WGs):

• WG 1 is responsible for the application of quality systems to medical devices
• WG 2 is responsible for general aspects stemming from the application of quality principles to medical devices
• WG 3 is responsible for symbols and nomenclature for medical devices

There is also a joint working group (IEC/SC 62A) that is working on the application of risk management to medical devices.

In 1996, ISO/TC 210 approved and published ISO 13485 and ISO 13488, which deal, respectively, with applying ISO 9001:1994 and ISO 9002:1994 to medical devices. (These two documents are the "successors" to EN 46001 and EN 46002.) In 1996, the committee published ISO 14969, a document providing guidance on the implementation of ISO 13485 and ISO 13488.

With the release of the 2000 revisions to the ISO 9000 series standards, upon which ISO 13485, ISO 13488, and ISO 14969 are no longer based, a tremendous amount of discussion and work has been thrust on ISO/TC 210. Current activities include the following:

• *Revision of ISO 13485 to a standard compatible with ISO 9001:2000.* The revision is planned to be titled *Quality management systems—Medical devices—System requirements for regulatory purposes.* The committee draft is scheduled to be released for vote and comment by April 2002 and will result in a stand-alone international standard that follows the format of ISO 9001:2000 but, where necessary and with clear rationale, establishes requirements specific to the medical device sector. Modifications to the langage in ISO 9001:2000 include those for "customer satisfaction" and "continual improvement." Even though members of ISO/TC 210 had significant influence and participated in the drafting committee of ISO/TC 176 for ISO 9001:2000, including the chairman of ISO/TC 210 and the convenor of WG 1, the official stance of ISO/TC 210 is that these concepts may be appropriate for a business excellence model but do not belong in a baseline quality system standard that will become a regulation in many countries. The early draft of a revised ISO 13485 omits any reference to customer satisfaction and continual improvement. This is a major departure from ISO 9001:2000. It is not clear how this controversy will be resolved over the next few years as ISO 13485 is finalized.

• *Revision of ISO 13488.* This is a standard for those device firms that do not require design controls, such as distributors and some original equipment manufacturers (OEMs). The current standard is a reference document for the soon-to-be-obsolete ISO 9002, and there is a great deal of discussion within the technical committee about whether ISO 13488 should be retained as a stand-alone document equivalent to ISO 9002:1994 for medical devices, or to scrap the standard.

• *Revision of ISO 14969 from a guidance standard to a stand-alone technical specification document.* A technical specification requires less consensus review than a standard. This change will allow for more latitude in drafting the document, but it will also mean that the final document will have less "standing" than its predecesor. The revised ISO 14969 will be significantly longer and more comprehensive than the current document, will provide guidance on refining quality systems, and will suggest alternatives. There will also be expanded text on design control, process validation, and quality planning. The document is expected to be issued in 2004.

• *The approval and publication of ISO 14971:2000.* Titled *Medical devices—Application of risk management to medical devices,* this is a dual ISO/IEC standard. The document was also adopted by CEN and CENELEC.

ISO 13485 AND ISO 13488

ISO 13485:1996 and ISO 13488:1996 provide particular requirements applicable to medical devices that are more specific than the general requirements contained in

ISO 9001 and ISO 9002. Many organizations are unclear about these documents; one would be wise to understand the following:

- These documents are *not* the same as ISO 9001 or ISO 9002. All requirements of ISO 9001 and ISO 9002 are included; ISO 13485/88 contains additional requirements for medical devices.
- These documents are *not* the same as the European Union Medical Device Directive.
- These documents are *not* the same as GMP regulations or the quality system regulation.
- These documents include *additional* requirements for medical devices beyond the requirements of an ISO 9001/ISO 9002 registered system.

The additional requirements included in ISO 13485/ISO 13488 are as follows:

For All Medical Devices

4.2 Quality System

- The supplier shall establish and document the specified requirements.
- The supplier must establish and maintain a file containing documents defining the product specifications, including complete manufacturing and quality assurance specifications for each type or model of medical device, or referring to the location of this information.

4.4 Design Control

- The supplier shall identify requirements that are related to the safety of the medical device and shall include such requirements as design input data.
- The supplier must document and maintain records of all design verification activities, including those involving clinical investigations.

4.5 Document and Data Control

- The supplier shall define the period for which at least one copy of an obsolete document shall be retained. This period shall ensure that specifications to which medical devices have been manufactured are available for at least the lifetime of the medical device, as defined by the supplier.

4.6 Purchasing

- To the extent required by the particular traceability requirements, the supplier shall retain copies of relevant purchasing documents.

4.8 Product Identification and Traceability

- The supplier shall establish and maintain procedures to ensure that medical devices received for refurbishing are identified and distinguished at all times from normal production.
- The supplier must establish, document, and maintain traceability procedures. The procedures must define the extent of traceability and facilitate corrective action.

4.9 Process Control

- *Personnel.* The supplier must establish, document, and maintain requirements for the health, cleanliness, and clothing of personnel if contact between such personnel and product or environment could adversely affect product quality.

- *Environmental control in manufacturing.* For medical devices that are supplied sterile *or* that are supplied nonsterile and intended for sterilization before use *or* where the microbiological and/or particulate cleanliness or other environmental conditions are of significance in their manufacture, the supplier must establish and document requirements for the environment to which the product is exposed. If appropriate, the environmental conditions must be controlled and/or monitored.

- *Cleanliness of the product.* The supplier must establish, document, and maintain requirements for cleanliness of the product if the product is cleaned by the supplier prior to sterilization and/or its use, *or* the product is supplied nonsterile to be subjected to a cleaning process prior to sterilization and/or its use, *or* the product is supplied to be used nonsterile and its cleanliness is of significance in use, *or* process agents are to be removed from the product during manufacture. If appropriate, any product cleaned prior to sterilization and/or its use will not be subject to the preceding personnel or environmental control requirements.

- *Maintenance.* The supplier must establish and document requirements for maintenance activities when such activities can affect product quality. Records of such maintenance shall be documented.

- *Installation.* If appropriate, the supplier must establish and document instructions and acceptance criteria for installing and checking the medical device. Records of installation and checking performed by the supplier or authorized representative must be retained. If the contract allows installation other than by the supplier or authorized representative, the supplier must provide the purchaser with written instructions for installation and checking.

- *Special processes.* The supplier must ensure that the quality records of special processes identify the work instruction used, the date that the special process was performed, and the identity of the operator of the special process.

4.13 Control of Nonconforming Product

- The supplier shall ensure that nonconforming product is accepted by concession (waiver) only if regulatory requirements are met. The identity of the person authorizing the concession shall be recorded.

- If the product needs to be reworked, the supplier must document the rework in a work instruction that has undergone the same authorization and approval procedure as the original work instruction.

4.14 Corrective and Preventive Action

- The supplier shall establish and maintain a documented feedback system to provide early warning of quality problems and for input into the corrective action system. If ISO 13485 is used for compliance with regulatory requirements for postmarketing surveillance, the surveillance shall form part of the feedback system.

- All feedback information, including reported customer complaints and returned product, must be documented, investigated, interpreted, collated, and communicated in accordance with defined procedures by a designated person. If any customer complaint is not followed by corrective action, the reason must be recorded.

- The supplier must maintain records of all complaint investigations. When the investigation determines that the activities at remote premises played a part in the complaint, a copy of the report must be sent to those premises. If ISO 13485 is used for compliance with regulatory requirements, the supplier must establish, document, and maintain procedures to notify the regulatory authority of those incidents that meet the reporting criteria.

- The supplier must establish, document, and maintain procedures for issuing advisory notices and recalling medical devices. These procedures must be capable of being implemented at any time.

4.15 Handling, Storage, Packaging, Preservation, and Delivery

- The supplier shall establish and maintain documented procedures for the control of the product with a limited shelf life or requiring special storage conditions. Such special storage conditions shall be controlled and recorded.

- If appropriate, special provisions must be made for handling used product to prevent contamination of other product, the manufacturing environment, or personnel.

4.16 Control of Quality Records

- The supplier shall retain quality records for a period at least equivalent to the lifetime of the medical device defined by the supplier, but not less than two years from the date of shipment from the supplier.

- The supplier must establish and maintain a record for each batch of medical devices that provides traceability to the extent required by element 4.8 and identifies the quality manufactured and quantity released to distribution. The batch record must be verified and authorized.

4.18 Training

- The supplier shall ensure that all personnel who are required to work under special environmental conditions or who perform special processes are appropriately trained or supervised by a trained person.

4.20 Statistical Techniquies

- The supplier shall establish and maintain procedures to ensure that sampling methods are regularly reviewed in the light of the occurrence of nonconforming product, quality audit reports, feedback information, and other appropriate considerations.

For Sterile Medical Devices

In addition to the requirements previously listed for all medical devices, the following supplementary provisions apply:

4.9 Process Control

- The supplier shall subject the medical device to a validated sterilization process and record all the control parameters of the sterilization process.

4.15 Handling, Storage, Packaging, Preservation, and Delivery

- The supplier shall establish and maintain procedures to ensure that the medical device is presented in a container that maintains the medical device's sterility, except for those medical devices for which only the inner surfaces are sterile and the medical device is such that the sterility of the inner surfaces is maintained.

- The supplier must establish and maintain procedures to ensure that the medical device can be presented in an aseptic manner, if its use so requires.

- The supplier must establish and maintain procedures to ensure that the package—or medical device, if only the inner surface is sterile—clearly reveals that it has been opened.

For Active Implantable Medical Devices

In addition to the requirements previously listed for all medical devices, the following supplementary provisions apply:

4.8 Product Identification and Traceability

- The extent of the traceability shall include all components and materials used and records of the environmental conditions that could cause the medical device not to satisfy its specified requirements.

4.10 Inspection and Testing

- The supplier shall record the identity of personnel performing any inspection or testing.

4.15 Handling, Storage, Packaging, Preservation, and Delivery

- The supplier shall record the identity of persons who perform the final labeling operation.

- The supplier must ensure that the name and address of the shipping package consignee is included in the quality records.

- The supplier must require that any authorized representative maintain records of medical device distribution and that such records be available for inspection.

For Implantable Medical Devices

In addition to the requirements previously listed for all medical devices, the following supplementary provisions apply:

4.8   Product Identification and Traceability

- The extent of the traceability shall include all components and materials used and records of the environmental conditions that could cause the medical device not to satisfy its specified requirements.

4.10   Inspection and Testing

- The supplier shall record the identity of personnel performing any inspection or testing.

4.15   Handling, Storage, Packaging, Preservation, and Delivery

- The supplier shall record the identity of persons who perform the final labeling operation.
- The supplier must ensure that the name and address of the shipping package consignee is included in the quality records.
- The supplier must require that any authorized representative maintain records of medical device distribution and that such records be available for inspection.

The Medical Device Directive and CE Marking

In 1985, the European Union implemented a new approach to the development of standards for products it considered critical to public health and safety. These new standards, which became known as directives, provide generic guidelines for those product lines and establish the basis for global marketing into the 21st century. These documents cover approximately 14 product lines from toys to electromagnetic equipment, heavy construction equipment, and medical devices. Their implementation dates range from having been completely effective during 1993 to being transitioned through 2007. Compliance with these directives is required to do business in Western Europe and the requirements contained in them are regulatory in nature.

Overview of the Medical Device Directive

One of the more important requirements that manufacturers of medical devices must meet is the European Union Medical Device Directive (MDD). The directive, officially known as 93/42/EEC, is one of the more frustrating mandates to decipher and understand, making compliance more difficult than it has to be. The MDD consists of 23 articles, 12 annexes, and 18 classification rules.

The MDD is intended to harmonize standards that benefit manufacturers, users, and patients and to define the requirements for the clinical testing, design, manufacture, testing/inspection, marketing, installation, and service of medical devices sold within the European Union. All medical devices sold within the European Union had to conform to this directive by 14 June 1998; however, this date was the end of the phase-in period, which began on 1 January 1995.

The Medical Device Directive in General

The main purpose of the MDD is to harmonize national controls to allow free movement of medical devices throughout the European Union and the European Free Trade Association while ensuring that all devices within the European Union are reasonably safe to use. Devices covered under the directive range from bandages and tongue depressors to knee and hip joints, X-ray equipment, and CAT scanners. The directive covers most medical devices other than active implantable medical devices and in-vitro diagnostic products; there is currently another directive (90/385/EEC) for active implantable medical devices and one (98/79/EC) for in-vitro diagnostics.

Another directive that may come into play for manufacturers of medical devices is the Electromedical Equipment Directive (84/549/EEC). There are also European Union good manufacturing practices, good laboratory practices, and the Human Medicinal Products and Risk Assessment Directives.

The Medical Device Directive does the following:

- Specifies essential requirements that must be met before any device can be placed on the market
- Introduces controls covering the safety, performance, specification, design, manufacture, and packaging of devices
- Specifies requirements for assessment of clinical investigative protocols and the evaluation of any adverse incidents that occur
- Introduces a system of classification of devices and applies a level of control that is matched to the degree of risk inherent in the device
- Empowers a competent authority to identify and designate notified bodies that check and verify that devices meet the relevant essential requirements

Intervention by a notified body is not required by manufacturers of Class I medical devices unless the devices are placed on the market in a sterile condition or have a measuring function. However, manufacturers (or their authorized representatives) of Class I devices must perform the following tasks:

- Review the device classification rules to confirm that their products fall within Class I (per Annex IX of the MDD)
- Check that their products meet all applicable essential requirements (per Annex I of the MDD);
- Prepare relevant technical documentation
- Prepare the EC Declaration of Conformity before applying the CE mark on their products
- Implement and maintain corrective action and vigilance procedures
- Obtain notified body approval for sterility or metrology aspects of their devices (if applicable)

- Make all relevant documentation available for inspection on the request of the competent authority
- Register with the competent authority
- Notify the competent authority, in advance, of any proposals to perform a clinical investigation to demonstrate safety and performance

Technical Documentation

The manufacturer of the medical device must retain technical documentation that demonstrates the conformity of the product with the requirements of the MDD. This technical documentation must be prepared prior to preparing the EC Declaration of Conformity and must be made available for review by the notified body and/or the competent authority.

The technical documentation should be prepared following review of the essential requirements in Annex I and must cover all of the following:

- *A general description of the product,* including any variations (for example, names, sizes, model numbers)
- *Raw material and component documentation,* including specifications (as applicable) of raw materials, drawings of components, quality control procedures, and/or master patterns
- *Intermediate product and subassembly documentation,* including specifications, appropriate drawings and master patterns, circuits, formulations, manufacturing procedures and methods, and quality control procedures
- *Final product documentation,* including specifications, appropriate drawings and master patterns, circuits, formulations, manufacturing procedures and methods, and quality control procedures
- *Packaging and labeling documentation,* including copies of all labels and instructions for use
- *Design verification,* including the results of qualification tests and design calculations relevant to the intended use of the product, including connections to other devices to allow the device to operate as intended
- *Risk analysis,* which substantiates that any risks associated with the use of the product are compatible with a high level of protection of health and safety and are weighed against the benefits to the patient and user
- *Compliance with the essential requirements and harmonized standards,* including a list of relevant harmonized standards that have been applied to the product
- *Clinical data,* if appropriate
- *Records* of manufacturing, inspection, and testing to show compliance with documented procedures and specifications

The Medical Device Directive Articles

Manufacturers of medical devices (or their authorized representatives) must be able to demonstrate compliance with the (applicable) articles and annexes of the MDD. Twenty-three articles comprise the portion of the MDD that sets the stage for compliance. Basically, this first section of the MDD provides definitions, defines the rules and routes for compliance, describes the classification of medical devices, and points the reader to the second section of the document—the 12 annexes that provide the detail. Readers interested in greater detail should refer to a publication on regulatory compliance.

The 23 articles in the MDD are as follows:

- Article 1: Definitions and Scope
- Article 2: Placing on the Market and Putting into Service
- Article 3: Essential Requirements
- Article 4: Free Movement, Devices Intended for Special Purposes
- Article 5: Reference to Standards
- Article 6: Committee of Standards and Technical Regulations
- Article 7: Committee on Medical Devices
- Article 8: Safeguard Clause
- Article 9: Classification
- Article 10: Information on Incidents Occurring Following Placing of Devices on the Market
- Article 11: Conformity Assessment Procedures
- Article 12: Particular Procedure for Systems and Procedure Packs
- Article 13: Decisions with Regard to Classification, Derogation Clause
- Article 14: Registration of Persons Responsible for Placing Devices on the Market
- Article 15: Clinical Investigation
- Article 16: Notified Bodies
- Article 17: CE Marking
- Article 18: Wrongly Affixed CE Marking
- Article 19: Decision in Respect of Refusal or Restriction
- Article 20: Confidentiality
- Article 21: Repeal and Amendment of Directives
- Article 22: Implementation and Transitional Provisions
- Article 23: Adoption of the Medical Device Directive

The Medical Device Directive Annexes

The 12 annexes of the MDD define the compliance requirements, providing the rules, requirements, and assessment routes that must be followed. As written, the annexes are complex and wordy and do not describe a clear path to reach the finish line—CE marking of the medical device.

The 12 annexes of the MDD are as follows:

- Annex I: The Essential Requirements
- Annex II: EC Declaration of Conformity (Full Quality Assurance System)
- Annex III: EC Type-Examination

- Annex IV: EC Verification
- Annex V: EC Declaration of Conformity (Production Quality Assurance)
- Annex VI: EC Declaration of Conformity (Product Quality Assurance)
- Annex VII: EC Declaration of Conformity
- Annex VIII: Statement Concerning Devices for Special Purposes
- Annex IX: Classification Criteria Rules
- Annex X: Clinical Evaluation
- Annex XI: Criteria to be Met for the Designation of Notified Bodies
- Annex XII: CE Marking of Conformity

Medical Device Classification

It would be extremely difficult to justify subjecting all medical devices to the same rigorous conformity assessment procedures. Rationally, a graduated system of controls corresponding to potential hazards would be more appropriate. Such classifications should be based on potential hazards related to the intended use of the device, possible failures, duration of contact with the human body, degree of invasiveness, and whether the device provides a local or systemic effect on the body.

Article 9 of the MDD places all medical devices into one of four classes of increasing risk to the patient according to their properties, function, and intended purpose. The level of control is proportionate to the level of risk to ensure protection of patient health. This device classification is as follows:

- *Class I devices* pose a low risk to the patient and, except for sterile products or measuring devices, can be self-certified by the manufacturer. Generally, these devices do not come into contact or interact with the body.
- *Class IIa devices* pose a medium risk and may require an assessed quality system. Generally, these devices are invasive in their interaction with the human body, but the methods of invasion are limited to natural body orifices. The category may also include therapeutic devices used in diagnosis or in wound management.
- *Class IIb devices* pose a medium risk and may require an assessed quality system; third-party certification is required. Generally, these devices are either partially or totally implantable within the human body and may modify the biological or chemical composition of body fluids.
- *Class III devices* pose a high risk and require design/clinical trial reviews, product certification, and an assessed quality system. All third-party product and system certification must be conducted by a European notified body (or designee through formal agreement). Generally, these devices affect the functioning of vital organs and/or life support systems.

Annex IX of the MDD includes three general sections: definitions, implementing rules, and the classification rules. The five implementing rules and 18 classification rules require interpretation to be understood, because there are no clear-cut categories.

Medical device classification is affected by the period that the device performs its intended function. Three definitions for duration of use apply to the directive:

transient (normally intended for continuous use for less than 60 minutes), *short term* (normally intended for continuous use for less than 30 days), and *long term* (normally intended for continuous use for more than 30 days).

Implementing Rules. There are five implementing rules that set the ground rules for further classification of the medical device:

- *Rule 1* states that the classification must be based on the intended purpose of the medical device.

- *Rule 2* states that if the medical device is intended to be used in conjunction with another medical device, the classification of each device must be separately performed. This rule also states that accessories are classified separately from any devices.

- *Rule 3* states that if any software is used to drive or influence a medical device, that software automatically falls in the same classification as the medical device.

- *Rule 4* states that if the medical device is not intended to be used solely or principally in a specific area of the body, the medical device must be classified on the basis of its most critical use.

- *Rule 5* states that if several rules apply to the same medical device, the most stringent rules resulting in the higher classification of the medical devices must be applied.

Classification Rules. There are 18 classification rules used to place the medical device into one of the four device classifications previously described. These are probably the least clearly defined rules and require a great deal of experience to understand and correctly apply; interpretation may become an issue due to the language used.

- *Rule 1:* All noninvasive devices are in Class I, unless one of the other following rules applies.

- *Rule 2:* All noninvasive devices intended for channeling or storing blood, body liquids or tissues, liquids, or gases for the purpose of eventual infusion, administration, or introduction into the body are in Class IIa if they are connected to an active medical device of Class IIa or higher intended for use in storing or channeling blood or other body fluids or for storing organs, parts of organs, or body tissues. In all other cases, they are in Class I.

- *Rule 3:* All noninvasive devices intended for modifying the biological or chemical composition of blood, other body liquids, or other liquids intended for infusion into the body are in Class IIb. If the treatment consists of filtration, centrifugation, or exchanges of gas or heat, the devices are in Class IIa.

- *Rule 4:* All noninvasive devices that come into contact with injured skin are in Class I if they are intended to be used as mechanical barriers, for compression, or for absorption of exudates. They are in Class IIb if they are intended to be used primarily with wounds that have breached the dermis and can only heal by secondary intent. They are in Class IIa in all other cases, including devices principally intended to manage the microenvironment of a wound.

- *Rule 5:* All invasive devices with respect to body orifices, other than devices that are surgically invasive and not intended for connection to an active medical device, are in Class I if they are intended for transient use. They are in Class IIa if they are intended for short-term use. If they are used in the oral cavity as far as the pharynx, in an ear canal up to the eardrum, or in a nasal cavity, they are in Class I. They are in Class IIb if they are intended for long-term use. If they are used in the oral cavity as far as the pharynx, in an ear canal up to the eardrum, or in a nasal cavity and are not likely to be absorbed by the mucus, they are in Class IIa. All invasive devices with respect to body orifices, other than surgically invasive devices, intended for connection to an active medical device in Class IIa or higher are in Class IIa.

- *Rule 6:* All surgically invasive devices intended for transient use are in Class IIa. If they are intended specifically to diagnose, monitor, or correct a defect of the heart or of the central circulatory system through direct contact with those parts of the body, they are in Class III. If they are reusable surgical instruments, they are in Class I. If they are intended to have a biological effect or to be wholly absorbed, they are in Class IIb. If they are intended to supply energy in the form of ionizing radiation, they are in Class IIb. If they are intended to administer medication by means of a delivery system in a manner that is potentially hazardous, taking account of the mode of application, they are in Class IIb.

- *Rule 7:* All surgically invasive devices intended for short-term use are in Class IIa. If they are intended either specifically to diagnose, monitor, or correct a defect of the heart or of the central circulatory system through direct contact with those parts of the body, they are in Class III. If they are intended specifically for use in direct contact with the central nervous system, they are in Class III. If they are intended to supply energy in the form of ionizing radiation, they are in Class IIb. If they are intended to have a biological effect or to be wholly absorbed, they are in Class III. If they are intended to undergo chemical change in the body, except if the devices are placed in the teeth or to administer medication, they are in Class IIb.

- *Rule 8:* All implantable devices and long-term surgically invasive devices are in Class IIb. If they are intended to be placed in the teeth, they are in Class IIa. If they are intended to be used in direct contact with the heart, the central circulatory system, or the central nervous system, they are in Class III. If they are intended to have a biological effect or to be wholly absorbed, they are in Class III. If they are intended to undergo chemical change in the body, except if the devices are placed in the teeth or to administer medication, they are in Class III.

- *Rule 9:* All active therapeutic devices intended to administer or exchange energy are in Class IIa. If their characteristics are such that they may administer or exchange energy to or from the human body in a potentially hazardous way, taking account of the nature, density, and site of application of the energy, they are in Class IIb. All active devices intended to control or monitor the performance of active therapeutic devices in Class IIb or intended to directly influence the performance of such devices are in Class IIb.

- *Rule 10:* Active devices intended for diagnosis are in Class IIa. If they are intended to supply energy that will be absorbed by the human body, except for devices used to illuminate the patient's body in the visible spectrum, they are in Class IIa. If they are intended to image in vivo distribution of radiopharmaceuticals, they are in Class IIa. If they are intended to allow direct diagnosis or monitoring of vital physiological processes, they are in Class IIa. If they are specifically intended to monitor vital physiological parameters where the nature of variability is such that it could result in immediate danger to the patient (for example, variation in cardiac performance, respiration, CNS activity), they are in Class IIb. Active devices intended to emit ionizing radiation and intended for diagnostic and therapeutic interventional radiology, including devices that control or monitor such devices or which directly influence their performance, are in Class IIb. Rule subtitle: "Active diagnostic devices."
- *Rule 11:* All active devices intended to administer and/or remove medicines, body liquids, or other substances to or from the body are in Class IIa. If this activity is performed in a manner that is potentially hazardous, taking into account the nature of the substances involved, the portion of the body concerned, and the mode of application, they are in Class IIb
- *Rule 12:* All other active devices are in Class I.
- *Rule 13:* All devices incorporating, as an integral part, a substance that, if used separately, can be considered to be a medicinal product and that is likely to act on the human body with action ancillary to that of the devices are in Class III.
- *Rule 14:* All devices used for contraception or the prevention of the transmission of sexually transmitted diseases are in Class IIb. If they are implantable or long-term invasive devices, they are in Class III.
- *Rule 15:* All devices intended specifically to be used for disinfecting, cleaning, rinsing, or hydrating contact lenses are in Class IIb. All devices intended specifically to be used for disinfecting medical devices are in Class IIa.
- *Rule 16:* Nonactive devices specifically intended for recording of X-ray diagnostic images are in Class IIa.
- *Rule 17:* All devices manufactured using animal tissues or derivatives rendered nonviable, except if they are intended to come into contact with intact skin only, are in Class III.
- *Rule 18:* Blood bags are in Class IIb.

Essential Requirements

The essential requirements (Annex I) are relatively straightforward and do not need significant interpretation. In some cases, compliance with other European Union directives may be required and are so defined in Annex I. It is important to reiterate that complying with the essential requirements is, well, essential! These are the *legal* requirements to place medical devices on the market in the European Union. As in other areas of the MDD, failure to comply can result in significant penalties to manufacturers or their authorized representatives.

Use of the CE Mark

The CE mark symbolizes conformity with all of the requirements and obligations incumbent on the manufacturer of the medical device relative to the product. The CE mark affixed to medical devices symbolizes the fact that the individual who has affixed or who is responsible for affixing the CE mark has verified that the product conforms to all of the European Union harmonization requirements that apply to the device and that the device has been assessed for compliance to the appropriate conformity assessment procedures. For any device subject to directives that concern other issues and require affixing the CE mark, there must be compliance to the requirements of those directives as well.

CE Mark Requirements

- The CE mark must consist of the initials CE, in the form shown in Figure 55.2. If the mark is reduced or enlarged, the proportions shown in Figure 55.2 must be met.
- For medical devices, the various components of the CE mark must have substantially the same vertical dimension, which may not be less than 5 millimeters. The minimum dimension may be waived for small devices.
- The CE mark must be affixed to the product or to its data plate. Where it is not possible or warranted due to the nature of the product, the CE mark must be affixed to the packaging (if any) and to any accompanying documents.
- The CE mark must be affixed visibly, legibly, and indelibly.
- The CE mark must be affixed at the end of the production control phase and must be followed by the identification number of the notified body.
- The CE mark and the identification number of the notified body *may* be followed by a pictogram or other mark indicating, for example, the category of use.
- The affixing of any other mark, sign, or indication that could deceive third parties as to the meaning and form of the CE mark is prohibited.
- A medical device may bear different marks (for example, indicating conformity with national or European standards or additional directives) if such marks do not cause confusion with the CE mark.

Figure 55.2 The CE mark.

- The CE mark must be affixed by the manufacturer or an authorized representative established within the European Union.

- Member states are authorized to take all required steps to exclude any possibility of confusion and to prevent abuse of the CE mark.

Notified Bodies

The MDD defines the criteria to be met for an organization to be designated as a notified body. A *notified body* is defined as "a government-sanctioned organization that can register and/or certify a quality system or product and determine that the system or products meets the European Union requirements." The notified body should not be confused with a registrar ("an accredited third party that evaluates an organization's [quality] system to verify compliance with the applicable requirements") or a competent authority ("the regulatory body within a member state that is charged with ensuring that the provisions of the Medical Device Directive are correctly implemented. As an example, for medical devices within the United Kingdom, the competent authority is the secretary of state for health acting through the Medical Devices Agency").

A notified body must comply with seven basic requirements, as follows:

- The notified body, its management, and assessment and verification staff cannot inspect any device for which they are the designer, manufacturer, supplier, installer, authorized representative, or user. They cannot be directly involved with the design, manufacture, marketing, or maintenance of the device or represent the parties involved with those activities.

- The notified body and its staff must perform its assessment and verification activities with professional integrity. Personnel must be competent in the field of medical devices and must be free from any pressures and inducements (particularly financial) that may influence their judgment or the results of the activities that they perform. If the notified body subcontracts specific tasks, it must ensure that the subcontractor meets the same provisions and criteria that must be met by the notified body.

- The notified body must be able to perform all activities in Annexes II through VI. It must have the necessary personnel, facilities, and equipment needed to properly perform the technical and administrative tasks entailed in assessment and verification activities.

- The notified body must have suitable training covering all assessment and verification activities for which it has been designated by the competent authority, satisfactory knowledge and experience in the products, standards, and applicable regulations for medical devices, and the ability to prepare and issue the necessary certificates, records, and reports to demonstrate that the activities have been performed.

- The notified body must be impartial, and fees cannot depend on the results of inspections or the number of inspections performed.

- The notified body must carry adequate insurance.
- Personnel of the notified body are required to maintain professional secrecy and confidentiality with respect to *all* information obtained during the course of their duties pursuant to the MDD.

The Active Implantable Medical Device Directive

One of the older requirements that manufacturers of active implantable medical devices must meet is the European Union Active Implantable Medical Device (AIMD) Directive, officially known as 90/385/EEC. Applicable medical devices sold within the European Union had to conform to this directive by 31 December 1994; however, this date was the end of the phase-in period, which began on 31 December 1992. Unfortunately, as the "oldest" of the directives relating to medical devices, the AIMD Directive is rather poorly written and is even more nebulous than the MDD. The document was amended on 22 July 1993, by directive 93/68/EEC. These amendments attempted to clarify the original document; unfortunately, the attempt was not very successful.

Seventeen articles of the AIMD Directive set the stage for compliance. This first section of the directive provides definitions, defines the rules and routes for compliance, describes the classification of medical devices, and points the reader to the second section of the document—the nine annexes that provide the detail. The AIMD Directive is an "unpolished" prequel to the MDD. The language is wordy and confusing and has little to add, in the author's opinion, over the content of the MDD. As such, it does not merit much comment.

Global Harmonization Task Force

The Global Harmonization Task Force (GHTF) was created in 1992 in response to the growing need for international harmonization in the regulation of medical devices. The five founding members of the organization were Australia, the United States, the European Union, Japan, and Canada. Chairmanship of the GHTF is rotated among the regulatory representatives of the five founding members; Australia's Therapeutic Goods Administration is the current chair.

The GHTF is a voluntary group of representatives from national medical device regulatory authorities and the regulated industry. Since its inception, the GHTF has comprised representatives from five founding members grouped into three geographical areas—Europe, Asia-Pacific, and North America—each of which actively regulates medical devices using their own regulatory framework.

The GHTF is charged with the following:

- Encouraging convergence in regulatory practices related to ensuring the safety, effectiveness/performance, and quality of medical devices
- Promoting technological innovation and facilitating international trade
- Publishing and disseminating harmonized guidance documents on basic regulatory practices

These documents, which are developed by four different GHTF study groups, can then be adopted by member national regulatory authorities.

The GHTF also serves as an information exchange forum through which countries with medical device regulatory systems under development can benefit from the experience of those with existing systems and/or pattern their practices on those of GHTF founding members.

GHTF Study Group 3 is responsible for examining existing quality system requirements in countries that have developed device regulatory systems and have identified areas suitable for harmonization. This group, currently chaired by the FDA, has been working closely with its counterpart in ISO/TC 210 (WG 1).

Study Group 3 has identified the same issues as those recognized by ISO/TC 210. Adoption of ISO 9000:2000 raised challenging issues for the medical device industry, forcing committee members to think "outside the box." Whatever the outcome, the goal is to maintain cooperation and harmonization among ISO/TC 176, ISO/TC 210, and the GHTF.

Chapter 56

Nuclear

Ron Cerzosimo
International Quality Consultants, Doylestown, Pennsylvania

INTRODUCTION

For almost five decades, nuclear power plant reactors have been in operation. At the end of 1999, there were 433 nuclear power plants in operation worldwide, with a total installed capacity of 349 GW (e) (billion watts electricity), and 37 nuclear power plants under construction.[1] The public is constantly reminded about the few troubled nuclear plants but rarely informed about the many that are operating properly and efficiently. Nor is the public informed about the attention paid to quality and safety in design and development, construction, and operation of the nuclear plants. Today's nuclear power reactors are safe, but the questions persist: Are they safe enough? How safe is safe enough? How is safety judged?

This chapter addresses the nature of the nuclear industry and the quality programs and systems that have been developed and implemented to assure the safety of the nuclear reactors and plant operations. Specifically, this chapter describes the current situation regarding nuclear power and what the industry sector requires in terms of quality and the assurance of quality. It describes the evolution of the quality assurance (QA) regulations, as well as industry codes and standards relevant to the design and development, construction, and operation of nuclear power plants in the United States of America and in other nations.

This chapter also describes the development of consensus standards, such as ASME's (American Society of Mechanical Engineers') NQA-1[2] and the International Organization for Standardization's ISO 9000 series quality management system standards (which are referred to throughout the chapter as ISO 9000 for 9001, 9002, and 9003),[3] the scope including the various project organizations, stakeholders, and their respective responsibilities for quality and safety. The relationship of ISO 9001:1994 to the International Atomic Energy Agency's (IAEA's) Code and Safety Guides contained in the Safety Series No. 50-C/SG-Q[4] on QA is addressed, focusing particularly on the application of these requirement standards and providing information and recommendations that may be considered when ISO 9001:1994 is utilized in the nuclear industry. Finally, the chapter provides insight on the potential use of ISO 9001:2000 in the nuclear industry and some thoughts on the future.

CURRENT SITUATION REGARDING NUCLEAR POWER

Nuclear power is an important contributor to the world's electricity needs. It supplies approximately one-sixth of global electricity, with 83 percent of its capacity concentrated in the industrialized nations, most notably Western Europe (France, Belgium, Germany, Sweden, and the United Kingdom), North America (Canada and the United States), and Asia (Japan and the Republic of Korea).[1] Despite this major contribution to electricity supply worldwide, there is no consensus on the future of nuclear power. In North America, there have been no new orders for nuclear power plants during the past two decades, and the number of operating reactors has started to decline. In Western Europe, nuclear capacity will likely remain the same for the next few years. In Asia, planning for an expansion of nuclear power continues, particularly in China, India, Japan, and the Republic of Korea. Any expansion of the contribution of nuclear power toward meeting global energy needs in a sustainable manner will require meeting a number of criteria— not the least of which is improvement of public confidence, especially in relation to the safety of power plant operations and waste disposal.[1]

Considering the safety of nuclear power plants, we need to address these questions: Are they safe? How safe is safe enough? How is safety judged, and by whom? If engineered safety—that is, with multiple redundant backup systems or defense in depth—is safe, how much enhancement is needed? How much is warranted? Or unwarranted? At what point should the cost of yet another marginal increment in safety be considered?

It is interesting to note that in the United States, approximately $200,000 is spent yearly on safety improvements in automobiles to save a single life in an automobile accident—and about 50,000 automobile accident deaths occur each year. In the nuclear industry, however, approximately $2 billion is spent yearly to save one life—and there have been no fatalities. Is there such a thing as "inherently safe" or an "inherently safe system"? These questions have been given considerable attention in the nuclear industry. Some years ago, a congressional report on a U.S. Department of Defense budget quoted court action on the U.S. Nuclear Regulatory Commission's (NRC's) required margin of safety for nuclear power plants. The report stated that the U.S. Court of Appeals (Washington, D.C.) held that under the adequate protection standard, "the NRC need ensure only an acceptable or adequate level of protection to public health and safety; the NRC need not demand that nuclear power plants present no risk of harm. The level of adequate protection need not, and almost certainly will not, be the level of zero risk. This court has long held that the adequate protection standard permits the acceptance of some level of risk."[5]

Major quality-related problems occurred in the nuclear industry during the 1960s, which prompted the establishment of QA regulations in the United States and other nations, including international guidance by the IAEA. Before discussing the application of ISO 9001:1994 and its relationship to these QA regulations and related initiatives, it is important to discuss the evolution of these programs for QA and understand the specific elements of these QA regulations and related initiatives. The next section of this chapter describes the programs for quality as they evolved within the United States and their commonalties with regulations in other nations, as well as the Codes of Practice and Safety Guides established by the IAEA for nuclear power plants .

EVOLUTION OF PROGRAMS FOR QUALITY ASSURANCE IN THE UNITED STATES

In July 1967 the Atomic Energy Commission (AEC) (now the NRC) published for public and industry comment Appendix A to 10 CFR 50, "General Design Criteria for Nuclear Power Plants." Following review, public comment, and subsequent revision, it was issued as an effective regulation in February 1971. The July 1967 draft included 55 criteria covering plant design (it currently includes 64 criteria). The 1967 draft included—and still includes—one criterion, Criterion 1: "Quality Standards and Records," which requires a QA program for certain structures, systems, and components. This criterion for QA was very general, although it was the first AEC proposal that would require nuclear power plant licensees to have a QA program. The lack of clearly defined requirements and criteria for QA was a key issue raised by the Atomic Safety and Licensing Board in the operating license hearings for the Zion, Illinois, plant in 1968. The board ruled that until the AEC developed criteria by which a licensee's QA program could be evaluated, the hearings would be halted.[7] Following the board's ruling, the AEC prepared and proposed a new regulation, Appendix B to 10 CFR Part 50, which would require licensees to develop programs to assure the quality of nuclear power plant design, construction, and operation.

Appendix B contained 18 criteria that must be a part of the QA program for safety-related systems and components. As used in Appendix B, "quality assurance" comprises all those planned and systematic actions necessary to provide adequate confidence that a structure, system, or component will perform satisfactorily in service. Appendix B was published for comment in April of 1969 and implemented in June 1970. The 18 criteria, by title, are as follows:

    I. Organization

    II. Quality Assurance Program

    III. Design Control

    IV. Procurement Document Control

    V. Instructions, Procedures, and Drawings

    VI. Document Control

    VII. Control of Purchased Material, Equipment, and Services

    VIII. Identification and Control of Materials, Parts, and Components

    IX. Control of Special Processes

    X. Inspection

    XI. Test Control

    XII. Control of Measuring and Test Equipment

    XIII. Handling, Storage, and Shipping

    XIV. Inspection, Test, and Operating Status

    XV. Nonconforming Materials, Parts, or Components

    XVI Corrective Action

    XVII. Quality Assurance Records

    XVIII. Audits

Clearly, Appendix B placed the burden of responsibility for QA on the licensee. The NRC is not directly responsible for nuclear power plant quality. Instead, it is the owner/licensee (a public or privately owned utility) that is responsible for achieving and assuring the quality and reliability of a nuclear power plant. The designers, constructors, labor contractors, and component vendors are responsible to the licensee to the extent that the owner/licensee delegates responsibility. While the establishment and execution of all or part of the QA program may be delegated to others, the licensee still retains responsibility for the program's adequacy and effectiveness.

In the early 1970s, the AEC and the industry began issuing guidance that provided acceptable methods and practices for satisfying the intent and requirements of the specific regulations (Appendices A and B). In October 1971, the American National Standards Institute (ANSI) issued N45.2, Quality Assurance Program Requirements for Nuclear Power Plants. This standard prescribed and described the QA requirements responsive to the 18 criteria mandated by Appendix A.

In late 1975 ANSI assigned overall responsibility for coordination (in the United States among technical societies) and for the development and maintenance of nuclear power QA standards to the ASME. The ASME Committee on Nuclear Quality Assurance (NQA) was constituted in October 1975. The NQA committee currently operates under the *ASME Operating Procedures and Practices for Nuclear Codes and Standards Development Committees*. The NQA committee prepared ANSI/ASME NQA-1, *Quality assurance program requirements for nuclear power plants,* and ANSI/ASME NQA-2, *Quality assurance program requirements for nuclear facilities*], which were first issued in 1979 and 1983, respectively, as American National Standards.

NQA-1-1979 was based upon the contents of ANSI/ASME N45.2-1977, *Quality assurance program requirements for nuclear facilities; N46.2, Revision 1, Quality assurance requirement for post reactor nuclear fuel cycle facilities;* and the following seven daughter standards of ANSI/ASME N45.2:

N45.2.6-1978: *Qualifications of inspection, examination, and testing personnel for nuclear power plants*

N45.2.9-1979: *Requirements for collection, storage, and maintenance of quality assurance records for nuclear power plants*

N45.2.10-1973: *Quality assurance terms and definitions*

N45.2.11-1974: *Quality assurance requirements for the design of nuclear power plants*

N45.2.12-1977: *Requirements for auditing of quality assurance programs for nuclear power plants*

N45.2.13-1976: *Quality assurance requirements for control of procurement of items and services for nuclear power plants*

N45.2.23-1978: *Qualification of quality assurance program audit personnel for nuclear power plants*

The ASME NQA-2-1983 standard incorporated the requirements of eight N45.2 daughter QA standards not included in ASME NQA-1:

N45.2.1-1980: *Cleaning of fluid systems and associated components for nuclear power plants*

N45.2.2-1978: *Packaging, shipping, receiving, storage, and handling of items for nuclear power plants*

N45.2.3-1973: *Housekeeping during the construction phase of nuclear power plants (R1978)*

N45.2.5-1978: *Supplementary quality assurance requirements for installation, inspection, and testing of structural concrete, structural steel, soils, and foundations during the construction phase of nuclear power plants*

N45.2.8-1975: *Supplementary quality assurance requirements for installation, inspection, and testing of mechanical equipment and systems for the construction phase of nuclear power plants (R1980)*

N45.2.15-1981: *Hoisting, rigging, and transporting of items for nuclear power plants*

N45.2.20-1979: *Supplementary quality assurance requirements for subsurface investigations for nuclear power plants*

Since the 1979 edition of NQA-1, it was revised in 1983, 1986, 1989, and 1994. Since the 1983 edition of NQA-2, it was revised in 1986 and 1989. In 1984, the NQA Subcommittee on Nuclear Waste Management was assigned responsibility for developing a QA program standard appropriate to site characterization of high-level nuclear waste repositories. This assignment resulted in ASME NQA-3, *Quality assurance requirements for the collection of scientific and technical information for the site characterization of high-level nuclear waste repositories.* This standard was issued in 1989.

In the early 1990s the NQA committee decided that the NQA-1, NQA-2, and NQA-3 standards were not structured in a way to enable users and potential users to easily understand and apply the requirements. The committee decided to restructure the NQA standards into a multipart document that would allow more rapid response to varied applications of NQA provisions and measures and permit judicious application of the entire standard or portions of the standard.

As a result, ASME NQA-1-1997, *Quality Assurance Requirements for Nuclear Facility Applications* was approved by ANSI in July 1997. This edition included requirements and nonmandatory guidance for the establishment and execution of QA programs for nuclear facility applications.

In May 2001, ASME NQA-1-1997 was revised and issued as ASME NQA-1-2001. It has four parts: Part I contains QA requirements for the siting, design, construction, operation, and decommissioning of nuclear power facilities. Part II contains QA requirements for the planning and execution of identified tasks during the fabrication, construction, modification, repair, maintenance, and testing of systems, components, and structures for nuclear facilities. Part III contains nonmandatory guidance and application appendices. Part IV is reserved for future NQA position papers and application matrices.

Another industry standard, developed by the American Nuclear Society (ANS), is the ANSI/ANS 3.2, *Administrative controls and quality assurance for the operational phase of nuclear power plants.* This standard was reaffirmed by ANS and ANSI in 1999. It is consistent with the 2001 version of NQA-1.

Since 1970, as the nuclear industry grew and gained experience in nuclear regulations, many AEC/NRC regulatory guides have been developed and published to address various aspects of quality and quality problems. The NRC's Advisory Committee on Reactor Safety (ACRS) and Advisory Committee on Waste Management (ACWM) have provided oversight and recommendations regarding nuclear industry issues and concerns in order to preserve consistency with the common defense and security and the public health and safety, as the NRC may by rule establish.

Over the last three decades, the nuclear power industry has developed programs to assure that information about problems and performance may be quickly exchanged. These programs have been supported by organizations such as the Atomic Industrial Forum (AIF), the Electric Power Research Institute (EPRI), the Institute for Nuclear Power Operations (INPO), the Nuclear Electric Institute (NEI), and the World Association of Nuclear Operations (WANO). The consensus standards identified in this chapter have continued to mature in response to numerous lessons learned from the accidents at Three Mile Island and Chernobyl.

While it is not specifically within the scope of this chapter, it should be mentioned that the U.S. Department of Energy (DOE) has prescribed its QA requirements for DOE nuclear facilities. Some, but not all, are included in the following:

10 CFR Part 71: *Packaging and transportation of radioactive material*

10 CFR Part 72: *Licensing requirements for the independent storage of spent nuclear fuel and high level radioactive waste*

10 CFR Part 830: *Nuclear safety management*

10 CFR Part 120: *Quality assurance requirements*

DOE Order 414.1 (formerly DOE 5700.6C): *Quality assurance*

DOE/RW-0333P: *Office of Civilian Radioactive Waste Management; Quality assurance requirements and description*

Note: The above list is not intended to be all-inclusive, but it is presented here for reference.

The DOE Guide 414.1.2, as an example, provides guidance on applying QA. It includes a provision where a single facility may adopt ISO 9001 for corporate reasons or ASME NQA-1 for an EPA/NRC regulation. The user is cautioned that, in tailoring to ISO 9001, the user may not circumvent the QA rule. Some facilities where this provision may be applied include National Laboratories (Argonne, Brookhaven, Lawrence Livermore, and Sandia) and the Princeton Plasma Physics Laboratory.

AN OVERVIEW OF QA REGULATIONS IN OTHER NATIONS

One study of QA regulatory programs have concluded that significant differences exist between programs of nations other than the United States.[6] Countries examined during the study included Canada, Germany, France, Japan, Sweden, and the United Kingdom. The study also concluded that there are some common elements:

1. Each has utilized the U.S. NRC's QA criteria (10 CFR Part 50, Appendix B) in developing its program.

2. Each has utilized the IAEA's Codes of Practice and Safety Guides for nuclear power.

3. Each has placed government regulatory functions for nuclear power plants with agencies or departments overseeing nonnuclear industries and activities not related to radioactive materials or devices.

This chapter will only briefly cover the nuclear QA regulations of Canada, Germany, and the United Kingdom.

In Canada, Atomic Energy of Canada Limited (AECL) sets basic criteria and requires licensees to design, construct, and operate power reactors that meet them. The AECL and CANDU industry have maintained and applied QA programs based on the Canadian Standards Association (CSA) N286 series of nuclear QA standards for nuclear lifecycle activities—such as design, procurement, construction, commissioning, and operation. For the manufacturing of equipment and components, the CSA CAN3 Z299 series and ASME standards are used. In particular, for pressure-retaining components, the QA programs based on N285 and ASME section III are used. In mid-1998, the AECL prepared a position paper on harmonization with ISO 9000 QA standards. Under the paper's recommendations, groups at AECL involved in manufacturing activities should do the following:

1. Migrate their QA program from CSA Z299 to ISO 9000, including obtaining certification.

2. Maintain the N286-based programs in their current state and show that CSA N286 programs comply with ISO 9000 requirements.

3. Maintain the CSA N285/ASME programs for pressure-retaining components in their current state and show that they comply with ISO 9000 requirements.

4. Plan to obtain ISO certification.

AECL has accomplished each of the above recommendations.

Previous to the paper's recommendations, in 1996, AECL prepared a procedure establishing the equivalence of some widely used QA standards, including ISO 9000. The procedure prescribes supplementary requirements that must be imposed in conjunction with some widely used international standards to achieve equivalence to CSA CAN3 Z299 standards. The procedure also provides guidance for when an ISO 9000 standard is used.

Germany's Department of Interior (BMI) has three major advisory bodies: the Committee on Reactor Safety (RSK), the Committee on Nuclear Safety Standards (KTA), and the Committee on Radiological Protection (SSK). While the SSK is an important advisory body to BMI, it has little direct involvement with QA programs.

In contrast, the RSK recommends guidelines which constitute the framework for safety-related standards that must be followed by an applicant for license. The KTA established and issued the Overall General Requirements for QA/QC, which have the force of regulation and are similar to the criteria in 10 CFR Part 50, Appendix B. They are, however, less prescriptive than the requirements of ISO 9001. With regard to licensing, an independent expert organization, TUV (Technische Uberwachungs-Vereine), performs various control functions, including review of design basis documents (such as system design descriptions, specifications and drawings), auditing, and inspection. As a requirement for certification, ISO 9000 and other requirements are imposed in procurement documents to suppliers.

In the United Kingdom there are only a few major participants in the nuclear power program, including the Central Electricity Generating Board (CEGB) and the Nuclear Installations Inspectorate (NII). The CEGB is the government-owned utility responsible for the design, construction, and operation of nuclear power plants. In recent years the CEGB has been reorganized and now consists of two groups: British Nuclear Fuel and British Energy. The NII acts as the regulatory agency and publishes the *Guide to the Quality Assurance Program for Nuclear Power Plants*. Interestingly, the NII does not mandate prescriptive QA requirements, only that a quality management system be established and implemented. The NII will, however, evaluate the system to determine its adequacy and suitability.

The QA requirements in the U.K. have been based primarily upon the BS 5882, Total Quality Assurance Programme for Nuclear Power Plants (including the BS 5750 which preceded ISO 9000), and the NII guidance document. The BS 5882 closely parallels 10 CFR Part 50, Appendix B. While the BS 5882 continues to be an active standard, it may be withdrawn in the near future. Current initiatives include replacing it with the IAEA Code 50-C-Q. A detailed description of the IAEA safety code is provided in the next section of this chapter.

SCOPE AND COVERAGE OF IAEA 50-C/SG-Q AND ISO 9001 DOCUMENTS

The agreement between IAEA and ISO regarding the scope and coverage of documents on quality in the nuclear sector published by IAEA and by ISO stipulates that standards of safety developed by IAEA are recommendations that member states use in the framework of national regulations for safe utilization of nuclear energy. Such standards should be considered as nuclear safety regulatory documents. The standards developed by ISO are complementary technical documents emphasizing industrial applications and contractual aspects.

The IAEA's Code and Safety Guides contained in Safety Series No. 50-C/SG-Q define basic QA requirements for ensuring safety and recommend how to fulfill them. The IAEA requirements and recommendations are generally used at the nuclear utility and regulator interface. ISO 9001:1994 specifies quality system requirements for use where any supplier's capability to design and supply a conforming product must be demonstrated. These requirements are aimed primarily at achieving customer satisfaction by preventing nonconformity at all stages of work, from design through servicing. ISO 9001:1994 is sometimes used at the nuclear utility and supplier interface.

The relationship between both standards is growing in significance owing to the impact on the owners and operators of nuclear facilities and their contractors and suppliers. The relationship between IAEA and ISO standards is considered critical, in particular regarding suppliers with a small range of nuclear supplies. These organizations are not willing to establish and implement special QA programs based on nuclear safety standards. On the other hand, these organizations may be qualified and capable based on ISO QA requirements. Any supplier that delivers nuclear items and services must comply with the nuclear regulatory safety regulations. Accordingly, the supplier has to demonstrate an acceptable degree of QA in relation to nuclear safety; this is achieved by imposing additional requirements on the supplier over and above requirements specified in ISO 9001:1994.

Before we discuss which additional requirements may be considered, we must examine the specific elements of the IAEA and ISO quality documents.

Let's first look at the IAEA's Code and Safety Guides contained in the Safety Series No. 50-C/SG-Q. The IAEA Safety Series includes one code—50-C-Q—on QA and 14 safety guides—50-SG-Q1 to Q14. Code 50-C-Q establishes the basic requirements that must be met to ensure adequate nuclear safety. The code consists of 10 basic requirements (BRs) and is prescribed in three functional categories:

1. Management.

    BR 1: Quality Assurance Programme

    BR 2: Training and Qualification

    BR 3: Non-Conformance Control and Corrective Action

    BR 4: Document Control and Records

2. Performance.

    BR 5: Work

    BR 6: Design

    BR 7: Procurement

    BR 8: Inspection and Testing

3. Assessment.

    BR 9: Management Self-Assessment

    BR 10: Independent Assessment

The code also includes an annex that provides guidance on the implementation of the basic requirements.

The safety guides describe acceptable methods for implementing particular elements of the code. Safety guides 50-SG-Q1 to Q14 are divided into two types: guides related to BRs and guides related to stages. BR-related safety guides provide recommendations and guidance on the relevance of the code's BRs to the lifecycle of nuclear power plants and other nuclear facilities. These are the BR-related safety guides:

Safety Guide Q1: *Establishing and implementing a quality assurance programme*

Safety Guide Q2: *Non-conformance control and corrective actions*

Safety Guide Q3: *Document control and records*

Safety Guide Q4: *Inspection and testing for acceptance*

Safety Guide Q5: *Assessment of the implementation of the quality assurance programme*

Safety Guide Q6: *Quality assurance in the procurement of items and services*

Safety Guide Q7: *Quality assurance in manufacturing*

Stage-related safety guides provide recommendations and guidance on how to implement the code during different lifecycle stages of nuclear power plants and other nuclear installations. These are the stage-related safety guides:

Safety Guide Q8: *Quality assurance in research and development*

Safety Guide Q9: *Quality assurance in siting*

Safety Guide Q10: *Quality assurance in design* (which may also be used as a BR-related guide when the design activities are carried out in any stage)

Safety Guide Q11: *Quality assurance in construction*

Safety Guide Q12: *Quality assurance in commissioning*

Safety Guide Q13: *Quality assurance in operation*

Safety Guide Q14: *Quality assurance in decommissioning*

Now let's look at the ISO 9001:1994 quality system standard, which has 20 clauses defining the requirements for a quality management system:

4.1   Management responsibility

4.2   Quality system

4.3   Contract review

4.4   Design control

4.5   Document and data control

4.6   Purchasing

4.7   Control of customer supplied product

4.8   Product identification and traceability

4.9   Process control

4.10   Inspection and testing

4.11   Control of inspection, measuring, and test equipment

4.12   Inspection and test status

4.13   Control of nonconforming product

4.14   Corrective and preventive action

4.15   Handling, storage, packaging, preservation, and delivery

4.16   Control of quality records

4.17   Internal quality audits

4.18   Training

4.19   Servicing

4.20   Statistical techniques

These clauses are sequentially numbered to reflect the sequence of events and activities from developing the quality policy to after-sales servicing.

RELATIONSHIP AND COMPARISON OF IAEA 50-C/SG-Q AND ISO 9001:1994

As stated previously, the relationship of IAEA 50-C/SG-Q and ISO 9001:1994 has increased in significance because of its impact on the owners and operators of nuclear facilities and their contractors and suppliers. As a result, the IAEA established a project to produce a guidance report identifying the major differences between the IAEA Safety Code and the ISO Quality Management System Standard and to provide recommendations for fulfilling nuclear safety requirements when ISO 9001:1994 is used.

In January 2000 an advisory group meeting was held in Vienna to draft revisions and finalize the IAEA technical document.[7] The report identified that while the 20 ISO 9001:1994 clauses are related to and comparable with the 10 basic requirements of IAEA Code 50-C-Q, they do not give any guidance or recommendations on how the specified requirements can be implemented to satisfy the IAEA code. The report concluded that there are major differences between the two standards and provided guidance by recommending additional requirements when applying ISO 9001:1994. The report also provides guidance to aid in the application of the additional requirements.

MAJOR DIFFERENCES BETWEEN IAEA 50-C-Q AND ISO 9001:1994

In general, the basic requirements of the IAEA Code 50-C-Q are addressed in one or more clauses of ISO 9001:1994. However, the IAEA safety guides provide more detailed and comprehensive guidance and recommendations on how to implement the basic requirements of the IAEA code. Additionally, each basic requirement of IAEA Code 50-C-Q addresses one or more of the clauses of ISO 9001:1994. Differences are evident in the underlying approaches, identification of the customer, and some additional requirements.

First, with regard to underlying approaches, IAEA 50-C-Q provides basic requirements to be adopted for establishing and implementing QA programs related to the safety of nuclear power plants and other nuclear installations. These basic requirements apply to the overall QA program of the responsible organization, as well as to any other separate QA programs in each stage of the life of a nuclear power plant. The code has the objective of enhancing nuclear safety by continually improving the methods employed to achieve quality. In contrast, the QA model established in ISO 9001:1994 provides the framework for a QA program that enables the supplier to demonstrate the capability to produce a quality product. While the requirements specified are aimed primarily at achieving customer satisfaction, they are generic and independent of any specific industry sector.

Second, with regard to identification of the customer, the nuclear utility satisfies the safety requirements of the national regulatory bodies (its customers) and society at large. The utility, acting as the customer to suppliers, may utilize, where appropriate, ISO 9001:1994 with additional requirements to define the QA program expected from the suppliers of items and services.

Third, with regard to additional requirements, the code defines specific requirements for management self-assessments. This is not an activity required by ISO 9001:1994. An effective management self-assessment evaluates such issues as the mission of the organization, whether employees understand the mission, what is expected of the organization, whether the expectations are met, opportunities for improving quality and enhancing safety, and how to make better use of human resources.

The code includes provisions for a graded approach in the application of QA during the various stages of a nuclear power plant lifecycle. The grading process provides a means for determining the types of controls and the extent to which they are applied to specific items, services, and processes. Accordingly, the highest grade should require the most stringent application of QA requirements; the lowest grade, the least stringent—each in relation to nuclear safety significance. Examples where grading should be applied are type and content of training, amount of detail and degree of review and approval of instructions, need for detail of inspection and test plans, degree of in-process reviews and controls, requirements for material traceability, type of assessment, and records to be generated and retained. Safety guide 50-SG-Q1 explains the graded approach in relation to nuclear safety. ISO 9001:1994 does not define or require a graded approach for applying the control elements of the quality system.

The code also requires the independence of inspection and testing personnel. ISO 9001:1994 does not specifically require this.

Interestingly enough, the IAEA safety guides do not directly consider the customer-related requirements of ISO 9001:1994 as defined in clauses 4.3, 4.7, and 4.19—"Contract review," "Control of customer supplied product," and "Servicing," respectively.

ADDITIONAL REQUIREMENTS AND GUIDANCE WHEN APPLYING ISO 9001:1994

Before we discuss the additional requirements and guidance when applying ISO 9001:1994 to satisfy the IAEA Safety Code, it must be presumed that the reader has an adequate knowledge and understanding of the specific requirements of both standards. It is not within the scope of this chapter to address the standards in such detail. One suggested source of information is the American Society for Quality (ASQ). In 1995, the Energy and Environmental Quality Division of ASQ published a document entitled *International Matrix of Nuclear Quality Assurance Program Requirements.*[8] The matrix compares specific direct quotes from regulations and standards, some of which include 10 CFR Part 50, Appendix B; IAEA 50-C-Q; BS 5882; and CAN3-N286.0. Others compared include selected IAEA safety guides; the BS-5750 series; the CSA Z299 series; and the ISO 9000 series. In this regard, only BRs where additional requirements are recommended are addressed in this chapter. Accordingly, BRs where no additional requirements are recommended are not addressed, including BR 3, Non-Conformance Control and Corrective Action; BR 4, Document Control and Records; and BR 5, Work. Additionally, most if not all of the IAEA safety guides provide sufficient detailed information and do not require much if any explanation.

The application of additional requirements or guidance from IAEA 50-C/SG-Q may be considered by the nuclear utility from two perspectives: (1) Should the utility address the difference or differences within its own QA program? and (2) Should the utility require its suppliers to address the difference or differences as an additional requirement in procurement documents? Certainly, such consideration should also take into account the respective national regulatory requirements.

The following will identify additional requirements and recommended application notes, where appropriate, when applying ISO 9001:1994. The additional requirements should be considered when applying ISO 9001:1994 where requirements are given in IAEA 50-C-Q and not found in ISO 9001:1994. Where the additional requirement or guidance is not self-explanatory, some additional notes on application are provided. The information presented will first show the section or sections, title, and additional requirements. Following this information, it will show the recommended application notes.

FROM IAEA 50-C-Q

Introduction, Sections 101–108; Section 104—The responsible organization has to demonstrate the effective fulfillment of the QA requirements to the satisfaction of the regulatory body.

Recommended Application Note: The utility should demonstrate that its quality program takes into account and incorporates any requirements from the regulatory body. The utility should require its supplier to apply any of these specific requirements where necessary.

BR 1: Quality Assurance Program, Sections 201–205; Section 204—Nuclear safety shall be the fundamental consideration in the identification of the items, services, and processes to which the QA program applies. A graded approach based on the relative importance to nuclear safety of each item, service, or process shall be used. The graded approach shall reflect a planned and recognized difference in the applications of specific QA requirements.

Recommended Application Note: The graded approach for activities and items, including procurement, should be described within the utility quality program. The application of grading to supplier activities should be clarified. The utility should consider whether its supplier should adopt complimentary grading and provide guidance.

BR 2: Training and Qualification, Section 206; Section 206—Personnel should be trained so that they are competent to perform their assigned work and understand the safety consequences of their activities.

Recommended Application Note: The utility should identify personnel involved with safety matters and provide the related training and qualification program. The utility should notify its suppliers when their personnel are involved with safety matters and ensure they are appropriately trained.

BR-3: Non-Conformance Control and Corrective Action—No additional requirements recommended.

BR-4: Document Control and Records—No additional requirements recommended.

BR-5: Work—No additional requirements recommended.

BR 6: Design, Sections 304–305; Section 305—The adequacy of the design, including design tools and design inputs and outputs shall be verified or validated by individuals or groups other than those who originally performed the work. Verification, validation, and approval shall be completed before implementation of the design.

Recommended Application Note: The utility quality program addressing design should specify that persons in charge of safety-related design verification and validation should be different from those performing the work. The utility should notify suppliers of the relevant requirements when they perform safety-related design activities. Any design verification and approval should be performed before the implementation of the design. Generally, design validation is performed through the commissioning under defined operating conditions, and specific dispositions should be applied for accident conditions.

Section Annex—Design inputs include all requirements for the design, such as the technical basis for the design (design basis), performance requirements, reliability requirements, and safety and security requirements. Computer programs used in the design are validated through testing or simulation prior to use if not proven through prior use. There is no recommended application note for this annex.

BR-7: Procurement, Sections 306–308; Section 308—The requirement for reporting deviations from procurement requirements shall be specified in the procurement documents.

Recommended Application Note: The reporting of deviations (nonconforming products) should be identified as necessary.

BR-8: Inspection and Testing for Acceptance, Sections 309–310; Section 309—Inspection and testing of specified items and processes shall be conducted using established acceptance and performance criteria. The level of inspection and testing and the degree of independence of personnel shall be established.

Recommended Application Note: Utilities should request suppliers to include this requirement in their quality program when appropriate.

BR-9: Management Self-Assessment, Section 401; Section 401—Management at all levels shall regularly assess the processes for which it is responsible. Management shall determine its effectiveness in establishing, promoting, and achieving nuclear safety objectives. Management process weaknesses and barriers that hinder the achievement of nuclear safety objectives shall be identified and corrected.

Recommended Application Note: Management self-assessment is more complex and detailed than the ISO management review process. Management self-assessment focuses on the achievement of nuclear safety objectives. The management review should include the assessment of nuclear safety–related processes. Nuclear safety objectives should be part of the quality objectives, with associated performance indicators. Weaknesses and barriers should be handled through corrective action. Management assessment should be carried out at all levels.

BR-10: Independent Assessment, Sections 402–405—Independent assessment, such as internal audits, external audits, surveillance, peer evaluation and technical review, should be focused on safety aspects and areas where problems have been found. Assessment objectives should be reviewed to reflect current management concerns and performance activities.

Recommended Application Note: Independent assessment includes quality systems internal audits, peer evaluation, technical review, design review, and inspection. Utilities should consider expanding the type of assessments that their suppliers perform.

As previously stated, most if not all of the IAEA safety guides provide sufficient detailed information, and they are considered as not requiring much, if any, explanation. However, some selected safety guides are discussed here only for the purpose of providing some specific examples of the extent of the detail described in the safety guides. The information shown below includes the safety guide number, title, a brief description of the SG's guidance, and application notes where SG guidance is not self-explanatory.

FROM IAEA SAFETY GUIDES 50-SG-Q

Safety Guide Q1: Establishing and Implementing a Quality Assurance Program. The responsible organization is required to establish a QA program at a time consistent with the schedule for accomplishing the stage-related activities for items, services, and processes important to safety. A graded approach shall be used. Design review, for example, requires consideration of inspectability, constructability, operability, maintainability, and ALARA (as low as reasonably achievable) before finalization of the design. Operations includes providing fully documented and detailed working documents; having a trained and qualified workforce; and ensuring that workshops, facilities, tools, and suitable working environments are in place.

Application Notes: The utility QA program should be developed according to the actual stages of the plant. The suppliers' quality systems should meet the QA requirements identified by the utility, including provisions for grading its own QA requirements to its sub-suppliers where necessary and for acceptance to the utility. When implementing the QA program, plans mentioned in the safety guides should be handled through quality planning.

Safety Guide Q2: Non-Conformance Control and Corrective Action. Nonconformances may be discovered during regulatory inspections. On being advised of a nonconformance, the line management should promptly inform the other nuclear plant personnel and the regulatory body, as required. Implementation of preventive actions may proceed in stages. Prior to implementation, all proposed actions should have been agreed to, documented, and authorized by appropriate personnel and the regulatory body, as required.

Application Notes: The utilities should determine how they address nonconformances and inform suppliers that the regulatory body may choose to conduct inspections. There may also be a need for suppliers to identify nonconformances that should be brought to the attention of the regulator via the utility representative.

Safety Guide Q3: Document Control and Records. During document preparation, activities described should be assessed using the grading system so that appropriate controls are considered and selected. Prior to issuance of a document, the acceptance or approval by the regulator should be obtained where required. The responsible organization should identify who is responsible for transferring and disposing of records.

Application Notes: QA documents should contain provisions to ensure that when documents are prepared they include the necessary controls for the activities to be implemented. This may apply to suppliers. Utilities should notify suppliers when regulatory approval is required. The utility is required to communicate records requirements to the supplier.

Safety Guide Q5: Assessment of the Implementation of the QA Program. The purpose of management self-assessment should be to evaluate known performance issues, identify contributing management aspects, and make improvements. Independent assessments, such as internal audits, peer evaluations, and technical review should focus on safety aspects, objectives, and problem areas that have been found. Appropriate combinations of various types of assessments should be used to provide the best balanced evaluation of performance.

Application Notes: Careful consideration should be given to imposing the requirement of management self-assessment on suppliers. Grading should help in this determination. Consideration may be given to recognizing that suppliers may adopt one or more methods for independent assessment.

Safety Guide Q6: Quality Assurance in Procurement of Items and Services. When a commercial-grade item is proposed for a safety function, a thorough technical evaluation of the complexity of the item and its safety significance should be completed. The critical characteristics required for the function should be included as acceptance criteria in procurement documents.

Application Notes: Methods to be used for such technical evaluations should be defined in the utility quality system and, where applicable, in the supplier's quality system.

THE FUTURE AND SOME INSIGHT ON THE POTENTIAL USE OF ISO 9001:2000 IN THE NUCLEAR INDUSTRY

In the nuclear industry, from a global perspective, utilities use national regulations for QA programs. ISO 9001:1994 is currently used on a very selective basis and only when additional requirements are imposed on suppliers. Within the United States, licensing is based on 10 CFR Part 50, Appendix B, and in some few instances, the ASME NQA-1 is used by utilities. However, the NRC endorses a version of the NQA-1 standard that is significantly earlier than the current NQA-1-2001 version.

IAEA Safety Code 50-C-Q and its related series of safety guides appears to provide the most prescriptive and descriptive requirements and guidance for quality. Certainly, due to the initiatives by the IAEA—specifically the work done by the Advisory Group on Quality—the use of ISO 9001:1994 may now be more easily considered and applied.

It is not likely that ISO 9001:1994 will be endorsed by regulatory bodies for nuclear power licensing in the United States. Nor will the United States, at least in the foreseeable future, endorse the ISO 9001:2000 standard. Some nations, such as Canada and Germany, appear to be actively linking ISO 9001 requirements with their regulatory requirements and applying ISO 9001 with appropriate additional requirements. The scheme for mutual recognition (that is, certification) is also utilized where appropriate and will most likely continue to be useful and beneficial.

Certainly, an evaluation and subsequent determination of the adequacy and suitability of an organization's quality system for application in the nuclear industry will continue on a case-by-case basis.

With regard to the future application of ISO 9001:2000, the IAEA has indicated that after ISO 9001:2000 is issued as an international standard, it plans to hold advisory group meetings to document and publish a comparative analysis of the new ISO 9001:2000 and the IAEA Safety Series No. 50-C/SG-Q Quality Assurance for Safety in Nuclear Power Plants and Other Nuclear Installations, Code and Safety Guides Q1-Q14.

ENDNOTES

1. "Overview," *1999 Annual Report* (Vienna: IAEA, 1999).
2. American Society of Mechanical Engineers, Three Park Avenue, New York, NY 10016-5990
3. International Organization for Standardization, Case Postale 56, CH-1211, Geneva 20, Switzerland.
4. International Atomic Energy Agency, Wagramer Strasse 5, A-1400, Vienna, Austria.
5. D. L. Ray, *Trashing the Planet* (Washington, DC: Regnery, Gateway, 1990): 134–36. [The congressional report was referenced in this book.]
6. NRC Office of Inspection and Enforcement, *NUREG-1055: Improving Quality and the Assurance of Quality in the Design and Construction of Nuclear Power Plants—A Report to Congress* (Washington, D.C.: NRC, 1984).
7. IAEA Technical Document No. 1182, *Quality Assurance Standards: Comparison between IAEA 50-C/SG-Q and ISO 9001:1994* (Vienna: IAEA, November 2000).
8. ASQC Energy & Environmental Quality Division, *International Matrix of Nuclear Quality Assurance Requirements* (Milwaukee: ASQC Quality Press, 1995).

SOURCES AND INTERVIEWS

Gustave E. Danielson, Jr., DOE, United States
Shami S. Dua, AECL, Canada
Dr. Ernst C. Glauser, Glauser Engineering, Switzerland
Owen Gormley, NRC, United States
Michael Hille, Siemens AG, Germany
Charles H. Moseley, Jr., Lockheed Martin Energy Systems, United States
Dr. Nestor Pieroni, Scientific Secretary (retired), IAEA, Austria
Neil Redman, Amethyst Management, United Kingdom
Youngjo Rim, KEPCO, Republic of Korea
Dr. William K. Sowder, Bechtel B&W,I, an operating division of Bechtel United States

Chapter 57

ISO 9001:2000 and Relationships: The Personal Business of Emotional Satisfaction

Mark Baker
Psychologist, QED Consulting Group, Lakeport, California

Judith Luchsinger
Owner, QED Consulting Group, Lakeport, California

It has been said that the only constant in life is change. That became most evident in the last half of the 20th century, as traditional ways of doing things fell away in the face of increasing technological and social innovations. Traditional concepts that formed the nature of the way we have done business for centuries proved ineffective in dealing with the modern global marketplace. Similarly, traditional concepts in the way that we have carried out relationships proved ineffective in dealing with modern relationship expectations. In short, we can no longer rely on what we "know" to attain success in life either professionally or personally.

Let us take a look at the changes we're seeing in the commercial workplace:

- Today, all employees are accountable for results; yesterday, for effort
- Today, companies must provide customer satisfaction; yesterday, sell a product
- Today, businesses strengthen competitiveness through the pursuit of operational excellence; yesterday, "If it works, don't fix it"
- Today, organizations are increasingly being reorganized to function as entrepreneurial companies; yesterday, bigger was better
- Today, the philosophy is collaboration and cooperation; yesterday, top-down management
- Today, problem solving focuses on the root cause; yesterday, status quo and cover up

Each of these changes involves movement toward quality. Businesses or organizations that have increased size, downsized, or reorganized but failed to preserve or improve the quality of their product(s) have lost ground or gone out of business. The same kind of trend can be observed in relationships.

Traditionally, marriages were an arrangement to provide political or financial stability. Then the notion of romantic love appeared, where the relationship arose out of choice even though the arrangement tended to remain out of necessity. With the influx of women into the labor force during World War II, financial independence became possible for women. With the advent of the birth control pill, women were freed from the reproductive cycle. Modern labor-saving devices freed people from the time-consuming tasks of maintaining a household. All this changed the traditional dependent nature of relationships to one where individuals could come together as independent equals.

In an effort to enhance that sense of equality, the cultural revolution of the 1960s started dismantling traditional rules and definitions of men, women, and relationships. Freed of the traditional policies and procedures of a relationship, so the theory went, men and women would be able to devise their own relationships based on a natural outflowing of their inherent goodness that would be more responsive to the genuine needs of those involved. What we have found, however, is that instead of gaining freedom, we have jumped from the frying pan of social constraints into the fire of indulged desires. We have gone from a social focus on the "other" to a social focus on the "I."

In today's marketplace, the businesses that have succeeded have documented and improved their processes to prevent defects that increase the costs of scrap, rework, reinspection, or retraining. They have analyzed their operations to root out the unnecessary work that adds no value for the customer. They have benchmarked other companies in an attempt to improve their own practices and make their operations more effective and efficient.

In this same way, for modern relationships to succeed with the current expectations of producing or increasing emotional satisfaction (the product), couples need to consciously examine their relationship for those processes that work to realize the product—that bring emotional satisfaction—and those processes that do not. They need to set in place *practices* and *processes* that allow the couple to be aware of those areas in their relationship that do not work to bring emotional satisfaction (nonconforming product) and develop the skills that allow them to make the decision to use as is, rework, or scrap. Even more important, they need to develop the awareness of those areas that do work to provide emotional satisfaction and develop the skills to bring them into place and maintain those practices.

The latter area (to focus on what is working) is actually much more difficult in a normal emotional relationship. Our brain unconsciously focuses on the pain of practices (processes) that do not bring emotional satisfaction (nonconforming product, otherwise known as the problem) and overlooks those areas that bring emotional satisfaction (taken for granted because they are not a problem and, anyway, they should be that way). So we tend to "know" we are in love but don't feel the need to demonstrate it; we tend to give to each other but not appreciate it as we measure our effort and minimize the other's; we tend to look not with tenderness but with expectations unmet.

In life there is no more free will than there is a free lunch. In order to create your relationship so that it addresses your personal needs (emotional satisfaction), you have to do it on purpose. It requires an effort, which makes it yours and valuable. A couple's ongoing documentation of their emotional business, saying what they are going to do and how they are going to do it, is essential to help develop the consensual cooperation that is the foundation of trust. Visible reminders of their commitment help the couple avoid the biological tendency to fixate on the immediate situation, so they can maintain their longer-range vision of the relationship in the emotional press of the present. It is important for couples to free themselves from the ego mandate to be right (which means the other must be wrong) and to focus on current needs and resources in order to develop an efficient and effective means to achieve relationship satisfaction.

Even though the traditional rules and roles of relationships were restrictive, they were clear-cut and provided women and men the concrete tasks that allowed them to feel that they were being good and honorable. The couple functioned by following an imposed prescriptive *policy* on how to make the relationship work. People had the self-discipline to try to be who they *should* be, to be good (to fill the defined role), but not a lot of freedom to define what *should* (the policy) was. In contrast, young people today have no clear-cut roles or rules defining what it is to be a man, a woman, or in a relationship. The goal has shifted from being good, which required self-discipline, to being happy, which is seen as requiring self-indulgence where impulsivity is mistaken for spontaneity. If a couple doesn't personally define their relationship, it will be unconsciously defined by their biology and the socialization they have experienced. Biology will define it as survival and propagation of genes, not personal emotional satisfaction or relationship happiness. And after a period of biochemical "in love," the couple will "awake" to the reality of being in a relationship with another human being who is not there to make them happy. And, finished with propagation, the couple will no longer have much in common.

In an attempt to balance the selfishness of the genes, the socialization process employs guilt to focus away from the needs of oneself and on the needs of the other. The socialized norm to place our needs last to avoid guilt tends to establish the barter mentality of an emotional marketplace where I will make you feel special if you will make me feel special. Unfortunately, if clear policies and processes are not communicated, we tend to be more aware of our own efforts than the efforts of our partner, resulting in feelings of deprivation and resentment.

People now have tremendous freedom to be who they want to be, but neither the self-discipline nor the tools to be able to define and pursue that freedom beyond the mood of the moment. As a result we are seeing a socially disastrous level of relationship failures. By some reports the failure rate for marriages begun after 1990 is 60 or 70 percent. We must remember that the mandate of our biology is to survive with the limited problem-solving tools of fight, flight, and panic (freezing). The mandate of the socialization process is to submerge our needs for the good of the whole. Neither our biology nor the socialization mandate engenders the kind of emotional satisfaction that is the expectation of most modern relationships.

Instead of changing partners, then, a quality management system (ISO 9001:2000) can provide the tools to change processes: to adapt along with the partner you have to the changing environment of emotional needs. Just as has been found in the business world, any quality system must know where it wants to go (*quality policy*), have controllable processes (*quality system*), and have the self-discipline, cooperation, and communication required for its operation and the achievement of its aims.

ISO 9001:2000 is a set of international standards for quality management. It consists of elements that, if addressed appropriately, provide a documented framework for bringing a product from inception through design and production to completion. If done well, it is nonbureaucratic. It streamlines. It brings inconsistent areas to attention for decision making. By taking the time up front to clarify customer requirements and establish consensus on the policies and procedures of the system, you enhance the efficiency and effectiveness of the relationship, thereby ensuring longer-term success, that is, emotional satisfaction.

While ISO 9001:2000 was originally designed for business application, we find ourselves in a cultural era when those very same needs exist for that more personal business, our emotional relationships. Lacking the traditional definitions of *self, the other,* and *relationship,* we tend to come to our emotional relationships with expectations formed by our childhood experiences and the cultural media. Time-hurried and feeling overwhelmed by the demands (the shoulds) in our life, we tend to transfer this lifestyle into our relationships, looking for that fast emotional fullness that requires minimal demand for participation on our part. In this atmosphere, the effort is not expended on being real; it is expended on gaining acceptance and love through presentations that push the boundaries of marketing ethics. And so the relationship is formed without real communication, or rather without communication that is real. This means that individuals enter into a relationship with assumptions and expectations that are either not shared or if shared are done so without real discussion about what the terms mean. We need to remember that the relationship is a process to be experienced together, shared, not a problem to be solved.

It is an irony of emotional relationships that when we have something precious (the feeling of being loved), it brings out our worst fears (the loss of that which is precious). That fear brings out all our personal insecurities about not being enough. We tend to become guarded with the memory of past hurts and hold back from saying what we really feel out of a concern for hurting the other and, in turn, being hurt or abandoned. In this atmosphere of best appearance and idealistic expectations, we make a contract and lifetime commitment without a frank discussion of how the product (emotional satisfaction) is going to be manufactured and distributed. With only individually assumed notions of how to create the product, it is inevitable that the relationship will run into problems with management responsibility, resource management, product realization, measurement, analysis, and improvement. Without those elements, there can be no assurance of quality. And, indeed, in the majority of cases there is not.

Much of the stuff of which a relationship is made is assumed and implied, and that is where the trouble starts. ISO doesn't tell you what to do, but it does require that the elements *be addressed* and documented. Going through such a process will bring to your attention areas where your relationship works and issues that need to be addressed, and it will guarantee that there is no "off-the-table-ism." When a couple is aware that the relationship crucible is intended to meet *her needs, his needs,* and *the couple's needs,* and they are dedicated to finding solutions to meet those multiple needs, then the odds move heavily in the favor of success. It takes sincere effort from a loving, heartfelt place. And it takes two. If both are not committed to making the relationship work for both parties, then it is not going to work for either. This is sometimes difficult to believe—that one person is not committed to making the relationship work for both—but it is the default perspective of the ego.

ISO 9001:2000 provides a tested, culture-free template for a couple to individualize their personal relationship to optimize their potential for emotional success. While it requires a paradigm shift to see your personal relationship as a business, the reality of a modern relationship is that it is a business, one of meeting emotional needs. (Note: If this personal business fails, it is costly in more ways than one!)

It is a business that generally entails three departments or functions. The first is the partnership, where the couple attends to the tasks of supporting and maintaining the household. The second is the friendship, where the couple attends to the needs of companionship and emotional sharing. And the third is the intimacy, where the couple attends to the needs of physical sharing. The product of emotional satisfaction must satisfy a minimum of three customers: her (and her needs), him (and his needs), and us (the relationship needs).

To achieve emotional satisfaction a couple must be willing to make the same level of commitment that has brought them professional success. It requires a mutual effort, collaboration, where both are committed to making the relationship work for both parties. The process requires a couple to make the commitment to sit down (ideally) at the beginning of their relationship and go through the rather laborious process of implementation, recognizing that the effort up front will provide a smoother, more harmonious relationship in the long run. The *quality policy* sets the aim and direction. The periodic *management review* meetings (herein called the weekly business meetings) enable the relationship to flexibly address the changing nature of personal needs. The *resource management* practices keep resources matched to budgets and needs. *Product realization* ensures needs and expectations are being met, bringing about emotional satisfaction. And *measurement, analysis, and improvement* processes bring about the continual improvement required of a quality management system.

In this chapter, we proceed through the standard ISO format explaining its application to relationships, setting out how to develop *management responsibility*, giving examples of a quality policy, and providing a high-level exposition of the ISO elements as applied to the personal realm. We include brief descriptions of what could be addressed in each of those areas. It is our intention to provide a detailed manual that will guide individuals and couples through the process just as ISO 9001:2000 is implemented in an organization. One of the mistakes that companies fall into when beginning their implementation is to think they can "copy" another company's *quality manual* and just change certain parts. That *never* works. Each company, like each family, has its own culture, its own processes, and its own goals. It takes longer and is only frustrating to try and match your own organization (or family, couple) to someone else's patterns and frequently leads to abandoning the attempt to implement a quality system—or in plainer terms, ends in failure or frustration. The manual will allow each couple to mutually design their unique relationship. (See ISO 9001:2000, clause 7.3, "Design and Development.")

Remember, ISO does not dictate what you do, only that you say what you do, do it, and (have evidence to) prove it. The international standard consists of minimum quality system requirements. When documented, they make up what is called the quality manual. In general, human beings would prefer to do away with the effort required in all paperwork. But impulsivity is not spontaneity. Most arguments arise because people's expectations are different and their memories of events and decisions are personal and rarely match. We all have had the experience where even our *own* personal memory sometimes betrays us when what we are sure is right turns out not to be real. Hence, any system that is going to provide a foundation for improvement and positive change *must* be documented. Take the example of verbal contracts. Unless they are very, very simple (and sometimes not even then), people get into arguments and disagree over the original agreement because our biology is continually looking for an advantage. Human brains perceive reality through the filters of our knowledge, fears, and instincts to create a personal perception of what is happening that often "rewrites history" in our favor—which is very convenient but not conducive to resolution, cooperation, and serenity. And destructive of trust—the linchpin of successful relationships. Remember, in a relationship, it is in each partner's best interest that the other is emotionally satisfied.

ISO 9001:2000, 2 Normative Reference

It seems cold when we're talking about the most private and personal processes in your life, but this section states that all standards are subject to revision. And as we all know but sometimes would rather not accept, everything is continually changing, either growing or dying. That applies to organisms as well as organizations. In your personal life you are not aiming to garner greater market share; nor are you in need of international certification that a quality management system is in place. But to expand your relationship beyond the policies determined by your knowledge, fears, and instincts, you must define, document, and implement a quality system. This chapter takes the quality management standards and applies them to the personal "marketplace" to demonstrate the process of producing emotional satisfaction.

If your relationship lacks mutuality and reciprocity, ISO will give you a way to address that emotional dissatisfaction as an alternative to the biological choices of fighting, fleeing, or freezing into a cold, parallel relationship. Embarking on the quality journey will certainly clarify where the problems lie and provide a forum for discussions, but without a commitment to be real (not right) and provide for each individual's needs and the couple's needs, emotional satisfaction is not possible.

One other caveat: implementing a quality system is a never-ending process of growth. We humans like to tie things up in neat little packages and be done with them so we can get to the next demand, but a relationship, like life, is a process to be experienced and not a problem to be solved. Your relationship is never finished; it is a work in process. As such, it is important to enjoy the journey, as the end of life is death. All of us are alive, but very few consciously live. A quality organization or relationship continually changes to reflect life (what is happening here and now). Change is inevitable and stimulating, one of the antidotes to the boredom of knowledge. We are only in denial if we think things are going to stay as they are today. We can count on change when things are going well or when things are going poorly—either way, they are going to cycle and change from one end of the continuum to the other. That is a comforting thought when things are going poorly and an irritating thought when things are going well.

As humans, we can take a step back to gain perspective on the immediate process, and thereby become aware of another constant in each situation. Each situation in life has an emotional resonance for us. Our emotions give us messages about reality, a feedback loop about what is happening here and now—like gages on a machine.

Our emotions are the unified field that reflects the current conditions in our body (actions), our brain (thoughts), and our environment (relationships), giving us the real (as opposed to right) feedback on what works and does not work. Taking a step back to gain perspective by understanding the messages that our emotions are communicating is a way of gaining the guidance necessary to make the decisions (effortful will) that are in the best interests of our family and ourselves.

ISO 9001:2000, 3   Terms and Definitions

In a business setting, the organization must first decide on the *scope* of the system to which it wants to apply quality principles. For example, does it want to include the production line but not the design function? Or does it want to include all departments except for administration or hospitality? Or does it want only its customer service arm certified?

For the purposes of this example, we will be talking about a committed couple. Now here is why it is difficult to translate the ISO quality management system. In a personal setting, the language appears specific to business organizations, but in the definitions of ISO 9000:2000, *Quality management systems – Fundamentals and vocabulary*, a *product* is defined as "result of a process." What does manufacturing have in common with your household? Both are systems. Both consist of processes, and it is the *processes* (not the people) that are required by ISO 9001:2000 to be controlled so that the system provides repeatability, thus ensuring consistent quality. An interesting statistic discovered by W. Edwards Deming and J. M. Juran is that in 85 percent of cases where there is a problem, it is a *process* problem, not a personnel problem. Can you imagine if 85 percent of your relationship problems were eliminated or solved?

So, a quick explanation may be needed here. In your household, you are the *supplier* as well as one of the internal *customers*. And your *product* is tangibly intangible: you feel emotional satisfaction.

QUALITY MANAGEMENT SYSTEM REQUIREMENTS (QUALITY RELATIONSHIP REQUIREMENTS)

ISO 9001:2000, 3   Management Responsibility

In an era when people emphasize relationship equality, management responsibility is often ignored, as it implies a hierarchical structure. We all have a prejudice against being dominated that stems from childhood experience, when our parents were dominant because we were still developing. Unfortunately, as with most fears, our concern about being controlled leads to an undefined relationship wherein either no one is in control or the stronger personality becomes controlling out of need. Both scenarios create the feared situation of being dominated by forces beyond our control and create the impression that the other is not cooperative or supportive. It is essential for a couple to sit down and address areas of responsibility in each of the three departments mentioned earlier—partnership, friendship, an intimacy. It is important for the couple to assess their respective skill levels and to recognize that in some areas one will lead and the other will provide support, and that the reverse will be true in other areas. It is by recognizing the shared responsibility of both leadership and support that the couple can clearly define a course of action in relationship situations and, with the reversal of roles, free themselves from the childhood prejudice of a dominant/submissive fear in the relationship.

Such sharing of responsibility may become a skill increasingly required in the business world as companies operate around the clock in a global workplace environment, and a single chief executive officer or chief operating officer, or department manager cannot physically be present or available at all locations at all times in all time zones.

So, who is *management*? Each individual in a couple is initially responsible for personal self-management. We are a socialized, biological organism with a primary need to survive and not be satisfied. According to that survivalist, top-of-the-food-chain mentality, the other is not seen as our partner but as someone who either is lunch (satisfying us), is going to make lunch out of us (frustrating us), or is a vehicle for perpetuating our genes. Our initial management responsibility is to maintain our own biological homeostatic balance of physical calmness, mental awareness, and a sense of being connected. At that point we can come to the relationship whole and giving rather than empty and seeking. In managing ourselves, we can see our partner as the customer for it is in our own best interest that our partner's needs are met. If he or she is happy, then life is more satisfying for us.

ISO 9002:2000, 5.2   Customer Focus

The couple must determine and convert to words the requirements (needs) of each as an individual and as a couple. This is a central area for a relationship to address. More than any other relationship in our life, our adult emotional relationships are loaded with historical expectations and fears that are often unknown even to ourselves. It is upon the rocks of these unconscious dynamics that relationships often flounder. While we obviously cannot express what we are not conscious of, we can honestly communicate that which we are aware of. This requires that we challenge the fear that the other will see us as imperfect and therefore undesirable. The failure to communicate honestly does not change those aspects we are ashamed of; it only lays the foundation for unpleasant surprises and unmet expectations resulting in "customer dissatisfaction."

In emotional relationships, it is particularly important to go beyond the dictionary definition of a word, to which the couple can usually agree, to the emotional experiences of that word, which are usually uniquely personal and much more defining. The emotional experience attached to the dictionary definition is the moving force that defines our thoughts and actions. By taking the time to communicate honestly and in detail about the expectations and assumptions each person brings to the relationship, the couple can start to develop the valuable relationship skill of empathy. With empathy and expectation clarification, the couple can then agree upon the exact quality and quantity of the product (emotional satisfaction) and the system of production.

ISO 9001:2000, 5.3   Quality Policy

First, the couple (the organization) needs what in ISO terms is called a quality policy. That policy states, "what you're in business for." It is usually a statement of one to 10 sentences that encapsulates your goal. The shorter (and more pithy) it is, the easier it is to remember. Have fun with this. Try and say what you as a couple stand for. Stephen Covey in his book *The 7 Habits of Highly Effective People* gives guidance, suggestions, examples, and exercises for writing a family mission statement and reviewing it periodically. His point is that if you don't know where you're going, any road will get you there. You just may not prefer the destination. So we're not going to argue the value of having a quality system. If you are uncertain that a quality system is necessary, then you are not ready to implement one.

Here are some examples of quality policies:

It is important that we be aware of our needs, communicate them appropriately, and realize that it is in our best interest that the other's needs are addressed.

It is important for us to be aware of our needs and our wants, to find a balance between the two, and to share that with each other.

In focusing on my needs I define me. In focusing on the other's needs I define we. The challenge is having me in we.

Once management has decided on a quality policy everyone must know what it is. It establishes the goal of your relationship and forms your commitment to quality. You can change your quality policy: you can refine it, you can tweak it, and you can throw it out and start over. ISO doesn't lock you in. It simply says you must have one, it must be documented, and everyone has to know what it is. It shall be understood and carried out throughout the relationship.

ISO 9001:2000, 5.4   Planning

Modern life is complicated as we attempt to gain a full life by filling our plate until it overflows. The resulting overstimulation often leads to forgetfulness, missed expectations, and lost opportunities. It is important for a couple to sit down and come to an agreement on the essential tasks involved in each of the (at least) three departments:

- In the partnership, what is required to maintain the household? Who is going to do what, when, and where? What preventive measures need to be taken to avoid costly repairs? How are the inevitable breakdowns going to be addressed?

- In the friendship, how is there going to be an equitable distribution of the giving and receiving of life experiences? In what individual and relationship ways are appreciation and correction, support and problem solving going to occur? What manner will be employed to decide in which activities to engage in the limited time frames available?

- In the intimacy, how will individual and relationship needs be recognized and addressed?

The couple shall establish quality objectives at each (relevant) level of the relationship. The quality objectives shall be consistent with the quality policy and the commitment to continual improvement. Quality objectives shall include those needed to meet requirements for emotional satisfaction.

ISO 9001:2000, 4.2.2   Quality Manual

The family needs to prepare a quality manual, which shall include a description of the elements of the quality management system and their interaction.

ISO 9001:2000, 4.2.4   Control of Records

Quality records appropriate to the family shall be maintained to demonstrate conformance to the requirements and the effective operation of the quality management system. The family shall establish and maintain quality management system–level procedures for the identification, storage, retrieval, protection, retention time, and disposition of quality records.

Given the relative and personal nature of human perception and memory, particularly in emotional areas, it is essential that the couple write down their understandings and agreements as to the quality and quantity of the product and the system of production. The more laborious process of writing engenders further clarification than a verbal expression provides. The commitment to paper allows for a better overview to ensure that input matches output. Having a written document allows for future review of current endeavors to ensure consistency with original agreements. In turn, the adaptive evolution of agreed procedures can then be compared and appreciated in review with the original plan of agreement.

At a time when we are flooded with information, it becomes important to discriminate between the information that must be filed and stored in an organized way and the information we can let go of. Someone shall be responsible for deciding how long to hold on to quality records and documents and where to store things so they will be both safe and accessible.

ISO 9001:2000, 5.5.1   Responsibility and Authority

Responsibility and authority need to be defined for household members. In business this looks like an organizational chart.

ISO 9001:2000, 5.5.2   Management Representative

Someone needs to be responsible for ensuring that the requirements of ISO 9001:2000 are met. It can be the responsibility of one person, shared, or rotated—but you need to agree on who this will be.

ISO 9001:2000, 5.5.3   Internal Communication

In a relationship, open, honest communication based on the structure of the quality management system (as opposed to personal you-message attacks) is essential to determine effectiveness. Unlike in business, in an emotional relationship the skill of empathy is essential. If you do not understand your partner's perspective, then it is difficult to attain and maintain the patience and tolerance necessary for an emotional relationship.

ISO 9001:2000, 5.6   Management Review

The couple "shall review the quality system at defined intervals sufficient to ensure its continuing suitability and effectiveness in satisfying the requirements of this . . . standard" and the stated quality policy and objectives. So, for example, on a weekly basis (management review), the couple will want to sit down at the table together and review lessons learned (results of audits), objectives accomplished (process performance and product conformance analyses), situations that need addressing (preventive and corrective action), procedures that need changing (customer feedback), and changing circumstances and follow-up actions from earlier meetings that will affect the need for further changes. It sounds so very formal in ISO language, but in reality, having a system with a requirement to do these things makes good sense. We often need a format to remind us to get around to doing these things or they are easily put off, sometimes indefinitely. We also need a format that allows us to appreciate what we have done and are doing that works, thereby forming the basis for a positive motivation based on pleasure (rather than the default guilt). Someone needs to take and keep simple notes as a record that this was done and to record the outcomes of the discussions.

ISO 9001:2000, 6.1   Provision of Resources

The couple shall determine and provide in a timely manner the resources needed to establish and maintain the quality management system.

ISO 9001:2000, 6.2.2   Competency, Awareness and Training

Given that an adult emotional relationship requires awareness and skill levels not required in any other relationship in our lives, it should be expected that specialized training would be needed initially and periodically throughout the relationship. Training could occur either individually or as a couple, and could focus on any of the three departments: partnership, friendship, and intimacy.

Three general skill areas common to all relationships are the need to develop empathy, the need to develop a problem-solving approach that focuses inclusively on the individual and relationship needs, and the need to reset back to an individual and relationship homeostatic balance of emotional satisfaction.

ISO 9001:2000, 7.2.1   Determination of Requirements Related to the Product

The couple shall define their wants and expectations regarding emotional satisfaction. It is important to be detailed in terms of expected actions (how, when, where). Another of the ironies of human nature is our brain's survivalist tendency to focus on what is wrong and to ignore what is going well. That problem-solving perspective can produce a skewed emotional picture of the relationship. It is important for the couple to clearly define the physical, mental, and relationship conditions that produce the desired feeling states of emotional satisfaction. Often those conditions are focused around the homeostatic balance of physical relaxation and energy, mental peace and clarity, and relationship connection and engagement.

ISO 9001:2000, 7.2.2   Review of Requirements Related to the Product

The couple will need to talk over their ability to supply the product to the customer (for example, how often they go out to dinner). In other words, the purpose of this step is to mutually define (quantify) "enough," which can be measured as a standard that can be maintained.

ISO 9001:2000, 7.2.3   Customer Communication

An unfortunate tendency in an emotional relationship is for us to take the ones we love for granted. We would never treat strangers the way we treat the ones we love or to whom we are close. After all, they love us and will forgive us. It is important for each person to continue to make the effort to be polite and cooperative in an emotional relationship. Curiously, this is more difficult than in a professional setting because of the memories and expectations our brain references in emotional situations. We learn to work as adults. We learn to be in emotional relationships as children, and if we do not make a conscious choice, those childhood expectations and skills determine our relationship style. It is through each individual's consistent and conscious effort to follow the agreed-upon contract every day that relationship skills are remembered and developed.

ISO 9001:2000, 7.3.1   Design and Development Planning

The couple shall plan and control the design and development of their emotional satisfaction. The need to understand each other's requirements for emotional satisfaction (the needs of each individual and the relationship needs). What do you want? "I want, need, expect to feel loved."

ISO 9001:2000, 7.3.2   Design and Development Inputs

The couple shall convert those needs into inputs. How do you want it produced? "I want you to tell me that you love me."

ISO 9001:2000, 7.3.3   Design and Development Outputs

The couple shall produce the requirement(s) of the input. What does it look like? The other says, "I love you."

ISO 9001:2000, 7.3.4   Design and Development Review

The couple shall evaluate the ability to fulfill requirements and identify problems and propose follow-up actions. How does it feel to produce it? The other says, "I can say that, but it's easier when I feel it."

ISO 9001:2000, 7.3.5   Design and Development Verification

The couple should openly appreciate the production. Does that meet your objective expectations? You say, "You did it the way I requested."

ISO 9001:2000, 7.3.6   Design and Development Validation

Next, the couple needs to validate that the product produced emotional satisfaction. Does that meet your subjective expectations? How does it feel? You say, "I feel loved."

Once customer requirements have been defined, it is essential for the couple to take a step back and regain an overall perspective. They must imagine going through the procedures they have agreed upon. Does the input (individual requirements) feel as if it matches the desired output (the other's effort), and does that in fact produce emotional satisfaction? Weekly emotional (business) meetings provide the opportunity to review conformity, a chance to upgrade plans, and a forum for feedback.

Once those conditions have been clearly defined, both individually and as a couple, it is valuable to have daily individual and relationship periods (self-assessments) for inspection and testing. Check it out at the source by asking, for example, "Is this as good for you as it is for me?" Or, "Any nigglings? Any knots?"

ISO 9001:2000, 7.4   Purchasing, and 7.4.1   Purchasing Process

Adequate resources shall be provided, including qualified people, materials, and equipment. It is difficult to provide quality meals if there isn't a working stove or cooking appliance. So if one of the elements of quality in your household includes tasty, nutritious meals, you need to provide the appropriate equipment and materials and possibly training.

ISO 9001:2000, 7.4.2   Purchasing Information

In the relationship it will be necessary to purchase materials to ensure product success in the three need areas (departments): partnership, friendship, and intimacy. The common area of the relationship needs often includes groceries, utilities, home improvements, and repairs. It is important for the couple to designate a fund account for these common needs, the means for accessing the funds, and areas of responsibility. Large-ticket items such as vacations, vehicles, and entertainment require an established means of research and acquisition. In addition, each partner needs a discretionary fund account with agreed-upon limits that allows him or her to address individual interests without the other's permission.

ISO 9001:2000, 7.5.1   Control of Production and Service Provision, and 7.5.3   Identification and Traceability

The value of studying history is that we can then recognize when a cycle comes around again. The purpose of a quality management system is to create a predictable, efficient, and continuously improving product cycle. There is a defined start, middle, and end to the product systems in each of the three departments. While those systems are laid out in the *contract*, that form of documentation is not readily available to assist at the time of emotional crisis. We must remember that the couple's efforts to implement their ISO 9001:2000 plan are the free choice that exists in contrast to the habits, fears, and instincts (old knowledge) that they brought into the relationship. Each partner in a couple has the potential to bring out the best and the worst in the other. According to human nature, habits, fears, and instincts are stronger and will come to consciousness sooner than new knowledge and good intentions. As such, it is helpful to lay out the production cycle for each of the major or crucial areas of the relationship.

One method is to take two pieces of paper, and on one piece draw a circle and, starting at the top, outline the agreed-upon systemic approach to the situation at hand. The linear sequence of decisions and areas of responsibility can be designated as points along the cycle proceeding in a clockwise fashion from the beginning to the end of the production cycle. This paper allows the couple to quickly see where they are in the production cycle. On the other sheet of paper, draw another circle. This circle is to represent the habits, fears, and instincts that emerge when this situation occurs in the relationship. As this is *old* knowledge, it will be a consistent pattern usually involving the fears of being controlled and dominated or of being rejected and abandoned. By using this design control in the weekly business meetings, the couple can begin to appreciate how their often-unconscious dynamics pull them into a dysfunctional approach when this situation occurs, preventing them from following their agreed-upon plan.

By outlining this dysfunctional approach to the situation with the same utilization of points representing irrational decisions and reactions, the couple has an opportunity to take a moment of emotional dissatisfaction and place it in the larger context of their dysfunctional systemic approach to a situation. With this awareness of where they are on the dysfunctional cycle, they then have the choice to look at the accompanying sheet of paper that describes the agreed-upon systemic approach to the functional cycle and to shift to the agreed-upon production cycle. This allows the couple to avoid the temptation to blame; it instead channels their frustration toward resolving the *process problem*, not the people problem.

By placing these graphs depicting satisfactory (functional) and unsatisfactory (dysfunctional) production cycles side by side in a visible place, a couple has a chance to be able to integrate this knowledge casually and consistently through everyday observation as well as at times of critical incidents.

It is this repeated exposure to the entire process that allows us to take a step back from the tendency to become target fixated (focused on the problem and not the solution) in times of stress or need deprivation. As this new knowledge becomes ingrained knowledge through daily practice, individual and relationship skill levels gradually become stronger than the habits, fears, and instincts. With daily exposure to the graphs and open communication between the couple, individual and relationship awareness and skill levels about the triggers increase, and preventive measures will become more efficient. (See also these sections: "Control of Measuring and Monitoring Devices" and "Preventive Action.")

ISO 9001:2000, 7.5.2   Validation of Processes

How can a couple ensure that their processes are capable of giving them emotional satisfaction? In relationships, as in all of life, there will be areas that work and areas that do not work in spite of all our plans and intentions. Often we see a shifting in the flow of what works and what does not work, providing the diversity and movement of life. Fortunately, life follows the logic of cause and effect with the emotions signaling whether or not current conditions work. Ongoing, open personal and relationship communication about current conditions provides for a validation assessment of emotional satisfaction.

The couple must be able to sit down and decide how to address nonconforming situations (emotional dissatisfaction). Through identifying the requirements and reviewing the degree of emotional satisfaction in the periodic business meetings (management review), the couple will be able to identify individual and relationship processes that do not work. In general, processes that do not work involve plans (old knowledge) that are being applied to current legitimate needs. The options available to the couple are to make a new plan that is more adaptive in meeting needs (rework it) or to accept that this is an inherent, individual way that cannot be changed (use as is or scrap the old one). The difficulty in these options involves the necessary courage to change, the serenity to accept, and the wisdom to tell the difference.

ISO 9001:2000, 7.5.4   Customer Property

Each person brings preferences to the relationship ("Don't give me an appliance for a present!" or "I need 30 minutes of solitude to unwind after work"), as well as favorite or sentimental items ("I want the stuffed fish mounted on the wall"). Such preferences often range from mild inclinations to sentimental identification, with the degree of attachment influencing the individual's ability to be cooperative in the three departments. It is important that each individual personally ascertains his or her degree of attachment to these personal preferences and communicates them honestly to enhance understanding of oneself and one's partner, develop realistic expectations, and avoid future resentment.

ISO 9001:2000, 7.5.5   Preservation of Product

It is said that your health is everything. This is never clearer than during an illness. Upon recovery, the emotional satisfaction of health is tangible. Without it nothing else matters. It is important for a couple to address their physical health through a regime of a balanced diet, regular exercise, and adequate sleep. Regular health checkups and maintenance of treatment/medication regimes is essential.

MEASUREMENT, ANALYSIS AND IMPROVEMENT

ISO 9001:2000, 8.2.2   Internal Audit

The couple shall conduct periodic internal audits to determine whether the quality management system conforms to requirements and has been implemented and maintained effectively. In a business setting, internal audits are conducted by personnel who are independent of the activity being audited. In a relationship setting, two levels of auditing need to take place. The first is the individual internal audit, and the second, the interpersonal relationship audit.

The interpersonal relationship audit shall be conducted at least once a year, and more frequently in crucial areas. It is important for the couple to review each aspect of the quality manual against what they are actually doing. This is the time to either adjust the contract (and the documentation in the quality manual) or their behavior so that there is again system agreement. The daily and weekly practices (internal audits) would provide more frequent monitoring. (See "Control of Measuring and Monitoring Devices.")

The goal here is to gradually master the personal and relationship until the processes become effortless actions. Nonconformance (variation from agreed-upon processes) will then be experienced personally and in the relationship as a felt sense (negative emotions) with corrective action arising out of personal management toward balance and emotional satisfaction. The collective development of these skills will come through the individual internal audit and interpersonal relationship audit.

ISO 9001:2000, 8.3   Control of Nonconformity

Once the couple has decided what to do in the area of emotional dissatisfaction, they need to decide how to carry out the decision. The person who does not have to make the change is often the one who is emotionally frustrated, so the couple must define a course that is a delicate balancing act between nagging and silent resentment. The partner changing the old habit or expectation needs to address the initial deprivation and unfamiliarity as a new skill level is developed to the point where it is able to satisfactorily address the underlying need. Appropriate support from the other partner at this point helps provide the emotional satisfaction and motivation to carry the individual through the period of skill development.

ISO 9001:2000, 8.4   Analysis of Data

One of the difficulties in experiencing growth and emotional satisfaction is the previously mentioned tendency for us to focus on the current problem and lose sight of the progress. It is important for the couple to create an easily accessible way to record their emotional state on a daily or at least a weekly basis. It is convenient if these data are easily transferable to a graph that can display over time the progress or lack thereof in their application of the system. Records can be as simple as happy/sad faces on each calendar day, to a simple recording form or a checklist. Whatever method of recording is appropriate for the situation. Such an overview often is necessary to be able to dispel situational perceptions of dissatisfaction and to provide the appreciation and motivation for long-term change.

ISO 9001:2000, 8.5   Improvement, and 8.5.2   Corrective Action

It is the nature of needs to constantly change. Relative needs such as hunger, sleep, and companionship are constantly shifting through the cycle of deprivation to satiety and back. The absolute needs of wholeness and union are met by opening up against the reactive survivalist tendency to contract. Having been civilized to try to be normal (a statistical term that defines an average that does not in reality exist), we have to make the effort to be natural. In life two forces—pain and pleasure—motivate us. Pain lets us know when we have done something that does not work, and it motivates us not to do it again. Unfortunately, if that is our knowledge of how to address the situation, in the absence of a conscious choice otherwise, we will find ourselves again doing what we know. Pleasure lets us know when we have done something that does work and motivates us to do it again. Unfortunately, pleasure, like pain, follows our actions and thoughts so that we first have to make the effort before we gain the pleasure. The development of an agreed-upon system of what to do if things work or do not work allows a couple to efficiently motivate themselves and avoid the tendency to lapse into laziness, guilt, and blame. Through their weekly emotional business meetings, a couple can consciously appreciate their individual and relationship successes. They also can develop a supportive corrective improvement plan to address areas of emotional dissatisfaction. With an objective examination of the individual and relationship successes and frustrations, a business meeting provides the forum for the couple to address expectations and to adjust them according to the reality of the current situation.

ISO 9001:2000, 8.5.3 Preventive Action

Our emotional satisfaction is a personal, relative experience. It is influenced by factors internal and external. As we have all experienced, when we are angry, hungry, tired, or sick, our perception of things is altered by the influences of those negative states.

It is important for each individual and the relationship that each partner has a consistent procedure or ritual by which he or she can bring him- or herself back to a measurable and replicable condition of psychophysiologic homeostatic balance. This is the emotional equivalent of bringing the individuals into calibration that is defined in the emotional arena as being calm, clear, and connected.

Individually, this could involve a 20-minute period at the beginning of the day during which the person sits in a quiet space and practices bringing about a psychophysiologic homeostatic balance. As their awareness and skill levels develop in attaining the conditions of emotional satisfaction, the individuals can visualize an image of themselves being that way. That image can be used to project into the anticipated day the sense of themselves being clear and connected as they see themselves addressing the situations before them.

At night before retiring, each individual could take a few moments to come back to that balanced way of experiencing him- or herself. This will preload knowledge of the satisfactory production cycle (preventive action). By reviewing the events of the day, and taking time to appreciate one's successes as well as being aware of those areas where one's awareness and skill levels need improving, each partner will be performing an individual audit. He or she could again use imagery to imagine him- or herself addressing the unsatisfactory situation in a more satisfactory fashion.

As a relationship, this could involve the partners sharing their individual practices and thereby forming a common relationship experience. This could be followed by an empathy talk to increase awareness of the current need states so that ensuing decisions can be made with the current individual and relationship needs in mind.

We, the authors, envision a concise, usable quality manual that helps focus the partners on processes and avoid blame. A great benefit will be realized from the frank discussion necessary to address the standard and the ability to laugh at one's own repeated "process nonconformities" (old neural circuits). We hope that by employing the ISO framework you are able to achieve the emotional nonattachment that you exercise in reviewing and improving processes in your businesses. One of the more difficult things for us to do is not to take our personal relationships personally.

Chapter 58

Printing and Graphic Arts

Ron Cerzosimo
International Quality Consultants (IQC), Doylestown, Pennsylvania

INTRODUCTION

Quality, like beauty, is in the eyes of the beholder. Someone once remarked, "Quality, I know it when I see it." Quality, or levels of quality, in the printing and graphic arts (hereafter referred to as printing) sector, may be directly related to the purchase price of the printed material. Acceptable quality of the printed material may at times be based on subjective acceptance criteria; and at times it may be based on very absolute and discriminating acceptance criteria. Fundamentally, whether or not the quality of the printed matter is judged acceptable is directly related to the customer's expectations and needs. Once a specification for quality is clearly defined, the achievement of quality is certainly a function of many factors, some of which include people, materials, processes, and management systems.

This chapter addresses how quality is achieved in the printing sector and provides examples for the application of a quality management system (QMS) using ISO 9001:1994. The chapter will specifically discuss the nature of the printing industry; identify and describe the unique and complex processes within the industry; describe the various approaches to quality and the assurance of quality; provide specific examples of ISO 9001:1994 as applied by a commercial direct mail advertising company; and offer some insight on the potential use of ISO 9001:2000 in the printing industry in the future.

NATURE OF THE PRINTING INDUSTRY WITH ITS UNIQUE AND COMPLEX PROCESSES

Based on data tracked by the U.S. Department of Commerce, it is estimated that the number of printing firms exceeds 50,000, and the number of printing facilities may well be more than 100,000. A large proportion of these firms (about 84 percent) employ fewer than 20 people. On the other hand, some of the firms in the smaller proportion have annual sales of between $2 billion and $4 billion. The industry produces a large variety of printed products as well as materials used in the printing process. Products include newspapers, books, magazines, direct mail advertisements, greeting cards, and much more. Products vary in print quality from newsprint to nationally recognized magazines. While it is difficult to characterize the processes in the printing industry because of the diversity of technologies and products, most printing activities can be categorized within a few different printing processes: lithography, gravure, flexography, letterpress, screen printing, and more recently, digitalography.

The fundamental steps in printing are referred to as imaging, prepress, printing, and postpress. Imaging produces an image of the material to be printed. Typically, this image is produced photographically; however, with increasing frequency, the image is produced electronically. The image on the film is transferred to the image carrier or plate. In prepress operations, an image carrier is produced that can transfer the ink in the image area and can repel the ink in a nonimage area. In printing, the ink is applied to the plate and the image is transferred to the substrate (for example, paper, plastic, ceramic, or metal). Depending on the desired form of final product, the postpress step may involve any number of finishing operations, including binding, stitching, foil stamping, labeling, inserting, packaging, mail sorting, and commingling (with postage applied) for the deliverable product to reach customers.

The state of the art in the printing industry with regard to technological advances has realized dramatic improvements. As an example, imaging operations begin with composition and typesetting, followed by the production of a photographic positive or negative. Composition involves the arrangement of art and text into the desired format. This composition task, historically performed manually, today is accomplished using computer systems. Pretyped material and images can be incorporated into the document being composed using computers equipped with both optical character recognition and photographic image scanners and digitizers. Most material and images today start as digital information and stay in that format until the output is produced (that is, proof, plate, and so on). Using computers, a direct to plate process is possible, eliminating the use of film (positive or negative). Computer to plate, direct to press, and related technologies, often considered a part of prepress, are now considered as a significant pressroom development.

While the digital revolution has been under development since the mid-1970s, digital print technology has moved toward mainstream utilization. And while some common phrases and topics include digital workflow and digital on-demand color laser printing, the industry currently is a mixture of traditional, or conventional, and digital printing.

It is not the purpose of this chapter to discuss the details of the various print processes and related applications. It is, however, appropriate that we discuss how printing organizations make quality certain. Making quality certain is addressed in the next section.

APPROACH TO QUALITY AND THE ASSURANCE OF QUALITY

Perhaps as early as the late 1700s to mid-1800s, one approach to achieving quality was a form of inspection known as proofreading. A galley, or a made-up page, would be checked against an original to ensure correctness. Today, because of the complex process equipment and the number and amount of raw materials used, quality and assurance of quality is approached by using process controls and management systems—and usually a combination of both.

For the purpose of this chapter, we consider *web offset* printing, commonly used in the printing of newspapers, magazine publications, and direct mail advertising. In web offset printing, variation is inherent in the complex processes and raw materials used. Defining the characteristics and attributes of the processes and materials is required to effect adequate controls that will ensure a quality product. Some materials used include substrates (for example, paper, plastics, glass, metal, and nylon), organic solvents, inks, ultraviolet (UV) coatings, and adhesives. Two material examples are provided here—paper and ink. A paper roll, or web, has important characteristics or attributes that affect the printing processes, including coating and finishing, grain, two-sidedness, density, flatness, and moisture content. Paper properties important to printability include color, brightness, opacity, smoothness, gloss, and reflectiveness. The working properties and performance characteristics of inks that affect press stability include body (consistency), length (viscosity and elasticity), thixotropy (the property of the ink to become more fluid as a result of working and less fluid on standing), tack (the force required to split an ink film between two surfaces), and drying.

To characterize the web offset lithographic press, we must think of the press as consisting of several sections. The elements, in order, are infeed, print unit or press, dryer, chill rolls, and delivery.

A blanket-to-blanket web offset lithographic press (or perfecting press—a press that prints on both sides of the paper in a single pass through the press) is commonly used in commercial printing. The web offset lithographic press has four basic elements: dampening system, inking system, plate cylinder, and blanket cylinder. Other elements to consider include folders, press controls, web tension, and image and web controls, as well as attributes such as print length, color, and registration, to mention just a few.

It is important to control all these characteristics and related process elements. In fact, most, if not all, require some form of monitoring and measuring to ensure process and product quality. In addition, there must be a system for quality and quality management that sustains continual quality improvement. Some approaches are described in the following sections.

THE DEMING PRINCIPLES

Dr. W. Edwards Deming, in a teleconference that reached across the United States in August 1987, suggested that faulty management practices were the reason why quality programs do not succeed. He also indicated that only management can take a process that is stable and reduce its variation. Further, he concluded that investing in machines rather than knowledge is not the answer; but that knowledge produces changes in quality, and quality is produced by working smarter.[1]

In his book *Out of the Crisis,* Dr. Deming proposed 14 principles for effective management.[2] Although these principles are familiar to most of us, they are listed here for reference purposes:

1. Create constancy of purpose for improvement of product and service.
2. Adopt the new philosophy.
3. Cease dependence on inspection to achieve quality.
4. End the practice of awarding business on the basis of price tag alone. Instead, minimize total cost by working with a single supplier.
5. Improve, constantly and forever, every process for planning, production, and service.
6. Institute training on the job.
7. Adopt and institute leadership.
8. Drive out fear.
9. Break down barriers between staff areas.
10. Eliminate slogans, exhortations, and targets for the workforce.
11. Eliminate numerical quotas for the workforce and numerical goals for management.
12. Remove barriers that rob people of pride of workmanship. Eliminate the annual rating or merit system.
13. Institute a vigorous program of education and self-improvement for everyone.
14. Put everyone in the company to work to accomplish the transformation.

Dr. Deming's principles have been applied in the printing industry to eliminate waste and inefficiency with continuous quality improvement.

ISO 9001:1994 AND A QUALITY MANAGEMENT SYSTEM (QMS)

ISO 9001:1994, *Quality systems—Model for quality assurance in design, development, production, installation and servicing,* is another approach to quality and the assurance of quality. This international standard prescribes the minimum requirements for a quality system in 20 elements, or clauses:

4.1   Management responsibility

4.2   Quality system

4.3   Contract review

4.4   Design control

4.5   Document and data control

4.6   Purchasing

4.7   Control of customer-supplied product

4.8   Product identification and traceability

4.9   Process control

4.10   Inspection and testing

4.11   Control of inspection, measuring, and test equipment

4.12   Inspection and test status

4.13   Control of nonconforming product

4.14   Corrective and preventive action

4.15   Handling, storage, packaging, preservation, and delivery

4.16   Control of quality records

4.17   Internal quality audits

4.18   Training

4.19   Servicing

4.20   Statistical techniques

These clauses are sequentially numbered to reflect the sequence of events and activities from developing the quality policy to after-sales servicing. As with most industry standards that prescribe requirements, ISO 9001:1994 states *what* must be done but not *how* to implement the requirements. A number of ISO 9000 series guidance-type standards offer information on implementation and "best current practice." These are certainly recommended reading, and a rather complete listing is shown on the last page of the ISO 9001 standard.

The requirements of ISO 9001 have been applied in the printing industry to eliminate waste and inefficiency with continuous quality improvement. Examples of this approach to quality and the assurance of quality are provided in the section of this chapter titled "Application of ISO 9001:1994 for Direct Mail and Advertising."

In the application of both the Deming and ISO 9001:1994 approaches, there are no restrictions regarding the specific techniques to be used. An organization may choose to implement ISO 9001:1994 and include concepts and practices prescribed by Dr. Deming.

THE SIX SIGMA INITIATIVE

Another quality initiative that has gained prominence in recent years is Six Sigma. This initiative can complement either of the two approaches previously discussed. Six Sigma has a customer focus and is considered a business strategy and philosophy based on statistical measurements. Somewhat simply stated, Six Sigma provides for the application of statistical tools for recognition and definition of a process as a result of characterization (measurement and analyses) and optimization (improvement and control) of the process. This would certainly appear to be beneficial to the printing industry, because printing processes are complex. The Six Sigma initiative attempts to minimize variation resulting from "drift and shift" in a given process and to ensure process capabilities. Theoretically, a process in control will yield a quality product. But to control, we must have some knowledge of industry-specific standards. Who develops these standards? What are they and what do they cover?

STANDARDS IN THE PRINTING INDUSTRY

Standards in the printing industry provide uniform, defined procedures and tools that help users produce quality products. The Association for Suppliers of Printing and Publishing Technologies (NPES) provides leadership worldwide in the development of such industry standards.[3] NPES serves as secretariat to the American National Standards Institute (ANSI) accredited Committee for Graphic Arts Technologies Standards (CGATS); the U.S. Technical Advisory Group to the ISO Technical Committee 130 (ISO/TC 130), Graphic Technology; and a new organization, the International Color Consortium (ICC) for developing a standard to enable different devices to translate their color definition information into a standard color interchange space.

The following are examples of ISO/TC 130 published standards:

- ISO 2836:1999, *Graphic technology—Prints and printing inks—Assessment of resistance to various agents*
- ISO 12634:1996, *Graphic technology—Determination of tack of paste inks and vehicles by a rotary tackmeter*
- ISO 12636:1998, *Graphic technology—Blankets for offset printing*
- ISO 13655:1996, *Graphic technology—Spectral measurement and colorimetric computation for graphic arts images*

Digital Distribution of Advertising for Publications (DDAP)[4] and Specifications for Web Offset Publications (SWOP)[5] also have printing industry endorsement in the United States for recommended specifications, guidance, and standards of practice. Another organization supporting the industry with research, testing, training, and the development of effective test images is the Graphic Arts Technical Foundation (GATF).[6]

Considering all these standards-development activities, there is no one standard for quality or quality management that is specific to the printing industry. Of course, there is ISO 9001:1994, which is not industry specific but certainly can and has been applied in the printing industry with beneficial results.

APPLICATION OF ISO 9001:1994 FOR DIRECT MAIL AND ADVERTISING

The examples provided in this section are based on the application of ISO 9001:1994 at Webcraft Direct Marketing Services, a division of Vertis. Webcraft provides fully integrated direct marketing programs, from planning, database management, in-line, and laser/lettershop production to full response management services, program analysis, and Internet integration. Webcraft is a multiplant operation and is certified to ISO 9001:1994 and ISO 14001:1996 for environmental management systems. Each plant location is independently certified.

Before establishing and developing the QMS, it was most important to ensure that executive management understood the benefits and values of the system. In addition, executive management at the highest levels had to commit to direct and active involvement with the system and its implementation. Given that these two conditions were satisfied, a quality management steering committee was formed to plan the process and ensure that sufficient maturity of the system's implementation could be demonstrated to achieve certification. In describing the application of ISO 9001:1994, let's consider each element or clause of the standard (by title) in sequence.

MANAGEMENT RESPONSIBILITY

The company's executive management defined and documented the quality policy as follows:

We will understand the needs and expectations of our customers.

We will stand by the commitments we make to our customers.

We will accomplish this through continuous improvement and
employee development.

The quality policy was signed by the most senior executives and posted and communicated to all Webcraft employees.

To ensure that the system would be sustained, objectives for quality were established and included as a part of the organization's operational planning process. Operational plans are established annually, consistent with the organization's strategic plan. Programs including responsibility assignment for achieving objectives and targets are documented and tracked. Performance indicators are reviewed quarterly.

For the system to function effectively, the organization had to understand that accountability is fundamental, and managers and supervisors had to take ownership of their own processes and be responsible as "process owners" for their respective processes. Adequate resources, including the assignment of trained personnel, are continuously monitored.

Executive management appointed a management representative for each plant. The management representatives, irrespective of other responsibilities, coordinate the planning and scheduling of the management review process. These review meetings are conducted quarterly and are integrated with operational reviews at each plant. Topics of discussion typically include action items and status from previous meetings; quality objectives and targets; results of audits; nonconformance; preventive and corrective actions; performance of suppliers; and evaluation of the quality system. Executive managers (president, senior vice presidents, and vice presidents) attend the review meetings and document their evaluation of the continuing suitability and effectiveness of the QMS in satisfying the requirements of the international standard (ISO 9001).

QUALITY SYSTEM

The QMS is documented at each plant with a quality system manual, quality system procedures, and department work instructions. These documents prescribe and describe activities, responsibilities, and actions required to be responsive to each element or clause of ISO 9001 and Webcraft's business practices. Planning is an important part of the QMS. Quality plans are developed and documented when a job is complex or when it has unusual customer requirements and conditions to be satisfied. These plans identify responsibilities and controls that are considered critical in nature.

CONTRACT REVIEW

Sales owns the contract review process. The nature of Webcraft's business is that there are many jobs (often on a fast track) and with many changes by the customer. It is extremely important that the customer's needs and expectations are clearly, accurately, and completely communicated to and within the organization. To fulfill the customer's requirements, sales works directly with a client services group, which consists of subgroups including business acquisition (including order confirmation, estimating and scheduling) and client/customer services. A project coordinator is assigned to be the client's in-house representative and is responsible for coordinating all preproduction and makeready activities. This includes ensuring that the latest client specifications are approved and all job-related materials (data, artwork, films, discs, paper, inks, adhesives, and so on) are available when the job is scheduled on press. Many checks and balances are incorporated for verifying the correctness and completeness of work as it progresses through each workflow stage of the internal design and manufacturing processes.

DESIGN CONTROL

The scope of design control activities extends beyond the normal creative services or product design groups. On the premise that process capability and reliability are significant contributors to making quality certain, design control activities are also implemented by the corporate and plant engineering organizations to ensure new and/or modified process equipment will perform their required functions as specified. The product design group works closely with sales and the client. The end result of this group's efforts may be a sample product (dummy) or creative services specification sheet (CSSS) that includes an end view showing dimensions, folds, piece insertion, and fit. The CSSS also defines the paper size and other paper attributes, inks, adhesives (such as remoist glues), and UV coatings as may be required for the job.

Often the design is complex and includes products such as phone cards using scratch off coating or fragrance oils that are encapsulated and applied to the printed product representing a client's fragrance or perfume. For these applications, not only is the visual quality of the printed product important, but also the quality of reproducing a specified fragrance (scent) must be consistent. Product design also defines and specifies a particular press to be used based on press capability. Designs are independently verified and validated to ensure the completeness and correctness of the final design.

DOCUMENT AND DATA CONTROL

There are more than a thousand documented procedures and instructions within the Webcraft organization. While these initially were issued and controlled as hard copy, most are now under electronic media control.

An effective review and approval process is used to ensure the adequacy and correctness of a document prior to its approval for use. Document originator(s) must obtain review and comments from users of the documents. All comments must be resolved before an approved, controlled document is issued. Control includes not only review and approval (including treating document changes the same as the original), but also the controlled distribution to ensure that only current revisions of documents are used and available where an activity is performed. A master document activity list reflects the current status at all times of the many documents that are under such control (that is, in preparation, review, revision, comments resolved, approved, and issued).

PURCHASING

To ensure that suppliers have the required capability, suppliers important to quality are evaluated and selected based on their ability to satisfy Webcraft's requirements. The basis for their selection and use (including their continued use) is documented. Purchase documents are reviewed and approved to ensure the inclusion of appropriate technical and quality requirements. Examples of requirements that may be included in purchase documents are technical specifications to be met; documents to be submitted with the purchased product or service (such as certificates of analysis and certified calibration reports); and access to the supplier's facility for the purpose of inspection, test, or audit by Webcraft, Webcraft's clients, and the client's representatives.

Although many Webcraft suppliers provide commodity items and materials (paper, inks, adhesives, calibration services, and so on), many outside service (OS) suppliers are used (such as, for bindery, insertion, and mailing) when and where Webcraft may have the need for such services. These OS suppliers are controlled in the same way as commodity suppliers. For the OS and critical commodity suppliers, an on-site evaluation or preaward assessment is normally performed to verify the supplier's capability.

CONTROL OF CUSTOMER-SUPPLIED PRODUCT

For Webcraft, customer-supplied products include preprint and inserts, envelopes, artwork, film, discs, labels, and data. Provisions for control of verification, storage, and maintenance are incorporated in daily business practices. It is important that such job-related materials are current and suitable for use. When such items are determined to be nonconforming, lost, or otherwise unsuitable for use, they are reported to the customer and handled in accordance with Webcraft's provisions for control of nonconforming product.

PRODUCT IDENTIFICATION AND TRACEABILITY

Webcraft uses a variety of methods for the identification and traceability of supplier and customer-supplied products as well as for Webcraft manufactured and processed products.

For example, bar coding is used for items and materials such as paper and inks. A computerized system allows tracking of the products throughout the process and provides information related to location, quantity, and use, including waste. Other job-related items, such as artwork, film, plates, and job-bag information (containing creative services specification sheets, press instructions, and bluelines) are identified by sales order and job numbers, including revision or version status.

Process-related items (perf wheels and slitters, blankets, rollers, and so on) are uniquely identified. Process-related materials (fountain solutions, solvents, and adhesives) are also uniquely identified, including shelf-life requirements when appropriate.

PROCESS CONTROL

Webcraft has documented provisions responsive to the requirements of this ISO 9001 clause. Particular attention is given to the use of qualified operators and the use of continuous monitoring and control of the product being processed, as well as the process itself. To determine what should be monitored and measured—or controlled—three questions must be answered: What are the critical characteristics of the product to be manufactured? What processes are used to ensure the critical characteristics of the product will be within the required tolerance or specification limits? What is critical about the processes that are used to ensure the critical characteristics of the product will be within the required tolerance or specification limits?

When these determinations are made, the focus can be on controlling the process ("a process in control is a product in control"). As an example, a press evaluation may be performed to analyze what is critical about the press operation. The expected result is to identify where variation (shift and drift) is introduced in the press equipment, including process control equipment, and taking appropriate actions (modify, control, monitor, and measure) to eliminate, or at least minimize, the variation that may be introduced. As a result of this analysis, it may be prudent and appropriate to control (calibrate) certain equipment and instrumentation that is judged critical to controlling the process. Such equipment and instruments may include temperature transmitters, recorders and controllers, infrared pyrometers, pressure and flow measuring devices, print length monitors, registration devices, imaging devices, and spectrophotometers.

It is important to recognize the importance of measuring and analyzing the most expensive piece of equipment in the print production process—the press. Current best practice includes press testing that takes into account the print production process as a whole. Information and data from press testing should yield the answers to the following questions:

- Is there any damage or deterioration to the main print system components of the press (such as the cylinders and gears)?
- Can the press print to industry-accepted ink densities and tone value increases?
- Can the press accurately achieve and maintain image register and fit from unit to unit?
- Can the press hold ink densities and tone value increase throughout a press run?

To this end, the use of preventive maintenance programs, training, and the qualification of people, including maintenance of qualifications, cannot be overemphasized.

INSPECTION AND TESTING

Webcraft performs inspection and testing for purchased products and during in-process and final stages of manufacturing.

Receiving inspection for some purchased products consists only of verification for damage and quantity. For many other products received, more-extensive verifications are performed. In most instances, if not all, when the purchased product is only checked for damage and quantity, a second-stage inspection is required to more suitably perform the test. Documents such as certificates of analysis or certified calibration reports, when submitted with the products, are evaluated for conformance to specification requirements. Frequently, samples of the materials are independently tested to verify and confirm that the actual material is consistent with the data shown in certificates of analysis.

In-process inspection and testing is performed as directly related to the process activities. In prepress, some verifications include checking color proofs, proofreading, and checking plates for coating applications. In data programming, some software verifications and validations check the coded data for format and correctness (names, addresses, and respective locations). In the pressroom, verifications include checking machine setup and makeready; first-piece operations; customer approvals; and quality control samples for imaging and registration, color, data, and glue tack and adhesion. In the bindery, verifications include checking for folds, trim, address position (for business reply envelopes), insertion sequence, and postal bar codes.

Final inspection and testing is a continuous process and critical because of dated material. Clients expect certain mail pieces to be in the mail and delivered by a specified date based on the client's prescheduled promotional activities (such as video rentals, new car rebates, airline promotions, U.S. tax return and census forms). In this regard, mailing operations check trays, sacks, and cartons for content, sequence numbers of mail pieces, and weight. Pallet weight is verified for reasonableness to expected piece count and to ensure compliance with postal regulations.

CONTROL OF INSPECTION, MEASURING, AND TEST EQUIPMENT

Based on evaluations of measurements to be made and the directly related measurement uncertainties, measuring devices are selected based on the measuring capability of the device. Controls consistent with the requirements of ISO 9001 are implemented, including calibration at suitable intervals with traceability to national or international standards, calibration status indicators, unique device identification, tamperproof seals to prevent invalidating calibration settings, appropriate preservation and storage to ensure fitness for use, and calibration records. Certified calibration reports, required by purchase documents, are reviewed to ensure that the data is appropriate and acceptable. Should the "as-found data" or precalibration data indicate that the measuring device was out of tolerance with the device specification limits, then an investigation is performed to determine where the device is used and what must be accomplished to resolve the potential nonconformities resulting from the use of the out-of-control device.

Provisions are also implemented for test software and comparative references. For example, software that is part of a measuring system must have evidence of verification, including continuing tracking of error reports or software bugs and evaluation of their impact on the measuring system. Postal templates are used throughout the Webcraft organization. Each template must be controlled and verified on a continuing basis.

Some examples of other measuring devices or equipment that Webcraft controls for use with product acceptance measurements include micrometers for paper thickness and cylinder blankets, densitometers for optical density of film and for ink density on the printed product, viewing stations for controlled lighting, and scales for checking weight of printed product compared with paid postage and postal regulations. In addition to the measuring devices used for product acceptance purposes, process control systems and equipment as described in this chapter under "Process Control" is considered critical to ensuring that the process is in control. These systems are also subject to calibration control requirements.

INSPECTION AND TEST STATUS

Various means are used to indicate conformance or nonconformance of the product. Press operators sign off on documents after quality control samples are verified as correct. Some press operations are continuously monitored electronically. In this case, a roll sheet (full impression) is pulled and examined for each finished roll of preprint. Other examples include indicating acceptance of first-piece inspections and color approvals and when press/image operators verify imager synchronization to indicate that imaging information is correct on the last good piece before the press or imager stops, and the first good piece after imaging has resumed.

CONTROL OF NONCONFORMING PRODUCT

At Webcraft, every employee is empowered to identify nonconforming product. When a product nonconformance is perceived (regardless of where may it be in the print production process), it is reported and validated to be an actual nonconformance. After this determination is made, the product is identified and segregated when practical, and the condition is documented on a nonconformance report (NCR) form. The nonconformance is evaluated and a disposition is made regarding the use of the nonconforming product. Additionally, the root cause contributing to the adverse-quality condition must be identified, and actions are required to correct the immediate condition that is adverse to quality and to preclude its recurrence. A supplier nonconformance is handled the same as an internal nonconformance. Every nonconformance is tracked to closure and measured as a measurement of quality (MOQ).

CORRECTIVE AND PREVENTIVE ACTION

Webcraft considers corrective and preventive action to be an inherent part of nonconformance control and the audit process (described later). In this regard, where and when corrective action is determined to be ineffective and/or inadequate, a corrective action request (CAR) is initiated and tracked to closure. Should Webcraft receive a customer complaint, it is processed similar to the CAR. Additionally, a CAR may also be issued as an "internal complaint" independent of an NCR for significant issues that have been identified. The process owner (that is, the manager responsible for the condition that caused the complaint) is assigned responsibility to resolve the complaint, including action to correct the immediate condition that is adverse to quality (customer dissatisfaction) as well as to preclude its recurrence.

Timeliness of corrective action is considered extremely important at Webcraft. Quality managers at each plant report on the status of open NCRs, audit nonconformance reports, and CARs at biweekly QMS steering committee meetings. These issues may also become topics of discussion at the quarterly management review meetings. When it appears that complex conditions and situations may not be resolved in a timely manner, teams are assigned to analyze the problems and recommend appropriate actions.

As discussed in the "Management Responsibility" section of this chapter, taking ownership of a process is fundamental to the system working effectively. In this regard, and as a matter of prevention, process owners are responsible for evaluating their processes and, as appropriate, performing potential problem analyses. In doing so, the process owner identifies where a potential problem exists and identifies the most probable cause. Accordingly, the process owner is then responsible for setting contingent action to eliminate the potential problem from occurring the first time, or at least for minimizing the resulting adverse effect.

HANDLING, STORAGE, PACKAGING, PRESERVATION, AND DELIVERY

Clause 4.15 of ISO 9001 has broad implications and affects all materials and products at the various Webcraft facilities. Provisions are documented to safeguard materials and products in inventory (temporary and nontemporary storage), during work in process, and when the product is at the final stage for delivery. Assessments of the condition of materials and products in storage is formally conducted at predetermined intervals, material handlers and fork lift truck drivers are trained, and when they have demonstrated their ability satisfactorily, they are considered qualified to fulfill their duties.

The deliverable product is packaged and delivered to meet the customer's requirements. Because of the nature of Webcraft's business, the packaging must be in compliance with U.S. postal regulations. Postal inspectors are located at some Webcraft facilities based on the volume of printed product to be delivered (approximately 40 million impressions per month).

CONTROL OF QUALITY RECORDS

To initiate the process for maintaining quality records to demonstrate conformance to specified requirements, Webcraft's process owners are responsible for evaluating the need and use of their respective quality records. The process owners also document their record needs in department work instructions, including the record type and other related information (such as identification, collection, indexing, storage, maintenance, and disposition). Record retention is specified as either lifetime or nonlifetime. When it is nonlifetime, the specific period is defined (number of months or years). Some examples of record types used and retained include records for training, supplier evaluations, contract reviews and order confirmations, inspections and tests, calibrations, internal and external quality system audits, product designs, NCRs and CARs, job-bag/press instructions, and management review.

The completeness and correctness of quality records are extremely important. Accordingly, the department instructions require the various process owners to review records for tasks and activities in progress and when completed. This review serves to ensure that records are being completed as required and that they are complete and correct.

INTERNAL QUALITY AUDITS

While each ISO 9001 clause is considered important, clause 4.17 is considered one of the most important. The issue of internal quality audits is also mentioned in clause 4.1, "Management responsibility" (assignment of trained personnel) and there are three guidance standards on the subject (ISO 10011, parts 1, 2, and 3).

Webcraft began the audit process early in the development stages of the QMS. This had obvious benefits. It provided for the process owners (auditees) to increase their knowledge of the QMS requirements and how to demonstrate conformance to the requirements. It also provided the classroom-trained auditors with on-the-job training and provided information regarding what was in place and what was not in place relative to conformance.

In one Webcraft plant of about 600 employees, approximately 10 percent of the employees were given three days of classroom training on the detailed requirements of ISO 9001 and the application principles of auditing. These candidate auditors volunteered and were interviewed before the training. They were representatives from every functional department (about 15) in the plant. After the classroom training, the candidate auditors were required to participate in three audits lasting five days each, including planning, auditing, reporting, and performing follow-up activities. When this requirement was satisfied, they were evaluated and, if judged qualified, certified by Webcraft as quality system auditors. In this capacity, they were then required to participate in two additional audits. In at least one of the two additional audits, they were required to act as lead auditor. They were then evaluated and, if judged qualified, certified by Webcraft as lead quality system auditors. Lead auditors and auditors must maintain their certifications by either continued active participation in the audit process or retraining.

Webcraft has found the audit process to be very beneficial. Audits are performed approximately every month by audit teams consisting of between three to seven auditors, depending on the audit scope. If an audit reveals an audit nonconformance, it is documented on an audit finding form. The information required includes the audit number and start date, organization audited, audit NCR number, location and date found or observed, controlling document, requirement (specific but brief description), observed condition (contrary to the requirement), auditor, and responsible person (process owner). Audit reports are comprehensive and issued within five working days after the post-audit or closing meeting. The process owners are required to provide a documented response stating the corrective action proposed or taken, including the actions to prevent recurrence along with the actual or anticipated completion date. The auditor evaluates the response and, if complete and satisfactory, accepts it. If the response is not complete, an additional response is required. The process owner is responsible for verifying the completed actions and notifying the auditor when completed. The auditor then independently verifies the actions as complete and satisfactory. When this entire process is completed, the audit nonconformance is closed. After each audit nonconformance for a given audit is closed, the audit itself is closed. All audit nonconformances are tracked to closure.

TRAINING

While the QMS is considered systems-based and not individual-based, it does, after all, depend on people. Webcraft considers its employees to be one of its most valuable resources. In this regard and responsive to ISO 9001, Webcraft's procedures require process owners to perform a training needs analysis (TNA) for each employee. The TNA identifies whether the training is mandatory or recommended, how it is to be accomplished, the expected benefit, any adverse condition should the training not be provided, estimated time and cost, and the date the training will be completed.

Some examples of training provided include training for QMS manual and procedural requirements, QMS documentation, QMS auditing, and department work instructions, problem solving and decision making, and a variety of training courses that are directly related to managerial and supervisory activities and responsibilities. Most press operators are trained through the Graphic Arts and Technical Foundation (GATF). Also, client services must have extensive training by the Society for Service Professionals in Printing (SSPP). As a minimum, each employee is expected to have at least 40 hours of training annually.

SERVICING

Since servicing is not a customer-specified requirement and not included as a part of Webcraft's scope of work, this element is considered a permissible exclusion.

STATISTICAL TECHNIQUES

This ISO 9001 requirement is quite short and simple. It requires an evaluation of the need for statistical techniques to establish, control, and verify process capability and product characteristics. Further, it requires documentation of procedures to implement and control the application of the statistical techniques identified. Despite being short and simply stated, clause 4.20 has broad implications.

Although it is helpful, one does not have to be a statistician to solve problems and present data. Minimal training can often provide an individual with the skills necessary to use cause-and-effect diagrams, Pareto analysis, basic sampling techniques, control charts, histograms, circular and bar charts, line graphs, and flowcharts. However, determining process capability and process variation is certainly a more challenging task, often requiring formal and extensive training in statistical analysis.

As Webcraft's QMS matures and continues to improve, it is evident that the statistical tools as used with Six Sigma are not only important but required for survival. Variability is everywhere around us. No two things are the same. To make quality certain in the print production process, process capability must be known, optimized, and controlled.

Some examples for the application of statistical techniques are related to the manufacturing or use of paper (the modulus of elasticity of paper), film and plates (uniform thickness, coatings), inks (for optical properties such as color, color strength, opacity, and gloss and for working properties such as body, length, and thixotropy), and adhesives and glues. Other examples include pressroom applications for ink density, print length monitoring, image registration, and product quality control.

THE FUTURE—ISO 9001:2000

Webcraft's QMS has already embraced the ISO/TC 176 consistent pair documents—ISO 9001:2000 and ISO 9004:2000. By the time this handbook is published, each plant will have their QMS aligned with the revised ISO 9001:2000 standard. Most of the changes and/or additions were already under consideration by Webcraft's quality staff. With the understanding that ISO 9001:1994 specified the minimum requirements for a QMS, Webcraft has always been proactive regarding the opportunity for improvement and enhancement of its QMS.

ISO 14001:1996, *Environmental management systems,* is integrated with the QMS at Webcraft. The results have been convincing, taking the QMS to a higher performance level with beneficial results.

Planning continues to be a significant contributor to the successful and effective implementation of the QMS. Regardless of the size of an organization, where there is real commitment, the concepts, values, and benefits of ISO 9001:2000 will enable any organization to improve its performance (both quality and productivity) and result in a higher degree of customer satisfaction.

ENDNOTES

1. W. E. Deming, "The Problems that Beset American Industry and Some Thoughts on Their Solution," a nationwide telecast via satellite from Minneapolis, MN, sponsored by the George Washington University Continuing Engineering Education Program, Washington, D.C., 1987.
2. W. E. Deming, *Out of the Crisis* (Cambridge, MA: MIT Press, 1986): 23–96.
3. The Association for Suppliers of Printing and Publishing Technologies (NPES), 1899 Preston White Drive, Reston, VA 22091-4368.
4. Digital Distribution of Advertising for Publications (DDAP), 1855 East Vista Way, Vista, CA 92804.
5. Specifications for Web Offset Publications (SWOP), 60 East 42nd Street, Suite 721, New York, NY 10165.
6. Graphic Arts Technical Foundation (GATF), 200 Deer Run Road, Sewickly, PA 15143-2328.

INTERVIEWS

Jeffrey Bittner, Webcraft, Direct Marketing Services
Michael E. Houser, Vertis, Inc.
Marlene Wolf, Webcraft, Direct Marketing Services

Chapter 59

Application of ISO 9001 to State Government

Curtis Ricketts
North Carolina Department of Labor, Raleigh, North Carolina

The ISO 9000 series of standards represents an international consensus for good management practices. The standards provide organizations with a systems model for meeting customer expectations and providing consistent delivery of services.

STATE GOVERNMENT

Today's state government organizations must wrestle with a number of factors that affect consistent service delivery. Three of these factors are the number and interrelationships of customers served, revolving staff doors, and organizational complexity.

A state agency in North Carolina must meet the customer expectations of the population of 7.7 million, the labor force of 3.9 million, and the 200,000 employers that provide jobs. In addition, executive branch agencies must meet expectations of the legislative (taxpayer representatives) branch, since they write the checks. Often these customers are at odds with each other over what services they want. All of them expect services to be consistent (fair, objective, timely), and each expects to receive personalized attention.

The very nature of the electoral process often results in frequent turnover of executive management. Management turnover can affect consistency of service delivery by altering objectives, priorities, institutional memory, and operational knowledge. Substantial turnover rates can also occur at levels other than management. Government continues to be a training ground and experience builder for the private sector and its higher salaries. This revolving door is particularly distressing for agencies with responsibilities in highly technical areas.

State agencies are typically complex organizations with a wide array of services. Services in the North Carolina Department of Labor (NCDOL) range from mechanical equipment inspections to wage and hour complaint investigations to apprenticeship program development. The department also administers a state occupational safety and health program. A total of 17 Standard Industrial Classification (SIC) codes are applicable to the work of the department.

A documented, accessible, utilized, and dynamically monitored system for operating government programs can and will assist a state agency in addressing these challenges.

WHY NCDOL?

On 3 September 1991, a fire erupted and spread throughout a chicken processing plant in Hamlet, North Carolina. Twenty-five people were killed. Fifty-six others were injured. This was the worst industrial accident in North Carolina history. In the aftermath of the fire, a perception arose in some quarters that the state agency charged with ensuring worker protection was neither as responsive nor as organized as it should be.

In 1993, newly elected NCDOL Commissioner Harry Payne began several initiatives to improve the effectiveness of agency services and enhance public confidence. One long-term initiative was the institution of a management system approach to agency operations. A quality management strategy was created based on the state quality award and the Baldrige model. Efforts in the first three years of Commissioner Payne's administration were centered on leadership, strategic planning, and customer focus. The next step in the plan was to address process management and human resource development.

Several process improvement projects were undertaken during those first three years, and most produced positive results. These efforts, however, did not lead to an institutional and ongoing focus on process management. Something different was needed. A solution emerged in the agency's boiler safety program. The boiler industry was interested in expanding its international markets. The department's boiler safety chief had encouraged the industry to pursue registration to ISO 9000 standards. He began to see potential benefits for his own inspection program and an opportunity to lead by example.

Commissioner Payne decided in December 1996 that the entire agency, including administrative services, would become registered to ISO 9001 by December 2000. The commissioner stated, "Our goal is to provide services that are consistent with our intentions." The effort would become one of the agency's major priorities during the four-year period.

The following pages describe one agency's experiences in development and implementation of quality systems based on the ISO 9001 standard. The first section provides some background information about the North Carolina Department of Labor.

NORTH CAROLINA DEPARTMENT OF LABOR

The North Carolina Department of Labor has statutory responsibilities for both regulatory and advisory services. The department's mission is to foster a safe, healthy, fair, and productive North Carolina. Specifically, it seeks to improve workplace safety and health; ensure the safety of boilers, elevators, and amusement devices; promote fairness in employment relationships; and encourage advanced worker training as a means to higher productivity. An independently elected commissioner of labor leads the agency. Three deputy commissioners charged with oversight of agency divisions assist the commissioner.

Advisory, consultative, and educational services include:

- Development and registration of apprenticeship programs
- Leading-edge initiatives in human resource management and technology
- Employment mediation
- Minerals industry safety evaluation and training
- Occupational safety and health consulting
- Occupational safety and health education, training, and technical assistance

Regulatory services include:

- Boiler safety inspections
- Elevator and amusement device safety inspections
- Wage and hour complaint resolution
- Retaliatory discrimination investigations
- Private personnel services regulation
- Agricultural housing inspections
- Occupational safety and health compliance inspections

The agency also maintains a full range of administrative services:

- Budget and accounting
- Human resources
- Information technology
- Labor statistics
- Legal affairs
- Public information
- Publications

The department has over 450 employees and maintains several offices throughout the state. Administrative and operational headquarters are located in Raleigh.

FEASIBILITY

The first step was to determine what the ISO 9001 standard required and how to implement the requirements. Feasibility research was conducted by collecting written materials on the standard and its application across sectors. Interviews were conducted with a number of consultants, registrars, and registered companies. This initial investigation suggested that there was much to be gained from implementation of an ISO 9001 quality management system. Formal structures for management reviews, clarification of customer requirements, process control, corrective action, and regular progress assessment are all fundamental needs for any management system. The research also suggested that adaptation to a governmental service organization would involve a certain amount of innovation.

A number of hurdles had to be overcome. The first major issue had to do with the standard itself. Whatever has been said or written about ISO 9001:1994, it was clearly designed with a manufacturing environment in mind. The project team struggled with questions of relevance in a service organization. They pondered whether the standard required inspection of inspectors and whether participants in worker training were a customer-supplied product. One early reaction was "Contract review: our customers don't contract with us for inspections; they'd just as soon we didn't visit them at all." Interpreting the various elements against a service environment, without overengineering or inventing unnecessary requirements, required a deliberative approach.

A second issue concerned the dispersion of departmental employees. The nature of the work requires that two-thirds of agency employees be positioned across the state's 300-mile wide and 200-mile deep geography. Third, each person provides one of 13 specialized services independently of the others. Some employees work from satellite offices, while others work out of their homes. Adequate control of documentation for all these people was potentially problematic.[1]

Cost was a major concern. At first glance, the diversity of departmental programs suggested that separate systems would have to be built. There were two problems with this approach. The cost to register multiple systems would be prohibitive, and separate systems would detract from organizational alignment rather than enhance it.

Finally, there was the issue of organizational commitment and perceived value. Would commitment at the top levels of management be sustainable over the long haul? What benefit would middle management perceive in trying to add 600 new elevators for annual inspection without increasing the travel budget, much less staffing? How could these systems be built without staff seeing it as just another management fad bringing extra work to an already overloaded workforce?

PROJECT DEVELOPMENT

Exploration and planning was conducted over a six-month period in the first half of 1997. This period included research activities and project design.

FRAMEWORK

The initial task was the development of a framework. The system structure had to adequately address the diversity of services. Adapting from a federal model used by the Property Management Section of the General Services Administration, the framework included a "corporate" system with almost autonomous and self-sustaining subsystems built around individual division needs. The departmental system is minimal in construction, addressing only requirements common across the agency. The strength of the quality system is in the division-level systems.

The project was structured in three overlapping phases. The first phase included four divisions from the three major service categories: advisory, regulatory, and administrative. Each division developed subsystems directly based on the standard. The common threads identified from these efforts provided the necessary input to create the corporate framework. From there, department-level requirements for key elements were defined and constructed, and the division-level subsystems were revised accordingly. The second and third phases each included eight additional divisions. In these subsequent phases, the subsystems received the benefit of building on a relevant departmental system. System development and registration of the initial phase was completed in 18 months. The remaining phases were completed in 11 months each (from planning to registration).

STANDARD INTERPRETATION

Standard interpretation required analysis on three levels. First, applicability of each of the 20 elements in ISO 9001 was determined within each phase one division. This led, secondly, to an understanding of element application for the major service categories (advisory, regulatory, and administrative). The information at the category level aided in designing the departmental system. Finally, each element was examined for significance at the department level.

In analyzing the standard's requirements, it became obvious that certain elements would apply in some divisions but not in others. One division might need to address design control while most others would not. The titles of several elements were changed when they did not seem appropriate to the organization. For instance, "contract review" became "clarification of customer requirements," and "design control" became "control of project development." These new titles reflected the intent of the standard in a way that was relevant to the work performed in the agency.

The final construction of the departmental system included two elements (purchasing and internal quality system assessment) administered only at the department level. Departmental procedures provide instruction on eight additional elements and are primarily general in nature. The remaining 10 elements are addressed for policy direction only, leaving the division-level subsystems to implement them as appropriate to the work performed.

DOCUMENT CONTROL AND STAFF DISPERSION

Electronic documentation was an almost obvious solution to matching staff dispersion and document control. The method of delivery was not so obvious. The agency decided to provide Internet access to all employees. A new intranet site then ensured quality system access; this decision provided a cost-effective solution while also creating even broader opportunities for improvement of communications.[2]

COST CONSIDERATIONS

The two most significant cost items were training and registration. A decision was made to build a "corporate" or departmental system and register in the name of the North Carolina Department of Labor. The scope of the registration would specifically define each individual subsystem as it was implemented. This approach reflected the "multisite" nature of the organization and its quality system. Initial registration included the first phase divisions and the departmental system. Additional divisions were phased into the scope, concurrent with the regular surveillance audits.

This approach minimizes registration costs because there is only one "registration." Further efficiency is gained by using the surveillance audits to add new divisions (sites) to the scope while the registrar is already on-site.

Training costs were contained by employing a cascading approach and redirecting the content to the needs of each group. This approach is explained in the next section.

ORGANIZATIONAL COMMITMENT

First, all managers attended a one-day orientation session in the second month of the exploration period. A 90-minute orientation session was presented to all employees at the end of the exploration period. These sessions were designed to reduce the potential anxiety associated with the unknown. Subsequent training was conducted on a "just in time" basis and directed only at those actively engaged in the development of systems.

Divisions were asked to apply for entry into the project. This approach increased the likelihood that those most committed to building quality systems would engage early and consequently increase the probability of success. Each selected division sent two representatives (including management) to a three-day training program on quality system development. The commissioner personally conveyed his vision and goals for the project at these sessions.

The department's chief of staff and deputy commissioners also attended the three-day programs. These executive leaders often attended and contributed to subsequent meetings on systems development.

Division employees received specific training after a division constructed its system. This training was provided by division management and oriented toward the content of the division system. The intention was to build transparent systems, focusing on the work that was done. In this way, employees related to the requirements for managing work processes rather than to the model (ISO 9001).

RESOURCES

Consulting resources were provided by an external vendor and by internal sources. An external consultant was selected to provide the three-day training and conduct a formal preassessment. Vendors were evaluated for their experience with government organizations, as well as their knowledge and experience of both the ISO 9000 model and the Baldrige model. These requirements ensured that someone who understood the broader considerations for implementation in a government environment would provide the training.

Overall project management and day-to-day consulting were provided by the department's quality office. These internal consultants possessed a working knowledge of the agency's services. This knowledge placed them in a better position to help the divisions understand the relevance of the standard's requirements.

Registrar selection was intentionally delayed until well into the project. This helped keep the project focused on meeting the needs of the organization first. After the preassessment, registrars were invited to submit proposals. A short presentation on the agency and its system structure was provided to potential vendors. The registrars were also asked to complete a questionnaire developed by the project team. Registrar proposals were evaluated on sector experience, flexibility of approach, assessment process, auditor qualifications, and cost.

SYSTEMS DEVELOPMENT

A number of lessons were learned in the development of the project's first phase. There were very few government examples, and NCDOL systems were constructed without benefit of a proven blueprint. One early design decision carried forward throughout the project relates to how systems development should begin.

PLANNING

Subsystem development plans include a two-month planning period to educate the divisions and collect the data necessary to build viable systems. The three-day training program is provided early in the planning period. It includes modules on the introduction and use of quality systems, the 20 elements of ISO 9001, procedure writing, flowcharting, and quality audits. The final module includes a specific pathway and time line for creating and implementing a quality system. Divisions are then asked to put aside almost all references to the ISO 9001 standard for the balance of the two-month planning period and focus on items that are most familiar to them.

CUSTOMERS → SERVICES → PROCESSES

System construction begins with an assessment of a division's customers and services. At the department level, major customer groups were identified as follows:

Those who *pay* for services	North Carolina general assembly and U.S. government (representing taxpayers)
Those who *receive* services	North Carolina businesses
Those who *benefit* from services	North Carolina workforce and general public

Each group carries relatively equal weight, and sometimes groups have competing interests. This is the nature of government, and balancing these interests goes with the territory.

The essential processes used to deliver services to customers are then identified and documented (including flowcharts). Divisions are strongly encouraged to engage staff most familiar with specific operations in documenting these processes. Current procedural or instructional documents related to work activities are identified and matched to the essential processes. These essential operational processes become the foundation of the quality system. All subsequent development is built around them.[3]

The next step is to determine which ISO 9001 elements are applicable to the division's services and key processes. A gap assessment is conducted to determine where a requirement exists and whether current documentation does or does not address the requirement.

REQUIRED ELEMENTS

At this point, the divisions begin work on the common elements. Eight elements are identified at the department level as required for all subsystems. (Process control is already addressed.) The other required elements have been sorted into two groups: management and infrastructure.

Management Elements	Infrastructure Elements
Management responsibility	Quality system
Clarification of customer requirements	Document and data control
Corrective and preventive action	Control of quality records
Training	

At this stage, 10 of the 20 elements have been addressed, including the eight required elements and the two department-only elements (purchasing and internal assessment).

OTHER ELEMENTS

Remaining elements, considered stabilizers, are addressed as appropriate to the work of the division. If applicable, design of project development (design control) is usually addressed next. This element is followed by product identification and traceability. Then these elements are addressed, in order:

- Inspection and testing
- Control of inspection, measuring, and testing equipment
- Inspection and test status
- Control of nonconforming product
- Handling, storage, packaging, preservation, and delivery
- Control of customer-supplied product
- Servicing
- Statistical techniques

SYSTEM ACTIVATION

A finished system includes a quality plan describing the relevance and level of commitment to each of the 20 elements. The system also includes documented procedures describing how each applicable requirement is executed. Specific work instructions related to tasks and activities are incorporated by reference within the procedures.

The final steps in system development are to initiate the document control mechanisms, produce the related records for system maintenance, train staff on the system's content and application, and activate the system.

ISO 9001:2000

Service-sector interpretation and implementation should be easier using the 2000 revision. This revision is constructed around a process model versus a functional model. The new process model describes the flow of an established system and provides a better illustration of how individual elements relate to each other.

Although the model helps to focus on how a system should perform, the creation of a system may be more easily accomplished by starting with the key operational processes.[4]

Table 59.1 converts the system development process used by NCDOL into the ISO 9001:2000 element structure.

Table 59.1 System development process.

Step 1:	7.0	Product realization	4.3	Contract review
			4.9	Process control
			4.4	Design control
			4.6	Purchasing
Step 2:	5.0	Management responsibility	4.1	Management responsibility
			4.2	Quality system
			4.3	Contract review
Step 3:	6.0	Resource management	4.1	Management responsibility
			4.2	Quality system
			4.9	Process control
			4.18	Training
	4.0	Quality management system	4.2	Quality system
			4.5	Document and data control
			4.16	Control of quality records
Step 4:	7.0	Product realization (remaining items)	4.7	Control of customer-supplied product
			4.8	Product identification and traceability
			4.10	Inspection and testing
			4.11	Control of inspection . . . equipment
			4.12	Inspection and test status
			4.15	Handling, . . . preservation and delivery
			4.19	Servicing
Step 5:	8.0	Measurement, analysis, and improvement	4.13	Control of nonconforming product
			4.14	Corrective and preventive action
			4.17	Internal quality audits
			4.10	Inspection and testing
			4.20	Statistical techniques

BENEFITS

Benefits realized during development and since implementation of the quality systems include:

- Streamlined processes
- Increased clarity of management priorities
- Better communication of operational needs and requirements
- Improved consistency in delivery of services

Quite often in the past, procedures for doing something were either established or changed by memo. Maybe the change in procedure was issued verbally. Early in one division's system development, a field supervisor and a manager were engaged in a discussion on how something should be done. The field supervisor finally said, "Well John Doe told me. . . ." Another manager, overhearing the exchange, remarked, "John Doe? John Doe's dead." ("John Doe" was commissioner of labor some 25 years ago.) The quality system approach ensures that the current rules are available to everyone who needs them and that obsolete rules remain obsolete. Managers appreciate this because it reduces inconsistency. Employees appreciate this because there is less confusion.

Another manager reported, "When we started this we didn't think our processes could be more streamlined and we found that they could." This is not just a one-time benefit. Operational processes and procedures are formally scheduled for review and adjustment. Regular management reviews and internal assessments help to ensure that methods for doing business are fresh and relevant. Corrective and preventive action mechanisms ensure that urgent problems are addressed in a timely manner.

Cross-unit exchange of ideas is becoming a standard fixture within the department. Systems administrators meet with each other regularly. Internal assessors not only make observations of other systems; they also take ideas for improvement back to their own divisions.

The project and the resulting systems have led to a greater sense of *esprit de corps* within the agency. All divisions have this objective in common. They each understand the efforts that others are required to exert. Since the systems are published on the intranet, staff members in any one division now have a convenient and user-friendly means for learning more about the way other divisions work.

Customers are assured that the relationship between the *consistency* and *flexibility* of the services they receive is more planned than accidental. Documented and controlled processes coupled with formal feedback loops provide this assurance.

These are examples of benefits already realized and leading to improved productivity and customer satisfaction. As the agency's system matures, additional benefits are certain to be ascribed to this management system.

RESULTS

Funding and staffing levels were increased significantly in the early 1990s but have remained nearly level for the past four years. The improvement results

Table 59.2 Summary of results

Item	Fiscal year 1992–93	Fiscal year 1999–00	Improvement
NCDOL budget	$20,490,834	$24,627,193	Increased by 20%
NCDOL staff levels	406.5 (full-time equivalent)	462 (full-time equivalent)	Increased by 13.7%
Apprenticeship programs (employer clients)	400	2263	Increased by 566%
Apprenticeship trainees (client employees)	2640	12,679	Increased by 480%
Boiler safety inspections	12,073	21,999	Increased by 82%
Elevator and amusement device inspections	15,934	24,747	Increased by 55%
Number of miners trained	8106	11,180	Increased by 38%
Occupational safety and health injury and illness rate (per 100,000 full-time workers)	8.0	6.0*	25% reduction in the rate of occupational injuries and illnesses
Occupational safety and health (number of people trained)	1173	12,397	Increased by 1,057%
Occupational safety and health (number of visits made)	2363	4315	Increased by 83%

* Fiscal year 1998–99 figures.

summarized in Table 59.2 far surpass the benefits gained from the relative increase of financial and human resources.

Agency results over the last eight years confirm the bottom-line effect that a management systems approach and continuous improvement efforts can produce. No one initiative, including the ISO 9001 effort, is singularly responsible for the progress made in the department. The agency focused on systematically improving its operations and took advantage of the tools that were available. These tools included management and staff training, technology implementation, best practice methods, strategic planning, and performance measurement, among others.

CONCLUSION

In 1993, the department set a strategy for implementing a management system approach to its operations. This strategy was based on the Baldrige model, and this model continues to be part of the vision. Implementation of ISO 9001 provided a solid foundation for a systematic approach to leadership, information and analysis, planning, human resource development, customer focus, and organizational results. With respect to process management, the progress is even more substantial. The agency continues to build a house of performance excellence.

ISO 9000 is not a management panacea. It does not create organizational utopia and was not designed with that intent. It can and does help an organization dynamically and systematically manage its operations and challenges. Poorly implemented, it can create a substantial amount of extra work.

The success of the ISO 9000 project in NCDOL is based on two key principles. First, all efforts were anchored to a focus on the major customer groups, the services provided to them, and the processes used to deliver the services. Second, the systems were designed, constructed, and implemented by the divisions themselves. The content is relevant to the way they work. ISO 9001 registration has consistently been viewed as an outcome measure rather than a goal.

The widespread acceptance of ISO 9001 across the private sector means that many agency customers understand the commitment made by the department. The third-party registration is an independent verification of the pledge to enhance public confidence. It is a measure of progress in the desire to be a model of a well-organized, consistent, and effective supplier of government services.

ENDNOTES

1. These last two issues were inherent to the structure of the agency. Improving communication and service consistency across the state was and is an ongoing priority for management.
2. The intranet site led to the formation of a comprehensive integrated management system within the agency. From an environmental perspective, it also dramatically reduced the reproduction of paper copies.
3. The process control element (4.9) has now been built without focusing on the standard. Participants found that this achievement provided them with a higher confidence level to build the rest of their system.
4. Build the system around the business, rather than the business around the system model. Operate the business by using the system.

Chapter 60

TL 9000: The Telecommunications Quality Management System

Sandford Liebesman
Lucent Technologies, Murray Hill, New Jersey

INTRODUCTION

In October 1997, Bell Atlantic, BellSouth, Pacific Bell, and Southwest Bell Communications (SBC) executives invited their leading suppliers to a meeting in Baltimore. The result was the formation of the QuEST Forum as a cooperative venture among the service providers and suppliers. Their goal was to create a quality management system standard for the telecommunications industry.

The QuEST Forum launched a worldwide supply-chain initiative to develop industry quality management system standards aimed at improving their products and services. The dynamic nature of telecommunications and the globalization of the industry highlighted a need for a single set of quality management system standards for telecommunications. The Forum brought together service providers and suppliers early in 1998 and produced the first two handbooks, *TL 9000 Quality System Requirements, Release 2.5* (QuEST Forum 1999a) and *TL 9000 Quality System Metrics Release 2.5* (1999b) by the end of 1999. Since then the two handbooks have been revised and published as issues 3.0 (QuEST Forum 2001 a and b).

The Forum started with 44 member companies of the telecommunications industry. As of 20 June 2001, there were 162 members. The goal is to have a membership of 200 by the end of 2001.

The industry makes annual purchases estimated at more than $125 billion worldwide. Of this, the cost of poor quality is estimated to be $10 billion to $15 billion. The potential savings from implementing TL 9000 are therefore considerable. This is especially important since it is estimated that the standards will be applicable to over 10,000 suppliers worldwide.

One major new aspect of TL 9000 is the metrics for hardware, software, and service quality. It is expected that the metrics will be a major benchmarking tool that will help the industry improve quality and hence drive down cost. Historically, the industry has benefited from improving hardware quality. Between 1985 and 1996, the annual cost of poor quality (COPQ) of hardware within the U.S. telecommunications industry was measured at $2.5 billion; but as the products improved, the annual COPQ was reduced to $750 million.

THE START OF TL 9000

Work began in January 1998 to draft a set of quality requirements to be incorporated into a TL 9000 handbook. Work groups consisting of industry experts in software, hardware, and services were formed and chartered with the development of the TL 9000 hardware, software, and service requirements to be added to the ISO 9001 requirements. These added requirements, or "adders," would be based on the historical needs of the industry. Additional work groups were formed to develop a second handbook consisting of hardware, software, and service metrics. A regular monthly schedule of team meetings was initiated with the goal of having a working implementation program by the end of 1999. It was understood from the beginning that cost- and performance-based metrics were especially important to the effort. This is because they can be used to quantify the benefits gained, assess progress in quality maturity, and identify areas where the quality process improvement will have the greatest cost impact and provide comparative benchmarking capabilities for the industry.

The QuEST Forum recognized the parallel between what they wanted to accomplish and what had been done by the automotive industry a few years earlier. The auto industry had created a standard based on ISO 9001 with adders called QS-9000 (AIAG 1998). The Forum consulted with the auto industry forum, the Automotive Industry Action Group (AIAG), during the start-up phase.

TELECOMMUNICATIONS INDUSTRY NEEDS

The working groups reviewed ISO 9001 and determined that supplemental requirements were needed in the following areas:

• *Reliability and associated costs.* The industry places a great emphasis on reliability because of demands placed on service providers by end users. The networks, switching systems, and local transmission equipment must operate continuously to accurately pass information between end users. In this high technology information age, the rapid transfer of data requires highly reliable products and services.

• *Software development and lifecycle management.* Software is an integral part of telecommunications product and service offerings. Although ISO 9000-3:1997 is a guide for applying ISO 9001:1994 to software quality management systems, it does not cover the software lifecycle needs of the industry (ISO 1997). TL 9000 developers used inputs from ISO 9000-3:1997, ISO/IEC 12207 (ISO 1995), TR-NWT-179 (Telcordia 1993), and other sources to satisfy most of these needs.

• *Specialized service functions.* Installation, engineering, maintenance, repair, call center, and support services are integral to the customer–supplier relationship in the telecommunications industry. In addition, the coverage of servicing in clause 4.19 of ISO 9001:1994 is extremely limited, and additional requirements are needed to provide "aftermarket" functions such as emergency service, problem notification, and supplier support (ISO 1994a).

• *Continuation and further development of the relationships between service providers and suppliers.* A unique characteristic of the telecommunications industry is the ongoing relationship between service providers and their suppliers. Service providers require new or improved features on a regular basis. Thus there is a need for continuous communication between customers and their suppliers.

These industry needs led to the development of the 83 adders and the 11 metrics defined in the two TL 9000 handbooks.

THE GOALS AND EXPECTATIONS OF TL 9000

There were five major goals defined by the QuEST Forum:

- To foster systems that will protect the integrity of telecommunications products, services, and networks
- To develop requirements that will help organizations more accurately assess the implementation of their quality management system
- To identify tools that will drive continuous improvement of products, services, and processes
- To develop standard metrics for use as a continuous improvement tool
- To implement an industry standard assessment process that will reduce the multiplicity of conflicting programs

There are a number of industry benefits that the QuEST Forum membership expects from the development of TL 9000, including:

- Improved service to end users
- Enhanced customer–supplier relationships (note that the QuEST Forum was designed as a cooperative effort among customers and suppliers)
- A reduction in the number of external second- and third-party audits and site visits
- Uniform performance- and cost-based metrics for use as benchmarks for improving product and service quality
- Enhanced supply-chain management, including second- and third-tier suppliers
- The creation of a platform for industry improvement initiatives

Specific expectations for Forum member products and services include:

- Reduced cycle time
- Improved on-time delivery
- Reduced lifecycle costs
- Superior products
- Defect reduction
- Increased profitability and market share

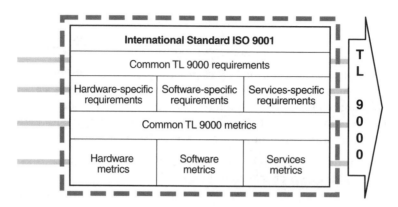

Figure 60.1   The TL 9000 model.
Source: QuEST, 1999a. Reproduced by permission of the QuEST Forum.

THE TL 9000 MODEL

The basic foundation of the TL 9000 model is ISO 9001:1994. TL 9000 incorporates the 20 elements of that standard and adds 83 new requirements, or adders, including the additional element 4.21, quality improvement and customer satisfaction. The adders are categorized as TL 9000 common requirements, hardware-specific requirements, software-specific requirements, service-specific requirements, or paired combinations of the specific types. A second set of requirements covers the metrics. Again, these are categorized into common, hardware-specific, software-specific, and service-specific metrics. Figure 60.1 depicts the TL 9000 model.

THE TL 9000 HANDBOOKS

The Forum developed two handbooks during 1998 and 1999. Book 1, Release 2.5 contains the verbatim ISO 9001 requirements, the 83 adders, and appendices covering accreditation, registration, and guidance for customer–supplier communication (QuEST 1999a). Release 3.0, published in 2001, reduced this number to 81 (QuEST 2001a). Book 2 contains a description of the metrics, responsibilities of all parties with respect to the metrics, and the product category and normalization tables (QuEST 1999b). Updated product category tables can be found on the QuEST Forum Web site (www.questForum.org).

SOURCES USED TO DEVELOP THE TL 9000 REQUIREMENTS HANDBOOK

At the start of the development of TL 9000, there were many industry documents to use as sources. The following are the publications that were chosen as sources for the adders:

- ISO 9001:1994, the basic quality management standard (ISO 1994a). Section 4 of this document contains requirements that were included verbatim in TL 9000, Book 1.
- ISO 9000-3:1997, the ISO document that provides guidance for applying ISO 9001 to software (ISO 1997).
- ISO/IEC 12207, the international standard that describes quality management system software lifecycle requirements (ISO 1995).
- TR-NWT-000179, the Telcordia Technologies document that describes telecommunications software requirements (Telcordia 1993).
- GR-1202, the Telcordia Technologies document that describes the Telcordia customer–supplier quality process (Telcordia 1995b).
- GR-1252, the Telcordia Technologies document that describes telecommunications hardware requirements (Telcordia 1995a).
- ISO 9004-2:1994, the ISO document that provides quality management system guidelines for service organizations (ISO 1994b).

In addition, the QuEST Forum membership provided an added set of requirements, and QS 9000 (AIAG 1998), ISO 10011-1 (ISO 1994c), ISO 10011-2 (ISO 1994d), and ISO 10011-3 (ISO 1994e) provided inputs for the appendices.

Table 60.1 contains a summary of the number of contributions to the requirements handbook from each source (QuEST 1999a). GR-1252, the Telcordia Technologies hardware requirements document, provided the largest number of inputs. However, three software requirements documents, TR-179, ISO/IEC 12207, and ISO 9000-3, collectively provided 32 requirements or parts of requirements.

Table 60.1 Sources of adders.

Source	Number of Requirements	Number of Notes
GR-1202	16 (15)+	0
GR-1252	23* (21)+	0
TR-179	13*	0
ISO 12207	13†	1
ISO 9000-3	6	1
ISO 9004-2	1	0
QuEST Forum membership	13 (14)+	0
Total	**83‡**	**2**

* This source contributed to one requirement jointly with one other source.
† This source contributed to two requirements jointly with one other source.
‡ Two requirements were developed from multiple sources (two sources in each case).
+ Changes in Release 3.0.

KEY DIFFERENCES FROM ISO 9001

The following areas are where the QuEST Forum focused its attention and expanded on the current ISO 9001 requirements:

- More emphasis on top management responsibilities
- More focus on proper/robust planning:
  - Quality planning
  - Project planning
  - Configuration management planning
  - Product planning
  - Lifecycle planning
  - Test planning
- Requirements for customer–supplier communication
- Requirements emphasizing quality improvement and customer satisfaction
- Requirements covering specialized service functions
- Training sanctioned by the QuEST Forum and delivered by two authorized training providers:
  - Excel Partnership
  - Stat-A-Matrix (The SAM Group)
- Metrics required for certification:
  - Objectives include a requirement to define metrics targets
  - Metrics must be defined, tracked, and reported to a central database
  - Metrics must be used to foster continuous quality improvement
  - Auditors responsibilities with respect to metrics are:
    - Ensuring that the suppliers' metrics processes are working
    - Ensuring that the results are used by the suppliers to improve products, services, and processes
- Unlike ISO 9001, *should* means the preferred approach. Suppliers choosing any other approach must be able to demonstrate that their approach meets the intent of TL 9000.

THE ADDED REQUIREMENTS (ADDERS)

TL 9000, Release 2.5, contains 83 adders developed to help ensure satisfaction of the industry needs. The number of adders in Release 3.0 has been reduced to 81. The adders apply to either hardware, software, service products, or combinations of these types of products. Common adders apply to all three types. Table 60.2 contains a summary of the adders by ISO 9001:1994 element and by the application. Table 60.3 contains the same summary for ISO 9001:2000 and by the application.

Table 60.2 Summary of Release 2.5 adders by ISO 9001:1994 element and application.

ISO 9000:1994 Element	Common	Software	Hardware	Service	Hardware and Service	Hardware and Software
4.1	1					
4.2	5	1				
4.3						
4.4	8	7	6	2		
4.5		1				
4.6	1					
4.7						
4.8			2			2
4.9		2	1	2	3	
4.10		1	2		2	
4.11			1			
4.12						
4.13	1					
4.14						
4.15	2	2	1			
4.16						
4.17						
4.18	6					
4.19	5	2	1			3
4.20	1					
4.21	7		1	1		
Total	**37**	**16**	**15**	**5**	**5**	**5**

The next sections contain a summary of the key adders under four categories:

- Quality management and improvement
- Product definition, design, and development
- Production
- Customer support

Release 2.5 will be used to summarize the information about adders contained in the next sections.

Table 60.3 Summary of Release 3.0 adders by ISO 9001:2000 element and application.

ISO 9000:2000 Element	Common	Software	Hardware	Service	Hardware and Service	Hardware and Software
4.2	1					
5.2	2					
5.4.1	1					
5.4.2	3					
5.5	1					
6.2	6				1	
6.4	1					
7.1	4	3		1		1
7.2	4		1			
7.3.1	3	2				
7.3.2	2	2	1			
7.3.3		1		1		
7.3.6		1				
7.3.7	2		1			1
7.4	1					
7.5.1	2	3		2		2
7.5.2					1	
7.5.3			2			1
7.5.5	1	1	1			1
7.6			1			
8.2.1	1					
8.2.3	1					
8.2.4		1	4		2	
8.4	1		1	1		
8.5.1	2					
8.5.2		1				
Total	**39**	**15**	**12**	**5**	**4**	**6**

Quality Management and Improvement

This section contains a description of adders applied to management responsibility (4.1), quality system (4.2), document and data control (4.5), training (4.18), and an added element, quality improvement and customer satisfaction (4.21).

4.1 Management Responsibility

- Management must include targets for the metrics in their objectives. This will help drive continuous quality improvement.
- Management with executive responsibility "should" demonstrate active involvement in long- and short-term planning.

4.2 Quality System

- Long- and short-term planning must address cycle time, customer service, training, cost, delivery commitments, and product reliability
- Design and development planning requires use of a lifecycle model
- Quality planning must include methods for soliciting customer and subcontractor input and methods for disaster recovery

4.5 Document and Data Control

- Customer-supplied documents relating to software development must be controlled

4.18 Training

The training organization must:

- Have a process for course development
- Teach quality improvement concepts, advanced quality training, and electrostatic discharge (ESD) training

4.21 Quality Improvement and Customer Satisfaction

The organization must:

- Have a quality improvement program
- Encourage employee participation in quality programs and provide performance feedback from customers
- Have management show its commitment to customer–supplier relationships
- Have a process for customer–supplier communication
- Collect and analyze customer satisfaction data, field performance data, and service performance data
- Have a new product introduction process.

Product Definition, Design, and Development

This section contains a description of adders applied to design control:

- Requirements must be traceable through design and test
- Project plans contain 17 specified "should" elements, such as roles and responsibilities, customer and subcontractor involvement, risk management, training, and post-project analysis
- "Should" requirements are specified for planning of tests, end of life, software integration, and software migration
- The organization must estimate and track project factors and computer resources

- The organization must solicit design input from customers and subcontractors
- Software design output must include architecture, source code, and user documentation
- Service design output must include service delivery procedures, resource and skill requirements, reliance on subcontractors, service characteristics, and standards of acceptability
- Products must be periodically retested
- Customers must be informed of design changes

Production

This section contains a description of adders applied to purchasing (4.6), process control (4.9), inspection and testing (4.10), handling, storage, packaging, preservation, and delivery (4.15), and statistical techniques (4.20).

The purchasing (4.6) adder contains 10 requirements, including risk analysis and management, future support of the product, and feedback from the supplier to key subcontractors.

4.9 Process Control

- The organization must have a process for replication and release of software. "Should" requirements are specified for both processes
- Hardware and service organizations must have processes covering operator qualification and employee skills list
- Service organizations must have a service delivery plan containing the 17 "should" requirements of the project plan in element 4.4

4.10 Inspection and Testing

- For hardware and service organizations, eight "should" parameters are specified for inspection and test documentation
- Four parameters are specified for software test documentation
- Repaired hardware products must be tested the same as new products
- Six parameters are specified for hardware and service inspection and test records
- A packaging and labeling audit is specified for hardware

4.15 Handling, Storage, Packaging, Preservation, and Delivery

- Work areas must be clean, safe, and organized
- The organization must provide ESD protection, control of materials that can deteriorate, software virus protection, and software patch documentation

Statistical techniques (4.20) must include process measurements.

Customer Support

This section contains a description of adders applied to product identification and traceability (4.8), control of nonconforming product (4.13), and servicing (4.19).

4.8 Product Identification and Traceability

- Hardware must be traceable for recall, and design changes must be traceable within lots
- Hardware and software products must be identified and controlled under a configuration management plan

The process for control of nonconforming product (4.13) must include trend analysis.

4.19 Servicing

Since servicing is such an important part of the customer–supplier relationship in the telecommunications industry, 11 adders were included in this element. The common requirements include:

- Supplier support program
- Service resources
- Notification about problems
- Problem severity
- Problem escalation

Other adders included:

- Supplier recall process (hardware)
- emergency service
- Problem resolution configuration management
- Installation plan
- Patching procedures
- Problem resolution

THE USE OF METRICS TO IMPROVE PRODUCT AND SERVICE QUALITY

The unique factor that makes TL 9000 different from the current ISO 9001 practice is the use of metrics for continuous quality improvement. These are measurements used to determine the quality level of product and services. Examples are circuit pack return rates, number of problem reports, and software update quality. It is expected that extending ISO 9000 in this direction will result in an industry drive to improve overall quality. Certainly, when suppliers know where their products stand relative to their competitors, and their customers know the quality level of "best in industry," there will be a drive by all to improve.

The QuEST Forum envisions multiple uses for the metrics. For example, they can be used to enhance customer–supplier communication that will be used to prioritize and solve the most costly problems. Metrics can also be used to bridge the gap between quality issues and business results. And they can be used to quantify the customers' views of their suppliers' quality. Some service providers have indicated that they will use the metrics to develop report cards for their suppliers.

The Forum has retained the University of Texas at Dallas (UTD) to gather the data and develop statistics for each product class. The statistics will identify the mean (or median) standard deviation (or range) and "best in industry." The data will be published on the QuEST Forum Web site (www.questForum.org). UTD was selected because of its long-standing role in telecommunications engineering education. It's expected that UTD will provide insight into benchmarking problems in industry quality and identifying quality trends and will help identify possible solutions to quality problems.

Output from the database consists of monthly or quarterly statistical summary reports derived from the TL 9000 metrics repository for each metric by product category as posted on the QuEST Forum Web site. These reports are posted on the Web site and distributed in hard copy form by the American Society for Quality (ASQ) as appropriate. However, the statistics for a product category is computed and posted only if it can be ensured that the statistical results will not in any way compromise supplier anonymity. There must be at least five sets of data from at least three companies before computations can be made.

THE METRICS IMPLEMENTATION PROCESS

The supplier gathers the data on a monthly basis and sends three months of data to UTD for inclusion in the industry database. A double-blind system has been set up to ensure that the data are secure and not available to competitors and other unauthorized persons. The process works as follows:

- When a supplier has gathered the data, a notification is sent to ASQ, which is the administrator of the QuEST Forum. ASQ is responsible for providing encryption keys back to the supplier to be used in sending the data to the industry database at the University of Texas at Dallas (UTD).

- The supplier encrypts the data and sends them to the metrics repository system (MRS) at UTD. Personnel transfer the data from the receiving server into the industry database without having access to the measurements. At least two individuals must be present during the transfer to ensure security of the data.

The double-blind process has alleviated a major concern of the QuEST Forum membership—the security of the data being supplied to UTD. As a result, the data will be safe from access by competitors. In addition, no single individual at UTD will be able to access the data alone. The whole process has been developed with a minimum cost to suppliers.

CONFIDENTIALITY OF SOURCE AND DATA

The QuEST Forum appointed a subteam to define requirements for the MRS. Confidentiality of source and data is the single most important concern of suppliers. UTD incorporated two key design elements:

- Separation of the administrative system and the data system
- Encryption

The administrative system, called the registration repository system (RRS), is managed by ASQ. A supplier who decides to apply for TL 9000 registration must notify ASQ of that intention. ASQ requires the supplier to define the scope (hardware, software, service, or any combination) and product categories. ASQ then assigns reporting IDs for each product category. The supplier submits the data to UTD using the reporting IDs. UTD does not know who is submitting the data, and ASQ does not know the content of the data. This is the essence of the double-blind system. Later in the process, ASQ issues a data submission confirmation to signify the supplier's successful submission of data to UTD.

The MRS database is managed by UTD. The supplier encrypts the data prior to submission, using the data submission software provided by UTD. The supplier chooses the encryption key that is 128 bits long. UTD receives the encrypted data from the supplier but does not know the owner of the data. This is because the data is transmitted from the incoming server directly into the MRS computer. UTD checks for a valid reporting ID transmitted with the data. UTD also performs a sanity check on the data. If the data are valid, UTD provides a qualitative data confirmation report to ASQ.

UTD developed a secure process to ensure that the database is backed up and recoverable in the event of natural disasters. UTD also instituted methods to protect the database from infection by software viruses.

UTD has complied with BS 7799, the document on information security management requirements developed by the British Standards Institute (BSI 1999). UTD is the first U.S. organization to be certified to this document by BSI.

APPROVED METRICS

The following 11 metrics in four categories have been approved:

- Common to hardware, software, and services:
  - Number of problem reports
  - Problem report fix response time
  - Overdue fix responsiveness
  - System outage measurement
  - On-time delivery
- Hardware only:
  - Return rates
- Software only:
  - Corrective patch quality
  - Feature patch quality
  - Software update quality
  - Release application aborts
- Service only:
  - Service quality

All suppliers are expected to establish a metrics system through which metrics collection, monitoring, and reporting takes place. The unique aspect of this system is that service providers also have a major role to play in that, for some metrics, the cooperation of service providers is a must. Unless they provide field data to the suppliers, the suppliers cannot generate certain metrics. In summary, the process requires cooperation between suppliers, service providers, and the Forum.

METRICS USAGE

The following principles for processing and usage of the metrics are meant to be consistent with the purpose of providing an environment where service providers and suppliers can work together to drive continuous improvement.

- Suppliers will provide TL 9000 metrics to the Forum administrator who will compile all the metric data and calculate an industry mean, standard deviation, and "best in industry" for each category. Forum results or reports produced by the Forum administrator will not identify individual suppliers.

- Service providers may request their suppliers to provide the TL 9000 metrics specific to that service provider. This information exchange will take place strictly between the supplier and the service provider per contractual agreements. The Forum administrator, ASQ, will not be involved in any way.

- There will be no ranking of suppliers by the QuEST Forum administrator.

The general uses of the metrics currently envisioned are as follows:

- The above statistics will be used by suppliers to improve products and services. The metrics provide data that are needed by suppliers to identify significant improvement areas. After improvement actions have been taken, the data will allow suppliers to determine the level of improvement and decide if additional significant improvement is needed.

- The statistics along with supplier-specific metrics may be used by service providers to evaluate and work with suppliers. By comparing a supplier's performance against the industry data, gaps in performance can be determined and the service provider and the supplier can address closing the gaps.

- Suppliers and service providers will use the metrics to determine if products, intercompany processes, and services meet the expectations of the end user.

- Suppliers will improve the industry products and services based on Forum initiatives and goals.

After the process and metrics have matured, they will be used to establish a telecommunication quality index to be published worldwide. In addition, the Forum may create an award program for the best in the industry.

COMMON METRICS

Common metrics are applicable to the hardware, software, and service categories. There are five common metrics defined in Release 2.5: (1) number of problem reports, (2) problem report fix response time, (3) overdue problem report fix responsiveness, (4) on-time delivery, and (5) system outage.

In Release 3.0, system outage has been moved to a new category, Hardware and Software Measurements (QuEST 2001b).

Number of Problem Reports (NPR)

The number of problem reports (NPR) metric is computed as the total problem reports per normalization unit per month. The purpose of this metric is to evaluate the number of problem reports or complaints during field operations in order to reduce their number, along with the associated costs and revenue losses. NPR provides a common means whereby customers and suppliers can evaluate the rate of problem reports, including engineering complaints (ECs) reported on the supplier's product.

Fix Response Time (FRT) and Overdue Problem Report Fix Responsiveness (OFR)

Fix response time (FRT) represents the responsiveness of suppliers to a subset of customer-reported problems that require a change to the product set. FRT measures the overall responsiveness of the supplier to all major and minor problems reported in hardware and software categories and all problems reported under service category. Overdue problem report fix responsiveness (OFR) measures the rate of closure of overdue reports of major and minor hardware and software problem and all service problem reports.

On-Time Delivery (OTD)

The purpose for measuring on-time delivery (OTD) is to evaluate the supplier's ability to meet the customer's needs for timely product and service delivery and to meet the expectations of the end users.

System Outage (SO)

The purpose of measuring system outage is to evaluate the downtime performance and outage frequency during field operation in order to reduce both the frequency and duration of outages and their associated cost and revenue impacts.

THE HARDWARE-ONLY METRIC: RETURN RATE

The purpose of collecting the return rate metric is threefold: (1) to provide a measure of quality of the product initially received by the customer and during subsequent in-service operation, (2) to determine areas that need corrective action or will most likely benefit from continuous improvement activity, and (3) to provide the input data needed to calculate equipment lifecycle costs.

SOFTWARE-ONLY METRICS

There are four metrics that apply to software only: (1) software update quality, (2) release application abort, (3) corrective patch quality, and (4) feature patch quality.

Software Update Quality (SUQ)

A software update is a set of changes to a release and is commonly referred to as dot or point release. It differs from a patch in the manner in which software changes are made to a system. A software update replaces the existing product with a new load as opposed to entering a subset of software (patch) into the current load.

Release Application Abort (RAA)

The release application abort (RAA) metric is the percentage of release applications that fail. It measures the percentage of systems with aborts for each of the last three most dominant releases per product category. The purpose of RAA is to minimize the service provider's risk of aborts when applying a software release.

Corrective Patch Quality (CPQ) and Feature Patch Quality (FPQ)

A feature patch adds functionality, while a corrective patch fixes a known problem. For each of these types of patches, errors can occur. Corrective patch quality is the percentage of official corrective patches that are determined to be defective. Feature patch quality is defined as the percentage of official feature patches that are determined to be defective. The purpose of tracking these metrics is to evaluate the percentage of defective official patches to minimize service provider risk of failure.

THE SERVICE-ONLY QUALITY METRIC

The service quality metric can be applied to any type of service provided by a supplier. Some of the metrics measured are:

- Percentage of conforming installation audits
- Percentage of successful maintenance visits without callbacks
- Percentage of successful repairs
- Percentage of calls to the conforming call center resolved within agreed-on time
- Percentage of support service transactions without a defect

The purpose of this metric is to provide quality measurement information for establishing the evaluation and continuous improvement of the service.

NORMALIZING FACTORS

A major issue during the development of these metrics was the identification of normalization factors, which allow comparison of similar products with different characteristics. For example, for circuit switching, the normalization factor for return rate is returns divided by 10,000 terminations per year. Thus products with a large number of terminations per circuit pack are measured fairly against those with fewer terminations per circuit pack.

Another issue was a result of a requirement of some service providers that the suppliers provide "Reliability and Quality Measurements for Telecommunications Systems" (RQMS) metrics defined in the Telcordia Technologies document GR-929-CORE (Telcordia 1998). In some cases, the supplier may provide the RQMS metrics in place of the corresponding TL 9000 metrics.

Other metrics and indicators are under consideration but have not been approved. Indicators are a separate category of measures used to "flag potential cost, schedule, productivity and quality issues," but are not reportable to UTD (Malec 1999).

The service providers have an important role with respect to certain metrics. They must provide the data necessary to calculate these metrics. If the data are not forthcoming, the supplier is excused from providing the associated metric. For example, in calculating the number of problem reports, the service providers must "report problems to the supplier and report normalizing information for hardware or software categories to the supplier according to the Product Category Table, Appendix A (QuEST 1999b, 5-5).

The registrar has an important role in ensuring compliance to the metrics requirements. "This includes assuring data validity and integrity, verifying [that] the benchmark metrics have been reported within the required time frame, and [assuring] that any metric-specific nonconformance is resolved in a timely manner" (Aycock 1999, 43). Also, because of the requirement in Book 1 that "objectives for quality shall include targets for the TL 9000 metrics defined in the *TL 9000 Quality System Metrics Handbook*", the registrar has a role in ensuring this use of the metrics (QuEST 1999b, 4-1). Finally, there are requirements for the supplier to collect and analyze customer satisfaction, field performance, and service performance data, some of which are metrics data (QuEST 1999b, 4-40–4-41).

PRODUCT AND SERVICE CATEGORIES

Official product and service categories are subject to change. Hence they are stored on the QuEST Forum Web site (www.questforum.org). The following are the product and service categories defined on the Web site as of 28 June 2001:

- *Switching*: equipment for the physical or virtual interconnection of communications channels in response to a signaling system. The switching category is broadly defined to include packet or circuit switched architectures.

- *Signaling*: equipment for the provisioning of signaling, that is, [network] states [that are] applied to operate and control the component groups of a telecommunications circuit to cause it to perform its intended function. . . . There are five basic categories of signals: . . . supervisory, information, address, control, and alerting . . . includes [only] signaling products that function within the telecommunications network (www.questforum.org).

- *Transmission*: equipment for the connection of the switched and interoffice networks with individual customers. An integral part of the distribution network is the loop, which connects the customer to the central office (CO), thus providing access to the interoffice network.

- *Operations and maintenance*: equipment, systems, and services for the management, upkeep, diagnosis, and repair of the communications network.
- *Common systems*: any of a variety of specialized generic, shared equipment to support network elements. Common systems include power systems and network equipment-building systems (NEBSs) (Telcordia 1995c) that provide space and environmental support for [the] network. These systems are located in central offices and remote building locations.
- *Customer premises*: equipment installed beyond the network demarcation point. Although commonly installed on the subscriber's premises, equipment with essentially identical functionality installed in the service provider's facility may also be classified as customer premises equipment.
- *Services (installation, engineering, maintenance, repair, call center, and support)*: results generated by activities at the interface between the supplier and the customer and by internal activities of the supplier to meet customer needs. Note the following:
  - The supplier or customer may be represented at the interface by personnel or equipment
  - Customer activities at the interface with the supplier may be essential to the service delivery
  - Delivery or use of tangible product may form part of the service delivery
  - A service may be linked with the manufacture and supply of tangible product
- *Components and subassemblies (includes component suppliers, contract manufacturers and original equipment manufacture [OEM] suppliers).* Includes individual components or assemblies provided for use in telecommunications systems excluding those already covered by a specific product category in another product family. These items would typically be used by other suppliers and not sold directly to service providers except as replacement parts.

PILOT PROGRAM

One of the QuEST Forum initiatives was the creation of a pilot program to validate TL 9000 and its associated activities. The goals of the program were to provide feedback on:

- The bottom-line value of the adders
- The processes that form the metrics reporting system
- The processes used to manage the registrar accreditation, and supplier assessment/certification system
- The sanctioned training courses
- The ability to audit the requirements and measurements

Feedback was accomplished through weekly conference calls, which included minutes posted on the Web site (www.questForum.org), monthly meetings, documented lessons learned, case studies, and commonly asked questions posted on the Web site.

Sixteen organizations from 11 companies participated in the program in four categories. Eight were hardware suppliers, three were software suppliers, four combined hardware and software suppliers, and one supplier of services. The participants are shown in Table 60.4.

The first step for each pilot organization was to make arrangement for its registrar to participate in the pilot program. Each registrar had to have its auditors take the QuEST Forum–sanctioned training and pass the auditor exam. Also, at least one member of the registrar's certification board with veto power or a majority of the board had to take the training and pass the exam. The registrar's accreditation agency also had to have at least one member of the registration decision-making body take the QuEST Forum–sanctioned training and pass the written exam. In addition, the accreditation agency had to witness at least one audit performed by each registrar using auditors who had completed the training and passed the exam.

Each pilot organization had to train its auditors and implementers, perform a gap analysis, develop processes for collection of the metrics, and submit the metrics data to UTD. The organizations that completed the process and were certified were not allowed to advertise the fact until the end of January 2000. They were honored at the 25 January 2000 Forum meeting in Dallas, Texas.

Table 60.4 Pilot participants.

Hardware (8)	Software (3)	Hardware and Software (4)	Service (1)
Adtran	Motorola	Fujitsu Network Communications	Nortel Networks
NEC America	Nortel Networks	Lucent Technologies	
Nortel Networks (2 organizations)	SBC–California	Nortel Networks	
Pirelli Cables & Systems		Marconi Access	
Siecor (2 organizations)			
Telllabs			

REGISTRATION PROCESS

The formal registration process started in the first quarter of 2000. The QuEST Forum established requirements for accreditation bodies to qualify registrars who will carry out TL 9000 certifications (QuEST 1999a, Appendixes A–E). A supplier must demonstrate conformance to TL 9000 by successfully completing a third-party certification audit from an accredited TL 9000 registrar. The supplier will obtain a certificate in any combination of hardware, software, and/or services:

- Hardware: TL 9000-HW
- Software: TL 9000-SW
- Service: TL 9000-SC

Note that the supplier must either be ISO 9001 or 9002 certified or must include certification to either of these standards as part of the TL 9000 certification.

The QuEST Forum has been working with the Registrar Accreditation Board (RAB)—the organization that oversees the competency of quality management system and environmental management system certification bodies in the United States—and the Standards Council of Canada (SCC) to pilot the procedures. Other accreditation agencies, such as the members of the International Accreditation Forum, will be invited to participate in the future. The following are the Web sites for these organizations:

- RAB: www.rabnet.com
- SCC: www.scc.ca

TRAINING

The QuEST Forum has authorized two organizations, Stat-A-Matrix (The SAM Group) and Excel Partnership, to develop and provide sanctioned TL 9000 training. The Forum retains the rights to the training intellectual property. The materials have been translated into French, Spanish, German, Japanese, and Portuguese. Translation into Chinese is in progress.

By selecting two training organizations to jointly provide training, the Forum expanded its philosophy of having competitors cooperate for the good of the industry. The two organizations should be commended for their joint effort and sharing of responsibilities and products. Also, the Forum should be commended for its foresight in taking this approach to providing sanctioned training. The results were better because two different perspectives were blended into the courses, making them stronger than the courses each trainer could have provided separately.

Four sanctioned courses have been developed by the two training providers:

- TL 9000 Quality System Overview: a half-day course aimed at the majority of company associates, including senior management, that describes the goals of TL 9000 and how it can aid the organization.
- TL 9000 Quality System Implementation: a three-day course that provides a road map for successful TL 9000 implementation and compliance.

- TL 9000 Quality System Requirements and Metrics Auditing: a four-day course that provides auditor training on the quality management system adders and the metrics requirements. A written exam is given at the completion of the course. Passage of the course and exam is required by QuEST to be certified as a TL 9000 auditor.
- TL 9000 Quality System Auditing for Registrars: a three-day course designed for auditors from registrar organizations. A test is given at the completion of the course. Passage is required by QuEST to be certified as a TL 9000 registrar auditor.

Excel Partnership is providing a fifth sanctioned course, TL 9000 Metrics Data Submission. This course describes the details of submitting data to the database at UTD.

The pilot organizations took early versions of the courses as part of the overall pilot program. They provided valuable input to the course developers that was later used to improve the courses.

ADMINISTRATION

An executive board consisting of six service providers and six suppliers governs the Forum. The chairmanship rotates on an annual basis between service providers and suppliers. The first chairman was Steve Welch, president of SBC Corporate and Administrative Services. Krish Prabhu, president and chief operating officer of Alcatel Telecom USA, succeeded him in 2000 and George Via, Senior Vice President–Operations, Verizon, succeeded them in 2001.

The Forum selected ASQ to be the Forum administrator and the University of Texas at Dallas to administer the MRS.

One reason for the selection of ASQ was its historical role in support of quality standards development that includes providing the secretariat for the United States Technical Advisory Groups to ISO Technical Committee 176 (ISO/TC 176), ISO/TC 207, ISO/TC 69, and IEC Technical Committee 56 (IEC/TC 56). Also, ASQ's role as a worldwide leader in the quality profession played an important part in the selection.

ASQ is responsible for many functions, including the following (Development 1999):

- Performance of general business functions
- Management of the program, including QuEST Forum and working meetings, board meetings and conference calls, membership, and Web site administration
- Management of accreditation bodies and registrar information
- Administration of membership responsibilities
- Distribution and publishing of marketing materials
- Administration of training and education responsibilities
- Publication and distribution of the quality system requirements and metrics handbooks and promotion of their use
- Arrangement of technical conferences and workshop programs

The Erik Jonsson School of Engineering and Computer Science at the University of Texas at Dallas administers the MRS. It is also expected that the university will provide research into the solutions of industry problems identified as a result of the analysis.

INFORMATION SOURCES

The main source of information is the QuEST Forum's Web site (http://www.quest Forum.org). The public portion of the Web site contains information on membership and meetings as well as a means of ordering books, materials, and merchandise. The member portion contains the metrics database summary results, individual membership information, presentations, minutes, product and service categories, and other QuEST Forum proprietary materials.

THE QUEST FORUM'S GLOBAL APPROACH

The QuEST Forum has made great strides in its goal to become a truly global telecommunications organization. It is the only global organization dealing with telecommunications quality management. The membership has grown internationally and includes service providers from the United Kingdom, South Africa, Australia, and Canada; suppliers from the United Kingdom, France, Israel, and Canada; and many multinational suppliers based in the United States. In addition, the QuEST Forum has established liaison status with organizations in Europe (including Russia), Japan, Korea, and Singapore.

The Forum has Liaison A status with ISO/TC 176, IEC/TC 56, and ISO/IEC JTC1/SC7. As a liaison member of ISO/TC 176, the Forum provided four members of task groups working on the year 2000 revisions to ISO 9001:1994 and ISO 9004:1994. These individuals have contributed to the verification, validation, transition, and implementation processes used by ISO/TC 176.

The Forum has also developed a cooperative relationship with the European IPQM and RQMS User Group (EIRUS), a European telecommunication metrics user group. EIRUS uses two sets of metrics based on Telcordia Technologies requirements: European In-Process Quality Metrics (E-IPQM) and European Reliability and Quality Measurements for Telecommunications Systems (E-RQMS) (Eurescom 1995). Joint working groups have been established to align the EIRUS and QuEST Forum metrics.

The QuEST Forum held Forum meetings in Brussels in June 1999, Paris in May 2000, Tokyo in June 2000, London in October 2000, and Buenos Aires in April 2000. Future meetings will be scheduled for other parts of the world.

FUTURE ACTIVITIES

The Forum is now in the process of working on the following new initiatives:

- Assessing the value of adding new metrics to the metrics handbook (QuEST 1999b)
- Extending TL 9000 requirements and metrics to the supply chain

- Developing the Business Excellence Acceleration Model (BEAM), a self-assessment industry guidance program based on regional, national, and state award criteria and aimed at continuous improvement of business processes, products, and services
- Revision of the training materials to align with changes due to alignment of the requirements handbook with ISO 9001:2000
- Expanding the global membership through Forum meetings in Europe, the Asia/Pacific region, and South America
- Expanding the industry membership to include new service providers, new suppliers, and the supply chain

REFERENCES

Automotive Industry Action Group (AIAG). *Quality System Requirements, QS-9000.* 3rd ed. Detroit, MI: March, 1998.

Aycock, G., J.-N. Drouen, and T. Yohe. "TL 9000 Performance Metrics to Drive Improvement." *Quality Progress* 32, no. 7 (July 1999):41–45.

British Standards Institute. BS 7799: 1999. *Information Security Management.* Part 1, *Code of Practice for Information Security Management.* Part 2, *Specification for Information Security Management.* London: 1999.

"Development of ASQ Role As TL 9000 Forum Administrator." *The Informed Outlook* 4, no. 5 (May 1999):1–2.

Eurescom GmbH. *European Quality Metrics: E-IPQM and E-RQMS.* Deliverable 5, Eurescom P307, Reliability engineering. Scloss Wolfsbrunnenweg 35, 69118 Heidelberg, Germany: November, 1995. URL: www.eurescom.de/.

International Organization for Standardization (ISO). ISO 9001:1994, *Quality systems—model for quality assurance in design/development, production, installation and servicing.* 2nd ed. Geneva, Switzerland: 1994a.

———. ISO 9004-2:1994, *Quality management and quality system elements.* Part 2, *Guidelines for services.* Geneva, Switzerland: 1994b.

———. ISO 10011-1:1994, *Guidelines for auditing quality systems—Auditing.* Geneva, Switzerland: 1994c.

———. ISO 10011-2:1994, *Guidelines for auditing quality systems—Qualification criteria for quality systems auditors.* Geneva, Switzerland: 1994d.

———. ISO 10011-3:1994, *Guidelines for auditing quality systems—Management of audit programs.* Geneva, Switzerland: 1994e.

———. ISO/IEC 12207, *Information technology software life cycle processes.* Geneva, Switzerland: February 1995.

———. ISO 9000-3:1997, *Quality management and quality assurance standards.* Part 3, *guidelines for the application of ISO 9001:1994 to the development, supply, installation, and maintenance of computer software.* 2nd ed. Geneva, Switzerland: 1997.

Liebesman, S., A. Jarvis, and A. Dandekar. *TL 9000: A Guide to Measuring Excellence in Telecommunications.* Milwaukee: ASQ Quality Press, 2001.

Malec, H. "TL 9000 Database Repository and Metrics." *The Informed Outlook* 4, no. 6 (June 1999): 4.

QuEST Forum. *TL 9000, Quality System Requirements.* Book 1, Release 2.5. Milwaukee: ASQ Quality Press, 1999a.

———. *TL 9000 Quality System Metrics.* Book 2, Release 2.5. Milwaukee: ASQ Quality Press, 1999b.

————. *TL 9000 Quality Management System Requirements Handbook.* Book 1, Release 3.0. Milwaukee: ASQ Quality Press, 2001a.

————. *TL 9000 Quality System Measurements Handbooks.* Book 2, Release 3.0. Milwaukee: ASQ Quality Press, 2001b.

Telcordia Technologies. TR-NWT-179, *Quality System Generic Requirements for Software.* Issue 2 (June 1993). Morristown, NJ.

————. GR-1252, *Quality System Generic Requirements for Hardware.* Issue 1 (May 1995a). Morristown, NJ.

————. GR-1202-CORE, *Generic Requirements for Customer Sensitive Quality Infrastructure.* Issue 1 (October 1995b). Morristown, NJ.

————. GR-63-CORE, *Network Equipment-Building System (NEBS) Requirements: Physical Protection.* Issue 1 (October 1995c). Morristown, NJ.

————. GR-929-CORE, *Reliability and Quality Measurements for Telecommunications Systems (RQMS).* Issue 4 (December 1998). Morristown, NJ.

Chapter 61

Achieving Certification in a Winery

Judith Luchsinger
Owner, QED Consulting Group, Lakeport, California

T his chapter discusses the first process to achieve compliance with ISO 9001:1994 standards by a U.S. winery: Fetzer Vineyards, located in Hopland, California, and owned by the Brown-Forman Corporation, Louisville, Kentucky.

MOTIVATION

The motivation of Brown-Forman, and Fetzer Vineyards to adopt the ISO model and seek ISO 9001 certification was primarily twofold. First, they intended to garner greater market share by the globalization of their business. Second, they realized that it is necessary to have processes in place from a business standpoint, not only for the repeatability of good business practices but also in their planning for continued success over generations.

SCOPE

The scope of the implementation included the winemaking (winery) and production functions of the organization. The production arm included quality control, logistics, bottling, and warehousing. Hospitality (the tasting room) was not included in the scope because it did not have a direct influence on the production of the wine nor the image of the winery in the marketplace.

So what is the comparison between winemaking and the more commonly encountered forms of manufacturing? Both consist of processes that can be documented and controlled. After the Fetzer implementation, the winemakers commented that having "a documented process is helpful. Not only does writing down the process help us understand the underlying system, it keeps everybody on the same page. The implementation of ISO does not create any limitation for us. It gives us guidelines from the initial receiving of the grapes to the end of the design. We have a clear understanding of what we need to do, so it speeds up the process."

During the implementation, an additional winemaker was hired, and the other winemakers said, "Having these design guidelines will save her five years of having to personally figure out the style of each brand and each variety in that brand."

LANGUAGE ISSUES

One of the interesting aspects of the Fetzer implementation was the challenge of dealing with their non-English-speaking employees. The issues they confronted were:

- Whether to have documentation in other languages
- If the documentation is entirely in English, how the non-English-speakers would have meaningful access to it
- How the ISO training would be handled
- What kinds of training would be necessary or helpful for these employees

The decision to document only in English was reached when the implementation team realized that if they translated all documents into Spanish, which is the most prevalent foreign language spoken by their non-English-speaking employees, in the future they might need to accommodate other foreign-language speakers as well. The upkeep of documentation in any language(s) other than English seemed too unwieldy a task as well as an unnecessary one that did not add value to their business.

Once the decision was made to keep documents only in English, the implementation team realized that the managers who have non-English-speaking employees in their departments communicate with them through a bilingual fellow employee. This system of using a colleague translator was already in place for most if not all non-English speakers. So, they decided that every non-English-speaking employee would have a designated translator who would translate all documentation necessary to read or review (for example, quality manual, procedures, and work instructions). The employees were already doing this in practice, so it was a painless decision on all parts to formalize the practice.

The initial ISO training for non-English speakers was presented in Spanish. The consultant-trainer felt the non-English speakers needed to recognize the documentation as it exists (in English) so they would know what it is, where it is, why they needed to be able to access it, and how to access it. Therefore, as they went through the English documentation, it was translated for them. Each individual's work instructions were translated verbally to that individual to double-check that he/she understood the instructions and corroborated that the instructions documented accurately what he/she does.

At the end of the training, each employee was asked if they had questions or concerns. The questions ranged from requesting clarity on the internal and certification audits to the Corrective Action form. It became clear that these questions were related: was this a Gestapo implementation? It had been carefully explained how the audits were audits of process, not people, and how the external audit was to ensure that the documentation was kept up-to-date to reflect the continuing changes that occur in every organization, and that the audit–corrective action–management review cycle was one of the engines that powered the improvement in the business practices. These answers were met with uneasiness.

Finally, one employee in quality control had the courage to ask the question to which the other questions were alluding: Was this ISO implementation for the purpose of disciplining employees? If not, why was the company using a Corrective Action form for employee suggestions (preventive actions)? They were assured that the process to correct a situation, rewrite a procedure, or put a new process in place required documentation and that it was simply efficient to use the same form. But the title of that form was a concern.

So, on the basis of worker input, Fetzer management made a new form entitled Employee Suggestion form (same form, different title) for employees to use to make suggestions. The workers were excited about having a process to make their suggestions and pleased that management made the commitment to ensure that their ideas would not be ignored or lost because of lack of a system.

Fetzer Vineyards already had a strong commitment to training for all employees. For their non-English speakers, they provide English As a Second Language (ESL) courses on-site on a semester basis (two hours, two times per week) and have done so for several years. Any employee can take preapproved classes to increase their skills and are reimbursed for tuition, fees, and textbooks on successful completion of the course.

THE DESIGN ELEMENT IN THE ART OF WINEMAKING

The issue of the art of winemaking was a consideration in the implementation. The initial reluctance of the winemakers was the fear that "capturing" and documenting processes might inhibit the creation of the many styles and complexities of the wines. Heath Dolan, Fetzer's cellar master, commented, "In doing the documentation of the creative process, we documented what we do based on the tasting notes of the winemakers; so this documenting did not and does not change how we go about creating the wine. We still preserve the ability to change a wine style midstream based on sensory evaluations that take place continually throughout the winemaking process. ISO doesn't require that the creativity or subjective choices regarding the ingredients, their timing, blending, cooperage or ultimate packaging be fixed, only that we keep track of the procedures and processes utilized in the design. We weren't asked to document our thoughts, only the processes that our decisions engendered."

Design and Development Planning

Customer requirements for the product are initially received from the brand managers in the form of Brand Positioning Statements. The winemakers "translate" these customer requirements into functional and performance requirements titled Design Guidelines and Finished Wine Specifications, which designate both the sourcing and the styles to be produced under each brand.

Design Input

All Fetzer wines have design inputs based on the Brand Positioning Statements and Bureau of Alcohol, Tobacco, and Firearms (BATF) regulations.

Design Output

During the creation of the wine, the winemaker of a particular varietal wine determines if the wine meets the Brand Positioning Statement and all regulatory and legal requirements, such as percentage of alcohol.

On receipt of all grapes or bulk wine, information is entered into the winemakers' database. This information includes vintage, variety, appellation, tax class, harvest Brix (where applicable), and analysis. At any point in the process, the winemakers' database can verify whether wine meets BATF and finished wine specifications.

Winemakers taste processing wine on a regular basis and take individual tasting notes. Based on these notes, action steps are communicated in document control, sections 9, 10, and 12 of ISO 9001:1994. All completed processes are entered into the winemakers' database. Continued blending and adjustment of a wine takes place until the wine, in the opinion of the winemaker, fulfills the requirements of the design to ensure that output meets input requirements.

Design Review

At appropriate stages of the winemaking process, as determined by the winemaker, formal tastings take place, and the results of these sensory evaluations are recorded in the winemakers' tasting notes database. These sensory evaluations provide the basis for any additional blending and quality decisions.

Design Verification

The tasting notes and winemakers' database provide verification that the Brand Positioning Statements, BATF regulations, and the finished wine specifications are being met.

The Pre-Bottling Report requires the signatures of two winemakers and verifies that each wine meets the design guidelines, BATF regulations, finished wine specifications, and label statements.

Design Validation

Design validation occurs when quality control performs chemical adjustments to the wine per the pre-bottling wine preparation to ensure that the wine meets bottling-line wine analysis parameters. The results are recorded on the Bottling Tank Report.

Control of Design Changes

Design changes are initiated by a brand manager through changes in existing Brand Positioning Statements or creation of new ones. For work in process, winemaker(s) determine the affectivity date of changes to wine.

Anyone can request a change in Brand Positioning Statements, but the brand manager must approve all changes. For all changes, the brand manager must create a new Brand Positioning Statement.

Thus, although there is flexibility in the subjective decision making of the winemakers, which constitutes an internal feedback loop for adjustments within parameters during wine creation, the results of those decisions are documented, and the process is sequential and repeatable. "We really didn't have to change our processes, just learn what they are. It was very subtle."

PARALLEL IMPLEMENTATION OF MULTIPLE PROJECTS

The decision to use SAP software (for tracking resources, inventory, making projections, and so on) was made at the corporate level. Many employees were receiving training during the same year the ISO implementation was proceeding. This resulted in updating some of the ISO documentation during the course of the implementation. For example, training was moving from the human resources department to a new training department, and not all employee files were complete. During the external audit, the training department manager was able to show that the department had a process in place for the move and were following it. Although not yet completed, the process was controlled.

James Sobbizadeh, the production manager who was responsible for the implementation of ISO, commented, "Every project is looked at on its own. When things happen like multiple project implementation, people get stressed. But, in my opinion, the stress is generated by confusion. If you have direction and specifics on the projects and clear outcome expectations, there is no stress. Everyone knows what needs to be done. And the key is to keep open and clear communication during the implementations on what needs to be done and the outcomes we want. We could have 6000 processes, but if you are clear and have proper specifications, you can do multiple projects. That is what stops the stress: the clarity. I don't mean to say that it eliminated all stress completely, but we could achieve these multiple goals because we were clear about where we wanted to go and were clear with what we wanted from our people. When you don't have clarity, ambiguity is the stressor and the unknown stressor is fear."

SELECTION OF CERTIFYING AGENCY

Fetzer management, in conjunction with the implementing consultants (Judith Luchsinger and George Zalatan of QED Consulting Group), selected Lloyd's Register Quality Assurance (LRQA) as the registrar. The consultants had previous good experience with LRQA. The goal was to find an auditor with previous experience in the food and beverage industry, as well as an appreciation of the complexities involved in winemaking in particular. The implementing consultant had heard from another consultant that LRQA's managing director based in New Jersey and Houston, Dave Hadlet, had both extensive auditing experience and knowledge of the wine industry, but was no longer doing audits. However, following a phone interview with him, he agreed to perform the audit, primarily to get an in-depth look, with his auditor's hat on, at a California winery and to be involved with the first winery in the United States to attempt ISO 9001 certification.

BEYOND ISO 9001

At this time, Fetzer Vineyards is reviewing and considering ISO 14000. They produce organic wines under the Bon Terra label and believe this is a wave of the future. James Sobbizadeh realizes that the industry will specify what it wants depending on the desires and needs of the consumer. As those customer wants, needs, and requirements become clear, Fetzer Vineyards is determined to stay open-minded to upcoming initiatives and to implement those that make good business sense. The company is on the cutting edge of this industry, and ISO implementation is indicative of their commitment to ensuring that Fetzer builds a system that can "last for generations and generations."

From a process-improvement point of view, their management review team has chosen to take a look at the number of "holds" in their production line. The first change they have made to reduce these holds was to take responsibility for surveillance out of the quality control department and place it in the hands of the operators on the line. They have only implemented this change for three weeks as of this writing, so no quantitative results are available yet.

Fetzer has also taken a look at its suppliers. The cork supplier from Portugal has an ISO 9002 certification, and the glass supplier is a sole source, so Fetzer has put in a procedure to evaluate, communicate, and work with suppliers.

As part of the continual improvement of their quality management system, Fetzer management will consider an upgrade to ISO 9001:2000 during the fiscal year 2001-02.

CONCLUSION

Sobbizadeh remarks that one of the biggest changes that has occurred since implementing ISO 9001 is that it has made Fetzer management aware that they can't impetuously make a change. Their process now is to suggest a change, get input and ideas from the people who will be affected, make a decision, and if indicated, make the change. "Ninety out of a hundred times we decide to go ahead with the changes, but the inclusive ISO procedure saves us the other ten times," said Sobbizadeh.

Appendix A

Common Acronyms

A

AACB—Australian Association of Certification Bodies

AAB—Argentine Accreditation Body

ABCB—Association of British Certification Bodies, U.K.

ABNT—Associacao Brasileira do Normas Tecnicas, Brazil

ACIL—American Council of Independent Laboratories

AECMA—European Association of Aerospace Manufacturers

AFAQ—Association Francaise pour l'Assurance de las Qualite, France

AIAG—Automotive Industry Action Group

AIB—Association des Industriels de Belgique (Belgian Organization for Quality System Assessement)

AICQ—Italian Association for Quality

AIHA—American Industrial Hygiene Association

ANSI—American National Standards Institute

AO—Accredited Organization

APEC—Asia Pacific Economic Cooperation

API—American Petroleum Institute

APLAC—Asia Pacific Laboratory Accreditation Cooperation

ASME—American Society of Mechanical Engineers
ASQ—American Society for Quality
ASTM—American Society for Testing and Materials
A2LA—American Association for Laboratory Accreditation

B
BOCA—Building Officials and Code Administrators International
BSA—Bulgarian System for Accreditation
BSI—British Standards Institution
BSR—Board of Standards Review

C
CAG—Chairmans Advisory Group
CAI—Cesky Institute pro Akreditaci (Czech Accreditation Institute)
CASE—Conformity Assessment Systems Evaluation, now NVCASE
CASCO—Committee on Conformity Assessment
CD—Committee Draft
CEAA—Canadian Environmental Auditing Association
CE—European Community
CE Mark—Conformité Européenne Mark of approval used by the European Union
CEN—Comité Européen de Normalisation (European Committee for Standardization)
CENELEC—European Committee for Electrotechnical Standardization
CEPAA—Council on Economic Priorities Accreditation Agency
CMA—Chemical Manufacturers Association
CNACR—China National Accreditation Committee for Quality System Registration Bodies
COPQ—Cost of Poor Quality

D
DAR—Deutscher Akkreditierungs Rat (German Accreditation Council)
DFQ—Danish Society for Quality
DGQ—German Society for Quality
DIN—Deutsches Institut fur Normung, German standards developing body
DQS—Deutsche Gesellschaft Zur Zertifizierung Qualitatssiche—Rungssystemen MBH (German Association for Certification of Quality Assurance Systems)
DIS—Draft International Standard
DS—Dansk Standardiseringsraad (Danish Standards Association)

E

EA—Environmental Audit

EA—European Cooperation for Accreditation

EARA—Environmental Auditors Registration Association

EC—European Community

ECTF—Electronic Communications Task Force

EFTA—European Free Trade Association

EMAS—Eco-Management and Auditing Scheme

EMS—Environmental Management System

EN—European Norm

ENAC—Entidad National de Acreditacion, Spain

EOQ—European Organization for Quality

EOTC—European Organization for Testing and Certification

EPA—Environmental Protection Agency

EPE—Environmental Performance Evaluation

EQS—EOTC Committee Responsible for Quality Assurance Assessment Certification

ETSI—European Telecommunications Standards Institute

EU—European Union

F

FAA—Federal Aviation Administration

FDIS—Final Draft International Standard

G

GATT—General Agreement on Tariffs and Trade

GDP—Gross Domestic Product

GMP—Good Manufacturing Practices

H

HACCP—Hazard Analysis Critical Control Points

I

IAAR—Independent Association of Accredited Registrars

IAF—International Accreditation Forum

IASG—International Automotive Sector Group

IATCA—International Auditor and Training Certification Association

IATF—International Automotive Task Force

ICSP—Interagency Council on Standards Policy, U.S.

IEAA—International Environmental Auditing Association

IEC—International Electrotechnical Commission

IETA—International Electrical Testing Association

IEEE—Institute of Electrical and Electronics Engineers

IGCC—Insulating Glass Certification Council

IIA—Institute of Internal Auditors

ILAC—International Laboratory Accreditation Cooperation

ILO—International Labor Organization

INMETRO—Instituto Nacional de Metrologia, Normalizaçâo e Qualidade Industrial (National Institute for Metrology, Standardization and Industrial Quality, Brazil)

IPQ—Instituto Português da Qualidade, Portugal

IQA—Institute for Quality Assurance, U.K.

IRCA—International Register of Certificated Auditors

IS—International Standard

ISC—International Standards Certification

ISO—International Organization for Standardization

IT—Information Technology

J

JAB—Japan Accreditation Board for Conformity Assessment

JCAHO—Joint Commission on the Accreditation of Healthcare Organizations

JAS-ANZ—Joint Accreditation Service of Australia and New Zealand

JRCA—Japanese Registration of Certified Auditors

K

KAB—Korea Accreditation Board

KEMA—Keuring Van Electrotechnische (Netherlands)

L

LCA—Lifecycle analysis or assessment

M

MLA—Multilateral Recognition Agreement

MoU—Memorandum of Understanding

MRA—Mutual Recognition Agreement

MRS—Metrics Repository System

N

NABL—National Accreditation Board for Testing and Calibration Laboratories, India

NACCB—National Accreditation Council for Certification Bodies, U.K.

NACE—Nomenclature Générale des Activités Économique dans les Communautés Européennes

NACLA—National Council on Laboratory Accreditation

NADCAP—National Aerospace and Defense Contractors Accreditation Program

NADL—National Board for Certification of Dental Laboratories

NAFTA—North American Free Trade Agreement

NAMI—National Accreditation and Management Institute

NAP—National Accreditation Program

NATA—National Association of Testing Authorities, Australia

NEMA—National Electrical Manufacturers Association

NEN—Netherlands Standardization Institute

NETA—(International) National Electrical Testing Association

NCSL—National Conference of Standards Laboratories

NIST—National Institute of Standards and Technology, U.S. Department of Commerce

NGO—Non-governmental organization

NQI—National Quality Institute, Canada

NRTL—Nationally Recognized Testing Laboratory

NSAI—National Standards Authority of Ireland

NSLAP—Naval Shipyard Laboratory Accreditation Program

NVCASE—National Voluntary Evaluation, formerly the CASE Program

NVLAP—National Voluntary Laboratory Accreditation Program, NIST

NWIP—New Work Item Proposal

O

OEM—Original Equipment Manufacturers

OH&S—Occupational Health & Safety

OMC—Organizational Member Council

OSHA—Occupational Safety and Health Administration, DOL

OVQ—Austrian Association for Quality

P

PAC—Pacific Accreditation Cooperation

PASC—Pacific Area Standards Cooperation

PL—Project Leader

Q

QA—Quality assurance

QM—Quality Management

QMS—Quality Management System

QSA—Quality Society of Australasia

QSM—Quality System Metrics

QSR—Quality System Requirements

QuEST—Quality Excellence for Suppliers of Telecommunications

R

RAB—Registrar Accreditation Board

S

SABS—South African Bureau of Standards

SAC—Singapore Accreditation Council

SAE—Society of Automotive Engineers

SANAS—South African National Accreditation System

SC—Subcommittee

SCC—Standards Council of Canada

SDO—Standards Development Organization

SGLC—Standards Group Leadership Council

SIC—Standard Industrial Classification code

SINCERT—Accreditamento Organismi Certificazione (Italian System for Accreditation of Certification Bodies)

SME—Small/Medium-Sized Enterprise

SME—Subject Matter Expert

SSG—Standards Study Group

T

TA—Technical Advisor

TAG—Technical Advisory Group

TC—Technical Committee

TELARC—Testing Laboratory Registration Council of New Zealand

TG—Task Group

TGC—Task Group Coordinator

TickIT—U.K. Quality System Registration Scheme for Software Companies

TMB—Technical Management Board, ISO

TQLS—Total Quality Learning Solution

TQM—Total Quality Management

TR—Technical Report

U

UKAS—United Kingdom Accreditation Service

UL—Underwriters Laboratories

UNIDO—United National Industrial Development Organization

USNC—United States National Committee

W

WD—Working Draft

WG—Working Group (international usage); Writing Group (national committee usage)

WTO—World Trade Organization

Appendix B

Sources for More Information

American National Standards Institute (ANSI)
Headquarters:
1819 L Street, NW
Washington, DC 20036
Tel: 202-293-8020; Fax: 202-293-9287
New York office:
11 West 42nd Street
New York, NY 10036
Tel: 212-642-4900; Fax: 212-398-0023
Web site: www.ansi.org

American Society for Quality (ASQ)
600 N. Plankinton Avenue
Milwaukee, WI 53203
Tel: 414-272-8575 or 800-248-1946; Fax: 414-272-1734
Web site: www.asq.org

American Society for Testing and Materials (ASTM)
100 Bar Harbor Drive
West Conshohocken, PA 19428-2959
Tel: 610-832-9500; Fax: 610-832-9555
Web site: www.astm.org

International Forum for Management Systems (INFORM)
Publisher of The Informed Outlook—*a twice-monthly newsletter on management systems—and other books and training videos*
15913 Edgewood Drive
Montclair, VA 22026
Tel: 703-680-1436; Fax: 703-680-1356
Web site: www.INFORMintl.com

International Organization for Standardization (ISO)
ISO Central Secretariat
1, rue de Varembé, Case postale 56
CH-1211 Geneva 20, Switzerland
Tel: 011-41-22-749-0111; Fax: 011-41-22-733-3430
Web site: www.iso.ch

NSF International (NSFI)
PO Box 130140
789 N. Dixboro Road
Ann Arbor, MI 48113-0140
Tel: 734-769-8010; Fax: 734-769-0109
Web site: www.nsf.org

QuEST Forum
c/o American Society for Quality (ASQ)
PO Box 422
Milwaukee, WI 53201-0422
Tel: 414-765-8672; Fax: 414-765-8665
Web site: http://questforum.asq.org

Appendix C

Further Readings

Arter, Dennis, and J. P. Russell. *ISO Lesson Guide 2000: Pocket Guide to Q9001-2000*, 2nd ed. (Milwaukee: ASQ Quality Press, 2001).

Cianfrani, Charles A., Joseph J. Tsiakals, and John E. (Jack) West. *ISO 9001:2000 Explained*, 2nd ed. (Milwaukee: ASQ Quality Press, 2001).

The Informed Outlook. Monthly Newsletter Published by ASQ and INFORM (International Forum for Management Systems)

Keeney, Kent A. *The ISO 9001 Auditor's Companion* (Milwaukee: ASQ Quality Press, 2002).

Ketola, Jeanne, and Kathy Roberts. *ISO 9000:2000 in a Nutshell: A Concise Guide to the Revisions*, 2nd ed. (Chico, CA: Paton Press, 2001).

Levinson, William A. *ISO 9000 at the Front Line* (Milwaukee: ASQ Quality Press, 2000).

Mehta, Praful (Paul) C. *ISO 9000 Audit Questionnaire and Registration Guidelines* (Milwaukee: ASQC Quality Press, 1994).

Russell, J. P., editing director. *The Quality Audit Handbook,* 2nd ed. (Milwaukee: ASQ Quality Press, 2000).

Taylor, C. Michael. *Meet the Registrar: Firsthand Accounts of ISO 9000 Success from the Registration Source* (Milwaukee: ASQC Quality Press, 1997).

West, John E. (Jack), and Charles A Cianfrani. *ISO 9000:2000—An Audio Workshop and Master Slide Set*, 2nd ed. (Milwaukee: ASQ Quality Press, 2001).

Wilson, Lawrence A. *Eight-Step Process to Successful ISO 9000 Implementation: A Quality Management System Approach* (Milwaukee: ASQC Quality Press, 1996).

Appendix D

Accredited Registrars in North America*

ISO 9000 Certificate Totals are for certificates issued in the United States, Canada and Mexico as of 8/1/2001

A2LA
American Association for Laboratory Accreditation
5301 Buckeystown Pike, Suite 350
Frederick, MD 21704
Phone: 301-644-3200; Fax: 301-662-2974
E-mail: krudd@a2la.org
Web site: www.a2la.org
ISO 9000 certificate total: 13

ABS QE
ABS Quality Evaluations, Inc.
16855 Northchase Drive
Houston, TX 77060
Phone: 281-877-6800; Fax: 281-877-6801
E-mail: qe_cust_serv@eagle.org
Web site: www.abs-qe.com/
ISO 9000 certificate total: 2,069

*Courtesy of QSU Publishing Company, which publishes Quality Systems Update newsletter on ISO 9000 and related standards as well as the ISO 9000 Registered Company Directory North America, which tracks third-party certifications to management systems standards such as ISO 9000, QS-9000, TS 16949, TL 9000 and AS9100. QSU Publishing Company, 3975 University Drive, Suite 230, Fairfax, VA 22030, Tel: 1-866-225-3122, Fax: 703-359-8462, URL: www.qsuonline.com.

AEA
AEA Quality Advantage Corporation
15 Myers Corner Road, Suite 1-S
Wappingers Falls, NY 12590-4117
Phone: 845-298-0032; Fax: 845-298-1253
E-mail: sales@aeaquality.com
Web site: www.aeaquality.com
ISO 9000 certificate total: 14

AENOR
Asociacion Espanola de Normalizacion y Certificacion
Génova, 628004 Madrid, Spain
Phone: +34 91 432 60 00; Fax: +34 91 310 40 32
E-mail: Certificacion@aenor.es
Web site: www.aenor.es
ISO 9000 certificate total: unknown

AFAQ-ASCERT
1054 31st Street, NW Suite 320
Washington, DC 20007
Phone: 800-241-3412; Fax: 202-337-3709
E-mail: info@afaq.org
Web site: www.afaq.org
ISO 9000 certificate total: 109

AGS
300 Esplande Drive, Suite 1120
Oxnard, CA 93030
Phone: 805-983-8200; Fax: 805-981-1034
E-mail: admin@americanglobalstandards.com
Web site: www.americanglobalstandards.com
ISO 9000 certificate total: unknown

AIB
AIB Registration Services
1213 Bakers Way
Manhattan, KS 66505
Phone: 785-537-4750; Fax: 785-537-1493
E-mail: information@aibonline.org
Web site: www.aibonline.org
ISO 9000 certificate total: 10

AOQC Moody
AOQC Moody International, Inc.
650 N Sam Houston Parkway E, Suite 228
Houston, TX 77060
Phone: 281-367-8764; Fax: 281-367-3496
E-mail: houston@aoqcmoody.com
Web site: www.aoqcmoody.com/
ISO 9000 certificate total: 67

AOQC Moody International, Ltd. (Canada)
57 Simcoe Street, Suite 2H
Oshawa, Ontario L1H 4G4
Phone: 905-433-2955; Fax: 905-432-9308
E-mail: mti@moodycanada.com
Web site: www.moodyint.com
ISO 9000 certificate total: 67

APIQR
American Petroleum Institute Quality Registrar
1220 L St. NW
Washington, DC 20005
Phone: 202-682-8129; Fax: 202-682-8070
E-mail: hahns@api.org
Web site: www.api.org
ISO 9000 certificate total: 28

AQA
American Quality Assessors
1107 Belleview Avenue Columbia, SC 29201
Phone: 803-779-8150; Fax: 803-779-8109
E-mail: kelly@aqausa.com
Web site: www.aqausa.com/
ISO 9000 certificate total: 568

ASME
American Society of Mechanical Engineers
Three Park Ave.
New York, NY 10016
Phone: 212-591-8033; Fax: 212-591-8599
E-mail: accreditation@asme.org
Web site: www.asme.org/codes
ISO 9000 certificate total: 15

AQSR
AQSR International
Automotive Quality Systems Registrar
3025 Boardwalk, Suite 120
Ann Arbor, MI 48108
Phone: 734-913-8055; Fax: 734-913-8152
E-mail: bkitchen@aqsr.com
Web site: www.aqsr.com
ISO 9000 certificate total: 418

ASQR Canada
ASQR International Canada
2560 Matheson Blvd. Suite 226
Mississauga, Ontario L4W 4Y9 Canada
Phone: 1-888-866-5666; Fax: 905-624-7213
E-mail: aqsrca@aqsr.com
Web site: www.aqsr.com
ISO 9000 certificate total: 5

ASR
American Systems Registrars
4550 Cascade Rd. SE Suite 202
Grand Rapids, MI 49546
Phone: 888-891-9002; Fax: 616-942-6409
E-mail: staff@asr.9000.net
Web site: www.asr.9000.net
ISO 9000 certificate total: 73

BNQ
Bureau de Normalisation du Quebec
Quality System Registration
333 rue Franquet
Sainte-Foy, Quebec G1P 4C7
Phone: 418-652-2238; Fax: 418-652-2292
E-mail: bnq@criq.qc.ca
Web site: www.criq.qc.ca/bnq
ISO 9000 certificate total: 653

BSI Inc.
12110 Sunset Hills Rd. Suite 140
Reston, VA 20190
Phone: 703-437-9000; Fax: 703-437-9001
E-mail: bsi_inc@compuserve.com
Web site: www.bsiamericas.com
ISO 9000 certificate total: 2,661

BQR
BestCERT Quality Registrars, Ltd.
714 River Street
Fitchburg, MA 01420
Phone: 978-665-0100; Fax: 978-665-0101
E-mail: bqriso@aol.com
Web site: www.bestcert.org
ISO 9000 certificate total: 74

BVQI
Bureau Veritas Quality International (North America), Inc.
509 N Main Street
Jamestown, NY 14701
Phone: 716-484-9002; Fax: 716-484-9003
E-mail: info@bvqi.com
Web site: www.bvqi.com/
ISO 9000 certificate total: 1,971

aerospace techniques

CGSB
Canadian General Standards Board
Place du Portage, Phase III, 6B1,
11 Laurier Street Hull,
Quebec K1A 1G6
Phone: 819-956-0398; Fax: 819-956-5740
E-mail: ncr.cgsb-ongc@pwgsc.gc.ca
Web site: www.pwgsc.gc.ca/cgsb
ISO 9000 certificate total: 244

CICS
Ceramic Industry Certification Scheme Ltd.
Queens Road, Penkhull
Stoke-On-Trent ST4 7LQ England
Phone: 44-1782-411-008; Fax: 44-1782-412-331
E-mail: info@cicsltd.com
Web site: www.cicsltd.com
ISO 9000 certificate total: 92

CRS
CRS Registrars, Inc.
Corporate Office
5515 Southwyck Boulevard, Suite 205
Toledo, OH 43614
Phone: 419-861-1689; Fax: 419-861-1696
E-mail: bned@crsregistrars.com
Web site: www.crsregistrars.com/
ISO 9000 certificate total: 306

DESC
Defense Electronics Supply Center
Quality Operations Division
1507 Wilmington Pike
Dayton, OH 45444-5764
Phone: 703-767-8736
E-mail: loppenheim@desc.dla.mil
Web site: www.desc.dla.mil/main/deschome.htm
ISO 9000 certificate total: unknown

DLS
DLS Quality Technology Associates, Inc.
100 Main Street
Camillus, NY 13031
Phone: 315-672-3598; Fax: 315-672-3596
E-mail: dlsqual@aol.com
Web site: http://hometown.aol.com/dlsqual
ISO 9000 certificate total: 43

DNV
Det Norske Veritas, DNV Certification, Inc.
16340 Park Ten Place, Suite 100
Houston, TX 77084
Phone: 281-721-6600; Fax: 281-721-6903
E-mail: les.smith@dnv.com
Web site: www.dnvcert.com/
ISO 9000 certificate total: 2,684

D&T
Deloitte & Touche Quality Registrar, Inc.
1666 Wyandotte St. E
Windsor, Ontario Canada N8Y 1CY
Phone: 888-258-2240 or 519-967-0388; Fax: 519-967-0324
E-mail: rtosti@deloitte.ca
Web site: www.deloitte.ca
ISO 9000 certificate total: 566

DQS
DQS-German American Registrar for Management Systems, Inc.
1000 Skokie Boulevard, Suite 360
Wilmette, IL 60091
Phone: 847-256-0523; Fax: 847-256-0572
E-mail: DQSofUSA@aol.com
Web site: www.dqscertus.com
ISO 9000 certificate total: 189

EAGLE
Eagle Registrations, Inc.
2242 W Schantz Ave.
Dayton, OH 45419
Phone: 937-293-2000 or 800-795-3641; Fax: 937-293-0220
E-mail: eagleiso@aol.com
Web site: www.Eagleregistrations.com
ISO 9000 certificate total: 73

EAQA
EAQA USA Registrars, Inc.
15475 Chemical Lane
Huntington Beach, CA 92649
Phone: 714-373-3773; Fax: 714-373-3775
E-mail: info@eaqausa.com
Web site: www.eaqausa.com
ISO 9000 certificate total: 7

ENTELA
Entela, Inc.,
Quality System Registration Division
3033 Madison Avenue SE
Grand Rapids, MI 49548-1289
Phone:616-248-9605; Fax: 616-574-9752
E-mail: tporter@entela.com
Web site: www.entela.com
ISO 9000 certificate total: 1,257

EQA
European Quality Assurance Ltd.
48 Millgate
Newark
Nottinghamshire, England NG24 4TY
Phone: 44-1636-611-226; Fax: 44-1636-611-704
E-mail: eqa@eqa.co.uk
Web site: www.eqa.co.uk
ISO 9000 certificate total: 47

EXCALIBUR
Excalibur Registrations Inc.
20740 Ryan Rd Suit 100
Warren, MI 48091-2738
Phone: 810-755-9100; Fax: 810-755-9110
E-mail: excalibur9000@ameritech.net
Web site: www.excaliburregistrations.com
ISO 9000 certificate total: 76

FM Global
PO Box 7500
Johnston, RI 02919
Phone: 781-255-4883; Fax: 781-762-9375
E-mail: information@fmglobal.com
Web site: www.fmglobal.com/
ISO 9000 certificate total: 77

GBJD
GBJD Registrars Limited
9251-8 Yonge Street,
Suite 310
Richmond Hill, Ontario L4C 9T3
Phone: 877-256-1967; Fax: 905-727-1730
ISO 9000 certificate total: unknown

GRI
Global Registrars, Inc.
4700 Clairton Boulevard
Pittsburgh, PA 15236
Phone: 412-884-2290; Fax: 412-884-2268
E-mail: info@globalregistrars.com
Web site: www.globalregistrars.com
ISO 9000 certificate total: 258

HSB
HSB Registration Services
610 Freedom Business Center Suite 300,
PO Box 61509
King of Prussia, PA 19406-0909
Phone: 800-345-1122 or 484-582-1866; Fax: 484-582-1802
E-mail: Dennis_Palmer@hsb.com
Web site: www.hsbiso.com
ISO 9000 certificate total: 155

ICL
International Certifications Ltd.
1854 S. MacDonald
Mesa, AZ 85210
Phone: 480-668-4302; Fax: 480-610-3501
E-mail: cindy@intlcert.com
Web site: www.intlcert.com
ISO 9000 certificate total: approximately 60

IMNC
Instituto Mexicano de Normalizacion y Certificacion
A.C.Manuel Maria Contreras No. 133,
1 er. Piso Col.
Cuauhtamoc, Mexico Distrito Federal 06470
Phone: 525-566-4750; Fax: 525-705-3686
E-mail: direccion@imnc.org.mx
Web site: www.imnc.org.mx
ISO 9000 certificate total: 31

IMS
International Management Systems
5420 Bay Center Dr. Suite 200
Tampa, FL 33609
Phone: 813-639-9876; Fax: 813-639-9875
E-mail: mriso9000@ims4iso.com
Web site: www.ims4iso.com
ISO 9000 certificate total: 31

ITS
ITS Intertek (Canada)
1829 32nd Avenue
Lachine, Quebec, H8T 3J1
Phone: 514-631-3100; Fax: 514-631-1133
E-mail: ddesilet@itsqs.com
Web site: www.etlsemko.com
ISO 9000 certificate total: 1,302

INTERTEK
ITS Intertek Services
70 Codman Hill Rd.
Boxborough, MA 01719
Phone: 978-929-2100 or 800-810-1195; Fax: 978-635-8595
E-mail: info@itsglobal.com
Web site: www.itsglobal.com/
ISO 9000 certificate total: 1,683

Sound mfg.

IOC
U.S. Army Munitions and
Armament Command
1 Rock Island Arsenal
Rock Island, IL 61299-5100
Attn: SOS MA-SNA
Phone: 309-782-6513; Fax: 309-782-6328
E-mail: maloneym@ioc.army.mil
Web site: www.ioc.army.mil (currently under construction)
ISO 9000 certificate total: 7

IQSR
International Quality System Registrars, Ltd.
7025 Tomken Road, Suite 271
Mississauga, Ontario L5S 1R6
Phone: 800-267-0861; Fax: 905-565-0117
E-mail: feedback@iqsr.com
Web site: www.iqsr.com
ISO 9000 certificate total: 360

ISOQAR
PO Box 850370
Braintree, MA 02185
Phone: 781-356-6572; Fax: 781-356-0444
E-mail: isoqarusa@isoqar.com
Web site: www.isoqar.com
ISO 9000 certificate total: 33

KEMA Registered Quality, Inc.
4377 County Line Road; Suite 202
Chalfont, PA 18914
Phone: 215-997-4519 ext. 310; Fax: 215-997-3810
E-mail: cpellegrino@krqusa.com
Web site: www.kemaregisteredquality.com
ISO 9000 certificate total: 399

KPMG Canada
KPMG Quality Registrar, LLP
4 Robert Speck Parkway
Suite 15000
Mississuaga, Ontario L4Z 1S1
Phone: 800-862-6752; Fax: 905-949-7997
E-mail: kgross@kpmg.ca
Web site: www.kpmg.ca/iso
ISO 9000 certificate total: 2,294

KPMG QR
KPMG Quality Registrar
150 John F. Kennedy Parkway
Short Hills, NJ 07078
Phone: 800-716-5595; Fax: 973-912-6050
E-mail: japanpract@kpmg.com
Web site: www.us.kpmg.com
ISO 9000 certificate total: 1,015

LPCB
Loss Prevention Certification Board Ltd.
BRE Certification Ltd.
Melrose Avenue
Borehamwood,
Hertfordshire WD6 2BJ England
Phone: 44-081-207-2345; Fax: 44-091-236-64335
E-mail: enquiries@brecertification.co.uk
Web site: www.brecertification.co.uk
ISO 9000 certificate total: 17

LRQA
Lloyd's Register Quality Assurance Limited
15810 Park Ten Place, Suite 330
Houston, TX 77084
Phone: 281-398-7370; Fax: 281-398-7337
E-mail: operations-usa@lrqa.com
Web site: www.lrqa.com
ISO 9000 certificate total: 2,059

NFFS
Non-Ferrous Founders Society
1480 Renaissance Drive; Suite 310
Park Ridge, IL 60068
Phone: 847-299-0950; Fax: 847-299-3598
E-mail: nqs9000@nffs.org
Web site: www.nffs.org
ISO 9000 certificate total: 21

NQA
National Quality Assurance Ltd.
4 Post Office Square Road
Acton, MA 01720
Phone: 800-649-5289 or 978-635-9256; Fax: 978-263-0785
E-mail: edupont@nqa-usa.com
Web site: www.nqa-usa.com
ISO 9000 certificate total: 1,621

NSAI
National Standards Authority of Ireland
402 Amherts St.
Nashua, NH 03063
Phone: 603-882-4412; Fax: 603-882-1985
E-mail: richb@nsaieast.com
Web site: www.nsaicert.com
ISO 9000 certificate total: 504

NSF
NSF International Strategic Registrations, Ltd.
789 N. Dixboro Rd.
Ann Arbor, MI 48105
Phone: 888-NSF-9000 or 734-827-6800; Fax: 734-827-6801
E-mail: information@nsf-isr.org
Web site: www.nsf-isr.org
ISO 9000 certificate total: 2,063

ORION
Orion Registrar, Inc.
PO Box 5070
Arvada, CO 80060
Phone: 303-456-6010; Fax: 303-456-6681
E-mail: pburck@orion-iso.com
Web site: www.orion-iso.com/index.htm
ISO 9000 certificate total: 167

OTS
OTS Quality Registrars, Inc.
3726 Dacoma Blvd.
Houston, TX 77092
Phone: 713-688-9494; Fax: 713-688-9590
E-mail: rplatt@bigcity.net
Web site: www.otsqr.com
ISO 9000 certificate total: 39

PJR
Perry Johnson Registrars, Inc.
26555 Evergreen Road; Suite 1430
Southfield, MI 48075
Phone: 1-800-800-7910; Fax: 248-358-0882
E-mail: pjr@pjr.com
Web site: www.pjr.com
ISO 9000 certificate total: 1,972

PRI
Performance Review Institute Registrar
161 Thornhill Road
Warrendale, PA 15086-7293
Phone: 724-772-1616; Fax: 724-772-1699
E-mail: pri@sae.org
Web site: www.pri.sae.org
ISO 9000 certificate total: 106

PRO
Professional Registrar Organization, Inc.
300 E. Long Lake Rd, Suite 275
Bloomfield Hills, MI 48304
Phone: 248-593-6511 or 800-793-4408; Fax: 248-593-4408
E-mail: proregistrar@aol.com
Web site: www.proregistrar.com
ISO 9000 certificate total: 244

QCB
Quality Certification Bureau, Inc.
9650 - 20 Avenue
Suite 103, Advanced Technology Centre
Edmonton, Alberta T6N 1G1
Phone: 800-268-7321; Fax: 780-496-2464
E-mail: qcbinc@qcbinc.com
Web site: www.qcbinc.com/
ISO 9000 certificate total: 1,320

QMI
Quality Management Institute
90 Burnhamthorpe Road W, Suite 300
Mississauga, Ontario L5B 3C3
Phone: 905-272-3920; Fax: 905-272-3942
E-mail: clientservices@qmi.com
Web site: www.qmi.com
ISO 9000 certificate total: 6,321

QMS
Quality Management Systems, Inc.
Suite 128
10811 Maple Chase
Boca Raton, Florida 33498
Phone: 561-883-9200; Fax: 561-852-7779
E-mail: info@qms.com
Web site: www.qms.net
ISO 9000 certificate total: unknown

QSR
Quality Systems Registrars, Inc.
13873 Park Center Road, Suite 217
Herndon, VA 22071-3279
Phone: 703-478-0241; Fax: 703-478-0645
E-mail: qsrdr@msn.com
Web site: www.qsr.com
ISO 9000 certificate total: 525

QUASAR
Quality Systems Assessment Registrar
Head Office 7250 W Credit Avenue
Mississauga, Ontario L5N 5N1
Phone: 905-542-0547; Fax: 905-542-1318
E-mail: info@cwbgroup.com
Web site: www.cwbgroup.com/english/quasar.htm
ISO 9000 certificate total: 93

SCS
Sira Certification Service/Sira Test and Certification Ltd.
480 D East Wilson Bridge Road
Worthington, OH 43085
Phone: 614-847-3988; Fax: 614-847-3980
E-mail: info@sira.co.uk
Web site: www.siraservices.co.uk/
ISO 9000 certificate total: 26

SGS ICS
SGS International Certification Services, Inc.
Meadows Office Complex,
201 Route 17 N
Rutherford, NJ 07070
Phone: 800-747-9047; Fax: 201-935-4555
E-mail: sgsics@attglobal.net
Web site: www.sgsicsus.com
ISO 9000 certificate total: 1,498

SGS ICS Canada
SGS International Certification Services Canada, Inc.
5925 Airport Road, Suite 300
Mississauga, Ontario L4V 1W1
Phone: 800-636-0847 or 905-676-9595; Fax: 905-676-9519
E-mail: info@sgsna.com
Web site: www.sgs.ca
ISO 9000 certificate total: 1,846

SQA
Smithers Quality Assessments, Inc.
425 W Market Street
Akron, OH 44303-2099
Phone: 330-762-4231; Fax: 330-762-7447
E-mail: sqa@smithersmail.com
Web site: www.smithersregistrar.com/
ISO 9000 certificate total: 401

SRI
Steel Related Industries Quality System Registrars
2000 Corporate Drive, Suite 580
Wexford, PA 15090-7605
Phone: 724-934-9000; Fax: 724-934-6825
E-mail: mail@SRIRegistrar.com
Web site: sriregistrar.com
ISO 9000 certificate total: 757

TELCORDIA
Telcordia Quality
3 Corporate Place
Piscataway, NJ 08854
Phone: 732-699-3739; Fax: 732-336-2244
E-mail: mfaccone@telcordia.com
Web site: www.telcordia.com
ISO 9000 certificate total: 25

TNR
The National Registry
3031 Javier Rd.
Fairfax, VA 22030
Phone: 800-222-9001; Fax: 703-205-0684
E-mail: info@thenationalregistry.com
Web site: www.thenationalregistry.com
ISO 9000 certificate total: unknown

TRA-CD
TRA Certification
700 E Beardsley Avenue,
PO Box 1081
Elkhart, IN 46515-1081
Phone: 800-398-9282 or 219-264-0745; Fax: 219-264-0740
E-mail: info@trarnold.com
Web site: www.tra-cd.com/
ISO 9000 certificate total: 137

TRC
The Registrar Company, Inc. (TRC)
PO Box 516186
Dallas, TX 75251-6186
Phone: 972-783-7194 or 800-966-3291; Fax: 972-783-8953
E-mail: trcquality@aol.com
Web site: www.theregistrarco.com
ISO 9000 certificate total: 53

TUV Essen
411 Dixon Landing Rd.
Milpitas, CA 95035
Phone: 408-586-6200 or 800-TUV-4630; Fax: 408-586-6299
E-mail: info@tuvessen.com
Web site: http://www.tuvessen.com
ISO 9000 certificate total: 293

TUV MS
TUV Management Service/TUV Product Service
(a division of TUV America Inc.)
5 Cherry Hill Drive
Danvers, MA 01923
Phone: 978-739-7000; Fax: 978-762-8414
E-mail: ddougherty@tuvam.com
Web site: www.tuvglobal.com
ISO 9000 certificate total: 1,372

TUV Rheinland
TUV Rheinland of North America, Inc.
12 Commerce Road
Newtown, CT 06470
Phone: 203-426-0888; Fax: 203-426-4009
E-mail: kmullaney@us.tuv.com
Web site: www.tuv.com/
ISO 9000 certificate total: 679

UL
Underwriters Laboratories, Inc.
1285 Walt Whitman Road
Melville, NY 11747-3081
Phone: 847-272-8800; Fax: 847-272-8129
E-mail: registrar@ul.com
Web site: www.ul.com/welcome/html
ISO 9000 certificate total: 3,171

UL Canada
Underwriters Laboratories of Canada
7 Crouse Road
Scarborough, Ontario M1R 3A9
Phone: 416-757-3611; Fax: 416-757-8915
E-mail: customerservice@ulc.ca
Web site: www.ulc.ca
ISO 9000 certificate total: 36

URS
United Registrar of Systems Ltd. Unit 4,
7 Lyndale Ave.
Webster, MA 01570
Phone: 508-943-1642; Fax: 508-943-1642
E-mail: bqa@os.com
Web site: www.urs.co.uk
ISO 9000 certificate total: 29

Vincotte USA
AIB-Vincotte (AV Qualite)
3276 Salem Dr.
Rochester-Hills, MI 48306
Phone: 248-370-9292; Fax: 248-377-3175
E-mail: homologation2@aib-vincotte.com
Web site: www.aib-vincotte.com
ISO 9000 certificate total: 51

VCA
Vehicle Certification Agency North America
17250 Newburgh Road, Suite 140
Livona, MI 48152
Phone: 734-591-1605; Fax: 734-591-1705
E-mail: vca@wwnet.com
Web site: www.vca.gov.uk
ISO 9000 certificate total: unknown

Appendix E
Author Biographies

Juhani Anttila, M.B.Ch.B., B.Med.Sci., FQSA is vice president of quality integration for Sonera Corporation, Helsinki, Finland. He was president of the Finnish Society for Quality from 1984–87 and honorary member since 1998; 1994–96 Vice President of the EOQ; and since 1995 Academician of the International Academy for Quality (IAQ). He is broadly involved with quality standardization, a member of ISO TC 176 since 1980. He was chairman of the criteria committee of the Finnish National Quality Award 1990–1994, and assessor of the European Quality Award in 1993. He is co-author of the book *ISO 9000 for the Creative Leader*.

Diane M. Baguley, PhD is a management services consultant in the New Zealand consulting engineering firm Beca Carter Hollings & Ferner Ltd., having retired as one of its principal shareholders in 2000. Ms. Baguley specializes in the service and project sectors. Originally qualified in medicine and microbiology, five years in research and ten years in manufacturing followed. Since 1997 she has led the New Zealand delegation to ISO/TC 176 and participated in its task groups on revision of ISO 9001:2000. She is an honorary life member and former president of the New Zealand Organisation for Quality and a fellow and member of the board of directors of the Quality Society of Australsia.

Mark A. Baker, PhD is a clinical psychologist at The Person Center, Lakeport, California. Dr. Baker has been in independent practice in clinical psychology in Northern California since 1982 with specialty areas in stress management, behavioral wellness, and coaching in human behavior and performance enhancement. He has an extensive clinical background in a variety of settings and organizational structures. He attained his PhD in Professional Psychology from United States

International University, San Diego, California. He also holds an MEd in Counseling Psychology from Lewis and Clark College, Portland, Oregon and a BA in Psychology, University of California, Berkeley, California.

Eugene M. Barker, CQE, CQM is a technical fellow at The Boeing Company, Commercial Airplanes Group, responsible for quality industry association interfaces. He leads Boeing's corporate Quality System Process Action Team and is a member of the Boeing Enterprise Quality Process Council. Gene is recognized within his company and across the aerospace industry as a visionary regarding quality systems. He led the industry writing team that drafted SAE AS9000 and chaired working group 11 of ISO TC20 that developed AS9100.

He is a fellow of the American Society for Quality, member of the Registrar Accreditation Board (RAB) board of directors, and a founding member of the International Aerospace Quality Group.

Robert W. Belfit, PhD is the founding president and chairman and is now chairman emeritus of Omni Tech International, Ltd., Midland, Michigan. Dr. Belfit worked for the Dow Chemical Company for 29 years as a chemist and Laboratory Leader and Director of Quality Standards and received three degrees in chemistry from Dartmouth College and the Pennsylvania State University. Since 1987 he has assisted many companies in implementation of quality management systems based on ISO 9000, TQM, and ISO 25, has served on the Board of A2LA, and is a member of the American Chemical Society and the American Society for Quality.

Malcolm H. Bird is director of process improvement in the Automotive Driveline Division of GKN PLC, Birmingham, England, the market leader in the design and manufacture of passenger car driveshafts.

Mr. Bird is a member of the drafting teams for ISO 9001:2000 and ISO 9004:2000 standards, and represents the U.K. automotive industry in the International Automotive Task Force, the group responsible for the first global automotive quality system standard, ISO/TS 16949. He also chairs the quality subcommission of CLEPA and also the SMMT Quality Panel in the U.K. Mr. Bird is a member of the Institute of Materials, The Royal Society for Chemistry, The Royal Aeronautical Society, and the Institute of Quality Assurance.

Russ Bloom is currently the sales and marketing manager for Smithers Quality Assessments, a leading registrar for quality management and environmental management systems headquartered in Akron, Ohio. He was an officer in the U.S. Army and attended Bowling Green State University. Russ has worked in the quality management field for the last 25 years as quality manager in the appliances, foundry, metal stamping, and plastics industries.

Mr. Bloom is also a senior lead auditor and has conducted over 100 certification audits to ISO 9000, AS9000, and QS-9000. He is an IRCA certified lead auditor, an environmental lead auditor for ISO 14001, and a member of ASQ.

Pat Buzek is a lead auditor with AOQC Moody International, Houston, Texas. Mr. Buzek earned a BS in Chemistry from St. Mary's University in San Antonio, Texas. Prior to becoming a lead auditor of the ISO and QS-9000 standards, he was the quality assurance manager at Miller Brewing Company's Irwindale, California brewery. He has conducted hundreds of audits, specializing in the chemical, plastics, and pulp and paper industries.

Ronald R. Cerzosimo is president of International Quality Consultants, Doylestown, Pennsylvania. He received his education in electrical engineering at Pennsylvania State University and in industrial management at LaSalle University, Philadelphia, Pennsylvania. He has served as a consultant to the U.S. Nuclear Regulatory Commission and currently is an advisor to the International Atomic Energy Agency.

Mr. Cerzosimo is a professional engineer, an ASQ fellow and Certified Quality Engineer, and an RAB QMS and EMS lead auditor. He has actively served the standards development community (including ASME, ANSI, U.S. Technical Advisory Groups to ISO Technical Committee 176 on QMS, and ISO Technical Committee 207 on EMS) for more than twenty years.

M. M. "Mickey" Christensen, PE is president of TQM Systems, Baton Rouge, Louisiana, a training and consulting company. Mr. Christensen is chair of the ASQ Healthcare Division Standards Committee, co-proposer to ISO for the first IWA-1 for healthcare organizations and has consulted with the first- and third-largest acute care hospitals certified to ISO 9000 in North America. He is a registered QMS lead auditor with RAB and IRCA, registered professional engineer, developer of a consortium program to certify small businesses to ISO 9000, chair of the Louisiana State Quality Award development committee, charter president of the Louisiana Quality Foundation, and a speaker on implementing ISO 9000 in healthcare.

Dr. Nigel H. Croft is chairman of the International Standardized Testing Organization, Zug, Switzerland, and works as an independent management systems consultant throughout Europe, Asia, and the Americas. A first class honors graduate of Cambridge University, Croft's career in quality began in 1974, and has included a number of senior management positions in England, Norway, and Brazil.

Dr. Croft has been active within ISO/TC176 since 1996, more recently as task group leader for the introduction of the ISO 9000:2000 standards, and member of the TC176/CASCO/IAF transition policy group. He is a fellow and council member of the Institute of Quality Assurance in the U.K.

Elio G. Di Maggio is suppliers qualification manager for ENI SpA, Milan, Italy. A nuclear engineer since 1978, Mr. DiMaggio was involved in the development of ISO 9001 clause 7 (Product realization) as a member of ISO/TC 176/SC 2/WG-18. He is presently governing board chairman of AOQC Moody International Certification, governing board vice chairman of ANGQ, Italy, governing board member of UNI Quality and Relaiability Commission, Italy, and AICQ member, Italy.

Joseph R. Dunbeck is the first chief executive officer of the Registrar Accreditation Board (RAB) in Milwaukee, Wisconsin. He holds a BA degree in Economics from Lawrence University in Appleton, Wisconsin, and an MBA in Marketing from Northwestern University in Evanston, Ilinois.

As CEO of RAB, Dunbeck directs the not-for-profit organization's ISO 9000 quality management systems and ISO 14000 environmental management systems programs for auditors, course providers, and registrars. RAB, through a joint agreement with ANSI, manages the National Accreditation Program for accrediting registrars and course providers for quality management systems (QMS) and environmental management systems (EMS). RAB directly operates the QMS and EMS auditor certification programs.

Donald N. Ekvall is president of Management Systems Analysis, Lansdale, Pennsylvania. He holds a BS in Electrical Engineering from the University of Pennsylvania, and an MBA in Industrial Management, from the Wharton School, University of Pennsylvania.

Mr. Ekvall has provided general consulting and problem solving in the fields of manufacturing management and quality assurance on an international basis. Mr. Ekvall has also conducted seminars in reengineering, process management, SPC made easy, failure mode and effects analysis (FMEA), implementation assistance for ISO 9000 series (Q90, QS-9000, and KSA 9000) requirements, ISO 14000, environmental management systems, and audit effectiveness of management systems.

Armando Espinosa is president of INLAC, Mexico City, Mexico. A graduate of Instituto Politécnico Nacional, Mexico City, Mexico, with a degree in Mechanical Engineering, Mr. Espinosa worked 37 years for Petróleos Mexicanos in various quality positions.

Mr. Espinosa has been president of the Mexican Society for Mechanical Engineers, and is currently president of the Latin American Institute for Quality Assurance and president of the Quality Council of Mexican College of Mechanical and Electrical Engineers. He has participated as Mexican delegate to technical committee ISO/TC 176 since 1992, and as INLAC liaison member representative since 1997. Over the years he has received numerous awards in recognition for his contribution in advancing quality culture, including the "Silver Medal of Paris City" presented in 1981 by Paris Lord Mayor Jacques Chirac.

James P. Gildersleeve is the publisher for the International Forum for Management Systems, Inc. (INFORM), Montclair, Virginia. Among other products produced by INFORM, he publishes a monthly newsletter titled *The Informed Outlook*, which has become a prominent voice for businesses worldwide on management system standards, their evolution, and uses. He has enjoyed a long association with quality management system standards and their offshoots, beginning with the development of marketing ventures for early training in the field and the production of various publications on the subject. Prior to introducing *The Informed Outlook* in 1996, he helped create other newsletters that reported on ISO 9000 and related standards.

Dr. A. Blanton Godfrey is dean and Joseph D. Moore Professor, College of Textiles, North Carolina State University, Raleigh, North Carolina. He received a BS in Physics from Virginia Tech and an MS and PhD in Statistics from Florida State University. Dr. Godfrey spent five years as head of the Quality Theory and Technology Department at Bell Laboratories and three years as chairman and CEO of the Juran Institute, Inc.

From 1979 until 1987 Dr. Godfrey was a member of the U.S. TAG to ISO TC 176 during the creation of the ISO 9000 series of standards. He is a fellow of ASQ, the American Statistical Association, and the World Academy of Productivity Sciences.

Dale K. Gordon is currently director of quality and business improvement for Rolls-Royce Allison's Defense North America unit, Indianapolis, Indiana. Mr. Gordon has been in the aerospace industy for over 20 years in various quality management positions within his company. He has co-authored a primer on quality systems and is currently the chairman of the American Aerospace Quality

Group (AAQG), an SAE subcommitee that is the owner of AS9000. Mr. Gordon was the U.S. lead for the recent effort to create a sector standard for aerospace, which is now an SAE standard known as AS9100 in the Americas and is published in Europe as EN9100 and in Asia as JIS Q9100.

Dr. Frank M. Gryna is distinguished professor of industrial engineering emeritus, Bradley University, Chesterfield, Missouri. Dr. Gryna has degrees in industrial engineering and over 50 years' experience in the managerial, technological, and statistical aspects of quality activities. He is a researcher and author on quality as associate editor of three editions of *Juran's Quality Handbook* and as co-author of the textbook, *Quality Planning and Analysis.*

His experience in quality has included university teaching, work in industry, and as a consultant. He was also senior vice president of the Juran Institute. His awards include the Edwards Medal and the E. L. Grant Award of the American Society for Quality.

Chris Hakes is chairman of two advisory organizations: Leadership Agenda Ltd., and BQC Performance Management Ltd., London, Nice, Pretoria, Singapore, and San Francisco. He is author of over ten international publications, including the widely used *Business Excellence Handbook* and the *Excellence Routefinder.* Chris was part of the original "Group of 10" that developed the framework for the first European Business Excellence Model some ten-plus years ago. He also led the team that created, for ISO/TC176, their ISO 9000 series guidelines on quality management principles. He can be contacted at chris@bqc-network.com and www.bqc-network.com .

Morgan Hall is senior manufacturing consultant at the University of Maryland Center for Quality and Productivity, College Park, Maryland. He holds degrees in mechanical and electrical engineering and a Master's from Johns Hopkins. Mr. Hall has 35 years experience with General Motors, holding senior management positions in production, engineering, and quality assurance. He holds IRCA and RAB ISO 9000 lead auditor certifications and is an RAB verifying auditor.

Mr. Hall is a member of the U.S. TAG and the U.S. delegate on WG 19, Interpretations. He manages the Maryland ISO Consortium Program for the Maryland Department of Business and Economic Development.

Dan J. Harper is a member of the U.S. TAG to ISO TC 176, the technical committee responsible for the ISO 9000 series standards, and is currently the U.S. TAG's head of delegation to subcommittee 3 of ISO TC176. He is convenor of ISO TC176/SC3 working group 1, which is responsible for the ISO 10012 standards.

Mr. Harper is a past chairman of the ASQ Measurement Quality Division, and is currently chairman of the ASQ Standards Committee. He served for three years as an awards judge for the Oregon Quality Initiative, a state program based on the Malcolm Balridge National Quality Award.

James Highlands is president of Management Systems Analysis, Inc., Royersford, Pennsylvania. He is certified by the RAB and the IRCA as a lead auditor and by ASQ as a quality auditor. For the past 3 years he has served as a lead delegate to TC 176/SC2 on quality management developing the ISO 9001:2000 standard. He has served as the vice chairman of the U.S. TAG to ISO TC 207 SC1 since 1993 and as a lead delegate in the development of ISO 14001 environmental management systems. He has authored two books on the subject of quality standards and management and is currently a member of ASME, ASQ, ANSI, and AMS.

Dr. Jeffrey H. Hooper is currently managing vice president of information services for Lucent Technologies Enhanced Services and Sales.

Prior to this assignment he was quality director of the AT&T Corporate Quality Office and head of Bell Laboratories Quality Theory and Technology Department. He has Bachelor and Master of Engineering degrees, and Master of Science and Doctor of Philosophy degrees in Operations Research, from Cornell University. Mr. Hooper has been actively involved in the development of national and international quality standards for 15 years. He is the project leader for the year 2000 revisions of the ISO 9001 and ISO 9004 standards, vice chair of the U.S. TAG to ISO/TC176, and leads the U.S. liaison effort between quality and environmental management system standards.

William (Bill) F. Houser is a principal of Integrated Productivity & Quality Systems (IPQS), a Spring, Texas–based consulting firm providing client support to achieve simultaneous productivity and quality improvement. He holds an electrical engineering degree, is a professional engineer, and a Certified Quality Engineer. Prior to joining IPQS Mr. Houser held general management, operations management, quality, and product service positions in diverse businesses including consumer and capital goods, automotive, electronics, ordnance, and aerospace. He has authored a number of publications covering such quality-related subjects as ISO 9000, QS-9000, AS9000, and management representative duties, is a frequent speaker at national conventions, and has had papers published in national publications.

Frank Houston is senior software quality consultant (software safety Black Belt) for EduQuest, Inc. He holds a BS, Engineering, (Johns Hopkins University, 1970), and an MS, Clinical Engineering, (Johns Hopkins, 1978). Career experiences have included digital design work for the defense industry, clinical engineering for Johns Hopkins Hospital, and biomedical engineering for the FDA. With FDA, Mr. Houston participated in the development of national and international software standards, supervised a group of CDRH software quality experts, and influenced the establishment of FDA software policies from 1982 until 1992. Since leaving the agency, has done software quality auditing and consulting for clients of all sizes in both the medical device and pharmaceutical industries.

Lorri Hunt is a management project specialist with Honeywell International, Federal Manufacturing & Technologies (operating for the U. S. Department of Energy), Kansas City, Missouri.

She is a voting member of the U.S. technical advisory group to TC 176, and supported the ISO 9004:2000 editing group during the revision process. She currently serves as the lead U.S. delegate for 10007, the international standard on configuration management. Ms. Hunt led the first successful ISO 9001 certification within the Department of Energy's Nuclear Weapon Complex. She currently serves as the lead facilitator for workshops offered through the state of New Mexico to assist small businesses in becoming ISO 9001 compliant.

ERRATA

The following author biography should have appeared in Appendix E, page 885.

ISO 9004 Group

Sandford Liebesman, PhD has had over 27 years of experience in quality at Bell Laboratories, Bellcore, and Lucent Technologies. He is author of the books: *Using ISO 9000 to Improve Business Processes* and *TL 9000: A Guide to Measuring Excellence in Telecommunications.* He is an RAB certified ISO 9000 Lead Auditor, has performed over thirty-five ISO 9000 and TL 9000 audits, and helped three Lucent organizations obtain certification. He led the US validation of ISO 9000:2000 as a member of ISO/TC 176. He also participated in the development of TL 9000 and the Business Excellence Acceleration Model.

Dr. Yoshinori Iizuka is a professor at the School of Engineering, the University of Tokyo. He graduated from the University of Tokyo in 1970, and received his doctor's degree in engineering from the University of Tokyo in 1981. His research has focused on quality management, including TQM, ISO 9000, new product development, software quality, system analysis/design, and statistical methods. He has been a member of Japanese delegations for ISO/TC176 since 1985, and an expert of SC2/WG18 and a member of POTG. His latest books are *ISO 9000 and Restructuring of TQC, Software ISO 9000, TQM—Total Quality Management in the 21st Century,* and *TQM 9000—Fusion of ISO 9000 and TQM.*

Knud E. Jensen is director of TQM—Team Quality Management I/S, Hovedgaard, Denmark. His educational background is in electronic engineering, supplemented by the International Quality Management and Quality Auditor courses and International Business Management course (INSEAD).

Mr. Jensen is chairman of the Danish National Committee—Quality, Danish delegation leader ISO/TC176, and chairman of the task force developing "Vision 2000." He has served within ISO/TC176/SC2 on WG5—ISO 9000-3 (application of ISO 9001 to software), WG11 revision of ISO 9001 resulting in ISO 9001:1994, the project team group that prepared a work program proposal for the 2000 revision of ISO 9001 and ISO 9004, and the WG18 revision of ISO 9001 and ISO 9004 that resulted in the 2000 issues.

Dr. F. Craig Johnson is professor emeritus at Florida State University, Tallahassee, Florida. He has been involved directly in ISO 9000 standards and American National Standards development as lead expert, ISO 9000 SC 1 Terminology WG 2 liaison; lead expert, ISO 10015 Quality Management—*Guidelines for Training;* lead expert, ISO 90013 Quality Management—*Guidelines for Quality Manuals;* chair, the ANSI/ASQ task group for the *American National Standard Z1.11— Guidelines for the Application of ISO 9001 to Education and Training Institutions;* standards representative and chair—ASQ Education Division; and chair—ASQ Freund–Marquardt Medal for Quality Management Standards Excellence.

Dr. Hitoshi Kume is a professor on the faculty of science and engineering at Chuo University, Tokyo, and professor emeritus, Tokyo University, Tokyo. He has served as Japanese chief delegate to ISO TC176 (1981–2000); chairman of the Accreditation Committee, The Japan Accreditation Board for Conformity Assessment (1994–2000); and is currently the chairman of the Board of Trustees, The Japan Accreditation Board for Conformity Assessment. He has written numerous articles on ISO 9000, including "The ISO 9000 Standards As Seen from the Standpoint of Continual Improvement" (2000); "The Scope and Depth of Quality Standards" (1999); "Effective Use of ISO 9000 in Quality Management" (1995); "ISO 9000 Implementation in Japan"(1993); "Quality Management by ISO 9000 and by TQC"(1993); "The Japanese Point of View on the ISO 9000 Standards" (1992); and "ISO 9000 Standards and Their Implementation" (1992).

Judith E. Luchsinger, PhD is the owner and principal consultant of QED Consulting Group, Lakeport, California. She has held a variety of positions in management and administration over the past 30 years, and for the past seven years has specialized exclusively in working with manufacturing, beverage, and service organizations to implement quality management systems, with emphasis on creating ISO 9001–compliant processes. Dr. Luchsinger's experience in this area has included training and implementation for both ISO 9001:1994 and ISO 9001:2000, including internal auditor training, workforce training, GAP analysis, pre-certification auditing and project management.

Noel Matthews is secretary and chief executive of International Accreditation Forum, Inc. (IAF). He has been a chartered professional engineer since 1956, with engineering experience in telecommunications, road, rail, and bridge construction. Mr. Matthews has also served as an assistant secretary in the federal government, chief executive of a national construction industry organization, secretary of Pacific International Cooperation, and secretary of the International Auditor and Training Certification Association.

Dale J. Misczynski is the president and CEO of The Isoagile Group, Austin, Texas, which provides strategic advice to senior management of businesses and organizations in the area of standards, international trade, and conformity assessment. He is a member of the board of directors of the International Accreditation Forum and has served on many IAF committees, including the TC 176/CASCO/IAF joint working group that established the transition guidance for ISO 9000:2000. Formerly the corporate vice president and director of quality for Motorola's global semiconductor operations, Mr. Misczynski has extensive experience in quality management systems in the high technology sector, international regulatory affairs, standardization, and conformity assessment.

Herbert C. Monnich, Jr. is the principal consultant with Herbert Monnich and Associates, Humble, Texas. He is the author of *ISO 9001:2000 for Small and Medium Sized Businesses* and numerous courses on quality subjects. He has over 15 years experience in the development of quality management standards. Mr. Monnich is an active member of the U.S. task group 18 to ISO/TC 176/SC2/WG 18 and other committees in the U.S. Standards Group on QEDS. He was deeply involved in the U.S. ISO 9001:2000 validation task group. He is a fellow of ASQ, Certified Quality Engineer, Certified Quality Auditor, and was the founding editor of the U.S. Standards Group newsletter.

Dr. Ennio Nicoloso, is a consultant for Sistemi Qualità, Roma, Italy. He was Italian delegation leader at ISO/TC 176; a member of WG18 and small business TG; and convenor of the forum WG on "Nuclear Quality Assurance." Dr. Nicoloso is president of the QMS Committee (Italian Association for Quality); a member of the Quality Commission (Italian Standard Body); and chairman of QTS Quality Systems Certification Committee; as well as a lecturer at university and QMS training courses in Italy and abroad, and editor of QMS Interpretation Sectoral Guidelines.

Jørgen Steen Petersen, is quality manager at Radiometer Medical A/S, Copenhagen, Denmark, a company developing, manufacturing, and marketing laboratory instruments and medical devices for hospitals. He holds an MS in Electronic Engineering and has 25 years experience developing and using quality management systems, 20 years experience with interpretation of FDA regulatory requirements, and participated in the training of quality engineers for many years.

Mr. Petersen participated in drafting ISO 9001:2000, and in drafting European standards for in-vitro diagnostic medical devices. He is a member of Danish

Standard S-216 Quality Systems and a consultant for medical device manufactures on FDA and EU regulatory requirements.

Dr. Klaus Petrick, DQS Deutsche Gesellschaft zur Zertifizierung von Management systemen mbH (DQS German Management System Registrar) Berlin, Germany, graduated from the aeronautical engineering program at Technical University, Berlin, and took his Doctorate at Technical University, Institute of Space Technology, Berlin. From 1973 to 1991 he served in the Deutsches Institut für Normung (DIN) e.V. as secretary of Standards Committee for Acoustics and Vibration (until 1988), and secretary of Standards Committee for Quality Management and Statistics (until 1991). From 1989 to 1993 Dr. Petrick served as chairman of EQS European Committee for Management System Assessment and Certification, since 1989 as managing director of DQS German Management System Registrar, from 1990 to 2001 as leader of the German delegation to ISO/TC 176 "Quality Management and Quality Assurance," and was 1997 and 1998 president of IQNet, the international certification network.

Ann W. Phillips is the vice president of management systems with Omni Tech International, Ltd., Huntsville, Alabama. Since August 1991, she has assisted numerous companies, ranging from small distributors to worldwide corporations, in their pursuit of ISO 9000/QS-9000 registration. Over 150 clients have achieved registration. Her emphasis is on implementing practical and effective management systems in a way that achieves measurable improvements in the business. Ms. Phillips has also served as an occupational health and safety supervisor where her primary responsibility was integrating quality, health, and safety management systems.

R. Dan Reid, MBS, MA, ASQ CQE, is purchasing manager for General Motors Powertrain Division, Pontiac, Michigan. He was the delegation leader of the International Automotive Task Force. He was an author of the three editions of QS-9000, the *Quality System Assessment (QSA), ISO TS 16949*, and the *ISO 9001:2000* revision (SC2/WG18/TG 1.7.7). He also worked on the Chrysler, Ford, and GM *Potential Failure Mode and Effects Analysis, Production Part Approval Process,* and *Advanced Product Quality Planning* manuals. Most recently, he was a principal author of an AIAG/ASQ ISO 9004–based document for healthcare, which was subsequently approved as the first ISO industry workshop agreement (IWA).

Curtis D. Ricketts is president of Synerplex Management Associates, Clayton, North Carolina. He is a former assistant commissioner of labor for the State of North Carolina, where he designed and led an ISO 9001 quality management system initiative, a first for a state agency. Mr. Ricketts has over 19 years experience in organizational performance and risk assessment, specializing in management systems, strategic planning, performance measurement, and continuous improvement. He holds quality manager and quality auditor certifications from ASQ and is a member of both the ANSI ASC Z1 Committee and the U.S. TAG to ISO/TC 176. He is also a former chairman of North Carolina's state quality award council.

Wayne G. Robertshaw is senior vice president of ARBOR, Inc., Media, Pennsylvania. He received his BA in Psychology from Hartwick College, and earned his MS in Experimental Psychology at Villanova University. Mr. Robertshaw has been designing, conducting, analyzing, and reporting on primary customer research studies for over 23 years. He has published in the *Journal of*

Advertising Research and has been an invited speaker at many conventions. He has developed a number of innovative techniques for studying customer satisfaction, which have been used by some of the country's largest corporations in setting corporate performance standards to maximize customer satisfaction.

J. P. Russell is president and owner of JP Russell & Associates, Gulf Breeze, Florida. He holds a BS in Engineering and a Masters of Business Administration. Mr. Russell is president of a Web-based training organization at www.QualityWBT.com. He is author or co-author of six books in the quality field and editor of *The Quality Audit Handbook*. He is a contributing author for *ASQ ISO 9000 Handbook* and Gower's *Handbook of Quality Management* (U.K.). He is a columnist for *Quality Progress* magazine. Mr. Russell's awards include the ASQ QAD's 1997 Quality Auditor of the Year award, the ISO/TC176's Outstanding Professional Achievement award, and ASQ's Testimonial Award in 2000. He is an ASQ fellow and CQA.

David Saunders is a vice president at ARBOR, Inc., Baltimore, Maryland, and a founder of ISOize.com. He provides training, consultation, and research for private companies and government agencies on how to achieve better quality at lower costs through customer-driven continuous improvement. A pioneer in innovative hands-on business-to-business customer research, Mr. Saunders has trained executives, managers, supervisors, and workers from a wide variety of engineering, design, and service functions in the art and science of customer interviewing, direct observation, and collection and analysis of linguistic data. He is the co-author of *Four Days with Dr. Deming* and a graduate of Hobart College.

Les Schnoll is director, quality assurance for Gliatech, Inc., Cleveland, Ohio. He has more than 25 years of experience in the FDA-regulated industries. Mr. Schnoll holds a BS in Biology from Ursinus College, Collegeville, Pennsylvania, an MS in Microbiology from Villanova University, Villanova, Pennsylvania, and an MBA from Central Michigan University. He is certified as a microbiologist by the U.K. MDA and authorized to perform assessments to the MDD, European sterilization standards, and EN 46000 standards.

Mr. Schnoll has written several articles for publications and is the author of two books. He is a senior member of ASQ and has actively participated on the U.S. TAG to TC 176, the U.S. TAG to TC 210, and the ANSI Z-1 Committee for many years.

Gordon Staples is a founder and managing partner of Excel Partnership Worldwide; Tokyo; Nantwich, Cheshire, U.K.; Buenos Aires; Sandy Hook, Connecticut. Mr. Staples has spent 25 years auditing more than 350 companies in 30 countries for the mechanical, electronic, service and software industries. He has specialized in ISO 9000, lead auditor, and TQM course development. Mr. Staples is also an original and continuing editorial advisor of *The Informed Outlook* newsletter. He is a fellow of the Institute of Quality Assurance and registered senior consultant, a fellow of the Association of Quality Management Consultants, senior member of ASQ, an RAB-certified quality systems lead auditor, and IRCA registered lead assessor.

John H. Stratton is a management systems consultant at Eastman Kodak (Retired), Rochester, New York. He has been actively implementing the ISO 9000 and 14000 standards since their introduction. He has worked to improve the ISO standards by representing the U.S. on several ISO committees including technical committee 176. He is currently helping to revise and improve the audit standards through writing the new ISO 19011. Mr. Stratton retired from Kodak after nearly thirty years in the field of quality and management systems. He now teaches auditors, helps organizations implement and improve ISO systems, and conducts audits for the U.S. Registrar Accreditation Board.

John G. Surak, PhD, is the coordinator of international programs for the College of Agriculture, Forestry, and Life Sciences; and a professor of food science at Clemson University, Clemson, South Carolina. He received his BS, MS, and PhD from the University of Wisconsin–Madison. Dr. Surak is a fellow in both the American Society for Quality and the Institute of Food Technologists. In addition, he serves on the ASQ Standards Committee. Dr. Surak teaches and lectures internationally on ISO 9000 and HACCP.

Steve Tokarz is director, quality and technical services, Packaging Corporation of America, Lake Forest, Illinois. Over the past 25 years, he has held leadership positions in quality and training with Packaging Corporation of America (PCA), Miller Brewing Co., and A&P. He earned a BS in Business Administration from Towson University and a Masters of Administrative Science from Johns Hopkins University, both located in the Baltimore, Maryland area. Steve was instrumental in having PCA adopt the ISO 9001 standard as the template for its quality/operating systems in its paper mills and converting facilities. Presently, 51 facilities are registered.

Dr. Harrison M. Wadsworth is professor emeritus in the School of Industrial and Systems Engineering at the Georgia Institute of Technology, Atlanta. He has BIE and MSIE degrees from Georgia Tech and a PhD in Statistics from Case Western Reserve University, Cleveland, Ohio. He is the author of numerous publications and technical reports, and is a fellow of ASQ, a member of the American Statistics Association, and a life member of the Institute of Industrial Engineers. He chairs subcommittee 1 of ISO TC 69 and is a U.S. delegate to ISO TC 176 where he participated in the development of ISO 9000:2000. He has received the Shewhart Medal and the Brumbaugh Award of the American Society for Quality.

Lawrence A. Wilson, PhD is president of Lawrence A. Wilson & Associates, an Atlanta-based consulting firm focusing on managing for quality. He earned his BS and MS from Kent State University, Dayton, Ohio, and his PhD at Emory University, Atlanta. Mr. Wilson was formerly director of quality assurance and safety at the Lockheed Aeronautical Systems Company, retiring in 1989 after 26 years. He was the lead U.S. delegate for the revision process for ISO 9001:2000/9004:2000 (1996–2000) and successfully performed as International Writing Group leader, responsible for ISO 9004:2000. Mr. Wilson is chair and honorary lifetime member of the National Security Industrial Association (now NDIA) Quality Committee, and chair of the Aerospace Industries Association Quality Committee.

Index